C000061509

THE
COLLECTED
NOVELS OF
VIRGINIA WOOLF

The Years, The Waves

VOLUME I

Read &' Co.

Copyright © 2021 Read & Co. Classics

This edition is published by Read & Co. Classics,
an imprint of Read & Co.

This book is copyright and may not be reproduced or copied in any
way without the express permission of the publisher in writing.

British Library Cataloguing-in-Publication Data
A catalogue record for this book is available
from the British Library.

Read & Co. is part of Read Books Ltd.
For more information visit
www.readandcobooks.co.uk

CONTENTS

Virginia Woolf

Virginia Woolf was born Adeline Virginia Stephen in Kensington, London, England in 1882. Her father, Leslie Stephen, was a respected man of letters, and as a young girl Woolf was introduced to many literary figures, including Henry James. Woolf also made great use of the family home's vast library, working her way through much of the English literary canon as a teenager. Her summers were spent in St. Ives, Cornwall, which would later form the setting for her famous novel, *To the Lighthouse*.

In 1895, when Woolf was just thirteen, her mother died, triggering the first of her many mental breakdowns. Despite this, between 1897 and 1901 she was able to take courses in Greek, Latin, German and history at the Ladies' Department of King's College London. She even began publishing work with the *Times Literary Supplement*. However, in 1904, following the death of her father, Woolf suffered another breakdown which saw her briefly institutionalised. Following her discharge, Woolf and her sisters moved from their family home to a new abode in Bloomsbury. It was here that Woolf met Lytton Strachey, John Maynard Keynes, E. M. Forster and various other writers and intellectuals, who together would form the famous Bloomsbury Set. In 1912, Woolf married author Leonard Woolf, who nursed her through another breakdown and suicide attempt. Woolf published her first novel, *The Voyage Out*, in 1915. This, as well as various essays, quickly established her as a major public intellectual.

During the twenties, Woolf published the novels that established her as a leading figure of modernism and one of the greatest British novelists of the 20th century: *Jacob's Room* (1922), *Mrs. Dalloway* (1925), *To the Lighthouse* (1927) and *Orlando* (1928). Stylistically, Woolf experimented with a lyrical stream-of-consciousness narrative mode, and is now considered – along with fellow modernist James Joyce – one of the finest innovators in the English language. Her work has been translated into fifty languages, and her major novels have never been out of print.

After completing her last novel, *Between the Acts*, Woolf fell into a period of deep depression – exacerbated by the the onset of World War ii and the destruction of her home during the Blitz. In 1941, fearing a total mental collapse, Woolf committed suicide. She was 59 years old.

THE
COLLECTED
NOVELS OF
VIRGINIA WOOLF

THE YEARS

1880

It was an uncertain spring. The weather, perpetually changing, sent clouds of blue and of purple flying over the land. In the country farmers, looking at the fields, were apprehensive; in London umbrellas were opened and then shut by people looking up at the sky. But in April such weather was to be expected. Thousands of shop assistants made that remark, as they handed neat parcels to ladies in flounced dresses standing on the other side of the counter at Whiteley's and the Army and Navy Stores. Interminable processions of shoppers in the West end, of business men in the East, paraded the pavements, like caravans perpetually marching,—so it seemed to those who had any reason to pause, say, to post a letter, or at a club window in Piccadilly. The stream of landaus, victorias and hansom cabs was incessant; for the season was beginning. In the quieter streets musicians doled out their frail and for the most part melancholy pipe of sound, which was echoed, or parodied, here in the trees of Hyde Park, here in St. James's by the twitter of sparrows and the sudden outbursts of the amorous but intermittent thrush.

The pigeons in the squares shuffled in the tree tops, letting fall a twig or two, and crooned over and over again the lullaby that was always interrupted. The gates at the Marble Arch and Apsley House were blocked in the afternoon by ladies in many-coloured dresses wearing bustles, and by gentlemen in frock coats carrying canes, wearing carnations. Here came the Princess, and as she passed hats were lifted. In the basements of the long avenues of the residential quarters servant girls in cap and apron prepared tea. Deviously ascending from the basement the silver teapot was placed on the table, and virgins and spinsters with hands that had staunched the sores of Bermondsey and Hoxton carefully measured out one, two, three, four spoonfuls of tea. When the sun went down a million little gaslights, shaped like the eyes in peacocks' feathers, opened in their glass cages, but nevertheless broad stretches of darkness were left on the pavement. The mixed light of the lamps and the setting sun was reflected equally in the placid waters of the Round Pond and the Serpentine. Diners-out, trotting over the Bridge in hansom cabs, looked for a moment at the charming vista. At length the moon rose and its polished coin, though obscured now and then by wisps of cloud, shone out with serenity, with severity, or perhaps with complete indifference. Slowly wheeling, like the rays of a searchlight, the days, the weeks, the years passed one after another across the sky.

Colonel Abel Pargiter was sitting after luncheon in his club talking. Since his companions in the leather armchairs were men of his own type, men who had been soldiers, civil servants, men who had now retired, they were reviving with old jokes and stories now their past in India, Africa, Egypt, and then, by a natural transition, they turned to the present. It was a question of some appointment, of some possible appointment.

Suddenly the youngest and the sprucest of the three leant forward. Yesterday he had lunched with . . . Here the voice of the speaker fell. The others bent towards him; with a brief wave of his hand Colonel Abel dismissed the servant who was removing the coffee cups. The three baldish and greyish heads remained close together for a few minutes. Then Colonel Abel threw himself back in his chair. The curious gleam which had come into all their eyes when Major Elkin began his story had faded

completely from Colonel Pargiter's face. He sat staring ahead of him with bright blue eyes that seemed a little screwed up, as if the glare of the East were still in them; and puckered at the corners as if the dust were still in them. Some thought had struck him that made what the others were saying of no interest to him; indeed, it was disagreeable to him. He rose and looked out of the window down into Piccadilly. Holding his cigar suspended he looked down on the tops of omnibuses, hansom cabs, victorias, vans and landaus. He was out of it all, his attitude seemed to say; he had no longer any finger in that pie. Gloom settled on his red handsome face as he stood gazing. Suddenly a thought struck him. He had a question to ask; he turned to ask it; but his friends were gone. The little group had broken up. Elkins was already hurrying through the door; Brand had moved off to talk to another man. Colonel Pargiter shut his mouth on the thing he might have said, and turned back again to the window overlooking Piccadilly. Everybody in the crowded street, it seemed, had some end in view. Everybody was hurrying along to keep some appointment. Even the ladies in their victorias and broughams were trotting down Piccadilly on some errand or other. People were coming back to London; they were settling in for the season. But for him there would be no season; for him there was nothing to do. His wife was dying; but she did not die. She was better today; would be worse tomorrow; a new nurse was coming; and so it went on. He picked up a paper and turned over the pages. He looked at a picture of the west front of Cologne Cathedral. He tossed the paper back into its place among the other papers. One of these days—that was his euphemism for the time when his wife was dead—he would give up London, he thought, and live in the country. But then there was the house; then there were the children; and there was also .
. . his face changed; it became less discontented; but also a little furtive and uneasy.

He had somewhere to go, after all. While they were gossiping he had kept that thought at the back of his mind. When he turned round and found them gone, that was the balm he clapped on his wound. He would go and see Mira; Mira at least would be glad to see him. Thus when he left the club he turned not East, where the busy men were going; nor West where his own house in Abercorn Terrace was; but took his way along the hard paths through the Green Park towards Westminster. The grass was very green; the leaves were beginning to shoot; little green claws, like birds' claws, were pushing out from the branches; there was a sparkle, an animation everywhere; the air smelt clean and brisk. But Colonel Pargiter saw neither the grass nor the trees. He marched through the Park, in his closely buttoned coat, looking straight ahead of him. But when he came to Westminster he stopped. He did not like this part of the business at all. Every time he approached the little street that lay under the huge bulk of the Abbey, the street of dingy little houses, with yellow curtains and cards in the window, the street where the muffin man seemed always to be ringing his bell, where children screamed and hopped in and out of white chalk-marks on the pavement, he paused, looked to the right, looked to the left; and then walked very sharply to Number Thirty and rang the bell. He gazed straight at the door as he waited with his head rather sunk. He did not wish to be seen standing on that door-step. He did not like waiting to be let in. He did not like it when Mrs Sims let him in. There was always a smell in the house; there were always dirty clothes hanging on a line in the back garden. He went up the stairs, sulkily and heavily, and entered the sitting-room.

Nobody was there; he was too early. He looked round the room with distaste. There were too many little objects about. He felt out of place, and altogether too large as he stood upright before the draped fireplace in front of a screen upon which was painted a kingfisher in the act of alighting on some bulrushes. Footsteps scurried about hither and thither on the floor above. Was there somebody with her? he asked himself listening. Children screamed in the street outside. It was sordid; it was mean; it was furtive. One of these days, he said to himself . . . but the door opened and his mistress, Mira, came in.

"Oh Bogy, dear!" she exclaimed. Her hair was very untidy; she was a little fluffy-looking; but she was very much younger than he was and really glad to see him, he thought. The little dog bounced up at her.

"Lulu, Lulu," she cried, catching the little dog in one hand while she put the other to her hair, "come and let Uncle Bogy look at you."

The Colonel settled himself in the creaking basket-chair. She put the dog on his knee. There was a red patch—possibly eczema—behind one of its ears. The Colonel put on his glasses and bent down to look at the dog's ear. Mira kissed him where his collar met his neck. Then his glasses fell off. She snatched them and put them on the dog. The old boy was out of spirits today, she felt. In that mysterious world of clubs and family life of which he never spoke to her something was wrong. He had come before she had done her hair, which was a nuisance. But her duty was to distract him. So she flitted—her figure, enlarging as it was, still allowed her to glide between table and chair—hither and thither; removed the fire-screen and set a light, before he could stop her, to the grudging lodging-house fire. Then she perched on the arm of his chair.

"Oh, Mira!" she said, glancing at herself in the looking-glass and shifting her hair-pins, "what a dreadfully untidy girl you are!" She loosed a long coil and let it fall over her shoulders. It was beautiful gold-glancing hair still, though she was nearing forty and had, if the truth were known, a daughter of eight boarded out with friends at Bedford. The hair began to fall of its own accord, of its own weight, and Bogy seeing it fall stooped and kissed her hair. A barrel-organ had begun to play down the street and the children all rushed in that direction, leaving a sudden silence. The Colonel began to stroke her neck. He began fumbling, with the hand that had lost two fingers, rather lower down, where the neck joins the shoulders. Mira slipped onto

13

the floor and leant her back against his knee.

Then there was a creaking on the stairs; someone tapped as if to warn them of her presence. Mira at once pinned her hair together, got up and shut the door.

The Colonel began in his methodical way to examine the dog's ears again. Was it eczema? or was it not eczema? He looked at the red patch, then set the dog on its legs in the basket and waited. He did not like the prolonged whispering on the landing outside. At length Mira came back; she looked worried; and when she looked worried she looked old. She began hunting about under cushions and covers. She wanted her bag, she said; where had she put her bag? In that litter of things, the Colonel thought, it might be anywhere. It was a lean, poverty-stricken-looking bag when she found it under the cushions in the corner of the sofa. She turned it upside down. Pocket handkerchiefs, screwed up bits of paper, silver and coppers fell out as she shook it. But there should have been a sovereign, she said. "I'm sure I had one yesterday," she murmured.

"How much?" said the Colonel.

It came to one pound—no, it came to one pound eight and sixpence, she said, muttering something about the washing. The Colonel slipped two sovereigns out of his little gold case and gave them to her. She took them and there was more whispering on the landing.

"Washing . . . ?" thought the Colonel, looking round the room. It was a dingy little hole; but being so much older than she was it did not do to ask questions about the washing. Here she was again. She flitted across the room and sat on the floor and put her head against his knee. The grudging fire which had been flickering feebly had died down now. "Let it be," he said impatiently, as she took up the poker. "Let it go out." She resigned the poker. The dog snored; the barrel organ played. His hand began its voyage up and down her neck, in and out of the long thick hair. In this small room, so close to the other houses, dusk came quickly; and the curtains were half drawn.

He drew her to him; he kissed her on the nape of the neck; and then the hand that had lost two fingers began to fumble rather lower down where the neck joins the shoulders.

A sudden squall of rain struck the pavement, and the children, who had been skipping in and out of their chalk cages, scudded away home. The elderly street singer, who had been swaying along the kerb, with a fisherman's cap stuck jauntily on the back of his head, lustily chanting "Count your blessings, Count your blessings—" turned up his coat collar and took refuge under the portico of a public house where he finished his injunction: "Count your blessings. Every One." Then the sun shone again; and dried the pavement.

"It's not boiling," said Milly Pargiter, looking at the tea-kettle. She was sitting at the round table in the front drawing-room of the house in Abercorn Terrace. "Not nearly boiling," she repeated.

The kettle was an old-fashioned brass kettle, chased with a design of roses that was almost obliterated. A feeble little flame flickered up and down beneath the brass bowl. Her sister Delia, lying back in a chair beside her, watched it too. "Must a kettle boil?" she asked idly after a moment, as if she expected no answer, and Milly did not answer. They sat in silence watching the little flame on a tuft of yellow wick. There were many plates and cups as if other people were coming; but at the moment they were alone. The room was full of furniture. Opposite them stood a Dutch cabinet with blue china on the shelves; the sun of the April evening made a bright stain here and there on the glass. Over the fireplace the portrait of a red-haired young woman in white muslin holding a basket of flowers on her lap smiled down on them.

Milly took a hairpin from her head and began to fray the wick into separate strands so as to increase the size of the flame.

"But that doesn't do any good," Delia said irritably as she

watched her. She fidgeted. Everything seemed to take such an intolerable time. Then Crosby came in and said, should she boil the kettle in the kitchen? and Milly said No. How can I put a stop to this fiddling and trifling, she said to herself, tapping a knife on the table and looking at the feeble flame that her sister was teasing with a hairpin. A gnat's voice began to wail under the kettle; but here the door burst open again and a little girl in a stiff pink frock came in.

"I think Nurse might have put you on a clean pinafore," said Milly severely, imitating the manner of a grown-up person. There was a green smudge on her pinafore as if she had been climbing trees.

"It hadn't come back from the wash," said Rose, the little girl, grumpily. She looked at the table, but there was no question of tea yet.

Milly applied her hairpin to the wick again. Delia leant back and glanced over her shoulder out of the window. From where she sat she could see the front door steps.

"Now, there's Martin," she said gloomily. The door slammed; books were slapped down on the hall table, and Martin, a boy of twelve, came in. He had the red hair of the woman in the picture, but it was rumpled.

"Go and make yourself tidy," said Delia severely. "You've plenty of time," she added. "The kettle isn't boiling yet."

They all looked at the kettle. It still kept up its faint melancholy singing as the little flame flickered under the swinging bowl of brass.

"Blast that kettle," said Martin, turning sharply away.

"Mama wouldn't like you to use language like that," Milly reproved him as if in imitation of an older person; for their mother had been ill so long that both sisters had taken to imitating her manner with the children. The door opened again.

"The tray, Miss . . ." said Crosby, keeping the door open with her foot. She had an invalid's tray in her hands.

"The tray," said Milly. "Now who's going to take up the tray?"

Again she imitated the manner of an older person who wishes to be tactful with children.

"Not you, Rose. It's too heavy. Let Martin carry it; and you can go with him. But don't stay. Just tell Mama what you've been doing; and then the kettle . . . the kettle. . . ."

Here she applied her hairpin to the wick again. A thin puff of steam issued from the serpent-shaped spout. At first intermittent, it gradually became more and more powerful, until, just as they heard steps on the stairs, one jet of powerful steam issued from the spout.

"It's boiling!" Milly exclaimed. "It's boiling!"

They ate in silence. The sun, judging from the changing lights on the glass of the Dutch cabinet, seemed to be going in and out. Sometimes a bowl shone deep blue; then became livid. Lights rested furtively upon the furniture in the other room. Here was a pattern; here was a bald patch. Somewhere there's beauty, Delia thought, somewhere there's freedom, and somewhere, she thought, *he* is—wearing his white flower. . . . But a stick grated in the hall.

"It's Papa!" Milly exclaimed warningly.

Instantly Martin wriggled out of his father's armchair; Delia sat upright. Milly at once moved forward a very large rose-sprinkled cup that did not match the rest. The Colonel stood at the door and surveyed the group rather fiercely. His small blue eyes looked round them as if to find fault; at the moment there was no particular fault to find; but he was out of temper; they knew at once before he spoke that he was out of temper.

"Grubby little ruffian," he said, pinching Rose by the ear as he passed her. She put her hand at once over the stain on her pinafore.

"Mama all right?" he said, letting himself down in one solid mass into the big armchair. He detested tea; but he always sipped a little from the huge old cup that had been his father's. He raised it and sipped perfunctorily.

"And what have you all been up to?" he asked.

He looked round him with the smoky but shrewd gaze that could be genial, but was surly now.

"Delia had her music lesson, and I went to Whiteley's—" Milly began, rather as if she were a child reciting a lesson.

"Spending money, eh?" said her father sharply, but not unkindly.

"No, Papa; I told you. They sent the wrong sheets—"

"And you, Martin?" Colonel Pargiter asked, cutting short his daughter's statement. "Bottom of the class as usual?"

"Top!" shouted Martin, bolting the word out as if he had restrained it with difficulty until this moment.

"Hm—you don't say so," said his father. His gloom relaxed a little. He put his hand into his trouser pocket and brought out a handful of silver. His children watched him as he tried to single out one sixpence from all the florins. He had lost two fingers of the right hand in the Mutiny, and the muscles had shrunk so that the right hand resembled the claw of some aged bird. He shuffled and fumbled; but as he always ignored the injury, his children dared not help him. The shiny knobs of the mutilated fingers fascinated Rose.

"Here you are, Martin," he said at length, handing the sixpence to his son. Then he sipped his tea again and wiped his moustaches.

"Where's Eleanor?" he said at last, as if to break the silence.

"It's her Grove day," Milly reminded him.

"Oh, her Grove day," muttered the Colonel. He stirred the sugar round and round in the cup as if to demolish it.

"The dear old Levys," said Delia tentatively. She was his favourite daughter; but she felt uncertain in his present mood how much she could venture.

He said nothing.

"Bertie Levy's got six toes on one foot," Rose piped up suddenly. The others laughed. But the Colonel cut them short.

"You hurry up and get off to your prep., my boy," he said,

glancing at Martin, who was still eating.

"Let him finish his tea, Papa," said Milly, again imitating the manner of an older person.

"And the new nurse?" the Colonel asked, drumming on the edge of the table. "Has she come?"

"Yes . . ." Milly began. But there was a rustling in the hall and in came Eleanor. It was much to their relief; especially to Milly's. Thank goodness, there's Eleanor she thought, looking up—the soother, the maker-up of quarrels, the buffer between her and the intensities and strifes of family life. She adored her sister. She would have called her goddess and endowed her with a beauty that was not hers, with clothes that were not hers, had she not been carrying a pile of little mottled books and two black gloves. Protect me, she thought, handing her a teacup, who am such a mousy, downtrodden inefficient little chit, compared with Delia, who always gets her way, while I'm always snubbed by Papa, who was grumpy for some reason. The Colonel smiled at Eleanor. And the red dog on the hearthrug looked up too and wagged his tail, as if he recognised her for one of those satisfactory women who give you a bone, but wash their hands afterwards. She was the eldest of the daughters, about twenty-two, no beauty, but healthy, and though tired at the moment, naturally cheerful.

"I'm sorry I'm late," she said. "I got kept. And I didn't expect—" She looked at her father.

"I got off earlier than I thought," he said hastily. "The meeting—" he stopped short. There had been another row with Mira.

"And how's your Grove, eh?" he added.

"Oh, my Grove—" she repeated; but Milly handed her the covered dish.

"I got kept," Eleanor said again, helping herself. She began to eat; the atmosphere lightened.

"Now tell us, Papa," said Delia boldly—she was his favourite daughter—"what you've been doing with yourself. Had any adventures?"

The remark was unfortunate.

"There aren't any adventures for an old fogy like me," said the Colonel surlily. He ground the grains of sugar against the walls of his cup. Then he seemed to repent of his gruffness; he pondered for a moment.

"I met old Burke at the Club; asked me to bring one of you to dinner; Robin's back, on leave," he said.

He drank up his tea. Some drops fell on his little pointed beard. He took out his large silk handkerchief and wiped his chin impatiently. Eleanor, sitting on her low chair, saw a curious look first on Milly's face, then on Delia's. She had an impression of hostility between them. But they said nothing. They went on eating and drinking until the Colonel took up his cup, saw there was nothing in it, and put it down firmly with a little chink. The ceremony of tea-drinking was over.

"Now, my boy, take yourself off and get on with your prep.," he said to Martin.

Martin withdrew the hand that was stretched towards a plate.

"Cut along," said the Colonel imperiously. Martin got up and went, drawing his hand reluctantly along the chairs and tables as if to delay his passage. He slammed the door rather sharply behind him. The Colonel rose and stood upright among them in his tightly buttoned frock-coat.

"And I must be off too," he said. But he paused a moment, as if there was nothing particular for him to be off to. He stood there very erect among them, as if he wished to give some order, but could not at the moment think of any order to give. Then he recollected.

"I wish one of you would remember," he said, addressing his daughters impartially, "to write to Edward. . . . Tell him to write to Mama."

"Yes," said Eleanor.

He moved towards the door. But he stopped.

"And let me know when Mama wants to see me," he remarked. Then he paused and pinched his youngest daughter by the ear.

"Grubby little ruffian," he said, pointing to the green stain on her pinafore. She covered it with her hand. At the door he paused again.

"Don't forget," he said, fumbling with the handle, "don't forget to write to Edward." At last he had turned the handle and was gone.

They were silent. There was something strained in the atmosphere, Eleanor felt. She took one of the little books that she had dropped on the table and laid it open on her knee. But she did not look at it. Her glance fixed itself rather absent-mindedly upon the farther room. The trees were coming out in the back garden; there were little leaves—little ear-shaped leaves on the bushes. The sun was shining, fitfully; it was going in and it was going out, lighting up now this, now—

"Eleanor," Rose interrupted. She held herself in a way that was oddly like her father's.

"Eleanor," she repeated in a low voice, for her sister was not attending.

"Well?" said Eleanor, looking at her.

"I want to go to Lamley's," said Rose.

She looked the image of her father, standing there with her hands behind her back.

"It's too late for Lamley's," said Eleanor.

"They don't shut till seven," said Rose.

"Then ask Martin to go with you," said Eleanor.

The little girl moved off slowly towards the door. Eleanor took up her account-books again.

"But you're not to go alone, Rose; you're not to go alone," she said, looking up over them as Rose reached the door. Nodding her head in silence, Rose disappeared.

She went upstairs. She paused outside her mother's bedroom and snuffed the sour-sweet smell that seemed to hang about the jugs, the tumblers, the covered bowls on the table outside the door. Up she went again, and stopped outside the schoolroom door. She did not want to go in, for she had quarrelled with Martin. They had quarrelled first about Erridge and the microscope and then about shooting Miss Pym's cats next door. But Eleanor had told her to ask him. She opened the door.

"Hullo, Martin—" she began.

He was sitting at a table with a book propped in front of him, muttering to himself—perhaps it was Greek, perhaps it was Latin.

"Eleanor told me—" she began, noting how flushed he looked, and how his hand closed on a bit of paper as if he were going to screw it into a ball. "To ask you . . ." she began, and braced herself and stood with her back against the door.

Eleanor leant back in her chair. The sun now was on the trees in the back garden. The buds were beginning to swell. The spring light of course showed up the shabbiness of the chair-covers. The large armchair had a dark stain on it where her father had rested his head, she noticed. But what a number of chairs there were—how roomy, how airy it was after that bedroom where old Mrs Levy—But Milly and Delia were both silent. It was the question of the dinner-party, she remembered. Which of them was to go? They both wanted to go. She wished people would not say, "Bring one of your daughters." She wished they would say, "Bring Eleanor," or "Bring Milly," or "Bring Delia," instead of lumping them all together. Then there could be no question.

"Well," said Delia abruptly, "I shall . . ."

She got up as if she were going somewhere. But she stopped. Then she strolled over to the window that looked out onto the street. The houses opposite all had the same little front gardens; the same steps; the same pillars; the same bow windows. But now dusk was falling and they looked spectral and insubstantial in the dim light. Lamps were being lit; a light glowed in the drawing-room opposite; then the curtains were drawn, and the room was blotted out. Delia stood looking down at the street.

22

A woman of the lower classes was wheeling a perambulator; an old man tottered along with his hands behind his back. Then the street was empty; there was a pause. Here came a hansom jingling down the road. Delia was momentarily interested. Was it going to stop at their door or not? She gazed more intently. But then, to her regret, the cabman jerked his reins, the horse stumbled on; the cab stopped two doors lower down.

"Someone's calling on the Stapletons," she called back, holding apart the muslin blind. Milly came and stood beside her sister, and together, through the slit, they watched a young man in a top-hat get out of the cab. He stretched his hand up to pay the driver.

"Don't be caught looking," said Eleanor warningly. The young man ran up the steps into the house; the door shut upon him and the cab drove away.

But for the moment the two girls stood at the window looking into the street. The crocuses were yellow and purple in the front gardens. The almond trees and privets were tipped with green. A sudden gust of wind tore down the street, blowing a piece of paper along the pavement; and a little swirl of dry dust followed after. Above the roofs was one of those red and fitful London sunsets that make window after window burn gold. There was a wildness in the spring evening; even here, in Abercorn Terrace the light was changing from gold to black, from black to gold. Dropping the blind, Delia turned, and coming back into the drawing-room, said suddenly:

"Oh my God!"

Eleanor, who had taken her books again, looked up disturbed.

"Eight times eight . . ." she said aloud. "What's eight times eight?"

Putting her finger on the page to mark the place, she looked at her sister. As she stood there with her head thrown back and her hair red in the sunset glow, she looked for a moment defiant, even beautiful. Beside her Milly was mouse-coloured and nondescript.

"Look here, Delia," said Eleanor, shutting her book, "you've only got to wait . . ." She meant but she could not say it, "until Mama dies."

"No, no, no," said Delia, stretching her arms out. "It's hopeless. . . ." she began. But she broke off, for Crosby had come in. She was carrying a tray. One by one with an exasperating little chink she put the cups, the plates, the knives, the jam-pots, the dishes of cake and the dishes of bread and butter, on the tray. Then, balancing it carefully in front of her, she went out. There was a pause. In she came again and folded the table-cloth and moved the tables. Again there was a pause. A moment or two later back she came carrying two silk-shaded lamps. She set one in the front room, one in the back room. Then she went, creaking in her cheap shoes, to the window and drew the curtains. They slid with a familiar click along the brass rod, and soon the windows were obscured by thick sculptured folds of claret-coloured plush. When she had drawn the curtains in both rooms, a profound silence seemed to fall upon the drawing-room. The world outside seemed thickly and entirely cut off. Far away down the next street they heard the voice of a street hawker droning; the heavy hooves of van horses clopped slowly down the road. For a moment wheels ground on the road; then they died out and the silence was complete.

Two yellow circles of light fell under the lamps. Eleanor drew her chair up under one of them, bent her head and went on with the part of her work that she always left to the last because she disliked it so much—adding up figures. Her lips moved and her pencil made little dots on the paper as she added eights to sixes, fives to fours.

"There!" she said at last. "That's done. Now I'll go and sit with Mama."

She stooped to pick up her gloves.

"No," said Milly, throwing aside a magazine she had opened, "I'll go . . ."

Delia suddenly emerged from the back room in which she had been prowling.

"I've nothing whatever to do," she said briefly. "I'll go."

She went upstairs, step by step, very slowly. When she came to the bedroom door with the jugs and glasses on the table outside, she paused. The sour-sweet smell of illness slightly sickened her. She could not force herself to go in. Through the little window at the end of the passage she could see flamingo-coloured curls of cloud lying on a pale-blue sky. After the dusk of the drawing-room, her eyes dazzled. She seemed fixed there for a moment by the light. Then on the floor above she heard children's voices—Martin and Rose quarrelling.

"Don't then!" she heard Rose say. A door slammed. She paused. Then she drew in a deep breath of air, looked once more at the fiery sky, and tapped on the bedroom door.

The nurse rose quietly; put her finger to her lips, and left the room. Mrs Pargiter was asleep. Lying in a cleft of the pillows with one hand under her cheek, Mrs Pargiter moaned slightly as if she wandered in a world where even in sleep little obstacles lay across her path. Her face was pouched and heavy; the skin was stained with brown patches; the hair which had been red was now white, save that there were queer yellow patches in it, as if some locks had been dipped in the yolk of an egg. Bare of all rings save her wedding ring, her fingers alone seemed to indicate that she had entered the private world of illness. But she did not look as if she were dying; she looked as if she might go on existing in this borderland between life and death for ever. Delia could see no change in her. As she sat down, everything seemed to be at full tide in her. A long narrow glass by the bedside reflected a section of the sky; it was dazzled at the moment with red light. The dressing-table was illuminated. The light struck on silver bottles and on glass bottles, all set out in the perfect order of things that are not used. At this hour of the evening the sick-room had an unreal cleanliness, quiet and order. There by the bedside was a little table set with spectacles, prayer-book and a vase of lilies of the valley. The flowers, too, looked unreal. There was nothing to do but to look.

She stared at the yellow drawing of her grandfather with the high light on his nose; at the photograph of her Uncle Horace in his uniform; at the lean and twisted figure on the crucifix to the right.

"But you don't believe in it!" she said savagely, looking at her mother sunk in sleep. "You don't want to die."

She longed for her to die. There she was—soft, decayed but everlasting, lying in the cleft of the pillows, an obstacle, a prevention, an impediment to all life. She tried to whip up some feeling of affection, of pity. For instance, that summer, she told herself, at Sidmouth, when she called me up the garden steps. . . . But the scene melted as she tried to look at it. There was the other scene of course—the man in the frock-coat with the flower in his button-hole. But she had sworn not to think of that till bedtime. What then should she think of? Grandpapa with the white light on his nose? The prayer-book? The lilies of the valley? Or the looking-glass? The sun had gone in; the glass was dim and reflected now only a dun-coloured patch of sky. She could resist no longer.

"Wearing a white flower in his button-hole," she began. It required a few minutes' preparation. There must be a hall; banks of palms; a floor beneath them crowded with people's heads. The charm was beginning to work. She became permeated with delicious starts of flattering and exciting emotion. She was on the platform; there was a huge audience; everybody was shouting, waving handkerchiefs, hissing and whistling. Then she stood up. She rose all in white in the middle of the platform; Mr Parnell was by her side.

"I am speaking in the cause of Liberty," she began, throwing out her hands, "in the cause of Justice. . . ." They were standing side by side. He was very pale but his dark eyes glowed. He turned to her and whispered. . . .

There was a sudden interruption. Mrs Pargiter had raised herself on her pillows.

"Where am I?" she cried. She was frightened and bewildered, as she often was on waking. She raised her hand; she seemed to appeal for help. "Where am I?" she repeated. For a moment Delia was bewildered too. Where was she?

"Here, Mama! Here!" she said wildly. "Here, in your own room."

She laid her hand on the counterpane. Mrs Pargiter clutched it nervously. She looked round the room as if she were seeking someone. She did not seem to recognise her daughter.

"What's happening?" she said. "Where am I?" Then she looked at Delia and remembered.

"Oh, Delia—I was dreaming," she murmured half apologetically. She lay for a moment looking out of the window. The lamps were being lit, and a sudden soft spurt of light came in the street outside.

"It's been a fine day . . ." she hesitated, "for . . ." It seemed as if she could not remember what for.

"A lovely day, yes, Mama," Delia repeated with mechanical cheerfulness.

". . . for . . ." her mother tried again.

What day was it? Delia could not remember.

". . . for your Uncle Digby's birthday," Mrs Pargiter at last brought out.

"Tell him from me—tell him how very glad I am."

"I'll tell him," said Delia. She had forgotten her uncle's birthday; but her mother was punctilious about such things.

"Aunt Eugénie—" she began.

But her mother was staring at the dressing-table. Some gleam from the lamp outside made the white cloth look extremely white.

"Another clean table-cloth!" Mrs Pargiter murmured peevishly. "The expense, Delia, the expense—that's what worries me—"

"That's all right, Mama," said Delia dully. Her eyes were fixed upon her grandfather's portrait; why, she wondered, had the artist put a dab of white chalk on the tip of his nose?

"Aunt Eugénie brought you some flowers," she said.

For some reason Mrs Pargiter seemed pleased. Her eyes rested contemplatively on the clean table-cloth that had suggested the washing bill a moment before.

"Aunt Eugénie . . ." she said. "How well I remember"—her voice seemed to get fuller and rounder—"the day the engagement was announced. We were all of us in the garden; there came a letter." She paused. "There came a letter," she repeated. Then she said no more for a time. She seemed to be going over some memory.

"The dear little boy died, but save for that . . ." She stopped again. She seemed weaker tonight, Delia thought; and a start of joy ran through her. Her sentences were more broken than usual. What little boy had died? She began counting the twists on the counterpane as she waited for her mother to speak.

"You know all the cousins used to come together in the summer," her mother suddenly resumed. "There was your Uncle Horace. . . ."

"The one with the glass eye," said Delia.

"Yes. He hurt his eye on the rocking-horse. The aunts thought so much of Horace. They would say . . ." Here there was a long pause. She seemed to be fumbling to find the exact words.

"When Horace comes . . . remember to ask him about the dining-room door."

A curious amusement seemed to fill Mrs Pargiter. She actually laughed. She must be thinking of some long-past family joke, Delia supposed, as she watched the smile flicker and fade away. There was complete silence. Her mother lay with her eyes shut; the hand with the single ring, the white and wasted hand, lay on the counterpane. In the silence they could hear a coal click in the grate and a street hawker droning down the road. Mrs Pargiter said no more. She lay perfectly still. Then she sighed profoundly.

The door opened, and the nurse came in. Delia rose and went

out. Where am I? she asked herself, staring at a white jug stained pink by the setting sun. For a moment she seemed to be in some borderland between life and death. Where am I? she repeated, looking at the pink jug, for it all looked strange. Then she heard water rushing and feet thudding on the floor above.

"Here you are, Rosie," said Nurse, looking up from the wheel of the sewing-machine as Rose came in.

The nursery was brightly lit; there was an unshaded lamp on the table. Mrs C., who came every week with the washing, was sitting in the armchair with a cup in her hand. "Go and get your sewing, there's a good girl," said Nurse as Rose shook hands with Mrs C., "or you'll never be done in time for Papa's birthday," she added, clearing a space on the nursery table.

Rose opened the table drawer and took out the boot-bag that she was embroidering with a design of blue and red flowers for her father's birthday. There were still several clusters of little pencilled roses to be worked. She spread it on the table and examined it as Nurse resumed what she was saying to Mrs C. about Mrs Kirby's daughter. But Rose did not listen.

Then I shall go by myself, she decided, straightening out the boot-bag. If Martin won't come with me, then I shall go by myself.

"I left my work-box in the drawing-room," she said aloud.

"Well, then, go and fetch it," said Nurse, but she was not attending; she wanted to go on with what she was saying to Mrs C. about the grocer's daughter.

Now the adventure has begun, Rose said to herself as she stole on tiptoe to the night nursery. Now she must provide herself with ammunition and provisions; she must steal Nurse's latchkey; but where was it? Every night it was hidden in a new place for fear of burglars. It would be either under the handkerchief-case or in the little box where she kept her mother's gold watch-chain. There it was. Now she had her pistol and her shot, she thought, taking her own purse from her own drawer, and enough provisions, she thought, as she hung her hat and coat over her arm, to last a fortnight.

She stole past the nursery, down the stairs. She listened intently as she passed the schoolroom door. She must be careful not to tread on a dry branch, or to let any twig crack under her, she told herself, as she went on tiptoe. Again she stopped and listened as she passed her mother's bedroom door. All was silent. Then she stood for a moment on the landing, looking down into the hall. The dog was asleep on the mat; the coast was clear; the hall was empty. She heard voices murmuring in the drawing-room.

She turned the latch of the front door with extreme gentleness, and closed it with scarcely a click behind her. Until she was round the corner she crouched close to the wall so that nobody could see her. When she reached the corner under the laburnum tree she stood erect.

"I am Pargiter of Pargiter's Horse," she said, flourishing her hand, "riding to the rescue!"

She was riding by night on a desperate mission to a besieged garrison, she told herself. She had a secret message—she clenched her fist on her purse—to deliver to the General in person. All their lives depended upon it. The British flag was still flying on the central tower—Lamley's shop was the central tower; the General was standing on the roof of Lamley's shop with his telescope to his eye. All their lives depended upon her riding to them through the enemy's country. Here she was galloping across the desert. She began to trot. It was growing dark. The street lamps were being lit. The lamplighter was poking his stick up into the little trap-door; the trees in the front gardens made a wavering network of shadow on the pavement; the pavement stretched before her broad and dark. Then there was the crossing; and then there was Lamley's shop on the little island of shops opposite. She had only to cross the desert, to ford the river, and she was safe. Flourishing the arm that held the pistol, she clapped spurs to her horse and galloped down Melrose Avenue. As she ran past the pillar-box the figure of a man suddenly emerged under the gas lamp.

"The enemy!" Rose cried to herself. "The enemy! Bang!" she cried, pulling the trigger of her pistol and looking him full in the face as she passed him. It was a horrid face: white, peeled, pock-marked; he leered at her. He put out his arm as if to stop her. He almost caught her. She dashed past him. The game was over.

She was herself again, a little girl who had disobeyed her sister, in her house shoes, flying for safety to Lamley's shop.

Fresh-faced Mrs Lamley was standing behind the counter folding up the newspapers. She was pondering among her twopenny watches, cards of tools, toy boats and boxes of cheap stationery something pleasant, it seemed; for she was smiling. Then Rose burst in. She looked up enquiringly.

"Hullo, Rosie!" she exclaimed. "What d'you want, my dear?"

She kept her hand on the pile of newspapers. Rose stood there panting. She had forgotten what she had come for.

"I want the box of ducks in the window," Rose at last remembered.

Mrs Lamley waddled round to fetch it.

"Isn't it rather late for a little girl like you to be out alone?" she asked, looking at her as if she knew she had come out in her house shoes, disobeying her sister.

"Good-night, my dear, and run along home," she said, giving her the parcel. The child seemed to hesitate on the doorstep: she stood there staring at the toys under the hanging oil lamp; then out she went reluctantly.

I gave my message to the General in person, she said to herself as she stood outside on the pavement again. And this is the trophy, she said, grasping the box under her arm. I am returning in triumph with the head of the chief rebel, she told herself, as she surveyed the stretch of Melrose Avenue before her.

I must set spurs to my horse and gallop. But the story no longer worked. Melrose Avenue remained Melrose Avenue. She looked down it. There was the long stretch of bare street in front of her. The trees were trembling their shadows over the pavement. The lamps stood at great distances apart, and there were pools of darkness between. She began to trot. Suddenly, as she passed the lamp-post, she saw the man again. He was leaning with his back against the lamp-post, and the light from the gas lamp flickered over his face. As she passed he sucked his lips in and out. He made a mewing noise. But he did not stretch his hands out at her; they were unbuttoning his clothes.

She fled past him. She thought that she heard him coming after her. She heard his feet padding on the pavement. Everything shook as she ran; pink and black spots danced before her eyes as she ran up the door-steps, fitted her key in the latch and opened the hall door. She did not care whether she made a noise or not. She hoped somebody would come out and speak to her. But nobody heard her. The hall was empty. The dog was asleep on the mat. Voices still murmured in the drawing-room.

"And when it does catch," Eleanor was saying, "it'll be much too hot."

Crosby had piled the coals into a great black promontory. A plume of yellow smoke was sullenly twining round it; it was beginning to burn, and when it did burn it would be much too hot.

"She can see Nurse stealing the sugar, she says. She can see her shadow on the wall," Milly was saying. They were talking about their mother.

"And then Edward," she added, "forgetting to write."

"That reminds me," said Eleanor. She must remember to write to Edward. But there would be time after dinner. She did not want to write; she did not want to talk; always when she came back from the Grove she felt as if several things were

32

going on at the same time. Words went on repeating themselves in her mind—words and sights. She was thinking of old Mrs Levy, sitting propped up in bed with her white hair in a thick flop like a wig and her face cracked like an old glazed pot.

"Them that's been good to me, them I remember . . . them that's ridden in their coaches when I was a poor widder woman scrubbing and mangling—" Here she stretched out her arm, which was wrung and white like the root of a tree. "Them that's been good to me, them I remember . . ." Eleanor repeated as she looked at the fire. Then the daughter came in who was working for a tailor. She wore pearls as big as hen's eggs; she had taken to painting her face; she was wonderfully handsome. But Milly made a little movement.

"I was thinking," said Eleanor on the spur of the moment, "the poor enjoy themselves more than we do."

"The Levys?" said Milly absent-mindedly. Then she brightened.

"Do tell me about the Levys," she added. Eleanor's relations with "the poor"—the Levys, the Grubbs, the Paravicinis, the Zwinglers and the Cobbs—always amused her. But Eleanor did not like talking about "the poor" as if they were people in a book. She had a great admiration for Mrs Levy, who was dying of cancer.

"Oh, they're much as usual," she said sharply. Milly looked at her. Eleanor's "broody" she thought. The family joke was, "Look out. Eleanor's broody. It's her Grove day." Eleanor was ashamed, but she always was irritable for some reason when she came back from the Grove—so many different things were going on in her head at the same time: Canning Place; Abercorn Terrace; this room; that room. There was the old Jewess sitting up in bed in her hot little room; then one came back here, and there was Mama ill; Papa grumpy; and Delia and Milly quarrelling about a party. . . . But she checked herself. She ought to try to say something to amuse her sister.

"Mrs Levy had her rent ready, for a wonder," she said. "Lily helps her. Lily's got a job at a tailor's in Shoreditch. She came in all covered with pearls and things. They do love finery—Jews," she added.

"Jews?" said Milly. She seemed to consider the taste of the Jews; and then to dimiss it.

"Yes," she said. "Shiny."

"She's extraordinarily handsome," said Eleanor, thinking of the red cheeks and the white pearls.

Milly smiled; Eleanor always would stick up for the poor. She thought Eleanor the best, the wisest, the most remarkable person she knew.

"I believe you like going there more than anything," she said. "I believe you'd like to go and live there if you had your way," she added, with a little sigh.

Eleanor shifted in her chair. She had her dreams, her plans, of course; but she did not want to discuss them.

"Perhaps you will, when you're married?" said Milly. There was something peevish yet plaintive in her voice. The dinner-party; the Burkes' dinner-party, Eleanor thought. She wished Milly did not always bring the conversation back to marriage. And what do they know about marriage? she asked herself. They stay at home too much, she thought; they never see anyone outside their own set. Here they are cooped up, day after day. . . . That was why she had said, "The poor enjoy themselves more than we do." It had struck her coming back into that drawing-room, with all the furniture and the flowers and the hospital nurses. . . . Again she stopped herself. She must wait till she was alone—till she was brushing her teeth at night. When she was with the others she must stop herself from thinking of two things at the same time. She took the poker and struck the coal.

"Look! What a beauty!" she exclaimed. A flame danced on top of the coal, a nimble and irrelevant flame. It was the sort of flame they used to make when they were children, by throwing salt on the fire. She struck again, and a shower of gold-eyed sparks went volleying up the chimney. "D'you remember," she said, "how we used to play at firemen, and Morris and I set the chimney on fire?"

"And Pippy went and fetched Papa," said Milly. She paused. There was a sound in the hall. A stick grated; someone was hanging up a coat. Eleanor's eyes brightened. That was Morris—yes; she knew the sound he made. Now he was coming in. She looked round with a smile as the door opened. Milly jumped up.

Morris tried to stop her.

"Don't go—" he began.

"Yes!" she exclaimed. "I shall go. I shall go and have a bath," she added on the spur of the moment. She left them.

Morris sat down in the chair she had left empty. He was glad to find Eleanor alone. Neither of them spoke for a moment. They watched the yellow plume of smoke, and the little flame dancing nimbly, irrelevantly, here and there on the black promontory of coals. Then he asked the usual question:

"How's Mama?"

She told him; there was no change: "except that she sleeps more," she said. He wrinkled his forehead. He was losing his boyish look, Eleanor thought. That was the worst of the Bar, everyone said; one had to wait. He was devilling for Sanders Curry; and it was dreary work, hanging about the Courts all day, waiting.

"How's old Curry?" she asked—old Curry had a temper.

"A bit liverish," said Morris grimly.

"And what have you been doing all day?" she asked.

"Nothing in particular," he replied.

"Still Evans v. Carter?"

"Yes," he said briefly.

"And who's going to win?" she asked.

"Carter, of course," he replied.

Why "of course" she wanted to ask? But she had said something silly the other day—something that showed that she had not been attending. She muddled things up; for example, what was the difference between Common Law and the other kind of law? She said nothing. They sat in silence, and watched the flame playing on the coals. It was a green flame, nimble, irrelevant.

"D'you think I've been an awful fool," he asked suddenly. "With all this illness, and Edward and Martin to be paid for— Papa must find it a bit of a strain." He wrinkled his brow up in the way that made her say to herself that he was losing his boyish look.

"Of course not," she said emphatically. Of course it would have been absurd for him to go into business; his passion was for the Law.

"You'll be Lord Chancellor one of these days," she said. "I'm sure of it." He shook his head, smiling.

"Quite sure," she said, looking at him as she used to look at him when he came back from school and Edward had all the prizes and Morris sat silent—she could see him now—bolting his food with nobody making a fuss of him. But even while she looked, a doubt came over her. Lord Chancellor, she had said. Ought she not to have said Lord Chief Justice? She never could remember which was which: and that was why he would not discuss Evans *v.* Carter with her.

She never told him about the Levys either, except by way of a joke. That was the worst of growing up, she thought; they couldn't share things as they used to share them. When they met they never had time to talk as they used to talk—about things in general—they always talked about facts—little facts. She poked the fire. Suddenly a blare of sound rang through the room. It was Crosby applying herself to the gong in the hall. She was like a savage wreaking vengeance upon some brazen victim. Ripples of rough sound rang through the room. "Lord, that's the dressing-bell!" said Morris. He got up and stretched himself. He raised his arms and held them for a moment suspended above his head. That's what he'll look like when he's the father of a family, Eleanor thought. He let his arms fall and left the room. She sat brooding for a moment; then she roused herself. What must I remember? she asked herself. To write to Edward, she mused, crossing over to her mother's writing-table. It'll be my table now, she thought, looking at the silver candlestick, the miniature of her grandfather, the tradesmen's books—one had a gilt cow stamped on it—and the spotted walrus with a brush in its back that Martin had given his mother on her last birthday.

Crosby held open the door of the dining-room as she waited for them to come down. The silver paid for polishing, she thought. Knives and forks rayed out round the table. The whole room, with its carved chairs, oil paintings, the two daggers on the mantel-piece, and the handsome sideboard—all the solid objects that Crosby dusted and polished every day—looked at its best in the evening. Meat-smelling and serge-curtained by day, it looked lit up, semi-transparent in the evening. And they were a handsome family, she thought as they filed in—the young ladies in their pretty dresses of blue and white sprigged muslin; the gentlemen so spruce in their dinner jackets. She pulled the Colonel's chair out for him. He was always at his best in the evening; he enjoyed his dinner; and for some reason his gloom had vanished. He was in his jovial mood. His children's spirits rose as they noted it.

"That's a pretty frock you're wearing," he said to Delia as he sat down.

"This old one?" she said, patting the blue muslin.

There was an opulence, an ease and a charm about him when he was in a good temper that she liked particularly. People always said she was like him; sometimes she was glad of it—tonight for instance. He looked so pink and clean and genial in his dinner-jacket. They became children again when he was in this mood, and were spurred on to make family jokes at which they all laughed for no particular reason.

"Eleanor's broody," said her father, winking at them. "It's her Grove day."

Everybody laughed; Eleanor had thought he was talking about Rover, the dog, when in fact he was talking about Mrs Egerton, the lady. Crosby, who was handing the soup, crinkled up her face because she wanted to laugh too. Sometimes the Colonel made Crosby laugh so much that she had to turn away and pretend to be doing something at the sideboard.

"Oh, Mrs Egerton—" said Eleanor, beginning her soup.

"Yes, Mrs Egerton," said her father, and went on telling his story about Mrs Egerton, "whose golden hair was said by the voice of slander not to be entirely her own."

Delia liked listening to her father's stories about India. They were crisp, and at the same time romantic. They conveyed an atmosphere of officers dining together in mess jackets on a very hot night with a huge silver trophy in the middle of the table.

He used always to be like this when we were small, she thought. He used to jump over the bonfire on her birthday, she remembered. She watched him flicking cutlets dexterously on to plates with his left hand. She admired his decision, his common sense. Flicking the cutlets on to plates, he went on—

"Talking of the lovely Mrs Egerton reminds me—did I ever tell you the story of old Badger Parkes and—"

"Miss—" said Crosby in a whisper, opening the door behind Eleanor's back. She whispered a few words to Eleanor privately.

"I'll come," said Eleanor, getting up.

"What's that—what's that?" said the Colonel, stopping in the middle of his sentence. Eleanor left the room.

"Some message from Nurse," said Milly.

The Colonel, who had just helped himself to cutlets, held his knife and fork in his hand. They all held their knives suspended. Nobody liked to go on eating.

"Well, let's get on with our dinner," said the Colonel, abruptly attacking his cutlet. He had lost his geniality. Morris helped himself tentatively to potatoes. Then Crosby reappeared.

She stood at the door, with her pale-blue eyes looking very prominent.

"What is it, Crosby? What is it?" said the Colonel.

"The Mistress, sir, taken worse, I think, sir," she said with a curious whimper in her voice. Everybody got up.

"You wait. I'll go and see," said Morris. They all followed him out into the hall. The Colonel was still holding his dinner napkin. Morris ran upstairs; in a moment he came down again.

"Mama's had a fainting-fit," he said to the Colonel. "I'm going to fetch Prentice." He snatched his hat and coat and ran down the front steps. They heard him whistling for a cab as they stood uncertainly in the hall.

"Finish your dinner, girls," said the Colonel peremptorily. But he paced up and down the drawing-room, holding his dinner napkin in his hand.

"It has come," Delia said to herself; "it has come!" An extraordinary feeling of relief and excitement possessed her. Her father was pacing from one drawing-room to the other; she followed him in; but she avoided him. They were too much alike; each knew what the other was feeling. She stood at the window looking up the street. There had been a shower of rain. The street was wet; the roofs were shining. Dark clouds were moving across the sky; the branches were tossing up and down in the light of the street lamps. Something in her was tossing up and down too.

Something unknown seemed to be approaching. Then a gulping sound behind her made her turn. It was Milly. She was standing by the mantelpiece under the picture of the white-robed girl with the flower-basket, and the tears slid slowly down her cheeks. Delia moved towards her; she ought to go up to her and put her arms round her shoulders; but she could not do it. Real tears were sliding down Milly's cheeks. But her own eyes were dry. She turned to the window again. The street was empty—only the branches were tossing up and down in the lamplight. The Colonel paced up and down; once he knocked against a table and said "Damn!" They heard steps moving about in the room upstairs. They heard voices murmuring. Delia turned to the window.

A hansom came trotting down the street. Morris jumped out directly the cab stopped. Dr. Prentice followed him. He went straight upstairs and Morris joined them in the drawing-room.

"Why not finish your dinner?" the Colonel said gruffly, coming to a halt and standing upright before them.

"Oh, after he's gone," said Morris irritably.

The Colonel resumed his pacing.

Then he stopped his pacing, and stood with his hands behind him in front of the fire. He had a braced look as if he were holding himself ready for an emergency.

We're both acting, Delia thought to herself, stealing a glance at him, but he's doing it better than I am.

She looked out of the window again. The rain was falling. When it crossed the lamplight it glanced in long strips of silver light.

"It's raining," she said in a low voice, but nobody answered her.

At last they heard footsteps on the stairs and Dr. Prentice came in. He shut the door quietly but said nothing.

"Well?" said the Colonel, facing up to him.

There was a prolonged pause.

"How d'you find her?" said the Colonel.

Dr. Prentice moved his shoulders slightly.

"She's rallied," he said. "For the moment," he added.

Delia felt as if his words struck her violently a blow on the head. She sank down on the arm of a chair.

So you're not going to die, she said, looking at the girl balanced on the trunk of a tree; she seemed to simper down at her daughter with smiling malice. You're not going to die— never, never! she cried clenching her hands together beneath her mother's picture.

"Now, shall we get on with our dinner?" said the

Colonel, taking up the napkin which he had dropped on the drawing-room table.

It was a pity—the dinner was spoilt, Crosby thought, bringing up the cutlets from the kitchen again. The meat was dried up, and the potatoes had a brown crust on top of them. One of the candles was scorching its shade too, she observed as she put the dish down in front of the Colonel. Then she shut the door on them, and they began to eat their dinner.

All was quiet in the house. The dog slept on its mat at the foot of the stairs. All was quiet outside the sickroom door. A faint sound of snoring came from the bedroom where Martin lay asleep. In the day nursery Mrs C. and the nurse had resumed their supper, which they had interrupted when they heard sounds in the hall below. Rose lay asleep in the night nursery. For some time she slept profoundly, curled round with the blankets tight twisted over her head. Then she stirred and stretched her arms out. Something had swum up on top of the blackness. An oval white shape hung in front of her dangling, as if it hung from a string. She half opened her eyes and looked at it. It bubbled with grey spots that went in and out. She woke completely. A face was hanging close to her as if it dangled on a bit of string. She shut her eyes; but the face was still there, bubbling in and out, grey, white, purplish and pock-marked. She put out her hand to touch the big bed next hers. But it was empty. She listened. She heard the clatter of knives and the chatter of voices in the day nursery across the passage. But she could not sleep.

She made herself think of a flock of sheep penned up in a hurdle in a field. She made one of the sheep jump the hurdle; then another. She counted them as they jumped. One, two, three, four—they jumped over the hurdle. But the fifth sheep would not jump. It turned round and looked at her. Its long narrow face was grey; its lips moved; it was the face of the man

41

at the pillar-box, and she was alone with it. If she shut her eyes there it was; if she opened them, there it was still.

She sat up in bed and cried out, "Nurse! Nurse!"

There was dead silence everywhere. The clatter of knives and forks in the next room had ceased. She was alone with something horrible. Then she heard a shuffling in the passage. It came closer and closer. It was the man himself. His hand was on the door. The door opened. An angle of light fell across the wash-stand. The jug and basin were lit up. The man was actually in the room with her . . . but it was Eleanor.

"Why aren't you asleep?" said Eleanor. She put down her candle and began to straighten the bedclothes. They were all crumpled up. She looked at Rose. Her eyes were very bright and her cheeks were flushed. What was the matter? Had they woken her, moving about downstairs in Mama's room?

"What's been keeping you awake?" she asked. Rose yawned again; but it was a sigh rather than a yawn. She could not tell Eleanor what she had seen. She had a profound feeling of guilt; for some reason she must lie about the face she had seen.

"I had a bad dream," she said. "I was frightened." A queer nervous jerk ran through her body as she sat up in bed. What was the matter? Eleanor wondered, again. Had she been fighting with Martin? Had she been chasing cats in Miss Pym's garden again?

"Have you been chasing cats again?" she asked. "Poor cats," she added; "they mind it just as much as you would," she said. But she knew that Rose's fright had nothing to do with the cats. She was grasping her finger tightly; she was staring ahead of her with a queer look in her eyes.

"What was your dream about?" she asked, sitting down on the edge of the bed. Rose stared at her; she could not tell her; but at all costs Eleanor must be made to stay with her.

"I thought I heard a man in the room," she brought out at last. "A robber," she added.

"A robber? Here?" said Eleanor. "But Rose, how could a robber get into your nursery? There's Papa, there's Morris—they would never let a robber come into your room."

"No," said Rose. "Papa would kill him," she added. There was something queer about the way she twitched.

"But what are you all doing?" she said restlessly. "Haven't you gone to bed yet? Isn't it very late?"

"What are we all doing?" said Eleanor. "We're sitting in the drawing-room. It's not very late." As she spoke a faint sound boomed through the room. When the wind was in the right direction they could hear St. Paul's. The soft circles spread out in the air: one, two, three, four—Eleanor counted eight, nine, ten. She was surprised that the strokes stopped so soon.

"There, it's only ten o'clock, you see," she said. It had seemed to her much later. But the last stroke dissolved in the air. "So now you'll go to sleep," she said. Rose clutched her hand.

"Don't go, Eleanor; not yet," she implored her.

"But tell me, what's frightened you?" Eleanor began. Something was being hidden from her, she was sure.

"I saw . . ." Rose began. She made a great effort to tell her the truth; to tell her about the man at the pillar-box. "I saw . . ." she repeated. But here the door opened and Nurse came in.

"I don't know what's come over Rosie tonight," she said, bustling in. She felt a little guilty; she had stayed downstairs with the other servants gossiping about the mistress.

"She sleeps so sound generally," she said, coming over to the bed.

"Now, here's Nurse," said Eleanor. "She's coming to bed. So you won't be frightened any more, will you?" She smoothed down the bed-clothes and kissed her. She got up and took her candle.

"Good-night, Nurse," she said, turning to leave the room.

"Good-night, Miss Eleanor," said Nurse, putting some sympathy into her voice; for they were saying downstairs that the mistress couldn't last much longer.

"Turn over and go to sleep, dearie," she said, kissing Rose on the forehead. For she was sorry for the little girl who would so soon be motherless. Then she slipped the silver links out of her cuffs and began to take the hairpins out of her hair, standing in her petticoats in front of the yellow chest of drawers.

"I saw," Eleanor repeated, as she shut the nursery door. "I saw . . ." What had she seen? Something horrible, something hidden. But what? There it was, hidden behind her strained eyes. She held the candle slightly slanting in her hand. Three drops of grease fell on the polished skirting before she noticed them. She straightened the candle and walked down the stairs. She listened as she went. There was silence. Martin was asleep. Her mother was asleep. As she passed the doors and went downstairs a weight seemed to descend on her. She paused, looking down into the hall. A blankness came over her. Where am I? she asked herself, staring at a heavy frame. What is that? She seemed to be alone in the midst of nothingness; yet must descend, must carry her burden—she raised her arms slightly, as if she were carrying a pitcher, an earthenware pitcher on her head. Again she stopped. The rim of a bowl outlined itself upon her eyeballs; there was water in it; and something yellow. It was the dog's bowl, she realised; that was the sulphur in the dog's bowl; the dog was lying curled up at the bottom of the stairs. She stepped carefully over the body of the sleeping dog and went into the drawing-room.

They all looked up as she came in; Morris had a book in his hand but he was not reading; Milly had some stuff in her hand but she was not sewing; Delia was lying back in her chair, doing nothing whatever. She stood there hesitating for a moment. Then she turned to the writing-table. "I'll write to Edward," she murmured. She took up the pen, but she hesitated. She found it difficult to write to Edward, seeing him before her, when she took up the pen, when she smoothed the notepaper on the writing-table. His eyes were too close together; he brushed up his crest before the looking-glass in the lobby in a way that irritated her. 'Nigs' was her nickname for him. "My dear Edward," she began to write, choosing 'Edward' not 'Nigs' on this occasion.

Morris looked up from the book he was trying to read. The scratching of Eleanor's pen irritated him. She stopped; then she wrote; then she put her hand to her head. All the worries were put on her of course. Still she irritated him. She always asked questions; she never listened to the answers. He glanced at his book again. But what was the use of trying to read? The atmosphere of suppressed emotion was distasteful to him. There was nothing that anybody could do, but there they all sat in attitudes of suppressed emotion. Milly's stitching irritated him, and Delia lying back in her chair doing nothing as usual. There he was cooped up with all these women in an atmosphere of unreal emotion. And Eleanor went on writing, writing, writing. There was nothing to write about—but here she licked the envelope and dabbed down the stamp.

"Shall I take it?" he said, dropping his book.

He got up as if he were glad to have something to do. Eleanor went to the front door with him and stood holding it open while he went to the pillar-box. It was raining gently, and as she stood at the door, breathing in the mild damp air, she watched the curious shadows that trembled on the pavement under the trees. Morris disappeared under the shadows round the corner. She remembered how she used to stand at the door when he was a small boy and went to a day school with a satchel in his hand. She used to wave to him; and when he got to the corner he always turned and waved back. It was a curious little ceremony, dropped now that they were both grown up. The shadows shook as she stood waiting; in a moment he emerged from the shadows. He came along the street and up the steps.

"He'll get that tomorrow," he said—"anyhow by the second post."

He shut the door and stooped to fasten the chain. It seemed

to her, as the chain rattled, that they both accepted the fact that nothing more was going to happen tonight. They avoided each other's eyes; neither of them wanted any more emotion tonight. They went back into the drawing-room.

"Well," said Eleanor, looking round her, "I think I shall go to bed. Nurse will ring," she said, "if she wants anything."

"We may as well all go," said Morris. Milly began to roll up her embroidery. Morris began to rake out the fire.

"What an absurd fire—" he exclaimed irritably. The coals were all stuck together. They were blazing fiercely.

Suddenly a bell rang.

"Nurse!" Eleanor exclaimed. She looked at Morris. She left the room hurriedly. Morris followed her.

But what's the good? Delia thought to herself. It's only another false alarm. She got up. "It's only Nurse," she said to Milly, who was standing up with a look of alarm on her face. She can't be going to cry again, she thought, and strolled off into the front room. Candles were burning on the mantelpiece; they lit up the picture of her mother. She glanced at the portrait of her mother. The girl in white seemed to be presiding over the protracted affair of her own deathbed with a smiling indifference that outraged her daughter.

"You're not going to die—you're not going to die!" said Delia bitterly, looking up at her. Her father, alarmed by the bell, had come into the room. He was wearing a red smoking-cap with an absurd tassel.

But it's all for nothing, Delia said silently, looking at her father. She felt that they must both check their rising excitement. "Nothing's going to happen—nothing whatever," she said, looking at him. But at that moment Eleanor came into the room. She was very white.

"Where's Papa?" she said, looking round. She saw him. "Come, Papa, come," she said, stretching out her hand. "Mama's dying. . . . And the children," she said to Milly over her shoulder.

Two little white patches appeared above her father's ears, Delia noticed. His eyes fixed themselves. He braced himself. He strode past them up the stairs. They all followed in a little procession behind. The dog, Delia noticed, tried to come upstairs with them; but Morris cuffed him back. The Colonel went first into the bedroom; then Eleanor; then Morris; then Martin came down, pulling on a dressing-gown; then Milly brought Rose wrapped in a shawl. But Delia hung back behind the others. There were so many of them in the room that she could get no further than the doorway. She could see two nurses standing with their backs to the wall opposite. One of them was crying— the one, she observed, who had only come that afternoon. She could not see the bed from where she stood. But she could see that Morris had fallen on his knees. Ought I to kneel too? she wondered. Not in the passage, she decided. She looked away; she saw the little window at the end of the passage. Rain was falling; there was a light somewhere that made the raindrops shine. One drop after another slid down the pane; they slid and they paused; one drop joined another drop and then they slid again. There was complete silence in the bedroom.

Is this death? Delia asked herself. For a moment there seemed to be something there. A wall of water seemed to gape apart; the two walls held themselves apart. She listened. There was complete silence. Then there was a stir, a shuffle of feet in the bedroom and out came her father, stumbling.

"Rose!" he cried. "Rose! Rose!" He held his arms with the fists clenched out in front of him.

You did that very well, Delia told him as he passed her. It was like a scene in a play. She observed quite dispassionately that the raindrops were still falling. One sliding met another and together in one drop they rolled to the bottom of the window-pane.

It was raining. A fine rain, a gentle shower, was peppering the pavements and making them greasy. Was it worth while opening an umbrella, was it necessary to hail a hansom, people coming out from the theatres asked themselves, looking up at the mild, milky sky in which the stars were blunted. Where it fell on earth, on fields and gardens, it drew up the smell of earth. Here a drop poised on a grass-blade; there filled the cup of a wild flower, till the breeze stirred and the rain was spilt. Was it worth while to shelter under the hawthorn, under the hedge, the sheep seemed to question; and the cows, already turned out in the grey fields, under the dim hedges, munched on, sleepily chewing with raindrops on their hides. Down on the roofs it fell—here in Westminster, there in the Ladbroke Grove; on the wide sea a million points pricked the blue monster like an innumerable shower bath. Over the vast domes, the soaring spires of slumbering University cities, over the leaded libraries, and the museums, now shrouded in brown holland, the gentle rain slid down, till, reaching the mouths of those fantastic laughers, the many-clawed gargoyles, it splayed out in a thousand odd indentations. A drunken man slipping in a narrow passage outside the public house, cursed it. Women in childbirth heard the doctor say to the midwife, "It's raining." And the walloping Oxford bells, turning over and over like slow porpoises in a sea of oil, contemplatively intoned their musical incantation. The fine rain, the gentle rain, poured equally over the mitred and the bareheaded with an impartiality which suggested that the god of rain, if there were a god, was thinking Let it not be restricted to the very wise, the very great, but let all breathing kind, the munchers and chewers, the ignorant, the unhappy, those who toil in the furnace making innumerable copies of the same pot, those who bore red hot minds through contorted letters, and also Mrs Jones in the alley, share my bounty.

It was raining in Oxford. The rain fell gently, persistently, making a little chuckling and burbling noise in the gutters. Edward, leaning out of the window, could still see the trees in the college garden, whitened by the falling rain. Save for the rustle of the trees and the rain falling, it was perfectly quiet. A damp, earthy smell came up from the wet ground. Lamps were being lit here and there in the dark mass of the college; and there was a pale-yellowish mound in one corner where lamplight fell upon a flowering tree. The grass was becoming invisible, fluid, grey, like water.

He drew in a long breath of satisfaction. Of all the moments in the day he liked this best, when he stood and looked out into the garden. He breathed in again the cool damp air, and then straightened himself and turned back into the room. He was working very hard. His day was parcelled out on the advice of his tutor into hours and half-hours; but he still had five minutes before he need begin. He turned up the reading-lamp. It was partly the green light that made him look a little pale and thin, but he was very handsome. With his clear-cut features and the fair hair that he brushed up with a flick of his fingers into a crest, he looked like a Greek boy on a frieze. He smiled. He was thinking as he watched the rain how, after the interview between his father and his tutor—when old Harbottle had said "Your son has a chance"—the old boy had insisted upon looking up the rooms that his own father had had when his father was at college. They had burst in and found a chap called Thompson on his knees blowing up the fire with a bellows.

"My father had these rooms, sir," the Colonel had said, by way of apology. The young man had got very red and said, "Don't mention it." Edward smiled. "Don't mention it," he repeated. It was time to begin. He turned the lamp a little higher. When the lamp was turned higher he saw his work cut out in a sharp circle of bright light from the surrounding dimness. He looked at the textbooks, at the dictionaries lying before him. He always had some doubts before he began. His father would be frightfully cut-up if he failed. His heart was set on it. He had sent him a dozen of fine old port "by way of a stirrup-cup," so he said. But after all Marsham was in for it; then there was the clever little Jew-boy from Birmingham—but it was time to begin. One after another the bells of Oxford began pushing their slow chimes through the air. They tolled ponderously, unequally, as if they had to roll the air out of their way and the air was heavy. He loved the sound of the bells. He listened till the last stroke had struck; then pulled his chair to the table; time was up; he must work now.

A little dint sharpened between his brows. He frowned as he read. He read; and made a note; then he read again. All sounds were blotted out. He saw nothing but the Greek in front of him. But as he read, his brain gradually warmed; he was conscious of something quickening and tightening in his forehead. He caught phrase after phrase exactly, firmly, more exactly, he noted, making a brief note in the margin, than the night before. Little negligible words now revealed shade of meaning which altered the meaning. He made another note; *that* was the meaning. His own dexterity in catching the phrase plumb in the middle gave him a thrill of excitement. There it was, clean and entire. But he must be precise; exact; even his little scribbled notes must be clear as print. He turned to this book; then that book. Then he leant back to see, with his eyes shut. He must let nothing dwindle off into vagueness. The clocks began striking. He listened. The clocks went on striking. The lines that had graved themselves on his face slackened; he leant back; his muscles relaxed; he looked up from his books into the dimness. He felt as if he had thrown himself down on the turf after running a race. But for a moment it seemed to him that he was still running; his mind went on without the book. It travelled by itself without impediments through a world of pure meaning; but gradually it lost its meaning. The books stood out on the wall: he saw the cream-coloured panels; a bunch of poppies in a blue vase. The last of the strokes had sounded. He gave a sigh and rose from the table.

He stood by the window again. It was raining, but the whiteness had gone. Save for a wet leaf shining here and there, the garden was all dark now—the yellow mound of the flowering tree had vanished. The college buildings lay round the garden in a low couched mass, here red-stained, here yellow-stained, where lights burnt behind curtains; and there lay the chapel, huddling its bulk against the sky which, because of the rain, seemed to tremble slightly. But it was no longer silent. He listened; there was no sound in particular; but, as he stood looking out, the building hummed with life. There was a sudden roar of laughter; then the tinkle of a piano; then a nondescript clatter and chatter—of china partly; then again the sound of rain falling, and the gutters chuckling and burbling as they sucked up the water. He turned back into the room.

It had grown chilly; the fire was almost out; only a little red glowed under the grey ash. Opportunely he remembered his father's gift—the wine that had come that morning. He went to the side table and poured himself out a glass of port. As he raised it against the light he smiled. He saw again his father's hand with two smooth knobs instead of fingers holding the glass, as he always held the glass, to the light before he drank.

"You can't drive a bayonet through a chap's body in cold blood," he remembered him saying.

"And you can't go in for an exam. without drinking," said Edward. He hesitated; he held the glass to the light in imitation of his father. Then he sipped. He set the glass on the table in front of him. He turned again to the *Antigone*. He read; then he sipped; then he read; then he sipped again. A soft glow spread over his spine at the nape of his neck. The wine seemed to press open little dividing doors in his brain. And whether it was the wine or the words or both, a luminous shell formed, a purple fume, from which out stepped a Greek girl; yet she was English. There she stood among the marble and the asphodel, yet there she was among the Morris wall-papers and the cabinets—his cousin Kitty, as he had seen her last time he dined at the lodge. She was both of them—Antigone and Kitty; here in the book; there in the room; lit up, risen, like a purple flower. No, he exclaimed, not in the least like a flower! For if ever a girl held herself upright, lived, laughed and breathed, it was Kitty, in the white and blue dress that she had worn last time he dined at the

Lodge. He crossed to the window. Red squares showed through the trees. There was a party at the Lodge. Who was she talking to? What was she saying? He went back to the table.

"Oh, damn!" he exclaimed, prodding the paper with his pencil. The point broke. Then there was a tap at the door, a sliding tap, not a commanding tap, the tap of one who passes, not of one who comes in. He went and opened the door. There on the stair above loomed the figure of a huge young man who was leaning over the banisters. "Come in," said Edward.

The huge young man came slowly down the stairs. He was very large. His eyes, which were prominent, became apprehensive at the sight of the books on the table. He looked at the books on the table. They were Greek. But there was wine after all.

Edward poured out wine. Beside Gibbs he looked what Eleanor called 'finicky.' He felt the contrast himself. The hand with which he lifted his glass was like a girl's beside Gibbs's great red paw. Gibbs's hand was burnt bright scarlet; it was like a piece of raw meat.

Hunting was the subject they had in common. They talked about hunting. Edward leant back and let Gibbs do the talking. It was all very pleasant, listening to Gibbs, riding through these English lanes. He was talking about cubbing in September; and a raw but handy hack. He was saying, "You remember that farm on the right as you go up to Stapleys? and the pretty girl?"—he winked—"worse luck, she's married to a keeper." He was saying—Edward watched him gulping down his port—how he wished this damned summer were over. Then, again, he was telling the old story about the spaniel bitch. "You'll come and stop with us in September," he was saying when the door opened so silently that Gibbs did not hear it, and in glided another man—quite another man.

It was Ashley who came in. He was the very opposite of Gibbs. He was neither tall nor short, neither dark nor fair. But he was not negligible—far from it. It was partly the way he moved, as if chair and table rayed out some influence which he could feel by means of some invisible antennae, or whiskers, like a cat. Now he sank down, cautiously, gingerly, and looked at the table and half read a line in a book. Gibbs stopped in the middle of his sentence.

"Hullo, Ashley," he said rather curtly. He stretched out and poured himself another glass of the Colonel's port. Now the decanter was empty.

"Sorry," he said, glancing at Ashley.

"Don't open another bottle for me," said Ashley quickly. His voice sounded a little squeaky, as if he were ill at ease.

"Oh, but we shall want some more too," said Edward casually. He went into the dining-room to fetch it.

"Damned awkward," he reflected as he stooped among the bottles. It meant, he reflected grimly as he chose his bottle, another row with Ashley, and he had had two rows with Ashley about Gibbs already this term.

He went back with the bottle and sat down on a low stool between them. He uncorked the wine and poured it out. They both looked at him, as he sat between them, admiringly. The vanity, which Eleanor always laughed at in her brother, was flattered. He liked to feel their eyes on him. And yet he was at his ease with both of them, he thought; the thought pleased him; he could talk hunting with Gibbs and books with Ashley. But Ashley could only talk about books, and Gibbs—he smiled— could only talk about girls. Girls and horses. He poured out three glasses of wine.

Ashley sipped gingerly, and Gibbs, with his great red hands on the glass, gulped rather. They talked about races; then they talked about examinations. Then Ashley, glancing at the books on the table, said:

"And what about you?"

"I've not the ghost of a chance," said Edward. His indifference was affected. He pretended to despise examinations; but it was pretence. Gibbs was taken in by him; but Ashley saw through him. He often caught Edward out in small vanities like this;

but they only served to endear him the more. How beautiful he looks, he was thinking: there he sat between them with the light falling on the top of his fair hair; like a Greek boy; strong; yet in some way, weak, needing his protection.

He ought to be rescued from brutes like Gibbs, he thought savagely. For how Edward could tolerate that clumsy brute, he thought looking at him, who always seemed to smell of beer and horses (he was listening to him) Ashley could not conceive. As he came in he had caught the tail of an infuriating sentence— of a sentence that seemed to show that they had made some plan together.

"Well, then, I'll see Storey about that hack," Gibbs was saying now, as if he were finishing some private talk that they had been having before he came in. A spasm of jealousy ran through Ashley. To hide it, he stretched out his hand and took up a book that lay open on the table. He pretended to read it.

He did it to insult him, Gibbs felt. Ashley, he knew, thought him a great hulking brute; the dirty little swine came in, spoilt the talk, and then began to give himself airs at Gibbs's expense. Very well; he had been going to go; now he would stay; he would twist his tail for him—he knew how. He turned to Edward and went on talking.

"You won't mind pigging it," he said. "My people will be up in Scotland."

Ashley turned a page viciously. They would be alone then. Edward began to relish the situation; he played up to it maliciously.

"All right," he said. "But you'll have to see I don't make a fool of myself," he added.

"Oh, it'll only be cubbing," said Gibbs. Ashley turned another page. Edward glanced at the book. It was being held upside down. But as he glanced at Ashley he caught his head against the panels and the poppies. How civilised he looked, he thought, compared with Gibbs; and how ironical. He respected him immensely. Gibbs had lost his glamour. There he was, telling the same old story of the spaniel bitch all over again. There would be a devil's own row tomorrow, he thought, and glanced surreptitiously at his watch. It was past eleven; and he must do an hour's work before breakfast. He swallowed down the last drops of his wine, stretched himself, yawned ostentatiously and rose.

"I'm off to bed," he said. Ashley looked at him appealingly. Edward could torture him horribly. Edward began unbuttoning his waistcoat; he had a perfect figure, Ashley thought, looking at him, standing between them.

"But don't you hurry" said Edward, yawning again. "Finish your drinks." He smiled at the thought of Ashley and Gibbs finishing their drinks together.

"There's plenty more in there if you want it." He indicated the next room and left them.

"Let 'em fight it out together," he thought as he shut the bedroom door. His own fight would come soon enough; he knew that from the look on Ashley's face. He was infernally jealous. He began to undress. He put his money methodically in two heaps on either side of the looking-glass, for he was a little near about money; folded his waistcoat carefully on a chair; then glanced at himself in the looking-glass, and brushed his crest up with the half-conscious gesture that irritated his sister. Then he listened.

A door slammed outside. One of them had gone—either Gibbs or Ashley. But one, he rather thought, was still there. He listened intently. He heard someone moving about in the sitting-room. Very quickly, very firmly, he turned the key in the door. A moment later the handle moved.

"Edward!" said Ashley. His voice was low and controlled.

Edward made no answer.

"Edward!" said Ashley, rattling the handle.

The voice was sharp and appealing.

"Good-night," said Edward sharply. He listened. There was a pause. Then he heard the door shut. Ashley was gone.

"Lord! What a row there'll be tomorrow," said Edward, going to the window and looking out at the rain that was still falling.

The party at the Lodge was over. The ladies stood in the doorway in their flowing gowns, and looked up at the sky from which a gentle rain was falling.

"Is that a nightingale?" said Mrs Larpent, hearing a bird twitter in the bushes. Then old Chuffy—the great Dr. Andrews—standing slightly behind her with his domed head exposed to the drizzle and his hirsute, powerful but not prepossessing countenance turned upward, gave a roar of laughter. It was a thrush, he said. The laughter was echoed back like a hyena laughing from the stone walls. Then, with a wave of the hand dictated by centuries of tradition, Mrs Larpent drew back her foot, as if she had encroached upon one of the chalk marks which decorate academic lintels and, signifying that Mrs Lathom, wife of the Divinity professor, should precede her, they passed out into the rain.

In the long drawing-room at the Lodge they were all standing up.

"I'm so glad Chuffy—Dr. Andrews—came up to your expectations," Mrs Malone was saying in her courteous manner. As residents they called the great Doctor "Chuffy"; he was Dr. Andrews to American visitors.

The other guests had gone. But the Howard Fripps, the Americans, were staying in the house. Mrs Howard Fripp was saying that Dr. Andrews had been perfectly charming to her. And her husband, the Professor, was saying something equally polite to the Master. Kitty, the daughter, standing a little in the background, wished that they would get it over and come to bed. But she had to stand there until her mother gave the signal for them to move.

"Yes, I never knew Chuffy in better form," her father continued, implying a compliment to the little American lady who had made such a conquest. She was small and vivacious, and Chuffy liked ladies to be small and vivacious.

"I adore his books," she said in her queer nasal voice.

"But I never expected to have the pleasure of sitting next him at dinner."

Did you really like the way he spits when he talks? Kitty wondered, looking at her. She was extraordinarily pretty and gay. All the other women had looked dowdy and dumpy beside her, except her mother. For Mrs Malone, standing by the fireplace with her foot on the fender, with her crisp white hair curled stiffly, never looked in the fashion or out of it. Mrs Fripp, on the contrary, looked in the fashion.

And yet they laughed at her, Kitty thought. She had caught the Oxford ladies lifting their eyebrows at some of Mrs Fripp's American phrases. But Kitty liked her American phrases; they were so different from what she was used to. She was American, a real American; but nobody would have taken her husband for an American, Kitty thought, looking at him. He might have been any professor, from any University, she thought, with his distinguished wrinkled face, his goatee beard and the black ribbon of his eyeglass crossing his shirt-front as if it were some foreign order. He spoke without any accent—at least without any American accent. Yet he too was different somehow. She had dropped her handkerchief. He stooped at once and gave it her with a bow that was almost too courteous—it made her shy. She bent her head and smiled at the Professor, rather shyly, as she took the handkerchief.

"Thank you so much," she said. He made her feel awkward. Beside Mrs Fripp she felt even larger than usual. Her hair, of the true Rigby red, never lay smooth as it should have done; Mrs Fripp's hair looked beautiful, glossy and tidy.

But now Mrs Malone, glancing at Mrs Fripp, said, "Well, ladies—?" and waved her hand.

There was something authoritative about her action—as if she had done it again and again; and been obeyed again and again. They moved towards the door. Tonight there was a little ceremony at the door; Professor Fripp bent very low over Mrs Malone's hand, not quite so low over Kitty's hand, and held the door wide open for them.

"He rather overdoes it," Kitty thought to herself as they passed out.

The ladies took their candles and went in single file up the wide low stairs. Portraits of former masters of Katharine's looked down on them as they mounted. The light of the candles flickered over the dark gold-framed faces as they went up stair after stair.

Now she'll stop, thought Kitty, following behind, and ask who *that* is.

But Mrs Fripp did not stop. Kitty gave her good marks for that. She compared favourably with most of their visitors, Kitty thought. She had never done the Bodleian quite so quick as she had done it that morning. Indeed, she had felt rather guilty. There were a great many more sights to be seen, had they wished it. But in less than an hour of it Mrs Fripp had turned to Kitty and had said in her fascinating, if nasal, voice:

"Well, my dear, I guess you're a bit fed-up with sights— what d'you say to an ice in that dear old bun-shop with the bow windows?"

And they had eaten ices when they ought to have been going round the Bodleian.

The procession had now reached the first landing, and Mrs Malone stopped at the door of the famous room where distinguished guests always slept when they stayed at the Lodge. She gave one look round as she held the door open.

"The bed where Queen Elizabeth did *not* sleep," she said, making the usual little joke as they looked at the great four-poster. The fire was burning; the water-jug was swaddled up like an old woman with the toothache; and the candles were lit on the dressing-table. But there was something strange about the room tonight, Kitty thought, glancing over her mother's shoulder; a dressing-gown flashed green and silver upon the bed. And on the dressing-table there were a number of little pots and jars and a large powder-puff stained pink. Could it be, was it possible, that the reason why Mrs Fripp looked so very bright and the Oxford ladies looked so very dingy was that Mrs Fripp—But Mrs Malone was saying, "You have everything you want?" with such extreme politeness that Kitty guessed that Mrs Malone too had seen the dressing-table. Kitty held out her hand. To her surprise, instead of taking it, Mrs Fripp pulled her down and kissed her.

"Thanks a thousand times for showing me all those sights," she said. "And remember, you're coming to stay with us in America," she added. For she had liked the big shy girl who had so obviously preferred eating ices to showing her the Bodleian; and she had felt sorry for her too for some reason.

"Good-night, Kitty," said her mother as she shut the door; and they touched each other perfunctorily on the cheek.

Kitty went on upstairs to her own room. She still felt the spot where Mrs Fripp had kissed her; the kiss had left a little glow on her cheek.

She shut the door. The room was very stuffy. It was a warm night, but they always shut the windows and drew the curtains. She opened the windows and drew the curtains. It was raining as usual. Arrows of silver rain crossed the dark trees in the garden. Then she kicked off her shoes. That was the worst of being so large—shoes were always too tight; white satin shoes in particular. Then she began to unhook her dress. It was difficult; there were so many hooks and all at the back; but at last the white satin dress was off and laid neatly across the chair; and then she began to brush her hair. It had been Thursday at its very worst, she reflected; sights in the morning; people for lunch; undergraduates for tea; and a dinner-party in the evening.

However, she concluded, tugging the comb through her hair, it's over . . . . it's over.

The candles flickered and then the muslin blind, blowing out in a white balloon, almost touched the flame. She opened her eyes with a start. She was standing at the open window with a light beside her in her petticoat.

"Anybody might see in," her mother had said, scolding her only the other day.

Now, she said, moving the candle to a table at the right, nobody can see in.

She began to brush her hair again. But with the light at the side instead of in front she saw her face from a different angle.

Am I pretty? she asked herself, putting down her comb and looking in the glass. Her cheek-bones were too prominent; her eyes were set too far apart. She was not pretty; no, her size was against her. What did Mrs Fripp think of me, she wondered?

She kissed me, she suddenly remembered with a start of pleasure, feeling again the glow on her cheek. She asked me to go with them in America. What fun that would be! she thought. What fun to leave Oxford and go to America! She tugged the comb through her hair, which was like a fuzz bush.

But the bells were making their usual commotion. She hated the sound of the bells; it always seemed to her a dismal sound; and then, just as one stopped, here was another beginning. They went walloping one over another, one after another, as if they would never be finished. She counted eleven, twelve, and then they went on thirteen, fourteen . . . clock repeating clock through the damp, drizzling air. It was late. She began to brush her teeth. She glanced at the calendar above the washstand and tore off Thursday and screwed it into a ball, as if she were saying "That's over! That's over!" Friday in large red letters confronted her. Friday was a good day; on Friday she had her lesson with Lucy; she was going to tea with the Robsons. "Blessed is he who has found his work" she read on the calendar. Calendars always seemed to be talking at you. She had not done her work. She glanced at a row of blue volumes, "The Constitutional History of England, by Dr. Andrews." There was a paper slip in volume three. She should have finished her chapter for Lucy; but not tonight. She was too tired tonight. She turned to the window. A roar of laughter floated out from the undergraduates' quarters.

What are they laughing at, she wondered as she stood by the window. It sounded as if they were enjoying themselves. They never laugh like that when they come to tea at the Lodge, she thought, as the laughter died away. The little man from Balliol sat twisting his fingers, twisting his fingers. He would not talk; but he would not go. Then she blew out the candle and got into bed. I rather like him, she thought, stretching out in the cool sheets, though he twists his fingers. As for Tony Ashton, she thought, turning on her pillow, I don't like him. He always seemed to be cross-examining her about Edward, whom Eleanor, she thought, calls 'Nigs'. His eyes were too close together. A bit of a barber's block, she thought. He had followed her at the picnic the other day—the picnic when the ant got into Mrs Lathom's skirts. There he was always beside her. But she didn't want to marry him. She didn't want to be a Don's wife and live in Oxford for ever. No, no, no! She yawned, turned on her pillow, and listening to a belated bell that went walloping like a slow porpoise through the thick drizzling air, yawned once more and fell asleep.

The rain fell steadily all night long, making a faint mist over the fields, chuckling and burbling in the gutters. In gardens it fell over flowering bushes of lilac and laburnum. It slipped gently over the leaden domes of libraries, and splayed out of the laughing mouths of gargoyles. It smeared the window where the Jew boy from Birmingham sat mugging up Greek with a wet towel round his head; where Dr. Malone sat up late writing another chapter in his monumental history of the college. And in the garden of the Lodge outside Kitty's window it sluiced the ancient tree under which Kings and poets had sat drinking three centuries ago, but now it was half fallen and had to be propped up by a stake in the middle.

"Umbrella, Miss?" said Hiscock, offering Kitty an umbrella as she left the house rather later than she should have left it the following afternoon. There was a chilliness in the air which made her glad, as she caught sight of a party with white and yellow frocks and cushions bound for the river, that she was not going to sit in a boat today. No parties today, she thought, no parties today. But she was late, the clock warned her.

She strode along until she came to the cheap red villas that her father disliked so much that he would always make a round to avoid them. But as it was in one of these cheap red villas that Miss Craddock lived, Kitty saw them haloed with romance. Her heart beat faster as she turned the corner by the new chapel and saw the steep steps of the house where Miss Craddock actually lived. Lucy went up those steps and down them every day; that was her window; this was her bell. The bell came out with a jerk when she pulled it; but it did not go back again, for everything was ramshackle in Lucy's house; but everything was romantic. There was Lucy's umbrella in the stand; and it too was not like other umbrellas; it had a parrot's head for a handle. But as she went up the steep shiny stairs excitement became mixed with fear: once more she had scamped her work; she had not "given her mind to it" again this week.

"She's coming!" thought Miss Craddock, holding her pen suspended. Her nose was red-tipped; there was something owl-like about the eyes, round which there was a sallow, hollow depression. There was the bell. The pen had been dipped in red ink; she had been correcting Kitty's essay. Now she heard her step on the stairs. "She's coming!" she thought with a little catch of her breath, laying down the pen.

"I'm awfully sorry, Miss Craddock," Kitty said, taking off her things and sitting down at the table. "But we had people staying in the house."

Miss Craddock brushed her hand over her mouth in a way she had when she was disappointed.

"I see," she said. "So you haven't done any work this week either."

Miss Craddock took up her pen and dipped it in the red ink.

Then she turned to the essay.

"It wasn't worth correcting," she remarked, pausing with her pen in the air.

"A child of ten would have been ashamed of it." Kitty blushed bright red.

"And the odd thing is," said Miss Craddock putting down her pen when the lesson was over, "that you've got quite an original mind."

Kitty flushed bright red with pleasure.

"But you don't use it," said Miss Craddock. "Why don't you use it?" she added, looking at her out of her fine grey eyes.

"You see, Miss Craddock," Kitty began eagerly, "my mother—"

"Hm . . . hm . . . hm . . ." Miss Craddock stopped her. Confidences were not what Dr. Malone paid her for. She got up.

"Look at my flowers," she said, feeling that she had snubbed her too severely. There was a bowl of flowers on the table; wild flowers, blue and white, stuck into a cushion of wet green moss.

"My sister sent them from the moors," she said.

"The moors?" said Kitty. "Which moors?" She stooped and touched the little flowers tenderly. How lovely she is, Miss Craddock thought; for she was sentimental about Kitty. But I will not be sentimental, she told herself.

"The Scarborough moors," she said aloud. "If you keep the moss damp but not too damp, they'll last for weeks," she added, looking at the flowers.

"Damp, but not too damp," Kitty smiled. "That's easy in Oxford, I should think. It's always raining here." She looked at the window. Mild rain was falling.

"If I lived up there, Miss Craddock—" she began, taking her umbrella. But she stopped. The lesson was over.

"You'd find it very dull," said Miss Craddock, looking at her. She was putting on her cloak. Certainly she looked very lovely, putting on her cloak.

"When I was your age," Miss Craddock continued, remembering her rôle as teacher, "I would have given my eyes to have the opportunities you have, to meet the people you meet; to know the people you know."

"Old Chuffy?" said Kitty, remembering Miss Craddock's profound admiration for that light of learning.

"You irreverent girl!" Miss Craddock expostulated. "The greatest historian of his age!"

"Well, he doesn't talk history to me," said Kitty, remembering the damp feel of a heavy hand on her knee.

She hesitated; but the lesson was over; another pupil was coming. She glanced round the room. There was a plate of oranges on the top of a pile of shiny exercise-books: a box that looked as if it contained biscuits. Was this her only room, she wondered? Did she sleep on the lumpy-looking sofa with the shawl thrown over it? There was no looking-glass, and she stuck her hat on rather to one side, thinking as she did so that Miss Craddock despised clothes.

But Miss Craddock was thinking how wonderful it was to be young and lovely and to meet brilliant men.

"I'm going to tea with the Robsons," said Kitty, holding out her hand. The girl, Nelly Robson, was Miss Craddock's favourite pupil; the only girl, she used to say, who knew what work meant.

"Are you walking?" said Miss Craddock, looking at her clothes. "It's some way, you know. Down Ringmer Road, past the gasworks."

"Yes, I'm walking," said Kitty, shaking hands.

"And I will try to work hard this week," she said, looking down on her with eyes full of love and admiration. Then she descended the steep stairs whose oilcloth shone bright with romance; and glanced at the umbrella that had a parrot for handle.

The son of the Professor, who had done it all off his own bat, "a most creditable performance", to quote Dr. Malone, was mending the hen coops in the back garden at Prestwich Terrace—a scratched up little place. Hammer, hammer, hammer, he went, fixing a board to the rotten roof. His hands

were white, unlike his father's, and long fingered too. He had no
love of doing these jobs himself. But his father mended the boots
on Sunday. Down came the hammer. He went at it, hammering
the long shiny nails that sometimes split the wood, or drove
outside. For it was rotten. He hated hens too, imbecile fowls, a
huddle of feathers, watching him out of their red beady eyes.
They scratched up the path; left little curls of feather here and
there on the beds, which were more to his fancy. But nothing
grew there. How grow flowers like other people if one kept hens?
A bell rang.

"Curse it! There's some old woman come to tea," he said,
holding his hammer suspended; and then brought it down
on the nail.

As she stood on the step, noting the cheap lace curtains and
the blue and orange glass, Kitty tried to remember what it was
that her father had said about Nelly's father. But a little maid
let her in. I'm much too large, Kitty thought, as she stood for a
moment in the room to which the maid had admitted her. It was
a small room, crowded with objects. And I'm too well dressed
she thought, looking at herself in the glass over the fireplace.
But here her friend Nelly came in. She was dumpy; over her
large grey eyes she wore steel spectacles, and her brown holland
overall seemed to increase her air of uncompromising veracity.

"We're having tea in the back room," she said, looking her up
and down. What has she been doing? Why is she dressed in an
overall? Kitty thought, following her into the room where tea
had already begun.

"Pleased to see you," said Mrs Robson formally, looking over
her shoulder. But nobody seemed in the least pleased to see her.
Two children were already eating. Slices of bread and butter
were in their hands, but they stayed the bread and butter and
stared at Kitty as she sat down.

She seemed to see the whole room at once. It was bare yet
crowded. The table was too large; there were hard green-plush

chairs; yet the table-cloth was coarse; darned in the middle; and the china was cheap with its florid red roses. The light was extraordinarily bright in her eyes. A sound of hammering came in from the garden outside. She looked at the garden; it was a scratched-up, earthy garden without flower-beds; and there was a shed at the end of the garden from which the sound of hammering came.

They're all so short too, Kitty thought, glancing at Mrs Robson. Only her shoulders came above the tea things; but her shoulders were substantial. She was a little like Bigge, the cook at the Lodge, but more formidable. She gave one brief look at Mrs Robson and then began to pull off her gloves secretly, swiftly, under the cover of the table-cloth. But why does nobody talk? she thought nervously. The children kept their eyes fixed upon her with a look of solemn amazement. Their owl-like stare went up and down over her uncompromisingly. Happily before they could express their disapproval, Mrs Robson told them sharply to go on with their tea; and the bread and butter slowly rose to their mouths again.

Why don't they say something? Kitty thought again, glancing at Nelly. She was about to speak when an umbrella grated in the hall; and Mrs Robson looked up and said to her daughter:

"There's Dad!"

Next moment in trotted a little man, who was so short that he looked as if his jacket should have been an Eton jacket, and his collar a round collar. He wore, too, a very thick watch-chain, made of silver, like a schoolboy's. But his eyes were keen and fierce, his moustache bristly, and he spoke with a curious accent.

"Pleased to see you," he said, and gripped her hand hard in his. He sat down, tucked a napkin under his chin so that it obscured his heavy silver watch-chain under its stiff white shield. Hammer, hammer, hammer came from the shed in the garden.

"Tell Jo tea's on the table," said Mrs Robson to Nelly, who had brought in a dish with a cover on it. The cover was removed. Actually they were going to eat fried fish and potatoes at tea-time, Kitty remarked.

But Mr Robson had turned his rather alarming blue eyes upon her. She expected him to say, "How is your father, Miss Malone?"

But he said:

"You're reading history with Lucy Craddock?"

"Yes," she said. She liked the way he said Lucy Craddock, as if he respected her. So many of the Dons sneered at her. She liked feeling too, as he made her feel, that she was nobody's daughter in particular.

"You're interested in history?" he said, applying himself to his fish and potatoes.

"I love it," she said. His bright blue eyes, gazing straight at her rather fiercely, seemed to make her say quite shortly what she meant.

"But I'm frightfully lazy," she added. Here Mrs Robson looked at her rather sternly, and handed her a thick slice of bread on the point of a knife.

Anyhow their taste is awful, she said by way of revenge for the snub that she felt was intended. She focussed her eyes on a picture opposite—an oily landscape in a heavy gilt frame. There was a blue and red Japanese plate on either side of it. Everything was ugly, especially the pictures.

"The moor at the back of our house," said Mr Robson, seeing her look at a picture.

It struck Kitty that the accent with which he spoke was a Yorkshire accent. In looking at the picture he had increased his accent.

"In Yorkshire?" she said. "We come from there too. My mother's family I mean," she added.

"Your mother's family?" said Mr Robson.

"Rigby," she said, and blushed slightly.

"Rigby?" said Mrs Robson, looking up.

"I wur-r-rked for a Miss Rigby before I married."

What sort of wur-r-rk had Mrs Robson done? Kitty wondered. Sam explained.

"My wife was a cook, Miss Malone, before we married," he said. Again he increased his accent as if he were proud of it. I had a great-uncle who rode in a circus, she felt inclined to say: and an Aunt who married . . . but here Mrs Robson interrupted her.

"The Hollies," she said. "Two very old ladies; Miss Ann and Miss Matilda." She spoke more gently.

"But they must be dead long ago," she concluded. For the first time she leant back in her chair and stirred her tea, just as old Snap at the farm, Kitty thought, stirred her tea round and round and round.

"Tell Jo we're not sparing the cake," said Mr Robson, cutting himself a slice of that craggy-looking object; and Nell went out of the room once more. The hammering stopped in the garden. The door opened. Kitty, who had altered the focus of her eyes to suit the smallness of the Robson family, was taken by surprise. The young man seemed immense in that little room. He was a handsome young man. He brushed his hand through his hair as came in, for a wood shaving had stuck in it.

"Our Jo," said Mrs Robson, introducing them. "Go and get the kittle, Jo," she added; and he went at once as if he were used to it. When he came back with the kettle, Sam began chaffing him about a hencoop.

"It takes you a long time, my son, to mend a hencoop," he said. There was some family joke which Kitty could not follow about mending boots and hencoops. She watched him eating steadily under his father's banter. He was not Eton or Harrow, or Rugby or Winchester; or reading or rowing. He reminded her of Alf, the farm hand up at Carter's, who had kissed her under the shadow of the haystack when she was fifteen, and old Carter loomed up leading a bull with a ring through its nose and said "Stop that!" She looked down again. She would rather like Jo to kiss her; better than Edward, she thought to herself suddenly. She remembered her own appearance, which she had forgotten. She liked him. Yes, she liked them all very much, she told herself; very much indeed. She felt as if she had given her nurse the slip and run off on her own.

Then the children began scrambling down off their chairs; the meal was over. She began to fish under the table for her gloves.

"These them?" said Jo, picking them up off the floor. She took them and crumpled them up in her hand.

He cast one quick sulky look at her as she stood in the doorway. She's a stunner, he said to himself, but my word, she gives herself airs!

Mrs Robson ushered her into the little room where, before tea, she had looked in the glass. It was crowded with objects. There were bamboo tables; velvet books with brass hinges; marble gladiators askew on the mantelpiece and innumerable pictures. . . . But Mrs Robson, with a gesture that was exactly like Mrs Malone's when she pointed to the Gainsborough that was not quite certainly a Gainsborough, was displaying a huge silver salver with an inscription.

"The salver my husband's pupils gave him," Mrs Robson began, pointing to the inscription. Kitty began to spell out the inscription.

"And this . . ." said Mrs Robson, when she had done, pointing to a document framed like a text on the wall.

But here Sam, who stood in the background fiddling with his watch-chain, stepped forward and indicated with his stubby forefinger the picture of an old woman looking rather over life size in the photographer's chair.

"My mother," he said and stopped. He gave a queer little chuckle.

"Your mother?" Kitty repeated, stooping to look. The unwieldy old lady, posed in all the stiffness of her best clothes, was plain in the extreme. And yet Kitty felt that admiration was expected.

"You're very like her, Mr Robson," was all she could find to say. Indeed they had something of the same sturdy look; the same piercing eyes; and they were both very plain. He gave an odd little chuckle.

"Glad you think so," he said. "Brought us all up. Not one of them a patch on her though." He gave his odd little chuckle again.

Then he turned to his daughter, who had come in and was standing there in her overall.

"Not a patch on her," he repeated, pinching Nell on the shoulder. As she stood there with her father's hand on her shoulder under the portrait of her grandmother, a sudden rush of self-pity came over Kitty. If she had been the daughter of people like the Robsons, she thought; if she had lived in the north—but it was clear they wanted her to go. Nobody ever sat down in this room. They were all standing up. Nobody pressed her to stay. When she said that she must go, they all came out into the little hall with her. They were all about to go on with what they were doing, she felt. Nell was about to go into the kitchen and wash up the tea things; Jo was about to return to his hencoops; the children were about to be put to bed by their mother; and Sam—what was he about to do? She looked at him standing there with his heavy watch-chain, like a schoolboy's. You are the nicest man I have ever met, she thought, holding out her hand.

"Pleased to have made your acquaintance," said Mrs Robson in her stately way.

"Hope you'll come again soon," said Mr Robson, grasping her hand very hard.

"Oh, I should love to!" she exclaimed, pressing their hands as hard as she could. Did they know how much she admired them? she wanted to say. Would they accept her in spite of her hat and her gloves? she wanted to ask. But they were all going off to their work. And I am going home to dress for dinner, she thought as she walked down the little front steps, pressing her pale kid gloves in her hands.

The sun was shining again; the damp pavements gleamed; a gust of wind tossed up the wet branches of the almond trees in the villa gardens; little twigs and tufts of blossom whirled onto the pavement and stuck there. As she stood still for a second at a crossing she too seemed to be tossed aloft out of her usual surroundings. She forgot where she was. The sky, blown into a blue open space, seemed to be looking down not here upon streets and houses, but upon open country, where the wind brushed the moors, and sheep, with grey fleeces ruffled, sheltered under stone walls. She could almost see the moors brighten and darken as the clouds passed over them.

But then in two strides the unfamiliar street became the street she had always known. Here she was again in the paved alley; there were the old curiosity shops with their blue china and their brass warming-pans; and next moment she was out in the famous crooked street with all the domes and steeples. The sun lay in broad stripes across it. There were the cabs and the awnings and the book-shops; the old men in black gowns billowing; the young women in pink and blue dresses flowing; and the young men in straw hats carrying cushions under their arms. But for a moment all seemed to her obsolete, frivolous, inane. The usual undergraduate in cap and gown with books under his arm looked silly. And the portentous old men with their exaggerated features, looked like gargoyles, carved, mediaeval, unreal. They were all like people dressed up and acting parts, she thought. Now she stood at her own door and waited for Hiscock, the butler, to take his feet off the fender and waddle upstairs. Why can't you talk like a human being? she thought, as he took her umbrella and mumbled his usual remark about the weather.

Slowly, as if a weight had got into her feet too, she went upstairs, seeing through open windows and open doors the smooth lawn, the recumbent tree and the faded chintzes. Down she sank on the edge of her bed. It was very stuffy. A bluebottle buzzed round and round; a lawn mower squeaked in the garden below. Far away pigeons were cooing—Take two coos, Taffy. Take two coos. Tak. . . . Her eyes half shut. It seemed to her that she was sitting on the terrace of an Italian inn. There was her

71

father pressing gentians on to a rough sheet of blotting paper. The lake below lapped and dazzled. She plucked up courage and said to her father: "Father . . ." He looked up very kindly over his spectacles. He held the little blue flower between his thumb and finger. "I want . . ." she began slipping off the balustrade upon which she was sitting. But here a bell struck. She rose and crossed to the washing-table. What would Nell think of this, she thought, tilting up the beautifully polished brass jug and dipping her hands in the hot water. Another bell tolled. She crossed to the dressing-table. The air from the garden outside was full of murmurings and cooings. Wood shavings, she said as she took up her brush and comb—he had wood shavings in his hair. A servant passed with a pile of tin dishes on his head. The pigeons were cooing Take two coos, Taffy. Take two coos. . . . But there was the dinner bell. In a moment she had pinned her hair up, hooked her dress on, and ran down the slippery stairs, sliding her palm along the banisters as she used to do when she was a child in a hurry. And there they all were.

Her parents were standing in the hall. A tall man was with them. His gown was thrown back and one last ray of sunshine lit up his genial, authoritative face. Who was he? Kitty could not remember.

"My word!" he exclaimed, looking up at her with admiration.

"It *is* Kitty, isn't it?" he said. Then he took her hand and pressed it.

"How you've grown!" he exclaimed. He looked at her as if he were looking not at her but at his own past.

"You don't remember me?" he added.

"Chingachgook!" she exclaimed, recalling some childish memory.

"But he is now Sir Richard Norton," said her mother, giving him a proud little pat on the shoulder; and they turned away, for the gentlemen were dining in Hall.

72

It was dull fish, Kitty thought; the plates were half cold. It was stale bread she thought, cut in meagre little squares; the colour, the gaiety of Prestwich Terrace was still in her eyes, in her ears. She granted, as she looked round, the superiority of the Lodge china and silver; and the Japanese plates and the picture had been hideous; but this dining-room with its hanging creepers and its vast cracked canvases was so dark. At Prestwich Terrace the room was full of light; the sound of hammer, hammer, hammer still rang in her ears. She looked out at the fading greens in the garden. For the thousandth time she echoed her childish wish that the tree would either lie down or stand up instead of doing neither. It was not actually raining, but gusts of whiteness seemed to blow about the garden as the wind stirred the thick leaves on the laurels.

"Didn't you notice it?" Mrs Malone suddenly appealed to her.

"What, Mama?" Kitty asked. She had not been attending.

"The odd taste in the fish," said her mother.

"I don't think I did," she said; and Mrs Malone went on talking to the butler. The plates were changed; another dish was brought in. But Kitty was not hungry. She bit one of the green sweets that were provided for her, and then the modest dinner, retrieved for the ladies from the relics of last night's party, was over and she followed her mother into the drawing-room.

It was too big when they were alone, but they always sat there. The pictures seemed to be looking down at the empty chairs, and the empty chairs seemed to be looking up at the pictures. The old gentleman who had ruled the college over a hundred years ago seemed to vanish in the daytime, but he came back when the lamps were lit. The face was placid, solid and smiling, and singularly like Dr. Malone, who, had a frame been set round him, might have hung over the fireplace too.

"It's nice to have a quiet evening once in a way," Mrs Malone was saying, "though the Fripps . . ." Her voice tailed off as she put on her spectacles and took up *The Times*. This was her moment of relaxation and recuperation after the day's work.

She suppressed a little yawn as she glanced up and down the columns of the newspaper.

"What a charming man he was," she observed casually, as she looked at the births and deaths. "One would hardly have taken him for an American."

Kitty recalled her thoughts. She was thinking of the Robsons. Her mother was talking about the Fripps.

"And I liked her too," she said rashly. "Wasn't she lovely?"

"Hum—m—m. A little overdressed for my taste," said Mrs Malone dryly. "And that accent—" she went on, looking through the paper, "I sometimes hardly understood what she said."

Kitty was silent. Here they differed; as they did about so many things.

Suddenly Mrs Malone looked up:

"Yes, just what I was saying to Bigge this morning," she said, laying down the paper.

"What, Mama?" said Kitty.

"This man—in the leading article," said Mrs Malone. She touched it with her finger.

"'With the best flesh, fish and fowl in the world,'" she read, "'we shall not be able to turn them to account because we have none to cook them'—what I was saying to Bigge this morning." She gave her quick little sigh. Just when one wanted to impress people, like those Americans, something went wrong. It had been the fish this time. She foraged for her work things, and Kitty took up the paper.

"It's the leading article," said Mrs Malone. That man almost always said the very thing that she was thinking, which comforted her, and gave her a sense of security in a world which seemed to her to be changing for the worse.

"'Before the rigid and now universal enforcement of school attendance?'" Kitty read out.

"Yes. That's it," said Mrs Malone, opening her work-box and looking for her scissors.

"'. . . the children saw a good deal of cooking which, poor as it was, yet gave them some taste and inkling of knowledge. They now see nothing and they do nothing but read, write, sum, sew or knit,'" Kitty read out.

"Yes, yes," said Mrs Malone. She unrolled the long strip of embroidery upon which she was working a design of birds pecking at fruit copied from a tomb at Ravenna. It was for the spare bedroom.

The leading article bored Kitty with its pompous fluency. She searched the paper for some little piece of news that might interest her mother. Mrs Malone liked someone to talk to her or read aloud to her as she worked. Night after night her embroidery served to weave the after-dinner talk into a pleasant harmony. One said something and stitched; looked at the design, chose another coloured silk, and stitched again. Sometimes Dr Malone read poetry aloud—Pope: Tennyson. Tonight she would have liked Kitty to talk to her. But she was becoming increasingly conscious of difficulty with Kitty. Why? She glanced at her. What was wrong? she wondered. She gave her quick little sigh.

Kitty turned over the large pages. Sheep had the fluke; Turks wanted religious liberty; there was the General Election.

"Mr Gladstone—" she began.

Mrs Malone had lost her scissors. It annoyed her.

"Who can have taken them again?" she began. Kitty went down on the floor to look for them. Mrs Malone ferreted in the work-box; then she plunged her hand into the fissure between the cushion and the chair frame and brought up not only the scissors but also a little mother-of-pearl paper-knife that had been missing for ever so long. The discovery annoyed her. It proved Ellen never shook up the cushions properly.

"Here they are, Kitty," she said. They were silent. There was always some constraint between them now.

"Did you enjoy your party at the Robsons', Kitty?" she asked, resuming her embroidery. Kitty did not answer. She turned the paper.

"There's been an experiment," she said. "An experiment with electric light. 'A brilliant light,'" she read, "'was seen to shoot forth suddenly shooting out a profound ray across the water to the Rock. Everything was lit up as if by daylight.'" She paused. She saw the bright light from the ships on the drawing-room chair. But here the door opened and Hiscock came in with a note on a salver.

Mrs Malone took it and read it in silence.

"No answer," she said. From the tone of her mother's voice Kitty knew that something had happened. She sat holding the note in her hand. Hiscock shut the door.

"Rose is dead!" said Mrs Malone. "Cousin Rose."

The note lay open on her knee.

"It's from Edward," she said.

"Cousin Rose is dead?" said Kitty. A moment before she had been thinking of a bright light on a red rock. Now everything looked dingy. There was a pause. There was silence. Tears stood in her mother's eyes.

"Just when the children most wanted her," she said, sticking the needle into her embroidery. She began to roll it up very slowly. Kitty folded *The Times* and laid it on a little table, slowly, so that it should not crackle. She had only seen Cousin Rose once or twice. She felt awkward.

"Fetch me my engagement book," said her mother at last. Kitty brought it.

"We must put off our dinner on Monday," said Mrs Malone, looking through her engagements.

"And the Lathoms' party on Wednesday," Kitty murmured, looking over her mother's shoulder.

"We can't put off everything," said her mother sharply, and Kitty felt rebuked.

But there were notes to be written. She wrote them at her mother's dictation.

Why is she so ready to put off all our engagements? thought Mrs Malone, watching her write. Why doesn't she enjoy going out with me any more? She glanced through the notes that her daughter brought her.

"Why don't you take more interest in things here, Kitty?" she said irritably, pushing the letters away.

"Mama, dear—" Kitty began, deprecating the usual argument.

"But what is it you want to do?" her mother persisted. She had put away her embroidery; she was sitting upright, she was looking rather formidable.

"Your father and I only want you to do what you want to do," she continued.

"Mama, dear—" Kitty repeated.

"You could help your father if it bores you helping me," said Mrs Malone. "Papa told me the other day that you never come to him now." She referred, Kitty knew, to his history of the college. He had suggested that she should help him. Again she saw the ink flowing—she had made an awkward brush with her arm— over five generations of Oxford men, obliterating hours of her father's exquisite penmanship; and could hear him say with his usual courteous irony, "Nature did not intend you to be a scholar, my dear," as he applied the blotting-paper.

"I know," she said guiltily. "I haven't been to Papa lately. But then there's always something—" She hesitated.

"Naturally," said Mrs Malone, "with a man in your father's position . . ." Kitty sat silent. They both sat silent. They both disliked this petty bickering; they both detested these recurring scenes; and yet they seemed inevitable. Kitty got up, took the letters she had written and put them in the hall.

What does she want? Mrs Malone asked herself, looking up at the picture without seeing it. When I was her age . . . she thought, and smiled. How well she remembered sitting at home on a spring evening like this up in Yorkshire, miles from anywhere. You could hear the beat of a horse's hoof on the road miles away. She could remember flinging up her bedroom window and looking down on the dark shrubs in the garden and crying out, "Is this life?" And in the winter there was the snow.

She could still hear the snow flopping off the trees in the garden. And here was Kitty, living in Oxford, in the midst of everything.

Kitty came back into the drawing-room and yawned very slightly. She raised her hand to her face with an unconscious gesture of fatigue that touched her mother.

"Tired, Kitty?" she said. "It's been a long day; you look pale."

"And you look tired too," said Kitty.

The bells came pushing forth one after another, one on top of another, through the damp, heavy air.

"Go to bed, Kitty," said Mrs Malone. "There! It's striking ten."

"But aren't you coming too, Mama?" said Kitty, standing beside her chair.

"Your father won't be back just yet," said Mrs Malone, putting on her spectacles again.

Kitty knew it was useless to try to persuade her. It was part of the mysterious ritual of her parents' lives. She bent down and gave her mother the little perfunctory peck that was the only sign they ever gave each other outwardly of their affection. Yet they were very fond of each other; yet they always quarrelled.

"Good-night, and sleep well," said Mrs Malone.

"I don't like to see your roses fade," she added, putting her arm round her for once in a way.

She sat still after Kitty had gone. Rose is dead, she thought—Rose who was about her own age. She read the note again. It was from Edward. And Edward, she mused, is in love with Kitty, but I don't know that I want her to marry him, she thought, taking up her needle. No, not Edward. . . . There was young Lord Lasswade. . . . That would be a nice marriage, she thought. Not that I want her to be rich, not that I care about rank, she thought, threading her needle. No, but he could give her what she wants. . . . What was it? . . . Scope, she decided, beginning to stitch. Then again her thoughts turned to Rose. Rose was dead. Rose who was about her own age. That must have been the first time he proposed to her, she thought, the day we had the picnic on the moors. It was a spring day. They were sitting on the grass. She could see Rose wearing a black hat with a cock's feather in it over her bright red hair. She could still see her blush and look extremely pretty when Abel rode up, much to their surprise— he was stationed at Scarborough—the day they had the picnic on the moors.

The house at Abercorn Terrace was very dark. It smelt strongly of spring flowers. For some days now wreaths had been piled one on top of another on the hall table. In the dimness— all the blinds were drawn—the flowers gleamed; and the hall smelt with the amorous intensity of a hot-house. Wreath after wreath, they kept arriving. There were lilies with broad bars of gold in them; others with spotted throats sticky with honey; white tulips, white lilac—flowers of all kinds, some with petals as thick as velvet, others transparent, paper-thin; but all white, and clubbed together, head to head, in circles, in ovals, in crosses so that they scarcely looked like flowers. Black-edged cards were attached to them, "With deep sympathy from Major and Mrs Brand"; "With love and sympathy from General and Mrs Elkin"; "For dearest Rose from Susan." Each card had a few words written on it.

Even now with the hearse at the door the bell rang; a messenger boy appeared bearing more lilies. He raised his cap, as he stood in the hall, for men were lurching down the stairs carrying the coffin. Rose, in deep black, prompted by her nurse, stepped forward and dropped her little bunch of violets on the coffin. But it slipped off as it swayed down the brilliant sunlit steps on the slanting shoulders of Whiteleys' men. The family followed after.

It was an uncertain day, with passing shadows and darting rays of bright sunshine. The funeral started at a walking pace. Delia, getting into the second carriage with Milly and Edward, noticed that the houses opposite had their blinds drawn in sympathy, but a servant peeped. The others, she noticed, did not seem to see her; they were thinking of their mother. When they got into the main road the pace quickened, for the drive to the cemetery was a long one. Through the slit of the blind, Delia noticed dogs playing; a beggar singing; men raising their hats as the hearse passed them. But by the time their own carriage passed, the hats were on again. Men walked briskly and unconcernedly along the pavement. The shops were already gay with spring clothing; women paused and looked in at the windows. But they would have to wear nothing but black all the summer, Delia thought, looking at Edward's coal-black trousers.

They scarcely spoke, or only in little formal sentences, as if they were already taking part in the ceremony. Somehow their relations had changed. They were more considerate, and a little important too, as if their mother's death had laid new responsibilities on them. But the others knew how to behave; it was only she who had to make an effort. She remained outside, and so did her father, she thought. When Martin suddenly burst out laughing at tea, and then stopped and looked guilty, she felt—that is what Papa would do, that is what I should do if we were honest.

She glanced out of the window again. Another man raised his hat—a tall man, a man in a frock-coat, but she would not allow herself to think of Mr Parnell until the funeral was over.

At last they reached the cemetery. As she took her place in the little group behind the coffin and walked up the church, she was relieved to find that she was overcome by some generalised and solemn emotion. People stood up on both sides of the church and she felt their eyes on her. Then the service began. A clergyman, a cousin, read it. The first words struck out with a rush of extraordinary beauty. Delia, standing behind her father, noticed how he braced himself and squared his shoulders.

"I am the resurrection and the life."

Pent up as she had been all these days in the half-lit house which smelt of flowers, the outspoken words filled her with glory. This she could feel genuinely; this was something that she said herself. But then, as Cousin James went on reading, something slipped. The sense was blurred. She could not follow with her reason. Then in the midst of the argument came another burst of familiar beauty. "And fade away suddenly like the grass, in the morning it is green, and groweth up; but in the evening it is cut down, dried up, and withered." She could feel the beauty of that. Again it was like music; but then Cousin James seemed to hurry, as if he did not altogether believe what he was saying. He seemed to pass from the known to the unknown; from what he believed to what he did not believe; even his voice altered. He looked clean, he looked starched and ironed like his robes. But what did he mean by what he was saying? She gave it up. Either one understood or one did not understand, she thought. Her mind wandered.

But I will not think of him, she thought, seeing a tall man who stood beside her on a platform and raised his hat, until it's over. She fixed her eyes upon her father. She watched him dab a great white pocket-handkerchief to his eyes and put it in his pocket; then he pulled it out and dabbed his eyes with it again. Then the voice stopped; he put his handkerchief finally in his pocket; and again they all formed up, the little group of the family, behind the coffin and again the dark people on either side rose, and watched them and let them go first and followed after.

It was a relief to feel the soft damp air blowing its leafy smell in her face again. But again now that she was out of doors, she began to notice things. She noticed how the black funeral horses were pawing the ground; they were scraping little pits with their hooves in the yellow gravel. She remembered hearing that funeral horses came from Belgium and were very vicious. They looked vicious she thought; their black necks were flecked with foam—but she recalled herself. They went straggling in ones and twos along a path until they reached a fresh mound

81

of yellow earth heaped beside a pit; and there again she noticed how the grave-diggers stood at a little distance, rather behind, with their spades.

There was a pause; people kept on arriving and took up their positions, some a little higher, some a little lower. She observed a poor-looking shabby woman prowling on the outskirts, and tried to think whether she were some old servant, but she could not put a name to her. Her Uncle Digby, her father's brother, stood directly opposite her, with his top-hat held like some sacred vessel between his hands, the image of grave decorum. Some of the women were crying; but not the men; the men had one pose; the women had another, she observed. Then it all began again. The splendid gust of music blew through them—"Man that is born of a woman": the ceremony had renewed itself; once more they were grouped, united. The family pressed a little closer to the graveside and looked fixedly at the coffin which lay with its polish and its brass handles there in the earth to be buried for ever. It looked too new to be buried for ever. She stared down into the grave. There lay her mother; in that coffin—the woman she had loved and hated so. Her eyes dazzled. She was afraid that she might faint; but she must look; she must feel; it was the last chance that was left her. Earth dropped on the coffin; three pebbles fell on the hard shiny surface; and as they dropped she was possessed by a sense of something everlasting; of life mixing with death, of death becoming life. For as she looked she heard the sparrows chirp quicker and quicker; she heard wheels in the distance sound louder and louder; life came closer and closer. . . .

"We give thee hearty thanks," said the voice, "for that it has pleased thee to deliver this our sister out of the miseries of this sinful world—"

What a lie! she cried to herself. What a damnable lie! He had robbed her of the one feeling that was genuine; he had spoilt her one moment of understanding.

She looked up. She saw Morris and Eleanor side by side; their faces were blurred; their noses were red; the tears were running down them. As for her father he was so stiff and so rigid that she had a convulsive desire to laugh aloud. Nobody can feel like that, she thought. He's overdoing it. None of us feel anything at all, she thought: we're all pretending.

Then there was a general movement; the attempt at concentration was over. People strolled off this way and that; there was no attempt now to form into a procession; little groups came together; people shook hands rather furtively, among the graves, and even smiled.

"How good of you to come!" said Edward, shaking hands with old Sir James Graham, who gave him a little pat on the shoulder. Ought she to go and thank him too? The graves made it difficult. It was becoming a shrouded and subdued morning party among the graves. She hesitated—she did not know what she ought to do next. Her father had walked on. She looked back. The grave-diggers had come forward; they were piling the wreaths one on top of another neatly; and the prowling woman had joined them and was stooping down to read the names on the cards. The ceremony was over; rain was falling.

1891

The autumn wind blew over England. It twitched the leaves off the trees, and down they fluttered, spotted red and yellow, or sent them floating, flaunting in wide curves before they settled. In towns coming in gusts round the corners, the wind blew here a hat off; there lifted a veil high above a woman's head. Money was in brisk circulation. The streets were crowded. Upon the sloping desks of the offices near St. Paul's, clerks paused with their pens on the ruled page. It was difficult to work after the holidays. Margate, Eastbourne and Brighton had bronzed them and tanned them. The sparrows and starlings, making their discordant chatter round the eaves of St. Martin's, whitened the heads of the sleek statues holding rods or rolls of paper in Parliament Square. Blowing behind the boat train, the wind ruffled the channel, tossed the grapes in Provence, and made the lazy fisher boy, who was lying on his back in his boat in the Mediterranean, roll over and snatch a rope.

But in England, in the North, it was cold. Kitty, Lady Lasswade, sitting on the terrace beside her husband and his spaniel, drew the cloak round her shoulders. She was looking at the hill top, where the snuffer-shaped monument raised by the old Earl made a mark for ships at sea. There was mist on the woods. Near at hand the stone ladies on the terrace had scarlet flowers in their urns. Thin blue smoke drifted across the flaming dahlias in the long beds that went down to the river. "Burning weeds," she said aloud. Then there was a tap on the window, and her little boy in a pink frock stumbled out, holding his spotted horse.

In Devonshire where the round red hills and the steep valleys

84

hoarded the sea air leaves were still thick on the trees—too thick, Hugh Gibbs said at breakfast. Too thick for shooting, he said, and Milly, his wife, left him to go to his meeting. With her basket on her arm she walked down the well-kept crazy pavement with the swaying movement of a woman with child. There hung the yellow pears on the orchard wall, lifting the leaves over them, they were so swollen. But the wasps had got at them—the skin was broken. With her hand on the fruit she paused. Pop, pop, pop sounded in the distant woods. Someone was shooting.

The smoke hung in veils over the spires and domes of the University cities. Here it choked the mouth of a gargoyle; there it clung to the walls that were peeled yellow. Edward, who was taking his brisk constitutional, noted smell, sound and colour; which suggested how complex impressions are; few poets compress enough; but there must be some line in Greek or Latin, he was thinking, which sums up the contrast,—when Mrs Lathom passed him and he raised his cap.

In the Law Courts the leaves lay dry and angular on the flagstones. Morris, remembering his childhood, shuffled his feet through them on his way to his chambers, and they scattered edgeways along the gutters. Not yet trodden down they lay in Kensington Gardens, and children, crunching the shells as they ran, scooped up a handful and scudded on through the mist down the avenues, with their hoops.

Racing over the hills in the country the wind blew vast rings of shadow that dwindled again to green. But in London the streets narrowed the clouds; mist hung thick in the East End by the river; made the voices of men crying "Any old iron to sell, any old iron," sound distant; and in the suburbs the organs were muted. The wind blew the smoke—for in every back garden in the angle of the ivy-grown wall that still sheltered a few last geraniums, leaves were heaped up; keen fanged flames were eating them—out into the street, into windows that stood open in the drawing-room in the morning. For it was October, the birth of the year.

Eleanor was sitting at her writing-table with her pen in her hand. It's awfully queer, she thought, touching the ink-corroded patch of bristle on the back of Martin's walrus with the point of her pen, that *that* should have gone on all these years. That solid object might survive them all. If she threw it away it would still exist somewhere or other. But she never had thrown it away because it was part of other things—her mother for example. . . . She drew on her blotting paper; a dot with strokes raying out round it. Then she looked up. They were burning weeds in the back garden; there was a drift of smoke; a sharp acrid smell; and leaves were falling. A barrel organ was playing up the street. "Sur le pont d'Avignon" she hummed in time to it. How did it go?—the song Pippy used to sing as she wiped your ears with a piece of slimy flannel?

"Ron, ron, ron, et plon, plon plon," she hummed. Then the tune stopped. The organ had moved further away. She dipped her pen in the ink.

"Three times eight," she murmured, "is twenty-four," she said decidedly; wrote a figure at the bottom of the page, swept together the little red and blue books and took them to her father's study.

"Here's the housekeeper!" he said good-humouredly as she came in. He was sitting in his leather armchair reading a pinkish financial paper.

"Here's the housekeeper," he repeated, looking up over his glasses. He was getting slower and slower, she thought; and she was in a hurry. But they got on extremely well; they were almost like brother and sister. He put down his paper and went to the writing-table.

But I wish you would hurry, Papa, she thought as she watched the deliberate way in which he unlocked the drawer in which he kept his cheque-book, or I shall be late.

"Milk's very high," he said, tapping the book with the gilt cow. "Yes. It's eggs in October," she said.

As he made out the cheque with extreme deliberation she glanced round the room. It looked like an office, with its files of papers and its deed-boxes, except that horses' bits hung by the fireplace, and there was the silver cup he had won at polo. Would he sit there all the morning reading the financial papers and considering his investments, she wondered? He stopped writing.

"And where are you off to now?" he asked with his shrewd little smile.

"A Committee," she said.

"A Committee," he repeated, signing his firm heavy signature. "Well, stand up for yourself; don't be sat on, Nell." He entered a figure in the ledger.

"Are you coming with me this afternoon, Papa?" she said as he finished writing the figure. "It's Morris's case you know; at the Law Courts."

He shook his head.

"No; I've got to be in the City at three," he said.

"Then I shall see you at lunch," she said, making a movement to go. But he held up his hand. He had something to say, but he hesitated. He was getting rather heavier in the face, she noted; there were little veins in his nose; he was getting rather too red and heavy.

"I was thinking of looking in at the Digbys'," he said, at length. He got up and walked to the window. He looked out at the back garden. She fidgeted.

"How the leaves are falling!" he remarked.

"Yes," she said. "They're burning weeds."

He stood looking at the smoke for a moment.

"Burning weeds," he repeated, and stopped.

"It's Maggie's birthday," at last he came out with it. "I thought I'd take her some little present—" He paused. He meant that he wished her to buy it, she knew.

"What would you like to give her?" she asked.

"Well," he said vaguely, "something pretty you know— something she could wear."

Eleanor reflected—Maggie, her little cousin; was she seven or eight?

"A necklace? A brooch? Something like that?" she asked quickly.

"Yes, something like that," said her father, settling down in his chair again. "Something pretty, something she could wear, you know." He opened the paper and gave her a little nod. "Thank you, my dear," he said as she left the room.

On the hall table, between a silver salver laden with visiting-cards—some with their corners turned down, some large, some small—and a piece of purple plush with which the Colonel polished his top hat—lay a thin foreign envelope with "England" marked in large letters in the corner. Eleanor, running down the stairs in a hurry, swept it into her bag as she passed. Then she ran at a peculiar ambling trot down the Terrace. At the corner she stopped and looked anxiously down the road. Among the other traffic she singled out one bulky form; mercifully, it was yellow; mercifully she had caught her bus. She hailed it and climbed on top. She sighed with relief as she pulled the leather apron over her knees. All responsibility now rested with the driver. She relaxed; she breathed in the soft London air; she heard the dull London roar with pleasure. She looked along the street and relished the sight of cabs, vans and carriages all trotting past with an end in view. She liked coming back in October to the full stir of life after the summer was over. She had been staying in Devonshire with the Gibbses. That's turned out very well, she thought, thinking of her sister's marriage to Hugh Gibbs, seeing Milly with her babies. And Hugh—she smiled. He rode about on a great white horse, breaking up litters. But there are too many trees and cows and too many little hills instead of one big one, she thought. She did not like Devonshire. She was glad to be back in London, on top of the yellow bus, with her bag stuffed with papers, and everything beginning again in October. They had left the residential quarter; the houses were changing; they were turning into shops. This was her world; here she was in her element. The streets were crowded; women were swarming in and out of shops with their shopping baskets. There was something customary, rhythmical about it, she thought, like rooks swooping in a field, rising and falling.

She, too, was going to her work—she turned her watch on her wrist without looking at it. After the Committee, Duffus; after Duffus, Dickson. Then lunch; and the Law Courts . . . then lunch and the Law Courts at two-thirty, she repeated. The bus trundled along the Bayswater Road. The streets were becoming poorer and poorer.

Perhaps I oughtn't to have given the job to Duffus, she said to herself—she was thinking of Peter Street where she had built houses; the roof was leaking again; there was a bad smell in the sink. But here the omnibus stopped; people got in and out; the omnibus went on again—but it's better to give the work to a small man, she thought, looking at the huge plate-glass windows of one of the large shops, instead of going to one of those big firms. There were always small shops side by side with big shops. It puzzled her. How did the small shops manage to make a living? she wondered. But if Duffus, she began—here the omnibus stopped; she looked up; she rose "—if Duffus thinks he can bully me," she said as she went down the steps, "he'll find he's mistaken."

She walked quickly up the cinder path to the galvanised iron shed in which the meeting took place. She was late; there they were already. It was her first meeting since the holidays, and they all smiled at her. Judd even took his toothpick out of his mouth—a sign of recognition that flattered her. Here we all are again, she thought, taking her place and laying her papers on the table.

But she meant "them", not herself. She did not exist; she was not anybody at all. But there they all were—Brocket, Cufnell, Miss Sims, Ramsden, Major Porter and Mrs Lazenby. The Major preaching organisation; Miss Sims (ex-mill hand) scenting condescension; Mrs Lazenby, offering to write to her cousin Sir John, upon which Judd, the retired shopkeeper, snubbed her. She smiled as she took her seat. Miriam Parrish was reading letters. But why starve yourself, Eleanor asked as she listened. She was thinner than ever.

She looked round the room as the letters were read. There had been a dance. Festoons of red and yellow paper were slung across the ceiling. The coloured picture of the Princess of Wales had loops of yellow roses at the corners; a sea-green ribbon across her breast, a round yellow dog on her lap, and pearls slung and knotted over her shoulders. She wore an air of serenity, of indifference; a queer comment upon their divisions, Eleanor thought; something that the Lazenbys worshipped; that Miss Sims derided; that Judd looked at cocking his eyebrows, picking his teeth. If he had had a son, he had told her, he would have sent him to the Varsity. But she recalled herself. Major Porter had turned to her.

"Now, Miss Pargiter," he said, drawing her in, because they were both of the same social standing, "you haven't given us your opinion."

She pulled herself together and gave him her opinion. She had an opinion—a very definite opinion. She cleared her throat and began.

The smoke blowing through Peter Street had condensed, between the narrowness of the houses, into a fine grey veil. But the houses on either side were clearly visible. Save for two in the middle of the street, they were all precisely the same— yellow-grey boxes with slate tents on top. Nothing whatever was happening; a few children were playing in the street, two cats turned something over in the gutter with their paws. Yet a woman leaning out of the windows searched this way, that way, up and down the street as if she were raking every cranny for something to feed on. Her eyes, rapacious, greedy, like the eyes of a bird of prey, were also sulky and sleepy, as if they

had nothing to feed their hunger upon. Nothing happened—
nothing whatever. Still she gazed up and down with her indolent
dissatisfied stare. Then a trap turned the corner. She watched it.
It stopped in front of the houses opposite which, since the sills
were green, and there was a plaque with a sunflower stamped
on it over the door, were different from the others. A little man
in a tweed cap got out and rapped at the door. It was opened by
a woman who was about to have a baby. She shook her head;
looked up and down the street; then shut the door. The man
waited. The horse stood patiently with the reins drooping and
its head bent. Another woman appeared at the window, with a
white many-chinned face, and an under lip that stood out like
a ledge. Leaning out of the window side by side the two women
watched the man. He was bandy-legged; he was smoking. They
passed some remark about him together. He walked up and
down as if he were waiting for somebody. Now he threw away
his cigarette. They watched him. What would he do next? Was
he going to give his horse a feed? But here a tall woman wearing
a coat and skirt of grey tweed came round the corner hastily;
and the little man turned and touched his cap.

"Sorry I'm late," Eleanor called out, and Duffus touched his
cap with the friendly smile that always pleased her.

"That's all right, Miss Pargiter," he said. She always hoped that
he did not feel that she was the ordinary employer.

"Now we'll go over it," she said. She hated the job, but it
had to be done.

The door was opened by Mrs Toms, the downstairs lodger.

Oh dear, thought Eleanor, observing the slant of her apron,
another baby coming, after all I told her.

They went from room to room of the little house, Mrs Toms
and Mrs Grove following after. There was a crack here; a stain
there. Duffus had a foot-rule in his hand with which he tapped
the plaster. The worst of it is, she thought, as she let Mrs Toms
do the talking, that I can't help liking him. It was his Welsh

accent largely; he was a charming ruffian. He was as supple as an eel, she knew; but when he talked like that, in that sing-song, which reminded her of Welsh valleys. . . . But he had cheated her at every point. There was a hole you could poke your finger through in the plaster.

"Look at that, Mr Duffus, there—" she said, stooping and poking her finger. He was licking his pencil. She loved going to his yard with him and seeing him size up planks and bricks; she loved his technical words for things, his little hard words.

"Now we'll go upstairs," she said. He seemed to her like a fly struggling to haul itself up out of a saucer. It was touch and go with small employers like Duffus; they might haul themselves up and become the Judds of their day and send their sons to the Varsity; or on the other hand they might fall in and then—He had a wife and five children; she had seen them in the room behind the shop, playing with reels of cotton on the floor. And she always hoped that they would ask her in. . . . But here was the top floor where old Mrs Potter lay bedridden. She knocked; she called out in a loud cheerful voice, "May we come in?"

There was no answer. The old woman was stone deaf; so in they went. There she was, as usual, doing nothing whatever, propped up in the corner of her bed.

"I've brought Mr Duffus to look at your ceiling," Eleanor shouted.

The old woman looked up and began plucking with her hands like a large tousled ape. She looked at them wildly, suspiciously.

"The ceiling, Mr Duffus," said Eleanor. She pointed to a yellow stain on the ceiling. The house had only been built five years; and yet everything wanted repairing. Duffus threw open the window and leant out. Mrs Potter clutched hold of Eleanor's hand, as if she suspected that they were going to hurt her.

"We've come to look at your ceiling," Eleanor repeated very loudly. But the words conveyed nothing. The old woman went off into a whining plaint; the words ran themselves together into a chant that was half plaint, half curse. If only the Lord would take her. Every night, she said, she implored Him to let her go. All her children were dead.

"When I wake in the morning . . ." she began.

"Yes, yes, Mrs Potter," Eleanor tried to soothe her; but her hands were firmly grasped.

"I pray Him to let me go," Mrs Potter continued.

"It's the leaves in the gutter," said Duffus, popping his head in again.

"And the pain—" Mrs Potter stretched out her hands; they were knotted and grooved like the gnarled roots of a tree.

"Yes, yes," said Eleanor. "But there's a leak; it's not only the dead leaves," she said to Duffus.

Duffus put his head out again.

"We're going to make you more comfortable," Eleanor shouted to the old woman. Now she was cringing and fawning; now she had pressed her hand to her lips.

Duffus drew his head in again.

"Have you found out what's wrong?" Eleanor said to him sharply. He was entering something in his pocket-book. She longed to go. Mrs Potter was asking her to feel her shoulder. She felt her shoulder. Her hand was still grasped. There was medicine on the table; Miriam Parrish came every week. Why do we do it? she asked herself as Mrs Potter went on talking. Why do we force her to live? she asked, looking at the medicine on the table. She could stand it no longer. She withdrew her hand.

"Good-bye, Mrs Potter," she shouted. She was insincere; she was hearty. "We're going to mend your ceiling," she shouted. She shut the door. Mrs Groves waddled in advance of her to show her the sink in the scullery. A wisp of yellow hair hung down behind her dirty ears. If I had to do this every day of my life, Eleanor thought, as she followed them down into the scullery, I should become a bag of bones like Miriam; with a string of beads. . . . And what's the use of that? she thought, stooping to smell the sink in the scullery.

"Well, Duffus," she said, facing him when the inspection

was over, with the smell of drains still in her nose. "What d'you propose to do about it?"

Her anger was rising; it was his fault largely. He had swindled her. But as she stood facing him and observed his little underfed body, and how his bow tie had worked up over his collar, she felt uncomfortable.

He shuffled and squirmed; she felt that she was going to lose her temper.

"If you can't make a good job of it," she said curtly, "I shall employ somebody else." She adopted the tone of the Colonel's daughter; the upper middle-class tone that she detested. She saw him turn sullen before her eyes. But she rubbed it in.

"You ought to be ashamed of it," she told him. He was impressed she could see. "Good morning," she said briefly.

The ingratiating smile was not produced for her benefit again, she observed. But you have to bully them or else they despise you, she thought as Mrs Toms let her out, and once more she observed the slant in her apron. A crowd of children stood round staring at Duffus's pony. But none of them, she noticed, dared stroke the pony's nose.

She was late. She gave one look at the sunflower on the terracotta plaque. That symbol of her girlish sentiment amused her grimly. She had meant it to signify flowers, fields in the heart of London; but now it was cracked. She broke into her usual ambling trot. The movement seemed to break up the disagreeable crust; to jolt off the grasp of the old woman's hand that was still on her shoulder. She ran; she dodged. Shopping women got in her way. She dashed into the road waving her hand among the carts and horses. The conductor saw her, curved his arm round her and hauled her up. She had caught her bus.

She trod on the toe of a man in the corner, and pitched down between two elderly women. She was panting slightly; her hair was coming down; she was red with running. She cast a glance at her fellow-passengers. They all looked settled, elderly, as if their minds were made up. For some reason she always felt that she was the youngest person in an omnibus, but today, since she had won her scrap with Judd, she felt that she was grown up. The grey line of houses jolted up and down before her eyes as the omnibus trundled along the Bayswater Road. The shops were turning into houses; there were big houses and little houses; public houses and private houses. And here a church raised its filigree spire. Underneath were pipes, wires, drains. . . . Her lips began moving. She was talking to herself. There's always a public house, a library and a church, she was muttering.

The man on whose toe she had trodden sized her up; a well-known type; with a bag; philanthropic; well nourished; a spinster; a virgin; like all the women of her class, cold; her passions had never been touched; yet not unattractive. She was laughing. . . . Here she looked up and caught his eye. She had been talking aloud to herself in an omnibus. She must cure herself of the habit. She must wait till she brushed her teeth. But luckily the bus was stopping. She jumped out. She began to walk quickly up Melrose Place. She felt vigorous and young. She noticed everything freshly after Devonshire. She looked down the long many-pillared vista of Abercorn Terrace. The houses, with their pillars and their front gardens, all looked highly respectable; in every front room she seemed to see a parlourmaid's arm sweep over the table, laying it for luncheon. In several rooms they were already sitting down to luncheon; she could see them between the tent-shaped opening made by the curtains. She would be late for her own luncheon, she thought as she ran up the front steps and fitted her latch-key in the door. Then, as if someone were speaking, words formed in her mind. "Something pretty, something to wear." She stopped with her key in the lock. Maggie's birthday; her father's present; she had forgotten it. She paused. She turned, she ran down the steps again. She must go to Lamley's.

Mrs Lamley, who had grown stout these last years, was

masticating a mouthful of cold mutton in the back room when she saw Miss Eleanor through the glass door.

"Good morning, Miss Eleanor," she began, coming out.

"Something pretty, something to wear," Eleanor panted. She was looking very well—quite brown after her holiday, Mrs Lamley noticed.

"For my niece—I mean cousin. Sir Digby's little girl," Eleanor brought out.

Mrs Lamley deprecated the cheapness of her goods.

There were toy boats; dolls; twopenny gold watches—but nothing nice enough for Sir Digby's little girl. But Miss Eleanor was in a hurry.

"There," she said, pointing to a card of bead necklaces. "That'll do."

It looked a little cheap, Mrs Lamley thought; reaching down a blue necklace with gold spots, but Miss Eleanor was in such a hurry that she wouldn't even have it wrapped in brown paper.

"I shall be late as it is, Mrs Lamley," she said, with a genial wave of her hand; and off she ran.

Mrs Lamley liked her. She always seemed so friendly. It was such a pity she didn't marry—such a mistake to let the younger sister marry before the elder. But then she had the Colonel to look after, and he was getting on now, Mrs Lamley concluded, going back to her mutton in the back shop.

"Miss Eleanor won't be a minute," said the Colonel as Crosby brought in the dishes. "Leave the covers on." He stood with his back to the fireplace waiting for her. Yes, he thought, I don't see why not. "I don't see why not," he repeated, looking at the dish-cover. Mira was on the scene again; the other fellow had turned out, as he knew he would, a bad egg. And what provision was he to make for Mira? What was he to do about it? It had struck him that he would like to put the whole thing before Eleanor. Why not after all? She's not a child any longer, he thought; and he didn't like this business of—of—shutting things up in drawers. But he felt some shyness at the thought of telling his own daughter.

"Here she is," he said abruptly to Crosby, who stood waiting mutely behind him.

No, no, he said to himself with sudden conviction, as Eleanor came in. I can't do it. For some reason when he saw her he realised that he could not tell her. And after all, he thought, seeing how bright-cheeked, how unconcerned she looked, she has her own life to live. A spasm of jealousy passed through him. She's got her own affairs to think about, he thought as they sat down.

She pushed a necklace across the table towards him.

"Hullo, what's that?" he said, looking at it blankly.

"Maggie's present, Papa," she said. "The best I could do. . . . I'm afraid it's rather cheap."

"Yes; that'll do very nicely," he said, glancing at it absentmindedly. "Just what she'll like," he added, shoving it to one side. He began to carve the chicken.

She was very hungry; she was still rather breathless. She felt a little "spun round," as she put it to herself. What did you spin things round on? she wondered, helping herself to bread sauce—a pivot? The scene had changed so often that morning; and every scene required a different adjustment; bringing this to the front; sinking that to the depths. And now she felt nothing; hungry merely; merely a chicken-eater; blank. But as she ate, the sense of her father imposed itself. She liked his solidity, as he sat opposite her munching his chicken methodically. What had he been doing, she wondered. Taking shares out of one company and putting them in another? He roused himself.

"Well, how was the Committee?" he asked. She told him, exaggerating her triumph with Judd.

"That's right. Stand up to 'em, Nell. Don't let yourself be sat on," he said. He was proud of her in his own way; and she liked him to be proud of her. At the same time she did not mention Duffus and Rigby Cottages. He had no sympathy with people who were foolish about money, and she never got a penny interest: it all went on repairs. She turned the conversation to Morris and his case at the Law Courts. She looked at her watch again. Her sister-in-law Celia had told her to meet her at the Law Courts at two-thirty sharp.

"I shall have to hurry," she said.

"Ah, but these lawyer chaps always know how to spin things out," said the Colonel. "Who's the Judge?"

"Sanders Curry," said Eleanor.

'Then it'll last till Domesday," said the Colonel.

"Which Court's he sitting in?" he asked.

Eleanor did not know.

"Here, Crosby—" said the Colonel. He sent Crosby for *The Times*. He began opening and turning the great sheets with his clumsy fingers as Eleanor swallowed her tart. By the time she had poured out coffee he had found out in which court the case was being heard.

"And you're going to the City, Papa?" she said as she put down her cup.

"Yes. To a meeting," he said. He loved going to the City, whatever he did there.

"Odd it should be Curry who's trying the case," she said, rising. They had dined with him not long ago in a dreary great house somewhere off Queen's Gate.

"D'you remember that party?" she said, getting up. "The old oak?" Curry collected oak chests.

"All shams I suspect," said her father. "Don't hurry," he expostulated. "Take a cab, Nell—if you want any change—" he began, fumbling with his curtailed fingers for silver. As she watched him Eleanor felt the old childish feeling that his pockets were bottomless silver mines from which half-crowns could be dug eternally.

"Well, then," she said, taking the coins, "we shall meet at tea."

"No," he reminded her, "I'm going round by the Digbys'."

He took the necklace in his large hairy hand. It looked a little cheap, Eleanor was afraid.

"And what about a box for this, eh?" he asked.

"Crosby, find a box for the necklace," said Eleanor. And Crosby, suddenly radiating importance, hurried off to the basement.

"It'll be dinner then," she said to her father. That'll mean, she thought with relief, that I needn't be back for tea.

"Yes, dinner," he said. He held a spill of paper in his hand which he was applying to the end of his cigar. He sucked. A little puff of smoke rose from the cigar. She liked the smell of cigars. She stood for a moment and drew it in.

"And give my love to Aunt Eugénie," she said. He nodded as he puffed at his cigar.

It was a treat to take a hansom—it saved fifteen minutes. She leant back in the corner, with a little sigh of content, as the flaps clicked above her knees. For a minute her mind was completely vacant. She enjoyed the peace, the silence, the rest from exertion as she sat there in the corner of the cab. She felt detached, a spectator, as it trotted along. The morning had been a rush; one thing on top of another. Now, until she reached the Law Courts, she could sit and do nothing. It was a long way; and the horse was a plodding horse, a red-coated hairy horse. It kept up its steady jog-trot all down the Bayswater Road. There was very little traffic; people were still at luncheon. A soft grey mist filled up the distance; the bells jingled; the houses passed. She ceased to notice what houses they were passing. She half shut her eyes, and then, involuntarily, she saw her own hand take a letter from the hall table. When? That very morning. What had she done with it? Put it in her bag? Yes. There it was, unopened; a letter from Martin in India. She would read it as they drove along. It was written on very thin paper in Martin's little hand. It was longer than usual; it was about an adventure with somebody called Renton. Who was Renton? She could not remember. "We started at dawn," she read.

She looked out of the window. They were being held up by

traffic at the Marble Arch. Carriages were coming out of the Park. A horse pranced; but the coachman had him well in hand.

She read again: "I found myself alone in the middle of the jungle. . . ."

But what were you doing? she asked.

She saw her brother; his red hair; his round face; and the rather pugnacious expression which always made her afraid that he would get himself into trouble one of these days. And so he had, apparently.

"I had lost my way; and the sun was sinking," she read.

"The sun was sinking . . ." Eleanor repeated, glancing ahead of her down Oxford Street. The sun shone on dresses in a window. A jungle was a very thick wood, she supposed; made of stunted little trees; dark green in colour. Martin was in the jungle alone, and the sun was sinking. What happened next? "I thought it better to stay where I was." So he stood in the midst of little trees alone, in the jungle; and the sun was sinking. The street before her lost its detail. It must have been cold, she thought, when the sun sank. She read again. He had to make a fire. "I looked in my pocket and found that I had only two matches . . . The first match went out." She saw a heap of dry sticks and Martin alone watching the match go out. "Then I lit the other, and by sheer luck it did the trick." The paper began to burn; the twigs caught; a fan of fire blazed up. She skipped on in her anxiety to reach the end . . . . —"once I thought I heard voices shouting, but they died away."

"They died away!" said Eleanor aloud.

They had stopped at Chancery Lane. An old woman was being helped across the road by a policeman; but the road was a jungle.

"They died away," she said. "And then?"

". . . I climbed a tree . . . I saw the track . . . the sun was rising. . . . They had given me up for dead."

The cab stopped. For a moment Eleanor sat still. She saw nothing but stunted little trees, and her brother looking at the sun rising over the jungle. The sun was rising. Flames for a moment danced over the vast funereal mass of the Law Courts. It was the second match that did the trick, she said to herself as she paid the driver and went in.

"Oh, there you are!" cried a little woman in furs, who was standing by one of the doors.

"I had given you up. I was just going in." She was a small cat-faced woman, worried, but very proud of her husband.

They pushed through the swing doors into the Court where the case was being tried. It seemed dark and crowded at first. Men in wigs and gowns were getting up and sitting down and coming in and going out like a flock of birds settling here and there on a field. They all looked unfamiliar; she could not see Morris. She looked about her, trying to find him.

"There he is," Celia whispered.

One of the barristers in the front row turned his head. It was Morris; but how odd he looked in his yellow wig! His glance passed over them without any sign of recognition. Nor did she smile at him; the solemn sallow atmosphere forbade personalities; there was something ceremonial about it all. From where she sat she could see his face in profile; the wig squared his forehead, and gave him a framed look, like a picture. Never had she seen him to such advantage; with such a brow, with such a nose. She glanced round. They all looked like pictures; all the barristers looked emphatic, cut out, like eighteenth-century portraits hung upon a wall. They were still rising and settling, laughing, talking. . . . Suddenly a door was thrown open. The usher demanded silence for his lordship. There was silence; everybody stood up; and the Judge came in. He made one bow and took his seat under the Lion and the Unicorn. Eleanor felt a little thrill of awe run through her. That was old Curry. But how transformed! Last time she had seen him he was sitting at the head of a dinner-table; a long yellow strip of embroidery went rippling down the middle; and he had taken her, with a candle, round the drawing-room to look at his old oak. But now, there he was, awful, magisterial, in his robes.

A barrister had risen. She tried to follow what the man with a big nose was saying; but it was difficult to pick it up now. She listened, however. Then another barrister rose—a chicken-breasted little man, wearing gold pince-nez. He was reading some document; then he too began to argue. She could understand parts of what he was saying; though how it bore on the case she did not know. When was Morris going to speak, she wondered? Not yet apparently. As her father had said, these lawyer chaps knew how to spin things out. There had been no need to hurry over luncheon; an omnibus would have done just as well. She fixed her eyes on Morris. He was cracking some joke with the sandy man next to him. Those were his cronies, she thought; this was his life. She remembered his passion for the Bar as a boy. It was she who had talked Papa round; one morning she had taken her life in her hand and gone to his study . . . but now, to her excitement, Morris himself got up.

She felt her sister-in-law stiffen with nervousness and clasp her little bag tightly. Morris looked very tall, and very black and white as he began. One hand was on the edge of his gown. How well she knew that gesture of Morris's, she thought—grasping something, so that you saw the white scar where he had cut himself bathing. But she did not recognise the other gesture— the way he flung his arm out. That belonged to his public life, his life in the Courts. And his voice was unfamiliar. But every now and then as he warmed to his speech, there was a tone in his voice that made her smile; it was his private voice. She could not help half turning to her sister-in-law as if to say, How like Morris! But Celia was looking with absolute fixity ahead of her at her husband. Eleanor, too, tried to fix her mind upon the argument. He spoke with extraordinary clearness; he spaced his words beautifully. Suddenly the Judge interrupted:

"Do I understand you to hold, Mr Pargiter . . . ?" he said in urbane yet awful tones; and Eleanor was thrilled to see how instantly Morris stopped short; how respectfully he bent his head as the Judge spoke.

But will he know the answer? she thought, as if he were a child, shifting in her seat with nervousness lest he might break down. But he had the answer at his finger-ends. Without hurry or flutter he opened a book; found his place; read out a passage, upon which old Curry nodded, and made a note in the great volume that lay open in front of him. She was immensely relieved.

"How well he did that!" she whispered. Her sister-in-law nodded; but she still grasped her bag tightly. Eleanor felt that she could relax. She glanced round her. It was an odd mixture of solemnity and licence. Barristers kept coming in and out. They stood leaning against the wall of the Court. In the pale top light all their faces looked parchment-coloured; all their features seemed cut out. They had lit the gas. She gazed at the Judge himself. He was now lying back in his great carved chair under the Lion and the Unicorn, listening. He looked infinitely sad and wise, as if words had been beating upon him for centuries. Now he opened his heavy eyes, wrinkled his forehead, and the little hand that emerged frailly from the enormous cuff wrote a few words in the great volume. Then again he lapsed with half-shut eyes into his eternal vigil over the strife of unhappy human beings. Her mind wandered. She leant back against the hard wooden seat and let the tide of oblivion flow over her. Scenes from her morning began to form themselves; to obtrude themselves. Judd at the Committee; her father reading the paper; the old woman plucking at her hand; the parlourmaid sweeping the silver over the table; and Martin lighting his second match in the jungle. . . .

She fidgeted. The air was fuggy; the light dim; and the Judge now that the first glamour had worn off, looked fretful; no longer immune from human weakness, and she remembered with a smile how very gullible he was, there in that hideous house in Queen's Gate, about old oak. "This I picked up at Whitby," he had said. And it was a sham. She wanted to laugh; she wanted to move. She rose and whispered:

"I'm going."

Her sister-in-law made a little murmur, perhaps of protest. But Eleanor made her way as silently as she could through the swing doors, out into the street.

The uproar, the confusion, the space of the Strand came upon her with a shock of relief. She felt herself expand. It was still daylight here; a rush, a stir, a turmoil of variegated life came racing towards her. It was as if something had broken loose— in her, in the world. She seemed, after her concentration, to be dissipated, tossed about. She wandered along the Strand, looking with pleasure at the racing street; at the shops full of bright chains and leather cases; at the white-faced churches; at the irregular jagged roofs laced across and across with wires. Above was the dazzle of a watery but gleaming sky. The wind blew in her face. She breathed in a gulp of fresh wet air. And that man, she thought, thinking of the dark little Court and its cut-out faces, has to sit there all day, every day. She saw Sanders Curry again, lying back in his great chair, with his face falling in folds of iron. Every day, all day, she thought, arguing points of law. How could Morris stand it? But he had always wanted to go to the Bar.

Cabs, vans and omnibuses streamed past; they seemed to rush the air into her face; they splashed the mud onto the pavement. People jostled and hustled and she quickened her pace in time with theirs. She was stopped by a van turning down one of the little steep streets that led to the river. She looked up and saw the clouds moving between the roofs, dark clouds, rain-swollen; wandering, indifferent clouds. She walked on.

Again she was stopped at the entrance to Charing Cross station. The sky was wide at that point. She saw a file of birds flying high, flying together; crossing the sky. She watched them. Again she walked on. People on foot, people in cabs were being sucked in like straws round the piers of a bridge; she had to wait.

Cabs piled with boxes went past her.

She envied them. She wished she were going abroad; to Italy, to India. . . . Then she felt vaguely that something was happening. The paper boys at the gates were dealing out papers with unusual rapidity. Men were snatching them and opening them and reading them as they walked on. She looked at a placard that was crumpled across a boy's legs. "Death" was written in very large black letters.

Then the placard blew straight, and she read another word: "Parnell."

"Dead" . . . she repeated. "Parnell." She was dazed for a moment. How could he be dead—Parnell? She bought a paper. They said so. . . .

"Parnell is dead!" she said aloud. She looked up and saw the sky again; clouds were passing; she looked down into the street. A man pointed at the news with his forefinger. Parnell is dead he was saying. He was gloating. But how could he be dead? It was like something fading in the sky.

She walked slowly along towards Trafalgar Square, holding the paper in her hand. Suddenly the whole scene froze into immobility. A man was joined to a pillar; a lion was joined to a man; they seemed stilled, connected, as if they would never move again.

She crossed into Trafalgar Square. Birds chattered shrilly somewhere. She stopped by the fountain and looked down into the large basin full of water. The water rippled black as the wind ruffled it. There were reflections in the water, branches and a pale strip of sky. What a dream, she murmured; what a dream . . . But someone jostled her. She turned. She must go to Delia. Delia had cared. Delia had cared passionately. What was it she used to say—flinging out of the house, leaving them all for the Cause, for this man? Justice, Liberty? She must go to her. This would be the end of all her dreams. She turned and hailed a cab.

She leant over the flaps of the cab looking out. The streets they were driving through were horribly poor; and not only poor, she thought, but vicious. Here was the vice, the obscenity, the reality of London. It was lurid in the mixed evening light. Lamps were being lit. Paper-boys were crying, Parnell . . . Parnell. He's dead, she said to herself, still conscious of the two worlds; one flowing in wide sweeps overhead, the other tip-tapping circumscribed upon the pavement. But here she was . . . She held up her hand. She stopped the cab opposite a little row of posts in an alley. She got out and made her way into the Square.

The sound of the traffic was dulled. It was very silent here. In the October afternoon, with dead leaves falling, the old faded Square looked dingy and decrepit and full of mist. The houses were let out in offices, to societies, to people whose names were pinned up on the door-posts. The whole neighbourhood seemed to her foreign and sinister. She came to the old Queen Anne doorway with its heavy carved eyebrows and pressed the bell at the top of six or seven bells. Names were written over them, sometimes only on visiting-cards. Nobody came. She pushed the door open and went in; she mounted the wooden stairs with carved banisters, that seemed to have been degraded from their past dignity. Jugs of milk with bills under them stood in the deep window-seats. Some of the panes were broken. Outside Delia's door, at the top, there was a milk-jug too, but it was empty. Her card was fixed by a drawing-pin to a panel. She knocked and waited. There was no sound. She turned the handle. The door was locked. She stood for a moment listening. A little window at the side gave on to the square. Pigeons crooned on the tree-tops. The traffic hummed far off; she could just hear paperboys crying death . . . death . . . death. The leaves were falling. She turned and went downstairs.

She strolled along the streets. Children had chalked the pavement into squares; women leant from the upper windows, raking the street with a rapacious, dissatisfied stare. Rooms were let out to single gentlemen only. There were cards in them which said "Furnished Apartments" or "Bed and Breakfast." She guessed at the life that went on behind those thick yellow curtains. This was the purlieus in which her sister lived, she thought, turning; she must often come back this way at night alone. Then she went back to the Square and climbed the stairs and rattled at the door again. But there was no sound within. She stood for a moment watching the leaves fall; she heard the paper-boys crying and the pigeons crooning in the tree-tops. Take two coos, Taffy; take two coos, Taffy; tak . . . Then a leaf fell.

The traffic at Charing Cross thickened as the afternoon wore on. People on foot, people in cabs were being sucked in at the gates of the station. Men swung along at a great pace as if there were some demon in the station who would be enraged if they kept him waiting. But even so they paused and snatched a paper as they passed. The clouds parting and massing let the light shine and then veiled it. The mud, now dark brown, now liquid gold, was splashed up by the wheels and hooves, and in the general churn and uproar the shrill chatter of the birds on the eaves was silenced. The hansoms jingled and passed; jingled and passed. At last among all the jingling cabs came one in which sat a stout red-faced man holding a flower wrapped in tissue-paper—the Colonel.

"Hi!" he cried as the cab passed the gates; and drove one hand through the trap-door in the roof. He leant out and a paper was thrust up at him.

"Parnell!" he exclaimed, as he fumbled for his glasses. "Dead, by Jove!"

The cab trotted on. He read the news two or three times over. He's dead, he said, taking off his glasses. A shock of something like relief, of something that had a tinge of triumph in it, went through him as he leant back in the corner. Well, he said to himself, he's dead—that unscrupulous adventurer— that agitator who had done all the mischief, that man . . . Some feeling connected with his own daughter here formed in him;

he could not say exactly what, but it made him frown. Anyhow he's dead now, he thought. How had he died? Had he killed himself? It wouldn't be surprising. . . . Anyhow he was dead and that was an end of it. He sat holding the paper crumpled in one hand, the flower wrapped in tissue paper in the other, as the cab drove down Whitehall. . . . One could respect him, he thought, as the cab passed the House of Commons, which was more than could be said for some of the other fellows . . . and there'd been a lot of nonsense talked about the divorce case. He looked out. The cab was driving near a certain street where he used to stop and look about him years ago. He turned and glanced down a street to the right. But a man in public life can't afford to do those things, he thought. He gave a little nod as the cab passed on. And now she's written to ask me for money, he thought. The other chap had turned out, as he knew he would, a bad egg. She'd lost all her looks, he was thinking; she had grown very stout. Well, he could afford to be generous. He put on his glasses again and read the City news.

It would make no difference, Parnell's death, coming now, he thought. Had he lived, had the scandal died down—he looked up. The cab was going the long way round as usual. "Left!" he shouted, "Left!" as the driver, as they always did, took the wrong turning.

In the rather dark basement at Browne Street, the Italian manservant was reading the paper in his shirt sleeves, when the housemaid waltzed in carrying a hat.

"Look what she's given me!" she cried. To atone for the mess in the drawing-room, Lady Pargiter had given her a hat. "Ain't I stylish?" she said, pausing in front of the glass with the great Italian hat that looked as if it were made of spun glass on one side of her head. And Antonio had to drop his paper and catch her round the waist from sheer gallantry, since she was no beauty, and her action was merely a parody of what he remembered in the hill towns of Tuscany. But a cab stopped in front of the railings; two legs stood still there, and he must detach himself, put on his jacket and go upstairs to answer the bell.

He takes his time, the Colonel thought, as he stood on the door-step waiting. The shock of the death had been absorbed almost; it still swept round in his system; but did not prevent him from thinking, as he stood there, that they had had the bricks re-pointed; but how had they money to spare, with the three boys to educate, and the two little girls? Eugénie was a clever woman of course; but he wished she would get a parlourmaid instead of these Italian dagoes who always seemed to be swallowing macaroni. Here the door opened, and as he went upstairs he thought he heard, from somewhere in the background, a shout of laughter.

He liked Eugénie's drawing-room, he thought, as he stood there waiting. It was very untidy. There was a litter of shavings from something that was being unpacked on the floor. They had been to Italy, he remembered. A looking-glass stood on the table. It was probably one of the things she had picked up there: the sort of thing that people did pick up in Italy; an old glass, covered with spots. He straightened his tie in front of it.

But I prefer a glass in which one can see oneself, he thought, turning away. There was the piano open; and the tea—he smiled—with the cup half full as usual; and branches stuck about the room, branches of withering red and yellow leaves. She liked flowers. He was glad he had remembered to bring her his usual gift. He held the flower wrapped in tissue paper in front of him. But why was the room so full of smoke? A gust blew in. Both windows in the back room were open, and the smoke was blowing in from the garden. Were they burning weeds, he wondered? He walked to the window and looked out. Yes, there they were—Eugénie and the two little girls. There was a bonfire. As he looked, Magdalena, the little girl who was his favourite, tossed a whole armful of dead leaves. She jerked them as high as she could, and the fire blazed up. A great fan of red flame flung out.

"That's dangerous!" he called out.

Eugénie pulled the children back. They were dancing with excitement. The other little girl, Sara, ducked under her mother's arm, seized another armful of leaves and flung them again. A great fan of red flame flung out. Then the Italian servant came and mentioned his name. He tapped on the window. Eugénie turned and saw him. She held the children back with one hand and raised the other in welcome.

"Stay where you are!" she cried. "We're coming!"

A cloud of smoke blew straight at him; it made his eyes water, and he turned and sat down in the chair by the sofa. In another second she came, hurrying towards him with both her hands stretched out. He rose and took them.

"We're having a bonfire," she said. Her eyes were glowing; her hair was looping down. "That's why I'm all so blown-about," she added, putting her hand to her head. She was untidy, but extremely handsome all the same, Abel thought. A fine large woman, growing ample, he noted as she shook hands; but it suited her. He admired that type more than the pink-and-white pretty Englishwoman. The flesh flowed over her like warm yellow wax; she had great dark eyes like a foreigner, and a nose with a ripple in it. He held out his camellia; his customary gift. She made a little exclamation as she took the flower from the tissue paper and sat down.

"How very good of you!" she said, and held it for a moment in front of her, and then did what he had often seen her do with a flower—put the stalk between her lips. Her movements charmed him as usual.

"Having a bonfire for the birthday?" he asked. . . . "No, no, no," he protested, "I don't want tea."

She had taken her cup, and sipped the cold tea that was left in it. As he watched her, some memory of the East came back to him; so women sat in hot countries in their doorways in the sun. But it was very cold at the moment with the window open and the smoke blowing in. He still had his newspaper in his hand; he laid it on the table.

"Seen the news?" he asked.

She put down her cup and slightly opened her large dark eyes. Immense reserves of emotion seemed to dwell in them. As she waited for him to speak, she raised her hand as if in expectation.

"Parnell," said Abel briefly. "He's dead."

"Dead?" Eugénie echoed him. She let her hand fall dramatically.

"Yes. At Brighton. Yesterday."

"Parnell is dead!" she repeated.

"So they say," said the Colonel. Her emotion always made him feel more matter-of-fact; but he liked it. She took up the paper.

"Poor thing!" she exclaimed, letting it fall.

"Poor thing?" he repeated. Her eyes were full of tears. He was puzzled. Did she mean Kitty O'Shea? He hadn't thought of her.

"She ruined his career for him," he said with a little snort.

"Ah, but how she must have loved him!" she murmured.

She drew her hand over her eyes. The Colonel was silent for a moment. Her emotion seemed to him out of all proportion to its object; but it was genuine. He liked it.

"Yes," he said, rather stiffly. "Yes, I suppose so." Eugénie picked up the flower again and held it, twirling it. She was oddly absentminded now and then, but he always felt at his ease with her. His body relaxed. He felt relieved of some obstruction in her presence.

"How people suffer! . . ." she murmured, looking at the flower. "How they suffer, Abel!" she said. She turned and looked straight at him.

A great gust of smoke blew in from the other room.

"You don't mind the draught?" he asked, looking at the window. She did not answer at once; she was twirling her flower. Then she roused herself and smiled.

"Yes, yes. Shut it!" she said with a wave of her hand. He went and shut the window. When he turned round, she had got up and was standing at the looking-glass, arranging her hair.

"We've had a bonfire for Maggie's birthday," she murmured, looking at herself in the Venetian glass that was covered with spots. "That's why, that's why—" she smoothed her hair and fixed the camellia in her dress. "I'm so very—"

She put her head a little on one side as if to observe the effect of the flower in her dress. The Colonel sat down and waited. He glanced at his paper.

"They seem to be hushing things up," he said.

"You don't mean—" Eugénie was beginning; but here the door opened and the children came in. Maggie, the elder, came first; the other little girl, Sara, hung back behind her.

"Hullo!" the Colonel exclaimed. "Here they are!" He turned round. He was very fond of children. "Many happy returns of the day to you, Maggie!" He felt in his pocket for the necklace that Crosby had done up in a cardboard box. Maggie came up to him to take it. Her hair had been brushed, and she was dressed in a stiff clean frock. She took the parcel and undid it; she held the blue-and-gold necklace dangling from her finger. For a moment the Colonel doubted whether she liked it. It looked a little garish as she held it dangling in her hand. And she was silent. Her mother at once supplied the words she should have spoken.

"How lovely, Maggie! How perfectly lovely!"

Maggie held the beads in her hand and said nothing.

"Thank Uncle Abel for the lovely necklace," her mother prompted her.

"Thank you for the necklace, Uncle Abel," said Maggie. She spoke directly and accurately, but the Colonel felt another twinge of doubt. A pang of disappointment out of all proportion to its object came over him. Her mother, however, fastened it round her neck. Then she turned away to her sister, who was peeping from behind a chair.

"Come, Sara," said her mother. "Come and say how-d'you-do."

She held out her hand partly to coax the little girl, partly, Abel guessed, in order to conceal the very slight deformity

112

that always made him uncomfortable. She had been dropped when she was a baby; one shoulder was slightly higher than the other; it made him feel squeamish; he could not bear the least deformity in a child. It did not affect her spirits, however. She skipped up to him, whirling round on her toe, and kissed him lightly on the cheek. Then she tugged at her sister's frock, and they both rushed away into the back room laughing.

"They are going to admire your lovely present, Abel," said Eugénie. "How you spoil them!—and me too," she added, touching the camellia on her breast.

"I hope she liked it?" he asked. Eugénie did not answer him. She had taken up the cup of cold tea again and was sipping it in her indolent Southern manner.

"And now," she said, leaning back comfortably, "tell me all your news."

The Colonel, too, lay back in his chair. He pondered for a moment. What was his news? Nothing occurred to him on the spur of the moment. With Eugénie, too, he always wanted to make a little splash; she put a shine on things. While he hesitated, she began:

"We've been having a wonderful time in Venice! I took the children. That's why we're all so brown. We had rooms not on the Grand Canal—I hate the Grand Canal—but just off it. Two weeks of blazing sun; and the colours"—she hesitated— "marvellous!" she exclaimed, "marvellous!" She threw out her hand. She had gestures of extraordinary significance. That's how she rigs things up, he thought. But he liked her for it.

He had not been to Venice for years.

"Any pleasant people there?" he asked.

"Not a soul," she said. "Not a soul. No one except a dreadful Miss—. One of those women who make one ashamed of one's country," she said energetically.

"I know 'em," he chuckled.

"But coming back from the Lido in the evening," she resumed, "with the clouds above and the water below—we had a balcony;

we used to sit there." She paused.

"Was Digby with you?" the Colonel asked.

"No, poor Digby. He took his holiday earlier, in August. He was up in Scotland with the Lasswades shooting. It does him good, you know." There she goes, rigging thing's up again, he thought.

But she resumed.

"Now tell me about the family. Martin and Eleanor, Hugh and Milly, Morris and . . ." She hesitated; he suspected that she had forgotten the name of Morris' wife.

"Celia," he said. He stopped. He wanted to tell her about Mira. But he told her about the family: Hugh and Milly; Morris and Celia. And Edward.

"They seem to think a lot of him at Oxford," he said gruffly. He was very proud of Edward.

"And Delia?" said Eugénie. She glanced at the paper. The Colonel at once lost his affability. He looked glum and formidable, like an old bull with his head down, she thought.

"Perhaps it will bring her to her senses," he said sternly. They were silent for a moment. There were shouts of laughter from the garden.

"Oh those children!" she exclaimed. She rose and went to the window. The Colonel followed her. The children had stolen back into the garden. The bonfire was burning fiercely. A clear pillar of flame rose in the middle of the garden. The little girls were laughing and shouting as they danced round it. A shabby old man, something like a decayed groom to look at, stood there with a rake in his hand. Eugénie flung up the window and cried out. But they went on dancing. The Colonel leant out too; they looked like wild creatures with their hair flying. He would have liked to go down and jump over the bonfire, but he was too old. The flames leapt high—clear gold, bright red.

"Bravo!" he cried, clapping his hands. "Bravo!"

"Little demons!" said Eugénie. She was as much excited as they were, he observed. She leant out of the window and cried to the old man with the rake:

"Make it blaze! Make it blaze!"

But the old man was raking out the fire. The sticks were scattered. The flames had sunk.

The old man pushed the children away.

"Well, that's over," said Eugénie, heaving a sigh. She turned. Someone had come into the room.

"Oh, Digby, I never heard you!" she exclaimed. Digby stood there with a case in his hands.

"Hullo, Digby!" said Abel, shaking hands.

"What's all this smoke?" said Digby, looking round him.

He's aged a bit, Abel thought. There he stood in his frock coat with the top buttons undone. His coat was a little threadbare; his hair was white on top. But he was very handsome; beside him the Colonel felt large, weather-beaten and rough. He was a little ashamed that he had been caught leaning out of the window clapping his hands. He looks older, he thought, as they stood side by side; yet he's five years younger than I am. He was a distinguished man in his way; the top of his tree; a knight and all the rest of it. But he's not as rich as I am, he remembered with satisfaction; for he had always been the failure of the two.

"You look so tired, Digby!" Eugénie exclaimed, sitting down. "He ought to take a real holiday," she said, turning to Abel. "I wish you'd tell him so." Digby brushed away a white thread that had stuck to his trousers. He coughed slightly. The room was full of smoke.

"What's all this smoke for?" he asked his wife.

"We've been having a bonfire for Maggie's birthday," she said as if excusing herself.

"Oh yes," he said. Abel was irritated; Maggie was his favourite; her father ought to have remembered her birthday.

"Yes," said Eugénie, turning to Abel again, "he lets everybody else take a holiday, but he never takes one himself. And then, when he's done a full day's work at the office, he comes back with his bag full of papers—" She pointed at the bag.

"You shouldn't work after dinner," said Abel. "That's a bad habit." Digby did look a bit off-colour, he thought. Digby brushed aside this feminine effusiveness.

"Seen the news?" he said to his brother, indicating the paper.

"Yes. By Jove!" said Abel. He liked talking politics with his brother, though he slightly resented his official airs as if he could say more but must not. And then it's all in the papers the day after, he thought. Still they always talked politics. Eugénie lying back in her corner always let them talk; she never interrupted. But at length she got up and began tidying the litter that had fallen from the packing-case. Digby stopped what he was saying and watched her. He was looking at the glass.

"Like it?" said Eugénie, with her hand on the frame.

"Yes," said Digby; but there was a hint of criticism in his voice. "Quite a pretty one."

"It's only for my bedroom," she said quickly. Digby watched her stuffing the bits of paper into the box.

"Remember," he said, "we're dining with the Chathams tonight."

"I know." She touched her hair again. "I shall have to make myself tidy," she said. Who were "the Chathams?" Abel wondered. Bigwigs, mandarins, he supposed half contemptuously. They moved a great deal in that world. He took it as a hint that he should go. They had come to the end of what they had to say to each other—he and Digby. He still hoped, however, that he might talk with Eugénie alone.

"About this African business—" he began, bethinking him of another question—when the children came in; they had come to say good-night. Maggie was wearing his necklace and it looked very pretty, he thought, or was it she who looked so pretty? But their frocks, their clean blue and pink frocks, were crumpled; they were smudged with the sooty London leaves that they had been holding in their arms.

"Grubby little ruffians!" he said, smiling at them. "Why d'you wear your best clothes to play in the garden?" said Sir Digby, as he kissed Maggie. He said it jokingly, but there was a hint of disapproval in his tones. Maggie made no answer. Her eyes were riveted on the camellia that her mother wore in the front of her dress. She went up and stood looking at her.

"And you—what a little sweep!" said Sir Digby, pointing to Sara.

"It's Maggie's birthday," said Eugénie, holding out her arm again as if to protect the little girl.

"That is a reason, I should have thought," said Sir Digby, surveying his daughters, "to—er—to—er—reform one's habits." He stumbled, trying to make his sentence sound playful; but it turned out as it generally did when he talked to the children, lame and rather pompous.

Sara looked at her father as if she were considering him.

"To—er—to—er—reform one's habits," she repeated. Emptied of all meaning, she had got the rhythm of his words exactly. The effect was somehow comic. The Colonel laughed; but Digby, he felt, was annoyed. He only patted Sara on the head when she came to say good-night; but he kissed Maggie as she passed him.

"Had a nice birthday?" he said, pulling her to him. Abel made it an excuse to go.

"But there is no need for you to go yet, Abel?" Eugénie protested as he held out his hand.

She kept hold of his hand as if to prevent him from going. What did she mean? Did she want him to stay, did she want him to go? Her eyes, her large dark eyes, were ambiguous.

"But you're dining out?" he said.

"Yes," she replied, letting his hand fall, and as she said no more there was nothing for it, he supposed—he must take himself off.

"Oh, I can find my way out alone," he said as he left the room.

He went downstairs rather slowly. He felt depressed and disappointed. He had not seen her alone; he had not told her anything. Perhaps he never would tell anybody anything. After all, he thought as he went downstairs, slowly, heavily, it was his own affair; it didn't matter to anybody else. One must burn one's own smoke, he thought as he took his hat. He glanced round.

Yes . . . the house was full of pretty things. He looked vaguely at a great crimson chair with gilt claws that stood in the hall. He envied Digby his house, his wife, his children. He was getting old, he felt. All his children were grown-up; they had left him. He paused on the doorstep and looked out into the street. It was quite dark; lamps were lit; the autumn was drawing in; and as he marched up the dark windy street, now spotted with raindrops, a puff of smoke blew full in his face; and leaves were falling.

1907

It was midsummer; and the nights were hot. The moon, falling on water, made it white, inscrutable, whether deep or shallow. But where the moonlight fell on solid objects it gave them a burnish and a silver plating, so that even the leaves in country roads seemed varnished. All along the silent country roads leading to London carts plodded; the iron reins fixed in the iron hands, for vegetables, fruit, flowers travelled slowly. Heaped high with round crates of cabbage, cherries, carnations, they looked like caravans piled with the goods of tribes migrating in search of water, driven by enemies to seek new pasturage. On they plodded, down this road, that road, keeping close to the kerb. Even the horses, had they been blind, could have heard the hum of London in the distance; and the drivers, dozing, yet saw through half shut eyes the fiery gauze of the eternally burning city. At dawn, at Covent Garden, they laid down their burdens; tables and trestles, even the cobbles were frilled as with some celestial laundry with cabbages, cherries and carnations.

All the windows were open. Music sounded. From behind crimson curtains, rendered semi-transparent and sometimes blowing wide came the sound of the eternal waltz—After the ball is over, after the dance is done—like a serpent that swallowed its own tail, since the ring was complete from Hammersmith to Shoreditch. Over and over again it was repeated by trombones outside public houses; errand boys whistled it; bands inside private rooms where people were dancing played it. There they sat at little tables at Wapping in the romantic Inn that overhung the river, between timber warehouses where barges were moored; and here again in Mayfair. Each table had its lamp; its canopy of tight red silk, and the flowers that had sucked damp from the earth that noon relaxed and spread their petals in vases. Each table had its pyramid of strawberries, its pale plump quail; and Martin, after India, after Africa, found it exciting to talk to a girl with bare shoulders, to a woman iridescent with green beetles wings in her hair in a manner that the waltz condoned and half concealed under its amorous blandishments. Did it matter what one said? For she looked over her shoulder, only half listening, as a man came in wearing decorations, and a lady, in black with diamonds, beckoned him to a private corner.

As the night wore on a tender blue light lay on the market carts still plodding close to the kerb, past Westminster, past the yellow round clocks, the coffee stalls and the statues that stood there in the dawn holding so stiffly their rods or rolls of paper. And the scavengers followed after, sluicing the pavements. Cigarette ends, little bits of silver paper, orange peel—all the litter of the day was swept off the pavement and still the carts plodded, and the cabs trotted, indefatigably, along the dowdy pavements of Kensington, under the sparkling lights of Mayfair, carrying ladies with high head dresses and gentlemen in white waistcoats along the hammered dry roads which looked in the moonlight as if they were plated with silver.

"Look!" said Eugénie as the cab trotted over the bridge in the summer twilight. "Isn't that lovely?"

She waved her hand at the water. They were crossing the Serpentine; but her exclamation was only an aside; she was listening to what her husband was saying. Their daughter Magdalena was with them; and she looked where her mother pointed. There was the Serpentine, red in the setting sun; the trees grouped together, sculptured, losing their detail; and the ghostly architecture of the little bridge, white at the end, composed the scene. The lights—the sun-light and the artificial light—were strangely mixed.

". . . of course it's put the Government in a fix," Sir Digby was saying. "But then that's what he wants."

"Yes . . . he'll make a name for himself, that young man," said Lady Pargiter.

The cab passed over the bridge. It entered the shadow of the trees. Now it left the Park and joined the long line of cabs, taking people in evening dress to plays, to dinner-parties, that was streaming towards the Marble Arch. The light grew more and more artificial; yellower and yellower. Eugénie leant across and touched something on her daughter's dress. Maggie looked up. She had thought that they were still talking politics.

"So," said her mother, arranging the flower in front of her dress. She put her head a little on one side and looked at her daughter approvingly. Then she gave a sudden laugh and threw her hand out. "D'you know what made me so late?" she said. "That imp, Sally . . ."

But her husband interrupted her. He had caught sight of an illuminated clock.

"We shall be late," he said.

"But eight-fifteen means eight-thirty," said Eugénie as they turned down a side street.

All was silent in the house at Browne Street. A ray from the street lamp fell through the fanlight and, rather capriciously, lit up a tray of glasses on the hall table; a top hat; and a chair with gilt paws. The chair, standing empty, as if waiting for someone, had a look of ceremony; as if it stood on the cracked floor of some Italian ante-room. But all was silent. Antonio, the man servant, was asleep; Mollie, the housemaid, was asleep; downstairs in the basement a door flapped to and fro—otherwise all was silent.

Sally in her bedroom at the top of the house turned on her side and listened intently. She thought she heard the front door click. A burst of dance music came in through the open window and made it impossible to hear.

She sat up in bed and looked out through the slit of the blind. Through the gap she could see a slice of the sky; then roofs; then the tree in the garden; then the backs of houses opposite standing in a long row. One of the houses was brilliantly lit and from the long open windows came dance music. They were waltzing. She saw shadows twirling across the blind. It was impossible to read; impossible to sleep. First there was the music; then a burst of talk; then people came out into the garden; voices chattered, then the music began again.

It was a hot summer's night, and though it was late, the whole world seemed to be alive; the rush of traffic sounded distant but incessant.

A faded brown book lay on her bed; as if she had been reading. But it was impossible to read; impossible to sleep. She lay back on the pillow with her hands behind her head.

"And he says," she murmured, "the world is nothing but . . ." She paused. What did he say? Nothing but thought, was it? she asked herself as if she had already forgotten. Well, since it was impossible to read and impossible to sleep, she would let herself *be* thought. It was easier to act things than to think them. Legs, body, hands, the whole of her must be laid out passively to take part in this universal process of thinking which the man said was the world living. She stretched herself out. Where did thought begin?

In the feet? she asked. There they were, jutting out under the single sheet. They seemed separated, very far away. She closed her eyes. Then against her will something in her hardened. It was impossible to act thought. She became something; a root; lying sunk in the earth; veins seemed to thread the cold mass; the tree put forth branches; the branches had leaves.

"—the sun shines through the leaves," she said, waggling her finger. She opened her eyes in order to verify the sun on the leaves and saw the actual tree standing out there in the garden. Far from being dappled with sunlight, it had no leaves at all. She felt for a moment as if she had been contradicted. For the tree was black, dead black.

She leant her elbow on the sill and looked out at the tree. A confused clapping sound came from the room where they were having the dance. The music had stopped; people began to come down the iron staircase into the garden which was marked out with blue and yellow lamps dotted along the wall. The voices grew louder. More people came and more people came. The dotted square of green was full of the flowing pale figures of women in evening dress; of the upright black-and-white figures of men in evening dress. She watched them moving in and out. They were talking and laughing; but they were too far off for her to hear what they were saying. Sometimes a single word or a laugh rose above the rest, and then there was a confused babble of sound. In their own garden all was empty and silent. A cat slid stealthily along the top of a wall; stopped; and then went on again as if drawn on some secret errand. Another dance struck up.

"Over again, over and over again!" she exclaimed impatiently. The air, laden with the curious dry smell of London earth, puffed in her face, blowing the blind out. Stretched flat on her bed, she saw the moon; it seemed immensely high above her. Little vapours were moving across the surface. Now they parted and she saw engravings chased over the white disc. What were they, she wondered—mountains? valleys? And if valleys, she said to herself half closing her eyes, then white trees; then icy hollows, and nightingales, two nightingales calling to each other, calling and answering each other across the valleys. The waltz music took the words "calling and answering each other" and flung them out; but as it repeated the same rhythm again and again, it coarsened them, it destroyed them. The dance music interfered with everything. At first exciting, then it became boring and finally intolerable. Yet it was only twenty minutes to one.

Her lip raised itself, like that of a horse that is going to bite. The little brown book was dull. She reached her hand above her head and took down another book from the shelf of battered books without looking at it. She opened the book at random; but her eye was caught by one of the couples who were still sitting

123

out in the garden though the others had gone in. What were they saying, she wondered? There was something gleaming in the grass, and, as far as she could see, the black-and-white figure stooped and picked it up.

"And as he picks it up," she murmured, looking out, "he says to the lady beside him: Behold, Miss Smith, what I have found on the grass—a fragment of my heart; of my broken heart, he says. I have found it in the grass; and I wear it on my breast"—she hummed the words in time to the melancholy waltz music—"my broken heart, this broken glass, for love—" she paused and glanced at the book. On the fly-leaf was written:

"Sara Pargiter from her Cousin Edward Pargiter."

". . . for love," she concluded, "is best."

She turned to the title-page.

"The Antigone of Sophocles, done into English verse by Edward Pargiter," she read.

Once more she looked out of the window. The couple had moved. They were going up the iron staircase. She watched them. They went into the ballroom. "And suppose in the middle of the dance," she murmured, "she takes it out; and looks at it and says, 'What is this?' and it's only a piece of broken glass—of broken glass. . . ." She looked down at the book again.

"The Antigone of Sophocles," she read. The book was brand-new; it cracked as she opened it; this was the first time she had opened it.

"The Antigone of Sophocles, done into English verse by Edward Pargiter," she read again. He had given it her in Oxford; one hot afternoon when they had been trailing through chapels and libraries. "Trailing and wailing," she hummed, turning over the pages, "and he said to me, getting up from the low armchair, and brushing his hand through his hair"—she glanced out of the window—"'my wasted youth, my wasted youth.'" The waltz was now at its most intense, its most melancholy. "Taking in his hand," she hummed in time to it, "this broken glass, this faded heart, he said to me . . ." Here the music stopped; there was a sound of clapping; the dancers once more came out into the garden.

She skipped through the pages. At first she read a line or two at random; then, from the litter of broken words, scenes rose, quickly, inaccurately, as she skipped. The unburied body of a murdered man lay like a fallen tree-trunk, like a statue, with one foot stark in the air. Vultures gathered. Down they flopped on the silver sand. With a lurch, with a reel, the top-heavy birds came waddling; with a flap of the grey throat swinging, they hopped—she beat her hand on the counterpane as she read— to that lump there. Quick, quick, quick with repeated jerks they struck the mouldy flesh. Yes. She glanced at the tree outside in the garden. The unburied body of the murdered man lay on the sand. Then in a yellow cloud came whirling—who? She turned the page quickly. Antigone? She came whirling out of the dust-cloud to where the vultures were reeling and flung white sand over the blackened foot. She stood there letting fall white dust over the blackened foot. Then behold! there were more clouds; dark clouds; the horsemen leapt down; she was seized; her wrists were bound with withies; and they bore her, thus bound—where?

There was a roar of laughter from the garden. She looked up. Where did they take her? she asked. The garden was full of people. She could not hear a word that they were saying. The figures were moving in and out.

"To the estimable court of the respected ruler?" she murmured, picking up a word or two at random, for she was still looking out into the garden. The man's name was Creon. He buried her. It was a moonlight night. The blades of the cactuses were sharp silver. The man in the loincloth gave three sharp taps with his mallet on the brick. She was buried alive. The tomb was a brick mound. There was just room for her to lie straight out. Straight out in a brick tomb, she said. And that's the end, she yawned, shutting the book.

She laid herself out, under the cold smooth sheets, and pulled the pillow over her ears. The one sheet and the one blanket fitted softly round her. At the bottom of the bed was a long stretch of cool fresh mattress. The sound of the dance music became dulled. Her body dropped suddenly; then reached ground. A dark wing brushed her mind, leaving a pause; a blank space. Everything—the music, the voices—became stretched and generalised. The book fell on the floor. She was asleep.

"It's a lovely night," said the girl who was going up the iron steps with her partner. She rested her hand on the balustrade. It felt very cold. She looked up; a slice of yellow light lay round the moon. It seemed to laugh round it. Her partner looked up too, and then mounted another step without saying anything for he was shy.

"Going to the match tomorrow?" he said stiffly, for they scarcely knew each other.

"If my brother gets off in time to take me," she said, and went up another step too. Then, as they entered the ballroom, he gave her a little bow and left her; for his partner was waiting.

The moon which was now clear of clouds lay in a bare space as if the light had consumed the heaviness of the clouds and left a perfectly clear pavement, a dancing ground for revelry. For some time the dappled iridescence of the sky remained unbroken. Then there was a puff of wind; and a little cloud crossed the moon.

There was a sound in the bedroom. Sara turned over.

"Who's that?" she murmured. She sat up and rubbed her eyes.

It was her sister. She stood at the door, hesitating. "Asleep?" she said in a low voice.

"No," said Sara. She rubbed her eyes. "I'm awake," she said, opening them.

Maggie came across the room and sat down on the edge of the bed. The blind was blowing out; the sheets were slipping off the bed. She felt dazed for a moment. After the ballroom, it looked so untidy. There was a tumbler with a toothbrush in it on the wash-stand; the towel was crumpled on the towel-horse;

and a book had fallen on the floor. She stooped and picked up the book. As she did so, the music burst out down the street. She held back the blind. The women in pale dresses, the men in black and white, were crowding up the stairs into the ballroom. Snatches of talk and laughter were blown across the garden.

"Is there a dance?" she asked.

"Yes. Down the street," said Sara.

Maggie looked out. At this distance the music sounded romantic, mysterious, and the colours flowed over each other, neither pink nor white nor blue.

Maggie stretched herself and unpinned the flower that she was wearing. It was drooping; the white petals were stained with black marks. She looked out of the window again. The mixture of lights was very odd; one leaf was a lurid green; another was a bright white. The branches crossed each other at different levels. Then Sally laughed.

"Did anybody give you a piece of glass," she said, "saying to you, Miss Pargiter . . . my broken heart?"

"No," said Maggie, "why should they?" The flower fell off her lap onto the floor.

"I was thinking," said Sara. "The people in the garden . . ."

She waved her hand at the window. They were silent for a moment, listening to the dance music.

"And who did you sit next?" Sara asked after a time.

"A man in gold lace," said Maggie.

"In gold lace?" Sara repeated.

Maggie was silent. She was getting used to the room; the discrepancy between this litter and the shiny ballroom was leaving her. She envied her sister lying in bed with the window open and the breeze blowing in.

"Because he was going to a party," she said. She paused. Something had caught her eye. A branch swayed up and down in the little breeze. Maggie held the blind so that the window was uncurtained. Now she could see the whole sky, and the houses and the branches in the garden.

"It's the moon," she said. It was the moon that was making the leaves white. They both looked at the moon, which shone like a silver coin, perfectly polished, very sharp and hard.

"But if they don't say O my broken heart," said Sara, "what do they say, at parties?"

Maggie flicked off a white fleck that had stuck to her arm from her gloves.

"Some people say one thing," she said, getting up, "and some people say another."

She picked up the little brown book which lay on the counterpane and smoothed out the bedclothes. Sara took the book out of her hand.

"This man," she said, tapping the ugly little brown volume, "says the world's nothing but thought, Maggie."

"Does he?" said Maggie, putting the book on the wash-stand. It was a device, she knew, to keep her standing there, talking.

"D'you think it's true?" Sara asked.

"Possibly," said Maggie, without thinking what she was saying. She put out her hand to draw the curtain.

"The world's nothing but thought, does he say?" she repeated, holding the curtain apart.

She had been thinking something of the kind when the cab crossed the Serpentine; when her mother interrupted her. She had been thinking, Am I that, or am I this? Are we one, or are we separate—something of the kind.

"Then what about trees and colours?" she said, turning round.

"Trees and colours?" Sara repeated.

"Would there be trees if we didn't see them?" said Maggie.

"What's 'I'? . . . 'I' . . ." She stopped. She did not know what she meant. She was talking nonsense.

"Yes," said Sara. "What's 'I'?" She held her sister tight by the skirt, whether she wanted to prevent her from going, or whether she wanted to argue the question.

"What's 'I'?" she repeated.

But there was a rustling outside the door and her mother came in.

"Oh my dear children!" she exclaimed, "still out of bed? Still talking?"

She came across the room, beaming, glowing, as if she were still under the influence of the party. Jewels flashed on her neck and her arms. She was extraordinarily handsome. She glanced round her.

"And the flower's on the floor, and everything's so untidy," she said. She picked up the flower that Maggie had dropped and put it to her lips.

"Because I was reading, Mama, because I was waiting," said Sara. She took her mother's hand and stroked the bare arm. She imitated her mother's manner so exactly that Maggie smiled. They were the very opposite of each other—Lady Pargiter so sumptuous; Sally so angular. But it's worked, she thought to herself, as Lady Pargiter allowed herself to be pulled down onto the bed. The imitation had been perfect.

"But you must go to sleep, Sal," she protested. "What did the doctor say? Lie straight, lie still, he said." She pushed her back onto the pillows.

"I am lying straight and still," said Sara. "Now"—she looked up at her—"tell me about the party."

Maggie stood upright in the window. She watched the couples coming down the iron staircase. Soon the garden was full of pale whites and pinks, moving in and out. She half heard them behind her talking about the party.

"It was a very nice party," her mother was saying.

Maggie looked out of the window. The square of the garden was filled with differently tinted colours. They seemed to ripple one over the other until they entered the angle where the light from the house fell, when they suddenly turned to ladies and gentlemen in full evening dress.

"No fish-knives?" she heard Sara saying.

She turned.

"Who was the man I sat next?" she asked.

"Sir Matthew Mayhew," said Lady Pargiter.

"Who is Sir Matthew Mayhew?" said Maggie.

"A most distinguished man, Maggie!" said her mother, flinging her hand out.

"A most distinguished man," Sara echoed her.

"But he is," Lady Pargiter repeated, smiling at her daughter whom she loved, perhaps because of her shoulder.

"It was a great honour to sit next him, Maggie," she continued. "A great honour," she said reprovingly. She paused, as if she saw a little scene. She looked up.

"And then," she resumed, "when Mary Palmer says to me, Which is your daughter? I see Maggie, miles away, at the other end of the room, talking to Martin, whom she might have met every day of her life in an omnibus!"

Her words were stressed so that they seemed to rise and fall. She emphasised the rhythm still further by tapping with her fingers on Sally's bare arm.

"But I don't see Martin every day," Maggie protested.

"I haven't seen him since he came back from Africa." Her mother interrupted her.

"But you don't go to parties, my dear Maggie, to talk to your own cousins. You go to parties to—"

Here the dance music crashed out. The first chords seemed possessed of frantic energy, as if they were summoning the dancers imperiously to return. Lady Pargiter stopped in the middle of her sentence. She sighed; her body seemed to become indolent and suave. The heavy lids lowered themselves slightly over her large dark eyes. She swayed her head slowly in time to the music.

"What's that they're playing?" she murmured. She hummed the tune, beating time with her hand. "Something I used to dance to."

"Dance it now, Mama," said Sara.

"Yes, Mama. Show us how you used to dance," Maggie urged her.

"But without a partner—?" Lady Pargiter protested.

Maggie pushed a chair away.

"Imagine a partner," Sara urged her.

"Well," said Lady Pargiter. She rose. "It was something like this," she said. She paused; she held her skirt out with one hand; she slightly crooked the other in which she held the flower; she twirled round and round in the space which Maggie had cleared. She moved with extraordinary stateliness. All her limbs seemed to bend and flow in the lilt and the curve of the music; which became louder and clearer as she danced to it. She circled in and out among the chairs and tables and then, as the music stopped, "There!" she exclaimed. Her body seemed to fold and close itself together as she sighed "There!" and sank all in one movement on the edge of the bed.

"Wonderful!" Maggie exclaimed. Her eyes rested on her mother with admiration.

"Nonsense," Lady Pargiter laughed, panting slightly. "I'm much too old to dance now; but when I was young; when I was your age—" She sat there panting.

"You danced out of the house onto the terrace and found a little note folded in your bouquet—" said Sara, stroking her mother's arm. "Tell us that story, Mama."

"Not tonight," said Lady Pargiter. "Listen—there's the clock striking!"

Since the Abbey was so near, the sound of the hour filled the room; softly, tumultuously, as if it were a flurry of soft sighs hurrying one on top of another, yet concealing something hard. Lady Pargiter counted. It was very late.

"I'll tell you the true story one of these days," she said as she bent to kiss her daughter goodnight.

"Now! Now!" cried Sara, holding her fast.

"No, not now—not now!" Lady Pargiter laughed, snatching away her hand. "There's Papa calling me!"

They heard footsteps in the passage outside, and then Sir Digby's voice at the door.

"Eugénie! It's very late, Eugénie!" they heard him say.

"Coming!" she cried. "Coming!"

Sara caught her by the train of her dress. "You haven't told us the story of the bouquet, Mamma!" she cried.

"Eugénie!" Sir Digby repeated. His voice sounded peremptory. "Have you locked—"

"Yes, yes, yes," said Eugénie. "I will tell you the true story another time," she said, freeing herself from her daughter's grasp. She kissed them both quickly and went out of the room.

"She won't tell us," said Maggie, picking up her gloves. She spoke with some bitterness.

They listened to the voices talking in the passage. They could hear their father's voice. He was expostulating. His voice sounded querulous and cross.

"Pirouetting up and down with his sword between his legs; with his opera hat under his arm and his sword between his legs," said Sara, pummelling her pillows viciously.

The voices went further away, downstairs.

"Who was the note from, d'you think?" said Maggie. She paused, looking at her sister burrowing into her pillows.

"The note? What note?" said Sara. "Oh, the note in the bouquet. I don't remember," she said. She yawned.

Maggie shut the window and pulled the curtain but she left a chink of light.

"Pull it tight, Maggie," said Sara irritably. "Shut out that din."

She curled herself up with her back to the window. She had raised a hump of pillow against her head as if to shut out the dance music that was still going on. She pressed her face into a cleft of the pillows.

She looked like a chrysalis wrapped round in the sharp white folds of the sheet. Only the tip of her nose was visible. Her hip and her feet jutted out at the end of the bed covered by a single sheet. She gave a profound sigh that was half a snore; she was asleep already.

Maggie went along the passage. Then she saw that there were lights in the hall beneath. She stopped and looked down over the banister. The hall was lit up. She could see the great Italian chair with the gilt claws that stood in the hall. Her mother had thrown her evening cloak over it, so that it fell in soft golden folds over the crimson cover. She could see a tray with whisky and a soda-water syphon on the hall table. Then she heard the voices of her father and mother as they came up the kitchen stairs. They had been down in the basement; there had been a burglary up the street; her mother had promised to have a new lock put on the kitchen door but had forgotten. She could hear her father say:

". . . they'd melt it down; we should never get it back again."

Maggie went on a few steps upstairs.

"I'm so sorry, Digby," Eugénie said as they came into the hall. "I will tie a knot in my handkerchief; I will go directly after breakfast tomorrow morning. . . . Yes," she said, gathering her cloak in her arms, "I will go myself, and I will say 'I've had enough of your excuses, Mr Toye. No, Mr Toye, you have deceived me once too often. And after all these years!'"

Then there was a pause. Maggie could hear soda-water squirted into a tumbler; the chink of a glass; and then the lights went out.

1908

It was March and the wind was blowing. But it was not "blowing." It was scraping, scourging. It was so cruel. So unbecoming. Not merely did it bleach faces and raise red spots on noses; it tweaked up skirts; showed stout legs; made trousers reveal skeleton shins. There was no roundness, no fruit in it. Rather it was like the curve of a scythe which cuts, not corn, usefully; but destroys, revelling in sheer sterility. With one blast it blew out colour—even a Rembrandt in the National Gallery, even a solid ruby in a Bond Street window: one blast and they were gone. Had it any breeding place it was in the Isle of Dogs among tin cans lying beside a workhouse drab on the banks of a polluted city. It tossed up rotten leaves, gave them another span of degraded existence; scorned, derided them, yet had nothing to put in the place of the scorned, the derided. Down they fell. Uncreative, unproductive, yelling its joy in destruction, its power to peel off the bark, the bloom, and show the bare bone, it paled every window; drove old gentlemen further and further into the leather smelling recesses of clubs; and old ladies to sit eyeless, leather cheeked, joyless among the tassels and antimacassars of their bedrooms and kitchens. Triumphing in its wantonness it emptied the streets; swept flesh before it; and coming smack against a dust cart standing outside the Army and Navy Stores, scattered along the pavement a litter of old envelopes; twists of hair; papers already blood smeared, yellow smeared, smudged with print and sent them scudding to plaster legs, lamp posts, pillar boxes, and fold themselves frantically against area railings.

Matty Stiles, the caretaker, huddled in the basement of the house in Browne Street, looked up. There was a rattle of dust along the pavement. It worked its way under the doors, through the window frames; on to chests and dressers. But she didn't care. She was one of the unlucky ones. She had been thinking it was a safe job, sure to last the summer out anyhow. The lady was dead; the gentleman too. She had got the job through her son the policeman. The house with its basement would never let this side of Christmas—so they told her. She had only to show parties round who came with orders to view from the agent. And she always mentioned the basement—how damp it was. "Look at that stain on the ceiling." There it was, sure enough. All the same, the party from China took a fancy to it. It suited him, he said. He had business in the city. She was one of the unlucky ones—after three months to turn out and lodge with her son in Pimlico.

A bell rang. Let him ring, ring, ring, she growled. She wasn't going to open the door any more. There he was standing on the door-step. She could see a pair of legs against the railing. Let him ring as much as he liked. The house was sold. Couldn't he see the notice on the board? Couldn't he read it? Hadn't he eyes? She huddled closer to the fire, which was covered with pale ash. She could see his legs there, standing on the door-step, between the canaries' cage and the dirty linen which she had been going to wash, but this wind made her shoulder ache cruel. Let him ring the house down, for all she cared.

Martin was standing there.

"Sold" was written on a strip of bright red paper pasted across the house-agent's board.

"Already!" said Martin. He had made a little circle to look at the house in Browne Street. And it was already sold. The red strip gave him a shock. It was sold already, and Digby had only been dead three months—Eugénie not much more than a year. He stood for a moment gazing at the black windows now grimed

135

with dust. It was a house of character; built some time in the eighteenth century. Eugénie had been proud of it. And I used to like going there, he thought. But now an old newspaper was on the door-step; wisps of straw had caught in the railings; and he could see, for there were no blinds, into an empty room. A woman was peering up at him from behind the bars of a cage in the basement. It was no use ringing. He turned away. A feeling of something extinguished came over him as he went down the street.

It's a grimy, it's a sordid end, he thought; I used to enjoy going there. But he disliked brooding over unpleasant thoughts. What's the good of it? he asked himself.

"The King of Spain's daughter," he hummed as he turned the corner, "came to visit me . . ."

"And how much longer," he asked himself, pressing the bell, as he stood on the door-step of the house in Abercorn Terrace, "is old Crosby going to keep me waiting?" The wind was very cold.

He stood there, looking at the buff-coloured front of the large, architecturally insignificant, but no doubt convenient family mansion in which his father and sister still lived.

"She takes her time nowadays," he thought, shivering in the wind. But here the door opened, and Crosby appeared.

"Hullo, Crosby!" he said.

She beamed on him so that her gold tooth showed. He was always her favourite, they said, and the thought pleased him today.

"How's the world treating you?" he asked, as he gave her his hat.

She was just the same—more shrivelled, more gnat-like, and her blue eyes were more prominent than ever.

"Feeling the rheumatics?" he asked, as she helped him off with his coat. She grinned, silently. He felt friendly; he was glad to find her much as usual. "And Miss Eleanor?" he asked, as he opened the drawing-room door. The room was empty. She was not there. But she had been there, for there was a book on the table. Nothing had been changed he was glad to see. He stood in front of the fire and looked at his mother's picture. In the course of the past few years it had ceased to be his mother; it had become a work of art. But it was dirty.

There used to be a flower in the grass, he thought, peering into a dark corner: but now there was nothing but dirty brown paint. And what's she been reading? he wondered. He took the book that was propped up against the teapot and looked at it. "Renan," he read. "Why Renan?" he asked himself, beginning to read as he waited.

"Mr Martin, Miss," said Crosby, opening the study door. Eleanor looked round. She was standing by her father's chair with her hands full of long strips of newspaper cuttings, as if she had been reading them aloud. There was a chess-board in front of him; the chess-men were set out for a game; but he was lying back in his chair. He looked lethargic, and rather gloomy.

"Put 'em away. . . . Keep 'em safe somewhere," he said, jerking his thumb at the cuttings. That was a sign that he had grown very old, Eleanor thought—wanting newspaper cuttings kept. He had grown inert and ponderous after his stroke; there were red veins in his nose and in his cheeks. She too felt old, heavy and dull.

"Mr Martin's called," Crosby repeated.

"Martin's come," Eleanor said. Her father seemed not to hear. He sat still with his head sunk on his breast. "Martin," Eleanor repeated. "Martin . . ."

Did he want to see him or did he not want to see him? She waited as if for some sluggish thought to rise. At last he gave a little grunt; but what it meant she was not certain.

"I'll send him in after tea," she said. She paused for a moment. He roused himself and began fumbling with his chess-men. He still had courage, she observed with pride. He still insisted upon doing things for himself.

She went into the drawing-room and found Martin standing in front of the placid, smiling picture of their mother. He held a book in his hand.

"Why Renan?" he said as she came in. He shut the book and kissed her. "Why Renan?" he repeated. She flushed slightly. It made her shy, for some reason, that he had found the book there, open. She sat down and laid the press cuttings on the tea-table.

"How's Papa?" he asked. She had lost something of her bright colour, he thought, glancing at her, and her hair had a tuft of grey in it.

"Rather gloomy," she said, glancing at the press cuttings.

"I wonder," she added, "who writes that sort of thing?"

"What sort of thing?" said Martin. He picked up one of the crinkled strips and began reading it: "'. . . an exceptionally able public servant . . . a man of wide interests. . . .' Oh, Digby," he said. "Obituaries. I passed the house this afternoon," he added. "It's sold."

"Already?" said Eleanor.

"It looked very shut-up and desolate," he added. "There was a dirty old woman in the basement."

Eleanor took out a hair-pin and began fraying the wick of the kettle. Martin watched her for a moment in silence.

"I liked going there," he said at length. "I liked Eugénie," he added.

Eleanor paused.

"Yes . . ." she said doubtfully. She had never felt at her ease with her. "She exaggerated," she added.

"Well of course," Martin laughed. He smiled, recalling some memory. "She had less sense of truth than . . . that's no sort of use, Nell," he broke off, irritated by her fumbling with the wick.

"Yes, yes," she protested. "It boils in time."

She paused. Stretching out towards the tea-caddy, she measured the tea. "One, two, three, four," she counted.

She still used the nice old silver tea-caddy, he noticed, with the sliding lid. He watched her measuring the tea methodically—

one, two, three, four. He was silent.

"We can't tell a lie to save our souls," he said abruptly.

What makes him say that? Eleanor wondered.

"When I was with them in Italy—," she said aloud. But here the door opened and Crosby came in carrying some sort of dish. She left the door ajar and a dog pushed in after her.

"I mean—" Eleanor added; but she could not say what she meant with Crosby in the room fidgeting about.

"It's time Miss Eleanor got a new kettle," said Martin, pointing to the old brass kettle, faintly engraved with a design of roses, which he had always hated.

"Crosby," said Eleanor, still poking with her pin, "doesn't hold with new inventions. Crosby won't trust herself in the Tube, will you, Crosby?"

Crosby grinned. They always spoke to her in the third person, because she never answered but only grinned. The dog snuffed at the dish she had just put down. "Crosby's letting that beast get much too fat," said Martin, pointing at the dog.

"That's what I'm always telling her," said Eleanor.

"If I were you, Crosby," said Martin, "I'd cut down his meals and take him for a brisk run round the park every morning." Crosby opened her mouth wide.

"Oh, Mr Martin!" she protested, shocked by his brutality into speech.

The dog followed her out of the room.

"Crosby's the same as ever," said Martin.

Eleanor had lifted the lid of the kettle and was looking in. There were no bubbles on the water yet.

"Damn that kettle," said Martin. He took up one of the newspaper cuttings and began to make it into a spill.

"No, no, Papa wants them kept," said Eleanor. "But he wasn't like that," she said, laying her hand on the newspaper cuttings. "Not in the least."

"What was he like?" Martin asked.

Eleanor paused. She could see her uncle clearly in her mind's eye; he held his top-hat in his hand; he laid his hand on her shoulder as they stopped in front of some picture. But how could she describe him?

"He used to take me to the National Gallery," she said.

"Very cultivated, of course," said Martin. "But he was such a damned snob."

"Only on the surface," said Eleanor.

"And always finding fault with Eugénie about little things," Martin added.

"But think of living with her," said Eleanor.

"That manner—" She threw her hand out; but not as Eugénie threw her hand out, Martin thought.

"I liked her," he said. "I liked going there." He saw the untidy room; the piano open; the window open; a wind blowing the curtains, and his aunt coming forward with her arms open. "What a pleasure, Martin! what a pleasure!" she would say. What had her private life been, he wondered—her love affairs? She must have had them—obviously, obviously.

"Wasn't there some story," he began, "about a letter?" He wanted to say, Didn't she have an affair with somebody? But it was more difficult to be open with his sister than with other women, because she treated him as if he were a small boy still. Had Eleanor ever been in love, he wondered, looking at her.

"Yes," she said. "There was a story—"

But here the electric bell rang sharply. She stopped.

"Papa," she said. She half rose.

"No," said Martin. "I'll go." He got up. "I promised him a game of chess."

"Thanks, Martin. He'll enjoy that," said Eleanor with relief as he left the room, and she found herself alone.

She leant back in her chair. How terrible old age was, she thought; shearing off all one's faculties, one by one, but leaving something alive in the centre: leaving—she swept up the press cuttings—a game of chess, a drive in the park, and a visit from old General Arbuthnot in the evening.

It was better to die, like Eugénie and Digby, in the prime of life with all one's faculties about one. But he wasn't like that, she thought, glancing at the press cuttings. "A man of singularly handsome presence . . . shot, fished, and played golf." No, not like that in the least. He had been a curious man; weak; sensitive; liking titles; liking pictures; and often depressed, she guessed, by his wife's exuberance. She pushed the cuttings away and took up her book. It was odd how different the same person seemed to two different people, she thought. There was Martin, liking Eugénie; and she, liking Digby. She began to read.

She had always wanted to know about Christianity—how it began; what it meant, originally. God is love, The kingdom of Heaven is within us, sayings like that she thought, turning over the pages, what did they mean? The actual words were very beautiful. But who said them—when? Then the spout of the tea-kettle puffed steam at her and she moved it away. The wind was rattling the windows in the back room; it was bending the little bushes; they still had no leaves on them. It was what a man said under a fig tree, on a hill, she thought. And then another man wrote it down. But suppose that what that man says is just as false as what this man—she touched the press cuttings with her spoon—says about Digby? And here am I, she thought, looking at the china in the Dutch cabinet, in this drawing-room, getting a little spark from what someone said all those years ago—here it comes (the china was changing from blue to livid) skipping over all those mountains, all those seas. She found her place and began to read.

But a sound in the hall interrupted her. Was someone coming in? She listened. No, it was the wind. The wind was terrific. It pressed on the house; gripped it tight, then let it fall apart. Upstairs a door slammed; a window must be open in the bedroom above. A blind was tapping. It was difficult to fix her mind on Renan. She liked it, though. French she could read easily of course; and Italian; and a little German. But what vast gaps there were, what blank spaces, she thought leaning back in her chair, in her knowledge! How little she knew about anything. Take this cup for instance; she held it out in front of her. What was it made of? Atoms? And what were atoms, and how did they stick together? The smooth hard surface of the china with its red flowers seemed to her for a second a marvellous mystery. But there was another sound in the hall. It was the wind, but it was also a voice, talking. It must be Martin. But who could he be talking to, she wondered? She listened, but she could not hear what he was saying because of the wind. And why, she asked herself, did he say We can't tell a lie to save our souls? He was thinking about himself; one always knew when people were thinking about themselves by their tone of voice. Perhaps he was justifying himself for having left the Army. That had been courageous, she thought; but isn't it odd, she mused, listening to the voices, that he should be such a dandy too? He was wearing a new blue suit with white stripes on it. And he had shaved off his moustache. He ought never to have been a soldier, she thought; he was much too pugnacious. . . . They were still talking. She could not hear what he was saying, but from the sound of his voice it came over her that he must have a great many love affairs. Yes—it became perfectly obvious to her, listening to his voice through the door, that he had a great many love affairs. But who with? and why do men think love affairs so important? she asked as the door opened.

"Hullo, Rose!" she exclaimed, surprised to see her sister come in too. "I thought you were in Northumberland!"

"You thought I was in Northumberland!" Rose laughed, kissing her. "But why? I said the eighteenth."

"But isn't today the eleventh?" said Eleanor.

"You're only a week behind the times, Nell," said Martin.

"Then I must have dated all my letters wrong!" Eleanor exclaimed. She glanced apprehensively at her writing-table. The walrus, with a worn patch in its bristles, no longer stood there.

"Tea, Rose?" she asked.

"No. It's a bath I want," said Rose. She threw off her hat and ran her fingers through her hair.

"You're looking very well," said Eleanor, thinking how handsome she looked. But she had a scratch on her chin.

"A positive beauty, isn't she?" Martin laughed at her.

Rose threw her head up rather like a horse. They always bickered, Eleanor thought—Martin and Rose. Rose was handsome, but she wished she dressed better. She was dressed in a green hairy coat and skirt with leather buttons, and she carried a shiny bag. She had been holding meetings in the North.

"I want a bath," Rose repeated. "I'm dirty. And what's all this?" she said, pointing to the press cuttings on the table. "Oh, Uncle Digby," she added casually, pushing them away. He had been dead some months now; they were already yellowish and curled.

"Martin says the house has been sold," said Eleanor.

"Has it?" she said indifferently. She broke off a piece of cake and began munching it. "Spoiling my dinner," she said. "But I had no time for lunch."

"What a woman of action she is!" Martin chaffed her.

"And the meetings?" Eleanor asked.

"Yes. What about the North?" said Martin.

They began to discuss politics. She had been speaking at a by-election. A stone had been thrown at her; she put her hand to her chin. But she had enjoyed it.

"I think we gave 'em something to think about," she said, breaking off another piece of cake.

She ought to have been the soldier, Eleanor thought. She was exactly like the picture of old Uncle Pargiter of Pargiter's Horse. Martin, now that he had shaved his moustache off and showed his lips, ought to have been—what? Perhaps an architect, she thought. He's so—she looked up. Now it was hailing. White rods came across the window in the back room. There was a great gust of wind; the little bushes blanched and bent under it. And a window banged upstairs in her mother's bedroom. Perhaps I ought to go and shut it, she thought. The rain must be coming in.

"Eleanor—"said Rose. "Eleanor"—she repeated.

Eleanor started.

"Eleanor's broody," said Martin.

"No, not at all—not at all," she protested. "What are you talking about?"

"I was asking you," said Rose. "Do you remember that row when the microscope was broken? Well, I met that boy—that horrid, ferret-faced boy—Erridge—up in the North."

"He wasn't horrid," said Martin.

"He was," Rose persisted. "A horrid little sneak. He pretended that it was I who broke the microscope and it was he who broke it. . . . D'you remember that row?" She turned to Eleanor.

"I don't remember that row," said Eleanor. "There were so many," she added.

"That was one of the worst," said Martin.

"It was," said Rose. She pursed her lips together. Some memory seemed to have come back to her. "And after it was over," she said, turning to Martin, "you came up into the nursery and asked me to go beetling with you in the Round Pond. D'you remember?"

She paused. There was something queer about the memory, Eleanor could see. She spoke with a curious intensity.

"And you said, 'I'll ask you three times; and if you don't answer the third time, I'll go alone.' And I swore, 'I'll let him go alone.'" Her blue eyes blazed.

"I can see you," said Martin. "Wearing a pink frock, with a knife in your hand."

"And you went," Rose said; she spoke with suppressed vehemence. "And I dashed into the bathroom and cut this gash"—she held out her wrist. Eleanor looked at it. There was a thin white scar just above the wrist joint.

When did she do that? Eleanor thought. She could not remember. Rose had locked herself into the bathroom with a knife and cut her wrist. She had known nothing about it. She looked at the white mark. It must have bled.

144

"Oh, Rose always was a firebrand!" said Martin. He got up. "She always had the devil's own temper," he added. He stood for a moment looking round the drawing-room, cluttered up with several hideous pieces of furniture that he would have got rid of had be been Eleanor, he thought, and forced to live there. But perhaps she did not mind things like that.

"Dining out?" she said. He dined out every night. She would like to have asked him where he was dining.

He nodded without saying anything. He met all sorts of people she did not know, she reflected; and he did not want to talk about them. He had turned to the fireplace.

"That picture wants cleaning," he said, pointing to the picture of their mother.

"It's a nice picture," he added, looking at it critically. "But usen't there to be a flower in the grass?"

Eleanor looked at it. She had not looked at it, so as to see it, for many years.

"Was there?" she said.

"Yes. A little blue flower," said Martin. "I can remember it when I was a child. . . ."

He turned. Some memory from his childhood came over him as he saw Rose sitting there at the tea table with her fist still clenched. He saw her standing with her back to the school-room door; very red in the face, with her lips tight shut as they were now. She had wanted him to do something. And he had crumpled a ball of paper in his hand and shied it at her.

"What awful lives children live!" he said, waving his hand at her as he crossed the room. "Don't they, Rose?"

"Yes," said Rose. "And they can't tell anybody," she added.

There was another gust and the sound of glass crashing.

"Miss Pym's conservatory?" said Martin, pausing with his hand on the door.

"Miss Pym?" said Eleanor. "She's been dead these twenty years!"

1910

In the country it was an ordinary day enough; one of the long reel of days that turned as the years passed from green to orange; from grass to harvest. It was neither hot nor cold, an English spring day, bright enough, but a purple cloud behind the hill might mean rain. The grasses rippled with shadow, and then with sunlight.

In London, however, the stricture and pressure of the season were already felt, especially in the West End, where flags flew; canes tapped; dresses flowed; and houses freshly painted had awnings spread and swinging baskets of red geraniums. The Parks too—St. James's, the Green Park, Hyde Park—were making ready. Already in the morning before there was a chance of a procession, the green chairs were ranged among the plump brown flower beds with their curled hyacinths, as if waiting for something to happen; for a curtain to rise; for Queen Alexandra to come, bowing through the gates. She had a face like a flower petal, and always wore her pink carnation.

Men lay flat on the grass reading newspapers with their shirts open; on the bald scrubbed space by the Marble Arch speakers congregated; nursemaids vacantly regarded them; and mothers, squatted on the grass, watched their children play.

Down Park Lane and Piccadilly vans, cars, omnibuses ran along the streets as if the streets were slots; stopped and jerked; as if a puzzle were solved, and then broken, for it was the season, and the streets were crowded. Over Park Lane and Piccadilly the clouds kept their freedom, wandering fitfully, staining windows gold, daubing them black, passed and vanished, though marble in Italy looked no more solid, gleaming in the quarries, veined with yellow, than the clouds over Park Lane.

If the bus stopped here, Rose thought, looking down over the side, she would get up. The bus stopped, and she rose. It was a pity, she thought, as she stepped onto the pavement and caught a glimpse of her own figure in a tailor's window, not to dress better, not to look nicer. Always reach-me-downs, coats and skirts from Whiteleys. But they saved time, and the years after all—she was over forty—made one care very little what people thought. They used to say, why don't you marry? Why don't you do this or that, interfering. But not any longer.

She paused in one of the little alcoves that were scooped out in the bridge, from habit. People always stopped to look at the river. It was running fast, a muddy gold this morning with smooth breadths and ripples, for the tide was high. And there was the usual tug and the usual barges with black tarpaulins and corn showing. The water swirled round the arches. As she stood there, looking down at the water, some buried feeling began to arrange the stream into a pattern. The pattern was painful. She remembered how she had stood there on the night of a certain engagement, crying; her tears had fallen, her happiness, it seemed to her, had fallen. Then she had turned—here she turned—and had seen the churches, the masts and roofs of the city. There's *that,* she had said to herself. Indeed it was a splendid view. . . . She looked, and then again she turned. There were the Houses of Parliament. A queer expression, half frown, half smile, formed on her face and she threw herself slightly backwards, as if she were leading an army.

"Damned humbugs!" she said aloud, striking her fist on the balustrade. A clerk who was passing looked at her with surprise. She laughed. She often talked aloud. Why not? That too was one of the consolations, like her coat and skirt, and the hat she stuck on without giving a look in the glass. If people chose to laugh, let them. She strode on. She was lunching in Hyams Place with her cousins. She had asked herself on the spur of the moment, meeting Maggie in a shop. First she had heard a voice; then seen a hand. And it was odd, considering how little she knew them— they had lived abroad—how strongly, sitting there at the counter before Maggie saw her, simply from the sound of her voice, she had felt—she supposed it was affection?—some feeling bred of blood in common. She had got up and said May I come and see you? busy as she was, hating to break her day in the middle. She walked on. They lived in Hyams Place, over the river—Hyams Place, that little crescent of old houses with the name carved in the middle which she used to pass so often when she lived down here. She used to ask herself in those far-off days Who was Hyam? But she had never solved the question to her satisfaction. She walked on, across the river.

The shabby street on the south side of the river was very noisy. Now and again a voice detached itself from the general clamour. A woman shouted to her neighbour; a child cried. A man trundling a barrow opened his mouth and bawled up at the windows as he passed. There were bedsteads, grates, pokers and odd pieces of twisted iron on his barrow. But whether he was selling old iron or buying old iron it was impossible to say; the rhythm persisted; but the words were almost rubbed out.

The swarm of sound, the rush of traffic, the shouts of the hawkers, the single cries and the general cries, came into the upper room of the house in Hyams Place where Sara Pargiter sat at the piano. She was singing. Then she stopped; she watched her sister laying the table.

"Go search the valleys," she murmured, as she watched her, "pluck up every rose." She paused. "That's very nice," she added, dreamily. Maggie had taken a bunch of flowers; had cut the tight little string which bound them, and had laid them side by side on the table; and was arranging them in an earthenware pot. They were differently coloured, blue, white and purple. Sara watched her arranging them. She laughed suddenly.

"What are you laughing at?" said Maggie absent-mindedly.

She added a purple flower to the bunch and looked at it.

"Dazed in a rapture of contemplation," said Sara, "shading her eyes with peacocks' feathers dipped in morning dew—" she pointed to the table. "Maggie said," she jumped up and pirouetted about the room, "three's the same as two, three's the same as two." She pointed to the table upon which three places had been laid.

"But we are three," said Maggie. "Rose is coming." Sara stopped. Her face fell.

"Rose is coming?" she repeated.

"I told you," said Maggie. "I said to you, Rose is coming to luncheon on Friday. It is Friday. And Rose is coming to luncheon. Any minute now," she said. She got up and began to fold some stuff that was lying on the floor.

"It is Friday, and Rose is coming to luncheon," Sara repeated.

"I told you," said Maggie. "I was in a shop. I was buying stuff. And somebody"—she paused to make her fold more accurately—"came out from behind a counter and said, 'I'm your cousin. I'm Rose,' she said. 'Can I come and see you? Any day, any time,' she said. So I said," she put the stuff on a chair, "lunch."

She looked round the room to see that everything was in readiness. Chairs were missing. Sara pulled up a chair.

"Rose is coming," she said, "and this is where she'll sit." She placed the chair at the table facing the window. "And she'll take off her gloves; and she'll lay one on this side, one on that. And she'll say, I've never been in this part of London before.'"

"And then?" said Maggie, looking at the table.

"You'll say 'It's so convenient for the theatres.'"

"And then?" said Maggie.

"And then she'll say rather wistfully, smiling, putting her head on one side, 'D'you often go to the theatre, Maggie?'"

"No," said Maggie. "Rose has red hair."

"Red hair?" Sara exclaimed. "I thought it was grey—a little wisp straggling from under a black bonnet," she added.

"No," said Maggie. "She has a great deal of hair; and it's red."

149

"Red hair; red Rose," Sara exclaimed. She spun round on her toe.

"Rose of the flaming heart; Rose of the burning breast; Rose of the weary world—red, red Rose!"

A door slammed below; they heard footsteps mounting the stairs. "There she is," said Maggie.

The steps stopped. They heard a voice saying, "Still further up? On the very top? Thank you." Then the steps began mounting the stairs again.

"This is the worst torture . . ." Sara began, screwing her hands together and clinging to her sister, "that life. . . ."

"Don't be such an ass," said Maggie, pushing her away, as the door opened.

Rose came in.

"It's ages since we met," she said, shaking hands.

She wondered what had made her come. Everything was different from what she expected. The room was rather poverty-stricken; the carpet did not cover the floor. There was a sewing-machine in the corner, and Maggie too looked different from what she had looked in the shop. But there was a crimson-and-gilt chair; she recognised it with relief.

"That used to stand in the hall, didn't it?" she said, putting her bag down on the chair.

"Yes," said Maggie.

"And that glass—" said Rose, looking at the old Italian glass blurred with spots that hung between the windows, "wasn't that there too?"

"Yes," said Maggie, "in my mother's bedroom."

There was a pause. There seemed to be nothing to say.

"What nice rooms you've found!" Rose continued, making conversation. It was a large room and the door-posts had little carvings on them. "But don't you find it rather noisy?" she continued.

The man was crying under the window. She looked out of

the window. Opposite there was a row of slate roofs, like half-opened umbrellas; and, rising high above them, a great building which, save for thin black strokes across it, seemed to be made entirely of glass. It was a factory. The man bawled in the street underneath.

"Yes, it's noisy," said Maggie. "But very convenient."

"Very convenient for the theatres," said Sara, as she put down the meat.

"So I remember finding," said Rose, turning to look at her, "when I lived here myself."

"Did you live here?" said Maggie, beginning to help the cutlets.

"Not here," she said. "Round the corner. With a friend."

"We thought you lived in Abercorn Terrace," said Sara.

"Can't one live in more places than one?" Rose asked, feeling vaguely annoyed, for she had lived in many places, felt many passions, and done many things.

"I remember Abercorn Terrace," said Maggie. She paused. "There was a long room; and a tree at the end; and a picture over the fireplace, of a girl with red hair?"

Rose nodded. "Mama when she was young," she said.

"And a round table in the middle?" Maggie continued.

Rose nodded.

"And you had a parlourmaid with very prominent blue eyes?"

"Crosby. She's still with us."

They ate in silence.

"And then?" said Sara, as if she were a child asking for a story.

"And then?" said Rose. "Well then"—she looked at Maggie, thinking of her as a little girl who had come to tea.

She saw them sitting round a table; and a detail that she had not thought of for years came back to her—how Milly used to take her hair-pin and fray the wick of the kettle. And she saw Eleanor sitting with her account books; and she saw herself go up to her and say: "Eleanor, I want to go to Lamley's."

Her past seemed to be rising above her present. And for some reason she wanted to talk about her past; to tell them something about herself that she had never told anybody—something hidden. She paused, gazing at the flowers in the middle of the table without seeing them. There was a blue knot in the yellow glaze she noticed.

"I remember Uncle Abel," said Maggie. "He gave me a necklace; a blue necklace with gold spots."

"He's still alive," said Rose.

They talked, she thought, as if Abercorn Terrace were a scene in a play. They talked as if they were speaking of people who were real, but not real in the way in which she felt herself to be real. It puzzled her; it made her feel that she was two different people at the same time; that she was living at two different times at the same moment. She was a little girl wearing a pink frock; and here she was in this room, now. But there was a great rattle under the windows. A dray went roaring past. The glasses jingled on the table. She started slightly, roused from her thoughts about her childhood, and separated the glasses.

"Don't you find it very noisy here?" she said.

"Yes. But very convenient for the theatres," said Sara.

Rose looked up. She had repeated herself. She thinks me an old fool, Rose thought, making the same remark twice over. She blushed slightly.

What is the use, she thought, of trying to tell people about one's past? What is one's past? She stared at the pot with the blue knot loosely tied in the yellow glaze. Why did I come, she thought, when they only laugh at me? Sally rose and cleared away the plates.

"And Delia—" Maggie began as they waited. She pulled the pot towards her, and began to arrange the flowers. She was not listening; she was thinking her own thoughts. She reminded Rose, as she watched her, of Digby—absorbed in the arrangement of a bunch of flowers, as if to arrange flowers, to put the white by the blue, were the most important thing in the world.

"She married an Irishman," she said aloud.

Maggie took a blue flower and placed it beside a white flower. "And Edward?" she asked.

"Edward . . ." Rose was beginning, when Sally came in with the pudding.

"Edward!" she exclaimed, catching the word.

"Oh blasted eyes of my deceased wife's sister—withered prop of my defunct old age . . ." She put down the pudding. "That's Edward," she said. "A quotation from a book he gave me. 'My wasted youth—my wasted youth' . . ." The voice was Edward's; Rose could hear him say it. For he had a way of belittling himself, when in fact he had a very good opinion of himself.

But it was not the whole of Edward. And she would not have him laughed at; for she was very fond of her brother and very proud of him.

"There's not much of 'my wasted youth' about Edward now," she said.

"I thought not," said Sara, taking her place opposite.

They were silent. Rose looked at the flower again. Why did I come? she kept asking herself. Why had she broken up her morning, and interrupted her day's work, when it was clear to her that they had not wished to see her?

"Go on, Rose," said Maggie, helping the pudding. "Go on telling us about the Pargiters."

"About the Pargiters?" said Rose. She saw herself running along the broad avenue in the lamplight.

"What could be more ordinary?" she said. "A large family, living in a large house . . ." And yet she felt that she had been herself very interesting. She paused. Sara looked at her.

"It's not ordinary," she said. "The Pargiters—" She was holding a fork in her hand, and she drew a line on the table-cloth. "The Pargiters," she repeated, "going on and on and on"—here her fork touched a salt-cellar—"until they come to a rock," she said; "and then Rose"—she looked at her again: Rose drew herself up slightly, "—Rose claps spurs to her horse, rides straight up to a man in a gold coat, and says 'Damn your eyes!' Isn't that

Rose, Maggie?" she said, looking at her sister as if she had been drawing her picture on the table-cloth.

That is true, Rose thought as she took her pudding. That is myself. Again she had the odd feeling of being two people at the same time.

"Well, that's done," said Maggie, pushing away her plate. "Come and sit in the armchair, Rose," she said.

She went over to the fireplace and pulled out an armchair, which had springs like hoops, Rose noticed, in the seat.

They were poor, Rose thought, glancing round her. That was why they had chosen this house to live in—because it was cheap. They cooked their own food—Sally had gone into the kitchen to make the coffee. She drew her chair up beside Maggie's.

"You make your own clothes?" she said, pointing to the sewing-machine in the corner. There was silk folded on it.

"Yes," said Maggie, looking at the sewing-machine.

"For a party?" said Rose. The stuff was silk, green, with blue rays on it.

"Tomorrow night," said Maggie. She raised her hand with a curious gesture to her face, as if she wanted to conceal something. She wants to hide herself from me, Rose thought, as I want to hide myself from her. She watched her; she had got up, had fetched the silk and the sewing-machine, and was threading the needle. Her hands were large and thin and strong, Rose noticed.

"I never could make my own clothes," she said, watching her arrange the silk smoothly under the needle. She was beginning to feel at her ease. She took off her hat and threw it on the floor. Maggie looked at her with approval. She was handsome, in a ravaged way; more like a man than a woman.

"But then," said Maggie, beginning to turn the handle rather cautiously, "you did other things." She spoke in the absorbed tones of someone who is using their hands.

The machine made a comfortable whirring sound as the needle pricked through the silk.

"Yes, I did other things," said Rose, stroking the cat that had stretched itself against her knee, "when I lived down here."

"But that was years ago," she added, "when I was young. I lived here with a friend," she sighed, "and taught little thieves."

Maggie said nothing; she was whirring the machine round and round.

"I always liked thieves better than other people," Rose added after a time.

"Yes," said Maggie.

"I never liked being at home," said Rose. "I liked being on my own much better."

"Yes," said Maggie.

Rose went on talking.

It was quite easy to talk, she found; quite easy. And there was no need to say anything clever; or to talk about one's self. She was talking about the Waterloo Road as she remembered it when Sara came in with the coffee.

"What was that about clinging to a fat man in the Campagna?" she asked, setting her tray down.

"The Campagna?" said Rose. "There was nothing about the Campagna."

"Heard through a door," said Sara, pouring out the coffee, "talk sounds very odd." She gave Rose her cup.

"I thought you were talking about Italy; about the Campagna, about the moonlight."

Rose shook her head. "We were talking about the Waterloo Road," she said. But what had she been talking about? Not simply about the Waterloo Road. Perhaps she had been talking nonsense. She had been saying the first thing that came into her head.

"All talk would be nonsense, I suppose, if it were written down," she said, stirring her coffee.

Maggie stopped the machine for a moment and smiled.

"And even if it isn't," she said.

"But it's the only way we have of knowing each other,"

Rose protested. She looked at her watch. It was later than she thought. She got up.

"I must go," she said. "But why don't you come with me?" she added on the spur of the moment.

Maggie looked up at her. "Where?" she said.

Rose was silent. "To a meeting," she said at length. She wanted to conceal the thing that interested her most; she felt extraordinarily shy. And yet she wanted them to come. But why? she asked herself, as she stood there awkwardly waiting. There was a pause.

"You could wait upstairs," she said suddenly. "And you'd see Eleanor; you'd see Martin—the Pargiters in the flesh," she added. She remembered Sara's phrase, "the caravan crossing the desert," she said.

She looked at Sara. She was balancing herself on the arm of a chair, sipping her coffee and swinging her foot up and down.

"Shall I come?" she asked, vaguely, still swinging her foot up and down.

Rose shrugged her shoulders. "If you like," she said.

"But should I like it?" Sara continued, still swinging her foot. ". . . this meeting? What do you think, Maggie?" she said, appealing to her sister. "Shall I go, or shan't I? Shall I go, or shan't I?" Maggie said nothing.

Then Sara got up, went to the window and stood there for a moment humming a tune. "Go search the valleys; pluck up every rose," she hummed. The man was passing; he was crying "Any old iron? Any old iron?" She turned round with a sudden jerk.

"I'll come," she said, as if she had made up her mind. "I'll fling on my clothes and come."

She sprang up and went into the bedroom. She's like one of those birds at the Zoo, Rose thought, that never flies but hops rapidly across the grass.

She turned to the window. It was a depressing little street, she thought. There was a public house at the corner. The houses opposite looked very dingy, and it was very noisy. "Any old iron to sell?" the man was crying under the window, "any old iron?" Children were screaming in the road; they were playing a game with chalk-marks on the pavement. She stood there looking down on them.

"Poor little wretches!" she said. She picked up her hat and ran two bonnet-pins sharply through it. "Don't you find it rather unpleasant," she said, giving her hat a little pat on one side as she looked in the looking-glass, "coming home late at night sometimes with that public house at the corner?"

"Drunken men, you mean?" said Maggie.

"Yes," said Rose. She buttoned the row of leather buttons on her tailor-made suit and gave herself a little pat here and there, as if she were making ready.

"And now what are you talking about?" said Sara, coming in carrying her shoes. "Another visit to Italy?"

"No," said Maggie. She spoke indistinctly because her mouth was full of pins. "Drunken men following one."

"Drunken men following one," said Sara. She sat down and began to put on her shoes.

"But they don't follow me," she said. Rose smiled. That was obvious. She was sallow, angular and plain. "I can walk over Waterloo Bridge at any hour of the day or night," she continued, tugging at her shoelaces, "and nobody notices." The shoe-lace was in a knot; she fumbled with it. "But I can remember," she continued, "being told by a woman—a very beautiful woman— she was like—"

"Hurry up," Maggie interrupted. "Rose is waiting."

". . . Rose is waiting—well, the woman told me, when she went into Regent's Park to have an ice"—she stood up, trying to fit her shoe on to her foot, "—to have an ice, at one of those little tables under the trees, one of those little round tables laid with a cloth under the trees"—she hopped about with one shoe off and one shoe on—"the eyes, she said, came through every leaf like the darts of the sun; and her ice was melted. . . . Her ice was melted!" she repeated, tapping her sister on the shoulder as she twirled round on her toe.

Rose held out her hand. "You're going to stay and finish your dress?" she said. "You won't come with us?" It was Maggie she wanted to come.

"No, I won't come," said Maggie, shaking hands. "I should hate it," she added, smiling at Rose with a candour that was baffling.

Did she mean me? thought Rose as she went down the stairs. Did she mean that she hated me? When I liked her so much?

In the alley that led into the old square off Holborn an elderly man, battered and red-nosed, as if he had weathered out many years at street corners, was selling violets. He had his pitch by a row of posts. The bunches, tightly laced, each with a green frill of leaves round the rather withered flowers, lay in a row on the tray; for he had not sold many.

"Nice vilets, fresh vilets," he repeated automatically as the people passed. Most of them went by without looking. But he went on repeating his formula automatically. "Nice vilets, fresh vilets," as if he scarcely expected any one to buy. Then two ladies came; and he held out his violets, and he said once more "Nice vilets, fresh vilets." One of them slapped down two coppers on his tray; and he looked up. The other lady stopped, put her hand on the post, and said, "Here I leave you." Upon which the one who was short and stout, struck her on the shoulder and said, "Don't be such an ass!" And the tall lady gave a sudden cackle of laughter, took a bunch of violets from the tray as if she had paid for it; and off they walked. She's an odd customer, he thought—she took the violets though she hadn't paid for them. He watched them walking round the square; then he began muttering again, "Nice vilets, sweet vilets."

"Is this the place where you meet?" said Sara as they walked along the square.

It was very quiet. The noise of the traffic had ceased. The

trees were not in full leaf yet, and pigeons were shuffling and crooning on the tree tops. Little bits of twig fell on the pavement as the birds fidgeted among the branches. A soft air puffed in their faces. They walked on round the square.

"That's the house over there," said Rose, pointing. She stopped when she reached a house with a carved doorway, and many names on the door-post. The windows on the ground floor were open; the curtains blew in and out, and through them they could see a row of heads, as if people were sitting round a table, talking.

Rose paused on the door-step.

"Are you coming in," she said, "or aren't you?"

Sara hesitated. She peered in. Then she brandished her bunch of violets in Rose's face and cried out, "All right!" she cried. "Ride on!"

Miriam Parrish was reading a letter. Eleanor was blackening the strokes on her blotting-paper. I've heard all this, I've done all this so often, she was thinking. She glanced round the table. People's faces even seemed to repeat themselves. There's the Judd type there's the Lazenby type, and there's Miriam, she thought, drawing on her blotting-paper. I know what he's going to say, I know what she's going to say, she thought, digging a little hole in the blotting-paper. Here Rose came in. But who's that with her, Eleanor asked? She did not recognise her. Whoever it was was waved by Rose to a seat in the corner, and the meeting went on. Why must we do it? Eleanor thought, drawing a spoke from the hole in the middle. She looked up. Someone was rattling a stick along the railings and whistling; the branches of a tree swung up and down in the garden outside. The leaves were already unfolding. . . . Miriam put down her papers; Mr Spicer rose.

There's no other way, I suppose, she thought, taking up her pencil again. She made a note as Mr Spicer spoke. She found that her pencil could take notes quite accurately while she herself thought of something else. She seemed able to divide herself into two. One person followed the argument—and he's putting it very well, she thought; while the other, for it was a fine afternoon, and she had wanted to go to Kew, walked down a green glade and stopped in front of a flowering tree. Is it a magnolia? she asked herself, or are they already over? Magnolias, she remembered, have no leaves, but masses of white blossom. . . . She drew a line on the blotting-paper.

Now Pickford . . . she said, looking up again. Mr Pickford spoke. She drew more spokes; blackened them. Then she looked up, for there was a change in the tone of voice.

"I know Westminster very well," Miss Ashford was saying.

"So do I!" said Mr Pickford. "I've lived there for forty years."

Eleanor was surprised. She had always thought he lived at Ealing. He lived at Westminster, did he? He was a clean-shaven, dapper little man, whom she had always seen in her mind's eye running to catch a train with a newspaper under his arm. But he lived at Westminster, did he? That was odd, she thought.

Then they went on arguing again. The cooing of the pigeons became audible. Take two coos, take two coos, tak . . . they were crooning. Martin was speaking. And he speaks very well, she thought . . . but he shouldn't be sarcastic; it puts people's backs up. She drew another stroke.

Then she heard the rush of a car outside; it stopped outside the window. Martin stopped speaking. There was a momentary pause. Then the door opened and in came a tall woman in evening dress. Everybody looked up.

"Lady Lasswade!" said Mr Pickford, getting up and scraping back his chair.

"Kitty!" Eleanor exclaimed. She half rose, but she sat down again. There was a little stir. A chair was found for her. Lady Lasswade took her place opposite Eleanor.

"I'm so sorry," she apologised, "to be so late. And for coming in these ridiculous clothes," she added, touching her cloak. She did look strange, dressed in evening dress in the broad daylight. There was something shining in her hair.

"The Opera?" said Martin as she sat down beside him.

"Yes," she said briefly. She laid her white gloves in a businesslike way on the table. Her cloak opened and showed the gleam of a silver dress beneath. She did look odd compared with the others; but it's very good of her to come, Eleanor thought, looking at her, considering she's going on to the Opera. The meeting began again.

How long has she been married? Eleanor wondered. How long is it since we broke the swing together at Oxford? She drew another stroke on the blotting-paper. The dot was now surrounded with strokes.

". . . and we discussed the whole matter perfectly frankly," Kitty was saying. Eleanor listened. That's the manner I like, she thought. She had been meeting Sir Edward at dinner. . . . It's the great ladies' manner, Eleanor thought . . . authoritative, natural. She listened again. The great ladies' manner charmed Mr Pickford; but it irritated Martin, she knew. He was pooh-poohing Sir Edward and his frankness. Then Mr Spicer was off again; and Kitty had joined in. Now there was Rose. They were all at loggerheads. Eleanor listened. She became more and more irritated. All it comes to is: I'm right and you're wrong, she thought. This bickering merely wasted time. If we could only get at something, something deeper, deeper, she thought, prodding her pencil on the blotting-paper. Suddenly she saw the only point that was of any importance. She had the words on the tip of her tongue. She opened her mouth to speak. But just as she cleared her throat, Mr Pickford swept his papers together and rose. Would they pardon him? he said. He had to be at the Law Courts. He rose and went.

The meeting dragged on. The ash-tray in the middle of the table became full of cigarette-stumps; the air became thick with smoke; then Mr Spicer went; Miss Bodham went; Miss Ashford wound a scarf tightly round her neck, snapped her attaché-case to, and strode out of the room. Miriam Parrish took off her pince-nez and fixed them to a hook that was sewn onto the front of her dress. Everybody was going; the meeting was over. Eleanor got up. She wanted to speak to Kitty. But Miriam intercepted her.

"About coming to see you on Wednesday," she began.

"Yes," said Eleanor.

"I've just remembered I've promised to take a niece to the dentist," said Miriam.

"Saturday would suit me just as well," said Eleanor.

Miriam paused. She pondered.

"Would Monday do instead?" she said.

"I'll write," said Eleanor with an irritation that she could never conceal, saint though Miriam was, and Miriam fluttered away with a guilty air as if she were a little dog caught stealing.

Eleanor turned. The others were still arguing.

"You'll agree with me one of these days," Martin was saying.

"Never! Never!" said Kitty, slapping her gloves on the table. She looked very handsome; at the same time rather absurd in her evening dress.

"Why didn't you speak, Nell?" she said, turning on her.

"Because—" Eleanor began, "I don't know," she added, rather feebly. She felt suddenly shabby and dowdy compared with Kitty, who stood there in full evening dress with something shining in her hair.

"Well," said Kitty, turning away. "I must be off. But can't I give anyone a lift?" she said, pointing to the window. There was her car.

"What a magnificent car!" said Martin, looking at it, with a sneer in his voice.

"It's Charlie's," said Kitty rather sharply.

"What about you, Eleanor?" she said, turning to her.

"Thanks," said Eleanor: "—one moment."

She had muddled her things up. She had left her gloves somewhere. Had she brought an umbrella, or hadn't she? She felt flustered and dowdy, as if she were a schoolgirl suddenly. There was the magnificent car waiting, and the chauffeur held the door open with a rug in his hand.

"Get in," said Kitty. And she got in and the chauffeur put the rug over her knees.

"We'll leave them," said Kitty, with a wave of her hand, "caballing." And the car drove off.

"What a pig-headed set they are!" said Kitty, turning to Eleanor.

"Force is always wrong—don't you agree with me?—always wrong!" she repeated, drawing the rug over her knees. She was still under the influence of the meeting. Yet she wanted to talk to Eleanor. They met so seldom; she liked her so much. But she was shy, sitting there in her absurd clothes, and she could not jerk her mind out of the rut of the meeting in which it was running.

"What a pig-headed set they are!" she repeated. Then she began: "Tell me. . . ."

There were many things that she wanted to ask; but the engine was so powerful; the car swept in and out of the traffic so smoothly; before she had time to say any of the things she wanted to say Eleanor had put her hand out because they had reached the Tube station.

"Would he stop here?" she said, rising.

"But must you get out?" Kitty began. She had wanted to talk to her. "I must, I must," said Eleanor. "Papa's expecting me." She felt like a child again beside this great lady and the chauffeur, who was holding the door open.

"Do come and see me—do let us meet again soon, Nell," said Kitty, taking her hand.

The car started on again. Lady Lasswade sat back in her corner. She wished she saw more of Eleanor, she thought; but she never could get her to come and dine. It was always "Papa's expecting me" or some other excuse, she thought rather bitterly. They had gone such different ways, they had lived such different lives, since Oxford. . . . The car slowed down. It had to take its place in the long line of cars that moved at a foot's pace, now stopping dead, now jerking on, down the narrow street, blocked by market carts, that led to the Opera House. Men and women in full evening dress were walking along the pavement. They looked uncomfortable and self-conscious as they dodged between costers' barrows, with their high piled hair and their evening cloaks; with their button-holes and their white waistcoats, in the glare of the afternoon sun. The ladies tripped uncomfortably on their high-heeled shoes; now and then they put their hands to their heads. The gentlemen kept close beside them as though protecting them. It's absurd, Kitty thought; it's ridiculous to come out in full evening dress at this time of day. She leant back in her corner. Covent Garden porters, dingy little clerks in their ordinary working clothes, coarse-looking women in aprons stared in at her. The air smelt strongly of oranges and bananas. But the car was coming to a standstill. It drew up under the archway; she pushed through the glass doors and went in.

She felt at once a sense of relief. Now that the daylight was extinguished and the air glowed yellow and crimson, she no longer felt absurd. On the contrary, she felt appropriate. The ladies and gentlemen who were mounting the stairs were dressed exactly as she was. The smell of oranges and bananas had been replaced by another smell—a subtle mixture of clothes and gloves and flowers that affected her pleasantly. The carpet was thick beneath her feet. She went along the corridor till she came to her own box with the card on it. She went in and the whole Opera House opened in front of her. She was not late after all. The orchestra was still tuning up; the players were laughing, talking and turning round in their seats as they fiddled busily with their instruments. She stood looking down at the stalls. The floor of the house was in a state of great agitation. People were passing to their seats; they were sitting down and getting up again; they were taking off their cloaks and signalling to friends. They were like birds settling on a field. In the boxes white figures were appearing here and there; white arms rested on the ledges of boxes; white shirt-fronts shone beside them. The whole house glowed—red, gold, cream-coloured, and smelt of clothes and flowers, and echoed with the squeaks and trills of the instruments and with the buzz and hum of voices. She glanced at the programme that was laid on the ledge of her box. It was *Siegfried*—her favourite opera. In a little space within the highly decorated border the names of the cast were given. She stooped to read them; then a thought struck her and she glanced at the royal box. It was empty. As she looked the door opened and two men came in; one was her cousin Edward; the other a boy, a cousin of her husband's.

"They haven't put it off?" he said as he shook hands. "I was afraid they might." He was something in the Foreign Office; with a handsome Roman head.

They all looked instinctively at the royal box. Programmes lay along the edge; but there was no bouquet of pink carnations. The box was empty.

"The doctors have given him up," said the young man, looking very important. They all think they know everything, Kitty thought, smiling at his air of private information.

"But if he dies?" she said, looking at the royal box, "d'you think they'll stop it?"

The young man shrugged his shoulders. About that he could not be positive apparently. The house was filling up. Lights winked on ladies' arms as they turned; ripples of light flashed, stopped, and then flashed the opposite way as they turned their heads.

But now the conductor pushed his way through the orchestra to his raised seat. There was an outburst of applause; he turned, bowed to the audience; turned again, all the lights sank down; the overture had begun.

Kitty leant back against the wall of the box; her face was shaded by the folds of the curtain. She was glad to be shaded. As they played the overture she looked at Edward. She could only see the outline of his face in the red glow; it was heavier than

165

it used to be; but he looked intellectual, handsome and a little remote as he listened to the overture. It wouldn't have done, she thought; I'm much too . . . she did not finish the sentence. He has never married, she thought; and she had. And I've three boys. I've been in Australia, I've been in India. . . . The music made her think of herself and her own life as she seldom did. It exalted her; it cast a flattering light over herself, her past. But why did Martin laugh at me for having a car? she thought. What's the good of laughing? she asked.

Here the curtain went up. She leant forward and looked at the stage. The dwarf was hammering at the sword. Hammer, hammer, hammer, he went with little short, sharp strokes. She listened. The music had changed. *He,* she thought, looking at the handsome boy, knows exactly what the music means. He was already completely possessed by the music. She liked the look of complete absorption that had swum up on top of his immaculate respectability, making him seem almost stern. . . . But here was Siegfried. She leant forward. Dressed in leopard-skins, very fat, with nut-brown thighs, leading a bear—here he was. She liked the fat bouncing young man in his flaxen wig: his voice was magnificent. Hammer, hammer, hammer he went. She leant back again. What did that make her think of? A young man who came into a room with shavings in his hair . . . when she was very young. In Oxford? She had gone to tea with them; had sat on a hard chair; in a very light room; and there was a sound of hammering in the garden. And then a boy came in with shavings in his hair. And she had wanted him to kiss her. Or was it the farm hand up at Carter's, when old Carter had loomed up suddenly leading a bull with a ring through its nose?

"That's the sort of life I like," she thought, taking up her opera-glasses. "That's the sort of person I am. . . ." she finished her sentence.

Then she put the opera-glasses to her eyes. The scenery suddenly became bright and close; the grass seemed to be made of thick green wool; she could see Siegfried's fat brown arms glistening with paint. His face was shiny. She put down the glasses and leant back in her corner.

And old Lucy Craddock—she saw Lucy sitting at a table; with her red nose, and her patient, kind eyes. "So you've done no work this week again, Kitty!" she said reproachfully. How I loved her! Kitty thought. And then she had gone back to the Lodge; and there was the tree, with a prop in the middle; and her mother sitting bolt upright. . . . I wish I hadn't quarrelled so much with my mother, she thought, overcome with a sudden sense of the passage of time and its tragedy. Then the music changed.

She looked at the stage again. The Wanderer had come in. He was sitting on a bank in a long grey dressing-gown; and a patch wobbled uncomfortably over one of his eyes. On and on he went; on and on. Her attention flagged. She glanced round the dim red house; she could only see white elbows pointed on the ledges of boxes; here and there a sharp pinpoint of light showed as some one followed the score with a torch. Edward's fine profile again caught her eye. He was listening, critically, intently. It wouldn't have done, she thought, it wouldn't have done at all.

At last the Wanderer had gone. And now? she asked herself, leaning forward. Siegfried burst in. Dressed in his leopard-skins, laughing and singing, here he was again. The music excited her. It was magnificent. Siegfried took the broken pieces of the sword and blew on the fire and hammered, hammered, hammered. The singing, the hammering and the fire leaping all went on at the same time. Quicker and quicker, more and more rhythmically, more and more triumphantly he hammered, until at last up he swung the sword high above his head and brought it down—crack! The anvil burst asunder. And then he brandished the sword over his head and shouted and sang; and the music rushed higher and higher; and the curtain fell.

The lights opened in the middle of the house. All the colour came back. The whole Opera House leapt into life again with its faces and its diamonds and its men and women. They were clapping and waving their programmes. The whole house seemed to be fluttering with white squares of paper. The curtains fell apart and were held back by tall footmen in knee-breeches. Kitty stood up and clapped. Again the curtains closed; again they parted. The footmen were almost pulled off their feet by the heavy folds that they had to hold back. Again and again they held the curtain back; and even when they had let it fall and the singers had disappeared and the orchestra were leaving their seats, the audience still stood clapping and waving their programmes.

Kitty turned to the young man in her box. He was leaning over the ledge. He was still clapping. He was shouting "Bravo! Bravo!" He had forgotten her. He had forgotten himself.

"Wasn't that marvellous?" he said at last, turning round.

There was an odd look on his face as if he were in two worlds at once and had to draw them together.

"Marvellous!" she agreed. She looked at him with a pang of envy.

"And now," she said, gathering her things together, "let us have dinner."

At Hyams Place they had finished dinner. The table was cleared; only a few crumbs remained, and the pot of flowers stood in the middle of the table like a sentry. The only sound in the room was the stitching of a needle, pricking through silk, for Maggie was sewing. Sara sat hunched on the music stool, but she was not playing.

"Sing something," said Maggie suddenly. Sara turned and struck the notes.

"Brandishing, flourishing my sword in my hand. . ." she sang. The words were the words of some pompous eighteenth century march, but her voice was reedy and thin. Her voice broke. She stopped singing.

She sat silent with her hands on the notes. "What's the good of singing if one hasn't any voice?" she murmured. Maggie went on sewing.

"What did you do today?" she said at length, looking up abruptly.

"Went out with Rose," said Sara.

"And what did you do with Rose?" said Maggie. She spoke absent-mindedly. Sara turned and glanced at her. Then she began to play again. "Stood on the bridge and looked into the water," she murmured.

"Stood on the bridge and looked into the water," she hummed, in time to the music. "Running water; flowing water. May my bones turn to coral; and fish light their lanthorns; fish light their green lanthorns in my eyes." She half turned and looked round at Maggie. But she was not attending. Sara was silent. She looked at the notes again. But she did not see the notes, she saw a garden; flowers; and her sister; and a young man with a big nose who stooped to pick a flower that was gleaming in the dark. And he held the flower out in his hand in the moonlight . . . Maggie interrupted her.

"You went out with Rose," she said. "Where to?"

Sara left the piano and stood in front of the fireplace.

"We got into a bus and went to Holborn," she said. "And we walked along a street," she went on; "and suddenly," she jerked her hand out, "I felt a clap on my shoulder." "Damned liar!" said Rose, "and took me and flung me against a public house wall!"

Maggie stitched on in silence.

"You got into a bus and went to Holborn," she repeated mechanically after a time. "And then?"

"Then we went in to a room," Sara continued, "and there were people—multitudes of people. And I said to myself . . ." she paused.

"A meeting?" Maggie murmured. "Where?"

"In a room," Sara answered. "A pale greenish light. A woman hanging clothes on a line in the back garden; and someone went by rattling a stick on the railings."

"I see," said Maggie. She stitched on quickly.

"I said to myself," Sara resumed, "whose heads are those" she paused.

"A meeting," Maggie interrupted her. "What for? What about?"

"There were pigeons cooing," Sara went on. "Take two coos, Taffy. Take two coos . . . Tak . . . And then a wing darkened the air, and in came Kitty clothed in starlight; and sat on a chair."

She paused. Maggie was silent. She went on stitching for a moment.

"Who came in?" she asked at length.

"Somebody very beautiful; clothed in starlight; with green in her hair," said Sara. "Whereupon"—here she changed her voice and imitated the tones in which a middle-class man might be supposed to welcome a lady of fashion, "up jumps Mr Pickford, and says 'Oh, Lady Lasswade, won't you take this chair?'"

She pushed a chair in front of her.

"And then," she went on, flourishing her hands, "Lady Lasswade sits down; puts her gloves on the table,"—she patted a cushion—"like that."

Maggie looked up over her sewing. She had a general impression of a room full of people; sticks rattling on the railings; clothes hanging out to dry, and someone coming in with beetles' wings in her hair.

"What happened then?" she asked.

"Then withered Rose, spiky Rose, tawny Rose, thorny Rose," Sara burst out laughing, "shed a tear."

"No, no," said Maggie. There was something wrong with the story; something impossible. She looked up. The light of a passing car slid across the ceiling. It was growing too dark to see. The lamp from the public-house opposite made a yellow glare in the room; the ceiling trembled with a watery pattern of fluctuating light. There was a sound of brawling in the street outside; a scuffling and trampling as if the police were hauling someone along the street against his will. Voices jeered and shouted after him.

"Another row?" Maggie murmured, sticking her needle in the stuff.

Sara got up and went to the window. A crowd had gathered outside the public house. A man was being thrown out. There he came, staggering. He fell against a lamp-post to which he clung. The scene was lit up by the glare of the lamp over the public house door. Sara stood for a moment at the window watching them. Then she turned; her face in the mixed light looked cadaverous and worn, as if she were no longer a girl, but an old woman worn out by a life of childbirth, debauchery and crime. She stood there hunched up, with her hands clenched together.

"In time to come," she said, looking at her sister, "people, looking into this room—this cave, this little antre, scooped out of mud and dung, will hold their fingers to their noses"—she held her fingers to her nose—"and say 'Pah! They stink!'" She fell down into a chair.

Maggie looked at her. Curled round, with her hair falling over her face and her hands screwed together she looked like some great ape, crouching there in a little cave of mud and dung. "Pah!" Maggie repeated to herself, "They stink" . . . She drove her needle through the stuff in a spasm of disgust. It was true, she thought; they were nasty little creatures, driven by uncontrollable lusts. The night was full of roaring and cursing; of violence and unrest, also of beauty and joy. She got up, holding the dress in her hands. The folds of silk fell down to the floor and she ran her hand over them.

"That's done. That's finished," she said, laying the dress on the table. There was nothing more she could do with her hands. She folded the dress up and put it away. Then the cat, which had been asleep, rose very slowly, arched its back and stretched itself to its full length.

"You want your supper, do you?" said Maggie. She went into the kitchen and came back with a saucer of milk. "There, poor puss," she said, putting the saucer down on the floor. She stood watching the cat lap up its milk, mouthful by mouthful; then it stretched itself out again with extraordinary grace.

Sara, standing at a little distance, watched her. Then she imitated her.

"There, poor puss, there, poor puss," she repeated. "As you rock the cradle, Maggie," she added.

Maggie raised her arms as if to ward off some implacable destiny; then let them fall. Sara smiled as she watched her; then tears brimmed, fell and ran slowly down her cheeks. But as she put up her hand to wipe them there was a sound of knocking; somebody was hammering on the door of the next house. The hammering stopped. Then it began again—hammer, hammer, hammer.

They listened.

"Upcher's come home drunk and wants to be let in," said Maggie. The knocking ceased. Then it began again.

Sara dried her eyes, roughly, energetically.

"Bring up your children on a desert island where the ships only come when the moon's full!" she exclaimed.

"Or have none?" said Maggie. A window was thrown open. A woman's voice was heard shrieking abuse at the man. He bawled back in a thick drunken voice from the doorstep. Then the door slammed.

They listened.

"Now he'll stagger against the wall and be sick," said Maggie. They could hear heavy footsteps lurching up the stairs in the next house. Then there was silence.

Maggie crossed the room to shut the window. The great windows of the factory opposite were all lit up; it looked like a palace of glass with thin black bars across it. A glaze of yellow light lit up the lower halves of the houses opposite; the slate roofs shone blue, for the sky hung down in a heavy canopy of yellow light. Footsteps tapped on the pavement, for people were still walking in the street. Far off a voice was crying hoarsely. Maggie leant out. The night was windy and warm.

"What's he crying?" she said.

The voice came nearer and nearer.

"Death . . . ?" she said.

"Death . . . ?" said Sara. They leant out. But they could not hear the rest of the sentence. Then a man who was wheeling a barrow along the street shouted up to them:

"The King's dead!"

1911

The sun was rising. Very slowly it came up over the horizon shaking out light. But the sky was so vast, so cloudless, that to fill it with light took time. Very gradually the clouds turned blue; leaves on forest trees sparkled; down below a flower shone; eyes of beasts—tigers, monkeys, birds—sparkled. Slowly the world emerged from darkness. The sea became like the skin of an innumerable scaled fish, glittering gold. Here in the South of France the furrowed vineyards caught the light; the little vines turned purple and yellow; and the sun coming through the slats of the blinds striped the white walls. Maggie, standing at the window, looked down on the courtyard, and saw her husband's book cracked across with shadow from the vine above; and the glass that stood beside him glowed yellow. Cries of peasants working came through the open window.

The sun, crossing the Channel, beat vainly on the blanket of thick sea mist. Light slowly permeated the haze over London; struck on the statues in Parliament Square, and on the Palace where the flag flew though the King, borne under a white and blue Union Jack, lay in the caverns at Frogmore. It was hotter than ever. Horses' noses hissed as they drank from the troughs; their hoofs made ridges hard and brittle as plaster on the country roads. Fires tearing over the moors left charcoal twigs behind them. It was August, the holiday season. The glass roofs of the great railway stations were globes incandescent with light. Travellers watched the hands of the round yellow clocks as they followed porters, wheeling portmanteaus, with dogs on leashes. In all the stations trains were ready to bore their way through England; to the North, to the South, to the West. Now the guard standing with his hand raised dropped his flag and the tea-urn slid past. Off the trains swung through the public gardens with asphalt paths; past the factories; into open country. Men standing on bridges fishing looked up; horses cantered; women came to doors and shaded their eyes; the shadow of the smoke floated over the corn, looped down and caught a tree. And on they passed.

In the station yard at Wittering, Mrs Chinnery's old victoria stood waiting. The train was late; it was very hot. William the gardener sat on the box in his buff-coloured coat with the plated buttons flicking the flies off. The flies were troublesome. They had gathered in little brown clusters on the horses' ears. He flicked his whip; the old mare stamped her hoofs; and shook her ears, for the flies had settled again. It was very hot. The sun beat down on the station yard, on the carts and flies and traps waiting for the train. At last the signal dropped; a puff of smoke blew over the hedge; and in a minute people came streaming out into the yard, and here was Miss Pargiter carrying her bag in her hand and a white umbrella. William touched his hat.

"Sorry to be so late," said Eleanor, smiling up at him, for she knew him; she came every year.

She put her bag on the seat and sat back under the shade of her white umbrella. The leather of the carriage was hot behind her back; it was very hot—hotter even than Toledo. They turned into the High Street; the heat seemed to make everything drowsy and silent. The broad street was full of traps and carts with the reins hanging loose and the horses' heads drooping. But after the din of the foreign market-places how quiet it seemed! Men in gaiters were leaning against the walls; the shops had their awnings out; the pavement was barred with shadow. They had parcels to fetch. At the fishmonger's they stopped; and a damp white parcel was handed out to them. At the ironmonger's they stopped; and William came back with a scythe. Then they stopped at the chemist's; but there they had to wait, because the lotion was not yet ready.

Eleanor sat back under the shade of her white umbrella. The air seemed to hum with the heat. The air seemed to smell of soap and chemicals. How thoroughly people wash in England, she thought, looking at the yellow soap, the green soap, and the pink soap in the chemist's window. In Spain she had hardly washed at all; she had dried herself with a pocket handkerchief standing among the white dry stones of the Guadalquivir. In Spain it was all parched and shrivelled. But here—she looked down the High Street—every shop was full of vegetables; of shining silver fish; of yellow-clawed, soft-breasted chickens; of buckets, rakes and wheel-barrows. And how friendly people were!

She noticed how often hats were touched; hands were grasped; people stopped, talking, in the middle of the road. But now the chemist came out with a large bottle wrapped in tissue paper. It was stowed away under the scythe.

"Midges very bad this year, William?" she asked, recognising the lotion.

"Tarrible bad, miss, tarrible," he said, touching his hat. There hadn't been such a drought since the Jubilee she understood him to say; but his accent, his singsong and Dorsetshire rhythm, made it difficult to catch what he said. Then he flicked his whip and they drove on; past the market cross; past the red brick town hall, with the arches under it; along a street of bow-windowed eighteenth-century houses, the residences of doctors and solicitors; past the pond with chains linking white posts together and a horse drinking; and so out into the country. The road was laid with soft white dust; the hedges, hung with wreaths of travellers' joy, seemed also thick with dust. The old horse settled down into his mechanical jog-trot, and Eleanor lay back under her white umbrella.

Every summer she came to visit Morris at his mother-in-law's house. Seven times, eight times she had come she counted; but this year it was different. This year everything was different. Her father was dead; her house was shut up; she had

176

no attachment at the moment anywhere. As she jolted through the hot lanes she thought drowsily, What shall I do now? Live there? she asked herself, as she passed a very respectable Georgian villa in the middle of a street. No, not in a village she said to herself; and they jogged through the village. What about that house then, she said to herself, looking at a house with a verandah among some trees. But then she thought, I should turn into a grey-haired lady cutting flowers with a pair of scissors and tapping at cottage doors. She did not want to tap at cottage doors. And the clergyman—a clergyman was wheeling his bicycle up the hill—would come to tea with her. But she did not want the clergyman to come to tea with her. How spick and span it all is she thought; for they were passing through the village. The little gardens were bright with red and yellow flowers. Then they began to meet village people; a procession. Some of the women carried parcels; there was a gleaming silver object on the quilt of a perambulator; and one old man clasped a hairy-headed coco-nut to his breast. There had been a Fête she supposed; here it was, returning. They drew to the side of the road as the carriage trotted past, and cast steady curious looks at the lady sitting under her green and white umbrella. Now they came to a white gate; trotted briskly down a short avenue; and drew up with a flourish of the whip in front of two slender columns; door-scrapers like bristling hedgehogs; and a wide open hall door.

She waited for a moment in the hall. Her eyes were dimmed after the glare of the road. Everything seemed pale and frail and friendly. The rugs were faded; the pictures were faded. Even the Admiral in his cocked hat over the fireplace wore a curious look of faded urbanity. In Greece one was always going back two thousand years. Here it was always the eighteenth century. Like everything English, she thought, laying down her umbrella on the refectory table beside the china bowl, with dried rose leaves in it, the past seemed near, domestic, friendly.

The door opened. "Oh Eleanor!" her sister-in-law exclaimed, running into the hall in her fly-away summer clothes, "How nice to see you! How brown you look! Come into the cool!"

She led her into the drawing-room. The drawing-room piano was strewn with white baby-linen; pink and green fruit glimmered in glass bottles.

"We're in such a mess," said Celia, sinking onto the sofa. "Lady St. Austell has only just this minute gone, and the Bishop."

She fanned herself with a sheet of paper.

"But it's been a great success. We had the bazaar in the garden. They acted." It was a programme with which she was fanning herself.

"A play?" said Eleanor.

"Yes, a scene from Shakespeare," said Celia. *"Midsummer-Night? As You Like It?* I forget which. Miss Green got it up. Happily it was so fine. Last year it poured. But how my feet are aching!" The long window opened onto the lawn. Eleanor could see people dragging tables.

"What an undertaking!" she said.

"It was!" Celia panted. "We had Lady St. Austell and the Bishop, coco-nut shies and a pig; but I think it all went off very well. They enjoyed it."

"For the Church?" Eleanor asked.

"Yes. The new steeple," said Celia.

"What a business!" said Eleanor again. She looked out onto the lawn. The grass was already scorched and yellow; the laurel bushes looked shrivelled. Tables were standing against the laurel bushes. Morris passed, dragging a table.

"Was it nice in Spain?" Celia was asking. "Did you see wonderful things?"

"Oh yes!" Eleanor exclaimed. "I saw . . ." She stopped. She had seen wonderful things—buildings, mountains, a red city in a plain. But how could she describe it?

"You must tell me all about it afterwards," said Celia getting up. "It's time we got ready. But I'm afraid," she said, toiling rather

178

painfully up the broad staircase, "I must ask you to be careful, because we're very short of water. The well. . . ." she stopped. The well, Eleanor remembered, always gave out in a hot summer. They walked together down the broad passage, past the old yellow globe which stood under the pleasant eighteenth-century picture of all the little Chinnerys in long drawers and nankeen trousers standing round their father and mother in the garden. Celia paused with her hand on the bedroom door. The sound of doves cooing came in through the open window.

"We're putting you in the Blue room this time," she said. Generally Eleanor had the Pink room.

She glanced in. "I hope you've got everything—" she began.

"Yes, I'm sure I've got everything," said Eleanor, and Celia left her.

The maid had already unpacked her things. There they were—laid on the bed. Eleanor took off her dress, and stood in her white petticoat washing herself, methodically but carefully, since they were short of water. The English sun still made her face prickle all over where the Spanish sun had burnt it. Her neck had been cut off from her chest as if it had been painted brown, she thought, as she slipped on her evening dress in front of the looking-glass. She twisted her thick hair, with the grey strand in it, rapidly into a coil; hung the jewel, a red blob like congealed raspberry jam with a gold seed in the centre, round her neck; and gave one glance at the woman who had been for fifty-five years so familiar that she no longer saw her—Eleanor Pargiter. That she was getting old was obvious; there were wrinkles across her forehead; hollows and creases where the flesh used to be firm.

And what was my good point? she asked herself, running the comb once more through her hair. My eyes? Her eyes laughed back at her as she looked at them. My eyes, yes, she thought. Somebody had once praised her eyes. She made herself open them instead of screwing them together. Round each eye were several little white strokes, where she had crinkled them up to avoid the glare on the Acropolis, at Naples, at Granada and Toledo. But that's over, she thought, people praising my eyes, and finished her dressing.

She stood for a moment looking at the burnt, dry lawn. The grass was almost yellow; the elm trees were beginning to turn brown; red-and-white cows were munching on the far side of the sunk hedge. But England was disappointing, she thought; it was small; it was pretty; she felt no affection for her native land— none whatever. Then she went down, for she wanted if possible to see Morris alone.

But he was not alone. He got up as she came in and introduced her to a stoutish, white-haired old man in a dinner-jacket.

"You know each other, don't you?" said Morris.

"Eleanor—Sir William Whatney." He put a little stress humorously upon the "Sir" which for a moment confused Eleanor.

"We used to know each other," said Sir William, coming forward and smiling as he took her hand.

She looked at him. Could it be William Whatney—old Dubbin—who used to come to Abercorn Terrace years ago? It was. She had not seen him since he went to India.

But are we all like that? she asked herself, looking from the grisled, crumpled red-and-yellow face of the boy she had known—he was almost hairless—at her own brother Morris. He looked bald and thin; but surely he was in the prime of life, as she was herself? Or had they all suddenly become old fogies like Sir William? Then her nephew North and her niece Peggy came in with their mother and they went in to dinner. Old Mrs Chinnery dined upstairs.

How has Dubbin become Sir William Whatney? she wondered, glancing at him as they ate the fish that had been brought up in the damp parcel. She had last seen him—in a boat on the river. They had gone for a picnic; they had supped on an island in the middle of the river. Maidenhead, was it?

They were talking about the Fête. Craster had won the pig; Mrs Grice had won the silver-plated salver.

"That's what I saw on the perambulator," said Eleanor. "I met the Fête coming back," she explained. She described the procession. And they talked about the Fête.

"Don't you envy my sister-in-law?" said Celia, turning to Sir William. "She's just back from a tour in Greece."

"Indeed!" said Sir William. "Which part of Greece?"

"We went to Athens, then to Olympia, then to Delphi," Eleanor began, reciting the usual formula. They were on purely formal terms evidently—she and Dubbin.

"My brother-in-law, Edward," Celia explained, "takes these delightful tours."

"You remember Edward?" said Morris. "Weren't you up with him?"

"No, he was junior to me," said Sir William. "But I've heard of him, of course. He's—let me think—what is he—a great swell, isn't he?"

"Oh, he's at the top of his tree," said Morris.

He was not jealous of Edward, Eleanor thought; but there was a certain note in his voice which told her that he was comparing his career with Edward's.

"They loved him," she said. She smiled; she saw Edward lecturing troops of devout school mistresses on the Acropolis. Out came their notebooks and down they scribbled every word he said. But he had been very generous; very kind; he had looked after her all the time.

"Did you meet anyone at the Embassy?" Sir William asked her. Then he corrected himself. "Not an Embassy though, is it?"

"No. Athens is not an Embassy," said Morris. Here there was a diversion; what was the difference between an Embassy and a Legation? Then they began to discuss the situation in the Balkans.

"There's going to be trouble there in the near future," Sir William was saying. He turned to Morris; they discussed the situation in the Balkans.

Eleanor's attention wandered. What's he done? she wondered. Certain words and gestures brought him back to her as he had been thirty years ago. There were relics of the old Dubbin if one half-shut one's eyes. She half-shut her eyes. Suddenly she remembered—it was *he* who had praised her eyes. "Your sister has the brightest eyes I ever saw," he had said. Morris had told her. And she had hidden her face behind a newspaper in the train going home to conceal her pleasure. She looked at him again. He was talking. She listened. He seemed too big for the quiet, English dining-room; his voice boomed out. He wanted an audience.

He was telling a story. He spoke in clipped, nervous sentences as if there were a ring round them—a style she admired, but she had missed the beginning. His glass was empty.

"Give Sir William some more wine," Celia whispered to the nervous parlour-maid. There was some juggling with decanters on the sideboard. Celia frowned nervously. A girl from the village who doesn't know her job, Eleanor reflected. The story was reaching its climax; but she had missed several links.

". . . and I found myself in an old pair of riding-breeches standing under a peacock umbrella; and all the good people were crouching with their heads to the ground. 'Good Lord,' I said to myself, 'if they only knew what a bally ass I feel!'" He held out his glass to be filled. "That's how we were taught our job in those days," he added.

He was boasting, of course; that was natural. He came back to England after ruling a district "about the size of Ireland," as they always said; and nobody had ever heard of him. She had a feeling that she would hear a great many more stories that sailed serenely to his own advantage, during the week-end. But he talked very well. He had done a great many interesting things. She wished that Morris would tell stories too. She wished that he would assert himself instead of leaning back and passing his hand—the hand with the cut on it—over his forehead.

Ought I to have urged him to go to the Bar? she thought. Her father had been against it. But once it's done there it is; he married; the children came; he had to go on, whether he wanted to or not. How irrevocable things are, she thought. We make our experiments, then they make theirs. She looked at her nephew North and at her niece Peggy. They sat opposite her with the sun on their faces. Their perfectly healthy egg-shell faces looked extraordinarily young. Peggy's blue dress stuck out like a child's muslin frock; North was still a brown-eyed cricketing boy. He was listening intently; Peggy was looking down at her plate. She had the non-committal look which well brought up children have when they listen to the talk of their elders. She might be amused; or bored? Eleanor could not be sure which it was.

"There he goes," Peggy said, suddenly looking up. "The owl . . . ." she said, catching Eleanor's eye. Eleanor turned to look out of the window behind her. She missed the owl; she saw the heavy trees, gold in the setting sun; and the cows slowly moving as they munched their way across the meadow.

"You can time him," said Peggy, "he's so regular." Then Celia made a move.

"Shall we leave the gentlemen to their politics," she said, "and have our coffee on the terrace?" and they shut the door upon the gentlemen and their politics.

"I'll fetch my glasses," said Eleanor, and she went upstairs.

She wanted to see the owl before it got too dark. She was becoming more and more interested in birds. It was a sign of old age, she supposed, as she went into her bedroom. An old maid who washes and watches birds, she said to herself as she looked in the glass. There were her eyes—they still seemed to her rather bright, in spite of the lines round them—the eyes she had shaded in the railway carriage because Dubbin praised them. But now I'm labelled, she thought—an old maid who washes and watches birds. That's what they think I am. But I'm not—I'm not in the least like that, she said. She shook her head, and turned away from the glass. It was a nice room; shady, civilised, cool after the bedrooms in foreign inns, with marks on the wall where someone had squashed bugs and men brawling under the window. But where were her glasses? Put away in some drawer? She turned to look for them.

"Did father say Sir William was in love with her?" Peggy asked as they waited on the terrace.

"Oh I don't know about that," said Celia. "But I wish they could have married. I wish she had children of her own. And then they could have settled here," she added. "He's such a delightful man."

Peggy was silent. There was a pause.

Celia resumed:

"I hope you were polite to the Robinsons this afternoon, dreadful as they are. . . ."

"They give ripping parties anyhow," said Peggy.

"'Ripping, ripping,'" her mother complained half laughing. "I wish you wouldn't pick up all North's slang, my dear. . . . Oh, here's Eleanor," she broke off.

Eleanor came out onto the terrace with her glasses, and sat down beside Celia. It was still very warm; it was still light enough to see the hills in the distance.

"He'll be back in a minute," said Peggy, drawing up a chair. "He'll come along that hedge."

She pointed to the dark line of hedge that went across the meadow. Eleanor focussed her glasses and waited.

"Now," said Celia, pouring out the coffee. "There are so many things I want to ask you." She paused. She always had a hoard of questions to ask; she had not seen Eleanor since April. In four months questions accumulated. Out they came drop by drop.

"In the first place," she began. "No. . . ." She rejected that question in favour of another.

"What's all this about Rose?" she asked.

"What?" said Eleanor absentmindedly, altering the focus of

her glasses. "It's getting too dark," she said; the field was blurred.

"Morris says she's been had up in a police-court," said Celia. She dropped her voice slightly though they were alone.

"She threw a brick—" said Eleanor. She focused her glasses on the hedge again. She held them poised in case the owl should come that way again.

"Will she be put in prison?" Peggy asked quickly.

"Not this time," said Eleanor. "Next time—Ah, here he comes!" she broke off. The blunt-headed bird came swinging along the hedge. He looked almost white in the dusk. Eleanor got him within the circle of her lens. He held a little black spot in front of him.

"He's got a mouse in his claws!" she exclaimed. "He's got a nest in the steeple," said Peggy. The owl swooped out of the field of vision.

"Now I can't see him any more," said Eleanor. She lowered her glasses. They were silent for a moment, sipping their coffee. Celia was thinking of her next question; Eleanor anticipated her.

"Tell me about William Whatney," she said. "When I last saw him he was a slim young man in a boat." Peggy burst out laughing.

"That must have been ages ago!" she said.

"Not so very long," said Eleanor. She felt rather nettled. "Well—" she reflected, "twenty years—twenty-five years perhaps."

It seemed a very short time to her; but then, she thought, it was before Peggy was born. She could only be sixteen or seventeen.

"Isn't he a delightful man?" Celia exclaimed. "He was in India, you know. Now he's retired, and we do hope he'll take a house here; but Morris thinks he'd find it too dull."

They sat silent for a moment, looking out over the meadow. The cows coughed now and then as they munched and moved a step further through the grass. A sweet scent of cows and grass was wafted up to them.

"It's going to be another hot day tomorrow," said Peggy. The sky was perfectly smooth; it seemed made of innumerable grey-blue atoms the colour of an Italian officer's cloak; until it reached the horizon where there was a long bar of pure green. Everything looked very settled; very still; very pure. There was not a single cloud, and the stars were not yet showing.

It was small; it was smug; it was petty after Spain, but still, now that the sun had sunk and the trees were massed together without separate leaves it had its beauty, Eleanor thought. The downs were becoming larger and simpler; they were becoming part of the sky.

"How lovely it is!" she exclaimed, as if she were making amends to England after Spain.

"If only Mr Robinson doesn't build!" sighed Celia; and Eleanor remembered—they were the local scourge; rich people who threatened to build. "I did my best to be polite to them at the bazaar today," Celia continued. "Some people won't ask them; but I say one must be polite to neighbours in the country. . . ."

Then she paused. "There are so many things I want to ask you," she said. The bottle was tilted on its end again. Eleanor waited obediently.

"Have you had an offer for Abercorn Terrace yet?" Celia demanded. Drop, drop, drop, out her questions came.

"Not yet," said Eleanor. "The agent wants me to cut it up into flats."

Celia pondered. Then she hopped on again.

"And now about Maggie—when's her baby going to be born?"

"In November, I think," said Eleanor. "In Paris," she added.

"I hope it'll be all right," said Celia. "But I do wish it could have been born in England." She reflected again. "Her children will be French, I suppose?" she said.

"Yes; French, I suppose," said Eleanor. She was looking at the green bar; it was fading; it was turning blue. It was becoming night.

"Everybody says he's a very nice fellow," said Celia. "But René—René," her accent was bad, "—it doesn't sound like a man's name."

"You can call him Renny," said Peggy, pronouncing it in the English way.

"But that reminds me of Ronny; and I don't like Ronny. We had a stable-boy called Ronny."

"Who stole the hay," said Peggy. They were silent again, "It's such a pity—" Celia began. Then she stopped. The maid had come to clear away the coffee.

"It's a wonderful night, isn't it?" said Celia, adapting her voice to the presence of servants. "It looks as if it would never rain again. In which case I don't know. . . ." And she went on prattling about the drought; about the lack of water. The well always ran dry. Eleanor, looking at the hills, hardly listened. "Oh, but there's quite enough for everybody at present," she heard Celia saying. And for some reason she held the sentence suspended without a meaning in her mind's ear, "—quite enough for everybody at present," she repeated. After all the foreign languages she had been hearing, it sounded to her pure English. What a lovely language, she thought, saying over to herself again the commonplace words, spoken by Celia quite simply, but with some indescribable burr in the r's, for the Chinnerys had lived in Dorsetshire since the beginning of time.

The maid had gone.

"What was I saying?" Celia resumed. "I was saying, It's such a pity. Yes. . . ." But there was a sound of voices; a scent of cigar smoke; the gentlemen were upon them. "Oh, here they are!" she broke off. And the chairs were pulled up and re-arranged.

They sat in a semicircle looking across the meadows at the fading hills. The broad bar of green that lay across the horizon had vanished. Only a tinge was left in the sky. It had become peaceful and cool; in them too something seemed to be smoothed out. There was no need to talk. The owl flew down the meadow again; they could just see the white of his wing against the dark of the hedge.

"There he goes," said North, puffing at a cigar which was his first, Eleanor guessed, Sir William's gift. The elm trees had

187

become dead black against the sky. Their leaves hung in a fretted pattern like black lace with holes in it. Through a hole Eleanor saw the point of a star. She looked up. There was another.

"It's going to be a fine day tomorrow," said Morris, knocking out his pipe against his shoe. Far away on a distant road there was a rattle of cart-wheels; then a chorus of voices singing—country people going home. This is England, Eleanor thought to herself; she felt as if she were slowly sinking into some fine mesh made of branches shaking, hills growing dark, and leaves hanging like black lace with stars among them. But a bat swooped low over their heads.

"I hate bats!" Celia exclaimed, raising her hand to her head nervously.

"Do you?" said Sir William. "I rather like them." His voice was quiet and almost melancholy. Now Celia will say, They get into one's hair, Eleanor thought.

"They get into one's hair," Celia said.

"But I haven't any hair," said Sir William. His bald head, his large face gleamed out in the darkness.

The bat swooped again, skimming the ground at their feet. A little cool air stirred at their ankles. The trees had become part of the sky. There was no moon, but the stars were coming out. There's another, Eleanor thought, gazing at a twinkling light ahead of her. But it was too low; too yellow; it was another house she realised, not a star. And then Celia began talking to Sir William, whom she wanted to settle near them; and Lady St. Austell had told her that the Grange was to let. Was that the Grange, Eleanor wondered, looking at a light, or a star? And they went on talking.

Tired of her own company, old Mrs Chinnery had come down early. There she sat in the drawing-room waiting. She had made a formal entry, but there was nobody there. Arrayed in her old lady's dress of black satin, with a lace cap on her head, she sat waiting. Her hawk-like nose was curved in her shrivelled cheeks;

a little red rim showed on one of her drooping eyelids.

"Why don't they come in?" she said peevishly to Ellen, the discreet black maid who stood behind her. Ellen went to the window and tapped on the pane.

Celia stopped talking and turned round. "That's Mama," she said. "We must go in." She got up and pushed back her chair.

After the dark, the drawing-room with its lamps lit had the effect of a stage. Old Mrs Chinnery sitting in her wheeled chair with her ear trumpet seemed to sit there awaiting homage. She looked exactly the same; not a day older; as vigorous as ever. As Eleanor bent to give her the customary kiss, life once more took on its familiar proportions. So she had bent, night after night, over her father. She was glad to stoop down; it made her feel younger herself. She knew the whole procedure by heart. They, the middle-aged, deferred to the very old; the very old were courteous to them; and then came the usual pause. They had nothing to say to her; she had nothing to say to them. What happened next? Eleanor saw the old lady's eyes suddenly brighten. What made the eyes of an old woman of ninety turn blue? Cards? Yes. Celia had fetched the green baize table; Mrs Chinnery had a passion for whist. But she too had her ceremony; she too had her manners.

"Not tonight," she said, making a little gesture as if to push away the table. "I am sure it will bore Sir William?" She gave a nod in the direction of the large man who stood there seeming a little outside the family party.

"Not at all. Not at all," he said with alacrity. "Nothing would please me more," he assured her.

You're a good fellow, Dubbin, Eleanor thought. And they drew up the chairs; and dealt the cards; and Morris chaffed his mother-in-law down her ear-trumpet and they played rubber after rubber. North read a book; Peggy strummed on the piano; and Celia, dozing over her embroidery, now and then gave a sudden start and put her hand over her mouth. At last the door opened stealthily. Ellen, the discreet black maid stood behind Mrs Chinnery's chair, waiting. Mrs Chinnery pretended to ignore her, but the others were glad to stop. Ellen stepped forward and Mrs Chinnery, submitting, was wheeled off to the mysterious upper chamber of extreme old age. Her pleasure was over.

Celia yawned openly.

"The bazaar," she said, rolling up her embroidery. "I shall go to bed. Come, Peggy. Come, Eleanor."

North jumped up with alacrity to open the door. Celia lit the brass candlesticks and began, rather heavily, to climb the stairs. Eleanor followed after. But Peggy lagged behind. Eleanor heard her whispering with her brother in the hall.

"Come along, Peggy," Celia called back over the banister as she toiled upstairs. When she got to the landing at the top she stopped under the picture of the little Chinnerys and called back again rather sharply:

"Come, Peggy." There was a pause. Then Peggy came, reluctantly. She kissed her mother obediently; but she did not look in the least sleepy. She looked extremely pretty and rather flushed. She did not mean to go to bed, Eleanor felt sure.

She went into her room and undressed. All the windows were open and she heard the trees rustling in the garden. It was so hot still that she lay in her nightgown on top of the bed with only the sheet over her. The candle burnt its little pear-shaped flame on the table by her side. She lay listening vaguely to the trees in the garden; and watched the shadow of a moth that dashed round and round the room. Either I must get up and shut the window or blow out the candle, she thought drowsily. She did not want to do either. She wanted to lie still. It was a relief to lie in the semi-darkness after the talk, after the cards. She could still see the cards falling; black, red and yellow; kings, queens and knaves; on a green baize table. She looked drowsily round her. A nice vase of flowers stood on the dressing-table; there was the polished wardrobe and a china box by her bedside. She lifted the lid. Yes; four biscuits and a pale piece of chocolate—in case she should be hungry in the night. Celia had provided books too, The Diary of a Nobody, Ruff's Tour in Northumberland and an odd volume of Dante, in case she should wish to read in the night. She took one of the books and laid it on the counterpane beside her. Perhaps because she had been travelling, it seemed as if the ship were still padding softly through the sea; as if the train were still swinging from side to side as it rattled across France. She felt as if things were moving past her as she lay stretched on the bed under the single sheet. But it's not the landscape any longer, she thought; it's people's lives, their changing lives.

The door of the pink bedroom shut. William Whatney coughed next door. She heard him cross the room. Now he was standing by the window, smoking a last cigar. What's he thinking, she wondered—about India?—how he stood under a peacock umbrella? Then he began moving about the room, undressing. She could hear him take up a brush and put it down again on his dressing-table. And it's to him, she thought, remembering the wide sweep of his chin and the floating stains of pink and yellow that lay underneath it, that I owe that moment, which had been more than pleasure, when she hid her face behind the newspaper in the corner of the third-class railway carriage.

Now there were three moths dashing round the ceiling. They made a little tapping noise as they dashed round and round from corner to corner. If she left the window open much longer the room would be full of moths. A board creaked in the passage outside. She listened. Peggy, was it, escaping, to join her brother? She felt sure there was some scheme on foot. But she could only hear the heavy-laden branches moving up and down in the garden; a cow lowing; a bird chirping, and then, to her delight, the liquid call of an owl going from tree to tree looping them with silver.

She lay looking at the ceiling. A faint water mark appeared

there. It was like a hill. It reminded her of one of the great desolate mountains in Greece or in Spain, which looked as if nobody had ever set foot there since the beginning of time.

She opened the book that lay on the counterpane. She hoped it was Ruff's Tour, or the Diary of a Nobody; but it was Dante, and she was too lazy to change it. She read a few lines, here and there. But her Italian was rusty; the meaning escaped her. There was a meaning however; a hook seemed to scratch the surface of her mind.

> chè per quanti si dice più lì nostro
> tanto possiede più di ben ciascuno.

What did that mean? She read the English translation.

> For by so many more there are who say 'ours'
> So much the more of good doth each possess.

Brushed lightly by her mind that was watching the moths on the ceiling, and listening to the call of the owl as it looped from tree to tree with its liquid cry, the words did not give out their full meaning, but seemed to hold something furled up in the hard shell of the archaic Italian. I'll read it one of these days, she thought, shutting the book. When I've pensioned Crosby off, when. . . . Should she take another house? Should she travel? Should she go to India, at last? Sir William was getting into bed next door, his life was over; hers was beginning. No, I don't mean to take another house, not another house, she thought, looking at the stain on the ceiling. Again the sense came to her of a ship padding softly through the waves; of a train swinging from side to side down a railway-line. Things can't go on for ever, she thought. Things pass, things change, she thought, looking up at the ceiling. And where are we going? Where? Where? . . . The moths were dashing round the ceiling; the book slipped on to the floor. Craster won the pig, but who was it won the silver salver? she mused; made an effort; turned round, and blew out the candle. Darkness reigned.

1913

It was January. Snow was falling; snow had fallen all day. The sky spread like a grey goose's wing from which feathers were falling all over England. The sky was nothing but a flurry of falling flakes. Lanes were levelled; hollows filled; the snow clogged the streams; obscured windows, and lay wedged against doors. There was a faint murmur in the air, a slight crepitation, as if the air itself were turning to snow; otherwise all was silent, save when a sheep coughed, snow flopped from a branch, or slipped in an avalanche down some roof in London. Now and again a shaft of light spread slowly across the sky as a car drove through the muffled roads. But as the night wore on, snow covered the wheel ruts; softened to nothingness the marks of the traffic, and coated monuments, palaces and statues with a thick vestment of snow.

It was still snowing when the young man came from the House Agents to see over Abercorn Terrace. The snow cast a hard white glare upon the walls of the bathroom, showed up the cracks on the enamel bath, and the stains on the wall. Eleanor stood looking out of the window. The trees in the back garden were heavily lined with snow; all the roofs were softly moulded with snow; it was still falling. She turned. The young man turned too. The light was unbecoming to them both, yet the snow— she saw it through the window at the end of the passage—was beautiful, falling.

Mr Grice turned to her as they went downstairs,

"The fact is, our clients expect more lavatory accommodation nowadays," he said, stopping outside a bedroom door.

Why can't he say "baths" and have done with it, she thought. Slowly she went downstairs. Now she could see the snow falling through the panels of the hall door. As he went downstairs, she noticed the red ears which stood out over his high collar; and the neck which he had washed imperfectly in some sink at Wandsworth. She was annoyed; as he went round the house, sniffing and peering, he had indicted their cleanliness, their humanity; and he used absurd long words. He was hauling himself up into the class above him, she supposed, by means of long words. Now he stepped cautiously over the body of the sleeping dog; took his hat from the hall table, and went down the front door-steps in his business man's buttoned boots, leaving yellow footprints in the thick white cushion of snow. A four-wheeler was waiting.

Eleanor turned. There was Crosby, dodging about in her best bonnet and mantle. She had been following Eleanor about the house like a dog all the morning; the odious moment could no longer be put off. Her four-wheeler was at the door; they had to say good-bye.

"Well, Crosby, it all looks very empty, doesn't it?" said Eleanor, looking in at the empty drawing-room. The white light of the snow glared in on the walls. It showed up the marks on the walls where the furniture had stood, where the pictures had hung.

"It does, Miss Eleanor," said Crosby. She stood looking too. Eleanor knew that she was going to cry. She did not want her to cry. She did not want to cry herself.

"I can still see you all sitting round that table, Miss Eleanor," said Crosby. But the table had gone. Morris had taken this; Delia had taken that; everything had been shared out and separated.

"And the kettle that wouldn't boil," said Eleanor. "D'you remember that?" She tried to laugh.

"Oh, Miss Eleanor," said Crosby, shaking her head, "I remember everything!" The tears were forming; Eleanor looked away into the further room.

There too were marks on the wall, where the bookcase had

stood, where the writing-table had stood. She thought of herself sitting there, drawing a pattern on the blotting-paper; digging a hole, adding up tradesmen's books. . . . Then she turned. There was Crosby. Crosby was crying. The mixture of emotions was positively painful; she was so glad to be quit of it all, but for Crosby it was the end of everything.

She had known every cupboard, flagstone, chair and table in that large rambling house, not from five or six feet of distance as they had known it; but from her knees, as she scrubbed and polished; she had known every groove, stain, fork, knife, napkin and cupboard. They and their doings had made her entire world. And now she was going off, alone, to a single room at Richmond.

"I should think you'd be glad to be out of that basement anyhow, Crosby," said Eleanor, turning into the hall again. She had never realised how dark, how low it was, until, looking at it with "our Mr Grice," she had felt ashamed.

"It was my home for forty years, Miss," said Crosby. The tears were running. For forty years! Eleanor thought with a start. She had been a little girl of thirteen or fourteen when Crosby came to them, looking so stiff and smart. Now her blue gnat's eyes protruded and her cheeks were sunk.

Crosby was stooping to put Rover on the chain.

"You're sure you want him?" said Eleanor, looking at the rather smelly, wheezy and unattractive old dog. "We could easily find a nice home for him in the country."

"Oh, miss, don't ask me to give him up!" said Crosby. Tears checked her speech. Tears were running freely down her cheeks. For all Eleanor could do to prevent it, tears formed in her eyes too.

"Dear Crosby, good-bye," she said. She bent and kissed her. She had a curious dry quality of skin she noticed. But her own tears were falling. Then Crosby, holding Rover on the chain, began to edge sideways down the slippery steps. Eleanor, holding the door open, looked after her. It was a dreadful moment; unhappy; muddled; altogether wrong. Crosby was so miserable; she was so glad. Yet as she held the door open her tears formed and fell. They had all lived here; she had stood here to wave Morris to school; there was the little garden in which they used to plant crocuses. And now Crosby, with flakes of snow falling on her black bonnet, climbed into the four-wheeler, holding Rover in her arms. Eleanor shut the door and went in.

Snow was falling as the cab trotted along the streets. There were long yellow ruts on the pavement where people, shopping, had pressed it into slush. It was beginning to thaw slightly; loads of snow slipped off the roofs and fell onto the pavement. Little boys, too, were snowballing; one of them threw a ball which struck the cab as it passed. But when it turned into Richmond Green the whole of the vast space was completely white. Nobody seemed to have crossed the snow there; everything was white. The grass was white; the trees were white; the railings were white; the only marks in the whole vista were the rooks, sitting huddled black on the tree tops. The cab trotted on.

The carts had churned the snow to a yellowish clotted mixture by the time the cab stopped in front of the little house off the Green. Crosby, carrying Rover in her arms lest his feet should mark the stairs, went up the steps. There was Louisa Burt standing to welcome her; and Mr Bishop, the lodger from the top floor who had been a butler. He lent a hand with the luggage, and Crosby followed after, to her little room.

Her room was at the top, and at the back, overlooking the garden. It was small, but when she had unpacked her things it was comfortable enough. It had a look of Abercorn Terrace. Indeed for many years she had been hoarding odds and ends with a view to her retirement. Indian elephants, silver vases, the walrus that she had found in the waste-paper basket one morning, when the guns were firing for the old Queen's funeral—there they all were. She ranged them askew on the mantelpiece, and when she had hung the portraits of the family—some in wedding-dress, some in wigs and gowns, and Mr Martin in his uniform in the middle because he was her favourite—it was quite like home.

But whether it was the change to Richmond, or whether he had caught cold in the snow, Rover sickened immediately. He refused his food. His nose was hot. His eczema broke out again. When she tried to take him shopping with her next morning he rolled over with his feet in the air as if he begged to be left alone. Mr Bishop had to tell Mrs Crosby—for she wore the courtesy title in Richmond—that in his opinion the poor old chap (here he patted his head) was better out of the way.

"Come along with me, my dear," said Mrs Burt, putting her arm on Crosby's shoulder, "and let Bishop do it."

"He won't suffer, I can assure you," said Mr Bishop, rising from his knees. He had put her Ladyship's dogs to sleep scores of time before this. "He'll just take one sniff"—Mr Bishop had his pocket-handkerchief in his hand—"and he'll be off in a jiffy."

"It'll be for his good, Annie," Mrs Burt added, trying to draw her away.

Indeed, the poor old dog looked very miserable. But Crosby shook her head. He had wagged his tail; his eyes were open. He was alive. There was a gleam of what she had long considered a smile on his face. He depended on her, she felt. She was not going to hand him over to strangers. She sat by his side for three days and nights; she fed him with a teaspoon on Brand's Essence; but at last he refused to open his lips; his body grew stiffer and stiffer; a fly walked across his nose without its twitching. This was in the early morning with the sparrows twittering on the trees outside.

"It's a mercy she's got something to distract her," said Mrs Burt as Crosby passed the kitchen window the day after the funeral in her best mantle and bonnet; for it was Thursday, when she fetched Mr Pargiter's socks from Ebury Street. "But he ought to have been put down long ago," she added, turning back to the sink. His breath had smelt.

Crosby took the District Railway to Sloane Square and then she walked. She walked slowly, with her elbows jutting out from her sides as if to protect herself from the haphazardry of the streets. She still looked sad; but the change from Richmond to Ebury Street did her good. She felt more herself in Ebury Street than in Richmond. A common sort of people lived in Richmond she always felt. Here the ladies and gentlemen had the same kind of way with them. She glanced approvingly into the shops as she passed. And General Arbuthnot, who used to visit the Master, lived in Ebury Street she reflected as she turned into that gloomy thoroughfare. He was dead now; Louisa had shown her the notice in the papers. But when he was alive, he had lived here. She had reached Mr Martin's lodgings. She paused on the steps and adjusted her bonnet. She always had a word with Martin when she came to fetch his socks; it was one of her pleasures; and she enjoyed a gossip with Mrs Briggs, his landlady. Today she would have the pleasure of telling her of the death of Rover. Sidling cautiously down the area steps which were slippery with sleet she stood at the back door and rang the bell.

Martin sat in his room reading his newspaper. The war in the Balkans was over; but there was more trouble brewing—that he was sure. Quite sure. He turned the page. The room was very dark with the sleet falling. And he could never read while he was waiting. Crosby was coming; he could hear voices in the hall. How they gossiped! How they chattered! he thought impatiently. He threw the paper down and waited. Now she was coming; her hand was on the door. But what was he to say to her? he wondered, as he saw the handle turning. He put down the paper. He made use of the usual formula: "Well, Crosby, how's the world treating you?" as she came in.

She remembered Rover; and the tears started to her eyes.

Martin listened to the story; he wrinkled his brow sympathetically. Then he got up, went into his bedroom, and came back holding a pyjama jacket in his hand.

"What d'you call *that*, Crosby?" he said. He pointed to a hole under the collar, fringed with brown. Crosby adjusted her gold-rimmed spectacles.

"A burn, sir," she said with conviction.

"Brand new pyjamas; only worn them twice," said Martin, holding them extended. Crosby touched them. They were made of the finest silk, she could tell.

"Tut—tut—tut!" she said, shaking her head.

"Will you please take this pyjama to Mrs What's-her-name," he went on, holding it out in front of him. He wanted to use a metaphor; but one had to be very literal and use only the simplest language, he remembered, when one talked to Crosby.

"Tell her to get another laundress," he concluded, "and send the old one to the devil."

Crosby gathered the injured pyjama tenderly to her breast; Mr Martin never could abide wool next the skin, she remembered. Martin paused. One must pass the time of the day with Crosby, but the death of Rover had seriously limited their topics of conversation.

"How's the rheumatics?" he asked, as she stood very upright at the door of the room with the pyjamas on her arm. She had grown distinctly smaller, he thought. She shook her head, Richmond was very low compared with Abercorn Terrace, she said. Her face dropped. She was thinking of Rover, he supposed. He must get her mind off that; he could not bear tears.

"Seen Miss Eleanor's new flat?" he asked. Crosby had. But she did not like flats. In her opinion Miss Eleanor wore herself out.

"And the people's not worth it, sir," she said, referring to the Zwinglers, Paravicinis and Cobbs who used to come to the back door for cast-off clothing in the old days.

Martin shook his head. He could not think what to say next. He hated talking to servants; it always made him feel insincere. Either one simpers, or one's hearty, he was thinking. In either case it's a lie.

"And are you keeping pretty well yourself, Master Martin?"

Crosby asked him, using the diminutive, which was a perquisite of her long service.

"Not married yet, Crosby," said Martin.

Crosby cast her eye round the room. It was a bachelor's apartment, with its leather chairs; its chessmen on top of a pile of books and its soda-water syphon on a tray. She ventured to say that she was sure that there were plenty of nice young ladies who would be very glad to take care of him.

"Ah, but I like lying in bed of a morning," said Martin.

"You always did, sir," she said, smiling. And then it was possible for Martin to take out his watch, step briskly to the window and exclaim as if he had suddenly remembered an appointment,

"By Jove, Crosby, I must be off!" and the door shut upon Crosby.

It was a lie. He had no engagement. One always lies to servants, he thought, looking out of the window. The mean outlines of the Ebury Street houses showed through the falling sleet. Everybody lies, he thought. His father had lied—after his death they had found letters from a woman called Mira tied up in his table-drawer. And he had seen Mira—a stout respectable lady who wanted help with her roof. Why had his father lied? What was the harm of keeping a mistress? And he had lied himself; about the room off the Fulham Road where he and Dodge and Erridge used to smoke cheap cigars and tell smutty stories. It was an abominable system, he thought; family life; Abercorn Terrace. No wonder the house would not let. It had one bathroom, and a basement; and there all those different people had lived, boxed up together, telling lies.

Then as he stood at the window looking at the little figures slinking along the wet pavement he saw Crosby come up the area steps with a parcel under her arm. She stood for a moment, like a frightened little animal, peering round her before she ventured to brave the dangers of the street. At last, off she trotted. He saw the snow falling on her black bonnet as she disappeared. He turned away.

1914

It was a brilliant spring; the day was radiant. Even the air seemed to have a burr in it as it touched the tree tops; it vibrated, it rippled. The leaves were sharp and green. In the country old church clocks rasped out the hour; the rusty sound went over fields that were red with clover, and up went the rooks as if flung by the bells. Round they wheeled; then settled on the tree tops.

In London all was gallant and strident; the season was beginning; horns hooted; the traffic roared; flags flew taut as trout in a stream. And from all the spires of all the London churches—the fashionable saints of Mayfair, the dowdy saints of Kensington, the hoary saints of the city—the hour was proclaimed. The air over London seemed a rough sea of sound through which circles travelled. But the clocks were irregular, as if the saints themselves were divided. There were pauses, silences. . . . Then the clocks struck again.

Here in Ebury Street some distant frail-voiced clock was striking. It was eleven. Martin, standing at his window, looked down on the narrow street. The sun was bright; he was in the best of spirits; he was going to visit his stockbroker in the city. His affairs were turning out well. At one time, he was thinking, his father had made a lot of money; then he lost it; then he made it; but in the end he had done very well.

He stood at the window for a moment admiring a lady of fashion in a charming hat who was looking at a pot in the curiosity shop opposite. It was a blue pot on a Chinese stand with green brocade behind it. The sloping symmetrical body, the depth of blue, the little cracks in the glaze pleased him. And the lady looking at the pot was also charming.

He took his hat and stick and went out into the street. He would walk part of the way to the City. "The King of Spain's daughter" he hummed as he turned up Sloane Street, "came to visit me. All for the sake of. . . ." He looked into the shop windows as he passed. They were full of summer dresses; charming confections of green and gauze, and there were flights of hats stuck on little rods. ". . . all for the sake of" he hummed as he walked on, "my silver nutmeg tree." But what was a silver nutmeg tree he wondered? An organ was fluting its merry little jig further down the street. The organ moved round and round, shifted this way and that, as if the old man who played it were half dancing to the tune. A pretty servant girl ran up the area steps and gave him a penny. His supple Italian face wrinkled all over as he whipped off his cap and bowed to her. The girl smiled and slipped back into the kitchen.

". . . all for the sake of my silver nutmeg tree" Martin hummed, peering down through the area railings into the kitchen where they were sitting. They looked very snug, with teapots and bread and butter on the kitchen table. His stick swung from side to side like the tail of a cheerful dog. Everybody seemed light-hearted and irresponsible, sallying out of their houses, flaunting along the streets with pennies for the organ-grinders and pennies for the beggars. Everybody seemed to have money to spend. Women clustered round the plate-glass windows. He too stopped, looked at the model of a toy boat; at dressing-cases, shining yellow with rows of silver bottles. But who wrote that song, he wondered, as he strolled on, about the King of Spain's daughter, the song that Pippy used to sing him, as she wiped his ears with a piece of slimy flannel? She used to take him on her knee and croak out in her wheezy rattle of a voice, "The King of Spain's daughter came to visit me, all for the sake of. . . ." And then suddenly her knee gave, and down he was tumbled onto the floor.

Here he was at Hyde Park Corner. The scene was extremely animated. Vans, motor-cars, motor omnibuses were streaming down the hill. The trees in the Park had little green leaves on them. Cars with gay ladies in pale dresses were already passing in at the gates. Everybody was going about their business. And somebody, he observed, had written the words "God is Love" in pink chalk on the gates of Apsley House. That must need some pluck, he thought, to write "God is love" on the gates of Apsley House when at any moment a policeman might nab you. But here came his bus; and he climbed on top.

"To St. Paul's," he said, handing the conductor his coppers.

The omnibuses swirled and circled in a perpetual current round the steps of St. Paul's. The statue of Queen Anne seemed to preside over the chaos and to supply it with a centre, like the hub of a wheel. It seemed as if the white lady ruled the traffic with her sceptre; directed the activities of the little men in bowler hats and round coats; of the women carrying attaché cases; of the vans, the lorries and the motor omnibuses. Now and then single figures broke off from the rest and went up the steps into the church. The doors of the Cathedral kept opening and shutting. Now and again a blast of faint organ music was blown out into the air. The pigeons waddled; the sparrows fluttered. Soon after midday a little old man carrying a paper bag took up his station half-way up the steps and proceeded to feed the birds. He held out a slice of bread. His lips moved. He seemed to be wheedling and coaxing them. Soon he was haloed by a circle of fluttering wings. Sparrows perched on his head and his hands. Pigeons waddled close to his feet. A little crowd gathered to watch him feeding the sparrows. He tossed his bread round him in a circle. Then there was a ripple in the air. The great clock, all the clocks of the city, seemed to be gathering their forces together; they seemed to be whirring a preliminary warning. Then the stroke struck. "One" blared out. All the sparrows fluttered up into the air; even the pigeons were frightened; some of them made a little flight round the head of Queen Anne.

As the last ripple of the stroke died away, Martin came out in the open space in front of the Cathedral.

He crossed over and stood with his back against a shop window looking up at the great dome. All the weights in his body seemed to shift. He had a curious sense of something moving in his body in harmony with the building; it righted itself: it came to a full stop. It was exciting—this change of proportion. He wished he had been an architect. He stood with his back pressed against the shop trying to get the whole of the cathedral clear. But it was difficult with so many people passing. They knocked against him and brushed in front of him. It was the rush hour, of course, when City men were making for their luncheons. They were taking short cuts across the steps. The pigeons were swirling up and then settling down again. The doors were opening and shutting as he mounted the steps. The pigeons were a nuisance, he thought, making a mess on the steps. He climbed up slowly.

"And who's that?" he thought, looking at someone who was standing against one of the pillars. "Don't I know her?"

Her lips were moving. She was talking to herself.

"It's Sally!" he thought. He hesitated; should he speak to her, or should he not? But she was company; and he was tired of his own.

"A penny for your thoughts, Sal!" he said, tapping her on the shoulder.

She turned; her expression changed instantly. "Just as I was thinking of you, Martin!" she exclaimed.

"What a lie!" he said, shaking hands.

"When I think of people, I always see them," she said. She gave her queer little shuffle as if she were a bird, a somewhat dishevelled fowl, for her cloak was not in the fashion. They stood for a moment on the steps, looking down at the crowded street beneath. A gust of organ music came out from the Cathedral behind them as the doors opened and shut. The faint ecclesiastical murmur was vaguely impressive, and the dark space of the Cathedral seen through the door.

"What were you thinking . . . ?" he began. But he broke off. "Come and lunch," he said. "I'll take you to a City chop house," and he shepherded her down the steps, along a narrow alley, blocked by carts, into which packages were being shot from the warehouses. They pushed through the swing doors into the chop house.

"Very full today, Alfred," said Martin affably, as the waiter took his coat and hat and hung them on the rack. He knew the waiter; he often lunched there; the waiter knew him too.

"Very full, Captain," he said.

"Now," he said, sitting down, "what shall we have?"

A vast brownish-yellow joint was being trundled from table to table on a lorry.

"That," said Sara, waving her hand at it.

"And drink?" said Martin. He took the wine-list and consulted it.

"Drink—" said Sara, "drink, I leave to you." She took off her gloves and laid them on a small reddish-brown book that was obviously a prayer-book.

"Drink you leave to me," said Martin. Why, he wondered, do prayer-books always have their leaves gilt with red and gold? He chose the wine.

"And what were you doing," he said, dismissing the waiter, "at St. Paul's?"

"Listening to the service," she said. She looked round her. The room was very hot and crowded. The walls were covered with gold leaves encrusted on a brown surface. People were passing them and coming in and out all the time. The waiter brought the wine. Martin poured her out a glass.

"I didn't know you went to services," he said, looking at her prayer-book.

She did not answer. She kept looking round her, watching the people come in and go out. She sipped her wine. The colour was coming into her cheeks. She took up her knife and fork and began to eat the admirable mutton. They ate in silence for a moment.

He wanted to make her talk.

"And what, Sal," he said, touching the little book, "d'you make of it?"

She opened the prayer-book at random and began to read:

"The father incomprehensible; the son incomprehensible—" she spoke in her ordinary voice.

"Hush!" he stopped her. "Somebody's listening."

In deference to him she assumed the manner of a lady lunching with a gentleman in a City restaurant.

"And what were you doing," she asked, "at St. Paul's?"

"Wishing I'd been an architect," he said. "But they sent me into the Army instead, which I loathed." He spoke emphatically.

"Hush," she whispered. "Somebody's listening."

He looked round quickly; then he laughed. The waiter was setting their tart in front of them. They ate in silence. He filled her glass again. Her cheeks were flushed; her eyes were bright. He envied her the generalised sensation of universal wellbeing that he used to get from a glass of wine. Wine was good—it broke down barriers. He wanted to make her talk.

"I didn't know you went to services," he said, looking at her prayer-book. "And what do you think of it?" She looked at it too. Then she tapped it with her fork.

"What do *they* think of it, Martin?" she asked. "The woman praying and the man with a long white beard?"

"Much what Crosby thinks when she comes to see me," he said. He thought of the old woman standing at the door of his room with the pyjama jacket over her arm, and the devout look on her face.

"I'm Crosby's God," he said, helping her to brussels sprouts.

"Crosby's God! Almighty, all-powerful Mr Martin!" She laughed.

She raised her glass to him. Was she laughing at him? he wondered. He hoped she did not think him very old. "You remember Crosby, don't you?" he said. "She's retired, and her dog's dead."

"Retired and her dog's dead?" she repeated. She looked again over her shoulder. Conversation in a restaurant was impossible; it was broken into little fragments. City men in their neat striped suits and bowler hats were brushing past them all the time.

"It's a fine church," she said, turning round. She had hopped back to St. Paul's, he supposed.

"Magnificent," he replied. "Were you looking at the monuments?"

Somebody had come in whom he recognised: Erridge, the stockbroker. He raised a finger and beckoned. Martin rose and went to speak to him. When he came back she had filled her glass again. She was sitting there, looking at the people, as if she were a child that he had taken to a pantomime.

"And what are you doing this afternoon?" he asked.

"The Round Pond at four," she said. She drummed on the table "The Round Pond at four." Now she had passed, he guessed, into the drowsy benevolence which waits on a good dinner and a glass of wine.

"Meeting somebody?" he asked.

"Yes. Maggie," she said.

They ate in silence. Fragments of other people's talk reached them in broken sentences. Then the man to whom Martin had spoken touched him on the shoulder as he went out.

"Wednesday at eight," he said.

"Right you are," said Martin. He made a note in his pocket-book.

"And what are you doing this afternoon?" she asked.

"Ought to see my sister in prison," he said, lighting a cigarette.

"In prison?" she asked.

"Rose. For throwing a brick," he said.

"Red Rose, tawny Rose," she began, reaching out her hand for the wine again, "wild Rose, thorny Rose—"

"No," he said, putting his hand over the mouth of the bottle,

209

"you've had enough." A little excited her. He must damp her excitement. There were people listening.

"A damned unpleasant thing," he said, "being in prison."

She drew back her glass and sat gazing at it, as if the engine of the brain were suddenly cut off. She was very like her mother—except when she laughed.

He would have liked to talk to her about her mother. But it was impossible to talk. Too many people were listening, and they were smoking. Smoke mixed with the smell of meat made the air heavy. He was thinking of the past when she exclaimed:

"Sitting on a three-legged stool having meat crammed down her throat!"

He roused himself. She was thinking of Rose, was she?

"Crash came a brick!" she laughed, flourishing her fork.

"'Roll up the map of Europe,' said the man to the flunkey. 'I don't believe in force'!" She brought down her fork. A plum-stone jumped. Martin looked round. People were listening. He got up.

"Shall we go?" he said, "—if you've had enough?"

She got up and looked for her cloak.

"Well, I've enjoyed it," she said, taking her cloak. "Thanks, Martin, for my good lunch."

He beckoned to the waiter who came with alacrity and totted up the bill. Martin laid a sovereign on the plate. Sara began to thrust her arms into the sleeves of her cloak.

"Shall I come with you," he said, helping her, "to the Round Pond at four?"

"Yes!" she said, spinning round on her heel. "To the Round Pond at four!"

She walked off, a little unsteadily he observed, past the City men who were still eating.

Here the waiter came up with the change and Martin began to slip it in his pocket. He kept back one coin for the tip. But as he was about to give it, he was struck by something shifty in Alfred's expression. He flicked up the flap of the bill; a two-shilling piece lay beneath.

It was the usual trick. He lost his temper.

"What's this?" he said angrily.

"Didn't know it was there, sir," the waiter stammered.

Martin felt his blood rise to his ears. He felt exactly like his father in a rage; as if he had white spots above his temples. He pocketed the coin that he had been going to give the waiter; and marched past him, brushing aside his hand. The man slunk back with a murmur.

"Let's be off," he said, hustling Sara along the crowded room. "Let's get out of this."

He hurried her into the street. The fug, the warm meaty smell of the City chop-house, had suddenly become intolerable.

"How I hate being cheated!" he said as he put on his hat.

"Sorry, Sara," he apologised. "I oughtn't to have taken you there. It's a beastly hole."

He drew in a breath of fresh air. The street noises, the unconcerned, business-like look of things, were refreshing after the hot steamy room. There were the carts waiting, drawn up along the street; and the packages sliding down into them from the warehouses. Again they came out in front of St. Paul's. He looked up. There was the same old man still feeding the sparrows. And there was the Cathedral. He wished he could feel again the sense of weights changing in his body and coming to a stop; but the queer thrill of some correspondence between his own body and the stone no longer came to him. He felt nothing except anger. Also, Sara distracted him. She was about to cross the crowded road. He put out his hand to stop her. "Take care," he said. Then they crossed.

"Shall we walk?" he asked. She nodded. They began to walk along Fleet Street. Conversation was impossible. The pavement was so narrow that he had to step on and off in order to keep beside her. He still felt the discomfort of anger, but the anger itself was cooling. What ought I to have done? he thought, seeing himself brush past the waiter without giving him a tip. Not that; he thought, no, not that. People pressing against him made him step off the pavement. After all, the poor devil had to make a living. He liked being generous: he liked to leave people smiling; and two shillings meant nothing to him. But what's the use, he thought, now it's done? He began to hum his little song— and then stopped, remembering that he was with someone.

"Look at that, Sal," he said, clutching at her arm. "Look at that!" He pointed at the splayed-out figure at Temple Bar; it looked as ridiculous as usual—something between a serpent and a fowl.

"Look at that!" he repeated laughing. They paused for a moment to look at the little flattened figures lodged so uncomfortably against the pediment of Temple Bar: Queen Victoria: King Edward. Then they walked on. It was impossible to talk because of the crowd. Men in wigs and gowns hurried across the street: some carried red bags, others blue bags.

"The Law Courts," he said, pointing at the cold mass of decorated stone. It looked very gloomy and funereal, ". . . where Morris spends his time," he said aloud.

He still felt uncomfortable at having lost his temper. But the feeling was passing. Only a little ridge of roughness remained in his mind.

"D'you think I ought to have been . . ." he began, a barrister he meant; but also Ought I to have done that—lost his temper with the waiter.

"Ought to have been—ought to have done?" she asked, bending towards him. She had not caught his meaning in the roar of the traffic. It was impossible to talk; but at any rate the feeling that he had lost his temper was diminishing. That little sting was being successfully smoothed over. Then back it came because he saw a beggar selling violets. And that poor devil, he thought, had to go without his tip because he cheated me. . . . He fixed his eyes on a pillar-box. Then he looked at a car. It was odd how soon one got used to cars without horses, he thought. They used to look ridiculous. They passed the woman selling violets. She wore a hat over her face. He dropped a sixpence in her tray to make amends to the waiter. He shook his head. No violets, he

212

meant; and indeed they were faded. But he caught sight of her face. She had no nose; her face was seamed with white patches; there were red rims for nostrils. She had no nose—she had pulled her hat down to hide that fact.

"Let's cross," he said, abruptly. He took Sara's arm and made her cross between the omnibuses. She must have seen such sights often; he had, often; but not together—that made a difference. He hurried her on to the further pavement.

"We'll get a bus," he said, "Come along."

He took her by the elbow to make her step out briskly. But it was impossible; a cart blocked the way; there were people passing. They were approaching Charing Cross. It was like the piers of a bridge; men and women were sucked in instead of water. They had to stop. Newspaper boys held placards against their legs. Men were buying papers: some loitered; others snatched them. Martin bought one and held it in his hand.

"We'll wait here," he said. "The bus'll come." An old straw hat with a purple ribbon round it, he thought opening his paper. The sight persisted. He looked up. The station clock's always fast, he assured a man who was hurrying to catch a train. Always fast, he said to himself as he opened the paper. But there was no clock. He turned to read the news from Ireland. Omnibus after omnibus stopped, then swooped off again. It was difficult to concentrate on the news from Ireland; he looked up.

"This is ours," he said, as the right bus came. They climbed on top and sat side by side overlooking the driver.

"Two to Hyde Park Corner," he said, producing a handful of silver, and looked through the pages of the evening paper; but it was only an early edition.

"Nothing in it," he said, stuffing the paper under the seat. "And now—" he began, filling his pipe. They were running smoothly down the incline of Piccadilly. "—where my old father used to sit," he broke off, waving his pipe at Club windows. ". . . and now"—he lit a match, "—and now, Sally, you can say whatever you like. Nobody's listening. Say something," he added, throwing his match overboard, "very profound."

He turned to her. He wanted her to speak. Down they dipped; up they swooped again. He wanted her to speak; or he must speak himself. And what could he say? He had buried his feeling. But some emotion remained. He wanted her to speak it: but she was silent. No, he thought, biting the stem of his pipe. I won't say it. If I did she'd think me . . .

He looked at her. The sun was blazing on the windows of St. George's Hospital. She was looking at it with rapture. But why with rapture? he wondered, as the bus stopped and he got down.

The scene since the morning had changed slightly. Clocks in the distance were just striking three. There were more cars; more women in pale summer dresses; more men in tail-coats and grey top-hats. The procession through the gates into the park was beginning. Everyone looked festive. Even the little dressmakers' apprentices with band-boxes looked as if they were taking part in some ceremonial. Green chairs were drawn up at the edge of the Row. They were full of people looking about them as if they had taken seats at a play. Riders cantered to the end of the Row; pulled up their horses; turned and cantered the other way. The wind, coming from the west, moved white clouds grained with gold across the sky. The windows of Park Lane shone with blue and gold reflections.

Martin stepped out briskly.

"Come along," he said; "come—come!" He walked on. I'm young, he thought; I'm in the prime of life. There was a tang of earth in the air; even in the Park there was some faint smell of spring, of the country.

"How I like—" he said aloud. He looked round. He had spoken to the empty air. Sara had lagged behind; there she was, tying her shoe-lace. But he felt as if he had missed a step going downstairs.

"What a fool one feels when one talks aloud to oneself," he said as she came up. She pointed.

214

"But look," she said, "they all do it."

A middle-aged woman was coming towards them. She was talking to herself. Her lips moved; she was gesticulating with her hand.

"It's the spring," he said, as she passed them.

"No. Once in winter I came here," she said, "and there was a negro, laughing aloud in the snow."

"In the snow," said Martin. "A negro." The sun was bright on the grass; they were passing a bed in which the many-coloured hyacinths were curled and glossy.

"Don't let's think of the snow," he said. "Let's think—" A young woman was wheeling a perambulator; a sudden thought came into his head. "Maggie," he said. "Tell me. I haven't seen her since her baby was born. And I've never met the Frenchman—what d'you call him?—René?"

"Renny," she said. She was still under the influence of the wine; of the wandering airs; of the people passing. He too felt the same distraction; but he wanted to end it.

"Yes. What's he like, this man René; Renny?"

He pronounced the word first in the French way; then as she did, in the English. He wanted to wake her. He took her arm.

"Renny!" Sara repeated. She threw her head back and laughed. "Let me see," she said. "He wears a red tie with white spots. And has dark eyes. And he takes an orange—suppose we're at dinner, and says, looking straight at you, 'This orange, Sara—'" She rolled her *r*'s. She paused.

"There's another person talking to himself," she broke off. A young man came past them in a closely buttoned-up coat as if he had no shirt. He was muttering as he walked. He scowled at them as he passed them.

"But Renny?" said Martin.

"We were talking about Renny," he reminded her. "He takes an orange—"

". . . and pours himself out a glass of wine," she resumed. "'Science is the religion of the future!'" she exclaimed, waving her hand as if she held a glass of wine.

"Of wine?" said Martin. Half listening, he had visualised an earnest French professor—a little picture to which now he must add inappropriately a glass of wine.

"Yes, wine," she repeated. "His father was a merchant," she continued. "A man with a black beard; a merchant at Bordeaux. And one day," she continued, "when he was a little boy, playing in the garden, there was a tap on the window. 'Don't make so much noise. Play further away,' said a woman in a white cap. His mother was dead. . . . And he was afraid to tell his father that the horse was too big to ride . . . and they sent him to England. . . ."

She was skipping over railings.

"And then what happened?" said Martin, joining her. "They became engaged?"

She was silent. He waited for her to explain—why they had married—Maggie and Renny. He waited, but she said no more. Well, she married him and they're happy he thought. He was jealous for a moment. The Park was full of couples walking together. Everything seemed fresh and full of sweetness. The air puffed soft in their faces. It was laden with murmurs; with the stir of branches; the rush of wheels; dogs barking, and now and again the intermittent song of a thrush.

Here a lady passed them, talking to herself. As they looked at her she turned and whistled, as if to her dog. But the dog she had whistled was another person's dog. It bounded off in the opposite direction. The lady hurried on pursing her lips together.

"People don't like being looked at," said Sara, "when they're talking to themselves." Martin roused himself.

"Look here," he said. "We've gone the wrong way." Voices floated out to them.

They had been walking in the wrong direction. They were near the bald rubbed space where the speakers congregate. Meetings were in full swing. Groups had gathered round the different orators. Mounted on their platforms, or sometimes only on boxes, the speakers were holding forth. The voices became louder, louder and louder as they approached.

"Let's listen," said Martin. A thin man was leaning forward holding a slate in his hand. They could hear him say, "Ladies and gentlemen . . ." They stopped in front of him. "Fix your eyes on me," he said. They fixed their eyes on him. "Don't be afraid," he said, crooking his finger. He had an ingratiating manner. He turned his slate over. "Do I look like a Jew?" he asked. Then he turned his slate and looked on the other side. And they heard him say that his mother was born in Bermondsey, as they strolled on, and his father in the Isle of—The voice died away.

"What about this chap?" said Martin. Here was a large man, banging on the rail of his platform.

"Fellow citizens!" he was shouting. They stopped. The crowd of loafers, errand-boys and nursemaids gaped up at him with their mouths falling open and their eyes gazing blankly. His hand raked in the line of cars that was passing with a superb gesture of scorn. His shirt appeared under his waistcoat.

"Joostice and liberty," said Martin, repeating his words, as the fist thumped on the railing. They waited. Then it all came over again.

"But he's a jolly good speaker," said Martin, turning. The voice died away. "And now, what's the old lady saying?" They strolled on.

The old lady's audience was extremely small. Her voice was hardly audible. She held a little book in her hand and she was saying something about sparrows. But her voice tapered off into a thin frail pipe. A chorus of little boys imitated her.

They listened for a moment. Then Martin turned again. "Come along, Sall," he said, putting his hand on her shoulder.

The voices grew fainter, fainter and fainter. Soon they ceased altogether. They strolled on across the smooth slope that rose and fell like a breadth of green cloth striped with straight brown paths in front of them. Great white dogs were gambolling; through the trees shone the waters of the Serpentine, set here and there with little boats. The urbanity of the Park, the gleam of the water, the sweep and curve and composition of the scene, as if somebody had designed it, affected Martin agreeably.

"Joostice and liberty," he said half to himself, as they came to the water's edge and stood a moment, watching the gulls cut the air into sharp white patterns with their wings.

"Did you agree with him?" he asked, taking Sara's arm to rouse her; for her lips were moving; she was talking to herself. "That fat man," he explained, "who flung his arm out." She started.

"Oi, oi, oi!" she exclaimed, imitating his cockney accent.

Yes, thought Martin, as they walked on. Oi, oi, oi, oi, oi, oi. It's always that. There wouldn't be much justice or liberty for the likes of him if the fat man had his way—or beauty either.

"And the poor old lady whom nobody listened to?" he said, "talking about the sparrows. . . ."

He could still see in his mind's eye the thin man persuasively crooking his finger; the fat man who flung his arms out so that his braces showed; and the little old lady who tried to make her voice heard above the cat-calls and whistles. There was a mixture of comedy and tragedy in the scene.

But they had reached the gate into Kensington Gardens. A long row of cars and carriages was drawn up by the kerb. Striped umbrellas were open over the little round tables where people were already sitting, waiting for their tea. Waitresses were hurrying in and out with trays; the season had begun. The scene was very gay.

A lady, fashionably dressed with a purple feather dipping down on one side of her hat, sat there sipping an ice. The sun dappled the table and gave her a curious look of transparency, as if she were caught in a net of light; as if she were composed of lozenges of floating colours. Martin half thought that he knew her; he half raised his hat. But she sat there looking in front of her; sipping her ice. No, he thought; he did not know her, and he stopped for a moment to light his pipe. What would the world be, he said to himself—he was still thinking of the fat man brandishing his arm—without "I" in it? He lit the match. He looked at the flame that had become almost invisible in the sun. He stood for a second drawing at his pipe. Sara had walked on. She too was netted with floating lights from between the leaves. A primal innocence seemed to brood over the scene. The birds made a fitful sweet chirping in the branches; the roar of London encircled the open space in a ring of distant but complete sound. The pink and white chestnut blossoms rode up and down as the branches moved in the breeze. The sun dappling the leaves gave everything a curious look of insubstantiality as if it were broken into separate points of light. He too, himself, seemed dispersed. His mind for a moment was a blank. Then he roused himself, threw away his match, and caught up Sally.

"Come along!" he said. "Come along. . . . The Round Pond at four!"

They walked on arm in arm in silence, down the long avenue with the Palace and the phantom church at the end of its vista. The size of the human figure seemed to have shrunk. Instead of full-grown people, children were now in the majority. Dogs of all sorts abounded. The air was full of barking and sudden shrill cries. Coveys of nursemaids pushed perambulators along the paths. Babies lay fast asleep in them like images of faintly tinted wax; their perfectly smooth eyelids fitted over their eyes as if they sealed them completely. He looked down; he liked children. Sally had looked like that the first time he saw her, asleep in her perambulator in the hall in Browne Street.

He stopped short. They had reached the Pond.

"Where's Maggie?" he said. "There—is that her?" He pointed to a young woman who was lifting a baby out of its perambulator under a tree.

"Where?" said Sara. She looked in the wrong direction.

He pointed.

"There, under that tree."

"Yes," she said, "that's Maggie."

They walked in that direction.

"But is it?" said Martin. He was suddenly doubtful; for she

had the unconsciousness of a person who is unaware that she is being looked at. It made her unfamiliar. With one hand she held the child; with the other she arranged the pillows of the perambulator. She too was dappled with lozenges of floating light.

"Yes," he said, noticing something about her gesture, "that's Maggie."

She turned and saw them.

She held up her hand as if to warn them to approach quietly. She put a finger to her lips. They approached silently. As they reached her, the distant sound of a clock striking was wafted on the breeze. One, two, three, four it struck. . . . Then it ceased.

"We met at St. Paul's," said Martin in a whisper. He dragged up two chairs and sat down. They were silent for a moment. The child was not asleep. Then Maggie bent over and looked at the child.

"You needn't talk in a whisper," she said aloud. "He's asleep."

"We met at St. Paul's," Martin repeated in his ordinary voice. "I'd been seeing my stockbroker." He took off his hat and laid it on the grass. "And when I came out," he resumed, "there was Sally. . . ." He looked at her. She had never told him, he remembered, what it was that she was thinking, as she stood there, with her lips moving, on the steps of St. Paul's.

Now she was yawning. Instead of taking the little hard green chair which he had pulled up for her, she had thrown herself down on the grass. She had folded herself like a grasshopper with her back against the tree. The prayer-book, with its red and gold leaves, was lying on the ground tented over with trembling blades of grass. She yawned; she stretched. She was already half asleep.

He drew his chair beside Maggie's; and looked at the scene in front of them.

It was admirably composed. There was the white figure of Queen Victoria against a green bank; beyond, was the red brick of the old palace; the phantom Church raised its spire, and the Round Pond made a pool of blue. A race of yachts was going forward. The boats leant on their sides so that the sails touched the water. There was a nice little breeze.

"And what did you talk about?" said Maggie.

Martin could not remember. "She was tipsy," he said, pointing to Sara. "And now she's going to sleep." He felt sleepy himself. The sun for the first time was almost hot on his head.

Then he answered her question.

"The whole world," he said, "Politics; religion; morality." He yawned. Gulls were screaming as they rose and sank over a lady who was feeding them. Maggie was watching them. He looked at her.

"I haven't seen you," he said, "since your baby was born." It's changed her, having a child, he thought. It's improved her, he thought. But she was watching the gulls; the lady had thrown a handful of fish. The gulls swooped round and round her head.

"D'you like having a child?" he said.

"Yes," she said, rousing herself to answer him. "It's a tie though."

"But it's nice having ties, isn't it?" he enquired. He was fond of children. He looked at the sleeping baby with its eyes sealed and its thumb in its mouth.

"D'you want them?" she asked.

"Just what I was asking myself," he said, "before—"

Here Sara made a click at the back of her throat; he dropped his voice to a whisper. "Before I met her at St. Paul's," he said. They were silent. The baby was asleep; Sara was asleep; the presence of the two sleepers seemed to enclose them in a circle of privacy. Two of the racing yachts were coming together as if they must collide; but one passed just ahead of the other. Martin watched them. Life had resumed its ordinary proportions. Everything once more was back in its place. The boats were sailing; the men walking; the little boys dabbled in the pond for minnows; the waters of the pond rippled bright blue. Everything was full of the stir, the potency, the fecundity of spring.

Suddenly he said aloud:

"Possessiveness is the devil."

Maggie looked at him. Did he mean herself—herself and the baby? No. There was a tone in his voice that told her he was thinking not of her.

"What are you thinking?" she asked.

"About the woman I'm in love with," he said. "Love ought to stop on both sides, don't you think, simultaneously?" He spoke without any stress on the words, so as not to wake the sleepers. "But it won't—that's the devil," he added in the same undertone.

"Bored, are you?" she murmured.

"Stiff," he said. "Bored stiff." He stooped and disinterred a pebble in the grass.

"And jealous?" she murmured. Her voice was very low and soft.

"Horribly," he whispered. It was true, now that she referred to it. Here the baby half woke and stretched out its hand. Maggie rocked the perambulator. Sara stirred. Their privacy was imperilled. It would be destroyed at any moment, he felt; and he wanted to talk.

He glanced at the sleepers. The baby's eyes were shut, and Sara's too. Still they seemed encircled in a ring of solitude. Speaking in a low voice without accent, he told her his story; the story of the lady; how she wanted to keep him, and he wanted to be free. It was an ordinary story, but painful—mixed. As he told it, however, the sting was drawn. They sat silent, looking in front of them.

Another race was starting; men crouched at the edge of the pond, each with his stick resting on a toy boat. It was a charming scene, gay, innocent and a trifle ridiculous. The signal was given; off the boats went. And will he, Martin thought, looking at the sleeping baby, go through the same thing too? He was thinking of himself—of his jealousy.

"My father," he said suddenly, but softly, "had a lady. . . . She called him 'Bogy'." And he told her the story of the lady who kept a boarding house at Putney—the very respectable lady, grown stout, who wanted help with her roof. Maggie laughed, but very gently, so as not to wake the sleepers. Both were still sleeping soundly.

"Was he in love," Martin asked her, "with your mother?"

She was looking at the gulls, cutting patterns on the blue distance with their wings. His question seemed to sink through what she was seeing; then suddenly it reached her.

"Are we brother and sister?" she asked; and laughed out loud. The child opened its eyes, and uncurled its fingers.

"We've woken him," said Martin. He began to cry. Maggie had to soothe him. Their privacy was over. The child cried; and the clocks began striking. The sound came wafted gently towards them on the breeze. One, two, three, four, five. . . .

"It's time to go," said Maggie, as the last stroke died away. She laid the baby back on its pillow, and turned. Sara was still asleep. She lay crumpled up with her back to the tree. Martin stooped and threw a twig at her. She opened her eyes but shut them again.

"No, no," she protested, stretching her arms over her head.

"It's time," said Maggie. She pulled herself up. "Time is it?" she sighed. "How strange . . . !" she murmured. She sat up and rubbed her eyes.

"Martin!" she exclaimed. She looked at him as he stood over her in his blue suit holding his stick in his hand. She looked at him as if she were bringing him back to the field of vision.

"Martin!" she said again.

"Yes, Martin!" he replied. "Did you hear what we've been saying?" he asked her.

"Voices," she yawned, shaking her head. "Only voices."

He paused for a moment, looking down at her. "Well, I'm off," he said, taking up his hat, "to dine with a cousin in Grosvenor Square," he added. He turned and left them.

He looked back at them after he had gone a little distance.

They were still sitting by the perambulator under the trees. He walked on. Then he looked back again. The ground sloped, and the trees were hidden. A very stout lady was being tugged along the path by a small dog on a chain. He could see them no longer.

The sun was setting as he drove across the Park, an hour or two later. He was thinking that he had forgotten something; but what, he did not know. Scene passed over scene; one obliterated another. Now he was crossing the bridge over the Serpentine. The water glowed with sunset light; twisted poles of lamp light lay on the water, and there, at the end the white bridge composed the scene. The cab entered the shadow of the trees, and joined the long line of cabs that was streaming towards the Marble Arch. People in evening dress were going to plays and parties. The light became yellower and yellower. The road was beaten to a metallic silver. Everything looked festive.

But I'm going to be late, he thought, for the cab was held up in a block by the Marble Arch. He looked at his watch—it was just on eight-thirty. But eight-thirty means eight-forty-five he thought, as the cab moved on. Indeed as it turned into the square there was a car at the door, and a man getting out. So I'm just on time, he thought, and paid the driver.

The door opened almost before he touched the bell, as if he had trod on a spring. The door opened, and two footmen started forward to take his things directly he entered the black-and-white paved hall. He followed another man up the imposing staircase of white marble, sweeping in a curve. A succession of large, dark pictures hung on the wall, and at the top outside the door was a yellow-and-blue picture of Venetian palaces and pale green canals.

"Canaletto or the school of?" he thought, pausing to let the other man precede him. Then he gave his name to the footman.

"Captain Pargiter," the man boomed out; and there was Kitty standing at the door. She was formal; fashionable; with a dash of red on her lips. She gave him her hand; but he moved on for other guests were arriving. "A saloon?" he said to himself, for the room with its chandeliers, yellow panels, and sofas and chairs dotted about had the air of a grandiose waiting-room. Seven or eight people were already there. It's not going to work this time, he said to himself as he chatted with his host, who had been racing. His face shone as if it had only that moment been taken out of the sun. One almost expected, Martin thought, as he stood talking, to see a pair of glasses slung round his shoulders, just as there was a red mark across his forehead where his hat had been. No, it's not going to work, Martin thought as they talked about horses. He heard a paper boy calling in the street below, and the hooting of horns. He preserved clearly his sense of the identity of different objects, and their differences. When a party worked all things, all sounds merged into one. He looked at an old lady with a wedge-shaped stone-coloured face sitting ensconced on a sofa. He glanced at Kitty's portrait by a fashionable portrait painter as he chatted, standing first on this foot, then on that, to the grizzled man with the bloodhound eyes and the urbane manner whom Kitty had married instead of Edward. Then she came up and introduced him to a girl all in white who was standing alone with her hand on the back of a chair.

"Miss Ann Hillier," she said. "My cousin, Captain Pargiter."

She stood for a moment beside them as if to facilitate their introduction. But she was a little stiff always; she did nothing but flick her fan up and down.

"Been to the races, Kitty?" Martin said, because he knew that she hated racing, and he always felt a wish to tease her.

"I? No; I don't go to races," she replied rather shortly. She turned away because somebody else had come in—a man in gold lace, with a star.

I should have been better off, Martin thought, reading my book.

"Have you been to the races?" he said aloud to the girl whom

225

he was to take down to dinner. She shook her head. She had white arms; a white dress; and a pearl necklace. Purely virginal, he said to himself; and only an hour ago I was lying stark naked in my bath in Ebury Street, he thought.

"I've been watching polo," she said. He looked down at his shoes, and noticed that they had creases across them; they were old; he had meant to buy a new pair, but had forgotten. That was what he had forgotten, he thought, seeing himself again in the cab, crossing the bridge over the Serpentine.

But they were going down to dinner. He gave her his arm. As they went down the stairs, and he watched the ladies' dresses in front of them trail from step to step, he thought, What on earth am I going to say to her? Then they crossed the black-and-white squares and went into the dining-room. It was harmoniously shrouded; pictures with hooded bars of light under them shone out; and the dinner table glowed; but no light shone directly on their faces.

If this doesn't work, he thought, looking at the portrait of a nobleman with a crimson cloak and a star that hung luminous in front of him, I'll never do it again. Then he braced himself to talk to the virginal girl who sat beside him. But he had to reject almost everything that occurred to him—she was so young.

"I've thought of three subjects to talk about," he began straight off, without thinking how the sentence was to end. "Racing; the Russian ballet; and"—he hesitated for a moment—"Ireland. Which interests you?" He unfolded his napkin.

"Please," she said, bending slightly towards him, "say that again."

He laughed. She had a charming way of putting her head on one side and bending towards him.

"Don't let's talk of any of them," he said. "Let's talk of something interesting. Do you enjoy parties?" he asked her. She was dipping her spoon in her soup. She looked up at him as she lifted it with eyes that seemed like bright stones under a film of water. They're like drops of glass under water, he thought. She was extraordinarily pretty.

"But I've only been to three parties in my life!" she said. She gave a charming little laugh.

"You don't say so!" he exclaimed. "This is the third, then; or is it the fourth?"

He listened to the sounds in the street. He could just hear the cars hooting; but they had gone far away; they made a continuous rushing noise. It was beginning to work. He held out his glass. He would like her to say, he thought, as his glass was filled, "What a charming man I sat next!" when she went to bed that night.

"This is my third *real* party," she said, stressing the word "real" in a way that seemed to him slightly pathetic. She must have been in the nursery three months ago, he thought, eating bread and butter.

"And I was thinking as I shaved," he said, "that I would never go to a party again." It was true; he had seen a hole in the bookcase. Who's taken my life of Wren? he had thought, holding his razor out; and had wanted to stay and read, alone. But now— what little piece of his vast experience could he break off and give to her, he wondered?

"Do you live in London?" she asked.

"Ebury Street," he told her. And she knew Ebury Street, because it was on the way to Victoria; she often went to Victoria, because they had a house in Sussex.

"And now tell me," he said, feeling that they had broken the ice—when she turned her head to answer some remark of the man on the other side. He was annoyed. The whole fabric that he had been building, like a game of spillikins in which one frail little bone is hooked on top of another, was dashed to the ground. Ann was talking as if she had known the other man all her life; he had hair that looked as if a rake had been drawn through it; he was very young. Martin sat silent. He looked at the great portrait opposite. A footman was standing beneath it; a row of decanters obscured the folds of the cloak on the floor.

That's the third Earl, or the fourth? he asked himself. He knew his eighteenth century; it was the fourth Earl who had made the great marriage. But after all, he thought, looking at Kitty at the head of the table, the Rigbys are a better family than they are. He smiled; he checked himself. I only think of "better families" when I dine in this sort of place, he thought. He looked at another picture; a lady in sea green; the famous Gainsborough. But here Lady Margaret, the woman on his left, turned to him.

"I'm sure you'll agree with me," she said, "Captain Pargiter"—he noticed that she swept her eyes over the name on his card before she spoke it, although they had met often before—"that it's a devilish thing to have done?"

She spoke so pouncingly that the fork she held upright seemed like a weapon with which she was about to pinion him. He threw himself into their conversation. It was about politics of course, about Ireland. "Tell me—what's your opinion?" she asked, with her fork poised. For a moment he had the illusion that he too was behind the scenes. The screen was down; the lights were up; and he too was behind the scenes. It was an illusion of course; they were only throwing him scraps from their larder; but it was an agreeable sensation while it lasted. He listened. Now she was holding forth to a distinguished old man at the end of the table. He watched him. He had let down a mask of infinitely wise tolerance over his face as she harangued them. He was arranging three crusts of bread by the side of his plate as if he were playing a mysterious little game of profound significance. "So," he seemed to be saying, "So," as if they were fragments of human destiny, not crusts, that he held in his fingers. The mask might conceal anything—or nothing? Anyhow it was a mask of great distinction. But here Lady Margaret pinioned him too with her fork; and he raised his eyebrows and moved one of the crusts a little to one side before he spoke. Martin leant forward to listen.

"When I was in Ireland," he began, "in 1880 . . ." He spoke very simply; he was offering them a memory; he told his story perfectly; it held its meaning without spilling a single drop. And he had played a great part. Martin listened attentively. Yes, it was absorbing. Here we are, he thought, going on and on and on. . . . He leant forward trying to catch every word. But he was conscious of some interruption; Ann had turned to him.

"Do tell me"—she was asking him—"who *he* is?" She bent her head to the right. She was under the impression that he knew everybody, apparently. He was flattered. He looked along the table. Who was it? Somebody he had met; somebody, he guessed, who was not quite at his ease.

"I know him," he said. "I know him—" He had a rather white, fat face; he was talking away at a great rate. And the young married woman to whom he was talking was saying "I see; I see," with little nods of her head. But there was a slight look of strain on her face. You needn't put yourself to all that trouble, my good fellow, Martin felt inclined to say to him. She doesn't understand a word you're saying.

"I can't put a name to him," he said aloud. "But I've met him—let me see—where? In Oxford or Cambridge?"

A faint look of amusement came into Ann's eyes. She had spotted the difference. She coupled them together. They were not her world—no.

"Have you seen the Russian dancers?" she was saying. She had been there with her young man, it seemed. And what's your world, Martin thought, as she rapped out her slender stock of adjectives—"heavenly," "amazing," "marvellous," and so on. Is it *"the"* world? he mused. He looked down the table. Anyhow no other world had a chance against it, he thought. And it's a good world too, he added; large; generous; hospitable. And very nice-looking. He glanced from face to face. Dinner was drawing to an end. They all looked as if they had been rubbed with wash leather, like precious stones; yet the bloom seemed ingrained; it went through the stone. And the stone was clear-cut; there was no blur, no indecision. Here a footman's white-gloved hand removing dishes knocked over a glass of wine. A red splash trickled onto the lady's dress. But she did not move a muscle;

she went on talking. Then she straightened the clean napkin that had been brought her, nonchalantly, over the stain.

That's what I like, Martin thought. He admired that. She would have blown her fingers on her nose like an applewoman if she wanted to, he thought. But Ann was talking.

"And when he gives that leap!" she exclaimed—she raised her hand with a lovely gesture in the air—"and then comes down!" She let her hand fall in her lap.

"Marvellous!" Martin agreed. He had got the very accent, he thought; he had got it from the young man whose hair looked as if a rake had gone through it.

"Yes: Nijinsky's marvellous," he agreed. "Marvellous," he repeated.

"And my aunt has asked me to meet him at a party," said Ann.

"Your aunt?" he said aloud.

She mentioned a well-known name.

"Oh, she's your aunt, is she?" he said. He placed her. So *that* was her world. He wanted to ask her—for he found her charming in her youth, her simplicity—but it was too late. Ann was rising.

"I hope—" he began. She bent her head towards him as if she longed to stay, catch his last word, his least word; but could not, since Lady Lasswade had risen; and it was time for her to go.

Lady Lasswade had risen; everybody rose. All the pink, grey, sea-coloured dresses lengthened themselves, and for a moment the tall women standing by the table looked like the famous Gainsborough hanging on the wall. The table, strewn with napkins and wine-glasses, had a derelict air as they left it. For a moment the ladies clustered at the door; then the little old woman in black hobbled past them with remarkable dignity; and Kitty, coming last, put her arm round Ann's shoulder and led her out. The door shut on the ladies.

Kitty paused for a moment.

"I hope you liked my old cousin?" she said to Ann as they walked upstairs together. She put her hand to her dress and straightened something as they passed a looking-glass.

"I thought him charming!" Ann exclaimed. "And what a lovely tree!" She spoke of Martin and the tree in exactly the same tone. They paused for a moment to look at a tree that was covered with pink blossoms in a china tub standing at the door. Some of the flowers were fully out; others were still unopened. As they looked a petal dropped.

"It's cruel to keep it here," said Kitty, "in this hot air."

They went in. While they dined the servants had opened the folding doors and lit lights in a further room so that it seemed as if they came into another room freshly made ready for them. There was a great fire blazing between two stately fire-dogs; but it seemed cordial and decorative rather than hot. Two or three of the ladies stood before it, opening and shutting their fingers as they spread them to the blaze; but they turned to make room for their hostess.

"How I love that picture of you, Kitty!" said Mrs Aislabie, looking up at the portrait of Lady Lasswade as a young woman. Her hair had been very red in those days; she was toying with a basket of roses. Fiery but tender, she looked, emerging from a cloud of white muslin.

Kitty glanced at it and then turned away.

"One never likes one's own picture," she said.

"But it's the image of you!" said another lady.

"Not now," said Kitty, laughing off the compliment rather awkwardly. Always after dinner women paid each other compliments about their clothes or their looks, she thought. She did not like being alone with women after dinner; it made her shy. She stood there, upright among them, while footmen went round with trays of coffee.

"By the way, I hope the wine—" she paused and helped herself to coffee, "the wine didn't stain your frock, Cynthia?" she said to the young married woman who had taken the disaster so coolly.

"And such a lovely frock," said Lady Margaret, fondling the folds of golden satin between her finger and thumb.

231

"D'you like it?" said the young woman.

"It's perfectly lovely! I've been looking at it the whole evening!" said Mrs Treyer, an Oriental-looking woman, with a feather floating back from her head in harmony with her nose, which was Jewish.

Kitty looked at them admiring the lovely frock. Eleanor would have found herself out of it, she thought. She had refused her invitation to dinner. That annoyed her.

"Do tell me," Lady Cynthia interrupted, "who was the man I sat next? One always meets such interesting people at your house," she added.

"The man you sat next?" said Kitty. She considered a moment. "Tony Ashton," she said.

"Is that the man who's been lecturing on French poetry at Mortimer House?" chimed in Mrs Aislabie. "I longed to go to those lectures. I heard they were wonderfully interesting."

"Mildred went," said Mrs Treyer.

"Why should we all stand?" said Kitty. She made a movement with her hands towards the seats. She did things like that so abruptly that they called her, behind her back, "The Grenadier." They all moved this way and that, and she herself, after seeing how the couples sorted themselves, sat down by old Aunt Warburton, who was enthroned in the great chair.

"Tell me about my delightful godson," the old lady began. She meant Kitty's second son, who was with the fleet at Malta.

"He's at Malta—" she began. She sat down on a low chair and began answering her questions. But the fire was too hot for Aunt Warburton. She raised her knobbed old hand.

"Priestley wants to roast us all alive," said Kitty. She got up and went to the window. The ladies smiled as she strode across the room and jerked up the top of the long window. Just for a moment, as the curtains hung apart, she looked at the square outside. There was a spatter of leaf-shadow and lamplight on the pavement; the usual policeman was balancing himself as he patrolled; the usual little men and women, foreshortened from this height, hurried along by the railings. So she saw them hurrying, the other way, when she brushed her teeth in the morning. Then she came back and sat down on a low stool beside old Aunt Warburton. The worldly old woman was honest, in her way.

"And the little red-haired ruffian whom I love?" she asked. He was her favourite; the little boy at Eton.

"He's been in trouble," said Kitty. "He's been swished." She smiled. He was her favourite too.

The old lady grinned. She liked boys who got into trouble. She had a wedge-shaped yellow face with an occasional bristle on her chin; she was over eighty; but she sat as if she were riding a hunter, Kitty thought, glancing at her hands. They were coarse hands, with big finger-joints; red and white sparks flashed from her rings as she moved them.

"And you, my dear," said the old lady, looking at her shrewdly under her bushy eyebrows, "busy as usual?"

"Yes. Much as usual," said Kitty, evading the shrewd old eyes; for she did things on the sly that they—the ladies over there— did not approve.

They were chattering together. Yet animated as it sounded, to Kitty's ear the talk lacked substance. It was a battledore and shuttlecock talk, to be kept going until the door opened and the gentlemen came in. Then it would stop. They were talking about a by-election. She could hear Lady Margaret telling some story that was rather coarse presumably, in the eighteenth-century way, since she dropped her voice.

"—turned her upside down and slapped her," she could hear her say. There was a twitter of laughter.

"I'm so delighted he got in in spite of them," said Mrs Treyer. They dropped their voices.

"I'm a tiresome old woman," said Aunt Warburton, raising one of her knobbed hands to her shoulder. "But now I'm going to ask you to shut that window." The draught was getting at her rheumatic joint.

Kitty strode to the window. "Damn these women!" she said to herself. She laid hold of the long stick with a beak at the end that stood in the window and poked; but the window stuck. She would have liked to fleece them of their clothes, of their jewels, of their intrigues, of their gossip. The window went up with a jerk. There was Ann standing about with nobody to talk to.

"Come and talk to us, Ann," she said, beckoning to her. Ann drew up a footstool and sat down at Aunt Warburton's feet. There was a pause. Old Aunt Warburton disliked young girls; but they had relations in common.

"Where's Timmy, Ann?" she asked.

"Harrow," said Ann.

"Ah, you've always been to Harrow," said Aunt Warburton. And then the old lady, with the beautiful breeding that simulated at least human charity, flattered the girl, likening her to her grandmother, a famous beauty.

"How I should love to have known her!" Ann exclaimed. "Do tell me—what was she like?"

The old lady began making a selection from her memoirs; it was only a selection; an edition with asterisks; for it was a story that could hardly be told to a girl in white satin. Kitty's mind wandered. If Charles stayed much longer downstairs, she thought, glancing at the clock, she would miss her train. Could Priestley be trusted to whisper a message in his ears? She would give them another ten minutes; she turned to Aunt Warburton again.

"She must have been wonderful!" Ann was saying. She sat with her hands clasped round her knees looking up into the face of the hairy old dowager. Kitty felt a moment's pity. Her face will be like their faces, she thought, looking at the little group at the other side of the room. Their faces looked harassed, worried; their hands moved restlessly. Yet they're brave, she thought; and generous. They gave as much as they took. Had Eleanor after all any right to despise them? Had she done more with her life than Margaret Marrable? And I? she thought. And I? . . . Who's right?

she thought. Who's wrong? . . . Here mercifully the door opened.

The gentlemen came in. They came in reluctantly, rather slowly, as if they had just stopped talking, and had to get their bearings in the drawing-room. They were a little flushed and still laughing, as if they had stopped in the middle of what they were saying. They filed in; and the distinguished old man moved across the room with the air of a ship making port, and all the ladies stirred without rising. The game was over; the battledores and shuttlecocks put away. They were like gulls settling on fish, Kitty thought. There was a rising and a fluttering. The great man let himself slowly down into a chair beside his old friend Lady Warburton. He put the tips of his fingers together and began "Well . . . ?" as if he were continuing a conversation left unfinished the night before. Yes, she thought, there was something—was it human? civilised? she could not find the word she wanted—about the old couple, talking, as they had talked for the past fifty years. . . . They were all talking. They had all settled in to add another sentence to the story that was just ending, or in the middle, or about to begin.

But there was Tony Ashton standing by himself without a sentence to add to the story. She went up to him therefore.

"Have you seen Edward lately?" he asked her as usual.

"Yes, today," she said. "I lunched with him. We walked in the Park. . . ." She stopped. They had walked in the Park. A thrush had been singing; they had stopped to listen. "That's the wise thrush that sings each song twice over . . ." he had said. "Does he?" she had asked innocently. And it had been a quotation.

She had felt foolish; Oxford always made her feel foolish. She disliked Oxford; yet she respected Edward and Tony too, she thought looking at him. A snob on the surface; underneath a scholar. . . . They had a standard. . . . But she roused herself.

He would like to talk to some smart woman—Mrs Aislabie, or Margaret Marrable. But they were both engaged—both were adding sentences with considerable vivacity. There was a pause. She was not a good hostess, she reflected; this sort of hitch always happened at her parties. There was Ann; Ann about to be captured by a youth she knew. But Kitty beckoned. Ann came instantly and submissively.

"Come and be introduced," she said, "to Mr Ashton. He's been lecturing at Mortimer House," she explained, "about—" She hesitated.

"Mallarmé," he said with his odd little squeak, as if his voice had been pinched off.

Kitty turned away. Martin came up to her.

"A very brilliant party, Lady Lasswade," he said with his usual tiresome irony.

"This? Oh, not at all," she said brusquely. This wasn't a party. Her parties were never brilliant. Martin was trying to tease her as usual. She looked down and saw his shabby shoes.

"Come and talk to me," she said, feeling the old family affection return. She noticed with amusement that he was a little flushed, a little, as the nurses used to say, "above himself". How many "parties" would it need, she wondered, to turn her satirical, uncompromising cousin into an obedient member of society?

"Let's sit down and talk sense," she said, sinking on to a little sofa. He sat down beside her.

"Tell me, what's Nell doing?" she asked.

"She sent her love," said Martin. "She told me to say how much she wanted to see you."

"Then why wouldn't she come tonight?" said Kitty. She felt hurt. She could not help it.

"She hasn't the right kind of hairpin," he said with a laugh, looking down at his shoes. Kitty looked down at them too.

"My shoes, you see, don't matter," he said. "But then I'm a man."

"It's such nonsense . . ." Kitty began. "What does it matter . . ."

But he was looking round him at the groups of beautifully dressed women; then at the picture.

"That's a horrid daub of you over the mantelpiece," he said, looking at the red-haired girl. "Who did it?"

"I forget . . . Don't let's look at it," she said.

"Let's talk . . ." Then she stopped.

He was looking round the room. It was crowded; there were little tables with photographs; ornate cabinets with vases of flowers; and panels of yellow brocade let into the walls. She felt that he was criticising the room and herself too.

"I always want to take a knife and scrape it all off," she said. But what's the use, she thought? If she moved a picture, "Where's Uncle Bill on the old cob?" her husband would say, and back it had to go again.

"Like a hotel, isn't it?" she continued.

"A saloon," he remarked. He did not know why he always wanted to hurt her; but he did; it was a fact.

"I was asking myself," he dropped his voice, "Why have a picture like that"—he nodded his head at the portrait—"when they've a Gainsborough . . ."

"And why," she dropped her voice, imitating his tone that was half sneering, half humorous, "come and eat their food when you despise them?"

"I don't! Not a bit!" he exclaimed. "I'm enjoying myself immensely. I like seeing you, Kitty," he added. It was true—he always liked her. "You haven't dropped your poor relations. That's very nice of you."

"It's they who've dropped me," she said.

"Oh, Eleanor," he said. "She's a queer old bird."

"It's all so . . ." Kitty began. But there was something wrong about the disposition of her party; she stopped in the middle of her sentence. "You've got to come and talk to Mrs Treyer," she said getting up.

Why does one do it? he wondered as he followed her. He had wanted to talk to Kitty; he had nothing to say to that Oriental-looking harpy with a pheasant's feather floating at the back of her head. Still, if you drink the good wine of the noble countess, he said bowing, you have to entertain her less desirable friends. He led her off.

Kitty went back to the fireplace. She dealt the coal a blow, and the sparks went volleying up the chimney. She was irritable; she was restless. Time was passing; if they stayed much longer she would miss her train. Surreptitiously she noted that the hands of the clock were close on eleven. The party was bound to break up soon; it was only the prelude to another party. Yet they were all talking, and talking, as if they would never go.

She glanced at the groups that seemed immovable. Then the clock chimed a succession of petulant little strokes, on the last of which the door opened and Priestley advanced. With his inscrutable butler's eyes and crooked forefinger he summoned Ann Hillier.

"That's Mama fetching me," said Ann, advancing down the room with a little flutter.

"She's taking you on?" said Kitty. She held her hand for a moment. Why? she asked herself, looking at the lovely face, empty of meaning, or character, like a page on which nothing has been written but youth. She held her hand for a moment.

"Must you go?" she said.

"I'm afraid I must," said Ann, withdrawing her hand.

There was a general rising and movement, like the flutter of white-winged gulls.

"Coming with us?" Martin heard Ann say to the youth through whose hair the rake seemed to have been passed. They turned to leave together. As she passed Martin, who stood with his hand out, Ann gave him the least bend of her head, as if his image had been already swept from her mind. He was dashed; his feeling was out of all proportion to its object. He felt a strong desire to go with them, wherever it was. But he had not been asked; Ashton had; he was following in their wake.

"What a toady!" he thought to himself with a bitterness that surprised him. It was odd how jealous he felt for a moment. They were all "going on," it seemed. He hung about a little awkwardly. Only the old fogies were left—no, even the great man was going on, it seemed. Only the old lady was left. She was hobbling across the room on Lasswade's arm. She wanted to confirm something that she had been saying about a miniature. Lasswade had taken it off the wall; he held it under a lamp so that she could pronounce her verdict. Was it Grandpapa on the cob, or was it Uncle William?

"Sit down, Martin, and let us talk," said Kitty. He sat down: but he had a feeling that she wanted him to go. He had seen her glance at the clock. They chatted for a moment. Now the old lady came back; she was proving, beyond a doubt, from her unexampled store of anecdotes, that it must be Uncle William on the cob; not Grandpapa. She was going. But she took her time. Martin waited till she was fairly in the doorway, leaning on her nephew's arm. He hesitated; they were alone now; should he stay, or should he go? But Kitty was standing up. She was holding out her hand.

"Come again soon and see me alone," she said. She had dismissed him, he felt.

That's what people always say, he said to himself as he made his way slowly downstairs behind Lady Warburton. Come again: but I don't know that I shall. . . . Lady Warburton went downstairs like a crab, holding on to the banisters with one hand, to Lasswade's arm with the other. He lingered behind her. He looked at the Canaletto once more. A nice picture: but a copy, he said to himself. He peered over the banisters and saw the black-and-white slabs on the hall beneath.

It did work, he said to himself, descending step by step into the hall. Off and on; by fits and starts. But was it worth it? he asked himself, letting the footman help him into his coat. The double doors stood wide open into the street. One or two people were passing; they peered in curiously, looking at the footmen, at the bright big hall; and at the old lady who paused for a moment on the black-and-white squares. She was robing herself. Now she was accepting her cloak with a violet slash in it; now her furs. A bag dangled from her wrist. She was hung about with chains; her fingers were knobbed with rings. Her sharp stone-coloured face, riddled with lines and wrinkled into creases, looked out from its soft nest of fur and laces. The eyes were still bright.

The nineteenth century going to bed, Martin said to himself as he watched her hobble down the steps on the arm of her footman. She was helped into her carriage. Then he shook hands with that good fellow his host, who had had quite as much wine as was good for him, and walked off through Grosvenor Square.

Upstairs in the bedroom at the top of the house Kitty's maid Baxter was looking out of the window, watching the guests drive off. There—that was the old lady going. She wished they would hurry; if the party went on much longer her own little jaunt would be done for. She was going up the river tomorrow with her young man. She turned and looked round her. She had everything ready—her ladyship's coat, skirt, and the bag with the ticket in it. It was long past eleven. She stood at the dressing-table waiting. The three-folded mirror reflected silver pots, powder puffs, combs and brushes. Baxter stooped down and smirked at herself in the glass—that was how she would look when she went up the river—then she drew herself up; she heard footsteps in the passage. Her ladyship was coming. Here she was.

Lady Lasswade came in, slipping the rings from her fingers. "Sorry to be so late, Baxter," she said. "Now I must hurry."

Baxter, without speaking, unhooked her dress; slipped it dexterously to her feet, and bore it away. Kitty sat down at her dressing-table and kicked off her shoes. Satin shoes were always too tight. She glanced at the clock on her dressing-table. She just had time.

Baxter was handing her coat. Now she was handing her bag.

"The ticket's in there, m'lady," she said, touching the bag.

"Now my hat," said Kitty. She stooped to settle it in front of the mirror. The little tweed travelling-hat poised on the top of her hair made her look quite a different person; the person she liked being. She stood in her travelling-dress, wondering if she had forgotten anything. Her mind was a perfect blank for a moment. Where am I? she wondered. What am I doing? Where am I going? Her eyes fixed themselves on the dressing-table; vaguely she remembered some other room, and some other time when she was a girl. At Oxford was it?

"The ticket, Baxter?" she said perfunctorily.

"In your bag, m'lady," Baxter reminded her. She was holding it in her hand.

"So that's everything," said Kitty, glancing round her.

She felt a moment's compunction.

"Thanks, Baxter," she said. "I hope you'll enjoy your. . ."— she hesitated: she did not know what Baxter did on her day off—". . . your play," she said at a venture. Baxter gave a queer little bitten-off smile. Maids bothered Kitty with their demure politeness; with their inscrutable, pursed-up faces. But they were very useful.

"Good-night!" she said to Baxter at the door of the bedroom; for there Baxter turned back as if her responsibility for her mistress ended. Somebody else had charge of the stairs.

Kitty looked in at the drawing-room, in case her husband should be there. But the room was empty. The fire was still blazing; the chairs, drawn out in a circle, still seemed to hold the skeleton of the party in their empty arms. But the car was waiting for her at the door.

"Plenty of time?" she said to the chauffeur as he laid the rug across her knees. Off they started.

It was a clear still night and every tree in the square was visible; some were black, others were sprinkled with strange patches of green artificial light. Above the arc lamps rose shafts of darkness. Although it was close on midnight, it scarcely seemed to be night; but rather some ethereal disembodied day, for there were so many lamps in the streets; cars passing; men in white mufflers with their light overcoats open walking along the clean dry pavements, and many houses were still lit up, for everyone was giving parties. The town changed as they drew smoothly through Mayfair. The public houses were closing; here was a group clustered round a lamp-post at the corner. A drunken man was bawling out some loud song; a tipsy girl with a feather bobbing in her eyes was swaying as she clung to the lamp-post . . . but Kitty's eyes alone registered what she saw. After the talk, the effort and the hurry, she could add nothing to what she saw. And they swept on quickly. Now they had turned, and the car was gliding at full speed up a long bright avenue of great shuttered shops. The streets were almost empty. The yellow station clock showed that they had five minutes to spare.

Just in time, she said to herself. The usual exhilaration mounted in her as she walked along the platform. Diffused light poured down from a great height. Men's cries and the clangour of shunting carriages echoed in the immense vacancy. The train was waiting; travellers were making ready to start. Some were standing with one foot on the step of the carriage drinking out of thick cups as if they were afraid to go far from their seats. She looked down the length of the train and saw the engine sucking water from a hose. It seemed all body, all muscle; even the neck had been consumed into the smooth barrel of the body. This was "the" train; the others were toys in comparison. She snuffed up the sulphurous air, which left a slight tinge of acid at the back of the throat, as if it already had a tang of the north.

The guard had seen her and was coming towards her with his whistle in his hand.

"Good evening, m'lady," he said.

"Good evening, Purvis. Run it rather fine," she said as he unlocked the door of her carriage.

"Yes, m'lady. Only just in time," he replied.

He locked the door. Kitty turned and looked round the small lighted room in which she was to spend the night. Everything was ready; the bed was made; the sheets were turned down; her bag was on the seat. The guard passed the window, holding his flag in his hand.

A man who had only just caught the train ran across the platform with his arms spread out. A door slammed.

"Just in time," Kitty said to herself as she stood there. Then the train gave a gentle tug. She could hardly believe that so great a monster could start so gently on so long a journey. Then she saw the tea-urn sliding past.

"We're off," she said to herself, sinking back onto the seat. "We're off!"

All the tension went out of her body. She was alone; and the train was moving. The last lamp on the platform slid away. The last figure on the platform vanished.

"What fun!" she said to herself, as if she were a little girl who had run away from her nurse and escaped. "We're off!"

She sat still for a moment in her brightly lit compartment; then she tugged the blind and it sprang up with a jerk. Elongated lights slid past; lights in factories and warehouses; lights in obscure back streets. Then there were asphalt paths; more lights in public gardens; and then bushes and a hedge in a field. They were leaving London behind them; leaving that blaze of light which seemed, as the train rushed into the darkness, to contract itself into one fiery circle. The train rushed with a roar through a tunnel. It seemed to perform an act of amputation; now she was cut off from that circle of light.

She looked round the narrow little compartment in which she was isolated. Everything shook slightly. There was a perpetual faint vibration. She seemed to be passing from one world to another; this was the moment of transition. She sat still for a moment; then undressed and paused with her hand on the blind. The train had got into its stride now; it was rushing at full speed through the country. A few distant lights twinkled here and there. Black clumps of trees stood in the grey summer fields; the fields were full of summer grasses. The light from the engine lit up a quiet group of cows; and a hedge of hawthorn. They were in open country now.

243

She pulled down the blind and climbed into her bed. She laid herself out on the rather hard shelf with her back to the carriage wall, so that she felt a faint vibration against her head. She lay listening to the humming noise which the train made, now that it had got into its stride. Smoothly and powerfully she was being drawn through England to the north. I need do nothing, she thought, nothing, nothing, but let myself be drawn on. She turned and pulled the blue shade over the lamp. The sound of the train became louder in the darkness; its roar, its vibration, seemed to fall into a regular rhythm of sound, raking through her mind, rolling out her thoughts.

Ah, but not all of them, she thought, turning restlessly on her shelf. Some still jutted up. One's not a child, she thought, staring at the light under the blue shade, any longer. The years changed things; destroyed things; heaped things up—worries and bothers; here they were again. Fragments of talk kept coming back to her; sights came before her. She saw herself raise the window with a jerk; and the bristles on Aunt Warburton's chin. She saw the women rising, and the men filing in. She sighed as she turned on her ledge. All their clothes are the same, she thought; all their lives are the same. And which is right? she thought, turning restlessly on her shelf. Which is wrong? She turned again.

The train rushed her on. The sound had deepened; it had become a continuous roar. How could she sleep? How could she prevent herself from thinking? She turned away from the light. *Now* where are we? she said to herself. Where is the train at this moment? *Now,* she murmured, shutting her eyes, we are passing the white house on the hill; *Now* we are going through the tunnel; *Now* we are crossing the bridge over the river. . . . A blank intervened; her thoughts became spaced; they became muddled. Past and present became jumbled together. She saw Margaret Marrable pinching the dress in her fingers, but she was leading a bull with a ring through its nose. . . . This is sleep, she said to herself, half opening her eyes; thank goodness, she said to herself, shutting them again, this is sleep. And she resigned herself to the charge of the train, whose roar now became dulled and distant.

There was a tap at her door. She lay for a moment, wondering why the room shook so; then the scene settled itself; she was in the train; she was in the country; they were nearing the station. She got up.

She dressed rapidly and stood in the corridor. It was still early. She watched the fields galloping past. They were the bare fields, the angular fields of the north. The spring was late here; the trees were not fully out yet. The smoke looped down and caught a tree in its white cloud. When it lifted, she thought how fine the light was; clear and sharp, white and grey. The land had none of the softness, none of the greenness of the land in the south. But here was the junction; here was the gasometer; they were running into the station. The train slowed down, and all the lamp-posts on the platform gradually came to a standstill.

She got out and drew in a deep breath of the cold raw air. The car was waiting for her; and directly she saw it she remembered—it was the new car; a birthday present from her husband. She had never driven in it yet. Cole touched his hat.

"Let's have it open, Cole," she said, and he opened the stiff new hood, and she got in beside him. Very slowly, for the engine seemed to beat intermittently, starting and stopping and then starting again, they moved off. They drove through the town; all the shops were still shut; women were on their knees scrubbing doorsteps; blinds were still drawn in bedrooms and sitting-rooms; there was very little traffic about. Only milk-carts rattled past. Dogs roamed down the middle of the street on private errands of their own. Cole had to hoot again and again.

"They'll learn in time, m'lady," he said as a great brindled cur slunk out of their way. In the town he drove carefully; but once they were outside he speeded up. Kitty watched the needle jump forward on the speedometer.

"She does it easily?" she asked, listening to the soft purr of the engine.

Cole lifted his foot to show how lightly it touched the accelerator. Then he touched it again and the car sped on. They were driving too fast, Kitty thought; but the road—she kept her eye on it—was still empty. Only two or three lumbering farm waggons passed them; the men went to the horses' heads and held them as they went by. The road stretched pearl-white in front of them; the hedges were decked with the little pointed leaves of early spring.

"Spring's very late up here," said Kitty; "cold winds I suppose?"

Cole nodded. He had none of the servile ways of the London flunkey; she was at her ease with him; she could be silent. The air seemed to have different grades of warmth and chill in it; now sweet; now—they were passing a farmyard—strong-smelling, acrid from the sour smell of manure. She leant back, holding her hat to her head as they rushed a hill. "You won't get her up this on top, Cole," she said. The pace slackened a little; they were climbing the familiar Crabbs hill, with the yellow streaks where carters had put on their brakes. In the old days, when she drove horses, they used to get out here and walk. Cole said nothing. He was going to show off his engine, she suspected. The car swept up finely. But the hill was long; there was a level stretch; then the road mounted again. The car faltered. Cole coaxed her on. Kitty saw him jerk his body slightly backwards and forwards as if he were encouraging horses. She felt the tension of his muscles. They slowed—they almost stopped. No, now they were on the crest of the hill. She had done it on top!

"Well done!" she exclaimed. He said nothing; but he was very proud, she knew.

"We couldn't have done that on the old car," she said.

"Ah, but it wasn't her fault," said Cole.

He was a very humane man; the kind of man she liked, she reflected—silent, reserved. On they swept again. Now they were passing the grey stone house where the mad lady lived alone with her peacocks and her bloodhounds. They had passed it. Now the woods were on their right hand and the air came singing through them. It was like the sea, Kitty thought, looking, as they passed, down a dark green drive patched with yellow sunlight. On they went again. Now heaps of ruddy brown leaves lay by the roadside staining the puddles red.

"It's been raining?" she said. He nodded. They came out on the high ridge with woods beneath and there, in a clearing among the trees, was the grey tower of the Castle. She always looked for it and greeted it as if she were raising a hand to a friend. They were on their own land now. Gateposts were branded with their initials; their arms swung above the doorways of inns; their crest was mounted over cottage doors. Cole looked at the clock. The needle leapt again.

Too fast, too fast! Kitty said to herself. But she liked the rush of the wind in her face. Now they reached the Lodge gate; Mrs Preedy was holding it open with a white-haired child on her arm. They rushed through the Park. The deer looked up and hopped away lightly through the fern.

"Two minutes under the quarter, m'lady," said Cole as they swept in a circle and drew up at the door. Kitty stood for a moment looking at the car. She laid her hand on the bonnet. It was hot. She gave it a little pat. "She did it beautifully, Cole," she said. "I'll tell his Lordship." Cole smiled; he was happy.

She went in. Nobody was about; they had arrived earlier than was expected. She crossed the great stone-flagged hall, with the armour and the busts, and went into the morning-room where breakfast was laid.

The green light dazzled her as she went in. It was as if she stood in the hollow of an emerald. All was green outside. The statues of grey French ladies stood on the terrace, holding their baskets; but the baskets were empty. In summer flowers would burn there. Green turf fell down in broad swaths between clipped yews; dipped to the river; and then rose again to the hill that was crested with woods. There was a curl of mist on the woods now—the light mist of early morning. As she gazed a bee buzzed in her ear; she thought she heard the murmur of the river over the stones; pigeons crooned in the tree tops. It was the voice of early morning, the voice of summer. But the door opened. Here was breakfast.

She breakfasted; she felt warm, stored, and comfortable as she lay back in her chair. And she had nothing to do— nothing whatever. The whole day was hers. It was fine too. The sunlight suddenly quickened in the room, and laid a broad bar of light across the floor. The sun was on the flowers outside. A tortoiseshell butterfly flaunted across the window; she saw it settle on a leaf, and there it sat, opening its wings and shutting them, opening and shutting them, as if it feasted on the sunlight. She watched it. The down was soft rust-red on its wings. Off it flaunted again. Then, admitted by an invisible hand, the chow stalked in; came straight up to her; sniffed at her skirt, and flung himself down in a bright patch of sunlight.

Heartless brute! she thought, but his indifference pleased her. He asked nothing of her either. She stretched her hand for a cigarette. And what would Martin say, she wondered, as she took the enamel box that turned from green to blue, as she opened it. Hideous? Vulgar? Possibly—but what did it matter what people said? Criticism seemed light as smoke this morning. What did it matter what he said, what they said, what anybody said, since she had a whole day to herself?—since she was alone? And there they are, still asleep, in their houses, she thought, standing at the window, looking at the green-grey grass, after their dances, after their parties . . . The thought pleased her. She threw away her cigarette and went upstairs to change her clothes.

The sun was much stronger when she came down again. The garden had already lost its look of purity; the mist was off the woods. She could hear the squeak of the lawn mower as she stepped out of the window. The rubber-shoed pony was pacing up and down the lawns leaving a pale wake in the grass behind him. The birds were singing in their scattered way. The starlings in their bright mail were feeding on the grass. Dew shone, red, violet, gold on the trembling tips of the grass blades. It was a perfect May morning.

She sauntered slowly along the terrace. As she passed she glanced in at the long windows of the library. Everything was shrouded and shut up. But the long room looked more than usually stately, its proportions seemly; and the brown books in their long rows seemed to exist silently, with dignity, by themselves, for themselves. She left the terrace and strolled down the long grass path. The garden was still empty; only a man in his shirt sleeves was doing something to a tree; but she need speak to nobody. The chow stalked after her; he too was silent. She walked on past the flower-beds to the river. There she always stopped, on the bridge, with the cannon-balls at intervals. The water always fascinated her. The quick northern river came down from the moors; it was never smooth and green, never deep and placid like southern rivers. It raced; it hurried. It splayed itself, red, yellow and clear brown, over the pebbles on the bed. Resting her elbows on the balustrade, she watched it eddy round the arches; she watched it make diamonds and sharp arrow streaks over the stones. She listened. She knew the different sounds it made in summer and winter; now it hurried, it raced.

But the chow was bored; he marched on. She followed him. She went up the green ride towards the snuffer-shaped monument on the crest of the hill. Every path through the woods had its name. There was Keepers' Path, Lovers' Walk, Ladies' Mile, and here was the Earl's Ride. But before she went into the woods, she stopped and looked back at the house. Times out of number she had stopped here; the Castle looked grey and stately; asleep this morning, with the blinds drawn, and no flag on the flagstaff. Very noble it looked, and ancient, and enduring. Then she went on into the woods.

The wind seemed to rise as she walked under the trees. It sang in their tops, but it was silent beneath. The dead leaves crackled under foot; among them sprang up the pale spring flowers, the loveliest of the year—blue flowers and white flowers, trembling on cushions of green moss. Spring was sad always, she thought; it brought back memories. All passes, all changes, she thought, as she climbed up the little path between the trees. Nothing of this belonged to her; her son would inherit; his wife would walk here after her. She broke off a twig; she picked a flower and put it to her lips. But she was in the prime of life; she was vigorous. She strode on. The ground rose sharply; her muscles felt strong and flexible as she pressed her thick-soled shoes to the ground. She threw away her flower. The trees thinned as she strode higher and higher. Suddenly she saw the sky between two striped tree trunks extraordinarily blue. She came out on the top. The wind ceased; the country spread wide all round her. Her body seemed to shrink; her eyes to widen. She threw herself on the ground, and looked over the billowing land that went rising and falling, away and away, until somewhere far off it reached the sea. Uncultivated, uninhabited, existing by itself, for itself, without towns or houses it looked from this height. Dark wedges of shadow, bright breadths of light lay side by side. Then, as she watched, light moved and dark moved; light and shadow went travelling over the hills and over the valleys. A deep murmur sang in her ears—the land itself, singing to itself, a chorus, alone. She lay there listening. She was happy, completely. Time had ceased.

1917

A very cold winter's night, so silent that the air seemed frozen, and, since there was no moon, congealed to the stillness of glass spread over England. Ponds and ditches were frozen; the puddles made glazed eyes in the roads, and on the pavement the frost had raised slippery knobs. Darkness pressed on the windows; towns had merged themselves in open country. No light shone, save when a searchlight rayed round the sky, and stopped, here and there, as if to ponder some fleecy patch.

"If that is the river," said Eleanor, pausing in the dark street outside the station, "Westminster must be there." The omnibus in which she had come, with its silent passengers looking cadaverous in the blue light, had already vanished. She turned.

She was dining with Renny and Maggie, who lived in one of the obscure little streets under the shadow of the Abbey. She walked on. The further side of the street was almost invisible. The lamps were shrouded in blue. She flashed her torch onto a name on a street corner. Again she flashed her torch. Here it lit up a brick wall; there a dark green tuft of ivy. At last the number thirty, the number she was looking for, shone out. She knocked and rang at the same moment, for the darkness seemed to muffle sound as well as sight. Silence weighed on her as she stood there waiting. Then the door opened and a man's voice said, "Come in!"

He shut the door behind him, quickly, as if to shut out the light. It looked strange after the streets—the perambulator in the hall; the umbrellas in the stand; the carpet, the pictures: they all seemed intensified.

"Come in!" said Renny again, and led her into the sitting-room ablaze with light. Another man was standing in the room, and she was surprised because she had expected to find them alone. But the man was somebody whom she did not know.

For a moment they stared at each other; then Renny said, "You know Nicholas . . ." but he did not speak the surname distinctly, and it was so long that she could not catch it. A foreign name, she thought. A foreigner. He was clearly not English. He shook hands with a bow like a foreigner, and he went on talking, as if he were in the middle of a sentence that he wished to finish . . . "we are talking about Napoleon—" he said, turning to her.

"I see," she said. But she had no notion what he was saying. They were in the middle of an argument, she supposed. But it came to an end without her understanding a word of it, except that it had to do with Napoleon. She took off her coat and laid it down. They stopped talking.

"I will go and tell Maggie," said Renny. He left them abruptly.

"You were talking about Napoleon?" Eleanor said. She looked at the man whose surname she had not heard. He was very dark; he had a rounded head and dark eyes. Did she like him or not? She did not know.

I've interrupted them, she felt, and I've nothing whatever to say. She felt dazed and cold. She spread her hands over the fire. It was a real fire; wood blocks were blazing; the flame ran along the streaks of shiny tar. A little trickle of feeble gas was all that was left her at home.

"Napoleon," she said, warming her hands. She spoke without any meaning.

"We were considering the psychology of great men," he said, "by the light of modern science," he added with a little laugh. She wished the argument had been more within her reach.

"That's very interesting," she said shyly.

"Yes—if we knew anything about it," he said.

"If we knew anything about it . . ." she repeated. There was a pause. She felt numb all over—not only her hands, but her brain.

"The psychology of great men—" she said, for she did not wish him to think her a fool, ". . . was that what you were discussing?"

"We were saying—" He paused. She guessed that he found it difficult to sum up their argument—they had evidently been talking for some time, judging by the newspapers lying about and the cigarette-ends on the table.

"I was saying," he went on, "I was saying we do not know ourselves, ordinary people; and if we do not know ourselves, how then can we make religions, laws, that—" he used his hands as people do who find language obdurate, "that—"

"That fit—that fit," she said, supplying him with a word that was shorter, she felt sure, than the dictionary word that foreigners always used.

"—that fit, that fit," he said, taking the word and repeating it as if he were grateful for her help.

". . . that fit," she repeated. She had no idea what they were talking about. Then suddenly, as she bent to warm her hands over the fire words floated together in her mind and made one intelligible sentence. It seemed to her that what he had said was, "We cannot make laws and religions that fit because we do not know ourselves."

"How odd that you should say that!" she said, smiling at him, "because I've so often thought it myself!"

"Why is that odd?" he said. "We all think the same things; only we do not say them."

"Coming along in the omnibus tonight," she began, "I was thinking about this war—I don't feel this, but other people do . . ." She stopped. He looked puzzled; probably she had misunderstood what he had said; she had not made her own meaning plain.

"I mean," she began again, "I was thinking as I came along in the bus—"

But here Renny came in.

He was carrying a tray with bottles and glasses.

"It is a great thing," said Nicholas, "being the son of a wine merchant."

It sounded like a quotation from the French grammar.

The son of the wine merchant, Eleanor repeated to herself, looking at his red cheeks, dark eyes and large nose. The other man must be Russian, she thought. Russian, Polish, Jewish?— she had no idea what he was, who he was.

She drank; the wine seemed to caress a knob in her spine. Here Maggie came in.

"Good evening," she said, disregarding the foreigner's bow as if she knew him too well to greet him.

"Papers," she protested, looking at the litter on the floor, "papers, papers." The floor was strewn with papers.

"We dine in the basement," she continued, turning to Eleanor, "because we've no servants." She led the way down the steep little stairs.

"But Magdalena," said Nicholas, as they stood in the little low-ceilinged room in which dinner was laid, "Sara said, 'We shall meet tomorrow night at Maggie's . . .' She is not here."

He stood; the others had sat down.

"She will come in time," said Maggie.

"I shall ring her up," said Nicholas. He left the room.

"Isn't it much nicer," said Eleanor, taking her plate, "not having servants . . ."

"We have a woman to do the washing-up," said Maggie.

"And we are extremely dirty," said Renny.

He took up a fork and examined it between the prongs.

"No, this fork, as it happens, is clean," he said, and put it down again.

Nicholas came back into the room. He looked perturbed. "She is not there," he said to Maggie. "I rang her up, but I could get no answer."

"Probably she's coming," said Maggie. "Or she may have forgotten. . . ."

She handed him his soup. But he sat looking at his plate

without moving. Wrinkles had come on his forehead; he made no attempt to hide his anxiety. He was without self-consciousness. "There!" he suddenly exclaimed, interrupting them as they talked. "She is coming!" he added. He put down his spoon and waited. Someone was coming slowly down the steep stairs.

The door opened and Sara came in. She looked pinched with the cold. Her cheeks were white here and red there, and she blinked as if she were still dazed from her walk through the blue-shrouded streets. She gave her hand to Nicholas and he kissed it. But she wore no engagement ring, Eleanor observed.

"Yes, we are dirty," said Maggie, looking at her; she was in her day clothes. "In rags," she added, for a loop of gold thread hung down from her own sleeve as she helped the soup.

"I was thinking how beautiful . . ." said Eleanor, for her eyes had been resting on the silver dress with gold threads in it. "Where did you get it?"

"In Constantinople, from a Turk," said Maggie.

"A turbaned and fantastic Turk," Sara murmured, stroking the sleeve as she took her plate. She still seemed dazed.

"And the plates," said Eleanor, looking at the purple birds on her plate, "Don't I remember them?" she asked.

"In the cabinet in the drawing-room at home," said Maggie. "But it seemed silly—keeping them in a cabinet."

"We break one every week," said Renny.

"They'll last the war," said Maggie.

Eleanor observed a curious mask-like expression come down over Renny's face as she said "the war." Like all the French, she thought, he cares passionately for his country. But contradictorily, she felt, looking at him. He was silent. His silence oppressed her. There was something formidable about his silence.

"And why were you so late?" said Nicholas, turning to Sara. He spoke gently, reproachfully, rather as if she were a child. He poured her out a glass of wine.

Take care, Eleanor felt inclined to say to her; the wine goes to one's head. She had not drunk wine for months. She was feeling already a little blurred; a little light-headed. It was the light after the dark; talk after silence; the war, perhaps, removing barriers.

But Sara drank. Then she burst out:

"Because of that damned fool."

"Damned fool?" said Maggie. "Which?"

"Eleanor's nephew," said Sara. "North. Eleanor's nephew, North." She held her glass towards Eleanor, as if she were addressing her. "North . . ." Then she smiled. "There I was, sitting alone. The bell rang. 'That's the wash,' I said. Footsteps came up the stairs. There was North—North," she raised her hand to her head as if in salute, "cutting a figure like this—'What the devil's that for?' I asked. 'I leave for the Front tonight,' he said, clicking his heels together. 'I'm a lieutenant in—' whatever it was—Royal Regiment of Rat-catchers or something. . . . And he hung his cap on the bust of our grandfather. And I poured out tea. 'How many lumps of sugar does a lieutenant in the Royal Rat-catchers require?' I asked. 'One. Two. Three. Four. . . .'"

She dropped pellets of bread on to the table. As each fell, it seemed to emphasise her bitterness. She looked older, more worn; though she laughed, she was bitter.

"Who is North?" Nicholas asked. He pronounced the word "North" as if it were a point on the compass.

"My nephew. My brother Morris's son," Eleanor explained.

"There he sat," Sara resumed, "in his mud-coloured uniform, with his switch between his legs, and his ears sticking out on either side of his pink, foolish face, and whatever I said, 'Good,' he said, 'Good,' 'Good,' until I took up the poker and tongs"— she took up her knife and fork—"and played 'God save the King, Happy and Glorious, Long to reign over us—'" She held her knife and fork as if they were weapons.

I'm sorry he's gone, Eleanor thought. A picture came before her eyes—the picture of a nice cricketing boy smoking a cigar on a terrace. I'm sorry. . . . Then another picture formed. She was sitting on the same terrace; but now the sun was setting; a maid came out and said, "The soldiers are guarding the line with fixed bayonets!" That was how she had heard of the war—three years ago. And she had thought, putting down her coffee-cup on a little table, Not if I can help it! overcome by an absurd but vehement desire to protect those hills; she had looked at the hills across the meadow. . . . Now she looked at the foreigner opposite.

"How unfair you are," Nicholas was saying to Sara. "Prejudiced; narrow; unfair," he repeated, tapping her hand with his finger.

He was saying what Eleanor felt herself.

"Yes. Isn't it natural . . ." she began. "Could you allow the Germans to invade England and do nothing?" she said, turning to Renny. She was sorry she had spoken; and the words were not the ones she had meant to use. There was an expression of suffering, or was it anger? on his face.

"I?" he said. "I help them to make shells."

Maggie stood behind him. She had brought in the meat. "Carve," she said. He was staring at the meat which she had put down in front of him. He took up the knife and began to carve mechanically.

"Now, Nurse," she reminded him. He cut another helping.

"Yes," said Eleanor awkwardly as Maggie took away the plate. She did not know what to say. She spoke without thinking. "Let's end it as quickly as possible and then . . ." She looked at him. He was silent. He turned away. He had turned to listen to what the others were saying, as if to take refuge from speaking himself.

"Poppycock, poppycock . . . don't talk such damned poppycock—that's what you really said," Nicholas was saying. His hands were large and clean and the finger-nails were trimmed very close, Eleanor noticed. He might be a doctor, she thought.

"What's 'poppy-cock'?" she asked, turning to Renny. For she did not know the word.

"American," said Renny. "He's an American," he said, nodding at Nicholas.

"No," said Nicholas, turning round, "I am a Pole."

"His mother was a Princess," said Maggie as if she were teasing him. That explains the seal on his chain, Eleanor thought. He wore a large old seal on his chain.

"She was," he said quite seriously. "One of the noblest families in Poland. But my father was an ordinary man—a man of the people. . . . You should have had more self-control," he added, turning again to Sara.

"So I should," she sighed. "But then he gave his bridle reins a shake and said, 'Adieu for evermore, adieu for evermore!'" She stretched out her hand and poured herself another glass of wine.

"You shall have no more to drink," said Nicholas, moving away the bottle. "She saw herself," he explained, turning to Eleanor, "on top of a tower, waving a white handkerchief to a knight in armour."

"And the moon was rising over a dark moor," Sara murmured, touching a pepper-pot.

The pepper-pot's a dark moor, Eleanor thought, looking at it. A little blur had come round the edges of things. It was the wine; it was the war. Things seemed to have lost their skins; to be freed from some surface hardness; even the chair with gilt claws, at which she was looking, seemed porous; it seemed to radiate out some warmth, some glamour, as she looked at it.

"I remember that chair," she said to Maggie. "And your mother . . ." she added. But she always saw Eugénie not sitting but in movement.

". . . dancing," she added.

"Dancing . . ." Sara repeated. She began drumming on the table with her fork.

"When I was young, I used to dance," she hummed.

"All men loved me when I was young. . . . Roses and syringas hung, when I was young, when I was young. D'you remember, Maggie?" She looked at her sister as if they both remembered the same thing.

Maggie nodded. "In the bedroom. A waltz," she said.

"A waltz . . ." said Eleanor. Sara was drumming a waltz rhythm on the table. Eleanor began to hum in time to it: "Hoity te, toity te, hoity te. . . ."

A long-drawn hollow sound wailed out.

"No, no!" she protested, as if somebody had given her the wrong note. But the sound wailed again.

"A fog-horn?" she said. "On the river?"

But as she said it she knew what it was.

The siren wailed again.

"The Germans!" said Renny. "Those damned Germans!" He put down his knife and fork with an exaggerated gesture of boredom.

"Another raid," said Maggie, getting up. She left the room; Renny followed her.

"The Germans . . ." said Eleanor as the door shut. She felt as if some dull bore had interrupted an interesting conversation. The colours began to fade. She had been looking at the red chair. It lost its radiance as she looked at it, as if a light had been extinguished underneath.

They heard the rush of wheels in the street. Everything seemed to be going past very quickly. There was the round of feet tapping on the pavement. Eleanor got up and drew the curtains slightly apart. The basement was sunk beneath the pavement, so that she only saw people's legs and skirts as they went past the area railings. Two men came by walking very quickly; then an old woman, with her skirt swinging from side to side, walked past.

"Oughtn't we to ask people in?" she said, turning round. But when she looked back the old woman had disappeared. So had the men. The street was now quite empty. The houses opposite were completely curtained. She drew their own curtain carefully. The table, with the gay china and the lamp, seemed ringed in a circle of bright light as she turned back.

She sat down again. "D'you mind air raids?" Nicholas asked, looking at her with his inquisitive expression. "People differ so much."

"Not at all," she said. She would have crumbled a piece of bread to show him that she was at her ease; but as she was not afraid, the action seemed to her unnecessary.

"The chances of being hit oneself are so small," she said. "What were we saying?" she added.

It seemed to her that they had been saying something extremely interesting; but she could not remember what. They sat silent for a moment. Then they heard a shuffling on the stairs.

"The children . . ." said Sara. They heard the dull boom of a gun in the distance.

Here Renny came in.

"Bring your plates," he said.

"In here." He led them into the cellar. It was a large cellar. With its crypt-like ceiling and stone walls it had a damp ecclesiastical look. It was used partly for coal, partly for wine. The light in the centre shone on glittering heaps of coal; bottles of wine wrapped in straw lay on their sides on stone shelves. There was a mouldy smell of wine, straw and damp. It was chilly after the dining-room. Sara came in carrying quilts and dressing-gowns which she had fetched from upstairs. Eleanor was glad to wrap herself in a blue dressing-gown; she wrapped it round her and sat holding her plate on her knees. It was cold.

"And now?" said Sara, holding her spoon erect.

They all looked as if they were waiting for something to happen. Maggie came in carrying a plum pudding.

"We may as well finish our dinner," she said. But she spoke too sensibly; she was anxious about the children, Eleanor guessed. They were in the kitchen. She had seen them as she passed.

"Are they asleep?" she asked.

"Yes. But if the guns . . ." she began, helping the pudding. Another gun boomed out. This time it was distinctly louder.

"They've got through the defences," said Nicholas.

They began to eat their pudding.

A gun boomed again. This time there was a bark in its boom.

"Hampstead," said Nicholas. He took out his watch. The silence was profound. Nothing happened. Eleanor looked at the blocks of stone arched over their heads. She noticed a spider's web in one corner. Another gun boomed. A sigh of air rushed up with it. It was right on top of them this time.

"The Embankment," said Nicholas. Maggie put down her plate and went into the kitchen.

There was profound silence. Nothing happened. Nicholas looked at his watch as if he were timing the guns. There was something queer about him, Eleanor thought; medical, priestly? He wore a seal that hung down from his watch-chain. The number on the box opposite was 1397. She noticed everything. The Germans must be overhead now. She felt a curious heaviness on top of her head. One, two, three, four, she counted, looking up at the greenish-grey stone. Then there was a violent crack of sound, like the split of lightning in the sky. The spider's web oscillated.

"On top of us," said Nicholas, looking up. They all looked up. At any moment a bomb might fall. There was dead silence. In the silence they heard Maggie's voice in the kitchen.

"That was nothing. Turn round and go to sleep." She spoke very calmly and soothingly.

One, two, three four, Eleanor counted. The spider's web was swaying. That stone may fall, she thought, fixing a certain stone with her eyes. Then a gun boomed again. It was fainter— further away.

"That's over," said Nicholas. He shut his watch with a click. And they all turned and shifted on their hard chairs as if they had been cramped.

Maggie came in.

"Well, that's over," she said. ("He woke for a moment, but he

261

went off to sleep again," she said in an undertone to Renny, "but the baby slept right through.") She sat down and took the plate that Renny was holding for her.

"Now let's finish our pudding," she said, speaking in her natural voice.

"Now we will have some wine," said Renny. He examined one bottle; then another; finally he took a third and wiped it carefully with the tail of his dressing-gown. He placed the bottle on a wooden case and they sat round in a circle.

"It didn't come to much, did it?" said Sara. She was tilting back her chair as she held out her glass.

"Ah, but we were frightened," said Nicholas. "Look—how pale we all are."

They looked at each other. Draped in their quilts and dressing-gowns, against the grey-green walls, they all looked whitish, greenish.

"It's partly the light," said Maggie. "Eleanor," she said, looking at her, "looks like an abbess."

The deep-blue dressing-gown which hid the foolish little ornaments, the tabs of velvet and lace on her dress, had improved her appearance. Her middle-aged face was crinkled like an old glove that has been creased into a multitude of fine lines by the gestures of a hand.

"Untidy, am I?" she said, putting her hand to her hair.

"No. Don't touch it," said Maggie.

"And what were we talking about before the raid?" Eleanor asked. Again she felt that they had been in the middle of saying something very interesting when they were interrupted. But there had been a complete break; none of them could remember what they had been saying.

"Well, it's over now," said Sara. "So let's drink a health— Here's to the New World!" she exclaimed. She raised her glass with a flourish. They all felt a sudden desire to talk and laugh.

"Here's to the New World!" they all cried, raising their glasses, and clinking them together.

The five glasses filled with yellow liquid came together in a bunch.

"To the New World!" they cried and drank. The yellow liquid swayed up and down in their glasses.

"Now, Nicholas," said Sara, setting her glass down with a tap on the box, "a speech! A speech!"

"Ladies and gentlemen!" he began, flinging his hand out like an orator. "Ladies and gentlemen . . ."

"We don't want speeches," Renny interrupted him.

Eleanor was disappointed. She would have liked a speech. But he seemed to take the interruption good-humouredly; he sat there nodding and smiling.

"Let's go upstairs," said Renny, pushing away the box.

"And leave this cellar," said Sara, stretching her arms out, "this cave of mud and dung. . . ."

"Listen!" Maggie interrupted. She held up her hand. "I thought I heard the guns again. . . ."

They listened. The guns were still firing, but far away in the distance. There was a sound like the breaking of waves on a shore far away.

"They're only killing other people," said Renny savagely. He kicked the wooden box.

"But you must let us think of something else," Eleanor protested. The mask had come down over his face.

"And what nonsense, what nonsense Renny talks," said Nicholas, turning to her privately. "Only children letting off fireworks in the back garden," he muttered as he helped her out of her dressing-gown. They went upstairs.

Eleanor came into the drawing-room. It looked larger than she remembered it, and very spacious and comfortable. Papers were strewn on the floor; the fire was burning brightly; it was warm; it was cheerful. She felt very tired. She sank down into an armchair. Sara and Nicholas had lagged behind. The others were helping the nurse to carry the children up to bed, she supposed. She lay back in the chair. Everything seemed to become quiet and natural again. A feeling of great calm possessed her. It was as if another space of time had been issued to her, but, robbed by the presence of death of something personal, she felt—she hesitated for a word; "immune?" Was that what she meant? Immune, she said, looking at a picture without seeing it. Immune, she repeated. It was a picture of a hill and a village perhaps in the South of France; perhaps in Italy. There were olive trees; and white roofs grouped against a hillside. Immune, she repeated, looking at the picture.

She could hear a gentle thudding on the floor above; Maggie and Renny were settling the children into their beds again, she supposed. There was a little squeak, like a sleepy bird chirping in its nest. It was very private and peaceful after the guns. But here the others came in.

"Did they mind it?" she said, sitting up, "—the children?"

"No," said Maggie. "They slept through it."

"But they may have dreamt," said Sara, pulling up a chair. Nobody spoke. It was very quiet. The clocks that used to boom out the hour in Westminster were silent.

Maggie took the poker and struck the wood blocks. The sparks went volleying up the chimney in a shower of gold eyes.

"How that makes me . . ." Eleanor began.

She stopped.

"Yes?" said Nicholas.

". . . think of my childhood," she added.

She was thinking of Morris and herself, and old Pippy; but had she told them nobody would know what she meant. They were silent. Suddenly a clear flute-like note rang out in the street below.

"What's that?" said Maggie. She started; she looked at the window; she half rose.

"The bugles," said Renny, putting out his hand to stop her.

The bugles blew again beneath the window. Then they heard them further down the street; then further away still down the next street.

Almost directly the hooting of cars began again, and the rushing of wheels as if the traffic had been released and the usual night life of London had begun again.

"It's over," said Maggie. She lay back in her chair; she looked very tired for a moment. Then she pulled a basket towards her and began to darn a sock.

"I'm glad I'm alive," said Eleanor. "Is that wrong, Renny?" she asked. She wanted him to speak. It seemed to her that he hoarded immense supplies of emotion that he could not express. He did not answer. He was leaning on his elbow, smoking a cigar and looking into the fire.

"I have spent the evening sitting in a coal cellar while other people try to kill each other above my head," he said suddenly. Then he stretched out and took up a paper.

"Renny, Renny, Renny," said Nicholas, as if he were expostulating with a naughty child. He went on reading. The rush of wheels and the hooting of motor cars had run themselves into one continuous sound.

As Renny was reading and Maggie was darning there was silence in the room. Eleanor watched the fire run along veins of tar and blaze and sink.

"What are you thinking, Eleanor?" Nicholas interrupted her. He calls me Eleanor, she thought; that's right.

"About the new world . . ." she said aloud. "D'you think we're going to improve?" she asked.

"Yes, yes," he said, nodding his head.

He spoke quietly as if he did not wish to rouse Renny who was reading, or Maggie who was darning, or Sara who was lying back in her chair half asleep. They seemed to be talking, privately, together.

"But how. . ." she began, "—how can we improve ourselves . . . live more. . ."—she dropped her voice as if she were afraid of waking sleepers—". . . live more naturally . . . better . . . How can we?"

"It is only a question," he said—he stopped. He drew himself close to her—"of learning. The soul . . ." Again he stopped.

"Yes—the soul?" she prompted him.

"The soul—the whole being," he explained. He hollowed his hands as if to enclose a circle. "It wishes to expand; to adventure; to form—new combinations?"

"Yes, yes," she said, as if to assure him that his words were right.

"Whereas now,"—he drew himself together; put his feet together; he looked like an old lady who is afraid of mice— "this is how we live, screwed up into one hard little, tight little—knot?"

"Knot, knot—yes, that's right," she nodded.

"Each is his own little cubicle; each with his own cross or holy book; each with his fire, his wife . . ."

"Darning socks," Maggie interrupted.

Eleanor started. She had seemed to be looking into the future. But they had been overheard. Their privacy was ended.

Renny threw down his paper. "It's all damned rot!" he said. Whether he referred to the paper, or to what they were saying, Eleanor did not know. But talk in private was impossible.

"Why d'you buy them then?" she said, pointing to the papers.

"To light fires with," said Renny.

Maggie laughed and threw down the sock she was mending. "There!" she exclaimed. "Mended. . . ."

Again they sat silent, looking at the fire. Eleanor wished that he would go on talking—the man she called Nicholas. When, she wanted to ask him, when will this new world come? When shall we be free? When shall we live adventurously, wholly, not like cripples in a cave? He seemed to have released something in her; she felt not only a new space of time, but new powers, something unknown within her. She watched his cigarette moving up and down. Then Maggie took the poker and struck the wood and again a shower of red-eyed sparks went volleying up the chimney. We shall be free, we shall be free, Eleanor thought.

"And what have you been thinking all this time?" said Nicholas, laying his hand on Sara's knee. She started. "Or have you been asleep?" he added.

"I heard what you were saying," she said.

"What were we saying?" he asked.

"The soul flying upwards like sparks up the chimney," she said. The sparks were flying up the chimney.

"Not such a bad shot," said Nicholas.

"Because people always say the same thing," she laughed. She roused herself and sat up. "There's Maggie—she says nothing. There's Renny—he says 'What damned rot!' Eleanor says 'That's just what I was thinking.' . . . And Nicholas, Nicholas,"—she patted him on the knee—"who ought to be in prison, says, 'Oh, my dear friends, let us improve the soul!'"

"Ought to be in prison?" said Eleanor, looking at him.

"Because he loves," Sara explained. She paused. "—the other sex, the other sex, you see," she said lightly, waving her hand in the way that was so like her mother's.

For a second a sharp shiver of repugnance passed over Eleanor's skin as if a knife had sliced it. Then she realised that it touched nothing of importance. The sharp shiver passed. Underneath was—what? She looked at Nicholas. He was watching her.

"Does that," he said, hesitating a little, "make you dislike me, Eleanor?"

"Not in the least! Not in the least!" she exclaimed spontaneously. All the evening, off and on, she had been feeling about him; this, that, and the other; but now all the feelings came together and made one feeling, one whole—liking. "Not in the least," she said again. He gave her a little bow. She returned it with a little bow. But the clock on the mantelpiece was striking. Renny was yawning. It was late. She got up. She went to the window and parted the curtains and looked out. All the houses were still curtained. The cold winter's night was almost black. It was like looking into the hollow of a dark-blue stone. Here and there a star pierced the blue. She had a sense of immensity and peace—as if something had been consumed. . . .

"Shall I get you a cab?" Renny interrupted.

"No, I'll walk," she said, turning. "I like walking in London."

"We will come with you," said Nicholas. "Come, Sara," he said. She was lying back in her chair swinging her foot up and down.

"But I don't want to come," she said, waving him away. "I want to stay; I want to talk; I want to sing—a hymn of praise—a song of thanksgiving. . . ."

"Here is your hat; here is your bag," said Nicholas, giving them to her.

"Come," he said, taking her by the shoulder and pushing her out of the room. "Come."

Eleanor went up to say good-night to Maggie.

"I should like to stay too," she said. "There are so many things I should like to talk about—"

"But I want to go to bed—I want to go to bed," Renny protested. He stood there with his hands stretched above his head, yawning.

Maggie rose. "So you shall," she laughed at him.

"Don't bother to come downstairs," Eleanor protested as he opened the door for her. But he insisted. He is very rude and at the same time very polite, she thought, as she followed him down the stairs. A man who feels many different things, and all passionately, all at the same time, she thought. . . . But they had reached the hall. Nicholas and Sara were standing there.

"Cease to laugh at me for once, Sara," Nicholas was saying as he put on his coat.

"And cease to lecture me," she said, opening the front door.

Renny smiled at Eleanor as they stood for a moment by the perambulator.

"Educating themselves!" he said.

"Good-night," she said, smiling as she shook hands. That is the man, she said to herself, with a sudden rush of conviction, as she came out into the frosty air, that I should like to have married. She recognised a feeling which she had never felt. But he's twenty years younger than I am, she thought, and married to my cousin. For a moment she resented the passage of time and the accidents of life which had swept her away—from all that, she said to herself. And a scene came before her; Maggie and Renny sitting over the fire. A happy marriage, she thought, that's what I was feeling all the time. A happy marriage. She looked up as she walked down the dark little street behind the others. A broad fan of light, like the sail of a windmill, was sweeping slowly across the sky. It seemed to take what she was feeling and to express it broadly and simply, as if another voice were speaking in another language. Then the light stopped and examined a fleecy patch of sky, a suspected spot.

The raid! she said to herself. I'd forgotten the raid!

The others had come to the crossing; there they stood.

"I'd forgotten the raid!" she said aloud as she came up with them. She was surprised; but it was true.

They were in Victoria Street. The street curved away, looking wider and darker than usual. Little figures were hurrying along the pavement; they emerged for a moment under a lamp, then vanished into darkness again. The street was very empty.

"Will the omnibuses be running as usual?" Eleanor asked as they stood there.

They looked round them. Nothing was coming along the street at the moment.

"I shall wait here," said Eleanor.

"Then I shall go," said Sara abruptly. "Goodnight!"

She waved her hand and walked away. Eleanor took it for granted that Nicholas would go with her.

"I shall wait here," she repeated.

But he did not move. Sara had already vanished. Eleanor looked at him. Was he angry? Was he unhappy? She did not

269

know. But here a great form loomed up through the darkness; its lights were shrouded with blue paint. Inside silent people sat huddled up; they looked cadaverous and unreal in the blue light. "Good-night," she said, shaking hands with Nicholas. She looked back and saw him still standing on the pavement. He still held his hat in his hand. He looked tall, impressive and solitary standing there alone, while the searchlights wheeled across the sky.

The omnibus moved on. She found herself staring at an old man in the corner who was eating something out of a paper bag. He looked up and caught her staring at him.

"Like to see what I've got for supper, lady?" he said, cocking one eyebrow over his rheumy, twinkling old eyes. And he held out for her inspection a hunk of bread on which was laid a slice of cold meat or sausage.

1918

A veil of mist covered the November sky; a many folded veil, so fine-meshed that it made one density. It was not raining, but here and there the mist condensed on the surface into dampness and made pavements greasy. Here and there on a grass blade or on a hedge leaf a drop hung motionless. It was windless and calm. Sounds coming through the veil—the bleat of sheep, the croak of rooks—were deadened. The uproar of the traffic merged into one growl. Now and then as if a door opened and shut, or the veil parted and closed, the roar boomed and faded.

"Dirty brute," Crosby muttered as she hobbled along the asphalt path across Richmond Green. Her legs were paining her. It was not actually raining, but the great open space was full of mist; and there was nobody near, so that she could talk aloud.

"Dirty brute," she muttered again. She had got into the habit of talking aloud. There was nobody in sight; the end of the path was lost in mist. It was very silent. Only the rooks gathered on the tree tops now and then let fall a queer little croak, and a leaf, spotted with black, fell to the ground. Her face twitched as she walked, as if her muscles had got into the habit of protesting, involuntarily, against the spites and obstacles that tormented her. She had aged greatly during the past four years. She looked so small and hunched that it seemed doubtful if she could make her way across the wide open space, shrouded in white mist. But she had to go to the High Street to do her shopping.

"The dirty brute," she muttered again. She had had some words that morning with Mrs Burt about the Count's bath. He spat in it, and Mrs Burt had told her to clean it.

"Count indeed—he's no more Count than you are," she continued. She was talking to Mrs Burt now. "I'm quite willing to oblige you," she went on. Even out here, in the mist, where she was free to say what she liked, she adopted a conciliatory tone, because she knew that they wanted to be rid of her. She gesticulated with the hand that was not carrying the bag as she told Louisa that she was quite ready to oblige her. She hobbled on. "And I shouldn't mind going either," she added bitterly, but this was spoken to herself only. It was no pleasure to her to live in the house any more; but there was nowhere else for her to go; that the Burts knew very well.

"And I'm quite ready to oblige you," she added aloud, as indeed she had said to Louisa herself. But the truth was that she was no longer able to work as she had done. Her legs pained her. It took all the strength out of her to do her own shopping, let alone to clean the bath. But it was all take-it-or-leave-it now. In the old days she would have sent the whole lot packing.

"Drabs . . . hussies," she muttered. She was now addressing the red-haired servant girl who had flung out of the house yesterday without warning. *She* could easily get another job. It didn't matter to her. So it was left to Crosby to clean the Count's bath.

"Dirty brute, dirty brute," she repeated; her pale-blue eyes glared impotently. She saw once more the blob of spittle that the Count had left on the side of his bath—the Belgian who called himself a Count. "I've been used to work for gentlefolk, not for dirty foreigners like you," she told him as she hobbled.

The roar of traffic sounded louder as she approached the ghostly line of trees. She could see houses now beyond the trees. Her pale-blue eyes peered forward through the mist as she made her way towards the railings. Her eyes alone seemed to express an unconquerable determination; she was not going to give in; she was bent on surviving. The soft mist was slowly lifting. Leaves lay damp and purple on the asphalt path. The rooks croaked and shuffled on the tree tops. Now a dark line of railings emerged from the mist. The roar of traffic in the High Street sounded louder and louder. Crosby stopped and rested her bag on the railing before she went on to do battle with the crowd of shoppers in the High Street. She would have to shove and push, and be jostled this way and that; and her feet pained her. They didn't mind if you bought or not, she thought; and often she was pushed out of her place by some bold-faced drab. She thought of the red-haired girl again, as she stood there, panting slightly, with her bag on the railing. Her legs pained her. Suddenly the long-drawn note of a siren floated out its melancholy wail of sound; then there was a dull explosion.

"Them guns again," Crosby muttered, looking up at the pale-grey sky with peevish irritation. The rooks, scared by the gun-fire, rose and wheeled round the tree tops. Then there was another dull boom. A man on a ladder who was painting the windows of one of the houses paused with his brush in his hand and looked round. A woman who was walking along carrying a loaf of bread that stuck half out of its paper wrapping stopped too. They both waited as if for something to happen. A topple of smoke drifted over and flopped down from the chimneys. The guns boomed again. The man on the ladder said something to the woman on the pavement. She nodded her head. Then he dipped his brush in the pot and went on painting. The woman walked on. Crosby pulled herself together and tottered across the road into the High Street. The guns went on booming and the sirens wailed. The war was over—so somebody told her as she took her place in the queue at the grocer's shop. The guns went on booming and the sirens wailed.

PRESENT DAY

It was a summer evening; the sun was setting; the sky was blue still, but tinged with gold, as if a thin veil of gauze hung over it, and here and there in the gold-blue amplitude an island of cloud lay suspended. In the fields the trees stood majestically caparisoned, with their innumerable leaves gilt. Sheep and cows, pearl white and parti-coloured, lay recumbent or munched their way through the half transparent grass. An edge of light surrounded everything. A red-gold fume rose from the dust on the roads. Even the little red brick villas on the high roads had become porous, incandescent with light, and the flowers in cottage gardens, lilac and pink like cotton dresses, shone veined as if lit from within. Faces of people standing at cottage doors or padding along pavements showed the same red glow as they fronted the slowly sinking sun.

Eleanor came out of her flat and shut the door. Her face was lit up by the glow of the sun as it sank over London, and for a moment she was dazzled and looked out over the roofs and spires that lay beneath. There were people talking inside her room, and she wanted to have a word with her nephew alone. North, her brother Morris's son, had just come back from Africa, and she had scarcely seen him alone. So many people had dropped in that evening—Miriam Parrish; Ralph Pickersgill; Antony Wedd; her niece Peggy, and on top of them all, that very talkative man, her friend Nicholas Pomjalovsky, whom they called Brown for short. She had scarcely had a word with North alone. For a moment they stood in the bright square of sunshine that fell on the stone floor of the passage. Voices were still talking within.

She put her hand on his shoulder.

"It's so nice to see you," she said. "And you haven't changed
. . ." She looked at him. She still saw traces of the brown-eyed
cricketing boy in the massive man, who was so burnt, and
a little grey too over the ears. "We sha'n't let you go back," she
continued, beginning to walk downstairs with him, "to that
horrid farm."

He smiled. "And you haven't changed either," he said.

She looked very vigorous. She had been in India. Her face was
tanned with the sun. With her white hair and her brown cheeks
she scarcely looked her age, but she must be well over seventy,
he was thinking. They walked downstairs arm-in-arm. There
were six flights of stone steps to descend, but she insisted upon
coming all the way down with him, to see him off.

"And North," she said, when they reached the hall, "you will be
careful. . . ." She stopped on the doorstep. "Driving in London,"
she said, "isn't the same as driving in Africa."

There was his little sports car outside; a man was going
past the door in the evening sunlight crying "Old chairs and
baskets to mend."

He shook his head; his voice was drowned by the voice of the
man crying. He glanced at a board that hung in the hall with
names on it. Who was in and who was out was signified with a
care that amused him slightly, after Africa. The voice of the man
crying "Old chairs and baskets to mend," slowly died away.

"Well, good-bye, Eleanor," he said turning. "We shall meet
later." He got into his car.

"Oh, but North—" she cried, suddenly remembering
something she wanted to say to him. But he had turned on the
engine; he did not hear her voice. He waved his hand to her—
there she stood at the top of the steps with her hair blowing in
the wind. The car started off with a jerk. She gave another wave
of her hand to him as he turned the corner.

Eleanor is just the same, he thought: more erratic perhaps.
With a room full of people—her little room had been crowded—

she had insisted upon showing him her new shower-bath. "You press that knob," she had said, "and look—" Innumerable needles of water shot down. He laughed aloud. They had sat on the edge of the bath together.

But the cars behind him hooted persistently; they hooted and hooted. What at? he asked. Suddenly he realised that they were hooting at him. The light had changed; it was green now, he had been blocking the way. He started off with a violent jerk. He had not mastered the art of driving in London.

The noise of London still seemed to him deafening, and the speed at which people drove was terrifying. But it was exciting after Africa. The shops even, he thought, as he shot past rows of plate-glass windows, were marvellous. Along the kerb, too, there were barrows of fruit and flowers. Everywhere there was profusion; plenty. . . . Again the red light shone out; he pulled up.

He looked about him. He was somewhere in Oxford Street; the pavement was crowded with people; jostling each other; swarming round the plate-glass windows which were still lit up. The gaiety, the colour, the variety, were amazing after Africa. All these years, he thought to himself, looking at a floating banner of transparent silk, he had been used to raw goods; hides and fleeces; here was the finished article. A dressing-case, of yellow leather fitted with silver bottles, caught his eye. But the light was green again. On he jerked.

He had only been back ten days, and his mind was a jumble of odds and ends. It seemed to him that he had never stopped talking: shaking hands; saying How-d'you-do? People sprang up everywhere; his father; his sister; old men got up from armchairs and said, You don't remember me? Children he had left in the nursery were grown-up men at college; girls with pigtails were now married women. He was still confused by it all; they talked so fast; they must think him very slow, he thought. He had to withdraw into the window and say, "What, what, what do they mean by it?"

For instance, this evening at Eleanor's there was a man

there with a foreign accent who squeezed lemon into his tea. Who might he be, he wondered? "One of Nell's dentists," said his sister Peggy, wrinkling her lip. For they all had lines cut; phrases ready-made. But that was the silent man on the sofa. It was the other one he meant—squeezing lemon in his tea. "We call him Brown," she murmured. Why Brown if he's a foreigner, he wondered. Anyhow they all romanticized solitude and savagery—"I wish I'd done what you did," said a little man called Pickersgill—except this man Brown, who had said something that interested him. "If we do not know ourselves, how can we know other people?" he had said. They had been discussing dictators; Napoleon; the psychology of great men. But there was the green light—"GO". He shot on again. And then the lady with the ear-rings gushed about the beauties of Nature. He glanced at the name of the street on the left. He was going to dine with Sara but he had not much notion how to get there. He had only heard her voice on the telephone saying, "Come and dine with me—Milton Street, fifty-two, my name's on the door." It was near the Prison Tower. But this man Brown—it was difficult to place him at once. He talked, spreading his fingers out with the volubility of a man who will in the end become a bore. And Eleanor wandered about, holding a cup, telling people about her shower-bath. He wished they would stick to the point. Talk interested him. Serious talk on abstract subjects. "Was solitude good; was society bad?" That was interesting; but they hopped from thing to thing. When the large man said, "Solitary confinement is the greatest torture we inflict," the meagre old woman with the wispy hair at once piped up, laying her hand on her heart, "It ought to be abolished!" She visited prisons, it seemed.

"Where the dickens am I now?" he asked, peering at the name on the street corner. Somebody had chalked a circle on the wall with a jagged line in it. He looked down the long vista. Door after door, window after window, repeated the same pattern. There was a red-yellow glow over it all, for the sun was sinking through the London dust. Everything was tinged with a warm yellow haze. Barrows full of fruit and flowers were drawn up at the kerb. The sun gilded the fruit; the flowers had a blurred brilliance; there were roses, carnations and lilies too. He had half a mind to stop and buy a bunch to take to Sally. But the cars were hooting behind him. He went on. A bunch of flowers, he thought, held in the hand would soften the awkwardness of meeting and the usual things that had to be said. "How nice to see you—you've filled out," and so on. He had only heard her voice on the telephone, and people changed after all these years. Whether this was the right street or not, he could not be sure; he filtered slowly round the corner. Then stopped; then went on again. This was Milton Street, a dusky street, with old houses, now let out as lodgings; but they had seen better days.

"The odds on that side; the evens on this," he said. The street was blocked with vans. He hooted. He stopped. He hooted again. A man went to the horse's head, for it was a coal-cart, and the horse slowly plodded on. Fifty-two was just along the row. He dribbled up to the door. He stopped.

A voice pealed out across the street, the voice of a woman singing scales.

"What a dirty," he said, as he sat still in the car for a moment—here a woman crossed the street with a jug under her arm—"sordid," he added, "low-down street to live in." He cut off his engine; got out, and examined the names on the door. Names mounted one above another; here on a visiting-card, here engraved on brass—Foster; Abrahamson; Roberts; S. Pargiter was near the top, punched on a strip of aluminium. He rang one of the many bells. No one came. The woman went on singing scales, mounting slowly. The mood comes, the mood goes, he thought. He used to write poetry; now the mood had come again as he stood there waiting. He pressed the bell two or three times sharply. But no one answered. Then he gave the door a push; it was open. There was a curious smell in the hall; of vegetables cooking; and the oily brown paper made it dark.

He went up the stairs of what had once been a gentleman's residence. The banisters were carved; but they had been daubed over with some cheap yellow varnish. He mounted slowly and stood on the landing, uncertain which door to knock at. He was always finding himself now outside the doors of strange houses. He had a feeling that he was no one and nowhere in particular. From across the road came the voice of the singer deliberately ascending the scale, as if the notes were stairs; and here she stopped indolently, languidly, flinging out the voice that was nothing but pure sound. Then he heard somebody inside, laughing.

That's her voice, he said. But there is somebody with her. He was annoyed. He had hoped to find her alone. The voice was speaking and did not answer when he knocked. Very cautiously he opened the door and went in.

"Yes, yes, yes," Sara was saying. She was kneeling at the telephone talking; but there was nobody there. She raised her hand when she saw him and smiled at him; but she kept her hand raised as if the noise he had made caused her to lose what she was trying to hear.

"What?" she said, speaking into the telephone. "What?" He stood silent, looking at the silhouettes of his grandparents on the mantelpiece. There were no flowers, he observed. He wished he had brought her some. He listened to what she was saying; he tried to piece it together.

"Yes, now I can hear. . . . Yes, you're right. Someone has come in. . . . Who? North. My cousin from Africa. . . ."

That's me, North thought. "My cousin from Africa." That's my label.

"You've met him?" she was saying. There was a pause. "D'you think so?" she said. She turned and looked at him. They must be discussing him, he thought. He felt uncomfortable.

"Good-bye," she said, and put down the telephone.

"He says he met you tonight," she said, going up to him and taking his hand. "And liked you," she added, smiling.

"Who was that?" he asked, feeling awkward; but he had no flowers to give her.

"A man you met at Eleanor's," she said.

"A foreigner?" he asked.

"Yes. Called Brown," she said, pushing up a chair for him.

He sat down on the chair she had pushed out for him, and she curled up opposite with her foot under her. He remembered the attitude; she came back in sections; first the voice; then the attitude; but something remained unknown.

"You've not changed," he said—the face he meant. A plain face scarcely changed; whereas beautiful faces wither. She looked neither young nor old; but shabby; and the room, with the pampas grass in a pot in the corner, was untidy. A lodging-house room tidied in a hurry he guessed.

"And you—" she said, looking at him. It was as if she were trying to put two different versions of him together; the one on the telephone perhaps and the one on the chair. Or was there some other? This half knowing people, this half being known, this feeling of the eye on the flesh, like a fly crawling—how uncomfortable it was, he thought; but inevitable, after all these years. The tables were littered; he hesitated, holding his hat in his hand. She smiled at him, as he sat there, holding his hat uncertainly.

"Who's the young Frenchman," she said, "with the top hat in the picture?"

"What picture?" he asked.

"The one who sits looking puzzled with his hat in his hand," she said. He put his hat on the table, but awkwardly. A book fell to the floor.

"Sorry," he said. She meant, presumably, when she compared him to the puzzled man in the picture, that he was clumsy; he always had been.

"This isn't the room where I came last time?" he asked.

He recognised a chair—a chair with gilt claws; there was the usual piano.

"No—that was on the other side of the river," she said, "when you came to say good-bye."

He remembered. He had come to her the evening before he left for the war; and he had hung his cap on the bust of their grandfather—that had vanished. And she had mocked him.

"How many lumps of sugar does a lieutenant in His Majesty's Royal Regiment of Rat-catchers require?" she had sneered. He could see her now dropping lumps of sugar into his tea. And they had quarrelled. And he had left her. It was the night of the raid, he remembered. He remembered the dark night; the searchlights that slowly swept over the sky; here and there they stopped to ponder a fleecy patch; little pellets of shot fell; and people scudded along the empty blue shrouded streets. He had been going to Kensington to dine with his family; he had said good-bye to his mother; he had never seen her again.

The voice of the singer interrupted. "Ah—h-h, oh-h-h, ah—h-h, oh—h-h," she sang, languidly climbing up and down the scale on the other side of the street.

"Does she go on like that every night?" he asked. Sara nodded. The notes coming through the humming evening air sounded slow and sensuous. The singer seemed to have endless leisure; she could rest on every stair.

And there was no sign of dinner, he observed; only a dish of fruit on the cheap lodging-house tablecloth, already yellowed with some gravy stain.

"Why d'you always choose slums—" he was beginning, for children were screaming in the street below, when the door opened and a girl came in carrying a bunch of knives and forks. The regular lodging-house skivvy, North thought; with red hands, and one of those jaunty white caps that girls in lodging-houses clap on top of their hair when the lodger has a party. In her presence they had to make conversation. "I've been seeing Eleanor," he said. "That was where I met your friend Brown. . . ."

The girl made a clatter laying the table with the knives and forks she held in a bunch.

"Oh, Eleanor," said Sara. "Eleanor—" But she watched the girl going clumsily round the table; she breathed rather hard as she laid it.

"She's just back from India," he said. He too watched the girl laying the table. Now she stood a bottle of wine among the cheap lodging-house crockery.

"Gallivanting round the world," Sara murmured.

"And entertaining the oddest set of old fogies," he added. He thought of the little man with the fierce blue eyes who wished he had been in Africa; and the wispy woman with beads who visited prisons it seemed.

". . . and that man, your friend—" he began. Here the girl went out of the room, but she left the door open, a sign that she was about to come back.

"Nicholas," said Sara, finishing his sentence. "The man you call Brown."

There was a pause. "And what did you talk about?" she asked. He tried to remember.

"Napoleon; the psychology of great men; if we don't know ourselves how can we know other people . . ." He stopped. It was difficult to remember accurately what had been said even one hour ago.

"And then," she said, holding out one hand and touching a finger exactly as Brown had done, "—how can we make laws, religions, that fit, that fit, when we don't know ourselves?"

"Yes! Yes!" he exclaimed. She had caught his manner exactly; the slight foreign accent; the repetition of the little word "fit", as if he were not quite sure of the shorter words in English.

"And Eleanor," Sara continued, "says . . . 'Can we improve— can we improve ourselves?' sitting on the edge of the sofa?"

"Of the bath," he laughed, correcting her.

"You've had that talk before," he said. That was precisely what he was feeling. They had talked before. "And then," he continued, "we discussed. . . ."

But here the girl burst in again. She had plates in her hand this time; blue-ringed plates, cheap lodging-house plates: "—society or solitude; which is best," he finished his sentence.

Sara kept looking at the table. "And which," she asked, in the distracted way of someone who with their surface senses watches what is being done, but at the same time thinks of something else "—which did you say? You who've been alone all these years," she said. The girl left the room again. "—among your sheep, North." She broke off; for now a trombone player had struck up in the street below, and as the voice of the woman practising her scales continued, they sounded like two people trying to express completely different views of the world in general at one and the same time. The voice ascended; the trombone wailed. They laughed.

". . . Sitting on the verandah," she resumed, "looking at the stars."

He looked up: was she quoting something? He remembered he had written to her when he first went out. "Yes, looking at the stars," he said.

"Sitting on the verandah in the silence," she added. A van went past the window. All sounds were for the moment obliterated.

"And then . . ." she said as the van rattled away—she paused as if she were referring to something else that he had written.

"—then you saddled a horse," she said, "and rode away!"

She jumped up, and for the first time he saw her face in the full light. There was a smudge on the side of her nose.

"D'you know," he said, looking at her, "that you've a smudge on your face?"

She touched the wrong cheek.

"Not that side—the other," he said.

She left the room without looking in the glass. From which we deduce the fact, he said to himself, as if he were writing a novel, that Miss Sara Pargiter has never attracted the love of men. Or had she? He did not know. These little snapshot pictures of people left much to be desired, these little surface pictures that one made, like a fly crawling over a face, and feeling, here's the nose, here's the brow.

He strolled to the window. The sun must be setting, for the brick of the house at the corner blushed a yellowish pink. One or two high windows were burnished gold. The girl was in the room, and she distracted him; also the noise of London still bothered him. Against the dull background of traffic noises, of wheels turning and brakes squeaking, there rose near at hand the cry of a woman suddenly alarmed for her child; the monotonous cry of a man selling vegetables; and far away a barrel organ was playing. It stopped; it began again. I used to write to her, he thought, late at night, when I felt lonely, when I was young. He looked at himself in the glass. He saw his sunburnt face with the broad cheek bones and the little brown eyes.

The girl had been sucked down into the lower portion of the house. The door stood open. Nothing seemed to be happening. He waited. He felt an outsider. After all these years, he thought, everyone was paired off; settled down; busy with their own affairs. You found them telephoning, remembering other conversations; they went out of the room; they left one alone. He took up a book and read a sentence.

"A shadow like an angel with bright hair . . ."

Next moment she came in. But there seemed to be some hitch in the proceedings. The door was open; the table laid; but nothing happened. They stood together, waiting, with their backs to the fireplace.

"How strange it must be," she resumed, "coming back after all these years—as if you'd dropped from the clouds in an aeroplane," she pointed to the table as if that were the field in which he had landed.

"On to an unknown land," said North. He leant forward and touched a knife on the table.

"—and finding people talking," she added.

"—talking, talking," he said, "about money and politics," he added, giving the fender behind him a vicious little kick with his heel.

Here the girl came in. She wore an air of importance derived apparently from the dish she carried, for it was covered with a great metal cover. She raised the cover with a certain flourish. There was a leg of mutton underneath. "Let's dine," said Sara.

"I'm hungry," he added.

They sat down and she took the carving-knife and made a long incision. A thin trickle of red juice ran out; it was underdone. She looked at it.

"Mutton oughtn't to be like that," she said. "Beef—but not mutton."

They watched the red juice running down into the well of the dish.

"Shall we send it back," she said, "or eat it as it is?"

"Eat it," he said. "I've eaten far worse joints than this," he added.

"In Africa . . ." she said, lifting the lids of the vegetable dishes. There was a slabbed-down mass of cabbage in one oozing green water; in the other, yellow potatoes that looked hard.

". . . in Africa, in the wilds of Africa," she resumed, helping him to cabbage, "in that farm you were on, where no one came for months at a time, and you sat on the verandah listening—"

"To sheep," he said. He was cutting his mutton into strips. It was tough.

"And there was nothing to break the silence," she went on, helping herself to potatoes, "but a tree falling, or a rock breaking from the side of a distant mountain—" She looked at him as if to verify the sentences that she was quoting from his letters.

"Yes," he said. "It was very silent."

"And hot," she added. "Blazing hot at midday: an old tramp tapped on your door . . . ?"

He nodded. He saw himself again, a young man, and very lonely.

"And then—" she began again. But a great lorry came crashing down the street. Something rattled on the table. The walls and the floor seemed to tremble. She parted two glasses that were jingling together. The lorry passed; they heard it rumbling away in the distance.

"And the birds," she went on. "The nightingales, singing in the moonlight?"

He felt uncomfortable at the vision she called up. "I must have written you a lot of nonsense!" he exclaimed. "I wish you'd torn them up—those letters!"

"No! They were beautiful letters! Wonderful letters!" she exclaimed, raising her glass. A thimbleful of wine always made her tipsy, he remembered. Her eyes shone; her cheeks glowed.

"And then you had a day off," she went on, "and jolted along a rough white road in a springless cart to the next town—"

"Sixty miles away," he said.

"And went to a bar; and met a man from the next—ranch?" She hesitated as if the word might be the wrong one.

"Ranch, yes, ranch," he confirmed her. "I went to the town and had a drink at the bar—"

"And then?" she said. He laughed. There were some things he had not told her. He was silent.

"Then you stopped writing," she said. She put her glass down.

"When I forgot what you were like," he said, looking at her.

"You gave up writing too," he said.

"Yes, I too," she said.

The trombone had moved his station and was wailing lugubriously under the window. The doleful sound, as if a dog had thrown back its head and were baying the moon, floated up to them. She waved her fork in time to it.

"Our hearts full of tears, our lips full of laughter, we passed on the stairs"—she dragged her words out to fit the wail of the trombone—"we passed on the stair-r-r-s"—but here the trombone changed its measure to a jig. "He to sorrow, I to bliss," she jigged with it, "he to bliss and I to sorrow, we passed on the stair-r-r-s."

She set her glass down.

"Another cut off the joint?" she asked.

"No, thank you," he said, looking at the rather stringy disagreeable object which was still bleeding into the well. The willow-pattern plate was daubed with gory streaks. She stretched her hand out and rang the bell. She rang; she rang a second time. No one came.

"Your bells don't ring," he said.

"No," she smiled. "The bells don't ring, and the taps don't run." She thumped on the floor. They waited. No one came. The trombone wailed outside.

"But there was one letter you wrote me," he continued as they waited. "An angry letter; a cruel letter."

He looked at her. She had lifted her lip like a horse that is going to bite. That, too, he remembered.

"Yes?" she said.

"The night you came in from the Strand," he reminded her.

Here the girl came in with the pudding. It was an ornate pudding, semi-transparent, pink, ornamented with blobs of cream.

"I remember," said Sara, sticking her spoon into the quivering jelly, "a still autumn night; the lights lit; and people padding along the pavement with wreaths in their hands?"

"Yes," he nodded. "That was it."

"And I said to myself," she paused, "this is Hell. We are the damned?" He nodded.

She helped him to pudding.

"And I," he said, as he took his plate, "was among the damned." He stuck his spoon into the quivering mass that she had given him.

"Coward; hypocrite, with your switch in your hand; and your cap on your head—" He seemed to quote from a letter that she had written him. He paused. She smiled at him.

"But what was the word—the word I used?" she asked, as if she were trying to remember.

"Poppycock!" he reminded her. She nodded.

"And then I went over the bridge," she resumed, raising her spoon half-way to her mouth, "and stopped in one of those little alcoves, bays, what d'you call 'em?—scooped out over the water, and looked down—" She looked down at her plate.

"When you lived on the other side of the river," he prompted her.

"Stood and looked down," she said, looking at her glass which she held in front of her, "and thought; Running water, flowing water, water that crinkles up the lights; moonlight; starlight—" She drank and was silent.

"Then the car came," he prompted her.

"Yes; the Rolls-Royce. It stopped in the lamplight and there they sat—"

"Two people," he reminded her.

"Two people. Yes," she said. "He was smoking a cigar. An upper-class Englishman with a big nose, in a dress suit. And she, sitting beside him, in a fur-trimmed cloak, took advantage of the pause under the lamplight to raise her hand"—she raised her hand—"and polish that spade, her mouth."

She swallowed her mouthful.

"And the peroration?" he prompted her.

She shook her head.

They were silent. North had finished his pudding. He took out his cigarette-case. Save for a dish of rather fly-blown fruit, apples and bananas, there was no more to eat apparently.

"We were very foolish when we were young, Sal," he said, as he lit his cigarette, "writing purple passages . . ."

"At dawn with the sparrows chirping," she said, pulling the plate of fruit towards her. She began peeling a banana, as if she were unsheathing some soft glove. He took an apple and peeled it. The curl of apple-skin lay on his plate, coiled up like a snake's skin, he thought; and the banana-skin was like the finger of a glove that had been ripped open.

The street was now quiet. The woman had stopped singing.

The trombone-player had moved off. The rush hour was over and nothing went down the street. He looked at her, biting little bits off her banana.

When she came to the fourth of June, he remembered, she wore her skirt the wrong way round. She was crooked in those days too; and they had laughed at her—he and Peggy. She had never married; he wondered why not. He swept up the broken coils of apple-peel on his plate.

"What does he do," he said suddenly, "—that man who throws his hands out?"

"Like this?" she said. She threw her hands out.

"Yes," he nodded. That was the man—one of those voluble foreigners with a theory about everything. Yet he had liked him—he gave off an aroma; a whirr; his flexible supple face worked amusingly; he had a round forehead; good eyes; and was bald.

"What does he do?" he repeated.

"Talks," she replied, "about the soul." She smiled. Again he felt an outsider; so many talks there must have been between them; such intimacy.

"About the soul," she continued, taking a cigarette. "Lectures," she added, lighting it. "Ten and six for a seat in the front row," she puffed her smoke out. "There's standing room at half a crown; but then," she puffed, "you don't hear so well. You only catch half the lesson of the Teacher, the Master," she laughed.

She was sneering at him now; she conveyed the impression that he was a charlatan. Yet Peggy had said that they were very intimate—she and this foreigner. The vision of the man at Eleanor's changed slightly like an air ball blown aside.

"I thought he was a friend of yours," he said aloud.

"Nicholas?" she exclaimed. "I love him!"

Her eyes certainly glowed. They fixed themselves upon a salt cellar with a look of rapture that made North feel once more puzzled.

"You love him. . ." he began. But here the telephone rang.

"There he is!" she exclaimed. "That's him! That's Nicholas!"

She spoke with extreme irritation.

The telephone rang again. "I'm not here!" she said. The telephone rang again. "Not here! Not here! Not here!" she repeated in time to the bell. She made no attempt to answer it. He could stand the stab of her voice and the bell no longer. He went over to the telephone. There was a pause as he stood with the receiver in his hand.

"Tell him I'm not here!" she said.

"Hullo," he said, answering the telephone. But there was a pause. He looked at her sitting on the edge of her chair, swinging her foot up and down. Then a voice spoke.

"I'm North," he answered the telephone. "I'm dining with Sara. . . . Yes, I'll tell her. . . ." He looked at her again. "She is sitting on the edge of her chair," he said, "with a smudge on her face, swinging her foot up and down."

Eleanor stood holding the telephone. She smiled, and for a moment after she had put the receiver back stood there, still smiling, before she turned to her niece Peggy who had been dining with her.

"North is dining with Sara," she said, smiling at the little telephone picture of two people at the other end of London, one of whom was sitting on the edge of her chair with a smudge on her face.

"He's dining with Sara," she said again. But her niece did not smile, for she had not seen the picture, and she was slightly irritated because, in the middle of what they were saying, Eleanor suddenly got up and said, "I'll just remind Sara."

"Oh, is he?" she said casually.

Eleanor came and sat down.

"We were saying—" she began.

"You've had it cleaned," said Peggy simultaneously. While Eleanor telephoned, she had been looking at the picture of her grandmother over the writing-table.

"Yes," Eleanor glanced back over her shoulder. "Yes. And do you see there's a flower fallen on the grass?" she said. She turned and looked at the picture. The face, the dress, the basket of flowers all shone softly melting into each other, as if the paint were one smooth coat of enamel. There was a flower—a little sprig of blue—lying in the grass.

"It was hidden by the dirt," said Eleanor. "But I can just remember it, when I was a child. That reminds me, if you want a good man to clean pictures—"

"But was it like her?" Peggy interrupted.

Somebody had told her that she was like her grandmother: and she did not want to be like her. She wanted to be dark and aquiline: but in fact she was blue-eyed and round-faced—like her grandmother.

"I've got the address somewhere," Eleanor went on.

"Don't bother—don't bother," said Peggy, irritated by her aunt's habit of adding unnecessary details. It was age coming on, she supposed: age that loosened screws and made the whole apparatus of the mind rattle and jingle.

"Was it like her?" she asked again.

"Not as I remember her," said Eleanor, glancing once more at the picture. "When I was a child perhaps—no, I don't think even as a child. What's so interesting," she continued, "is that what they thought ugly—red hair for instance—we think pretty; so that I often ask myself," she paused, puffing at her cheroot, "'What is pretty?'"

"Yes," said Peggy. "That's what we were saying."

For when Eleanor suddenly took it into her head that she must remind Sara of the party, they had been talking about Eleanor's childhood—how things had changed; one thing seemed good to one generation, another to another. She liked getting Eleanor to talk about her past; it seemed to her so peaceful and so safe.

"Is there any standard, d'you think?" she said, wishing to bring her back to what they were saying.

"I wonder," said Eleanor absentmindedly. She was thinking of something else.

"How annoying!" she exclaimed suddenly. "I had it on the tip of my tongue—something I want to ask you. Then I thought of Delia's party: then North made me laugh—Sally sitting on the edge of her chair with a smudge on her nose; and that's put it out of my head." She shook her head.

"D'you know the feeling when one's been on the point of saying something, and been interrupted; how it seems to stick *here*," she tapped her forehead, "so that it stops everything else? Not that it was anything of importance," she added. She wandered about the room for a moment. "No, I give it up; I give it up," she said, shaking her head.

"I shall go and get ready now, if you'll call a cab."

She went into the bedroom. Soon there was the sound of running water.

Peggy lit another cigarette. If Eleanor were going to wash, as seemed likely from the sounds in the bedroom, there was no need to hurry about the cab. She glanced at the letters on the mantelpiece. An address stuck out on the top of one of them—"Mon Repos, Wimbledon." One of Eleanor's dentists, Peggy thought to herself. The man she went botanising with on Wimbledon Common perhaps. A charming man. Eleanor had described him. "He says every tooth is quite unlike every other tooth. And he knows all about plants. . . ." It was difficult to get her to stick to her childhood.

She crossed to the telephone; she gave the number. There was a pause. As she waited she looked at her hands holding the telephone. Efficient, shell-like, polished but not painted, they're a compromise, she thought, looking at her finger-nails, between science and . . . But here a voice said "Number, please," and she gave it.

Again she waited. As she sat where Eleanor had sat she saw the telephone picture that Eleanor had seen—Sally sitting on the edge of her chair with a smudge on her face. What a fool, she thought bitterly, and a thrill ran down her thigh. Why was she bitter? For she prided herself upon being honest—she was a doctor—and that thrill she knew meant bitterness. Did she envy her because she was happy, or was it the croak of some ancestral prudery—did she disapprove of these friendships with men who did not love women? She looked at the picture of her grandmother as if to ask her opinion. But she had assumed the immunity of a work of art; she seemed as she sat there, smiling at her roses, to be indifferent to our right and wrong.

"Hullo," said a gruff voice, which suggested sawdust and a shelter, and she gave the address and put down the telephone just as Eleanor came in—she was wearing a red-gold Arab cloak with a silver veil over her hair.

"One of these days d'you think you'll be able to see things at the end of the telephone?" Peggy said, getting up. Eleanor's hair was her beauty, she thought; and her silver-washed dark eyes—a fine old prophetess, a queer old bird, venerable and funny at one and the same time. She was burnt from her travels so that her hair looked whiter than ever.

"What's that?" said Eleanor, for she had not caught her remark about the telephone. Peggy did not repeat it. They stood at the window waiting for the cab. They stood there side by side, silent, looking out, because there was a pause to fill up, and the view from the window, which was so high over the roofs, over the squares and angles of back gardens to the blue line of hills in the distance served, like another voice speaking, to fill up the pause. The sun was setting; one cloud lay curled like a red feather in the blue. She looked down. It was queer to see cabs turning corners, going round this street and down the other, and not to hear the sound they made. It was like a map of London; a section laid beneath them. The summer day was fading; lights were being lit, primrose lights, still separate, for the glow of the sunset was still in the air. Eleanor pointed at the sky.

"That's where I saw my first aeroplane—there between those chimneys," she said. There were high chimneys, factory chimneys, in the distance; and a great building—Westminster Cathedral was it?—over there riding above the roofs.

"I was standing here, looking out," Eleanor went on. "It must have been just after I'd got into the flat, a summer's day, and I saw a black spot in the sky, and I said to whoever it was— Miriam Parrish, I think, yes, for she came to help me to get into the flat—I hope Delia, by the way, remembered to ask her—" . . . that's old age, Peggy noted, bringing in one thing after another.

"You said to Miriam—" she prompted her.

"I said to Miriam, 'Is it a bird? No, I don't think it can be a bird. It's too big. Yet it moves.' And suddenly it came over me, that's an aeroplane! And it was! You know they'd flown the Channel not so very long before. I was staying with you in Dorset at the time: and I remember reading it out in the paper, and someone—your father, I think—said: 'The world will never be the same again!'"

"Oh, well—" Peggy laughed. She was about to say that aeroplanes hadn't made all that difference, for it was her line to disabuse her elders of their belief in science, partly because their credulity amused her, partly because she was daily impressed by the ignorance of doctors—when Eleanor sighed.

"Oh dear," she murmured.

She turned away from the window.

Old age again, Peggy thought. Some gust blew open a door: one of the many millions in Eleanor's seventy-odd years; out came a painful thought; which she at once concealed—she had gone to her writing-table and was fidgeting with papers—with the humble generosity, the painful humility of the old.

"What, Nell—?" Peggy began.

"Nothing, nothing," said Eleanor. She had seen the sky; and that sky was laid with pictures—she had seen it so often; any one of which might come uppermost when she looked at it. Now, because she had been talking to North, it brought back the war; how she had stood there one night, watching the searchlights. She had come home, after a raid; she had been dining in

Westminster with Renny and Maggie. They had sat in a cellar; and Nicholas—it was the first time she had met him—had said that the war was of no importance. "We are children playing with fireworks in the back garden" . . . she remembered his phrase; and how, sitting round a wooden packing-case, they had drunk to a new world. "A new world—a new world!" Sally had cried, drumming with her spoon on top of the packing-case. She turned to her writing-table, tore up a letter and threw it away.

"Yes," she said, fumbling among her papers, looking for something. "Yes—I don't know about aeroplanes, I've never been up in one; but motor cars—I could do without motor cars. I was almost knocked down by one, did I tell you? In the Brompton Road. All my own fault—I wasn't looking. . . . And wireless—that's a nuisance—the people downstairs turn it on after breakfast; but on the other hand—hot water; electric light; and those new—" She paused. "Ah, there it is!" she exclaimed. She pounced upon some paper that she had been hunting for. "If Edward's there tonight, do remind me—I'll tie a knot in my handkerchief. . . ."

She opened her bag, took out a silk handkerchief, and proceeded solemnly to tie it into a knot . . . "to ask him about Runcorn's boy."

The bell rang.

"The taxi," she said.

She glanced about to make sure that she had forgotten nothing. She stopped suddenly. Her eye had been caught by the evening paper, which lay on the floor with its broad bar of print and its blurred photograph. She picked it up.

"What a face!" she exclaimed, flattening it out on the table.

As far as Peggy could see, but she was short-sighted, it was the usual evening paper's blurred picture of a fat man gesticulating.

"Damned—" Eleanor shot out suddenly, "bully!" She tore the paper across with one sweep of her hand and flung it on the floor. Peggy was shocked. A little shiver ran over her skin as the paper tore. The word "damned" on her aunt's lips had shocked her.

Next moment she was amused; but still she had been shocked. For when Eleanor, who used English so reticently, said "damned" and then "bully," it meant much more than the words she and her friends used. And her gesture, tearing the paper . . . What a queer set they are, she thought, as she followed Eleanor down the stairs. Her red-gold cloak trailed from step to step. So she had seen her father crumple *The Times* and sit trembling with rage because somebody had said something in a newspaper. How odd!

And the way she tore it! she thought, half laughing, and she flung out her hand as Eleanor had flung hers. Eleanor's figure still seemed erect with indignation. It would be simple, she thought, it would be satisfactory, she thought, following her down flight after flight of stone steps, to be like that. The little knob on her cloak tapped on the stairs. They descended rather slowly.

"Take my aunt," she said to herself, beginning to arrange the scene into an argument she had been having with a man at the hospital, "take my aunt, living alone in a sort of workman's flat at the top of six flights of stairs . . ." Eleanor stopped.

"Don't tell me," she said, "that I left the letter upstairs—Runcorn's letter that I want to show Edward, about the boy?" She opened her bag. "No: here it is." There it was in her bag. They went on downstairs.

Eleanor gave the address to the cabman and sat down with a jerk in her corner. Peggy glanced at her out of the corner of her eye.

It was the force that she had put into the words that impressed her, not the words. It was as if she still believed with passion—she, old Eleanor—in the things that man had destroyed. A wonderful generation, she thought, as they drove off. Believers . . .

"You see," Eleanor interrupted, as if she wanted to explain her words, "it means the end of everything we cared for."

"Freedom?" said Peggy perfunctorily.

"Yes," said Eleanor. "Freedom and justice."

The cab drove off down the mild respectable little streets where every house had its bow window, its strip of garden, its private name. As they drove on, into the big main street, the scene in the flat composed itself in Peggy's mind as she would tell it to the man in the hospital. "Suddenly she lost her temper," she said, "took the paper and tore it across—my aunt, who's over seventy." She glanced at Eleanor to verify the details. Her aunt interrupted her.

"That's where we used to live," she said. She waved her hand towards a long lamp-starred street on the left. Peggy, looking out, could just see the imposing unbroken avenue with its succession of pale pillars and steps. The repeated columns, the orderly architecture, had even a pale pompous beauty as one stucco column repeated another stucco column all down the street.

"Abercorn Terrace," said Eleanor; ". . . the pillar-box," she murmured as they drove past. Why the pillar-box? Peggy asked herself. Another door had been opened. Old age must have endless avenues, stretching away and away down its darkness, she supposed, and now one door opened and then another.

"Aren't people—" Eleanor began. Then she stopped. As usual, she had begun in the wrong place.

"Yes?" said Peggy. She was irritated by this inconsequence.

"I was going to say—the pillar-box made me think," Eleanor began; then she laughed. She gave up the attempt to account for the order in which her thoughts came to her. There was an order, doubtless; but it took so long to find it, and this rambling, she knew, annoyed Peggy, for young people's minds worked so quickly.

"That's where we used to dine," she broke off, nodding at a big house at the corner of a square. "Your father and I. The man he used to read with. What was his name? He became a Judge. . . . . . . We used to dine there, the three of us. Morris, my father and I . . . They had very large parties in those days. Always legal people. And he collected old oak. Mostly shams," she added with a little chuckle.

"You used to dine . . ." Peggy began. She wished to get her back to her past. It was so interesting; so safe; so unreal—that past of the 'eighties; and to her, so beautiful in its unreality.

"Tell me about your youth . . ." she began.

"But your lives are much more interesting than ours were," said Eleanor. Peggy was silent.

They were driving along a bright crowded street; here stained ruby with the light from picture palaces; here yellow from shop windows gay with summer dresses, for the shops, though shut, were still lit up, and people were still looking at dresses, at flights of hats on little rods, at jewels.

When my Aunt Delia comes to town, Peggy continued the story of Eleanor that she was telling her friend at the hospital, she says, We must have a party. Then they all flock together. They love it. As for herself, she hated it. She would far rather have stayed at home or gone to the pictures. It's the sense of the family, she added, glancing at Eleanor as if to collect another little fact about her to add to her portrait of a Victorian spinster. Eleanor was looking out of the window. Then she turned.

"And the experiment with the guinea-pig—how did that go off?" she asked. Peggy was puzzled.

Then she remembered and told her.

"I see. So it proved nothing. So you've got to begin all over again. That's very interesting. Now I wish you'd explain to me . . ." There was another problem that puzzled her.

The things she wants explained, Peggy said to her friend at the Hospital, are either as simple as two and two make four, or so difficult that nobody in the world knows the answer. And if you say to her, "What's eight times eight?"—she smiled at the profile of her aunt against the window—she taps her forehead and says . . . but again Eleanor interrupted her.

"It's so good of you to come," she said, giving her a little pat on the knee. (But did I show her, Peggy thought, that I hate coming?)

"It's a way of seeing people," Eleanor continued. "And now that we're all getting on—not you, us—one doesn't like to miss chances."

They drove on. And how does one get *that* right? Peggy thought, trying to add another touch to the portrait. "Sentimental" was it? Or, on the contrary, was it good to feel like that . . . natural . . . right? She shook her head. I'm no use at describing people, she said to her friend at the Hospital. They're too difficult. . . . She's not like that—not like that at all, she said, making a little dash with her hand as if to rub out an outline that she had drawn wrongly. As she did so, her friend at the Hospital vanished.

She was alone with Eleanor in the cab. And they were passing houses. Where does she begin, and where do I end? she thought. . . . On they drove. They were two living people, driving across London; two sparks of life enclosed in two separate bodies; and those sparks of life enclosed in two separate bodies are at this moment, she thought, driving past a picture palace. But what is this moment; and what are we? The puzzle was too difficult for her to solve it. She sighed.

"You're too young to feel that," said Eleanor.

"What?" Peggy asked with a little start.

"About meeting people. About not missing chances of seeing them."

"Young?" said Peggy. "I shall never be as young as you are!" She patted her Aunt's knee in her turn. "Gallivanting off to India . . ." she laughed.

"Oh, India. India's nothing nowadays," said Eleanor. "Travel's so easy. You just take a ticket; just get on board ship. . . . But what I want to see before I die," she continued, "is something different. . . ." She waved her hand out of the window. They were passing public buildings; offices of some sort. ". . . another kind of civilisation. Tibet, for instance. I was reading a book by a man called—now what was he called?"

She paused, distracted by the sights in the street. "Don't

people wear pretty clothes nowadays?" she said, pointing to a girl with fair hair and a young man in evening dress.

"Yes," said Peggy perfunctorily, looking at the painted face and the bright shawl; at the white waistcoat and the smoothed back hair. Anything distracts Eleanor, everything interests her, she thought.

"Was it that you were suppressed when you were young?" she said aloud, recalling vaguely some childish memory; her grandfather with the shiny stumps instead of fingers; and a long dark drawing-room. Eleanor turned. She was surprised.

"Suppressed?" she repeated. She so seldom thought about herself now that she was surprised.

"Oh, I see what you mean," she added after a moment. A picture—another picture—had swum to the surface. There was Delia standing in the middle of the room; Oh my God! Oh my God! she was saying; a hansom cab had stopped at the house next door; and she herself was watching Morris—was it Morris?—going down the street to post a letter. . . . She was silent. I do not want to go back into my past, she was thinking. I want the present.

"Where's he taking us?" she said, looking out. They had reached the public part of London; the illuminated. The light fell on broad pavements; on white brilliantly lit-up public offices; on a pallid, hoary-looking church. Advertisements popped in and out. Here was a bottle of beer: it poured: then stopped: then poured again. They had reached the theatre quarter. There was the usual garish confusion. Men and women in evening dress were walking in the middle of the road. Cabs were wheeling and stopping. Their own taxi was held up. It stopped dead under a statue: the lights shone on its cadaverous pallor.

"Always reminds me of an advertisement of sanitary towels," said Peggy, glancing at the figure of a woman in nurse's uniform holding out her hand.

Eleanor was shocked for a moment. A knife seemed to slice her skin, leaving a ripple of unpleasant sensation; but what was solid in her body it did not touch, she realised after a moment. That she said because of Charles, she thought, feeling the bitterness in her tone—her brother, a nice dull boy who had been killed.

"The only fine thing that was said in the war," she said aloud, reading the words cut on the pedestal.

"It didn't come to much," said Peggy sharply.

The cab remained fixed in the block.

The pause seemed to hold them in the light of some thought that they both wished to put away.

"Don't people wear pretty clothes nowadays?" said Eleanor, pointing to another girl with fair hair in a long bright cloak and another young man in evening dress.

"Yes," said Peggy briefly.

But why don't you enjoy yourself more? Eleanor said to herself. Her brother's death had been very sad, but she had always found North much the more interesting of the two. The cab threaded its way through the traffic and passed into a back street. He was stopped now by a red light. "It's nice, having North back again," Eleanor said.

"Yes," said Peggy. "He says we talk of nothing but money and politics," she added. She finds fault with him because he was not the one to be killed; but that's wrong, Eleanor thought.

"Does he?" she said. "But then . . ." A newspaper placard, with large black letters, seemed to finish her sentence for her. They were approaching the square in which Delia lived. She began to fumble with her purse. She looked at the metre which had mounted rather high. The man was going the long way round.

"He'll find his way in time," she said. They were gliding slowly round the square. She waited patiently, holding her purse in her hand. She saw a breadth of dark sky over the roofs. The sun had sunk. For a moment the sky had the quiet look of the sky that lies above fields and woods in the country.

"He'll have to turn, that's all," she said. "I'm not despondent," she added, as the taxi turned. "Travelling, you see: when one has to mix up with all sorts of other people on board ship, or in one of those little places where one has to stay—off the beaten track—" The taxi was sliding tentatively past house after house—"You ought to go there, Peggy," she broke off; "you ought to travel: the natives are so beautiful you know; half naked: going down to the river in the moonlight;—that's the house over there—" She tapped on the window—the taxi slowed down. "What was I saying? I'm not despondent, no, because people are so kind, so good at heart. . . . So that if only ordinary people, ordinary people like ourselves . . ."

The cab drew up at a house whose windows were lit up. Peggy leant forward and opened the door. She jumped out and paid the driver. Eleanor bundled out after her. "No, no, no, Peggy," she began.

"It's my cab. It's my cab," Peggy protested.

"But I insist on paying my share," said Eleanor, opening her purse.

"That's Eleanor," said North. He left the telephone and turned to Sara. She was still swinging her foot up and down.

"She told me to tell you to come to Delia's party," he said.

"To Delia's party? Why to Delia's party?" she asked.

"Because they're old and want you to come," he said, standing over her.

"Old Eleanor; wandering Eleanor; Eleanor with the wild eyes . . ." she mused. "Shall I, shan't I, shall I, shan't I?" she hummed, looking up at him. "No," she said, putting her feet to the ground, "I shan't."

"You must," he said. For her manner irritated him—Eleanor's voice was still in his ears.

"I must, must I?" she said, making the coffee.

"Then," she said, giving him his cup and picking up the book at the same time, "read until we must go."

She curled herself up again, holding her cup in her hand.

It was still early, it was true. But why, he thought as he opened the book again and turned over the pages, won't she come? Is she afraid? he wondered. He looked at her crumpled in her chair. Her dress was shabby. He looked at the book again, but he could hardly see to read. She had not lit the lamp.

"I can't see to read without a light," he said. It grew dark soon in this street; the houses were so close. Now a car passed and a light slid across the ceiling.

"Shall I turn on the light?" she asked.

"No," he said. "I'll try to remember something." He began to say aloud the only poem he knew by heart. As he spoke the words out into the semi-darkness they sounded extremely beautiful, he thought, because they could not see each other, perhaps.

He paused at the end of the verse.

"Go on," she said.

He began again. The words going out into the room seemed like actual presences, hard and independent; yet as she was listening they were changed by their contact with her. But as he reached the end of the second verse—

> Society is all but rude—
> To this delicious solitude . . .

he heard a sound. Was it in the poem or outside of it, he wondered? Inside, he thought, and was about to go on, when she raised her hand. He stopped. He heard heavy footsteps outside the door. Was someone coming in? Her eyes were on the door.

"The Jew," she murmured.

"The Jew?" he said. They listened. He could hear quite distinctly now. Somebody was turning on taps; somebody was having a bath in the room opposite.

"The Jew having a bath," she said.

"The Jew having a bath?" he repeated.

"And tomorrow there'll be a line of grease round the bath," she said.

"Damn the Jew!" he exclaimed. The thought of a line of grease

303

from a strange man's body on the bath next door disgusted him.

"Go on—" said Sara: "Society is all but rude," she repeated the last lines, "to this delicious solitude."

"No," he said.

They listened to the water running. The man was coughing and clearing his throat as he sponged.

"Who is this Jew?" he asked.

"Abrahamson, in the tallow trade," she said.

They listened.

"Engaged to a pretty girl in a tailor's shop," she added.

They could hear the sounds through the thin walls very distinctly.

He was snorting as he sponged himself.

"But he leaves hairs in the bath," she concluded.

North felt a shiver run through him. Hairs in food, hairs on basins, other people's hairs made him feel physically sick.

"D'you share a bath with him?" he asked.

She nodded.

He made a noise like "Pah!"

"'Pah.' That's what I said," she laughed. "'Pah!'—when I went into the bathroom on a cold winter's morning—'Pah!'—she threw her hand out—"'Pah!'" She paused.

"And then—?" he asked.

"And then," she said, sipping her coffee, "I came back into the sitting-room. And breakfast was waiting. Fried eggs and a bit of toast. Lydia with her blouse torn and her hair down. The unemployed singing hymns under the window. And I said to myself—" she flung her hand out, "'Polluted city, unbelieving city, city of dead fish and worn-out frying-pans'—thinking of a river's bank, when the tide's out," she explained.

"Go on," he nodded.

"So I put on my hat and coat and rushed out in a rage," she continued, "and stood on the bridge, and said, 'Am I a weed, carried this way, that way, on a tide that comes twice a day without a meaning?'"

"Yes?" he prompted her.

"And there were people passing; the strutting; the tiptoeing; the pasty; the ferret-eyed; the bowler-hatted, servile innumerable army of workers. And I said, 'Must I join your conspiracy? Stain the hand, the unstained hand,'"—he could see her hand gleam as she waved it in the half-light of the sitting-room, "'—and sign on, and serve a master; all because of a Jew in my bath, all because of a Jew?'"

She sat up and laughed, excited by the sound of her own voice which had run in to a jog-trot rhythm.

"Go on, go on," he said.

"But I had a talisman, a glowing gem, a lucent emerald"— she picked up an envelope that lay on the floor—"a letter of introduction. And I said to the flunkey in peach-blossom trousers, 'Admit me, sirrah,' and he led me along corridors piled with purple till I came to a door, a mahogany door, and knocked; and a voice said, 'Enter.' And what did I find?" She paused. "A stout man with red cheeks. On his table three orchids in a vase. Pressed into your hand, I thought, as the car crunches the gravel by your wife at parting. And over the fireplace the usual picture—"

"Stop!" North interrupted her. "You have come to an office," he tapped the table. "You are presenting a letter of introduction— but to whom?"

"Oh, to whom?" she laughed. "To a man in sponge-bag trousers. 'I knew your father at Oxford,' he said, toying with the blotting-paper, ornamented in one corner with a cartwheel. But what do *you* find insoluble, I asked him, looking at the mahogany man, the clean-shaven, rosy-gilled, mutton-fed man—"

"The man in a newspaper office," North checked her, "who knew your father. And then?"

"There was a humming and a grinding. The great machines went round; and little boys popped in with elongated sheets; black sheets; smudged; damp with printer's ink. 'Pardon me a moment,' he said, and made a note in the margin. But the Jew's in my bath, I said—the Jew . . . the Jew—" She stopped suddenly and emptied her glass.

Yes, he thought, there's the voice; there's the attitude; and the reflection in other people's faces; but then there's something true—in the silence perhaps. But it was not silent. They could hear the Jew thudding in the bathroom; he seemed to stagger from foot to foot as he dried himself. Now he unlocked the door, and they heard him go upstairs. The pipes began to give forth hollow gurgling sounds.

"How much of that was true?" he asked her. But she had lapsed into silence. The actual words he supposed—the actual words floated together and formed a sentence in his mind—meant that she was poor; that she must earn her living, but the excitement with which she had spoken, due to wine perhaps, had created yet another person; another semblance, which one must solidify into one whole.

The house was quiet now, save for the sound of the bath water running away. A watery pattern fluctuated on the ceiling. The street lamps jiggering up and down outside made the houses opposite a curious pale red. The uproar of the day had died away; no carts were rattling down the street. The vegetable-sellers, the organ-grinders, the woman practising her scales, the man playing the trombone, had all trundled away their barrows, pulled down their shutters, and closed the lids of their pianos. It was so still that for a moment North thought he was in Africa, sitting on the verandah in the moonlight; but he roused himself. "What about this party?" he said. He got up and threw away his cigarette. He stretched himself and looked at his watch. "It's time to go," he said. "Go and get ready," he urged her. For if one went to a party, he thought, it was absurd to go just as people were leaving. And the party must have begun.

"What were you saying—what were you saying, Nell?" said Peggy, in order to distract Eleanor from paying her share of the cab, as they stood on the doorstep. "Ordinary people—ordinary people ought to do what?" she asked.

Eleanor was still fumbling with her purse and did not answer.

"No, I can't allow that," she said. "Here, take this—"

But Peggy brushed aside the hand, and the coins rolled on the doorstep. They both stooped simultaneously and their heads collided.

"Don't bother," said Eleanor as a coin rolled away. "It was all my fault." The maid was holding the door open.

"And where do we take our cloaks off?" she said. "In here?"

They went into a room on the ground floor which, though an office, had been arranged so that it could be used as a cloak-room. There was a looking-glass on the table: and in front of it trays of pins and combs and brushes. She went up to the glass and gave herself one brief glance.

"What a gipsy I look!" she said, and ran a comb through her hair. "Burnt as brown as a nigger!" Then she gave way to Peggy and waited.

"I wonder if this was the room . . ." she said.

"What room?" said Peggy abstractedly: she was attending to her face.

". . . where we used to meet," said Eleanor. She looked about her. It was still used as an office apparently; but now there were house-agents' placards on the wall.

"I wonder if Kitty'll come tonight," she mused.

Peggy was gazing into the glass and did not answer.

"She doesn't often come to town now. Only for weddings and christenings and so on," Eleanor continued.

Peggy was drawing a line with a tube of some sort round her lips.

"Suddenly you meet a young man six-foot-two and you realise this is the baby," Eleanor went on.

Peggy was still absorbed in her face.

"D'you have to do that fresh every time?" said Eleanor.

"I should look a fright if I didn't," said Peggy. The tightness round her lips and eyes seemed to her visible. She had never felt less in the mood for a party.

"Oh, how kind of you . . ." Eleanor broke off. The maid had brought in a sixpence.

"Now, Peggy," said she, proffering the coin, "let me pay my share."

"Don't be an ass," said Peggy, brushing away her hand.

"But it was my cab," Eleanor insisted. Peggy walked on. "Because I hate going to parties," Eleanor continued, following her, still holding out the coin, "on the cheap. You don't remember your grandfather? He always said, 'Don't spoil a good ship for a ha'porth of tar.' If you went shopping with him," she went on as they began mounting the stairs, "'Show me the very best thing you've got,' he'd say."

"I remember him," said Peggy.

"Do you?" said Eleanor. She was pleased that anyone should remember her father. "They've lent these rooms, I suppose," she added as they walked upstairs. Doors were open. "That's a solicitor's," she said, looking at some deed-boxes with white names painted on them.

"Yes, I see what you mean about painting—making-up," she continued, glancing at her niece. "You do look nice. You look lit-up. I like it on young people. Not for myself. I should feel bedizened—bedizzened?—how d'you pronounce it? And what am I to do with these coppers if you won't take them? I ought to have left them in my bag downstairs." They mounted higher and higher. "I suppose they've opened all these rooms," she continued—they had now reached a strip of red carpet—"so that if Delia's little room gets too full—but of course the party's hardly begun yet. We're early. Everybody's upstairs. I hear them talking. Come along. Shall I go first?"

A babble of voices sounded behind a door. A maid intercepted them.

"Miss Pargiter," said Eleanor.

"Miss Pargiter!" the maid called out, opening the door.

"Go and get ready," said North. He crossed the room and fumbled with the switch.

He touched the switch, and the electric light in the middle of the room came on. The shade had been taken off, and a cone of greenish paper had been twisted round it.

"Go and get ready," he repeated. Sara did not answer. She had pulled a book towards her and pretended to read it.

"He's killed the king," she said. "So what'll he do next?" She held her finger between the pages of the book and looked up at him; a device, he knew, to put off the moment of action. He did not want to go either. Still, if Eleanor wanted them to go—he hesitated, looking at his watch.

"What'll he do next?" she repeated.

"Comedy," he said briefly, "Contrast," he said, remembering something he had read. "The only form of continuity," he added at a venture.

"Well, go on reading," she said, handing him the book.

He opened it at random.

"The scene is a rocky island in the middle of the sea," he said. He paused.

Always before reading he had to arrange the scene; to let this sink; that come forward. A rocky island in the middle of the sea, he said to himself—there were green pools, tufts of silver grass, sand, and far away the soft sigh of waves breaking. He opened his mouth to read. Then there was a sound behind him; a presence—in the play or in the room? He looked up.

"Maggie!" Sara exclaimed. There she was standing at the open door in evening dress.

"Were you asleep?" she said, coming into the room. "We've been ringing and ringing."

She stood smiling at them, amused, as if she had wakened sleepers.

"Why d'you trouble to have a bell when it's always broken?" said a man who stood behind her.

North rose. At first he scarcely remembered them. The surface sight was strange on top of his memory of them, as he had seen them years ago.

"The bells don't ring, and the taps don't run," he said, awkwardly. "Or they don't stop running," he added, for the bath water was still gurgling in the pipes.

"Luckily the door was open," said Maggie. She stood at the table looking at the broken apple peel and the dish of fly-blown fruit. Some beauty, North thought, withers; some, he looked at her, grows more beautiful with age. Her hair was grey; her children must be grown up now, he supposed. But why do women purse their lips up when they look in the glass? he wondered. She was looking in the glass. She was pursing her lips. Then she crossed the room, and sat down in the chair by the fireplace.

"And why has Renny been crying?" said Sara. North looked at him. There were wet marks on either side of his large nose.

"Because we've been to a very bad play," he said, "and should like something to drink," he added.

Sara went to the cupboard and began clinking glasses. "Were you reading?" said Renny, looking at the book which had fallen on the floor.

"We were on a rocky island in the middle of the sea," said Sara, putting the glasses on the table. Renny began to pour out whisky.

Now I remember him, North thought. Last time they had met was before he went to the war. It was in a little house in Westminster. They had sat in front of the fire. And a child had played with a spotted horse. And he had envied them their happiness. And they had talked about science. And Renny had said, "I help them to make shells," and a mask had come down over his face. A man who made shells; a man who loved peace; a man of science; a man who cried. . . .

"Stop!" cried Renny. "Stop!" Sara had spurted the soda water over the table.

"When did you get back?" Renny asked him, taking his glass

and looking at him with eyes still wet with tears.

"About a week ago," he said.

"You've sold your farm?" said Renny. He sat down with his glass in his hand.

"Yes, sold it," said North. "Whether I shall stay, or go back," he said, taking his glass and raising it to his lips, "I don't know."

"Where was your farm?" said Renny, bending towards him. And they talked about Africa.

Maggie looked at them drinking and talking. The twisted cone of paper over the electric light was oddly stained. The mottled light made their faces look greenish. The two grooves on each side of Renny's nose were still wet. His face was all peaks and hollows; North's face was round and snub-nosed and rather blueish about the lips. She gave her chair a little push so that she got the two heads in relation side by side. They were very different. And as they talked about Africa their faces changed, as if some twitch had been given to the fine network under the skin and the weights fell into different sockets. A thrill ran through her as if the weights in her own body had changed too. But there was something about the light that puzzled her. She looked round. A lamp must be flaring in the street outside. Its light, flickering up and down, mixed with the electric light under the greenish cone of mottled paper. It was that which. . . . She started; a voice had reached her.

"To Africa?" she said, looking at North.

"To Delia's party," he said. "I asked if you were coming. . . ." She had not been listening.

"One moment . . ." Renny interrupted. He held up his hand like a policeman stopping traffic. And again they went on, talking about Africa.

Maggie lay back in her chair. Behind their heads rose the curve of the mahogany chair back. And behind the curve of the chair back was a crinkled glass with a red lip; then there was the straight line of the mantelpiece with little black-and-white squares on it; and then three rods ending in soft yellow plumes. She ran her eye from thing to thing. In and out it went, collecting, gathering, summing up into one whole, when, just as she was about to complete the pattern, Renny exclaimed:

"We must—we must!"

He had got up. He had pushed away his glass of whisky. He stood there like somebody commanding a troop, North thought; so emphatic was his voice, so commanding his gesture. Yet it was only a question of going round to an old woman's party. Or was there always, he thought, as he too rose and looked for his hat, something that came to the surface, inappropriately, unexpectedly, from the depths of people, and made ordinary actions, ordinary words, expressive of the whole being, so that he felt, as he turned to follow Renny to Delia's party, as if he were riding to the relief of a besieged garrison across a desert?

He stopped with his hand on the door. Sara had come in from the bedroom. She had changed; she was in evening dress; there was something odd about her—perhaps it was the effect of the evening dress estranging her?

"I am ready," she said, looking at them.

She stooped and picked up the book that North had let fall.

"We must go—" she said, turning to her sister.

She put the book on the table; she gave it a sad little pat as she shut it.

"We must go," she repeated, and followed them down the stairs.

Maggie rose. She gave one more look at the cheap lodging-house room. There was the pampas grass in its terra-cotta pot; the green vase with the crinkled lip; and the mahogany chair. On the dinner table lay the dish of fruit; the heavy sensual apples lay side by side with the yellow spotted bananas. It was an odd combination—the round and the tapering, the rosy and the yellow. She switched off the light. The room now was almost dark, save for a watery pattern fluctuating on the ceiling. In this phantom evanescent light only the outlines showed; ghostly apples, ghostly bananas, and the spectre of a chair. Colour was slowly returning, as her eyes grew used to the darkness, and substance. . . . She stood there for a moment looking. Then a voice shouted:

"Maggie! Maggie!"

"I'm coming!" she cried, and followed them down the stairs.

"And your name, miss?" said the maid to Peggy as she hung back behind Eleanor.

"Miss Margaret Pargiter," said Peggy.

"Miss Margaret Pargiter!" the maid called out into the room.

There was a babble of voices; lights opened brightly in front of her, and Delia came forward. "Oh, Peggy!" she exclaimed. "How nice of you to come!"

She went in; but she felt plated, coated over with some cold skin. They had come too early—the room was almost empty. Only a few people stood about, talking too loudly, as if to fill the room. Making believe, Peggy thought to herself as she shook hands with Delia and passed on, that something pleasant is about to happen. She saw with extreme clearness the Persian rug and the carved fireplace, but there was an empty space in the middle of the room.

What is the tip for this particular situation? she asked herself, as if she were prescribing for a patient. Take notes, she added. Do them up in a bottle with a glossy green cover, she thought. Take notes and the pain goes. Take notes and the pain goes, she repeated to herself as she stood there alone. Delia hurried past her. She was talking, but talking at random.

"It's all very well for you people who live in London—" she was saying. But the nuisance of taking notes of what people say, Peggy went on as Delia passed her, is that they talk such nonsense . . . such complete nonsense, she thought, drawing herself back against the wall. Here her father came in. He paused at the door; put his head up as if he were looking for someone, and advanced with his hand out.

And what's this? she asked, for the sight of her father in his rather worn shoes had given her a direct spontaneous feeling. This sudden warm spurt? she asked, examining it. She watched him cross the room. His shoes always affected her strangely. Part sex; part pity, she thought. Can one call it "love"? But she forced herself to move. Now that I have drugged myself into a state of comparative insensibility, she said to herself, I will walk across the room boldly; I will go to Uncle Patrick, who is standing by the sofa picking his teeth, and I will say to him— what shall I say?

A sentence suggested itself for no rhyme or reason as she crossed the room: "How's the man who cut his toes off with the hatchet?"

"How's the man who cut his toes off with the hatchet?" she said, speaking the words exactly as she thought them. The handsome old Irishman bent down, for he was very tall, and hollowed his hand, for he was hard of hearing.

"Hacket? Hacket?" he repeated. She smiled. The steps from brain to brain must be cut very shallow, if thought is to mount them, she noted.

"Cut his toes off with the hatchet when I was staying with you," she said. She remembered how when she last stayed with them in Ireland the gardener had cut his foot with a hatchet.

"Hacket? Hacket?" he repeated. He looked puzzled. Then understanding dawned.

"Oh, the Hackets!" he said. "Dear old Peter Hacket—yes." It seemed that there were Hackets in Galway, and the mistake, which she did not trouble to explain, was all to the good, for it set him off, and he told her stories about the Hackets as they sat side by side on the sofa.

A grown woman, she thought, crosses London to talk to a deaf old man about the Hackets, whom she's never heard of, when she meant to ask after the gardener who cut his toe off with a hatchet. But does it matter? Hackets or hatchets? She laughed, happily in time with a joke, so that it seemed appropriate. But one wants somebody to laugh with, she thought. Pleasure is increased by sharing it. Does the same hold good of pain? she mused. Is that the reason why we all talk so much of ill-health—because sharing things lessens things? Give pain, give pleasure an outer body, and by increasing the surface diminish them. . . . But the thought slipped. He was off telling his old stories. Gently, methodically, like a man setting in motion some still serviceable but rather weary nag, he was off remembering old days, old dogs, old memories that slowly shaped themselves, as he warmed, into little figures of country house life. She fancied as she half listened that she was looking at a faded snapshot of cricketers; of shooting parties on the many steps of some country mansion.

How many people, she wondered, listen? This "sharing," then, is a bit of a farce. She made herself attend.

"Ah yes, those were fine old days!" he was saying. The light came into his faded eyes.

She looked once more at the snapshot of the men in gaiters, and the women in flowing skirts on the broad white steps with the dogs curled up at their feet. But he was off again.

"Did you ever hear from your father of a man called Roddy Jenkins who lived in the little white house on the right-hand side as you go along the road?" he asked. "But you must know that story?" he added.

"No," she said, screwing up her eyes as if she referred to the files of memory. "Tell me."

And he told her the story.

I'm good, she thought, at fact-collecting. But what makes up a person—, (she hollowed her hand), the circumference,—no, I'm not good at that. There was her Aunt Delia. She watched her moving quickly about the room. What do I know about her? That she's wearing a dress with gold spots; has wavy hair, that was red, is white; is handsome; ravaged; with a past. But what past? She married Patrick. . . . The long story that Patrick was telling her kept breaking up the surface of her mind like oars

315

dipping into water. Nothing could settle. There was a lake in the story too, for it was a story about duck-shooting.

She married Patrick, she thought, looking at his battered weather-worn face with the single hairs on it. Why did Delia marry Patrick? she wondered. How do they manage it—love, childbirth? The people who touch each other and go up in a cloud of smoke: red smoke? His face reminded her of the red skin of a gooseberry with the little stray hairs. But none of the lines on his face was sharp enough, she thought, to explain how they came together and had three children. They were lines that came from shooting; lines that came from worry; for the old days were over, he was saying. They had to cut things down.

"Yes, we're all finding that," she said perfunctorily. She turned her wrist cautiously so that she could read her watch. Fifteen minutes only had passed. But the room was filling with people she did not know. There was an Indian in a pink turban.

"Ah, but I'm boring you with these old stories," said her uncle, wagging his head. He was hurt, she felt.

"No, no, no!" she said, feeling uncomfortable. He was off again, but out of good manners this time, she felt. Pain must outbalance pleasure by two parts to one, she thought; in all social relations. Or am I the exception, the peculiar person? she continued, for the others seemed happy enough. Yes, she thought, looking straight ahead of her, and feeling again the stretched skin round her lips and eyes tight from the tiredness of sitting up late with a woman in childbirth, I'm the exception; hard; cold; in a groove already; merely a doctor.

Getting out of grooves is damned unpleasant, she thought, before the chill of death has set in, like bending frozen boots. . . . She bent her head to listen. To smile, to bend, to make believe you're amused when you're bored, how painful it is, she thought. All ways, every way's painful, she thought; staring at the Indian in the pink turban.

"Who's that fellow?" Patrick asked, nodding his head in his direction.

"One of Eleanor's Indians I expect," she said aloud, and thought, If only the merciful powers of darkness would obliterate the external exposure of the sensitive nerve and I could get up and. . . . There was a pause.

"But I mustn't keep you here, listening to my old stories," said Uncle Patrick. His weather-beaten nag with the broken knees had stopped.

"But tell me, does old Biddy still keep the little shop," she asked, "where we used to buy sweets?"

"Poor old body—" he began. He was off again. All her patients said that, she thought. Rest—rest—let me rest. How to deaden; how to cease to feel; that was the cry of the woman bearing children; to rest, to cease to be. In the Middle Ages, she thought, it was the cell; the monastery; now it's the laboratory; the professions; not to live; not to feel; to make money, always money, and in the end, when I'm old and worn like a horse, no, it's a cow —for part of old Patrick's story had imposed itself upon her mind: ". . . for there's no sale for the beasts at all," he was saying, "no sale at all. Ah, there's Julia Cromarty—" he exclaimed, and waved his hand, his large loose-jointed hand, at a charming compatriot.

She was left sitting alone on the sofa. For her uncle rose and went off with both hands outstretched to greet the bird-like old woman who had come in chattering.

She was left alone. She was glad to be alone. She had no wish to talk. But next moment somebody stood beside her. It was Martin. He sat down beside her. She changed her attitude completely.

"Hullo, Martin!" she greeted him cordially.

"Done your duty by the old mare, Peggy?" he said. He referred to the stories that old Patrick always told them.

"Did I look very glum?" she asked.

"Well," he said, glancing at her, "not exactly enraptured."

"One knows the end of his stories by now," she excused herself, looking at Martin. He had taken to brushing his hair up like a waiter's. He never looked her fully in the face. He never felt entirely at his ease with her. She was his doctor; she knew that he dreaded cancer. She must try to distract him from thinking, Does she see any symptoms?

"I was wondering how they came to marry," she said. "Were they in love?" She spoke at random to distract him.

"Of course he was in love," he said. He looked at Delia. She was standing by the fireplace talking to the Indian. She was still a very handsome woman, with her presence, with her gestures.

"We were all in love," he said, glancing sideways at Peggy. The younger generation were so serious.

"Oh, of course," she said, smiling. She liked his eternal pursuit of one love after another love—his gallant clutch upon the flying tail, the slippery tail of youth—even he, even now.

"But you," he said, stretching his feet out, hitching up his trousers, "your generation I mean—you miss a great deal . . . you miss a great deal," he repeated. She waited.

"Loving only your own sex," he added.

He liked to assert his own youth in that way, she thought; to say things that he thought up to date.

"I'm not that generation," she said.

"Well, well, well," he chuckled, shrugging his shoulder and glancing at her sideways. He knew very little about her private life. But she looked serious; she looked tired. She works too hard, he thought.

"I'm getting on," said Peggy. "Getting into a groove. So Eleanor told me tonight."

Or was it she, on the other hand, who had told Eleanor she was "suppressed"? One or the other.

"Eleanor's a gay old dog," he said. "Look!" He pointed.

There she was, talking to the Indian in her red cloak.

"Just back from India," he added. "A present from Bengal, eh?" he said, referring to the cloak.

"And next year she's off to China," said Peggy.

"But Delia—" she asked; Delia was passing them. "Was she in

love?" (What you in your generation called "in love," she added to herself.)

He wagged his head from side to side and pursed his lips. He always liked his little joke, she remembered.

"I don't know—I don't know about Delia," he said. "There was the cause, you know—what she called in those days The Cause." He screwed his face up. "Ireland, you know. Parnell. Ever heard of a man called Parnell?" he asked.

"Yes," said Peggy.

"And Edward?" she added. He had come in; he looked very distinguished, too, in his elaborate, if conscious simplicity.

"Edward—yes," said Martin. "Edward was in love. Surely you know that old story—Edward and Kitty?"

"The one who married—what was his name?—Lasswade?" Peggy murmured as Edward passed them.

"Yes, she married the other man—Lasswade. But he was in love—he was very much in love," Martin murmured. "But you," he gave her a quick little glance. There was something in her that chilled him. "Of course, you have your profession," he added. He looked at the ground. He was thinking of his dread of cancer, she supposed. He was afraid that she had noted some symptom.

"Oh, doctors are great humbugs," she threw out at random.

"Why? People live longer than they used, don't they?" he said. "They don't die so painfully anyhow," he added.

"We've learnt a few little tricks," she conceded. He stared ahead of him with a look that moved her pity.

"You'll live to be eighty—if you want to live to be eighty," she said. He looked at her.

"Of course I'm all in favour of living to be eighty!" he exclaimed. "I want to go to America. I want to see their buildings. I'm on that side, you see. I enjoy life." He did, enormously.

He must be over sixty himself, she supposed. But he was wonderfully got up; as sprig and spruce as a man of forty, with his canary-coloured lady in Kensington.

"I don't know," she said aloud.

"Come, Peggy, come," he said. "Don't tell me you don't enjoy—here's Rose."

Rose came up. She had grown very stout.

"Don't you want to be eighty?" he said to her. He had to say it twice over. She was deaf.

"I do. Of course I do!" she said when she understood him. She faced them. She made an odd angle with her head thrown back, Peggy thought, as if she were a military man.

"Of course I do," she said, sitting down abruptly on the sofa beside them.

"Ah, but then—" Peggy began. She paused. Rose was deaf, she remembered. She had to shout. "People hadn't made such fools of themselves in your day," she shouted. But she doubted if Rose heard.

"I want to see what's going to happen," said Rose. "We live in a very interesting world," she added.

"Nonsense," Martin teased her. "You want to live," he bawled in her ear, "because you enjoy living."

"And I'm not ashamed of it," she said. "I like my kind— on the whole."

"What you like is fighting them," he bawled.

"D'you think you can get a rise out of me at this time o' day?" she said, tapping him on the arm.

Now they'll talk about being children; climbing trees in the back garden, thought Peggy, and how they shot somebody's cats. Each person had a certain line laid down in their minds, she thought, and along it came the same old sayings. One's mind must be crisscrossed like the palm of one's hand, she thought, looking at the palm of her hand.

"She always was a spitfire," said Martin, turning to Peggy.

"And they always put the blame on me," Rose said. *"He* had the school-room. Where was I to sit? 'Oh, run away and play in the nursery!'" she waved her hand.

"And so she went into the bathroom and cut her wrist with a

knife," Martin jeered.

"No, that was Erridge: that was about the microscope," she corrected him.

It's like a kitten catching its tail, Peggy thought; round and round they go in a circle. But it's what they enjoy, she thought; it's what they come to parties for. Martin went on teasing Rose.

"And where's your red ribbon?" he was asking.

Some decoration had been given her, Peggy remembered, for her work in the war.

"Aren't we worthy to see you in your war paint?" he teased her.

"This fellow's jealous," she said, turning to Peggy again. "He's never done a stroke of work in his life."

"I work—I work," Martin insisted. "I sit in an office all day long—"

"Doing what?" said Rose.

Then they became suddenly silent. That turn was over—the old-brother-and-sister turn. Now they could only go back and repeat the same thing over again.

"Look here," said Martin, "we must go and do our duty." He rose. They parted.

"Doing what?" Peggy repeated, as she crossed the room. "Doing what?" she repeated. She was feeling reckless; nothing that she did mattered. She walked to the window and twitched the curtain apart. There were the stars pricked in little holes in the blue-black sky. There was a row of chimney-pots against the sky. Then the stars. Inscrutable, eternal, indifferent—those were the words; the right words. But I don't feel it, she said, looking at the stars. So why pretend to? What they're really like, she thought, screwing up her eyes to look at them, is little bits of frosty steel. And the moon—there it was—is a polished dish-cover. But she felt nothing, even when she had reduced moon and stars to that. Then she turned and found herself face to face with a young man she thought she knew but could not put a name to.

He had a fine brow, but a receding chin and he was pale, pasty.

"How-d'you-do?" she said. Was his name Leacock or Laycock?

"Last time we met," she said, "was at the races." She connected him, incongruously, with a Cornish field, stone walls, farmers and rough ponies jumping.

"No, that's Paul," he said. "My brother Paul." He was tart about it. What did he do, then, that made him superior in his own esteem to Paul?

"You live in London?" she said.

He nodded.

"You write?" she hazarded. But why, because he was a writer—she remembered now seeing his name in the papers— throw your head back when you say "Yes"? She preferred Paul; he looked healthy; this one had a queer face; knit up; nerve-drawn; fixed.

"Poetry?" she said.

"Yes." But why bite off that word as if it were a cherry on the end of a stalk? she thought. There was nobody coming; they were bound to sit down side by side, on chairs by the wall.

"How do you manage, if you're in an office?" she said. Apparently in his spare time.

"My uncle," he began. ". . . You've met him?"

Yes, a nice commonplace man; he had been very kind to her about a passport once. This boy, of course, though she only half listened, sneered at him. Then why go into his office? she asked herself. My people, he was saying . . . hunted. Her attention wandered. She had heard it all before. I, I, I—he went on. It was like a vulture's beak pecking, or a vacuum-cleaner sucking, or a telephone bell ringing. I, I, I. But he couldn't help it, not with that nerve-drawn egotist's face, she thought, glancing at him. He could not free himself, could not detach himself. He was bound on the wheel with tight iron hoops. He had to expose, had to exhibit. But why let him? she thought, as he went on talking. For what do I care about his "I, I, I"? Or his poetry? Let me shake him off then, she said to herself, feeling like a person whose blood has been sucked, leaving all the nerve-centres pale. She paused. He noted her lack of sympathy. He thought her stupid, she supposed.

"I'm tired," she apologised. "I've been up all night," she explained. "I'm a doctor—"

The fire went out of his face when she said "I." That's done it—now he'll go, she thought. He can't be "you"—he must be "I." She smiled. For up he got and off he went.

She turned round and stood at the window. Poor little wretch, she thought; atrophied, withered; cold as steel; hard as steel; bald as steel. And I too, she thought, looking at the sky. The stars seemed pricked haphazard in the sky, except that there, to the right over the chimney-pots, hung that phantom wheel-barrow—what did they call it? The name escaped her. I will count them, she thought, returning to her notebook, and had begun one, two, three, four . . . when a voice exclaimed behind her: "Peggy! Aren't your ears tingling?" She turned. It was Delia of course, with her genial ways, her imitation Irish flattery: "—because they ought to be," said Delia, laying a hand on her shoulder, "considering what *he's* been saying"—she pointed to a grey-haired man—"what praises he's been singing of you."

Peggy looked where she pointed. There was her teacher over there, her master. Yes, she knew he thought her clever. She was, she supposed. They all said so. Very clever.

"He's been telling me—" Delia began. But she broke off.

"Just help me open this window," she said. "It's getting hot."

"Let me," said Peggy. She gave the window a jerk, but it stuck, for it was old and the frames did not fit.

"Here, Peggy," said somebody, coming behind her. It was her father. His hand was on the window, his hand with the scar. He pushed; the window went up.

"Thanks, Morris, that's better," said Delia. "I was telling Peggy her ears ought to be tingling," she began again: "'My most brilliant pupil!' That's what *he* said," Delia went on. "I assure you I felt quite proud. 'But she's my niece,' I said. He hadn't known it—"

There, said Peggy, that's pleasure. The nerve down her spine seemed to tingle as the praise reached her father. Each emotion touched a different nerve. A sneer rasped the thigh; pleasure thrilled the spine; and also affected the sight. The stars had softened; they quivered. Her father brushed her shoulder as he dropped his hand; but neither of them spoke.

"D'you want it open at the bottom too?" he said.

"No, that'll do," said Delia. "The room's getting hot," she said. "People are beginning to come. They must use the rooms downstairs," she said. "But who's that out there?" she pointed. Opposite the house against the railings of the square was a group in evening dress.

"I think I recognise one of them," said Morris, looking out. "That's North, isn't it?"

"Yes, that's North," said Peggy, looking out.

"Then why don't they come in?" said Delia, tapping on the window.

"But you must come and see it for yourselves," North was saying. They had asked him to describe Africa. He had said that there were mountains and plains; it was silent, he had said, and birds sang. He stopped; it was difficult to describe a place to people who had not seen it. Then curtains in the house opposite parted, and three heads appeared at the window. They looked at the heads outlined on the window opposite them. They were standing with their backs to the railings of the square. The trees hung dark showers of leaves over them. The trees had become part of the sky. Now and then they seemed to shift and shuffle slightly as a breeze went through them. A star shone among the leaves. It was silent too; the murmur of the traffic was run together into one far hum. A cat slunk past; for a second they saw the luminous green of the eyes; then it was extinguished. The cat crossed the lighted space and vanished. Someone tapped again on the window and cried, "Come in!"

"Come!" said Renny, and threw his cigar into the bushes behind him. "Come, we must."

They went upstairs, past the doors of offices, past long windows that opened on to back gardens that lay behind houses. Trees in full leaf stretched their branches across at different levels; the leaves, here bright green in the artificial light, here dark in shadow, moved up and down in the little breeze. Then they came to the private part of the house, where the red carpet was laid; and a roar of voices sounded from behind a door as if a flock of sheep were penned there. Then music, a dance, swung out.

"Now," said Maggie, pausing for a moment, outside the door. She gave their names to the servant.

"And you, sir?" said the maid to North, who hung behind.

"Captain Pargiter," said North, touching his tie.

"And Captain Pargiter!" the maid called out.

Delia was upon them instantly. "And Captain Pargiter!" she exclaimed, as she came hurrying across the room. "How very nice of you to come!" she exclaimed. She took their hands at random, here a left hand, there a right hand, in her left hand, in her right hand.

"I thought it was you," she exclaimed, "standing in the square. I thought I could recognise Renny—but I wasn't sure about North. Captain Pargiter!" she wrung his hand, "you're quite a stranger—but a very welcome one! Now who d'you know? Who don't you know?"

She glanced round, twitching her shawl rather nervously.

"Let me see, there's all your uncles and aunts; and your cousins; and your sons and daughters—yes, Maggie, I saw your lovely couple not long ago. They're somewhere. . . . Only all the generations in our family are so mixed; cousins and aunts, uncles and brothers—but perhaps it's a good thing."

She stopped rather suddenly as if she had used up that vein. She twitched her shawl.

"They're going to dance," she said, pointing at the young man who was putting another record on the gramophone. "It's all right for dancing," she added, referring to the gramophone. "Not for music." She became simple for a moment. "I can't bear music on the gramophone. But dance music—that's another thing. And young people—don't you find that?—must dance. It's right they should. Dance or not—just as you like." She waved her hand.

"Yes, just as you like," her husband echoed her. He stood beside her, dangling his hands in front of him like a bear on which coats are hung in a hotel.

"Just as you like," he repeated, shaking his paws.

"Help me to move the tables, North," said Delia. "If they're going to dance, they'll want everything out of the way—and the rugs rolled up." She pushed a table out of the way. Then she ran across the room to whisk a chair against the wall.

Now one of the vases was upset, and a stream of water flowed across the carpet.

"Don't mind it, don't mind it—it doesn't matter at all!" Delia exclaimed, assuming the manner of a harum-scarum Irish hostess. But North stooped and swabbed up the water.

"And what are you going to do with that pocket handkerchief?" Eleanor asked him; she had joined them in her flowing red cloak.

"Hang it on a chair to dry," said North, walking off.

"And you, Sally?" said Eleanor, drawing back against the wall since they were going to dance. "Going to dance?" she asked, sitting down.

"I?" said Sara, yawning. "I want to sleep." She sank down on a cushion beside Eleanor.

"But you don't come to parties," Eleanor laughed, looking down at her, "to sleep, do you?" Again she saw the little picture she had seen at the end of the telephone. But she could not see her face; only the top of her head.

"Dining with you, wasn't he?" she said, as North passed them with his handkerchief.

"And what did you talk about?" she asked. She saw her, sitting on the edge of a chair, swinging her foot up and down, with a smudge on her nose.

"Talk about?" said Sara. "You, Eleanor." People were passing them all the time; they were brushing against their knees; they were beginning to dance. It made one feel a little dizzy, Eleanor thought, sinking back in her chair.

"Me?" she said. "What about me?"

"Your life," said Sara.

"My life?" Eleanor repeated. Couples began to twist and turn slowly past them. It was a fox-trot that they were dancing, she supposed.

My life, she said to herself. That was odd, it was the second time that evening that somebody had talked about her life. And I haven't got one, she thought. Oughtn't a life to be something you could handle and produce?—a life of seventy odd years. But I've only the present moment, she thought. Here she was alive, now, listening to the fox-trot. Then she looked round. There was Morris; Rose; Edward with his head thrown back talking to a man she did not know. I'm the only person here, she thought, who remembers how he sat on the edge of my bed that night, crying—the night Kitty's engagement was announced. Yes, things came back to her. A long strip of life lay behind her. Edward crying, Mrs. Levy talking; snow falling; a sunflower with a crack in it; the yellow omnibus trotting along the Bayswater Road. And I thought to myself, I'm the youngest person in this omnibus; now I'm the oldest. . . . Millions of things came back to her. Atoms danced apart and massed themselves. But how did they compose what people called a life? She clenched her hands and felt the hard little coins she was holding. Perhaps there's "I" at the middle of it, she thought; a knot; a centre; and again she saw herself sitting at her table drawing on the blotting-paper, digging little holes from which spokes radiated. Out and out they went; thing followed thing, scene obliterated scene. And then they say, she thought, "We've been talking about you!"

"My life . . ." she said aloud, but half to herself.

"Yes?" said Sara, looking up.

Eleanor stopped. She had forgotten her. But there was somebody listening. Then she must put her thoughts into order; then she must find words. But no, she thought, I can't find words; I can't tell anybody.

"Isn't that Nicholas?" she said, looking at a rather large man who stood in the doorway.

"Where?" said Sara. But she looked in the wrong direction. He had disappeared. Perhaps she had been mistaken. My life's been other people's lives, Eleanor thought—my father's; Morris's; my friends' lives; Nicholas's. . . . Fragments of a conversation with him came back to her. Either I'd been lunching with him or dining with him, she thought. It was in a restaurant. There was a parrot with a pink feather in a cage on the counter. And they had sat there talking—it was after the war—about the future; about education. And he wouldn't let me pay for the wine, she suddenly remembered, though it was I who ordered it. . . .

Here somebody stopped in front of her. She looked up. "Just as I was thinking of you!" she exclaimed.

It was Nicholas.

"Good-evening, madame!" he said, bending over her in his foreign way.

"Just as I was thinking of you!" she repeated. Indeed it was like a part of her, a sunk part of her, coming to the surface. "Come and sit beside me," she said, and pulled up a chair.

"D'you know who that chap is, sitting by my aunt?" said North to the girl he was dancing with. She looked round; but vaguely.

"I don't know your aunt," she said. "I don't know anybody here."

The dance was over and they began walking towards the door.

"I don't even know my hostess," she said. "I wish you'd point her out to me."

"There—over there," he said. He pointed to Delia in her black dress with the gold spangles.

"Oh, that," she said, looking at her. "That's my hostess, is it?" He had not caught the girl's name, and she knew none of them either. He was glad of it. It made him seem different to himself—it stimulated him. He shepherded her towards the door. He wanted to avoid his relations. In particular he wanted to avoid his sister Peggy; but there she was, standing alone by the door. He looked the other way; he conveyed his partner out of the door. There must be a garden or a roof somewhere, he thought, where they could sit, alone. She was extraordinarily pretty and young.

"Come along," he said, "downstairs."

"And what were you thinking about me?" said Nicholas, sitting down beside Eleanor.

She smiled. There he was in his rather ill-assorted dress-clothes, with the seal engraved with the arms of his mother the princess, and his swarthy wrinkled face that always made her think of some loose-skinned, furry animal, savage to others but kind to herself. But what was she thinking about him? She was thinking of him in the lump; she could not break off little fragments. The restaurant had been smoky she remembered.

"How we dined together once in Soho," she said. ". . . d'you remember?"

"All the evenings with you I remember, Eleanor," he said. But his glance was a little vague. His attention was distracted. He was looking at a lady who had just come in; a well-dressed lady, who stood with her back to the bookcase equipped for every emergency. If I can't describe my own life, Eleanor thought, how can I describe him? For what he was she did not know; only that it gave her pleasure when he came in; relieved her of the need of thinking; and gave her mind a little jog. He was looking at the lady. She seemed upheld by their gaze; vibrating under it. And suddenly it seemed to Eleanor that it had all happened before. So a girl had come in that night in the restaurant: had stood, vibrating, in the door. She knew exactly what he was going to say. He had said it before, in the restaurant. He is going to say, She is like a ball on the top of a fishmonger's fountain. As she thought it, he said it. Does everything then come over again a little differently? she thought. If so, is there a pattern; a theme, recurring, like music; half remembered, half foreseen? . . . a gigantic pattern, momentarily perceptible? The thought gave her extreme pleasure: that there was a pattern. But who makes it? Who thinks it? Her mind slipped. She could not finish her thought.

"Nicholas . . ." she said. She wanted him to finish it; to take her thought and carry it out into the open unbroken; to make it whole, beautiful, entire.

"Tell me, Nicholas . . ." she began; but she had no notion how she was going to finish her sentence, or what it was that she wanted to ask him. He was talking to Sara. She listened. He was laughing at her. He was pointing at her feet.

". . . coming to a party," he was saying, "with one stocking that is white, and one stocking that is blue."

"The Queen of England asked me to tea;" Sara hummed in time to the music; "and which shall it be; the gold or the rose; for all are in holes, my stockings, said she." This is their love-making, Eleanor thought, half listening to their laughter, to their bickering. Another inch of the pattern, she thought, still using her half-formulated idea to stamp the immediate scene. And if this love-making differs from the old, still it has its charm; it was "love," different from the old love, perhaps, but worse, was it? Anyhow, she thought, they are aware of each other; they live in each other; what else is love, she asked, listening to their laughter.

". . . Can you never act for yourself?" he was saying. "Can you never even choose stockings for yourself?"

"Never! Never!" Sara was laughing.

". . . Because you have no life of your own," he said. "She lives in dreams," he added, turning to Eleanor, "alone."

"The professor preaching his little sermon," Sara sneered, laying her hand on his knee.

"Sara singing her little song," Nicholas laughed, pressing her hand.

But they are very happy, Eleanor thought: they laugh at each other.

"Tell me, Nicholas . . ." she began again. But another dance was beginning. Couples came flocking back into the room. Slowly, intently, with serious faces, as if they were taking part in some mystic rite which gave them immunity from other feelings, the dancers began circling past them, brushing against their knees, almost treading on their toes. And then someone stopped in front of them.

"Oh, here's North," said Eleanor, looking up.

"North!" Nicholas exclaimed. "North! We met this evening," he stretched out his hand to North, "—at Eleanor's."

"We did," said North warmly. Nicholas crushed his fingers; he felt them separate again when the hand was removed. It was effusive; but he liked it. He was feeling effusive himself. His eyes shone. He had lost his puzzled look completely. His adventure had turned out well. The girl had written her name in his pocket-book. "Come and see me tomorrow at six," she had said.

"Good-evening again, Eleanor," he said, bowing over her hand. "You're looking very young. You're looking extraordinarily handsome. I like you in those clothes," he said, looking at her Indian cloak.

"The same to you, North," she said. She looked up at him. She thought she had never seen him look so handsome, so vigorous.

"Aren't you going to dance?" she asked. The music was in full swing.

"Not unless Sally will honour me," he said, bowing to her with exaggerated courtesy. What has happened to him? Eleanor thought. He looks so handsome, so happy. Sally rose. She gave her hand to Nicholas.

"I will dance with you," she said. They stood for a moment

waiting; and then they circled away.

"What an odd-looking couple!" North exclaimed. He screwed his face up into a grin as he watched them. "They don't know how to dance!" he added. He sat down by Eleanor in the chair that Nicholas had left empty.

"Why don't they marry?" he asked.

"Why should they?" she said.

"Oh, everybody ought to marry," he said. "And I like him, though he's a bit of a—shall we say 'bounder?'" he suggested, as he watched them circling rather awkwardly in and out.

"'Bounder'?" Eleanor echoed him.

"Oh it's his fob, you mean," she added, looking at the gold seal which swung up and down as Nicholas danced.

"No, not a bounder," she said aloud. "He's—"

But North was not attending. He was looking at a couple at the further end of the room. They were standing by the fireplace. Both were young; both were silent; they seemed held still in that position by some powerful emotion. As he looked at them, some emotion about himself, about his own life, came over him, and he arranged another background for them or for himself—not the mantelpiece and the bookcase, but cataracts roaring, clouds racing, and they stood on a cliff above a torrent. . . .

"Marriage isn't for everyone," Eleanor interrupted.

He started. "No. Of course not," he agreed. He looked at her. She had never married. Why not? he wondered. Sacrificed to the family, he supposed—old Grandpapa without any fingers. Then some memory came back to him of a terrace, a cigar and William Whatney. Was not that her tragedy, that she had loved him? He looked at her with affection. He felt fond of everyone at the moment.

"What luck to find you alone, Nell!" he said, laying his hand on her knee.

She was touched; the feel of his hand on her knee pleased her.

"Dear North!" she exclaimed. She felt his excitement through her dress; he was like a dog on a leash; straining forward with all his nerves erect, she felt, as he laid his hand on her knee.

"But don't marry the wrong woman!" she said.

"I?" he asked. "What makes you say that?" Had she seen him, he wondered, shepherding the girl downstairs?

"Tell me—" she began. She wanted to ask him, coolly and sensibly, what his plans were, now that they were alone; but as she spoke she saw his face change; an exaggerated expression of horror came over it.

"Milly!" he muttered. "Damn her!"

Eleanor glanced quickly over her shoulder. Her sister Milly, voluminous in draperies proper to her sex and class, was coming towards them. She had grown very stout. In order to disguise her figure, veils with beads on them hung down over her arms. They were so fat that they reminded North of asparagus; pale asparagus tapering to a point.

"Oh, Eleanor!" she exclaimed. For she still kept relics of a younger sister's doglike devotion.

"Oh, Milly!" said Eleanor, but not so cordially.

"How nice to see you, Eleanor!" said Milly, with her little old-woman's chuckle; yet there was something deferential in her manner. "And you too, North!"

She gave him her fat little hand. He noticed how the rings were sunk in her fingers, as if the flesh had grown over them. Flesh grown over diamonds disgusted him.

"How very nice that you're back again!" she said, settling slowly down into her chair. Everything, he felt, became dulled. She cast a net over them; she made them all feel one family; he had to think of their relations in common; but it was an unreal feeling.

"Yes, we're staying with Connie," she said; they had come up for a cricket match.

He sunk his head. He looked at his shoes.

"And I've not heard a word about your travels, Nell," she went on. They fall and fall, and cover all, he went on, as he listened to the damp falling patter of his aunt's little questions. But he was in such a superfluity of high spirits that he could still make her words jingle. Did the tarantulas bite, she was asking him, and were the stars bright? And where shall I spend tomorrow night? he added, for the card in his waistcoat pocket rayed out of its own accord without regard for the context scenes which obliterated the present moment. They were staying with Connie, she went on, who was expecting Jimmy, who was home from Uganda . . . his mind slipped a few words, for he was seeing a garden, a room, and the next word he heard was "adenoids"— which is a good word, he said to himself, separating it from its context; wasp-waisted; pinched in the middle; with a hard, shining, metallic abdomen, useful to describe the appearance of an insect—but here a vast bulk approached; chiefly white waistcoat, lined with black; and Hugh Gibbs stood over them. North sprang up to offer him his chair.

"My dear boy, you don't expect me to sit on *that?*" said Hugh, deriding the rather spindly seat that North offered him.

"You must find me something—" he looked about him, holding his hands to the sides of his white waistcoat, "more substantial."

North pulled a stuffed seat towards him. He lowered himself cautiously.

"Chew, chew, chew," he said as he sat down.

And Milly said, "Tut-tut-tut," North observed.

That was what it came to—thirty years of being husband and wife—tut-tut-tut—and chew-chew-chew. It sounded like the half-inarticulate munchings of animals in a stall. Tut-tut-tut, and chew-chew-chew—as they trod out the soft steamy straw in the stable; as they wallowed in the primeval swamp, prolific, profuse, half-conscious, he thought; listening vaguely to the good-humoured patter, which suddenly fastened itself upon him.

"What d'you weigh, North?" his uncle was asking, sizing him

up. He looked him up and down as if he were a horse.

"We must get you to fix a date," Milly added, "when the boys are home."

They were inviting him to stay with them at the Towers in September for cub-hunting. The men shot, and the women—he looked at his aunt as if she might be breaking into young even there, on that chair—the women broke off into innumerable babies. And those babies had other babies; and the other babies had—adenoids. The word recurred; but it now suggested nothing. He was sinking; he was falling under their weight; the name in his pocket even was fading. Could nothing be done about it? he asked himself. Nothing short of revolution, he thought. The idea of dynamite, exploding dumps of heavy earth, shooting earth up in a tree-shaped cloud, came to his mind, from the War. But that's all poppy-cock, he thought; war's poppy-cock, poppy-cock. Sara's word "poppy-cock" returned. So what remains? Peggy caught his eye, where she stood talking to an unknown man. You doctors, he thought, you scientists, why don't you drop a little crystal into a tumbler, something starred and sharp, and make them swallow it? Common sense; reason; starred and sharp. But would they swallow it? He looked at Hugh. He had a way of blowing his cheeks in and out, as he said tut-tut-tut and chew-chew-chew. Would you swallow it? he said silently to Hugh.

Hugh turned to him again.

"And I hope you're going to stay in England now, North," he said, "though I dare say it's a fine life out there?"

And so they turned to Africa and the paucity of jobs. His exhilaration was oozing. The card no longer rayed out pictures. The damp leaves were falling. They fall and fall and cover all, he murmured to himself and looked at his aunt, colourless save for a brown stain on her forehead; and her hair colourless save for a stain like the yolk of egg on it. All over he suspected she must be soft and discoloured like a pear that has gone sleepy. And Hugh himself—his great hand was on his knee—was bound round with raw beef-steak. He caught Eleanor's eye. There was a strained look in it.

"Yes, how they've spoilt it," she was saying.

But the resonance had gone out of her voice.

"Brand-new villas everywhere," she was saying. She had been down in Dorsetshire apparently.

"Little red villas all along the road," she went on.

"Yes, that's what strikes me," he said, rousing himself to help her, "how you've spoilt England while I've been away."

"But you won't find many changes in our part of the world, North," said Hugh. He spoke with pride.

"No. But then we're lucky," said Milly. "We have several large estates. We're very lucky," she repeated. "Except for Mr Phipps," she added. She gave a tart little laugh.

North woke up. She meant that, he thought. She spoke with an acerbity that made her real. Not only did she become real, but the village, the great house, the little house, the church and the circle of old trees also appeared before him in complete reality. He would stay with them.

"That's our parson," Hugh explained. "Quite a good chap in his way; but high—very high. Candles—that sort of thing."

"And his wife . . ." Milly began.

Here Eleanor sighed. North looked at her. She was dropping off to sleep. A glazed look, a fixed expression, had come over her face. She looked terribly like Milly for a moment; sleep brought out the family likeness. Then she opened her eyes wide; by an effort of will she kept them open. But obviously she saw nothing.

"You must come down and see what you make of us," Hugh said. "What about the first week in September, eh?" He swayed from side to side as if his benevolence rolled about in him. He was like an old elephant who may be going to kneel. And if he does kneel, how will he ever get up again, North asked himself. And if Eleanor falls sound asleep and snores, what am I going to do, left sitting here between the knees of the elephant?

He looked round for an excuse to go.

There was Maggie coming along, not looking where she was going. They saw her. He felt a strong desire to cry out, "Take care! Take care!" for she was in the danger zone. The long white tentacles that amorphous bodies leave floating so that they can catch their food, would suck her in. Yes, they saw her: she was lost.

"Here's Maggie!" Milly exclaimed, looking up.

"Haven't seen you for an age!" said Hugh, trying to heave himself up.

She had to stop; to put her hand into that shapeless paw. Using the last ounce of energy that remained to him, from the address in his waistcoat pocket, North rose. He would carry her off. He would save her from the contamination of family life.

But she ignored him. She stood there, answering their greetings with perfect composure as if using an outfit provided for emergencies. Oh Lord, North said to himself, she's as bad as they are. She was glazed; insincere. They were talking about *her* children now.

"Yes. That's the baby," she was saying, pointing to a boy who was dancing with a girl.

"And your daughter, Maggie?" Milly asked, looking round.

North fidgeted. This is the conspiracy, he said to himself; this is the steam roller that smooths, obliterates; rounds into identity; rolls into balls. He listened. Jimmy was in Uganda; Lily was in Leicestershire; *my* boy—*my* girl . . . they were saying. But they're not interested in other people's children, he observed. Only in their own; their own property; their own flesh and blood, which they would protect with the unsheathed claws of the primeval swamp, he thought, looking at Milly's fat little paws, even Maggie, even she. For she too was talking about my boy, my girl. How then can we be civilised, he asked himself?

Eleanor snored. She was nodding off, shamelessly, helplessly. There was an obscenity in unconsciousness, he thought. Her mouth was open; her head was on one side.

But now it was his turn. Silence gaped. One has to egg it on, he thought; somebody has to say something, or human society would cease. Hugh would cease; Milly would cease; and he was about to apply himself to find something to say, something with which to feed the immense vacancy of that primeval maw, when Delia, either from the erratic desire of a hostess always to interrupt, or divinely inspired by human charity—which he could not say—came beckoning.

"The Ludbys!" she exclaimed. "The Ludbys!"

"Oh where? The dear Ludbys!" said Milly, and up they heaved and off they went, for the Ludbys, it appeared, seldom left Northumberland.

"Well, Maggie?" said North, turning to her—but here Eleanor made a little click at the back of her throat. Her head pitched forward. Sleep, now that she slept soundly, had given her dignity. She looked peaceful, far from them, rapt in the calm which sometimes gives the sleeper the look of the dead. They sat silent, for a moment, alone together, in private.

"Why—why—why—" he said at last, making a gesture as if he were plucking tufts of grass from the carpet.

"Why?" Maggie asked. "Why what?"

"The Gibbses," he murmured. He jerked his head at them, where they stood talking by the fireplace. Gross, obese, shapeless, they looked to him like a parody, a travesty, an excrescence that had overgrown the form within, the fire within.

"What's wrong?" he asked. She looked too. But she said nothing. Couples came dancing slowly past them. A girl stopped, and her gesture as she raised her hand, unconsciously, had the seriousness of the very young anticipating life in its goodness which touched him.

"Why—?" he jerked his thumb in the direction of the young, "when they're so lovely—"

She too looked at the girl, who was fastening a flower that

had come undone in the front of her frock. She smiled. She said nothing. Then half consciously she echoed his question without a meaning in her echo, "Why?"

He was dashed for a moment. It seemed to him that she refused to help him. And he wanted her to help him. Why should she not take the weight off his shoulders and give him what he longed for—assurance, certainty? Because she too was deformed like the rest of them? He looked down at her hands. They were strong hands; fine hands; but if it were a question, he thought, watching the fingers curl slightly, of "my" children, of "my" possessions, it would be one rip down the belly; or teeth in the soft fur of the throat. We cannot help each other, he thought, we are all deformed. Yet, disagreeable as it was to him to remove her from the eminence upon which he placed her, perhaps she was right, he thought, and we who make idols of other people, who endow this man, that woman, with power to lead us, only add to the deformity, and stoop ourselves.

"I'm going to stay with them," he said aloud.

"At the Towers?" she asked.

"Yes," he said. "For cubbing in September."

She was not listening. Her eyes were on him. She was getting him into relation with something else he felt. It made him uneasy. She was looking at him as if he were not himself but somebody else. He felt again the discomfort that he had felt when Sally described him on the telephone.

"I know," he said, stiffening the muscles of his face, "I'm like the picture of a Frenchman holding his hat."

"Holding his hat?" she asked.

"And getting fat," he added.

". . . Holding a hat . . . who's holding a hat?" said Eleanor, opening her eyes.

She glanced about her in bewilderment. Since her last recollection, and it seemed only a second ago, was of Milly talking of candles in a church, something must have happened.

Milly and Hugh had been there; but they were gone. There had been a gap—a gap filled with the golden light of lolling candles, and some sensation which she could not name.

She woke up completely.

"What nonsense are you talking?" she said. "North's not holding a hat! And he's not fat," she added. "Not at all, not at all," she repeated, patting him affectionately on the knee.

She felt extraordinarily happy. Most sleep left some dream in one's mind—some scene or figure remained when one woke up. But this sleep, this momentary trance, in which the candles had lolled and lengthened themselves, had left her with nothing but a feeling; a feeling, not a dream.

"He's not holding a hat," she repeated.

They both laughed at her.

"You've been dreaming, Eleanor," said Maggie.

"Have I?" she said. A deep gulf had been cut in the talk, it was true. She could not remember what they had been saying. There was Maggie; but Milly and Hugh had gone.

"Only a second's nap," she said. "But what are you going to do, North? What are your plans?" she said, speaking rather quickly.

"We musn't let him go back, Maggie," she said. "Not to that horrid farm."

She wished to appear extremely practical, partly to prove that she had not slept, partly to protect the extraordinary feeling of happiness that still remained with her. Covered up from observation it might survive, she felt.

"You've saved enough, haven't you?" she said aloud.

"Saved enough?" he said. Why, he wondered, did people who had been asleep always want to make out that they were extremely wide-awake? "Four or five thousand," he added at random.

"Well, that's enough," she insisted. "Five per cent; six per cent—" She tried to do the sum in her head. She appealed to Maggie for help. "Four or five thousand—how much would that be, Maggie? Enough to live on, wouldn't it?"

"Four or five thousand," repeated Maggie.

"At five or six per cent . . ." Eleanor put in. She could never do sums in her head at the best of times; but for some reason it seemed to her very important to bring things back to facts. She opened her bag, found a letter, and produced a stubby little pencil.

"There—work it out on that," she said. Maggie took the paper and drew a few lines with the pencil as if to test it. North glanced over her shoulder. Was she solving the problem before her—was she considering his life, his needs? No. She was drawing, apparently a caricature—he looked—of a big man opposite in a white waistcoat. It was a farce. It made him feel slightly ridiculous.

"Don't be so silly," he said.

"That's my brother," she said, nodding at the man in the white waistcoat. "He used to take us for rides on an elephant. . . ." She added a flourish to the waistcoat.

"And we're being very sensible," Eleanor protested.

"If you want to live in England, North—if you want—"

He cut her short.

"I don't know what I want," he said.

"Oh, I see!" she said. She laughed. Her feeling of happiness returned to her, her unreasonable exaltation. It seemed to her that they were all young, with the future before them. Nothing was fixed; nothing was known; life was open and free before them.

"Isn't that odd?" she exclaimed. "Isn't that queer? Isn't that why life's a perpetual—what shall I call it?—miracle? . . . I mean," she tried to explain, for he looked puzzled, "old age they say is like this; but it isn't. It's different; quite different. So when I was a child; so when I was a girl; it's been a perpetual discovery, my life. A miracle." She stopped. She was rambling on again. She felt rather light-headed, after her dream.

"There's Peggy!" she exclaimed, glad to attach herself to something solid. "Look at her! Reading a book!"

Peggy, marooned when the dance started, over by the bookcase, stood as close to it as she could. In order to cover her loneliness she took down a book. It was bound in green leather; and had, she noted as she turned it in her hands, little gilt stars tooled upon it. Which is all to the good, she thought, turning it over, because then it'll seem as if I were admiring the binding. . . . But I can't stand here admiring the binding, she thought. She opened it. He'll say what I'm thinking, she thought as she did so. Books opened at random always did.

"La médiocrité de l'univers m'étonne et me révolte" she read. That was it. Precisely. She read on. *". . . la petitesse de toutes choses m'emplit de dégoût . . ."* She lifted her eyes. They were treading on her toes. *". . . la pauvreté des êtres humains m'anéantit."* She shut the book and put it back on the shelf.

Precisely, she said.

She turned her watch on her wrist and looked at it surreptitiously. Time was getting on. An hour is sixty minutes, she said to herself; two hours are one hundred and twenty minutes. How many have I still to stay here? Could she go yet? She saw Eleanor beckoning. She put the book back on the shelf. She went towards them.

"Come, Peggy, come and talk to us," Eleanor called out, beckoning.

"D'you know what time it is, Eleanor?" said Peggy, coming up to them. She pointed to her watch. "Don't you think it's time to be going?" she said.

"I'd forgotten the time," said Eleanor.

"But you'll be so tired tomorrow," Peggy protested, standing beside her.

"How like a doctor!" North twitted her. "Health, health, health!" he exclaimed. "But health's not an end in itself," he said, looking up at her.

She ignored him.

"D'you mean to stay to the end?" she said to Eleanor. "This'll go on all night." She looked at the twisting couples gyrating in time to the tune on the gramophone, as if some animal were dying in a slow but exquisite anguish.

"But we're enjoying ourselves," said Eleanor. "Come and enjoy yourself too."

She pointed to the floor at her side. Peggy let herself down onto the floor at her side. Give up brooding, thinking, analysing, Eleanor meant she knew. Enjoy the moment—but could one? she asked, pulling her skirts round her feet as she sat down. Eleanor bent over and tapped her on the shoulder.

"I want you to tell me," she said, drawing her into the conversation, since she looked so glum, "you're a doctor—you know these things—what do dreams mean?"

Peggy laughed. Another of Eleanor's questions. Does two and two make four—and what is the nature of the universe?

"I don't mean dreams exactly," Eleanor went on. "Feelings—feelings that come when one's asleep?"

"My dear Nell," said Peggy, glancing up at her, "how often have I told you? Doctors know very little about the body; absolutely nothing about the mind." She looked down again.

"I always said they were humbugs!" North exclaimed.

"What a pity!" said Eleanor. "I was hoping you'd be able to explain to me—" She was bending down. There was a flush on her cheek, Peggy noted; she was excited; but what was there to be excited about?

"Explain—what?" she asked.

"Oh, nothing," said Eleanor. Now I've snubbed her, Peggy thought.

She looked at her again. Her eyes were bright; her cheeks were flushed, or was it only the tan from her voyage to India? And a little vein stood out on her forehead. But what was there to be excited about? She leant back against the wall. From her seat on the floor she had a queer view of people's feet; feet pointing this way, feet pointing that way; patent leather pumps; satin slippers; silk stockings and socks. They were dancing rhythmically, insistently, to the tune of the fox-trot. And what about the cocktail and the tea, said he to me, said he to me—the tune seemed to repeat over and over again. And voices went on over her head. Odd little gusts of inconsecutive conversations reached her . . . down in Norfolk where my brother-in-law has a boat . . . Oh, a complete washout, yes I agree. . . . People talked nonsense at parties. And beside her Maggie was talking; North was talking; Eleanor was talking. Suddenly Eleanor swept her hand out.

"There's Renny!" she was saying. "Renny, whom I never see. Renny whom I love. . . . Come and talk to us, Renny." And a pair of pumps crossed Peggy's field of vision and stopped in front of her. He sat down beside Eleanor. She could just see the line of his profile; the big nose; the thin cheek. And what about the cocktails and the tea, said he to me, said he to me, the music ground out; the couples danced past. But the little group on the chairs above her were talking; they were laughing.

"I know you'll agree with me . . ." Eleanor was saying. Through her half-shut eyes Peggy could see Renny turn towards her. She saw his thin cheek; his big nose; his nails, she noticed, were very close cut.

"Depends what you were saying . . ." he said.

"What were we saying?" Eleanor pondered. She's forgotten already, Peggy suspected.

". . . That things have changed for the better," she heard Eleanor's voice.

"Since you were a girl?" That she thought was Maggie's voice.

Then a voice from a skirt with a pink bow on the hem interrupted. ". . . I don't know how it is but the heat doesn't affect me as much as it used to do. . . ." She looked up. There were fifteen pink bows on the dress, accurately stitched, and wasn't that Miriam Parrish's little saint-like, sheep-like head on top?

"What I mean is, we've changed in ourselves," Eleanor was saying. "We're happier—we're freer—"

What does she mean by "happiness," by "freedom"? Peggy

asked herself, lapsing against the wall again.

"Take Renny and Maggie," she heard Eleanor saying. And then she stopped. And then she went on again:

"D'you remember, Renny, the night of the raid? When I met Nicholas for the first time . . . when we sat in the cellar? . . . Going downstairs I said to myself, That's a happy marriage—" There was another pause. "I said to myself," she continued, and Peggy saw her hand laid on Renny's knee, "If I'd known Renny when I was young. . . ." She stopped. Does she mean she would have fallen in love with him? Peggy wondered. Again the music interrupted . . . said he to me, said he to me. . . .

"No, never . . ." she heard Eleanor say. "No, never. . . ." Was she saying she had never been in love, never wanted to marry? Peggy wondered. They were laughing.

"Why, you look like a girl of eighteen!" she heard North say.

"And I feel like one!" Eleanor exclaimed. But you'll be a wreck tomorrow morning Peggy thought, looking at her. She was flushed, the veins stood out on her forehead.

"I feel . . ." she stopped. She put her hand to her head: "as if I'd been in another world! So happy!" she exclaimed.

"Tosh, Eleanor, tosh," said Renny.

I thought he'd say that, Peggy said to herself with some queer satisfaction. She could see his profile as he sat on the other side of her aunt's knee. The French are logical; they are sensible, she thought. Still, she added, why not let Eleanor have her little flutter if she enjoys it?

"Tosh? What d'you mean by 'tosh'?" Eleanor was asking. She was leaning forward; she held her hand up as if she wanted him to speak.

"Always talking of the other world," he said. "Why not this one?"

"But I meant this world!" she said. "I meant, happy in this world—happy with living people." She waved her hand as if to embrace the miscellaneous company, the young, the old, the dancers, the talkers; Miriam with her pink bows, and the Indian in his turban. Peggy sank back against the wall. Happy in this world, she thought, happy with living people!

The music stopped. The young man who had been putting records on the gramophone had walked off. The couples broke apart and began to push their way through the door. They were going to eat perhaps; they were going to stream out into the back garden and sit on hard sooty chairs. The music which had been cutting grooves in her mind had ceased. There was a lull—a silence. Far away she heard the sounds of the London night; a horn hooted; a siren wailed on the river. The far-away sounds, the suggestion they brought in of other worlds, indifferent to this world, of people toiling, grinding, in the heart of darkness, in the depths of night, made her say over Eleanor's words, Happy in this world, happy with living people. But how can one be "happy"? she asked herself, in a world bursting with misery. On every placard at every street corner was Death; or worse— tyranny; brutality; torture; the fall of civilisation; the end of freedom. We here, she thought, are only sheltering under a leaf, which will be destroyed. And then Eleanor says the world is better, because two people out of all those millions are "happy." Her eyes had fixed themselves on the floor; it was empty now save for a wisp of muslin torn from some skirt. But why do I notice everything? she thought. She shifted her position. Why must I think? She did not want to think. She wished that there were blinds like those in railway carriages that came down over the light and hooded the mind. The blue blind that one pulls down on a night journey, she thought. Thinking was torment; why not give up thinking, and drift and dream? But the misery of the world, she thought, forces me to think. Or was that a pose? Was she not seeing herself in the becoming attitude of one who points to his bleeding heart? to whom the miseries of the world are misery, when in fact, she thought, I do not love my kind. Again she saw the ruby-splashed pavement, and faces mobbed at the door of a picture palace; apathetic, passive faces; the faces of people drugged with cheap pleasures; who had not even the courage to be themselves, but must dress up, imitate, pretend. And here, in this room, she thought, fixing her eyes on a couple. . . . But I will not think, she repeated; she would force her mind to become a blank and lie back, and accept quietly, tolerantly, whatever came.

She listened. Scraps reached her from above. ". . . flats in Highgate have bathrooms," they were saying. ". . . Your mother . . . Digby. . . . Yes, Crosby's still alive—" It was family gossip, and they were enjoying it. But how can I enjoy it? she said to herself. She was too tired; the skin round her eyes felt taut; a hoop was bound tight over her head; she tried to think herself away into the darkness of the country. But it was impossible; they were laughing. She opened her eyes, exacerbated by their laughter.

That was Renny laughing. He held a sheet of paper in his hand; his head was flung back; his mouth was wide open. From it came a sound like Ha! Ha! Ha! That is laughter, she said to herself. That is the sound people make when they are amused.

She watched him. Her muscles began to twitch involuntarily. She could not help laughing too. She stretched out her hand and Renny gave her the paper. It was folded; they had been playing a game. Each of them had drawn a different part of a picture. On top there was a woman's head like Queen Alexandra, with a fuzz of little curls; then a bird's neck; the body of a tiger; and stout elephant's legs dressed in child's drawers completed the picture.

"I drew that—I drew that!" said Renny pointing to the legs from which a long trail of ribbon depended. She laughed, laughed, laughed; she could not help laughing.

"The face that launched a thousand ships!" said North, pointing to another part of the monster's person. They all laughed again. She stopped laughing; her lips smoothed themselves out. But her laughter had had some strange effect on her. It had relaxed her, enlarged her. She felt, or rather she saw, not a place, but a state of being, in which there was real laughter, real happiness, and this fractured world was whole; whole, and free. But how could she say it?

"Look here . . ." she began. She wanted to express something that she felt to be very important; about a world in which people were whole, in which people were free . . . But they were laughing; she was serious. "Look here . . ." she began again.

Eleanor stopped laughing.

"Peggy wants to say something," she said. The others stopped talking, but they had stopped at the wrong moment. She had nothing to say when it came to the point, and yet she had to speak.

"Here," she began again, "here you all are—talking about North—" He looked up at her in surprise. It was not what she had meant to say, but she must go on now that she had begun. Their faces gaped at her like birds with their mouths open. ". . . How he's to live, where he's to live," she went on. ". . . But what's the use, what's the point of saying that?"

She looked at her brother. A feeling of animosity possessed her. He was still smiling, but his smile smoothed itself out as she looked at him.

"What's the use?" she said, facing him. "You'll marry. You'll have children. What'll you do then? Make money. Write little books to make money. . . ."

She had got it wrong. She had meant to say something impersonal, but she was being personal. It was done now however; she must flounder on now.

"You'll write one little book, and then another little book," she said viciously, "instead of living . . . living differently, differently."

She stopped. There was the vision still, but she had not grasped it. She had broken off only a little fragment of what she meant to say, and she had made her brother angry. Yet there it hung before her, the thing she had seen, the thing she had not said. But as she fell back with a jerk against the wall, she felt relieved of some oppression; her heart thumped; the veins on her forehead stood out. She had not said it, but she had tried to say it. Now she could rest; now she could think herself away under the shadow of their ridicule, which had no power to hurt her, into the country. Her eyes half shut; it seemed to her that she was on a terrace, in the evening; an owl went up and down, up and down; its white wing showed on the dark of the hedge; and she heard country people singing and the rattle of wheels on a road.

Then gradually the blur became distinct; she saw the line of the bookcase opposite; the wisp of muslin on the floor; and two large feet, in tight shoes, so that the bunions showed, stopped in front of her.

For a moment nobody moved; nobody spoke. Peggy sat still. She did not want to move, or to speak. She wanted to rest, to lean, to dream. She felt very tired. Then more feet stopped, and the hem of a black skirt.

"Aren't you people coming down to supper?" said a chuckling little voice. She looked up. It was her aunt Milly, with her husband by her side.

"Supper's downstairs," said Hugh. "Supper's downstairs." And they passed on.

"How prosperous they've grown!" said North's voice, laughing at them.

"Ah, but they're so good to people . . ." Eleanor protested. The sense of the family again, Peggy noted.

Then the knee against which she was sheltering herself moved.

"We must go," said Eleanor. Wait, wait, Peggy wanted to implore her. There was something she wanted to ask her; something she wanted to add to her outburst, since nobody had attacked her, and nobody had laughed at her. But it was useless; the knees straightened themselves; the red cloak elongated itself; Eleanor had risen. She was hunting for her bag or her handkerchief; she was ferreting in the cushions of her chair. As usual, she had lost something.

"I'm sorry to be such an old muddler," she apologised. She shook a cushion; coins rolled out onto the floor. A sixpenny bit spun on its edge across the carpet, reached a pair of silver shoes on the floor and fell flat.

"There!" Eleanor exclaimed. "There! . . . But that's Kitty! isn't it?" she exclaimed.

Peggy looked up. A handsome elderly woman, with curled white hair and something shining in her hair was standing in the doorway looking round her, as if she had just come in and were looking for her hostess, who was not there. It was at her feet that the sixpence had fallen.

"Kitty!" Eleanor repeated. She went towards her with her hands stretched out. They all got up. Peggy got up. Yes, it was over; it was destroyed she felt. Directly something got together, it broke. She had a feeling of desolation. And then you have to pick up the pieces, and make something new, something different, she thought, and crossed the room, and joined the foreigner, the man she called Brown, whose real name was Nicholas Pomjalovsky.

"Who is that lady," Nicholas asked her, "who appears to come into a room as if the whole world belonged to her?"

"That's Kitty Lasswade," said Peggy. As she stood in the door, they could not pass.

"I'm afraid I'm dreadfully late," they heard her saying in her clear, authoritative tones. "But I've been to the ballet."

That's Kitty, is it? North said to himself, looking at her. She was one of those well-set-up rather masculine old ladies who repelled him slightly. He thought he remembered that she was the wife of one of our governors; or was it the Viceroy of India? He could see her, as she stood there, doing the honours of Government House. "Sit here. Sit there. And you, young man, I hope you take plenty of exercise?" He knew the type. She had a short straight nose and blue eyes very wide apart. She might have looked very dashing in the eighties, he thought; in a tight riding-habit; worn a small hat, with a cock's feather in it; perhaps had an affair with an aide-de-camp; and then settled down, become dictatorial, and told stories about her past. He listened.

"Ah, but he's not a patch on Nijinsky!" she was saying.

The sort of thing she would say, he thought. He examined the books in the bookcase. He took one out and held it upside down. One little book, and then another little book—Peggy's taunt returned to him. The words had stung him out of all proportion to their surface meaning. She had turned on him with such violence, as if she despised him; she had looked as if she were going to burst into tears. He opened the little book. Latin, was it? He broke off a sentence and let it swim in his mind. There the words lay, beautiful, yet meaningless, yet composed in a pattern—*nox est perpetua una dormienda*. He remembered his master saying, Mark the long word at the end of the sentence. There the words floated; but just as they were about to give out their meaning, there was a movement at the door. Old Patrick had come ambling up, had given his arm gallantly to the widow of the Governor-General, and they were proceeding with a curious air of antiquated ceremony down the stairs. The others began to follow them. The younger generation following in the wake of the old, North said to himself as he put the book back on the shelf and followed. Only, he observed, they were not so very young; Peggy—there were white hairs on Peggy's head— she must be thirty-seven, thirty-eight?

"Enjoying yourself, Peg?" he said as they hung back behind the others. He had a vague feeling of hostility towards her. She seemed to him bitter, disillusioned, and very critical of everyone, especially of himself.

"You go first, Patrick," they heard Lady Lasswade boom out in her genial loud voice. "These staircases are not adapted . . ." she paused, as she advanced what was probably a rheumatic leg, "for old people who. . ." there was another pause as she descended another step, "'ve been kneeling on damp grass killing slugs."

North looked at Peggy and laughed. He had not expected the sentence to end like that, but the widows of viceroys, he thought, always have gardens, always kill slugs. Peggy smiled too. But he felt uncomfortable with her. She had attacked him. There they stood, however, side by side.

"Did you see old William Whatney?" she said, turning to him.

"No!" he exclaimed. *"He* still alive? That old white walrus with the whiskers?"

"Yes—that's him," she said. There was an old man in a white waistcoat standing in the door.

"The old Mock Turtle," he said. They had to fall back on childish slang, on childish memories, to cover their distance, their hostility.

"D'you remember . . ." he began.

"The night of the row?" she said. "The night I let myself out of the window by a rope."

"And we picnicked in the Roman camp," he said.

"We should never have been found out if that horrid little scamp hadn't told on us," she said, descending a step.

"A little beast with pink eyes," said North.

They could think of nothing else to say, as they stood blocked, waiting for the others to move on, side by side. And he used to read her his poetry in the apple-loft, he remembered, and as they walked up and down by the rose bushes. And now they had nothing to say to each other.

"Perry," he said, descending another step, suddenly remembering the name of the pink-eyed boy who had seen them coming home that morning and had told on them.

"Alfred," she added.

She still knew certain things about him, he thought; they still had something very profound in common. That was why, he thought, she had hurt him by what she had said, before the others, about his "writing little books." It was their past condemning his present. He glanced at her.

Damn women, he thought, they're so hard; so unimaginative. Curse their little inquisitive minds. What did their "education" amount to? It only made her critical, censorious. Old Eleanor, with all her rambling and stumbling, was worth a dozen of Peggy any day. She was neither one thing nor the other, he thought, glancing at her; neither in the fashion nor out of it.

She felt him look at her and look away. He was finding fault with something about her, she knew. Her hands? Her dress? No, it was because she criticised him, she thought. Yes, she thought as she descended another step, now I'm going to be trounced; now I'm going to be paid back for telling him he'd write "little books." It takes from ten to fifteen minutes, she thought, to get an answer; and then it'll be something off the point but disagreeable—very, she thought. The vanity of men was immeasurable. She waited. He looked at her again. And now he's comparing me with the girl I saw him talking to, she thought, and saw again the lovely, hard face. He'll tie himself up with a red-lipped girl, and become a drudge. He must, and I can't, she thought. No, I've a sense of guilt always. I shall pay for it, I shall pay for it, I kept saying to myself even in the Roman camp, she thought. She would have no children, and he would produce little Gibbses, more little Gibbses, she thought, looking in at the door of a solicitor's office, unless she leaves him at the end of the year for some other man. . . . The solicitor's name was Alridge, she noted. But I will take no more notes; I will enjoy myself, she thought suddenly. She put her hand on his arm.

"Met anybody amusing tonight?" she said.

He guessed that she had seen him with the girl.

"One girl," he said briefly.

"So I saw," she said.

She looked away.

"I thought her lovely," she said, carefully observing a tinted picture of a bird with a long beak that hung on the stairs.

"Shall I bring her to see you?" he asked.

So he cared for her opinion, did he? Her hand was still on his arm; she felt something hard and taut beneath the sleeve, and the touch of his flesh, bringing back to her the nearness of human beings and their distance, so that if one meant to help one hurt, yet they depended on each other, produced in her such a tumult of sensation that she could scarcely keep herself from

353

crying out, North! North! North! But I mustn't make a fool of myself again, she said to herself.

"Any evening after six," she said aloud, carefully descending another step, and they reached the bottom of the stairs.

A roar of voices sounded from behind the door of the supper room. She withdrew her hand from his arm. The door burst open.

"Spoons! spoons! spoons!" cried Delia, brandishing her arms in a rhetorical manner as if she were still declaiming to someone inside. She caught sight of her nephew and niece. "Be an angel, North, and fetch spoons!" she cried, throwing her hands out towards him.

"Spoons for the widow of the Governor-General!" North cried, catching her manner, imitating her dramatic gesture.

"In the kitchen, in the basement!" Delia cried, waving her arm at the kitchen stairs. "Come, Peggy, come," she said, catching Peggy's hand in hers, "we're all sitting down to supper." She burst into the room where they were having supper. It was crowded. People were sitting on the floor, on chairs, on office stools. Long office tables, little typewriting tables, had been pressed into use. They were strewn with flowers, frilled with flowers. Carnations, roses, daisies, were flung down higgledy-piggledy. "Sit on the floor, sit anywhere," Delia commanded, waving her hand promiscuously.

"Spoons are coming," she said to Lady Lasswade, who was drinking her soup out of a mug.

"But I don't want a spoon," said Kitty. She tilted the mug and drank.

"No, you wouldn't," said Delia, "but other people do."

North brought in a bunch of spoons and she took them from him.

"Now who wants a spoon and who doesn't?" she said, brandishing the bunch of spoons in front of her. Some people do and some don't, she thought.

Her sort of people, she thought, did not want spoons; the

others—the English—did. She had been making that distinction between people all her life.

"A spoon? A spoon?" she said, looking round her at the crowded room with some complacency. All sorts of people were there, she noted. That had always been her aim; to mix people; to do away with the absurd conventions of English life. And she had done it tonight, she thought. There were nobles and commoners; people dressed and people not dressed; people drinking out of mugs, and people waiting with their soup getting cold for a spoon to be brought to them.

"A spoon for me," said her husband, looking up at her.

She wrinkled her nose. For the thousandth time he had dashed her dream. Thinking to marry a wild rebel, she had married the most King-respecting, Empire-admiring of country gentlemen, and for that very reason partly—because he was, even now, such a magnificent figure of a man. "A spoon for your Uncle," she said dryly, and sent North off with the bunch. Then she sat down beside Kitty, who was gulping her soup like a child at a school treat. She set down her mug empty, among the flowers.

"Poor flowers," she said, taking up a carnation that lay on the table-cloth and putting it to her lips. "They'll die, Delia—they want water."

"Roses are cheap today," said Delia. "Twopence a bunch off a barrow in Oxford Street," she said. She took up a red rose and held it under the light, so that it shone, veined, semi-transparent.

"What a rich country England is!" she said, laying it down again. She took up her mug.

"What I'm always telling you," said Patrick, wiping his mouth. "The only civilised country in the whole world," he added.

"I thought we were on the verge of a smash," said Kitty. "Not that it looked much like it at Covent Garden tonight," she added.

"Ah, but it's true," he sighed, going on with his own thoughts. "I'm sorry to say it—but we're savages compared with you."

"He won't be happy till he's got Dublin Castle back again,"

Delia twitted him.

"You don't enjoy your freedom?" said Kitty, looking at the queer old man whose face always made her think of a hairy gooseberry. But his body was magnificent.

"It seems to me that our new freedom is a good deal worse than our old slavery," said Patrick, fumbling with his toothpick.

Politics as usual, money and politics, North thought, overhearing them, as he went round with the last of his spoons.

"You're not going to tell me that all that struggle has been in vain, Patrick?" said Kitty.

"Come to Ireland and see for yourself, m'lady," he said grimly.

"It's too early—too early to tell," said Delia.

Her husband looked past her with the sad innocent eyes of an old sporting dog whose hunting days are over. But they could not keep their fixity for long. "Who's this chap with the spoons?" he said, resting his eyes on North, who stood just behind them, waiting.

"North," said Delia. "Come and sit by us, North."

"Good-evening to you, Sir," said Patrick. They had met already, but he had already forgotten.

"What, Morris's son?" said Kitty, turning round abruptly. She shook hands cordially. He sat down and took a gulp of soup.

"He's just back from Africa. He's been on a farm there," said Delia.

"And how does the old country strike you?" said Patrick, leaning towards him genially.

"Very crowded," he said, looking round the room. "And you all talk," he added, "about money and politics." That was his stock phrase. He had said it twenty times already.

"You were in Africa?" said Lady Lasswade. "And what made you give up your farm?" she demanded. She looked him in the eyes and spoke just as he expected she would speak; too imperiously for his liking. What business is that of yours, old lady? he asked himself.

"I'd had about enough of it," he said aloud.

"And I'd have given anything to be a farmer!" she exclaimed. That was a little out of the picture, North thought. So were her eyes; she ought to have worn a pince-nez; but she did not.

"But in my youth," she said, rather fiercely—her hands were rather stubby, and the skin was rough, but she gardened, he remembered—"that wasn't allowed."

"No," said Patrick. "And it's my belief," he continued, drumming on the table with a fork, "that we should all be very glad, very glad, to go back to things as they were. What's the War done for us, eh? Ruined me for one." He wagged his head with melancholy tolerance from side to side.

"I'm sorry to hear that," said Kitty. "But speaking for myself, the old days were bad days, wicked days, cruel days. . . ." Her eyes turned blue with passion.

What about the aide-de-camp, and the hat with a cock's feather in it? North asked himself.

"Don't you agree with me, Delia?" said Kitty, turning to her.

But Delia was talking across her, using her rather exaggerated Irish sing-song to someone at the next table. Don't I remember this room, Kitty thought; a meeting; an argument. But what was it about? Force . . .

"My dear Kitty," Patrick interrupted, patting her hand with his great paw. "That's another instance of what I'm telling you. Now these ladies have got the vote," he said, turning to North, "are they any better off?"

Kitty looked fierce for a moment; then she smiled.

"We won't argue, my old friend," she said, giving him a little pat on the hand.

"And it's just the same with the Irish," he went on. North saw that he was bent on treading out the round of his familiar thoughts like an old broken-winded horse. "They'd be glad enough to join the Empire again, I assure you. I come of a family," he said to North, "that has served its king and country for three hundred—"

"English settlers," said Delia, rather shortly, returning to her soup. That's what they quarrel about when they're alone, North thought.

"We've been three hundred years in the country," old Patrick continued, padding out his round—he laid a hand on North's arm, "and what strikes an old fellow like me, an old fogy like me—"

"Nonsense, Patrick," Delia struck in, "I've never seen you look younger. Might be fifty, mightn't he, North?"

But Patrick shook his head.

"I shan't see seventy again," he said simply. ". . . But what strikes an old fellow like me," he continued, patting North's arm, "is with such a lot of good feeling about," he nodded rather vaguely at a placard that was pinned to the wall—"and nice things too,"—he referred perhaps to the flowers, but his head jerked involuntarily as he talked—"what do these fellows want to be shooting each other for? I don't join any societies; I don't sign any of these"—he pointed to the placard—"what d'you call 'em? manifestoes—I just go to my friend Mike, or it may be Pat—they're all good friends of mine, and we—"

He stooped and pinched his foot.

"Lord, these shoes!" he complained.

"Tight, are they?" said Kitty. "Kick 'em off."

Why had the poor old boy been brought over here, North wondered, and stuck into those tight shoes? He was clearly talking to his dogs. There was a look in his eyes now when he raised them again and tried to recover the drift of what he had been saying that was like the look of a sportsman who saw the birds rising in a semicircle over the wide green bog. But they were out of shot. He could not remember where he had got to. ". . . We talk things over," he said, "round a table." His eyes became mild and vacant as if the engine were cut off, and his mind glided on silently.

"The English talk too," said North perfunctorily. Patrick nodded, and looked vaguely at a group of young people. But he was not interested in what other people were saying. His mind could no longer stretch beyond its beat. His body was still beautifully proportioned; it was his mind that was old. He would say the same thing all over again, and when he had said it he would pick his teeth and sit gazing in front of him. There he sat now, holding a flower between his finger and thumb, loosely, without looking at it, as if his mind were gliding on—But Delia interrupted.

"North must go and talk to his friends," she said. Like so many wives, she saw when her husband was becoming a bore, North thought, as he got up.

"Don't wait to be introduced," said Delia, waving her hand. "Do just what you like—just what you like," her husband echoed her, beating on the table with his flower.

North was glad to go; but where was he to go now? He was an outsider, he felt again, as he glanced round the room. All these people knew each other. They called each other—he stood on the outskirts of a little group of young men and women—by their Christian names, by their nicknames. Each was already part of a little group, he felt as he listened, keeping on the outskirts. He wanted to hear what they were saying; but not to be drawn in himself. He listened. They were arguing. Politics and money, he said to himself; money and politics. That phrase came in handy. But he could not understand the argument, which was already heated. Never have I felt so lonely, he thought. The old platitude about solitude in a crowd was true; for hills and trees accept one; human beings reject one. He turned his back and pretended to read the particulars of a desirable property at Bexhill which Patrick had called for some reason "a manifesto." "Running water in all the bedrooms," he read. He overheard scraps of talk. That's Oxford, that's Harrow, he continued, recognising the tricks of speech that were caught at school and college. It seemed to him that they were still cutting little private jokes about Jones minor winning the long jump; and old Foxy, or whatever the headmaster's name was. It was like hearing small boys at a private school, hearing these young men talk politics. "I'm right . . . you're wrong." At their age, he thought, he had been in the trenches; he had seen men killed. But was that a good education? He shifted from one foot to another. At their age, he thought, he had been alone on a farm sixty miles from a white man, in control of a herd of sheep. But was that a good education? Anyhow it seemed to him, half hearing their argument, looking at their gestures, catching their slang, that they were all the same sort. Public school and university, he sized them up as he looked over his shoulder. But where are the Sweeps and the Sewer-men, the Seamstresses and the Stevedores? he thought, making a list of trades that began with the letter S. For all Delia's pride in her promiscuity, he thought, glancing at the people, there were only Dons and Duchesses, and what other words begin with D? he asked himself, as he scrutinised the placard again—Drabs and Drones?

He turned. A nice fresh-faced boy with a freckled nose in ordinary day clothes was looking at him. If he didn't take care he would be drawn in too. Nothing would be easier than to join a society, to sign what Patrick called "a manifesto." But he did not believe in joining societies, in signing manifestoes. He turned back to the desirable residence with its three-quarters of an acre of garden and running water in all the bedrooms. People met, he thought, pretending to read, in hired halls. And one of them stood on a platform. There was the pump-handle gesture; the wringing-wet-clothes gesture; and then the voice, oddly detached from the little figure and tremendously magnified by the loudspeaker, went booming and bawling round the hall: Justice! Liberty! For a moment, of course, sitting among knees, wedged in tight, a ripple, a nice emotional quiver, went over the skin; but next morning, he said to himself as he glanced again at the house-agents' placard, there's not an idea, not a phrase that would feed a sparrow. What do they mean by Justice and Liberty? he asked, all these nice young men with two or three hundred a year. Something's wrong, he thought; there's a gap, a dislocation, between the word and the reality. If they want to reform the world, he thought, why not begin there, at the centre, with themselves? He turned on his heel and ran straight into an old man in a white waistcoat.

"Hullo!" he said, holding out his hand.

It was his Uncle Edward. He had the look of an insect whose body has been eaten out, leaving only the wings, the shell.

"Very glad to see you back, North," said Edward, and shook him warmly by the hand.

"Very glad," he repeated. He was shy. He was spare and thin. He looked as if his face had been carved and graved by a multitude of fine instruments; as if it had been left out on a frosty night and frozen over. He threw his head back like a horse champing a bit; but he was an old horse, a blue-eyed horse whose bit no longer irked him. His movements were from habit, not from feeling. What had he been doing all these years? North wondered, as they stood there surveying each other. Editing Sophocles? What would happen if Sophocles one of these days were edited? What would they do then, these eaten out hollow-shelled old men?

"You've filled out," said Edward, looking him up and down. "You've filled out," he repeated.

There was a subtle deference in his manner. Edward, the scholar, paid tribute to North, the soldier. Yes, but they found it difficult to talk. He had the air of being stamped, North thought; he had kept something, after all, out of the hubbub.

"Shan't we sit down?" said Edward, as if he wished to talk to him seriously about interesting things. They looked about for a quiet place. He had not frittered his time away talking to old red setters and raising his gun, North thought, glancing about him, to see if by chance there was a quiet place in the room where they could sit down and talk. But there were only two office stools empty beside Eleanor over there in the corner.

She saw them and called out, "Oh, there's Edward! I know

there was something I wanted to ask. . ." she began.

It was a relief that the interview with the headmaster should be broken up by this impulsive, foolish old woman. She was holding out her pocket-handkerchief.

"I made a knot," she was saying. Yes, there it was, a knot in her pocket-handkerchief.

"Now what did I make a knot for?" she said, looking up.

"It is an admirable habit to make a knot," said Edward in his courteous, clipped way, lowering himself a little stiffly onto the chair beside her. "But at the same time it is advisable. . . ." He stopped. That's what I like about him, North thought, taking the other chair: he left half his sentence unfinished.

"It was to remind me—" said Eleanor putting her hand to her thick crop of white hair. Then she stopped. What is it that makes him look so calm, so carved, North thought, stealing a look at Edward, who waited with admirable serenity for his sister to remember why she had made a knot in her handkerchief. There was something final about him; he left half his sentences unfinished. He hadn't worried himself about politics and money, he thought. There was something sealed up, stated, about him. Poetry and the past, was it? But as he fixed his eyes upon him, Edward smiled at his sister.

"Well, Nell?" he said.

It was a quiet smile, a tolerant smile.

North broke in, for Eleanor was still ruminating over her knot. "I met a man at the Cape who was a tremendous admirer of yours, Uncle Edward," he said. The name came back to him— "Arbuthnot," he said.

"R. K.?" said Edward. And he raised his hand to his head and smiled. It pleased him, that compliment. He was vain; he was touchy; he was—North stole a glance to add another impression—established. Glazed over with the smooth glossy varnish that those in authority wear. For he was now—what? North could not remember. A professor? A master? Somebody who had an attitude fixed on him, from which he could not relax any longer. Still, Arbuthnot, R. K., had said, with emotion, that he owed more to Edward than to any man.

"He said he owed more to you than to any man," he said aloud.

Edward brushed aside the compliment; but it pleased him. He had a way of putting his hand to his head that North remembered. And Eleanor called him "Nigs." She laughed at him; she preferred failures, like Morris. There she sat holding her pocket-handkerchief in her hand, smiling, ironically, covertly, at some memory.

"And what are your plans?" said Edward. "You deserve a holiday."

There was something flattering in his manner, North thought, like a schoolmaster welcoming back to school an old boy who had won distinction. But he meant it; he doesn't say what he doesn't mean, North thought, and that was alarming too. They were silent.

"Delia's got a wonderful lot of people here tonight, hasn't she?" said Edward, turning to Eleanor. They sat looking at the different groups. His clear blue eyes surveyed the scene amiably but sardonically. But what's he thinking, North asked himself. He's got something behind that mask, he thought. Something that's kept him clear of this muddle. The past? Poetry? he thought, looking at Edward's distinct profile. It was finer than he remembered.

"I'd like to brush up my classics," he said suddenly. "Not that I ever had much to brush," he added, foolishly, afraid of the schoolmaster.

Edward did not seem to be listening. He was raising his eyeglass and letting it fall, as he looked at the queer jumble. There his head rested with the chin thrown up, on the back of his chair. The crowd, the noise, the clatter of knives and forks, made it unnecessary to talk. North stole another glance at him. The past and poetry, he said to himself, that's what I want to talk about, he thought. He wanted to say it aloud. But Edward was too formed and idiosyncratic; too black and white and linear, with his head tilted up on the back of his chair, to ask him questions easily.

Now he was talking about Africa, and North wanted to talk about the past and poetry. There it was, he thought, locked up in that fine head, the head that was like a Greek boy's head grown white; the past and poetry. Then why not prise it open? Why not share it? What's wrong with him, he thought, as he answered the usual intelligent Englishman's questions about Africa and the state of the country. Why can't he flow? Why can't he pull the string of the shower bath? Why's it all locked up, refrigerated? Because he's a priest, a mystery monger, he thought; feeling his coldness; this guardian of beautiful words.

But Edward was speaking to him.

"We must arrange a date," he was saying, "next autumn." He meant it too.

"Yes," North said aloud, "I'd love to. . . . In the autumn. . . ." And he saw before him a house with creeper-shaded rooms, butlers creeping, decanters, and some one handing a box of good cigars.

Unknown young men coming round with trays pressed different eatables upon them.

"How very kind of you!" said Eleanor, taking a glass. He himself took a glass of some yellow liquid. It was some kind of claret cup, he supposed. The little bubbles kept rising to the top and exploding. He watched them rise and explode.

"Who's that pretty girl," said Edward, inclining his head, "over there, standing in the corner, talking to the youth?"

He was benignant and urbane.

"Aren't they lovely?" said Eleanor. "Just what I was thinking. . . . Everyone looks so young. That's Maggie's daughter. . . . But who's that talking to Kitty?"

"That's Middleton," said Edward. "What, don't you remember him? You must have met him in the old days."

They chatted, basking there at their ease. Spinners and sitters in the sun, North thought, taking their ease when the day's work is over; Eleanor and Edward each in his own niche, with his hands on the fruit, tolerant, assured.

He watched the bubbles rising in the yellow liquid. For them it's all right, he thought; they've had their day: but not for him, not for his generation. For him a life modelled on the jet (he was watching the bubbles rise), on the spring, of the hard leaping fountain; another life; a different life. Not halls and reverberating megaphones; not marching in step after leaders, in herds, groups, societies, caparisoned. No; to begin inwardly, and let the devil take the outer form, he thought, looking up at a young man with a fine forehead and a weak chin. Not black shirts, green shirts, red shirts—always posing in the public eye; that's all poppycock. Why not down barriers and simplify? But a world, he thought, that was all one jelly, one mass, would be a rice pudding world, a white counterpane world. To keep the emblems and tokens of North Pargiter—the man Maggie laughs at; the Frenchman holding his hat; but at the same time spread out, make a new ripple in human consciousness, be the bubble and the stream, the stream and the bubble—myself and the world together—he raised his glass. Anonymously, he said, looking at the clear yellow liquid. But what do I mean, he wondered—I, to whom ceremonies are suspect, and religion's dead; who don't fit, as the man said, don't fit in anywhere? He paused. There was the glass in his hand; in his mind a sentence. And he wanted to make other sentences. But how can I, he thought—he looked at Eleanor, who sat with a silk handkerchief in her hands—unless I know what's solid, what's true; in my life, in other people's lives?

"Runcorn's boy," Eleanor suddenly ejaculated. "The son of the porter at my flat," she explained. She had untied the knot in her handkerchief.

"The son of the porter at your flat," Edward repeated. His eyes were like a field on which the sun rests in winter, North thought, looking up—the winter's sun, that has no heat left in it but some pale beauty.

"Commissionaire they call him, I think," she said.

"How I hate that word!" said Edward with a little shudder. "Porter's good English, isn't it?"

"That's what I say," said Eleanor. "The son of the *porter* at my flat. . . . Well, he wants, they want him to go to college. So I said if I saw you, I'd ask you—"

"Of course, of course," said Edward kindly.

And that's all right, North said to himself. That's the human voice at its natural speaking level. Of course, of course, he repeated.

"He wants to go to college, does he?" Edward went on. "What examinations has he passed, eh?"

What examinations has he passed, eh? North repeated. He repeated that too, but critically, as if he were actor and critic; he listened but he commented. He surveyed the thin yellow liquid in which the bubbles rose more slowly, one by one. Eleanor did not know what examinations he had passed. And what was I thinking? North asked himself. He felt that he had been in the middle of a jungle; in the heart of darkness; cutting his way towards the light; but provided only with broken sentences, single words, with which to break through the briar-bush of human bodies, human wills and voices, that bent over him, binding him, blinding him. . . . He listened.

"Well then, tell him to come and see me," said Edward, briskly.

"But that's asking too much of you, Edward?" Eleanor protested.

"That's what I'm for," said Edward.

That's the right tone of voice too, North thought. Not carapaced—the words "caparison" and "carapace" collided in his mind, and made a new word that was no word. What I mean is, he added, taking a drink of his claret cup, underneath there's the fountain; the sweet nut. The fruit, the fountain that's in all of us; in Edward; in Eleanor; so why caparison ourselves on top? He looked up.

A big man had stopped in front of them. He bent over and very politely gave Eleanor his hand. He had to bend, for his white waistcoat enclosed so magnificent a sphere. "Alas," he was saying in a voice that was oddly mellifluous for one of his bulk, "I'd love nothing more; but I have a meeting at ten tomorrow morning." They were inviting him to sit down and talk. He was tittupping up and down on his little feet in front of them.

"Throw it over!" said Eleanor, smiling up at him, just as she used to smile when she was a girl with her brother's friends, thought North. Then why hadn't she married one of them, he wondered. Why do we hide all the things that matter? he asked himself.

"And leave my directors cooling their heels? As much as my place is worth!" the old friend was saying, and swung round on his heel with the agility of a trained elephant.

"Seems a long time since he acted in the Greek play, doesn't it?" said Edward. ". . . in a toga," he added with a grin, following the well-rounded person of the great railway magnate as he went with a certain celerity, for he was a perfect man of the world, through the crowd to the door.

"That's Chipperfield, the great railway man," he explained to North. "A very remarkable fellow," he went on. "Son of a railway porter." He made little pauses between each sentence. "Done it all off his own bat. . . . A delightful house . . . Perfectly restored. . . . Two or three hundred acres, I suppose. . . . Has his shooting. . . . Asks me to direct his reading. . . . And buys old masters."

"And buys old masters," North repeated. The deft little sentences seemed to build up a pagoda; sparely but accurately; and through it all ran some queer breath of mockery tinged with affection.

"Shams, I should think," Eleanor laughed.

"Well, we needn't go into that," Edward chuckled. Then they were silent. The pagoda floated off. Chipperfield had vanished through the door.

"How nice this drink is," Eleanor said above his head. North could see her glass held at the level of his head on her knee. A thin green leaf floated on top of it. "I hope it's not intoxicating?" she said, raising it.

North took up his glass again. What was I thinking last time I looked at it? he asked himself. A block had formed in his forehead as if two thoughts had collided and had stopped the passage of the rest. His mind was a blank. He swayed the liquid from side to side. He was in the middle of a dark forest.

"So, North . . ." His own name roused him with a start. It was Edward speaking. He jerked forward. ". . . you want to brush up your classics, do you?" Edward went on. "I'm glad to hear you say that. There's a lot in those old fellows. But the younger generation," he paused, ". . . don't seem to want 'em."

"How foolish!" said Eleanor. "I was reading one of them the other day . . . the one you translated. Now which was it?" She paused. She never could remember names. "The one about the girl who . . ."

"The Antigone?" Edward suggested.

"Yes! The Antigone!" she exclaimed. "And I thought to myself, just what you say, Edward—how true—how beautiful. . . ."

She broke off, as if afraid to continue.

Edward nodded. He paused. Then suddenly he jerked his head back and said some words in Greek: "[Greek text]."

North looked up.

"Translate it," he said.

Edward shook his head. "It's the language," he said.

Then he shut up. It's no go, North thought. He can't say what he wants to say; he's afraid. They're all afraid; afraid of being laughed at; afraid of giving themselves away. He's afraid too, he thought, looking at the young man with a fine forehead and a weak chin who was gesticulating too emphatically. We're all afraid of each other, he thought; afraid of what? Of criticism; of laughter; of people who think differently. . . . He's afraid of me because I'm a farmer (and he saw again his round face;

high cheek-bones and small brown eyes). And I'm afraid of him because he's clever. He looked at the big forehead, from which the hair was already receding. That's what separates us; fear, he thought.

He shifted his position. He wanted to get up and talk to him. Delia had said, "Don't wait to be introduced." But it was difficult to speak to a man whom he did not know, and say: "What's this knot in the middle of my forehead? Untie it." For he had had enough of thinking alone. Thinking alone tied knots in the middle of the forehead; thinking alone bred pictures, foolish pictures. The man was moving off. He must make the effort. Yet he hesitated. He felt repelled and attracted, attracted and repelled. He began to rise; but before he had got on his feet somebody thumped on a table with a fork.

A large man sitting at a table in the corner was thumping on the table with his fork. He was leaning forward as if he wanted to attract attention, as if he were about to make a speech. It was the man Peggy called Brown; the others called Nicholas; whose real name he did not know. Perhaps he was a little drunk.

"Ladies and gentlemen!" he said. "Ladies and gentlemen!" he repeated rather more loudly.

"What, a speech?" said Edward quizzically. He half turned his chair; he raised his eyeglass, which hung on a black silk ribbon as if it were a foreign order.

People were buzzing about with plates and glasses. They were stumbling over cushions on the floor. A girl pitched head foremost.

"Hurt yourself?" said a young man, stretching out his hand.

No, she had not hurt herself. But the interruption had distracted attention from the speech. A buzz of talk had risen like the buzz of flies over sugar. Nicholas sat down again. He was lost apparently in contemplation of the red stone in his ring; or of the strewn flowers; the white, waxy flowers, the pale, semi-transparent flowers, the crimson flowers that were so full-blown that the gold heart showed, and the petals had fallen and lay among the hired knives and forks, the cheap tumblers on the table. Then he roused himself.

"Ladies and gentlemen!" he began. Again he thumped the table with his fork. There was a momentary lull. Rose marched across the room.

"Going to make a speech, are you?" she demanded. "Go on, I like hearing speeches." She stood beside him, with her hand hollowed round her ear like a military man. Again the buzz of talk had broken out.

"Silence!" she exclaimed. She took a knife and rapped on the table.

"Silence! Silence!" She rapped again.

Martin crossed the room.

"What's Rose making such a noise about?" he asked.

"I'm asking for silence!" she said, flourishing her knife in his face. "This gentleman wants to make a speech!"

But he had sat down and was regarding his ring with equanimity.

"Isn't she the very spit and image," said Martin, laying his hand on Rose's shoulder and turning to Eleanor as if to confirm his words, "of old Uncle Pargiter of Pargiter's Horse?"

"Well, I'm proud of it!" said Rose, brandishing her knife in his face. "I'm proud of my family; proud of my country; proud of . . ."

"Your sex?" he interrupted her.

"I am," she asseverated. "And what about you?" she went on, tapping him on the shoulder. "Proud of yourself, are you?"

"Don't quarrel, children, don't quarrel!" cried Eleanor, giving her chair a little edge nearer. "They always would quarrel," she said, "always . . . always. . . ."

"She was a horrid little spitfire," said Martin, squatting down on the floor, and looking up at Rose, "with her hair scraped off her forehead . . ."

". . . wearing a pink frock," Rose added. She sat down abruptly, holding her knife erect in her hand. "A pink frock; a pink frock," she repeated, as if the words recalled something.

"But go on with your speech, Nicholas," said Eleanor, turning to him. He shook his head.

"Let us talk about pink frocks," he smiled.

". . . in the drawing-room at Abercorn Terrace, when we were children," said Rose. "D'you remember?" She looked at Martin. He nodded his head.

"In the drawing-room at Abercorn Terrace . . ." said Delia. She was going from table to table with a great jug of claret cup. She stopped in front of them. "Abercorn Terrace!" she exclaimed, filling a glass. She flung her head back and looked for a moment astonishingly young, handsome, and defiant.

"It was Hell!" she exclaimed. "It was Hell!" she repeated.

"Oh come, Delia . . ." Martin protested, holding out his glass to be filled.

"It was Hell," she said, dropping her Irish manner, and speaking quite simply, as she poured out the drink.

"D'you know," she said, looking at Eleanor, "when I go to Paddington, I always say to the man, 'Drive the other way round!'"

"That's enough . . ." Martin stopped her; his glass was full. "I hated it too . . ." he began.

But here Kitty Lasswade advanced upon them. She held her glass in front of her as though it were a bauble.

"What's Martin hating now?" she said, facing him.

A polite gentleman pushed forward a little gilt chair upon which she sat down.

"He always was a hater," she said, holding her glass out to be filled.

"What was it you hated that night, Martin, when you dined with us?" she asked him. "I remember how angry you made me. . . ."

She smiled at him. He had grown cherubic; pink and plump; with his hair brushed back like a waiter's.

"Hated? I never hated anybody," he protested.

"My heart's full of love; my heart's full of kindness," he laughed, waving his glass at her.

"Nonsense," said Kitty. "When you were young you hated . . . everything!" she flung her hand out. "My house . . . my friends. . . ." She broke off with a quick little sigh. She saw them again— the men filing in; the women pinching some dress between their thumbs and fingers. She lived alone now, in the north.

". . . and I daresay I'm better off as I am," she added, half to herself, "with just a boy to chop up wood."

There was a pause.

"Now let him get on with his speech," said Eleanor.

"Yes. Get on with your speech!" said Rose. Again she rapped her knife on the table; again he half rose.

"Going to make a speech, is he?" said Kitty, turning to Edward who had drawn his chair up beside her.

"The only place where oratory is now practised as an art . . ." Edward began. Then he paused, drew his chair a little closer, and adjusted his glasses, ". . . is the church," he added.

That's why I didn't marry you, Kitty said to herself. How the voice, the supercilious voice, brought it back! the tree half fallen; rain falling; undergraduates calling; bells tolling; she and her mother. . . .

But Nicholas had risen. He took a deep breath which expanded his shirt front. With one hand he fumbled with his fob; the other he flung out with an oratorical gesture.

"Ladies and gentlemen!" he began again. "In the name of all who have enjoyed themselves tonight. . . ."

"Speak up! Speak up!" the young men cried who were standing in the window.

("Is he a foreigner?" Kitty whispered to Eleanor.)

". . . in the name of all who have enjoyed themselves tonight," he repeated more loudly, "I wish to thank our host and hostess. . . ."

"Oh, don't thank me!" said Delia brushing past them with her empty jug.

Again the speech was brought to the ground. He must be a foreigner, Kitty thought to herself, because he has no self-consciousness. There he stood holding his wine-glass and smiling.

"Go on, go on," she urged him. "Don't mind them." She was in the mood for a speech. A speech was a good thing at parties. It gave them a fillip. It gave them a finish. She rapped her glass on the table.

"It's very nice of you," said Delia, trying to push past him, but he had laid his hand on her arm, "but don't thank me."

"But Delia," he expostulated, still holding her, "it's not what *you* want; it's what *we* want. And it is fitting," he continued, waving his hand out, "when our hearts are full of gratitude. . ."

Now he's getting into his stride, Kitty thought. I daresay he's a bit of an orator. Most foreigners are.

". . . when our hearts are full of gratitude," he repeated, touching one finger.

"What for?" said a voice abruptly.

Nicholas stopped again.

("Who is that dark man?" Kitty whispered to Eleanor. "I've been wondering all the evening."

"Renny," Eleanor whispered. "Renny," she repeated.)

"What for?" said Nicholas. "That is what I am about to tell you. . . ." He paused, and drew a deep breath which again expanded his waistcoat. His eyes beamed; he seemed full of spontaneous subterraneous benevolence. But here a head popped up over the edge of the table; a hand swept up a fistful of flower petals; and a voice cried:

"Red Rose, thorny Rose, brave Rose, tawny Rose!" The petals were thrown, fan-shape, over the stout old woman who was sitting on the edge of her chair. She looked up in surprise. Petals had fallen on her. She brushed them where they had lodged upon the prominences of her person. "Thank you! Thank you!" she exclaimed. Then she took up a flower and beat it energetically upon the edge of the table. "But I want my speech!" she said, looking at Nicholas.

"No, no," he said. "This is not a time for making speeches," and sat down again.

"Let's drink then," said Martin. He raised his glass. "Pargiter of Pargiter's Horse!" he said. "I drink to her!" He put his glass down with a thump on the table.

"Oh, if you're all drinking healths," said Kitty, "I'll drink too. Rose, your health. Rose is a fine fellow," she said, raising her glass. "But Rose was wrong," she added. "Force is always wrong,—don't you agree with me, Edward?" She tapped him on the knee. I'd forgotten the War, she muttered half to herself. "Still," she said aloud, "Rose had the courage of her convictions. Rose went to prison. And I drink to her!" She drank.

"The same to you, Kitty," said Rose, bowing to her.

"She smashed his window," Martin jeered at her, "and then she helped him to smash other people's windows. Where's your decoration, Rose?"

"In a cardboard box on the mantelpiece," said Rose. "You can't get a rise out of me at this time of day, my good fellow."

"But I wish you had let Nicholas finish his speech," said Eleanor.

Down through the ceiling, muted and far away, came the preliminary notes of another dance. The young people, hastily swallowing what remained in their glasses, rose and began to move off upstairs. Soon there was the sound of feet thudding, rhythmically, heavily on the floor above.

"Another dance?" said Eleanor. It was a waltz. "When we were young," she said, looking at Kitty, "we used to dance. . . ." The tune seemed to take her words and to repeat them—when I was young I used to dance—I used to dance. . . .

"And how I hated it!" said Kitty, looking at her fingers, which were short and pricked. "How nice it is," she said, "not to be young! How nice not to mind what people think! Now one can live as one likes," she added, ". . . now that one's seventy."

She paused. She raised her eyebrows as if she remembered something. "Pity one can't live again," she said. But she broke off.

"Aren't we going to have our speech after all, Mr—?" she said, looking at Nicholas, whose name she did not know. He sat gazing benevolently in front of him, paddling his hands among the flower petals.

"What's the good?" he said. "Nobody wants to listen." They listened to the feet thudding upstairs, and to the music repeating, it seemed to Eleanor, when I was young I used to dance, all men loved me when I was young. . . .

"But I want a speech!" said Kitty in her authoritative manner. It was true; she wanted something—something that gave a fillip, a finish—what she scarcely knew. But not the past—not memories. The present; the future; that was what she wanted.

"There's Peggy!" said Eleanor, looking round. She was sitting on the edge of a table, eating a ham sandwich.

"Come, Peggy!" she called out. "Come and talk to us!"

"Speak for the younger generation, Peggy!" said Lady Lasswade, shaking hands.

"But I'm not the younger generation," said Peggy. "And I've made my speech already," she said. "I made a fool of myself upstairs," she said, sinking down on the floor at Eleanor's feet.

"Then, North . . ." said Eleanor, looking down on the parting of North's hair as he sat on the floor beside her.

"Yes, North," said Peggy, looking at him across her aunt's knee. "North says we talk of nothing but money and politics," she added. "Tell us what we ought to do." He started. He had been dozing off, dazed by the music and voices. What we ought to do? he said to himself, waking up. What ought we to do?

He jerked up into a sitting posture. He saw Peggy's face looking at him. Now she was smiling; her face was gay; it reminded him of his grandmother's face in the picture. But he saw it as he had seen it upstairs—scarlet, puckered—as if she were about to burst into tears. It was her face that was true; not her words. But only her words returned to him—to live differently—differently. He paused. This is what needs courage, he said to himself; to speak the truth. She was listening. The old people were already gossiping about their own affairs.

". . . It's a nice little house," Kitty was saying. "An old mad woman used to live there. . . . You'll have to come and stay with me, Nell. In the spring. . . ."

Peggy was watching him over the rim of her ham sandwich.

"What you said was true," he blurted out, ". . . quite true." It was what she meant that was true, he corrected himself; her feeling, not her words. He felt her feeling now; it was not about him; it was about other people; about another world, a new world. . . .

The old aunts and uncles were gossiping above him.

"What was the name of the man I used to like so much at Oxford?" Lady Lasswade was saying. He could see her silver body bending towards Edward.

"The man you liked at Oxford?" Edward was repeating. "I thought you never liked anyone at Oxford. . . ." And they laughed.

But Peggy was waiting, she was watching him. He saw again the glass with the bubbles rising; he felt again the constriction of a knot in his forehead. He wished there were someone, infinitely wise and good, to think for him, to answer for him. But the young man with the receding forehead had vanished.

". . . To live differently . . . differently," he repeated. Those were her words; they did not altogether fit his meaning; but he had to use them. Now I've made a fool of myself too, he thought, as a ripple of some disagreeable sensation went across his back as if a knife had sliced it, and he leant against the wall.

"Yes, it was Robson!" Lady Lasswade exclaimed. Her trumpet voice rang out over his head.

"How one forgets things!" she went on. "Of course—Robson. That was his name. And the girl I used to like—Nelly? The girl who was going to be a doctor?"

"Died, I think," said Edward.

"Died, did she—died—" said Lady Lasswade. She paused

for a moment. "Well, I wish you'd make your speech," she said, turning and looking down at North.

He drew himself back. No more speech-making for me, he thought. He had his glass in his hand still. It was still half full of pale yellow liquid. The bubbles had ceased to rise. The wine was clear and still. Stillness and solitude, he thought to himself; silence and solitude . . . that's the only element in which the mind is free now.

Silence and solitude, he repeated; silence and solitude. His eyes half closed themselves. He was tired; he was dazed; people talked; people talked. He would detach himself, generalise himself, imagine that he was lying in a great space on a blue plain with hills on the rim of the horizon. He stretched out his feet. There were the sheep cropping; slowly tearing the grass; advancing first one stiff leg and then another. And babbling— babbling. He made no sense of what they were saying. Through his half-open eyes he saw hands holding flowers—thin hands, fine hands; but hands that belonged to no one. And were they flowers the hands held? Or mountains? Blue mountains with violet shadows? Then petals fell. Pink, yellow, white with violet shadows, the petals fell. They fall and fall and cover all, he murmured. And there was the stem of a wine-glass; the rim of a plate; and a bowl of water. The hands went on picking up flower after flower; that was a white rose; that was a yellow rose; that was a rose with violet valleys in its petals. There they hung, many folded, many coloured, drooping over the rim of the bowl. And petals fell. There they lay, violet and yellow, little shallops, boats on a river. And he was floating, and drifting, in a shallop, in a petal, down a river into silence, into solitude . . . which is the worst torture, the words came back to him as if a voice had spoken them, that human beings can inflict. . . .

"Wake up, North . . . we want your speech!" a voice interrupted him. Kitty's red handsome face was hanging over him.

"Maggie!" he exclaimed, pulling himself up. It was she who was sitting there, putting flowers into water. "Yes, it's Maggie's turn to speak," said Nicholas, putting his hand on her knee.

"Speak, speak!" Renny urged her.

But she shook her head. Laughter took her and shook her. She laughed, throwing her head back as if she were possessed by some genial spirit outside herself that made her bend and rise, as a tree, North thought, is tossed and bent by the wind. No idols, no idols, no idols, her laughter seemed to chime as if the tree were hung with innumerable bells, and he laughed too.

Their laughter ceased. Feet thudded, dancing on the floor above. A siren hooted on the river. A van crashed down the street in the distance. There was a rush and quiver of sound; something seemed to be released; it was as if the life of the day were about to begin, and this were the chorus, the cry, the chirp, the stir, which salutes the London dawn.

Kitty turned to Nicholas.

"And what was your speech going to have been about, Mr . . . I'm afraid I don't know your name?" she said.

". . . the one that was interrupted?"

"My speech?" he laughed. "It was to have been a miracle!" he said. "A masterpiece! But how can one speak when one is always interrupted? I begin: I say, Let us give thanks. Then Delia says, Don't thank me. I begin again: I say, Let us give thanks to someone, to somebody . . . And Renny says, What for? I begin again, and look—Eleanor is sound asleep." (He pointed at her.) "So what's the good?"

"Oh, but there is some good—" Kitty began.

She still wanted something—some finish, some fillip—what she did not know. And it was getting late. She must go.

"Tell me, privately, what you were going to have said, Mr—?" she asked him.

"What I was going to have said? I was going to have said—" he paused and stretched his hand out; he touched each finger separately.

"First I was going to have thanked our host and hostess.

Then I was going to have thanked this house—" he waved his hand round the room hung with the placards of the house agent, "—which has sheltered the lovers, the creators, the men and women of goodwill. And finally—" he took his glass in his hand, "I was going to drink to the human race. The human race," he continued, raising his glass to his lips, "which is now in its infancy, may it grow to maturity! Ladies and gentlemen!" he exclaimed, half rising and expanding his waistcoat, "I drink to that!"

He brought his glass down with a thump on the table. It broke.

"That's the thirteenth glass broken tonight!" said Delia, coming up and stopping in front of them. "But don't mind— don't mind. They're very cheap—glasses."

"What's very cheap?" Eleanor murmured. She half opened her eyes. But where was she? In what room? In which of the innumerable rooms? Always there were rooms; always there were people. Always from the beginning of time. . . . She shut her hands on the coins she was holding, and again she was suffused with a feeling of happiness. Was it because this had survived— this keen sensation (she was waking up) and the other thing, the solid object—she saw an ink-corroded walrus—had vanished? She opened her eyes wide. Here she was; alive; in this room, with living people. She saw all the heads in a circle. At first they were without identity. Then she recognised them. That was Rose; that was Martin; that was Morris. He had hardly any hair on the top of his head. There was a curious pallor on his face.

There was a curious pallor on all their faces as she looked round. The brightness had gone out of the electric lights; the table-cloths looked whiter. North's head—he was sitting on the floor at her feet—was rimmed with whiteness. His shirt-front was a little crumpled.

He was sitting on the floor at Edward's feet with his hands bound round his knees, and he gave little jerks and looked up at him as if he appealed to him about something.

"Uncle Edward," she heard him say, "tell me this . . ."

He was like a child asking to be told a story.

"Tell me this," he repeated, giving another little jerk. "You're a scholar. About the classics now. Aeschylus. Sophocles. Pindar."

Edward bent towards him.

"And the chorus," North jerked on again. She leant towards them. "The chorus—" North repeated.

"My dear boy," she heard Edward say as he smiled benignly down at him, "don't ask me. I was never a great hand at that. No, if I'd had my way"—he paused and passed his hand over his forehead—"I should have been . . . . " A burst of laughter drowned his words. She could not catch the end of the sentence. What had he said—what had he wished to be? She had lost his words.

There must be another life, she thought, sinking back into her chair, exasperated. Not in dreams; but here and now, in this room, with living people. She felt as if she were standing on the edge of a precipice with her hair blown back; she was about to grasp something that just evaded her. There must be another life, here and now, she repeated. This is too short, too broken. We know nothing, even about ourselves. We're only just beginning, she thought, to understand, here and there. She hollowed her hands in her lap, just as Rose had hollowed hers round her ears. She held her hands hollowed; she felt that she wanted to enclose the present moment; to make it stay; to fill it fuller and fuller, with the past, the present and the future, until it shone, whole, bright, deep with understanding.

"Edward," she began, trying to attract his attention. But he was not listening to her; he was telling North some old college story. It's useless, she thought, opening her hands. It must drop. It must fall. And then? she thought. For her too there would be the endless night; the endless dark. She looked ahead of her as though she saw opening in front of her a very long dark tunnel. But, thinking of the dark, something baffled her; in fact it was growing light. The blinds were white.

There was a stir in the room.

Edward turned to her.

"Who are *they?*" he asked her, pointing to the door.

She looked. Two children stood in the door. Delia had her hands on their shoulders as if to encourage them. She was leading them over to the table in order to give them something to eat. They looked awkward and clumsy.

Eleanor glanced at their hands, at their clothes, at the shape of their ears. "The children of the caretaker, I should think," she said. Yes, Delia was cutting slices of cake for them, and they were larger slices of cake than she would have cut had they been the children of her own friends. The children took the slices and stared at them with a curious fixed stare as if they were fierce. But perhaps they were frightened, because she had brought them up from the basement into the drawing-room.

"Eat it!" said Delia, giving them a little pat.

They began to munch slowly, gazing solemnly round them.

"Hullo, children!" cried Martin, beckoning to them. They stared at him solemnly.

"Haven't you got a name?" he said. They went on eating in silence. He began to fumble in his pocket.

"Speak!" he said. "Speak!"

"The younger generation," said Peggy, "don't mean to speak."

They turned their eyes on her now; but they went on munching. "No school tomorrow?" she said. They shook their heads from side to side.

"Hurrah!" said Martin. He held the coins in his hand; pressed between his thumb and finger. "Now—sing a song for sixpence!" he said.

"Yes. Weren't you taught something at school?" Peggy asked.

They stared at her but remained silent. They had stopped eating. They were a centre of a little group. They swept their eyes over the grown-up people for a moment, then, each giving the other a little nudge, they burst into song:

Etho passo tanno hai,
Fai donk to tu do,
Mai to, kai to, lai to see
Toh dom to tuh do—

That was what it sounded like. Not a word was recognisable. The distorted sounds rose and sank as if they followed a tune. They stopped.

They stood with their hands behind their backs. Then with one impulse they attacked the next verse:

Fanno to par, etto to mar,
Timin tudo, tido,
Foll to gar in, mitno to par,
Eido, teido, meido—

They sang the second verse more fiercely than the first. The rhythm seemed to rock and the unintelligible words ran themselves together almost into a shriek. The grown-up people did not know whether to laugh or to cry. Their voices were so harsh; the accent was so hideous.

They burst out again:

Chree to gay ei, Geeray didax. . . .

Then they stopped. It seemed to be in the middle of a verse. They stood there grinning, silent, looking at the floor. Nobody knew what to say. There was something horrible in the noise they made. It was so shrill, so discordant, and so meaningless. Then old Patrick ambled up.

"Ah, that's very nice, that's very nice. Thank you, my dears," he said in his genial way, fiddling with his toothpick. The children grinned at him. Then they began to make off. As they sidled past Martin, he slipped coins into their hands. Then they made a dash for the door.

"But what the devil were they singing?" said Hugh Gibbs. "I couldn't understand a word of it, I must confess." He held his hands to the sides of his large white waistcoat.

"Cockney accent, I suppose," said Patrick. "What they teach 'em at school, you know."

"But it was . . ." Eleanor began. She stopped. What was it? As they stood there they had looked so dignified; yet they had made this hideous noise. The contrast between their faces and their voices was astonishing; it was impossible to find one word for the whole. "Beautiful?" she said, with a note of interrogation, turning to Maggie.

"Extraordinarily," said Maggie.

But Eleanor was not sure that they were thinking of the same thing.

She gathered together her gloves, her bag and two or three coppers, and got up. The room was full of a queer pale light. Objects seemed to be rising out of their sleep, out of their disguise, and to be assuming the sobriety of daily life. The room was making ready for its use as an estate agent's office. The tables were becoming office tables; their legs were the legs of office tables, and yet they were still strewn with plates and glasses, with roses, lilies and carnations.

"It's time to go," she said, crossing the room. Delia had gone to the window. Now she jerked the curtains open.

"The dawn!" she exclaimed rather melodramatically.

The shapes of houses appeared across the square. Their blinds were all drawn; they seemed fast asleep still in the morning pallor.

"The dawn!" said Nicholas, getting up and stretching himself. He too walked across to the window. Renny followed him.

"Now for the peroration," he said, standing with him in the window. "The dawn—the new day—"

He pointed at the trees, at the roofs, at the sky.

"No," said Nicholas, holding back the curtain. "There you are mistaken. There is going to be no peroration—no peroration!" he exclaimed, throwing his arm out, "because there was no speech."

"But the dawn has risen," said Renny, pointing at the sky.

It was a fact. The sun had risen. The sky between the chimneys looked extraordinarily blue.

"And I am going to bed," said Nicholas after a pause. He turned away.

"Where is Sara?" he said, looking round him. There she was curled up in a corner with her head against a table asleep apparently.

"Wake your sister, Magdalena," he said, turning to Maggie. Maggie looked at her. Then she took a flower from the table and tossed it at her. She half-opened her eyes. "It's time," said Maggie, touching her on the shoulder. "Time, is it?" she sighed. She yawned and stretched herself. She fixed her eyes on Nicholas as if she were bringing him back to the field of vision. Then she laughed.

"Nicholas!" she exclaimed.

"Sara!" he replied. They smiled at each other. Then he helped her up and she balanced herself uncertainly against her sister, and rubbed her eyes.

"How strange," she murmured, looking round heir, ". . . how strange. . . ."

There were the smeared plates, and the empty wine-glasses; the petals and the bread crumbs. In the mixture of lights they looked prosaic but unreal; cadaverous but brilliant. And there against the window, gathered in a group, were the old brothers and sisters.

"Look, Maggie," she whispered, turning to her sister, "Look!" She pointed at the Pargiters, standing in the window.

The group in the window, the men in their black-and-white evening dress, the women in their crimsons, golds and silvers, wore a statuesque air for a moment, as if they were carved in stone. Their dresses fell in stiff sculptured folds. Then they moved; they changed their attitudes; they began to talk.

"Can't I give you a lift back, Nell?" Kitty Lasswade was saying. "I've a car waiting."

Eleanor did not answer. She was looking at the curtained houses across the square. The windows were spotted with gold. Everything looked clean swept, fresh and virginal. The pigeons were shuffling on the tree tops.

"I've a car . . ." Kitty repeated.

"Listen . . ." said Eleanor, raising her hand. Upstairs they were playing "God save the King" on the gramophone; but it was the pigeons she meant; they were crooning.

"That's wood pigeons, isn't it?" said Kitty. She put her head on one side to listen. Take two coos, Taffy, take two coos . . . tak . . . they were crooning.

"Wood pigeons?" said Edward, putting his hand to his ear.

"There on the tree tops," said Kitty. The green-blue birds were shuffling about on the branches, pecking and crooning to themselves.

Morris brushed the crumbs off his waistcoat.

"What an hour for us old fogies to be out of bed!" he said. "I haven't seen the sun rise since . . . since. . . ."

"Ah, but when we were young," said old Patrick, slapping him on the shoulder, "we thought nothing of making a night of it! I remember going to Covent Garden and buying roses for a certain lady. . ."

Delia smiled as if some romance, her own or another's, had been recalled to her.

"And I . . ." Eleanor began. She stopped. She saw an empty milk jug and leaves falling. Then it had been autumn. Now it was summer. The sky was a faint blue; the roofs were tinged purple against the blue; the chimneys were a pure brick red. An air of ethereal calm and simplicity lay over everything.

"And all the tubes have stopped, and all the omnibuses," she said turning round. "How are we going to get home?"

"We can walk," said Rose. "Walking won't do us any harm."

"Not on a fine summer morning," said Martin.

A breeze went through the square. In the stillness they could hear the branches rustle as they rose slightly, and fell, and shook a wave of green light through the air.

Then the door burst open. Couple after couple came flocking in, dishevelled, gay, to look for their cloaks and their hats, to say good-night.

"It's been so good of you to come!" Delia exclaimed, turning towards them with her hands outstretched.

"Thank you—thank you for coming!" she cried.

"And look at Maggie's bunch!" she said, taking a bunch of many coloured flowers that Maggie held out to her.

"How beautifully you've arranged them!" she said. "Look, Eleanor!" She turned to her sister.

But Eleanor was standing with her back to them. She was watching a taxi that was gliding slowly round the square. It stopped in front of a house two doors down.

"Aren't they lovely?" said Delia, holding out the flowers.

Eleanor started.

"The roses? Yes . . ." she said. But she was watching the cab. A young man had got out; he paid the driver. Then a girl in a tweed travelling suit followed him. He fitted his latch-key to the door. "There," Eleanor murmured, as he opened the door and they stood for a moment on the threshold. "There!" she repeated, as the door shut with a little thud behind them.

Then she turned round into the room. "And now?" she said, looking at Morris, who was drinking the last drops of a glass of wine. "And now?" she asked, holding out her hands to him.

The sun had risen, and the sky above the houses wore an air of extraordinary beauty, simplicity and peace.

THE WAVES

The sun had not yet risen. The sea was indistinguishable from the sky, except that the sea was slightly creased as if a cloth had wrinkles in it. Gradually as the sky whitened a dark line lay on the horizon dividing the sea from the sky and the grey cloth became barred with thick strokes moving, one after another, beneath the surface, following each other, pursuing each other, perpetually.

As they neared the shore each bar rose, heaped itself, broke and swept a thin veil of white water across the sand. The wave paused, and then drew out again, sighing like a sleeper whose breath comes and goes unconsciously. Gradually the dark bar on the horizon became clear as if the sediment in an old wine-bottle had sunk and left the glass green. Behind it, too, the sky cleared as if the white sediment there had sunk, or as if the arm of a woman couched beneath the horizon had raised a lamp and flat bars of white, green and yellow spread across the sky like the blades of a fan. Then she raised her lamp higher and the air seemed to become fibrous and to tear away from the green surface flickering and flaming in red and yellow fibres like the smoky fire that roars from a bonfire. Gradually the fibres of the burning bonfire were fused into one haze, one incandescence which lifted the weight of the woollen grey sky on top of it and turned it to a million atoms of soft blue. The surface of the sea slowly became transparent and lay rippling and sparkling until the dark stripes were almost rubbed out. Slowly the arm that held the lamp raised it higher and then higher until a broad flame became visible; an arc of fire burnt on the rim of the horizon, and all round it the sea blazed gold.

The light struck upon the trees in the garden, making one leaf transparent and then another. One bird chirped high up; there was a pause; another chirped lower down. The sun sharpened the walls of the house, and rested like the tip of a fan upon a white

387

*blind and made a blue finger-print of shadow under the leaf by
the bedroom window. The blind stirred slightly, but all within was
dim and unsubstantial. The birds sang their blank melody outside.*

'I see a ring,' said Bernard, 'hanging above me. It quivers and
hangs in a loop of light.'

'I see a slab of pale yellow,' said Susan, 'spreading away until it
meets a purple stripe.'

'I hear a sound,' said Rhoda, 'cheep, chirp; cheep chirp; going
up and down.'

'I see a globe,' said Neville, 'hanging down in a drop against
the enormous flanks of some hill.'

'I see a crimson tassel,' said Jinny, 'twisted with gold threads.'

'I hear something stamping,' said Louis. 'A great beast's foot is
chained. It stamps, and stamps, and stamps.'

'Look at the spider's web on the corner of the balcony,' said
Bernard. 'It has beads of water on it, drops of white light.'

'The leaves are gathered round the window like pointed
ears,' said Susan.

'A shadow falls on the path,' said Louis, 'like an elbow bent.'

'Islands of light are swimming on the grass,' said Rhoda.
'They have fallen through the trees.'

'The birds' eyes are bright in the tunnels between the leaves,'
said Neville.

'The stalks are covered with harsh, short hairs,' said Jinny,
'and drops of water have stuck to them.'

'A caterpillar is curled in a green ring,' said Susan, 'notched
with blunt feet.'

'The grey-shelled snail draws across the path and flattens the
blades behind him,' said Rhoda.

'And burning lights from the window-panes flash in and out
on the grasses,' said Louis.

'Stones are cold to my feet,' said Neville. 'I feel each one, round
or pointed, separately.'

'The back of my hand burns,' said Jinny, 'but the palm is

clammy and damp with dew.'

'Now the cock crows like a spurt of hard, red water in the white tide,' said Bernard.

'Birds are singing up and down and in and out all round us,' said Susan.

'The beast stamps; the elephant with its foot chained; the great brute on the beach stamps,' said Louis.

'Look at the house,' said Jinny, 'with all its windows white with blinds.'

'Cold water begins to run from the scullery tap,' said Rhoda, 'over the mackerel in the bowl.'

'The walls are cracked with gold cracks,' said Bernard, 'and there are blue, finger-shaped shadows of leaves beneath the windows.'

'Now Mrs Constable pulls up her thick black stockings,' said Susan.

'When the smoke rises, sleep curls off the roof like a mist,' said Louis.

'The birds sang in chorus first,' said Rhoda. 'Now the scullery door is unbarred. Off they fly. Off they fly like a fling of seed. But one sings by the bedroom window alone.'

'Bubbles form on the floor of the saucepan,' said Jinny. 'Then they rise, quicker and quicker, in a silver chain to the top.'

'Now Billy scrapes the fish-scales with a jagged knife on to a wooden board,' said Neville.

'The dining-room window is dark blue now,' said Bernard, 'and the air ripples above the chimneys.'

'A swallow is perched on the lightning-conductor,' said Susan. 'And Biddy has smacked down the bucket on the kitchen flags.'

'That is the first stroke of the church bell,' said Louis. 'Then the others follow; one, two; one, two; one, two.'

'Look at the table-cloth, flying white along the table,' said Rhoda. 'Now there are rounds of white china, and silver streaks beside each plate.'

'Suddenly a bee booms in my ear,' said Neville. 'It is here;

it is past.'

'I burn, I shiver,' said Jinny, 'out of this sun, into this shadow.'

'Now they have all gone,' said Louis. 'I am alone. They have gone into the house for breakfast, and I am left standing by the wall among the flowers. It is very early, before lessons. Flower after flower is specked on the depths of green. The petals are harlequins. Stalks rise from the black hollows beneath. The flowers swim like fish made of light upon the dark, green waters. I hold a stalk in my hand. I am the stalk. My roots go down to the depths of the world, through earth dry with brick, and damp earth, through veins of lead and silver. I am all fibre. All tremors shake me, and the weight of the earth is pressed to my ribs. Up here my eyes are green leaves, unseeing. I am a boy in grey flannels with a belt fastened by a brass snake up here. Down there my eyes are the lidless eyes of a stone figure in a desert by the Nile. I see women passing with red pitchers to the river; I see camels swaying and men in turbans. I hear tramplings, tremblings, stirrings round me.

'Up here Bernard, Neville, Jinny and Susan (but not Rhoda) skim the flower-beds with their nets. They skim the butterflies from the nodding tops of the flowers. They brush the surface of the world. Their nets are full of fluttering wings. "Louis! Louis! Louis!" they shout. But they cannot see me. I am on the other side of the hedge. There are only little eye-holes among the leaves. Oh Lord, let them pass. Lord, let them lay their butterflies on a pocket-handkerchief on the gravel. Let them count out their tortoise-shells, their red admirals and cabbage whites. But let me be unseen. I am green as a yew tree in the shade of the hedge. My hair is made of leaves. I am rooted to the middle of the earth. My body is a stalk. I press the stalk. A drop oozes from the hole at the mouth and slowly, thickly, grows larger and larger. Now something pink passes the eyehole. Now an eye-beam is slid through the chink. Its beam strikes me. I am a boy in a grey flannel suit. She has found me. I am struck on the nape of the neck. She has kissed me. All is shattered.'

'I was running,' said Jinny, 'after breakfast. I saw leaves moving in a hole in the hedge. I thought "That is a bird on its nest." I parted them and looked; but there was no bird on a nest. The leaves went on moving. I was frightened. I ran past Susan, past Rhoda, and Neville and Bernard in the tool-house talking. I cried as I ran, faster and faster. What moved the leaves? What moves my heart, my legs? And I dashed in here, seeing you green as a bush, like a branch, very still, Louis, with your eyes fixed. "Is he dead?" I thought, and kissed you, with my heart jumping under my pink frock like the leaves, which go on moving, though there is nothing to move them. Now I smell geraniums; I smell earth mould. I dance. I ripple. I am thrown over you like a net of light. I lie quivering flung over you.'

'Through the chink in the hedge,' said Susan, 'I saw her kiss him. I raised my head from my flower-pot and looked through a chink in the hedge. I saw her kiss him. I saw them, Jinny and Louis, kissing. Now I will wrap my agony inside my pocket-handkerchief. It shall be screwed tight into a ball. I will go to the beech wood alone, before lessons. I will not sit at a table, doing sums. I will not sit next Jinny and next Louis. I will take my anguish and lay it upon the roots under the beech trees. I will examine it and take it between my fingers. They will not find me. I shall eat nuts and peer for eggs through the brambles and my hair will be matted and I shall sleep under hedges and drink water from ditches and die there.'

'Susan has passed us,' said Bernard. 'She has passed the tool-house door with her handkerchief screwed into a ball. She was not crying, but her eyes, which are so beautiful, were narrow as cats' eyes before they spring. I shall follow her, Neville. I shall go gently behind her, to be at hand, with my curiosity, to comfort her when she bursts out in a rage and thinks, "I am alone."

'Now she walks across the field with a swing, nonchalantly, to deceive us. Then she comes to the dip; she thinks she is unseen; she begins to run with her fists clenched in front of her. Her nails meet in the ball of her pocket-handkerchief. She is making for the beech woods out of the light. She spreads her arms as she comes to them and takes to the shade like a swimmer. But she is blind after the light and trips and flings herself down on the roots under the trees, where the light seems to pant in and out, in and out. The branches heave up and down. There is agitation and trouble here. There is gloom. The light is fitful. There is anguish here. The roots make a skeleton on the ground, with dead leaves heaped in the angles. Susan has spread her anguish out. Her pocket-handkerchief is laid on the roots of the beech trees and she sobs, sitting crumpled where she has fallen.'

'I saw her kiss him,' said Susan. 'I looked between the leaves and saw her. She danced in flecked with diamonds light as dust. And I am squat, Bernard, I am short. I have eyes that look close to the ground and see insects in the grass. The yellow warmth in my side turned to stone when I saw Jinny kiss Louis. I shall eat grass and die in a ditch in the brown water where dead leaves have rotted.'

'I saw you go,' said Bernard. 'As you passed the door of the tool-house I heard you cry "I am unhappy." I put down my knife. I was making boats out of firewood with Neville. And my hair is untidy, because when Mrs Constable told me to brush it there was a fly in a web, and I asked, "Shall I free the fly? Shall I let the fly be eaten?" So I am late always. My hair is unbrushed and these chips of wood stick in it. When I heard you cry I followed you, and saw you put down your handkerchief, screwed up, with its rage, with its hate, knotted in it. But soon that will cease. Our bodies are close now. You hear me breathe. You see the beetle too carrying off a leaf on its back. It runs this way, then that way, so that even your desire while you watch the beetle, to possess one single thing (it is Louis now) must waver, like the light in and out of the beech leaves; and then words, moving darkly, in the depths of your mind will break up this knot of hardness, screwed in your pocket-handkerchief.'

'I love,' said Susan, 'and I hate. I desire one thing only. My eyes are hard. Jinny's eyes break into a thousand lights. Rhoda's are like those pale flowers to which moths come in the evening. Yours grow full and brim and never break. But I am already set on my pursuit. I see insects in the grass. Though my mother still knits white socks for me and hems pinafores and I am a child, I love and I hate.'

'But when we sit together, close,' said Bernard, 'we melt into each other with phrases. We are edged with mist. We make an unsubstantial territory.'

'I see the beetle,' said Susan. 'It is black, I see; it is green, I see; I am tied down with single words. But you wander off; you slip away; you rise up higher, with words and words in phrases.'

'Now,' said Bernard, 'let us explore. There is the white house lying among the trees. It lies down there ever so far beneath us. We shall sink like swimmers just touching the ground with the tips of their toes. We shall sink through the green air of the leaves, Susan. We sink as we run. The waves close over us, the beech leaves meet above our heads. There is the stable clock with its gilt hands shining. Those are the flats and heights of the roofs of the great house. There is the stable-boy clattering in the yard in rubber boots. That is Elvedon.

'Now we have fallen through the tree-tops to the earth. The air no longer rolls its long, unhappy, purple waves over us. We touch earth; we tread ground. That is the close-clipped hedge of the ladies' garden. There they walk at noon, with scissors, clipping roses. Now we are in the ringed wood with the wall round it. This is Elvedon. I have seen signposts at the cross-roads with one arm pointing "To Elvedon". No one has been there. The ferns smell very strong, and there are red funguses growing beneath them. Now we wake the sleeping daws who have never seen a human form; now we tread on rotten oak apples, red with age and slippery. There is a ring of wall round this wood; nobody comes here. Listen! That is the flop of a giant toad in the undergrowth; that is the patter of some primeval fir-cone falling to rot among the ferns.

'Put your foot on this brick. Look over the wall. That is

393

Elvedon. The lady sits between the two long windows, writing. The gardeners sweep the lawn with giant brooms. We are the first to come here. We are the discoverers of an unknown land. Do not stir; if the gardeners saw us they would shoot us. We should be nailed like stoats to the stable door. Look! Do not move. Grasp the ferns tight on the top of the wall.'

'I see the lady writing. I see the gardeners sweeping,' said Susan. 'If we died here, nobody would bury us.'

'Run!' said Bernard. 'Run! The gardener with the black beard has seen us! We shall be shot! We shall be shot like jays and pinned to the wall! We are in a hostile country. We must escape to the beech wood. We must hide under the trees. I turned a twig as we came. There is a secret path. Bend as low as you can. Follow without looking back. They will think we are foxes. Run!

'Now we are safe. Now we can stand upright again. Now we can stretch our arms in this high canopy, in this vast wood. I hear nothing. That is only the murmur of the waves in the air. That is a wood-pigeon breaking cover in the tops of the beech trees. The pigeon beats the air; the pigeon beats the air with wooden wings.'

'Now you trail away,' said Susan, 'making phrases. Now you mount like an air-ball's string, higher and higher through the layers of the leaves, out of reach. Now you lag. Now you tug at my skirts, looking back, making phrases. You have escaped me. Here is the garden. Here is the hedge. Here is Rhoda on the path rocking petals to and fro in her brown basin.'

'All my ships are white,' said Rhoda. 'I do not want red petals of hollyhocks or geranium. I want white petals that float when I tip the basin up. I have a fleet now swimming from shore to shore. I will drop a twig in as a raft for a drowning sailor. I will drop a stone in and see bubbles rise from the depths of the sea. Neville has gone and Susan has gone; Jinny is in the kitchen garden picking currants with Louis perhaps. I have a short time alone, while Miss Hudson spreads our copy-books on the schoolroom table. I have a short space of freedom. I have picked all the fallen petals and made them swim. I have put raindrops in some. I will plant a lighthouse here, a head of Sweet Alice. And I will now rock the brown basin from side to side so that my ships may ride the waves. Some will founder. Some will dash themselves against the cliffs. One sails alone. That is my ship. It sails into icy caverns where the sea-bear barks and stalactites swing green chains. The waves rise; their crests curl; look at the lights on the mastheads. They have scattered, they have foundered, all except my ship, which mounts the wave and sweeps before the gale and reaches the islands where the parrots chatter and the creepers . . .'

'Where is Bernard?' said Neville. 'He has my knife. We were in the tool-shed making boats, and Susan came past the door. And Bernard dropped his boat and went after her taking my knife, the sharp one that cuts the keel. He is like a dangling wire, a broken bell-pull, always twangling. He is like the seaweed hung outside the window, damp now, now dry. He leaves me in the lurch; he follows Susan; and if Susan cries he will take my knife and tell her stories. The big blade is an emperor; the broken blade a Negro. I hate dangling things; I hate dampish things. I hate wandering and mixing things together. Now the bell rings and we shall be late. Now we must drop our toys. Now we must go in together. The copy-books are laid out side by side on the green baize table.'

'I will not conjugate the verb,' said Louis, 'until Bernard has said it. My father is a banker in Brisbane and I speak with an Australian accent. I will wait and copy Bernard. He is English. They are all English. Susan's father is a clergyman. Rhoda has no father. Bernard and Neville are the sons of gentlemen. Jinny lives with her grandmother in London. Now they suck their pens. Now they twist their copy-books, and, looking sideways at Miss Hudson, count the purple buttons on her bodice. Bernard has a chip in his hair. Susan has a red look in her eyes. Both are flushed. But I am pale; I am neat, and my knickerbockers are drawn together by a belt with a brass snake. I know the lesson by heart. I know more than they will ever know. I knew my cases and my genders; I could know everything in the world if I wished. But I do not wish to come to the top and say my lesson. My roots are threaded, like fibres in a flower-pot, round and round about the world. I do not wish to come to the top and live in the light of this great clock, yellow-faced, which ticks and ticks. Jinny and Susan, Bernard and Neville bind themselves into a thong with which to lash me. They laugh at my neatness, at my Australian accent. I will now try to imitate Bernard softly lisping Latin.'

'Those are white words,' said Susan, 'like stones one picks up by the seashore.'

'They flick their tails right and left as I speak them,' said Bernard. 'They wag their tails; they flick their tails; they move through the air in flocks, now this way, now that way, moving all together, now dividing, now coming together.'

'Those are yellow words, those are fiery words,' said Jinny. 'I should like a fiery dress, a yellow dress, a fulvous dress to wear in the evening.'

'Each tense,' said Neville, 'means differently. There is an order in this world; there are distinctions, there are differences in this world, upon whose verge I step. For this is only a beginning.'

'Now Miss Hudson,' said Rhoda, 'has shut the book. Now the terror is beginning. Now taking her lump of chalk she draws figures, six, seven, eight, and then a cross and then a line on the blackboard. What is the answer? The others look; they look with understanding. Louis writes; Susan writes; Neville writes; Jinny writes; even Bernard has now begun to write. But I cannot write. I see only figures. The others are handing in their answers, one by one. Now it is my turn. But I have no answer. The others are allowed to go. They slam the door. Miss Hudson goes. I am left alone to find an answer. The figures mean nothing now. Meaning has gone. The clock ticks. The two hands are convoys marching through a desert. The black bars on the clock face are green oases. The long hand has marched ahead to find water. The other, painfully stumbles among hot stones in the desert. It will die in the desert. The kitchen door slams. Wild dogs bark far away. Look, the loop of the figure is beginning to fill with time; it holds the world in it. I begin to draw a figure and the world is looped in it, and I myself am outside the loop; which I now join—so—and seal up, and make entire. The world is entire, and I am outside of it, crying, "Oh save me, from being blown for ever outside the loop of time!"'

'There Rhoda sits staring at the blackboard,' said Louis, 'in the schoolroom, while we ramble off, picking here a bit of thyme, pinching here a leaf of southernwood while Bernard tells a story. Her shoulder-blades meet across her back like the wings of a small butterfly. And as she stares at the chalk figures, her mind lodges in those white circles, it steps through those white loops into emptiness, alone. They have no meaning for her. She has no answer for them. She has no body as the others have. And I, who speak with an Australian accent, whose father is a banker in Brisbane, do not fear her as I fear the others.'

'Let us now crawl,' said Bernard, 'under the canopy of the currant leaves, and tell stories. Let us inhabit the underworld. Let us take possession of our secret territory, which is lit by pendant currants like candelabra, shining red on one side, black on the other. Here, Jinny, if we curl up close, we can sit under the canopy of the currant leaves and watch the censers swing. This is our universe. The others pass down the carriage-drive. The skirts of Miss Hudson and Miss Curry sweep by like candle extinguishers. Those are Susan's white socks. Those are Louis' neat sand-shoes firmly printing the gravel. Here come warm gusts of decomposing leaves, of rotting vegetation. We are in a swamp now; in a malarial jungle. There is an elephant white with maggots, killed by an arrow shot dead in its eye. The bright eyes of hopping birds—eagles, vultures—are apparent. They take us for fallen trees. They pick at a worm—that is a hooded cobra—and leave it with a festering brown scar to be mauled by lions. This is our world, lit with crescents and stars of light;

and great petals half transparent block the openings like purple windows. Everything is strange. Things are huge and very small. The stalks of flowers are thick as oak trees. Leaves are high as the domes of vast cathedrals. We are giants, lying here, who can make forests quiver.'

'This is here,' said Jinny, 'this is now. But soon we shall go. Soon Miss Curry will blow her whistle. We shall walk. We shall part. You will go to school. You will have masters wearing crosses with white ties. I shall have a mistress in a school on the East Coast who sits under a portrait of Queen Alexandra. That is where I am going, and Susan and Rhoda. This is only here; this is only now. Now we lie under the currant bushes and every time the breeze stirs we are mottled all over. My hand is like a snake's skin. My knees are pink floating islands. Your face is like an apple tree netted under.'

'The heat is going,' said Bernard, 'from the Jungle. The leaves flap black wings over us. Miss Curry has blown her whistle on the terrace. We must creep out from the awning of the currant leaves and stand upright. There are twigs in your hair, Jinny. There is a green caterpillar on your neck. We must form, two by two. Miss Curry is taking us for a brisk walk, while Miss Hudson sits at her desk settling her accounts.'

'It is dull,' said Jinny, 'walking along the high road with no windows to look at, with no bleared eyes of blue glass let into the pavement.'

'We must form into pairs,' said Susan, 'and walk in order, not shuffling our feet, not lagging, with Louis going first to lead us, because Louis is alert and not a wool-gatherer.'

'Since I am supposed,' said Neville, 'to be too delicate to go with them, since I get so easily tired and then am sick, I will use this hour of solitude, this reprieve from conversation, to coast round the purlieus of the house and recover, if I can, by standing on the same stair half-way up the landing, what I felt when I heard about the dead man through the swing-door last night when cook was shoving in and out the dampers. He was found with his throat cut. The apple-tree leaves became fixed in the sky; the moon glared; I was unable to lift my foot up the stair. He was found in the gutter. His blood gurgled down the gutter. His jowl was white as a dead codfish. I shall call this stricture, this rigidity, "death among the apple trees" for ever. There were the floating, pale-grey clouds; and the immitigable tree; the implacable tree with its greaved silver bark. The ripple of my life was unavailing. I was unable to pass by. There was an obstacle. "I cannot surmount this unintelligible obstacle," I said. And the others passed on. But we are doomed, all of us, by the apple trees, by the immitigable tree which we cannot pass.

'Now the stricture and rigidity are over; and I will continue to make my survey of the purlieus of the house in the late afternoon, in the sunset, when the sun makes oleaginous spots on the linoleum, and a crack of light kneels on the wall, making the chair legs look broken.'

'I saw Florrie in the kitchen garden,' said Susan, 'as we came back from our walk, with the washing blown out round her, the pyjamas, the drawers, the night-gowns blown tight. And Ernest kissed her. He was in his green baize apron, cleaning silver; and his mouth was sucked like a purse in wrinkles and he seized her with the pyjamas blown out hard between them. He was blind as a bull, and she swooned in anguish, only little veins streaking her white cheeks red. Now though they pass plates of bread and butter and cups of milk at tea-time I see a crack in the earth and hot steam hisses up; and the urn roars as Ernest roared, and I am blown out hard like the pyjamas, even while my teeth meet in the soft bread and butter, and I lap the sweet milk. I am not afraid of heat, nor of the frozen winter. Rhoda dreams, sucking a crust soaked in milk; Louis regards the wall opposite with snail-green eyes; Bernard moulds his bread into pellets and calls them "people". Neville with his clean and decisive ways has finished. He has rolled his napkin and slipped it through the silver ring. Jinny spins her fingers on the table-cloth, as if they were dancing in the sunshine, pirouetting. But I am not afraid of the heat or of the frozen winter.'

'Now,' said Louis, 'we all rise; we all stand up. Miss Curry spreads wide the black book on the harmonium. It is difficult not to weep as we sing, as we pray that God may keep us safe while we sleep, calling ourselves little children. When we are sad and trembling with apprehension it is sweet to sing together, leaning slightly, I towards Susan, Susan towards Bernard, clasping hands, afraid of much, I of my accent, Rhoda of figures; yet resolute to conquer.'

'We troop upstairs like ponies,' said Bernard, 'stamping, clattering one behind another to take our turns in the bathroom. We buffet, we tussle, we spring up and down on the hard, white beds. My turn has come. I come now.

'Mrs Constable, girt in a bath-towel, takes her lemon-coloured sponge and soaks it in water; it turns chocolate-brown; it drips; and, holding it high above me, shivering beneath her, she squeezes it. Water pours down the runnel of my spine. Bright arrows of sensation shoot on either side. I am covered with warm flesh. My dry crannies are wetted; my cold body is warmed; it is sluiced and gleaming. Water descends and sheets me like an eel. Now hot towels envelop me, and their roughness, as I rub my back, makes my blood purr. Rich and heavy sensations form on the roof of my mind; down showers the day—the woods; and Elvedon; Susan and the pigeon. Pouring down the walls of my mind, running together, the day falls copious, resplendent. Now I tie my pyjamas loosely round me, and lie under this thin sheet afloat in the shallow light which is like a film of water drawn over my eyes by a wave. I hear through it far off, far away, faint and far, the chorus beginning; wheels; dogs; men shouting; church bells; the chorus beginning.'

'As I fold up my frock and my chemise,' said Rhoda, 'so I put off my hopeless desire to be Susan, to be Jinny. But I will stretch my toes so that they touch the rail at the end of the bed; I will assure myself, touching the rail, of something hard. Now I cannot sink; cannot altogether fall through the thin sheet now. Now I spread my body on this frail mattress and hang suspended. I am above the earth now. I am no longer upright, to be knocked against and damaged. All is soft, and bending. Walls and cupboards whiten and bend their yellow squares on top of which a pale glass gleams. Out of me now my mind can pour. I can think of my Armadas sailing on the high waves. I am relieved of hard contacts and collisions. I sail on alone under the white cliffs. Oh, but I sink, I fall! That is the corner of the cupboard; that is the nursery looking-glass. But they stretch, they elongate. I sink down on the black plumes of sleep; its thick wings are pressed to my eyes. Travelling through darkness I see the stretched flower-beds, and Mrs Constable runs from behind the corner of the pampas-grass to say my aunt has come to fetch me in a carriage. I mount; I escape; I rise on spring-heeled boots over the tree-tops. But I am now fallen into the carriage at the hall door, where she sits nodding yellow plumes with eyes hard like glazed marbles. Oh, to awake from dreaming! Look, there is the chest of drawers. Let me pull myself out of these waters. But they heap themselves on me; they sweep me between their great shoulders; I am turned; I am tumbled; I am stretched, among these long lights, these long waves, these endless paths, with people pursuing, pursuing.'

The sun rose higher. Blue waves, green waves swept a quick fan over the beach, circling the spike of sea-holly and leaving shallow pools of light here and there on the sand. A faint black rim was left behind them. The rocks which had been misty and soft hardened and were marked with red clefts.

Sharp stripes of shadow lay on the grass, and the dew dancing on the tips of the flowers and leaves made the garden like a mosaic of single sparks not yet formed into one whole. The birds, whose breasts were specked canary and rose, now sang a strain or two together, wildly, like skaters rollicking arm-in-arm, and were suddenly silent, breaking asunder.

The sun laid broader blades upon the house. The light touched

something green in the window corner and made it a lump of
emerald, a cave of pure green like stoneless fruit. It sharpened
the edges of chairs and tables and stitched white table-cloths with
fine gold wires. As the light increased a bud here and there split
asunder and shook out flowers, green veined and quivering, as
if the effort of opening had set them rocking, and pealing a faint
carillon as they beat their frail clappers against their white walls.
Everything became softly amorphous, as if the china of the plate
flowed and the steel of the knife were liquid. Meanwhile the
concussion of the waves breaking fell with muffled thuds, like logs
falling, on the shore.

'Now,' said Bernard, 'the time has come. The day has come.
The cab is at the door. My huge box bends George's bandy-legs
even wider. The horrible ceremony is over, the tips, and the
good-byes in the hall. Now there is this gulping ceremony with
my mother, this hand-shaking ceremony with my father; now I
must go on waving, I must go on waving, till we turn the corner.
Now that ceremony is over. Heaven be praised, all ceremonies
are over. I am alone; I am going to school for the first time.

'Everybody seems to be doing things for this moment only;
and never again. Never again. The urgency of it all is fearful.
Everybody knows I am going to school, going to school for
the first time. "That boy is going to school for the first time,"
says the housemaid, cleaning the steps. I must not cry. I must
behold them indifferently. Now the awful portals of the station
gape; "the moon-faced clock regards me." I must make phrases
and phrases and so interpose something hard between myself
and the stare of housemaids, the stare of clocks, staring faces,
indifferent faces, or I shall cry. There is Louis, there is Neville, in
long coats, carrying handbags, by the booking-office. They are
composed. But they look different.'

'Here is Bernard,' said Louis. 'He is composed; he is easy.
He swings his bag as he walks. I will follow Bernard, because
he is not afraid. We are drawn through the booking-office on

to the platform as a stream draws twigs and straws round the piers of a bridge. There is the very powerful, bottle-green engine without a neck, all back and thighs, breathing steam. The guard blows his whistle; the flag is dipped; without an effort, of its own momentum, like an avalanche started by a gentle push, we start forward. Bernard spreads a rug and plays knuckle-bones. Neville reads. London crumbles. London heaves and surges. There is a bristling of chimneys and towers. There a white church; there a mast among the spires. There a canal. Now there are open spaces with asphalt paths upon which it is strange that people should now be walking. There is a hill striped with red houses. A man crosses a bridge with a dog at his heels. Now the red boy begins firing at a pheasant. The blue boy shoves him aside. "My uncle is the best shot in England. My cousin is Master of Foxhounds." Boasting begins. And I cannot boast, for my father is a banker in Brisbane, and I speak with an Australian accent.'

'After all this hubbub,' said Neville, 'all this scuffling and hubbub, we have arrived. This is indeed a moment—this is indeed a solemn moment. I come, like a lord to his halls appointed. That is our founder; our illustrious founder, standing in the courtyard with one foot raised. I salute our founder. A noble Roman air hangs over these austere quadrangles. Already the lights are lit in the form rooms. Those are laboratories perhaps; and that a library, where I shall explore the exactitude of the Latin language, and step firmly upon the well-laid sentences, and pronounce the explicit, the sonorous hexameters of Virgil, of Lucretius; and chant with a passion that is never obscure or formless the loves of Catullus, reading from a big book, a quarto with margins. I shall lie, too, in the fields among the tickling grasses. I shall lie with my friends under the towering elm trees.

'Behold, the Headmaster. Alas, that he should excite my ridicule. He is too sleek, he is altogether too shiny and black, like some statue in a public garden. And on the left side of his waistcoat, his taut, his drum-like waistcoat, hangs a crucifix.'

'Old Crane,' said Bernard, 'now rises to address us. Old Crane, the Headmaster, has a nose like a mountain at sunset, and a blue cleft in his chin, like a wooded ravine, which some tripper has fired; like a wooded ravine seen from the train window. He sways slightly, mouthing out his tremendous and sonorous words. I love tremendous and sonorous words. But his words are too hearty to be true. Yet he is by this time convinced of their truth. And when he leaves the room, lurching rather heavily from side to side, and hurls his way through the swing-doors, all the masters, lurching rather heavily from side to side, hurl themselves also through the swing-doors. This is our first night at school, apart from our sisters.'

'This is my first night at school,' said Susan, 'away from my father, away from my home. My eyes swell; my eyes prick with tears. I hate the smell of pine and linoleum. I hate the wind-bitten shrubs and the sanitary tiles. I hate the cheerful jokes and the glazed look of everyone. I left my squirrel and my doves for the boy to look after. The kitchen door slams, and shot patters among the leaves when Percy fires at the rooks. All here is false; all is meretricious. Rhoda and Jinny sit far off in brown serge, and look at Miss Lambert who sits under a picture of Queen Alexandra reading from a book before her. There is also a blue scroll of needlework embroidered by some old girl. If I do not purse my lips, if I do not screw my handkerchief, I shall cry.'

'The purple light,' said Rhoda, 'in Miss Lambert's ring passes to and fro across the black stain on the white page of the Prayer Book. It is a vinous, it is an amorous light. Now that our boxes are unpacked in the dormitories, we sit herded together under maps of the entire world. There are desks with wells for the ink. We shall write our exercises in ink here. But here I am nobody. I have no face. This great company, all dressed in brown serge, has robbed me of my identity. We are all callous, unfriended. I will seek out a face, a composed, a monumental face, and will endow it with omniscience, and wear it under my dress like a talisman and then (I promise this) I will find some dingle in a

404

wood where I can display my assortment of curious treasures. I promise myself this. So I will not cry.'

'That dark woman,' said Jinny, 'with high cheek-bones, has a shiny dress, like a shell, veined, for wearing in the evening. That is nice for summer, but for winter I should like a thin dress shot with red threads that would gleam in the firelight. Then when the lamps were lit, I should put on my red dress and it would be thin as a veil, and would wind about my body, and billow out as I came into the room, pirouetting. It would make a flower shape as I sank down, in the middle of the room, on a gilt chair. But Miss Lambert wears an opaque dress, that falls in a cascade from her snow-white ruffle as she sits under a picture of Queen Alexandra pressing one white finger firmly on the page. And we pray.'

'Now we march, two by two,' said Louis, 'orderly, processional, into chapel. I like the dimness that falls as we enter the sacred building. I like the orderly progress. We file in; we seat ourselves. We put off our distinctions as we enter. I like it now, when, lurching slightly, but only from his momentum, Dr Crane mounts the pulpit and reads the lesson from a Bible spread on the back of the brass eagle. I rejoice; my heart expands in his bulk, in his authority. He lays the whirling dust clouds in my tremulous, my ignominiously agitated mind—how we danced round the Christmas tree and handing parcels they forgot me, and the fat woman said, "This little boy has no present," and gave me a shiny Union Jack from the top of the tree, and I cried with fury—to be remembered with pity. Now all is laid by his authority, his crucifix, and I feel come over me the sense of the earth under me, and my roots going down and down till they wrap themselves round some hardness at the centre. I recover my continuity, as he reads. I become a figure in the procession, a spoke in the huge wheel that turning, at last erects me, here and now. I have been in the dark; I have been hidden; but when the wheel turns (as he reads) I rise into this dim light where I just perceive, but scarcely, kneeling boys, pillars and memorial

405

brasses. There is no crudity here, no sudden kisses.'

'The brute menaces my liberty,' said Neville, 'when he prays. Unwarmed by imagination, his words fall cold on my head like paving-stones, while the gilt cross heaves on his waistcoat. The words of authority are corrupted by those who speak them. I gibe and mock at this sad religion, at these tremulous, grief-stricken figures advancing, cadaverous and wounded, down a white road shadowed by fig trees where boys sprawl in the dust—naked boys; and goatskins distended with wine hang at the tavern door. I was in Rome travelling with my father at Easter; and the trembling figure of Christ's mother was borne niddle-noddling along the streets; there went by also the stricken figure of Christ in a glass case.

'Now I will lean sideways as if to scratch my thigh. So I shall see Percival. There he sits, upright among the smaller fry. He breathes through his straight nose rather heavily. His blue and oddly inexpressive eyes are fixed with pagan indifference upon the pillar opposite. He would make an admirable churchwarden. He should have a birch and beat little boys for misdemeanours. He is allied with the Latin phrases on the memorial brasses. He sees nothing; he hears nothing. He is remote from us all in a pagan universe. But look—he flicks his hand to the back of his neck. For such gestures one falls hopelessly in love for a lifetime. Dalton, Jones, Edgar and Bateman flick their hands to the back of their necks likewise. But they do not succeed.'

'At last,' said Bernard, 'the growl ceases. The sermon ends. He has minced the dance of the white butterflies at the door to powder. His rough and hairy voice is like an unshaven chin. Now he lurches back to his seat like a drunken sailor. It is an action that all the other masters will try to imitate; but, being flimsy, being floppy, wearing grey trousers, they will only succeed in making themselves ridiculous. I do not despise them. Their antics seem pitiable in my eyes. I note the fact for future reference with many others in my notebook. When I am grown up I shall carry a notebook—a fat book with many pages, methodically lettered. I shall enter my phrases. Under B shall come "Butterfly powder". If, in my novel, I describe the sun on the window-sill, I shall look under B and find butterfly powder. That will be useful. The tree "shades the window with green fingers". That will be useful. But alas! I am so soon distracted— by a hair like twisted candy, by Celia's Prayer Book, ivory covered. Louis' can contemplate nature, unwinking, by the hour. Soon I fail, unless talked to. "The lake of my mind, unbroken by oars, heaves placidly and soon sinks into an oily somnolence." That will be useful.'

'Now we move out of this cool temple, into the yellow playing-fields,' said Louis. 'And, as it is a half-holiday (the Duke's birthday) we will settle among the long grasses, while they play cricket. Could I be "they" I would choose it; I would buckle on my pads and stride across the playing-field at the head of the batsmen. Look now, how everybody follows Percival. He is heavy. He walks clumsily down the field, through the long grass, to where the great elm trees stand. His magnificence is that of some mediaeval commander. A wake of light seems to lie on the grass behind him. Look at us trooping after him, his faithful servants, to be shot like sheep, for he will certainly attempt some forlorn enterprise and die in battle. My heart turns rough; it abrades my side like a file with two edges: one, that I adore his magnificence; the other I despise his slovenly accents—I who am so much his superior—and am jealous.'

'And now,' said Neville, 'let Bernard begin. Let him burble on, telling us stories, while we lie recumbent. Let him describe what we have all seen so that it becomes a sequence. Bernard says there is always a story. I am a story. Louis is a story. There is the story of the boot-boy, the story of the man with one eye, the story of the woman who sells winkles. Let him burble on with his story while I lie back and regard the stiff-legged figures of the padded batsmen through the trembling grasses. It seems as if the whole world were flowing and curving—on the earth the trees, in the sky the clouds. I look up, through the trees, into

407

the sky. The match seems to be played up there. Faintly among the soft, white clouds I hear the cry "Run", I hear the cry "How's that?" The clouds lose tufts of whiteness as the breeze dishevels them. If that blue could stay for ever; if that hole could remain for ever; if this moment could stay for ever—

'But Bernard goes on talking. Up they bubble—images. "Like a camel," . . . "a vulture." The camel is a vulture; the vulture a camel; for Bernard is a dangling wire, loose, but seductive. Yes, for when he talks, when he makes his foolish comparisons, a lightness comes over one. One floats, too, as if one were that bubble; one is freed; I have escaped, one feels. Even the chubby little boys (Dalton, Larpent and Baker) feel the same abandonment. They like this better than the cricket. They catch the phrases as they bubble. They let the feathery grasses tickle their noses. And then we all feel Percival lying heavy among us. His curious guffaw seems to sanction our laughter. But now he has rolled himself over in the long grass. He is, I think, chewing a stalk between his teeth. He feels bored; I too feel bored. Bernard at once perceives that we are bored. I detect a certain effort, an extravagance in his phrase, as if he said "Look!" but Percival says "No." For he is always the first to detect insincerity; and is brutal in the extreme. The sentence tails off feebly. Yes, the appalling moment has come when Bernard's power fails him and there is no longer any sequence and he sags and twiddles a bit of string and falls silent, gaping as if about to burst into tears. Among the tortures and devastations of life is this then—our friends are not able to finish their stories.'

'Now let me try,' said Louis, 'before we rise, before we go to tea, to fix the moment in one effort of supreme endeavour. This shall endure. We are parting; some to tea; some to the nets; I to show my essay to Mr Barker. This will endure. From discord, from hatred (I despise dabblers in imagery—I resent the power of Percival intensely) my shattered mind is pieced together by some sudden perception. I take the trees, the clouds, to be witnesses of my complete integration. I, Louis, I, who shall walk the earth these seventy years, am born entire, out of hatred, out of discord. Here on this ring of grass we have sat together, bound by the tremendous power of some inner compulsion. The trees wave, the clouds pass. The time approaches when these soliloquies shall be shared. We shall not always give out a sound like a beaten gong as one sensation strikes and then another. Children, our lives have been gongs striking; clamour and boasting; cries of despair; blows on the nape of the neck in gardens.

'Now grass and trees, the travelling air blowing empty spaces in the blue which they then recover, shaking the leaves which then replace themselves, and our ring here, sitting, with our arms binding our knees, hint at some other order, and better, which makes a reason everlastingly. This I see for a second, and shall try tonight to fix in words, to forge in a ring of steel, though Percival destroys it, as he blunders off, crushing the grasses, with the small fry trotting subservient after him. Yet it is Percival I need; for it is Percival who inspires poetry.'

'For how many months,' said Susan, 'for how many years, have I run up these stairs, in the dismal days of winter, in the chilly days of spring? Now it is midsummer. We go upstairs to change into white frocks to play tennis—Jinny and I with Rhoda following after. I count each step as I mount, counting each step something done with. So each night I tear off the old day from the calendar, and screw it tight into a ball. I do this vindictively, while Betty and Clara are on their knees. I do not pray. I revenge myself upon the day. I wreak my spite upon its image. You are dead now, I say, school day, hated day. They have made all the days of June—this is the twenty-fifth—shiny and orderly, with gongs, with lessons, with orders to wash, to change, to work, to eat. We listen to missionaries from China. We drive off in brakes along the asphalt pavement, to attend concerts in halls. We are shown galleries and pictures.

'At home the hay waves over the meadows. My father leans

upon the stile, smoking. In the house one door bangs and then another, as the summer air puffs along the empty passages. Some old picture perhaps swings on the wall. A petal drops from the rose in the jar. The farm wagons strew the hedges with tufts of hay. All this I see, I always see, as I pass the looking-glass on the landing, with Jinny in front and Rhoda lagging behind. Jinny dances. Jinny always dances in the hall on the ugly, the encaustic tiles; she turns cartwheels in the playground; she picks some flower forbiddenly, and sticks it behind her ear so that Miss Perry's dark eyes smoulder with admiration, for Jinny, not me. Miss Perry loves Jinny; and I could have loved her, but now love no one, except my father, my doves and the squirrel whom I left in the cage at home for the boy to look after.'

'I hate the small looking-glass on the stairs,' said Jinny. 'It shows our heads only; it cuts off our heads. And my lips are too wide, and my eyes are too close together; I show my gums too much when I laugh. Susan's head, with its fell look, with its grass-green eyes which poets will love, Bernard said, because they fall upon close white stitching, put mine out; even Rhoda's face, mooning, vacant, is completed, like those white petals she used to swim in her bowl. So I skip up the stairs past them, to the next landing, where the long glass hangs and I see myself entire. I see my body and head in one now; for even in this serge frock they are one, my body and my head. Look, when I move my head I ripple all down my narrow body; even my thin legs ripple like a stalk in the wind. I flicker between the set face of Susan and Rhoda's vagueness; I leap like one of those flames that run between the cracks of the earth; I move, I dance; I never cease to move and to dance. I move like the leaf that moved in the hedge as a child and frightened me. I dance over these streaked, these impersonal, distempered walls with their yellow skirting as firelight dances over teapots. I catch fire even from women's cold eyes. When I read, a purple rim runs round the black edge of the textbook. Yet I cannot follow any word through its changes. I cannot follow any thought from present to past. I do not stand lost, like Susan, with tears in my eyes remembering home; or lie, like Rhoda, crumpled among the ferns, staining my pink cotton green, while I dream of plants that flower under the sea, and rocks through which the fish swim slowly. I do not dream.

'Now let us be quick. Now let me be the first to pull off these coarse clothes. Here are my clean white stockings. Here are my new shoes. I bind my hair with a white ribbon, so that when I leap across the court the ribbon will stream out in a flash, yet curl round my neck, perfectly in its place. Not a hair shall be untidy.'

'That is my face,' said Rhoda, 'in the looking-glass behind Susan's shoulder—that face is my face. But I will duck behind her to hide it, for I am not here. I have no face. Other people have faces; Susan and Jinny have faces; they are here. Their world is the real world. The things they lift are heavy. They say Yes, they say No; whereas I shift and change and am seen through in a second. If they meet a housemaid she looks at them without laughing. But she laughs at me. They know what to say if spoken to. They laugh really; they get angry really; while I have to look first and do what other people do when they have done it.

'See now with what extraordinary certainty Jinny pulls on her stockings, simply to play tennis. That I admire. But I like Susan's way better, for she is more resolute, and less ambitious of distinction than Jinny. Both despise me for copying what they do; but Susan sometimes teaches me, for instance, how to tie a bow, while Jinny has her own knowledge but keeps it to herself. They have friends to sit by. They have things to say privately in corners. But I attach myself only to names and faces; and hoard them like amulets against disaster. I choose out across the hall some unknown face and can hardly drink my tea when she whose name I do not know sits opposite. I choke. I am rocked from side to side by the violence of my emotion. I imagine these nameless, these immaculate people, watching me from behind bushes. I leap high to excite their admiration. At night, in bed, I excite their complete wonder. I often die pierced with arrows to win their tears. If they should say, or I should

411

see from a label on their boxes, that they were in Scarborough last holidays, the whole town runs gold, the whole pavement is illuminated. Therefore I hate looking-glasses which show me my real face. Alone, I often fall down into nothingness. I must push my foot stealthily lest I should fall off the edge of the world into nothingness. I have to bang my head against some hard door to call myself back to the body.'

'We are late,' said Susan. We must wait our turn to play. We will pitch here in the long grass and pretend to watch Jinny and Clara, Betty and Mavis. But we will not watch them. I hate watching other people play games. I will make images of all the things I hate most and bury them in the ground. This shiny pebble is Madame Carlo, and I will bury her deep because of her fawning and ingratiating manners, because of the sixpence she gave me for keeping my knuckles flat when I played my scales. I buried her sixpence. I would bury the whole school: the gymnasium; the classroom; the dining-room that always smells of meat; and the chapel. I would bury the red-brown tiles and the oily portraits of old men—benefactors, founders of schools. There are some trees I like; the cherry tree with lumps of clear gum on the bark; and one view from the attic towards some far hills. Save for these, I would bury it all as I bury these ugly stones that are always scattered about this briny coast, with its piers and its trippers. At home, the waves are mile long. On winter nights we hear them booming. Last Christmas a man was drowned sitting alone in his cart.'

'When Miss Lambert passes,' said Rhoda, 'talking to the clergyman, the others laugh and imitate her hunch behind her back; yet everything changes and becomes luminous. Jinny leaps higher too when Miss Lambert passes. Suppose she saw that daisy, it would change. Wherever she goes, things are changed under her eyes; and yet when she has gone is not the thing the same again? Miss Lambert is taking the clergyman through the wicket-gate to her private garden; and when she comes to the pond, she sees a frog on a leaf, and that will change. All is solemn, all is pale where she stands, like a statue in a grove. She lets her tasselled silken cloak slip down, and only her purple ring still glows, her vinous, her amethystine ring. There is this mystery about people when they leave us. When they leave us I can companion them to the pond and make them stately. When Miss Lambert passes, she makes the daisy change; and everything runs like streaks of fire when she carves the beef. Month by month things are losing their hardness; even my body now lets the light through; my spine is soft like wax near the flame of the candle. I dream; I dream.'

'I have won the game,' said Jinny. 'Now it is your turn. I must throw myself on the ground and pant. I am out of breath with running, with triumph. Everything in my body seems thinned out with running and triumph. My blood must be bright red, whipped up, slapping against my ribs. My soles tingle, as if wire rings opened and shut in my feet. I see every blade of grass very clear. But the pulse drums so in my forehead, behind my eyes, that everything dances—the net, the grass; your faces leap like butterflies; the trees seem to jump up and down. There is nothing staid, nothing settled, in this universe. All is rippling, all is dancing; all is quickness and triumph. Only, when I have lain alone on the hard ground, watching you play your game, I begin to feel the wish to be singled out; to be summoned, to be called away by one person who comes to find me, who is attracted towards me, who cannot keep himself from me, but comes to where I sit on my gilt chair, with my frock billowing round me like a flower. And withdrawing into an alcove, sitting alone on a balcony we talk together.

'Now the tide sinks. Now the trees come to earth; the brisk waves that slap my ribs rock more gently, and my heart rides at anchor, like a sailing-boat whose sails slide slowly down on to the white deck. The game is over. We must go to tea now.'

'The boasting boys,' said Louis, 'have gone now in a vast team to play cricket. They have driven off in their great brake, singing in chorus. All their heads turn simultaneously at the corner by the laurel bushes. Now they are boasting. Larpent's brother played football for Oxford; Smith's father made a century at Lords. Archie and Hugh; Parker and Dalton; Larpent and Smith; then again Archie and Hugh; Parker and Dalton; Larpent and Smith—the names repeat themselves; the names are the same always. They are the volunteers; they are the cricketers; they are the officers of the Natural History Society. They are always forming into fours and marching in troops with badges on their caps; they salute simultaneously passing the figure of their general. How majestic is their order, how beautiful is their obedience! If I could follow, if I could be with them, I would sacrifice all I know. But they also leave butterflies trembling with their wings pinched off; they throw dirty pocket-handkerchiefs clotted with blood screwed up into corners. They make little boys sob in dark passages. They have big red ears that stand out under their caps. Yet that is what we wish to be, Neville and I. I watch them go with envy. Peeping from behind a curtain, I note the simultaneity of their movements with delight. If my legs were reinforced by theirs, how they would run! If I had been with them and won matches and rowed in great races, and galloped all day, how I should thunder out songs at midnight! In what a torrent the words would rush from my throat!'

'Percival has gone now,' said Neville. 'He is thinking of nothing but the match. He never waved his hand as the brake turned the corner by the laurel bush. He despises me for being too weak to play (yet he is always kind to my weakness). He despises me for not caring if they win or lose except that he cares. He takes my devotion; he accepts my tremulous, no doubt abject offering, mixed with contempt as it is for his mind. For he cannot read. Yet when I read Shakespeare or Catullus, lying in the long grass, he understands more than Louis. Not the words—but what are words? Do I not know already how to rhyme, how to imitate Pope, Dryden, even Shakespeare? But I cannot stand all day in the sun with my eyes on the ball; I cannot feel the flight of the ball through my body and think only of the ball. I shall be a clinger to the outsides of words all my life. Yet I could not live with him and suffer his stupidity. He will coarsen and snore. He will marry and there will be scenes of tenderness at breakfast. But now he is young. Not a thread, not a sheet of paper lies between him and the sun, between him and the rain, between him and the moon as he lies naked, tumbled, hot, on his bed. Now as they drive along the high road in their brake his face is mottled red and yellow. He will throw off his coat and stand with his legs apart, with his hands ready, watching the wicket. And he will pray, "Lord let us win"; he will think of one thing only, that they should win.

'How could I go with them in a brake to play cricket? Only Bernard could go with them, but Bernard is too late to go with them. He is always too late. He is prevented by his incorrigible moodiness from going with them. He stops, when he washes his hands, to say, "There is a fly in that web. Shall I rescue that fly; shall I let the spider eat it?" He is shaded with innumerable perplexities, or he would go with them to play cricket, and would lie in the grass, watching the sky, and would start when the ball was hit. But they would forgive him; for he would tell them a story.'

'They have bowled off,' said Bernard, 'and I am too late to go with them. The horrid little boys, who are also so beautiful, whom you and Louis, Neville, envy so deeply, have bowled off with their heads all turned the same way. But I am unaware of these profound distinctions. My fingers slip over the keyboard without knowing which is black and which white. Archie makes easily a hundred; I by a fluke make sometimes fifteen. But what is the difference between us? Wait though, Neville; let me talk. The bubbles are rising like the silver bubbles from the floor of a saucepan; image on top of image. I cannot sit down to my book, like Louis, with ferocious tenacity. I must open the little trap-door and let out these linked phrases in which I run together whatever happens, so that instead of incoherence there is perceived a wandering thread, lightly joining one thing to another. I will tell you the story of the doctor.

'When Dr Crane lurches through the swing-doors after prayers he is convinced, it seems, of his immense superiority; and indeed Neville, we cannot deny that his departure leaves us not only with a sense of relief, but also with a sense of something removed, like a tooth. Now let us follow him as he heaves through the swing-door to his own apartments. Let us imagine him in his private room over the stables undressing. He unfastens his sock suspenders (let us be trivial, let us be intimate). Then with a characteristic gesture (it is difficult to avoid these ready-made phrases, and they are, in his case, somehow appropriate) he takes the silver, he takes the coppers from his trouser pockets and places them there, and there, on his dressing-table. With both arms stretched on the arms of his chair he reflects (this is his private moment; it is here we must try to catch him): shall he cross the pink bridge into his bedroom or shall he not cross it? The two rooms are united by a bridge of rosy light from the lamp at the bedside where Mrs Crane lies with her hair on the pillow reading a French memoir. As she reads, she sweeps her hand with an abandoned and despairing gesture over her forehead, and sighs, "Is this all?" comparing herself with some French duchess. Now, says the doctor, in two years I shall retire. I shall clip yew hedges in a west country garden. An admiral I might have been; or a judge; not a schoolmaster. What forces, he asks, staring at the gas-fire with his shoulders hunched up more hugely than we know them (he is in his shirt-sleeves remember), have brought me to this? What vast forces? he thinks, getting into the stride of his majestic phrases as he looks over his shoulder at the window. It is a stormy night; the branches of the chestnut trees are ploughing up and down. Stars flash between them. What vast forces of good and evil have brought me here? he asks, and sees with sorrow that his chair has worn a little hole in the pile of the purple carpet. So there he sits, swinging his braces. But stories that follow people into their private rooms are difficult. I cannot go on with this story. I twiddle a piece of string; I turn over four or five coins in my trouser pocket.'

'Bernard's stories amuse me,' said Neville, 'at the start. But when they tail off absurdly and he gapes, twiddling a bit of string, I feel my own solitude. He sees everyone with blurred edges. Hence I cannot talk to him of Percival. I cannot expose my absurd and violent passion to his sympathetic understanding. It too would make a "story". I need someone whose mind falls like a chopper on a block; to whom the pitch of absurdity is sublime, and a shoe-string adorable. To whom I can expose the urgency of my own passion? Louis is too cold, too universal. There is nobody here among these grey arches, and moaning pigeons, and cheerful games and tradition and emulation, all so skilfully organized to prevent feeling alone. Yet I am struck still as I walk by sudden premonitions of what is to come. Yesterday, passing the open door leading into the private garden, I saw Fenwick with his mallet raised. The steam from the tea-urn rose in the middle of the lawn. There were banks of blue flowers. Then suddenly descended upon me the obscure, the mystic sense of adoration, of completeness that triumphed over chaos. Nobody saw my poised and intent figure as I stood at the open door. Nobody guessed the need I had to offer my being to one god; and perish, and disappear. His mallet descended; the vision broke.

'Should I seek out some tree? Should I desert these form rooms and libraries, and the broad yellow page in which I read Catullus, for woods and fields? Should I walk under beech trees, or saunter along the river bank, where the trees meet united like lovers in the water? But nature is too vegetable, too vapid. She has only sublimities and vastitudes and water and leaves. I begin to wish for firelight, privacy, and the limbs of one person.'

'I begin to wish,' said Louis, 'for night to come. As I stand here with my hand on the grained oak panel of Mr Wickham's door I think myself the friend of Richelieu, or the Duke of St Simon holding out a snuff-box to the King himself. It is my privilege. My witticisms "run like wildfire through the court". Duchesses tear emeralds from their earrings out of admiration—but these rockets rise best in darkness, in my cubicle at night. I am now a boy only with a colonial accent holding my knuckles against Mr Wickham's grained oak door. The day has been full of ignominies and triumphs concealed from fear of laughter. I am the best scholar in the school. But when darkness comes I put off this unenviable body—my large nose, my thin lips, my colonial accent—and inhabit space. I am then Virgil's companion, and Plato's. I am then the last scion of one of the great houses of France. But I am also one who will force himself to desert these windy and moonlit territories, these midnight wanderings, and confront grained oak doors. I will achieve in my life—Heaven grant that it be not long—some gigantic amalgamation between the two discrepancies so hideously apparent to me. Out of my suffering I will do it. I will knock. I will enter.'

'I have torn off the whole of May and June,' said Susan, 'and twenty days of July. I have torn them off and screwed them up so that they no longer exist, save as a weight in my side. They have been crippled days, like moths with shrivelled wings unable to fly. There are only eight days left. In eight days' time I shall get out of the train and stand on the platform at six twenty five. Then my freedom will unfurl, and all these restrictions that wrinkle and shrivel—hours and order and discipline, and being here and there exactly at the right moment—will crack asunder. Out the day will spring, as I open the carriage-door and see my father in his old hat and gaiters. I shall tremble. I shall burst into tears. Then next morning I shall get up at dawn. I shall let myself out by the kitchen door. I shall walk on the moor. The great horses of the phantom riders will thunder behind me and stop suddenly. I shall see the swallow skim the grass. I shall throw myself on a bank by the river and watch the fish slip in and out among the reeds. The palms of my hands will be printed with pine-needles. I shall there unfold and take out whatever it is I have made here; something hard. For something has grown in me here, through the winters and summers, on staircases, in bedrooms. I do not want, as Jinny wants, to be admired. I do not want people, when I come in, to look up with admiration. I want to give, to be given, and solitude in which to unfold my possessions.

'Then I shall come back through the trembling lanes under the arches of the nut leaves. I shall pass an old woman wheeling a perambulator full of sticks; and the shepherd. But we shall not speak. I shall come back through the kitchen garden, and see the curved leaves of the cabbages pebbled with dew, and the house in the garden, blind with curtained windows. I shall go upstairs to my room, and turn over my own things, locked carefully in the wardrobe: my shells; my eggs; my curious grasses. I shall feed my doves and my squirrel. I shall go to the kennel and comb my spaniel. So gradually I shall turn over the hard thing that has grown here in my side. But here bells ring; feet shuffle perpetually.'

'I hate darkness and sleep and night,' said Jinny, 'and lie longing for the day to come. I long that the week should be all one day without divisions. When I wake early—and the birds wake me—I lie and watch the brass handles on the cupboard grow clear; then the basin; then the towel-horse. As each thing in the bedroom grows clear, my heart beats quicker. I feel my body harden, and become pink, yellow, brown. My hands pass over my legs and body. I feel its slopes, its thinness. I love to hear the gong roar through the house and the stir begin—here a thud, there a patter. Doors slam; water rushes. Here is another day, here is another day, I cry, as my feet touch the floor. It may be a bruised day, an imperfect day. I am often scolded. I am often in disgrace for idleness, for laughing; but even as Miss Matthews grumbles at my feather-headed carelessness, I catch sight of something moving—a speck of sun perhaps on a picture, or the donkey drawing the mowing-machine across the lawn; or a sail that passes between the laurel leaves, so that I am never cast down. I cannot be prevented from pirouetting behind Miss Matthews into prayers.

'Now, too, the time is coming when we shall leave school and wear long skirts. I shall wear necklaces and a white dress without sleeves at night. There will be parties in brilliant rooms; and one man will single me out and will tell me what he has told no other person. He will like me better than Susan or Rhoda. He will find in me some quality, some peculiar thing. But I shall not let myself be attached to one person only. I do not want to be fixed, to be pinioned. I tremble, I quiver, like the leaf in the hedge, as I sit dangling my feet, on the edge of the bed, with a new day to break open. I have fifty years, I have sixty years to spend. I have not yet broken into my hoard. This is the beginning.'

'There are hours and hours,' said Rhoda, 'before I can put out the light and lie suspended on my bed above the world, before I can let the day drop down, before I can let my tree grow, quivering in green pavilions above my head. Here I cannot let it grow. Somebody knocks through it. They ask questions, they interrupt, they throw it down.

'Now I will go to the bathroom and take off my shoes and wash; but as I wash, as I bend my head down over the basin, I will let the Russian Empress's veil flow about my shoulders. The diamonds of the Imperial crown blaze on my forehead. I hear the roar of the hostile mob as I step out on to the balcony. Now I dry my hands, vigorously, so that Miss, whose name I forget, cannot suspect that I am waving my fist at an infuriated mob. "I am your Empress, people." My attitude is one of defiance. I am fearless. I conquer.

'But this is a thin dream. This is a papery tree. Miss Lambert blows it down. Even the sight of her vanishing down the corridor blows it to atoms. It is not solid; it gives me no satisfaction—this Empress dream. It leaves me, now that it has fallen, here in the passage rather shivering. Things seem paler. I will go now into the library and take out some book, and read and look; and read again and look. Here is a poem about a hedge. I will wander down it and pick flowers, green cowbind and the moonlight-coloured May, wild roses and ivy serpentine. I will clasp them in my hands and lay them on the desk's shiny surface. I will sit by the river's trembling edge and look at the water-lilies, broad and bright, which lit the oak that overhung the hedge with moonlight beams of their own watery light. I will pick flowers; I will bind flowers in one garland and clasp them and present them—Oh! to whom? There is some check in the flow of my being; a deep stream presses on some obstacle; it jerks; it tugs; some knot in the centre resists. Oh, this is pain, this is anguish! I faint, I fail. Now my body thaws; I am unsealed, I am incandescent. Now the stream pours in a deep tide fertilizing, opening the shut, forcing the tight-folded, flooding free. To whom shall I give all that now flows through me, from my warm, my porous body? I will gather my flowers and present them—Oh! to whom?

'Sailors loiter on the parade, and amorous couples; the omnibuses rattle along the sea front to the town. I will give; I will enrich; I will return to the world this beauty. I will bind my flowers in one garland and advancing with my hand outstretched will present them—Oh! to whom?'

'Now we have received,' said Louis, 'for this is the last day of the last term—Neville's and Bernard's and my last day—whatever our masters have had to give us. The introduction has been made; the world presented. They stay, we depart. The great Doctor, whom of all men I most revere, swaying a little from side to side among the tables, the bound volumes, has dealt out Horace, Tennyson, the complete works of Keats and Matthew Arnold, suitably inscribed. I respect the hand which gave them. He speaks with complete conviction. To him his words are true, though not to us. Speaking in the gruff voice of deep emotion, fiercely, tenderly, he has told us that we are about to go. He has bid us "quit ourselves like men". (On his lips quotations from the Bible, from *The Times*, seem equally magnificent.) Some will do this; others that. Some will not meet again. Neville, Bernard and I shall not meet here again. Life will divide us. But we have formed certain ties. Our boyish, our irresponsible years are over. But we have forged certain links. Above all, we have inherited traditions. These stone flags have been worn for six hundred years. On these walls are inscribed the names of men of war, of statesmen, of some unhappy poets (mine shall be among them). Blessings be on all traditions, on all safeguards and circumscriptions! I am most grateful to you men in black gowns, and you, dead, for your leading, for your guardianship; yet after all, the problem remains. The differences are not yet solved. Flowers toss their heads outside the window. I see wild birds, and impulses wilder than the wildest birds strike from my wild heart. My eyes are wild; my lips tight pressed. The bird flies; the flower dances; but I hear always the sullen thud of the waves; and the chained beast stamps on the beach. It stamps and stamps.'

'This is the final ceremony,' said Bernard. This is the last of all our ceremonies. We are overcome by strange feelings. The guard holding his flag is about to blow his whistle; the train breathing steam in another moment is about to start. One wants to say something, to feel something, absolutely appropriate to the occasion. One's mind is primed; one's lips are pursed. And then a bee drifts in and hums round the flowers in the bouquet which Lady Hampton, the wife of the General, keeps smelling to show her appreciation of the compliment. If the bee were to sting her nose? We are all deeply moved; yet irreverent; yet penitent; yet anxious to get it over; yet reluctant to part. The bee distracts us; its casual flight seems to deride our intensity. Humming vaguely, skimming widely, it is settled now on the carnation. Many of us will not meet again. We shall not enjoy certain pleasures again, when we are free to go to bed, or to sit up, when I need no longer smuggle in bits of candle-ends and immoral literature. The bee now hums round the head of the great Doctor. Larpent, John, Archie, Percival, Baker and Smith—I have liked them enormously. I have known one mad boy only. I have hated one mean boy only. I enjoy in retrospect my terribly awkward breakfasts at the Headmaster's table with toast and marmalade. He alone does not notice the bee. If it were to settle on his nose he would flick it off with one magnificent gesture. Now he has made his joke; now his voice has almost broken but not quite. Now we are dismissed—Louis, Neville and I for ever. We take our highly polished books, scholastically inscribed in a little crabbed hand. We rise, we disperse; the pressure is removed. The bee has become an insignificant, a disregarded insect, flown through the open window into obscurity. Tomorrow we go.'

'We are about to part,' said Neville. 'Here are the boxes; here are the cabs. There is Percival in his billycock hat. He will forget me. He will leave my letters lying about among guns and dogs unanswered. I shall send him poems and he will perhaps reply with a picture post card. But it is for that that I love him. I shall propose meeting—under a clock, by some Cross; and shall wait, and he will not come. It is for that that I love him. Oblivious, almost entirely ignorant, he will pass from my life. And I shall pass, incredible as it seems, into other lives; this is only an escapade perhaps, a prelude only. I feel already, though I cannot endure the Doctor's pompous mummery and faked emotions, that things we have only dimly perceived draw near. I shall be free to enter the garden where Fenwick raises his mallet. Those who have despised me shall acknowledge my sovereignty. But by some inscrutable law of my being sovereignty and the possession of power will not be enough; I shall always push through curtains to privacy, and want some whispered words alone. Therefore I go, dubious, but elate; apprehensive of intolerable pain; yet I think bound in my adventuring to conquer after huge suffering, bound, surely, to discover my desire in the end. There, for the last time, I see the statue of our pious founder with the doves about his head. They will wheel for ever about his head, whitening it, while the organ moans in the chapel. So I take my seat; and, when I have found my place in the comer of our reserved compartment, I will shade my eyes with a book to hide one tear; I will shade my eyes to observe; to peep at one face. It is the first day of the summer holidays.'

'It is the first day of the summer holidays,' said Susan. 'But the day is still rolled up. I will not examine it until I step out on to the platform in the evening. I will not let myself even smell it until I smell the cold green air off the fields. But already these are not school fields; these are not school hedges; the men in these fields are doing real things; they fill carts with real hay; and those are real cows, not school cows. But the carbolic smell of corridors and the chalky smell of schoolrooms is still in my nostrils. The glazed, shiny look of matchboard is still in my eyes. I must wait for fields and hedges, and woods and fields, and steep railway cuttings, sprinkled with gorse bushes, and trucks in sidings, and tunnels and suburban gardens with women hanging out washing, and then fields again and children swinging on gates, to cover it over, to bury it deep, this school that I have hated.

'I will not send my children to school nor spend a night all my life in London. Here in this vast station everything echoes and booms hollowly. The light is like the yellow light under an awning. Jinny lives here. Jinny takes her dog for walks on these pavements. People here shoot through the streets silently. They look at nothing but shop-windows. Their heads bob up and down all at about the same height. The streets are laced together with telegraph wires. The houses are all glass, all festoons and glitter; now all front doors and lace curtains, all pillars and white steps. But now I pass on, out of London again; the fields begin again; and the houses, and women hanging washing, and trees and fields. London is now veiled, now vanished, now crumbled, now fallen. The carbolic and the pitch-pine begin to lose their savour. I smell corn and turnips. I undo a paper packet tied with a piece of white cotton. The egg shells slide into the cleft between my knees. Now we stop at station after station, rolling out milk cans. Now women kiss each other and help with baskets. Now I will let myself lean out of the window. The air rushes down my nose and throat—the cold air, the salt air with the smell of turnip fields in it. And there is my father, with his back turned, talking to a farmer. I tremble, I cry. There is my father in gaiters. There is my father.'

'I sit snug in my own corner going North,' said Jinny, 'in this roaring express which is yet so smooth that it flattens hedges, lengthens hills. We flash past signal-boxes; we make the earth rock slightly from side to side. The distance closes for ever in a point; and we for ever open the distance wide again. The telegraph poles bob up incessantly; one is felled, another rises. Now we roar and swing into a tunnel. The gentleman pulls up the window. I see reflections on the shining glass which lines the tunnel. I see him lower his paper. He smiles at my reflection in the tunnel. My body instantly of its own accord puts forth a frill under his gaze. My body lives a life of its own. Now the black window glass is green again. We are out of the tunnel. He reads his paper. But we have exchanged the approval of our bodies. There is then a great society of bodies, and mine is introduced; mine has come into the room where the gilt chairs are. Look— all the windows of the villas and their white-tented curtains dance; and the men sitting in the hedges in the cornfields with knotted blue handkerchiefs are aware too, as I am aware, of heat and rapture. One waves as we pass him. There are bowers and arbours in these villa gardens and young men in shirt-sleeves on ladders trimming roses. A man on a horse canters over the field. His horse plunges as we pass. And the rider turns to look at us. We roar again through blackness. And I lie back; I give myself up to rapture; I think that at the end of the tunnel I enter a lamp-lit room with chairs, into one of which I sink, much admired, my dress billowing round me. But behold, looking up, I meet the eyes of a sour woman, who suspects me of rapture. My body shuts in her face, impertinently, like a parasol. I open my body, I shut my body at my will. Life is beginning. I now break into my hoard of life.'

'It is the first day of the summer holidays,' said Rhoda. 'And now, as the train passes by these red rocks, by this blue sea, the term, done with, forms itself into one shape behind me. I see its colour. June was white. I see the fields white with daisies, and white with dresses; and tennis courts marked with white. Then there was wind and violent thunder. There was a star riding through clouds one night, and I said to the star, "Consume me." That was at midsummer, after the garden party and my humiliation at the garden party. Wind and storm coloured July. Also, in the middle, cadaverous, awful, lay the grey puddle in the courtyard, when, holding an envelope in my hand, I carried a message. I came to the puddle. I could not cross it. Identity failed me. We are nothing, I said, and fell. I was blown like a feather, I was wafted down tunnels. Then very gingerly, I pushed my foot across. I laid my hand against a brick wall. I returned very painfully, drawing myself back into my body over the grey, cadaverous space of the puddle. This is life then to which I am committed.

'So I detach the summer term. With intermittent shocks, sudden as the springs of a tiger, life emerges heaving its dark crest from the sea. It is to this we are attached; it is to this we are bound, as bodies to wild horses. And yet we have invented devices for filling up the crevices and disguising these fissures. Here is the ticket collector. Here are two men; three women; there is a cat in a basket; myself with my elbow on the window-sill—this is here and now. We draw on, we make off, through whispering fields of golden corn. Women in the fields are surprised to be left behind there, hoeing. The train now stamps heavily, breathes stertorously, as it climbs up and up. At last we are on the top of the moor. Only a few wild sheep live here; a few shaggy ponies; yet we are provided with every comfort; with tables to hold our newspapers, with rings to hold our tumblers. We come carrying these appliances with us over the top of the moor. Now we are on the summit. Silence will close behind us. If

I look back over that bald head, I can see silence already closing and the shadows of clouds chasing each other over the empty moor; silence closes over our transient passage. This I say is the present moment; this is the first day of the summer holidays. This is part of the emerging monster to whom we are attached.'

'Now we are off,' said Louis. 'Now I hang suspended without attachments. We are nowhere. We are passing through England in a train. England slips by the window, always changing from hill to wood, from rivers and willows to towns again. And I have no firm ground to which I go. Bernard and Neville, Percival, Archie, Larpent and Baker go to Oxford or Cambridge, to Edinburgh, Rome, Paris, Berlin, or to some American University. I go vaguely, to make money vaguely. Therefore a poignant shadow, a keen accent, falls on these golden bristles, on these poppy-red fields, this flowing corn that never overflows its boundaries; but runs rippling to the edge. This is the first day of a new life, another spoke of the rising wheel. But my body passes vagrant as a bird's shadow. I should be transient as the shadow on the meadow, soon fading, soon darkening and dying there where it meets the wood, were it not that I coerce my brain to form in my forehead; I force myself to state, if only in one line of unwritten poetry, this moment; to mark this inch in the long, long history that began in Egypt, in the time of the Pharaohs, when women carried red pitchers to the Nile. I seem already to have lived many thousand years. But if I now shut my eyes, if I fail to realize the meeting-place of past and present, that I sit in a third-class railway carriage full of boys going home for the holidays, human history is defrauded of a moment's vision. Its eye, that would see through me, shuts—if I sleep now, through slovenliness, or cowardice, burying myself in the past, in the dark; or acquiesce, as Bernard acquiesces, telling stories; or boast, as Percival, Archie, John, Walter, Lathom, Larpent, Roper, Smith boast—the names are the same always, the names of the boasting boys. They are all boasting, all talking, except Neville, who slips a look occasionally over the edge of a French novel, and so will always slip into cushioned firelit rooms, with many books and one friend, while I tilt on an office chair behind a counter. Then I shall grow bitter and mock at them. I shall envy them their continuance down the safe traditional ways under the shade of old yew trees while I consort with cockneys and clerks, and tap the pavements of the city.

'But now disembodied, passing over fields without lodgment— (there is a river; a man fishes; there is a spire, there is the village street with its bow-windowed inn)—all is dreamlike and dim to me. These hard thoughts, this envy, this bitterness, make no lodgment in me. I am the ghost of Louis, an ephemeral passer-by, in whose mind dreams have power, and garden sounds when in the early morning petals float on fathomless depths and the birds sing. I dash and sprinkle myself with the bright waters of childhood. Its thin veil quivers. But the chained beast stamps and stamps on the shore.'

'Louis and Neville,' said Bernard, 'both sit silent. Both are absorbed. Both feel the presence of other people as a separating wall. But if I find myself in company with other people, words at once make smoke rings—see how phrases at once begin to wreathe off my lips. It seems that a match is set to a fire; something burns. An elderly and apparently prosperous man, a traveller, now gets in. And I at once wish to approach him; I instinctively dislike the sense of his presence, cold, unassimilated, among us. I do not believe in separation. We are not single. Also I wish to add to my collection of valuable observations upon the true nature of human life. My book will certainly run to many volumes, embracing every known variety of man and woman. I fill my mind with whatever happens to be the contents of a room or a railway carriage as one fills a fountain-pen in an inkpot. I have a steady unquenchable thirst. Now I feel by imperceptible signs, which I cannot yet interpret but will later, that his defiance is about to thaw. His solitude shows signs of cracking. He has passed a remark about a country house. A smoke ring issues from my lips (about crops) and circles him, bringing him into contact. The human voice has a disarming quality—(we are not single, we are one). As we exchange these few but amiable remarks about country houses, I furbish him up and make him concrete. He is indulgent as a husband but not faithful; a small builder who employs a few men. In local society he is important; is already a councillor, and perhaps in time will be mayor. He wears a large ornament, like a double tooth torn up by the roots, made of coral, hanging at his watch-chain. Walter J. Trumble is the sort of name that would fit him. He has been in America, on a business trip with his wife, and a double room in a smallish hotel cost him a whole month's wages. His front tooth is stopped with gold.

'The fact is that I have little aptitude for reflection. I require the concrete in everything. It is so only that I lay hands upon the world. A good phrase, however, seems to me to have an independent existence. Yet I think it is likely that the best are made in solitude. They require some final refrigeration which I cannot give them, dabbling always in warm soluble words. My method, nevertheless, has certain advantages over theirs. Neville is repelled by the grossness of Trumble. Louis, glancing, tripping with the high step of a disdainful crane, picks up words as if in sugar-tongs. It is true that his eyes—wild, laughing, yet desperate—express something that we have not gauged. There is about both Neville and Louis a precision, an exactitude, that I admire and shall never possess. Now I begin to be aware that action is demanded. We approach a junction; at a junction I have to change. I have to board a train for Edinburgh. I cannot precisely lay fingers on this fact—it lodges loosely among my thoughts like a button, like a small coin. Here is the jolly old boy who collects tickets. I had one—I had one certainly. But it does not matter. Either I shall find it, or I shall not find it. I examine my note-case. I look in all my pockets. These are the things that for ever interrupt the process upon which I am eternally engaged of finding some perfect phrase that fits this very moment exactly.'

'Bernard has gone,' said Neville, 'without a ticket. He has escaped us, making a phrase, waving his hand. He talked as easily to the horse-breeder or to the plumber as to us. The plumber accepted him with devotion. "If he had a son like that," he was thinking, "he would manage to send him to Oxford." But what did Bernard feel for the plumber? Did he not only wish to continue the sequence of the story which he never stops telling himself? He began it when he rolled his bread into pellets as a child. One pellet was a man, one was a woman. We are all pellets. We are all phrases in Bernard's story, things he writes down in his notebook under A or under B. He tells our story with extraordinary understanding, except of what we most feel. For he does not need us. He is never at our mercy. There he is, waving his arms on the platform. The train has gone without him. He has missed his connection. He has lost his ticket. But that does not matter. He will talk to the barmaid about the nature of human destiny. We are off; he has forgotten us already; we pass out of his view; we go on, filled with lingering sensations, half bitter, half sweet, for he is somehow to be pitied, breasting the world with half-finished phrases, having lost his ticket: he is also to be loved.

'Now I pretend again to read. I raise my book, till it almost covers my eyes. But I cannot read in the presence of horse-dealers and plumbers. I have no power of ingratiating myself. I do not admire that man; he does not admire me. Let me at least be honest. Let me denounce this piffling, trifling, self-satisfied world; these horse-hair seats; these coloured photographs of piers and parades. I could shriek aloud at the smug self-satisfaction, at the mediocrity of this world, which breeds horse-dealers with coral ornaments hanging from their watch-chains. There is that in me which will consume them entirely. My laughter shall make them twist in their seats; shall drive them howling before me. No; they are immortal. They triumph. They will make it impossible for me always to read Catullus in a third-class railway carriage. They will drive me in October to take refuge in one of the universities, where I shall become a don; and go with schoolmasters to Greece; and lecture on the ruins of the Parthenon. It would be better to breed horses and live in one of those red villas than to run in and out of the skulls of Sophocles and Euripides like a maggot, with a high-minded wife, one of those University women. That, however, will be my fate. I shall suffer. I am already at eighteen capable of such contempt that horse-breeders hate me. That is my triumph; I do not compromise. I am not timid; I have no accent. I do not finick about fearing what people think of "my father a banker at Brisbane" like Louis.

'Now we draw near the centre of the civilized world. There are the familiar gasometers. There are the public gardens intersected by asphalt paths. There are the lovers lying shamelessly mouth to mouth on the burnt grass. Percival is now almost in Scotland; his train draws through the red moors; he sees the long line of the Border hills and the Roman wall. He reads a detective novel, yet understands everything.

The train slows and lengthens, as we approach London, the centre, and my heart draws out too, in fear, in exultation. I am about to meet—what? What extraordinary adventure waits me, among these mail vans, these porters, these swarms of people calling taxis? I feel insignificant, lost, but exultant. With a soft shock we stop. I will let the others get out before me. I will sit still one moment before I emerge into that chaos, that tumult. I will not anticipate what is to come. The huge uproar is in my ears. It sounds and resounds, under this glass roof like the surge of a sea. We are cast down on the platform with our handbags. We are whirled asunder. My sense of self almost perishes; my contempt. I become drawn in, tossed down, thrown sky-high. I step out on to the platform, grasping tightly all that I possess—one bag.'

The sun rose. Bars of yellow and green fell on the shore, gilding

431

the ribs of the eaten-out boat and making the sea-holly and its mailed leaves gleam blue as steel. Light almost pierced the thin swift waves as they raced fan-shaped over the beach. The girl who had shaken her head and made all the jewels, the topaz, the aquamarine, the water-coloured jewels with sparks of fire in them, dance, now bared her brows and with wide-opened eyes drove a straight pathway over the waves. Their quivering mackerel sparkling was darkened; they massed themselves; their green hollows deepened and darkened and might be traversed by shoals of wandering fish. As they splashed and drew back they left a black rim of twigs and cork on the shore and straws and sticks of wood, as if some light shallop had foundered and burst its sides and the sailor had swum to land and bounded up the cliff and left his frail cargo to be washed ashore.

In the garden the birds that had sung erratically and spasmodically in the dawn on that tree, on that bush, now sang together in chorus, shrill and sharp; now together, as if conscious of companionship, now alone as if to the pale blue sky. They swerved, all in one flight, when the black cat moved among the bushes, when the cook threw cinders on the ash heap and startled them. Fear was in their song, and apprehension of pain, and joy to be snatched quickly now at this instant. Also they sang emulously in the clear morning air, swerving high over the elm tree, singing together as they chased each other, escaping, pursuing, pecking each other as they turned high in the air. And then tiring of pursuit and flight, lovelily they came descending, delicately declining, dropped down and sat silent on the tree, on the wall, with their bright eyes glancing, and their heads turned this way, that way; aware, awake; intensely conscious of one thing, one object in particular.

Perhaps it was a snail shell, rising in the grass like a grey cathedral, a swelling building burnt with dark rings and shadowed green by the grass. Or perhaps they saw the splendour of the flowers making a light of flowing purple over the beds, through which dark tunnels of purple shade were driven between

432

the stalks. Or they fixed their gaze on the small bright apple leaves, dancing yet withheld, stiffly sparkling among the pink-tipped blossoms. Or they saw the rain drop on the hedge, pendent but not falling, with a whole house bent in it, and towering elms; or, gazing straight at the sun, their eyes became gold beads.

Now glancing this side, that side, they looked deeper, beneath the flowers, down the dark avenues into the unlit world where the leaf rots and the flower has fallen. Then one of them, beautifully darting, accurately alighting, spiked the soft, monstrous body of the defenceless worm, pecked again and yet again, and left it to fester. Down there among the roots where the flowers decayed, gusts of dead smells were wafted; drops formed on the bloated sides of swollen things. The skin of rotten fruit broke, and matter oozed too thick to run. Yellow excretions were exuded by slugs, and now and again an amorphous body with a head at either end swayed slowly from side to side. The gold-eyed birds darting in between the leaves observed that purulence, that wetness, quizzically. Now and then they plunged the tips of their beaks savagely into the sticky mixture.

Now, too, the rising sun came in at the window, touching the red-edged curtain, and began to bring out circles and lines. Now in the growing light its whiteness settled in the plate; the blade condensed its gleam. Chairs and cupboards loomed behind so that though each was separate they seemed inextricably involved. The looking-glass whitened its pool upon the wall. The real flower on the window-sill was attended by a phantom flower. Yet the phantom was part of the flower, for when a bud broke free the paler flower in the glass opened a bud too.

The wind rose. The waves drummed on the shore, like turbaned warriors, like turbaned men with poisoned assegais who, whirling their arms on high, advance upon the feeding flocks, the white sheep.

'The complexity of things becomes more close,' said Bernard, 'here at college, where the stir and pressure of life are so extreme, where the excitement of mere living becomes daily more urgent. Every hour something new is unburied in the great bran pie. What am I? I ask. This? No, I am that. Especially now, when I have left a room, and people talking, and the stone flags ring out with my solitary footsteps, and I behold the moon rising, sublimely, indifferently, over the ancient chapel—then it becomes clear that I am not one and simple, but complex and many. Bernard, in public, bubbles; in private, is secretive. That is what they do not understand, for they are now undoubtedly discussing me, saying I escape them, am evasive. They do not understand that I have to effect different transitions; have to cover the entrances and exits of several different men who alternately act their parts as Bernard. I am abnormally aware of circumstances. I can never read a book in a railway carriage without asking, Is he a builder? Is she unhappy? I was aware today acutely that poor Simes, with his pimple, was feeling, how bitterly, that his chance of making a good impression upon Billy Jackson was remote. Feeling this painfully, I invited him to dinner with ardour. This he will attribute to an admiration which is not mine. That is true. But "joined to the sensibility of a woman" (I am here quoting my own biographer) "Bernard possessed the logical sobriety of a man." Now people who make a single impression, and that, in the main, a good one (for there seems to be a virtue in simplicity), are those who keep their equilibrium in mid-stream. (I instantly see fish with their noses one way, the stream rushing past another.) Canon, Lycett, Peters, Hawkins, Larpent, Neville—all fish in mid-stream. But you understand, *you*, my self, who always comes at a call (that would be a harrowing experience to call and for no one to come; that would make the midnight hollow, and explains the expression of old men in clubs—they have given up calling for a self who does not come), you understand that I am only superficially represented by what I was saying tonight. Underneath, and, at the moment when I am most disparate, I am also integrated. I sympathize effusively; I also sit, like a toad in a hole, receiving with perfect coldness whatever comes. Very few of you who are now discussing me have the double capacity to feel, to reason. Lycett, you see, believes in running after hares; Hawkins has spent a most industrious afternoon in the library. Peters has his young lady at the circulating library. You are all engaged, involved, drawn in, and absolutely energized to the top of your bent—all save Neville, whose mind is far too complex to be roused by any single activity. I also am too complex. In my case something remains floating, unattached.

'Now, as a proof of my susceptibility to atmosphere, here, as I come into my room, and turn on the light, and see the sheet of paper, the table, my gown lying negligently over the back of the chair, I feel that I am that dashing yet reflective man, that bold and deleterious figure, who, lightly throwing off his cloak, seizes his pen and at once flings off the following letter to the girl with whom he is passionately in love.

'Yes, all is propitious. I am now in the mood. I can write the letter straight off which I have begun ever so many times. I have just come in; I have flung down my hat and my stick; I am writing the first thing that comes into my head without troubling to put the paper straight. It is going to be a brilliant sketch which, she must think, was written without a pause, without an erasure. Look how unformed the letters are—there is a careless blot. All must be sacrificed to speed and carelessness. I will write a quick, running, small hand, exaggerating the down stroke of the "y" and crossing the "t" thus—with a dash. The date shall be only Tuesday, the 17th, and then a question mark. But also I must give her the impression that though he—for this is not myself— is writing in such an off-hand, such a slap-dash way, there is some subtle suggestion of intimacy and respect. I must allude to talks we have had together—bring back some remembered scene. But I must seem to her (this is very important) to be passing from thing to thing with the greatest ease in the world. I shall pass from the service for the man who was drowned (I have a phrase for that) to Mrs Moffat and her sayings (I have a note of them), and so to some reflections apparently casual but full of profundity (profound criticism is often written casually) about some book I have been reading, some out-of-the-way book. I want her to say as she brushes her hair or puts out the candle, "Where did I read that? Oh, in Bernard's letter." It is the speed, the hot, molten effect, the laval flow of sentence into sentence that I need. Who am I thinking of? Byron of course. I am, in some ways, like Byron. Perhaps a sip of Byron will help to put me in the vein. Let me read a page. No; this is dull; this is scrappy. This is rather too formal. Now I am getting the hang of it. Now I am getting his beat into my brain (the rhythm is the main thing in writing). Now, without pausing I will begin, on the very lilt of the stroke—.

'Yet it falls flat. It peters out. I cannot get up steam enough to carry me over the transition. My true self breaks off from my assumed. And if I begin to re-write it, she will feel "Bernard is posing as a literary man; Bernard is thinking of his biographer" (which is true). No, I will write the letter tomorrow directly after breakfast.

'Now let me fill my mind with imaginary pictures. Let me suppose that I am asked to stay at Restover, King's Laughton, Station Langley three miles. I arrive in the dusk. In the courtyard of this shabby but distinguished house there are two or three dogs, slinking, long-legged. There are faded rugs in the hall; a military gentleman smokes a pipe as he paces the terrace. The note is of distinguished poverty and military connections. A hunter's hoof on the writing table—a favourite horse. "Do you ride?" "Yes, sir, I love riding." "My daughter expects us in the drawing-room." My heart pounds against my ribs. She is standing at a low table; she has been hunting; she munches sandwiches like a tomboy. I make a fairly good impression on the Colonel. I am not too clever, he thinks; I am not too raw. Also I play billiards. Then the nice maid who has been with the family thirty years comes in. The pattern on the plates is of Oriental long-tailed birds. Her mother's portrait in muslin hangs over the fireplace. I can sketch the surroundings up to a point with extraordinary ease. But can I make it work? Can I hear her voice—the precise tone with which, when we are alone, she says "Bernard"? And then what next?

'The truth is that I need the stimulus of other people. Alone, over my dead fire, I tend to see the thin places in my own stories. The real novelist, the perfectly simple human being, could go on, indefinitely, imagining. He would not integrate, as I do. He would not have this devastating sense of grey ashes in a burnt-out grate. Some blind flaps in my eyes. Everything becomes impervious. I cease to invent.

'Let me recollect. It has been on the whole a good day. The drop that forms on the roof of the soul in the evening is round, many-coloured. There was the morning, fine; there was the afternoon, walking. I like views of spires across grey fields. I like glimpses between people's shoulders. Things kept popping into my head. I was imaginative, subtle. After dinner, I was dramatic. I put into concrete form many things that we had dimly observed about our common friends. I made my transitions easily. But now let me ask myself the final question, as I sit over this grey fire, with its naked promontories of black coal, which of these people am I? It depends so much upon the room. When I say to myself, "Bernard", who comes? A faithful, sardonic man, disillusioned, but not embittered. A man of no particular age or calling. Myself, merely. It is he who now takes the poker and rattles the cinders so that they fall in showers through the grate. "Lord," he says to himself, watching them fall, "what a pother!" and then he adds, lugubriously, but with some sense of consolation, "Mrs Moffat will come and sweep it all up—" I fancy I shall often repeat to myself that phrase, as I rattle and bang through life, hitting first this side of the carriage, then the other, "Oh, yes, Mrs Moffat will come and sweep it all up." And so to bed.'

'In a world which contains the present moment,' said Neville, 'why discriminate? Nothing should be named lest by so doing we change it. Let it exist, this bank, this beauty, and I, for one instant, steeped in pleasure. The sun is hot. I see the river. I see trees specked and burnt in the autumn sunlight. Boats float past, through the red, through the green. Far away a bell tolls, but not for death. There are bells that ring for life. A leaf falls, from joy. Oh, I am in love with life! Look how the willow shoots its fine sprays into the air! Look how through them a boat passes, filled with indolent, with unconscious, with powerful young men. They are listening to the gramophone; they are eating fruit out of paper bags. They are tossing the skins of bananas, which then sink eel-like, into the river. All they do is beautiful. There are cruets behind them and ornaments; their rooms are full of oars and oleographs but they have turned all to beauty. That boat passes under the bridge. Another comes. Then another. That is Percival, lounging on the cushions, monolithic, in giant repose. No, it is only one of his satellites, imitating his monolithic, his giant repose. He alone is unconscious of their tricks, and when he catches them at it he buffets them good-humouredly with a blow of his paw. They, too, have passed under the bridge through 'the fountains of the pendant trees', through its fine strokes of yellow and plum colour. The breeze stirs; the curtain quivers; I see behind the leaves the grave, yet eternally joyous buildings, which seem porous, not gravid; light, though set so immemorially on the ancient turf. Now begins to rise in me the familiar rhythm; words that have lain dormant now lift, now toss their crests, and fall and rise, and fall and rise again. I am a poet, yes. Surely I am a great poet. Boats and youth passing and distant trees, "the falling fountains of the pendant trees". I see it all. I feel it all. I am inspired. My eyes fill with tears. Yet even as I feel this, I lash my frenzy higher and higher. It foams. It becomes artificial, insincere. Words and words and words, how they gallop—how they lash their long manes and tails, but for some fault in me I cannot give myself to their backs; I cannot fly with them, scattering women and string bags. There is some flaw in me—some fatal hesitancy, which, if I pass it over, turns to foam and falsity. Yet it is incredible that I should not be a great poet. What did I write last night if it was not good poetry? Am I too fast, too facile? I do not know. I do not know myself sometimes, or how to measure and name and count out the grains that make me what I am.

'Something now leaves me; something goes from me to meet that figure who is coming, and assures me that I know him before I see who it is. How curiously one is changed by the addition, even at a distance, of a friend. How useful an office one's friends perform when they recall us. Yet how painful to be recalled, to be mitigated, to have one's self adulterated, mixed up, become part of another. As he approaches I become not myself but Neville mixed with somebody—with whom?—with Bernard? Yes, it is Bernard, and it is to Bernard that I shall put the question, Who am I?'

'How strange,' said Bernard, 'the willow looks seen together. I was Byron, and the tree was Byron's tree, lachrymose, down-showering, lamenting. Now that we look at the tree together, it has a combined look, each branch distinct, and I will tell you what I feel, under the compulsion of your clarity.

'I feel your disapproval, I feel your force. I become, with you, an untidy, an impulsive human being whose bandanna handkerchief is for ever stained with the grease of crumpets. Yes, I hold Gray's *Elegy* in one hand; with the other I scoop out the bottom crumpet, that has absorbed all the butter and sticks to the bottom of the plate. This offends you; I feel your distress acutely. Inspired by it and anxious to regain your good opinion, I proceed to tell you how I have just pulled Percival out of bed; I describe his slippers, his table, his guttered candle; his surly and complaining accents as I pull the blankets off his feet; he burrowing like some vast cocoon meanwhile. I describe all this in such a way that, centred as you are upon some private sorrow (for a hooded shape presides over our encounter), you give way, you laugh and delight in me. My charm and flow of language, unexpected and spontaneous as it is, delights me too.

I am astonished, as I draw the veil off things with words, how much, how infinitely more than I can say, I have observed. More and more bubbles into my mind as I talk, images and images. This, I say to myself, is what I need; why, I ask, can I not finish the letter that I am writing? For my room is always scattered with unfinished letters. I begin to suspect, when I am with you, that I am among the most gifted of men. I am filled with the delight of youth, with potency, with the sense of what is to come. Blundering, but fervid, I see myself buzzing round flowers, humming down scarlet cups, making blue funnels resound with my prodigious booming. How richly I shall enjoy my youth (you make me feel). And London. And freedom. But stop. You are not listening. You are making some protest, as you slide, with an inexpressibly familiar gesture, your hand along your knee. By such signs we diagnose our friends' diseases. "Do not, in your affluence and plenty," you seem to say, "pass me by." "Stop," you say. "Ask me what I suffer."

'Let me then create you. (You have done as much for me.) You lie on this hot bank, in this lovely, this fading, this still bright October day, watching boat after boat float through the combed-out twigs of the willow tree. And you wish to be a poet; and you wish to be a lover. But the splendid clarity of your intelligence, and the remorseless honesty of your intellect (these Latin words I owe you; these qualities of yours make me shift a little uneasily and see the faded patches, the thin strands in my own equipment) bring you to a halt. You indulge in no mystifications. You do not fog yourself with rosy clouds, or yellow.

'Am I right? Have I read the little gesture of your left hand correctly? If so, give me your poems; hand over the sheets you wrote last night in such a fervour of inspiration that you now feel a little sheepish. For you distrust inspiration, yours or mine. Let us go back together, over the bridge, under the elm trees, to my room, where, with walls round us and red serge curtains drawn, we can shut out these distracting voices, scents and savours of lime trees, and other lives; these pert shop-girls, disdainfully tripping, these shuffling, heavy-laden old women; these furtive glimpses of some vague and vanishing figure—it might be Jinny, it might be Susan, or was that Rhoda disappearing down the avenue? Again, from some slight twitch I guess your feeling; I have escaped you; I have gone buzzing like a swarm of bees, endlessly vagrant, with none of your power of fixing remorselessly upon a single object. But I will return.'

'When there are buildings like these,' said Neville, 'I cannot endure that there should be shop-girls. Their titter, their gossip, offends me; breaks into my stillness, and nudges me, in moments of purest exultation, to remember our degradation.

'But now we have regained our territory after that brief brush with the bicycles and the lime scent and the vanishing figures in the distracted street. Here we are masters of tranquillity and order; inheritors of proud tradition. The lights are beginning to make yellow slits across the square. Mists from the river are filling these ancient spaces. They cling, gently, to the hoary stone. The leaves now are thick in country lanes, sheep cough in the damp fields; but here in your room we are dry. We talk privately. The fire leaps and sinks, making some knob bright.

'You have been reading Byron. You have been marking the passages that seem to approve of your own character. I find marks against all those sentences which seem to express a sardonic yet passionate nature; a moth-like impetuosity dashing itself against hard glass. You thought, as you drew your pencil there, "I too throw off my cloak like that. I too snap my fingers in the face of destiny." Yet Byron never made tea as you do, who fill the pot so that when you put the lid on the tea spills over. There is a brown pool on the table—it is running among your books and papers. Now you mop it up, clumsily, with your pocket-handkerchief. You then stuff your handkerchief back into your pocket—that is not Byron; that is you; that is so essentially you that if I think of you in twenty years' time, when we are both famous, gouty and intolerable, it will be by that scene: and if you are dead, I shall weep. Once you were Tolstoi's young man;

now you are Byron's young man; perhaps you will be Meredith's young man; then you will visit Paris in the Easter vacation and come back wearing a black tie, some detestable Frenchman whom nobody has ever heard of. Then I shall drop you.

'I am one person—myself. I do not impersonate Catullus, whom I adore. I am the most slavish of students, with here a dictionary, there a notebook in which I enter curious uses of the past participle. But one cannot go on for ever cutting these ancient inscriptions clearer with a knife. Shall I always draw the red serge curtain close and see my book, laid like a block of marble, pale under the lamp? That would be a glorious life, to addict oneself to perfection; to follow the curve of the sentence wherever it might lead, into deserts, under drifts of sand, regardless of lures, of seductions; to be poor always and unkempt; to be ridiculous in Piccadilly.

'But I am too nervous to end my sentence properly. I speak quickly, as I pace up and down, to conceal my agitation. I hate your greasy handkerchiefs—you will stain your copy of *Don Juan.* You are not listening to me. You are making phrases about Byron. And while you gesticulate, with your cloak, your cane, I am trying to expose a secret told to nobody yet; I am asking you (as I stand with my back to you) to take my life in your hands and tell me whether I am doomed always to cause repulsion in those I love?

'I stand with my back to you fidgeting. No, my hands are now perfectly still. Precisely, opening a space in the bookcase, I insert *Don Juan;* there. I would rather be loved, I would rather be famous than follow perfection through the sand. But am I doomed to cause disgust? Am I a poet? Take it. The desire which is loaded behind my lips, cold as lead, fell as a bullet, the thing I aim at shop-girls, women, the pretence, the vulgarity of life (because I love it) shoots at you as I throw—catch it—my poem.'

'He has shot like an arrow from the room,' said Bernard. 'He has left me his poem. O friendship, I too will press flowers between the pages of Shakespeare's sonnets! O friendship, how piercing are your darts—there, there, again there. He looked at me, turning to face me; he gave me his poem. All mists curl off the roof of my being. That confidence I shall keep to my dying day. Like a long wave, like a roll of heavy waters, he went over me, his devastating presence—dragging me open, laying bare the pebbles on the shore of my soul. It was humiliating; I was turned to small stones. All semblances were rolled up. "You are not Byron; you are your self." To be contracted by another person into a single being—how strange.

'How strange to feel the line that is spun from us lengthening its fine filament across the misty spaces of the intervening world. He is gone; I stand here, holding his poem. Between us is this line. But now, how comfortable, how reassuring to feel that alien presence removed, that scrutiny darkened and hooded over! How grateful to draw the blinds, and admit no other presence; to feel returning from the dark corners in which they took refuge, those shabby inmates, those familiars, whom, with his superior force, he drove into hiding. The mocking, the observant spirits who, even in the crisis and stab of the moment, watched on my behalf now come flocking home again. With their addition, I am Bernard; I am Byron; I am this, that and the other. They darken the air and enrich me, as of old, with their antics, their comments, and cloud the fine simplicity of my moment of emotion. For I am more selves than Neville thinks. We are not simple as our friends would have us to meet their needs. Yet love is simple.

'Now they have returned, my inmates, my familiars. Now the stab, the rent in my defences that Neville made with his astonishing fine rapier, is repaired. I am almost whole now; and see how jubilant I am, bringing into play all that Neville ignores in me. I feel, as I look from the window, parting the curtains, "That would give him no pleasure; but it rejoices me." (We use our friends to measure our own stature.) My scope embraces what Neville never reaches. They are shouting hunting-songs over the way. They are celebrating some run with the beagles.

The, little boys in caps who always turned at the same moment when the brake went round the corner are clapping each other on the shoulder and boasting. But Neville, delicately avoiding interference, stealthily, like a conspirator, hastens back to his room. I see him sunk in his low chair gazing at the fire which has assumed for the moment an architectural solidity. If life, he thinks, could wear that permanence, if life could have that order—for above all he desires order, and detests my Byronic untidiness; and so draws his curtain; and bolts his door. His eyes (for he is in love; the sinister figure of love presided at our encounter) fill with longing; fill with tears. He snatches the poker and with one blow destroys that momentary appearance of solidity in the burning coals. All changes. And youth and love. The boat has floated through the arch of the willows and is now under the bridge. Percival, Tony, Archie, or another, will go to India. We shall not meet again. Then he stretches his hand for his copy-book—a neat volume bound in mottled paper—and writes feverishly long lines of poetry, in the manner of whomever he admires most at the moment.

'But I want to linger; to lean from the window; to listen. There again comes that rollicking chorus. They are now smashing china—that also is the convention. The chorus, like a torrent jumping rocks, brutally assaulting old trees, pours with splendid abandonment headlong over precipices. On they roll; on they gallop, after hounds, after footballs; they pump up and down attached to oars like sacks of flour. All divisions are merged—they act like one man. The gusty October wind blows the uproar in bursts of sound and silence across the court. Now again they are smashing the china—that is the convention. An old, unsteady woman carrying a bag trots home under the fire-red windows. She is half afraid that they will fall on her and tumble her into the gutter. Yet she pauses as if to warm her knobbed, her rheumaticky hands at the bonfire which flares away with streams of sparks and bits of blown paper. The old woman pauses against the lit window. A contrast. That I see and Neville does not see; that I feel and Neville does not feel. Hence he will reach perfection and I shall fail and shall leave nothing behind me but imperfect phrases littered with sand.

'I think of Louis now. What malevolent yet searching light would Louis throw upon this dwindling autumn evening, upon this china-smashing and trolling of hunting-songs, upon Neville, Byron and our life here? His thin lips are somewhat pursed; his cheeks are pale; he pores in an office over some obscure commercial document. "My father, a banker at Brisbane"—being ashamed of him he always talks of him—failed. So he sits in an office, Louis the best scholar in the school. But I seeking contrasts often feel his eye on us, his laughing eye, his wild eye, adding us up like insignificant items in some grand total which he is for ever pursuing in his office. And one day, taking a fine pen and dipping it in red ink, the addition will be complete; our total will be known; but it will not be enough.

'Bang! They have thrown a chair now against the wall. We are damned then. My case is dubious too. Am I not indulging in unwarranted emotions? Yes, as I lean out of the window and drop my cigarette so that it twirls lightly to the ground, I feel Louis watching even my cigarette. And Louis says, "That means something. But what?"'

'People go on passing,' said Louis. They pass the window of this eating-shop incessantly. Motor-cars, vans, motor-omnibuses; and again motor-omnibuses, vans, motor-cars—they pass the window. In the background I perceive shops and houses; also the grey spires of a city church. In the foreground are glass shelves set with plates of buns and ham sandwiches. All is somewhat obscured by steam from a tea-urn. A meaty, vapourish smell of beef and mutton, sausages and mash, hangs down like a damp net in the middle of the eating-house. I prop my book against a bottle of Worcester sauce and try to look like the rest.

'Yet I cannot. (They go on passing, they go on passing in disorderly procession.) I cannot read my book, or order my beef,

445

with conviction. I repeat, "I am an average Englishman; I am an average clerk", yet I look at the little men at the next table to be sure that I do what they do. Supple-faced, with rippling skins, that are always twitching with the multiplicity of their sensations, prehensile like monkeys, greased to this particular moment, they are discussing with all the right gestures the sale of a piano. It blocks up the hall; so he would take a Tenner. People go on passing; they go on passing against the spires of the church and the plates of ham sandwiches. The streamers of my consciousness waver out and are perpetually torn and distressed by their disorder. I cannot therefore concentrate on my dinner. "I would take a tenner. The case is handsome; but it blocks up the hall." They dive and plunge like guillemots whose feathers are slippery with oil. All excesses beyond that norm are vanity. That is the mean; that is the average. Meanwhile the hats bob up and down; the door perpetually shuts and opens. I am conscious of flux, of disorder; of annihilation and despair. If this is all, this is worthless. Yet I feel, too, the rhythm of the eating-house. It is like a waltz tune, eddying in and out, round and round. The waitresses, balancing trays, swing in and out, round and round, dealing plates of greens, of apricot and custard, dealing them at the right time, to the right customers. The average men, including her rhythm in their rhythm ("I would take a tenner; for it blocks up the hall") take their greens, take their apricots and custard. Where then is the break in this continuity? What the fissure through which one sees disaster? The circle is unbroken; the harmony complete. Here is the central rhythm; here the common mainspring. I watch it expand, contract; and then expand again. Yet I am not included. If I speak, imitating their accent, they prick their ears, waiting for me to speak again, in order that they may place me—if I come from Canada or Australia, I, who desire above all things to be taken to the arms with love, am alien, external. I, who would wish to feel close over me the protective waves of the ordinary, catch with the tail of my eye some far horizon; am aware of hats bobbing up and down in perpetual disorder. To me is addressed the plaint of the wandering and distracted spirit (a woman with bad teeth falters at the counter), "Bring us back to the fold, we who pass so disjectedly, bobbing up and down, past windows with plates of ham sandwiches in the foreground." Yes; I will reduce you to order.

'I will read in the book that is propped against the bottle of Worcester sauce. It contains some forged rings, some perfect statements, a few words, but poetry. You, all of you, ignore it. What the dead poet said, you have forgotten. And I cannot translate it to you so that its binding power ropes you in, and makes it clear to you that you are aimless; and the rhythm is cheap and worthless; and so remove that degradation which, if you are unaware of your aimlessness, pervades you, making you senile, even while you are young. To translate that poem so that it is easily read is to be my endeavour. I, the companion of Plato, of Virgil, will knock at the grained oak door. I oppose to what is passing this ramrod of beaten steel. I will not submit to this aimless passing of billycock hats and Homburg hats and all the plumed and variegated head-dresses of women. (Susan, whom I respect, would wear a plain straw hat on a summer's day.) And the grinding and the steam that runs in unequal drops down the window pane; and the stopping and the starting with a jerk of motor-omnibuses; and the hesitations at counters; and the words that trail drearily without human meaning; I will reduce you to order.

'My roots go down through veins of lead and silver, through damp, marshy places that exhale odours, to a knot made of oak roots bound together in the centre. Sealed and blind, with earth stopping my ears, I have yet heard rumours of wars; and the nightingale; have felt the hurrying of many troops of men flocking hither and thither in quest of civilization like flocks of birds migrating seeking the summer; I have seen women carrying red pitchers to the banks of the Nile. I woke in a garden, with a blow on the nape of my neck, a hot kiss, Jinny's; remembering all this as one remembers confused cries and toppling pillars and shafts of red and black in some nocturnal conflagration. I am for ever sleeping and waking. Now I sleep; now I wake. I see the gleaming tea-urn; the glass cases full of pale-yellow sandwiches; the men in round coats perched on stools at the counter; and also behind them, eternity. It is a stigma burnt on my quivering flesh by a cowled man with a red-hot iron. I see this eating-shop against the packed and fluttering birds' wings, many feathered, folded, of the past. Hence my pursed lips, my sickly pallor; my distasteful and uninviting aspect as I turn my face with hatred and bitterness upon Bernard and Neville, who saunter under yew trees; who inherit armchairs; and draw their curtains close, so that lamplight falls on their books.

'Susan, I respect; because she sits stitching. She sews under a quiet lamp in a house where the corn sighs close to the window and gives me safety. For I am the weakest, the youngest of them all. I am a child looking at his feet and the little runnels that the stream has made in the gravel. That is a snail, I say; that is a leaf. I delight in the snails; I delight in the leaf, I am always the youngest, the most innocent, the most trustful. You are all protected. I am naked. When the waitress with the plaited wreaths of hair swings past, she deals you your apricots and custard unhesitatingly, like a sister. You are her brothers. But when I get up, brushing the crumbs from my waistcoat, I slip too large a tip, a shilling, under the edge of my plate, so that she may not find it till I am gone, and her scorn, as she picks it up with laughter, may not strike on me till I am past the swing-doors.'

'Now the wind lifts the blind,' said Susan, 'jars, bowls, matting and the shabby arm-chair with the hole in it are now become distinct. The usual faded ribbons sprinkle the wallpaper. The bird chorus is over, only one bird now sings close to the bedroom window. I will pull on my stockings and go quietly past the bedroom doors, and down through the kitchen, out through the garden past the greenhouse into the field. It is still early morning. The mist is on the marshes. The day is stark and stiff as a linen shroud. But it will soften; it will warm. At this hour, this still early hour, I think I am the field, I am the barn, I am the trees; mine are the flocks of birds, and this young hare who leaps, at the last moment when I step almost on him. Mine is the heron that stretches its vast wings lazily; and the cow that creaks as it pushes one foot before another munching; and the wild, swooping swallow; and the faint red in the sky, and the green when the red fades; the silence and the bell; the call of the man fetching cart-horses from the fields—all are mine.

'I cannot be divided, or kept apart. I was sent to school; I was sent to Switzerland to finish my education. I hate linoleum; I hate fir trees and mountains. Let me now fling myself on this flat ground under a pale sky where the clouds pace slowly. The cart grows gradually larger as it comes along the road. The sheep gather in the middle of the field. The birds gather in the middle of the road—they need not fly yet. The wood smoke rises. The starkness of the dawn is going out of it. Now the day stirs. Colour returns. The day waves yellow with all its crops. The earth hangs heavy beneath me.

'But who am I, who lean on this gate and watch my setter nose in a circle? I think sometimes (I am not twenty yet) I am not a woman, but the light that falls on this gate, on this ground. I am the seasons, I think sometimes, January, May, November; the mud, the mist, the dawn. I cannot be tossed about, or float gently, or mix with other people. Yet now, leaning here till the gate prints my arm, I feel the weight that has formed itself in my side. Something has formed, at school, in Switzerland, some hard thing. Not sighs and laughter, not circling and ingenious phrases; not Rhoda's strange communications when she looks past us, over our shoulders; nor Jinny's pirouetting, all of a piece, limbs and body. What I give is fell. I cannot float gently, mixing with other people. I like best the stare of shepherds met in the road; the stare of gipsy women beside a cart in a ditch suckling their children as I shall suckle my children. For soon in the hot

449

midday when the bees hum round the hollyhocks my lover will come. He will stand under the cedar tree. To his one word I shall answer my one word. What has formed in me I shall give him. I shall have children; I shall have maids in aprons; men with pitchforks; a kitchen where they bring the ailing lambs to warm in baskets, where the hams hang and the onions glisten. I shall be like my mother, silent in a blue apron locking up the cupboards.

'Now I am hungry. I will call my setter. I think of crusts and bread and butter and white plates in a sunny room. I will go back across the fields. I will walk along this grass path with strong, even strides, now swerving to avoid the puddle, now leaping lightly to a clump. Beads of wet form on my rough skirt; my shoes become supple and dark. The stiffness has gone from the day; it is shaded with grey, green and umber. The birds no longer settle on the high road.

'I return, like a cat or fox returning, whose fur is grey with rime, whose pads are hardened by the coarse earth. I push through the cabbages, making their leaves squeak and their drops spill. I sit waiting for my father's footsteps as he shuffles down the passage pinching some herb between his fingers. I pour out cup after cup while the unopened flowers hold themselves erect on the table among the pots of jam, the loaves and the butter. We are silent.

'I go then to the cupboard, and take the damp bags of rich sultanas; I lift the heavy flour on to the clean scrubbed kitchen table. I knead; I stretch; I pull, plunging my hands in the warm inwards of the dough. I let the cold water stream fanwise through my fingers. The fire roars; the flies buzz in a circle. All my currants and rices, the silver bags and the blue bags, are locked again in the cupboard. The meat is stood in the oven; the bread rises in a soft dome under the clean towel. I walk in the afternoon down to the river. All the world is breeding. The flies are going from grass to grass. The flowers are thick with pollen. The swans ride the stream in order. The clouds, warm now, sun-spotted, sweep over the hills, leaving gold in the water, and gold on the necks of the swans. Pushing one foot before the other, the cows munch their way across the field. I feel through the grass for the white-domed mushroom; and break its stalk and pick the purple orchid that grows beside it and lay the orchid by the mushroom with the earth at its root, and so home to make the kettle boil for my father among the just reddened roses on the tea-table.

'But evening comes and the lamps are lit. And when evening comes and the lamps are lit they make a yellow fire in the ivy. I sit with my sewing by the table. I think of Jinny; of Rhoda; and hear the rattle of wheels on the pavement as the farm horses plod home; I hear traffic roaring in the evening wind. I look at the quivering leaves in the dark garden and think "They dance in London. Jinny kisses Louis".'

'How strange,' said Jinny, 'that people should sleep, that people should put out the lights and go upstairs. They have taken off their dresses, they have put on white nightgowns. There are no lights in any of these houses. There is a line of chimney-pots against the sky; and a street lamp or two burning, as lamps burn when nobody needs them. The only people in the streets are poor people hurrying. There is no one coming or going in this street; the day is over. A few policemen stand at the corners. Yet night is beginning. I feel myself shining in the dark. Silk is on my knee. My silk legs rub smoothly together. The stones of a necklace lie cold on my throat. My feet feel the pinch of shoes. I sit bolt upright so that my hair may not touch the back of the seat. I am arrayed, I am prepared. This is the momentary pause; the dark moment. The fiddlers have lifted their bows.

'Now the car slides to a stop. A strip of pavement is lighted. The door is opening and shutting. People are arriving; they do not speak; they hasten in. There is the swishing sound of cloaks falling in the hall. This is the prelude, this is the beginning. I glance, I peep, I powder. All is exact, prepared. My hair is swept in one curve. My lips are precisely red. I am ready now to join

451

men and women on the stairs, my peers. I pass them, exposed to their gaze, as they are to mine. Like lightning we look but do not soften or show signs of recognition. Our bodies communicate. This is my calling. This is my world. All is decided and ready; the servants, standing here, and again here, take my name, my fresh, my unknown name, and toss it before me. I enter.

'Here are gilt chairs in the empty, the expectant rooms, and flowers, stiller, statelier, than flowers that grow, spread green, spread white, against the walls. And on one small table is one bound book. This is what I have dreamt; this is what I have foretold. I am native here. I tread naturally on thick carpets. I slide easily on smooth-polished floors, I now begin to unfurl, in this scent, in this radiance, as a fern when its curled leaves unfurl. I stop. I take stock of this world. I look among the groups of unknown people. Among the lustrous green, pink, pearl-grey women stand upright the bodies of men. They are black and white; they are grooved beneath their clothes with deep rills. I feel again the reflection in the window of the tunnel; it moves. The black-and-white figures of unknown men look at me as I lean forward; as I turn aside to look at a picture, they turn too. Their hands go fluttering to their ties. They touch their waistcoats, their pocket-handkerchiefs. They are very young. They are anxious to make a good impression. I feel a thousand capacities spring up in me. I am arch, gay, languid, melancholy by turns. I am rooted, but I flow. All gold, flowing that way, I say to this one, "Come." Rippling black, I say to that one, "No." One breaks off from his station under the glass cabinet. He approaches. He makes towards me. This is the most exciting moment I have ever known. I flutter. I ripple. I stream like a plant in the river, flowing this way, flowing that way, but rooted, so that he may come to me. "Come," I say, "come." Pale, with dark hair, the one who is coming is melancholy, romantic. And I am arch and fluent and capricious; for he is melancholy, he is romantic. He is here; he stands at my side.

'Now with a little jerk, like a limpet broken from a rock, I am

452

broken off: I fall with him; I am carried off. We yield to this slow flood. We go in and out of this hesitating music. Rocks break the current of the dance; it jars, it shivers. In and out, we are swept now into this large figure; it holds us together; we cannot step outside its sinuous, its hesitating, its abrupt, its perfectly encircling walls. Our bodies, his hard, mine flowing, are pressed together within its body; it holds us together; and then lengthening out, in smooth, in sinuous folds, rolls us between it, on and on. Suddenly the music breaks. My blood runs on but my body stands still. The room reels past my eyes. It stops.

'Come, then, let us wander whirling to the gilt chairs. The body is stronger than I thought. I am dizzier than I supposed. I do not care for anything in the world. I do not care for anybody save this man whose name I do not know. Are we not acceptable, moon? Are we not lovely sitting together here, I in my satin; he in black and white? My peers may look at me now. I look straight back at you, men and women. I am one of you. This is my world. Now I take this thin-stemmed glass and sip. Wine has a drastic, an astringent taste. I cannot help wincing as I drink. Scent and flowers, radiance and heat, are distilled here to a fiery, to a yellow liquid. Just behind my shoulder-blades some dry thing, wide-eyed, gently closes, gradually lulls itself to sleep. This is rapture; this is relief. The bar at the back of my throat lowers itself. Words crowd and cluster and push forth one on top of another. It does not matter which. They jostle and mount on each other's shoulders. The single and the solitary mate, tumble and become many. It does not matter what I say. Crowding, like a fluttering bird, one sentence crosses the empty space between us. It settles on his lips. I fill my glass again. I drink. The veil drops between us. I am admitted to the warmth and privacy of another soul. We are together, high up, on some Alpine pass. He stands melancholy on the crest of the road. I stoop. I pick a blue flower and fix it, standing on tiptoe to reach him, in his coat. There! That is my moment of ecstasy. Now it is over.

'Now slackness and indifference invade us. Other people

brush past. We have lost consciousness of our bodies uniting under the table. I also like fair-haired men with blue eyes. The door opens. The door goes on opening. Now I think, next time it opens the whole of my life will be changed. Who comes? But it is only a servant, bringing glasses. That is an old man—I should be a child with him. That is a great lady—with her I should dissemble. There are girls of my own age, for whom I feel the drawn swords of an honourable antagonism. For these are my peers. I am a native of this world. Here is my risk, here is my adventure. The door opens. O come, I say to this one, rippling gold from head to heels. "Come," and he comes towards me.'

'I shall edge behind them,' said Rhoda, 'as if I saw someone I know. But I know no one. I shall twitch the curtain and look at the moon. Draughts of oblivion shall quench my agitation. The door opens; the tiger leaps. The door opens; terror rushes in; terror upon terror, pursuing me. Let me visit furtively the treasures I have laid apart. Pools lie on the other side of the world reflecting marble columns. The swallow dips her wing in dark pools. But here the door opens and people come; they come towards me. Throwing faint smiles to mask their cruelty, their indifference, they seize me. The swallow dips her wings; the moon rides through the blue seas alone. I must take his hand; I must answer. But what answer shall I give? I am thrust back to stand burning in this clumsy, this ill-fitting body, to receive the shafts of his indifference and his scorn, I who long for marble columns and pools on the other side of the world where the swallow dips her wings.

'Night has wheeled a little further over the chimney-pots. I see out of the window over his shoulder some unembarrassed cat, not drowned in light, not trapped in silk, free to pause, to stretch, and to move again. I hate all details of the individual life. But I am fixed here to listen. An immense pressure is on me. I cannot move without dislodging the weight of centuries. A million arrows pierce me. Scorn and ridicule pierce me. I, who could beat my breast against the storm and let the hail choke me joyfully, am pinned down here; am exposed. The tiger leaps. Tongues with their whips are upon me. Mobile, incessant, they flicker over me. I must prevaricate and fence them off with lies. What amulet is there against this disaster? What face can I summon to lay cool upon this heat? I think of names on boxes; of mothers from whose wide knees skirts descend; of glades where the many-backed steep hills come down. Hide me, I cry, protect me, for I am the youngest, the most naked of you all. Jinny rides like a gull on the wave, dealing her looks adroitly here and there, saying this, saying that, with truth. But I lie; I prevaricate.

'Alone, I rock my basins; I am mistress of my fleet of ships. But here, twisting the tassels of this brocaded curtain in my hostess's window, I am broken into separate pieces; I am no longer one. What then is the knowledge that Jinny has as she dances; the assurance that Susan has as, stooping quietly beneath the lamplight, she draws the white cotton through the eye of her needle? They say, Yes; they say, No; they bring their fists down with a bang on the table. But I doubt; I tremble; I see the wild thorn tree shake its shadow in the desert.

'Now I will walk, as if I had an end in view, across the room, to the balcony under the awning. I see the sky, softly feathered with its sudden effulgence of moon. I also see the railings of the square, and two people without faces, leaning like statues against the sky. There is, then, a world immune from change. When I have passed through this drawing-room flickering with tongues that cut me like knives, making me stammer, making me lie, I find faces rid of features, robed in beauty. The lovers crouch under the plane tree. The policeman stands sentinel at the corner. A man passes. There is, then, a world immune from change. But I am not composed enough, standing on tiptoe on the verge of fire, still scorched by the hot breath, afraid of the door opening and the leap of the tiger, to make even one sentence. What I say is perpetually contradicted. Each time the door opens I am interrupted. I am not yet twenty-one. I am to be broken. I am to be derided all my life. I am to be cast up and down among these men and women, with their twitching faces, with their lying tongues, like a cork on a rough sea. Like a ribbon of weed I am flung far every time the door opens. I am the foam that sweeps and fills the uttermost rims of the rocks with whiteness; I am also a girl, here in this room.'

The sun, risen, no longer couched on a green mattress darting a fitful glance through watery jewels, bared its face and looked straight over the waves. They fell with a regular thud. They fell with the concussion of horses' hooves on the turf. Their spray rose like the tossing of lances and assegais over the riders' heads. They swept the beach with steel blue and diamond-tipped water. They drew in and out with the energy, the muscularity, of an engine which sweeps its force out and in again. The sun fell on cornfields and woods, rivers became blue and many-plaited, lawns that sloped down to the water's edge became green as birds' feathers softly ruffling their plumes. The hills, curved and controlled, seemed bound back by thongs, as a limb is laced by muscles; and the woods which bristled proudly on their flanks were like the curt, clipped mane on the neck of a horse.

In the garden where the trees stood, thick over flowerbeds, ponds, and greenhouses the birds sang in the hot sunshine, each alone. One sang under the bedroom window; another on the topmost twig of the lilac bush; another on the edge of the wall. Each sang stridently, with passion, with vehemence, as if to let the song burst out of it, no matter if it shattered the song of another bird with harsh discord. Their round eyes bulged with brightness; their claws gripped the twig or rail. They sang, exposed without shelter, to the air and the sun, beautiful in their new plumage, shell-veined or brightly mailed, here barred with soft blues, here splashed with gold, or striped with one bright feather. They sang as if the song were urged out of them by the pressure of the morning. They sang as if the edge of being were sharpened and must cut, must split the softness of the blue-green light, the dampness of the wet earth; the fumes and steams of the greasy kitchen vapour; the hot breath of mutton and beef; the richness of pastry and fruit; the damp shreds and peelings thrown from the kitchen bucket, from which a slow steam oozed on the rubbish heap. On all the sodden, the damp-spotted, the curled with wetness, they descended, dry-beaked, ruthless, abrupt. They swooped suddenly from the lilac bough or the fence. They spied a snail and tapped the shell against a stone. They tapped furiously, methodically, until the shell broke and something slimy oozed from the crack. They swept and soared sharply in flights high into the air, twittering short, sharp notes, and perched in the upper branches of some tree, and looked down upon leaves and spires beneath, and the country white with blossom, flowing with grass, and the sea which beat like a drum that raises a regiment of plumed and turbaned soldiers. Now and again their songs ran together in swift scales like the interlacings of a mountain stream whose waters, meeting, foam and then mix, and hasten quicker and quicker down the same channel, brushing the same broad leaves. But there is a rock; they sever.

The sun fell in sharp wedges inside the room. Whatever the light touched became dowered with a fanatical existence. A plate was like a white lake. A knife looked like a dagger of ice. Suddenly tumblers revealed themselves upheld by streaks of light. Tables and chairs rose to the surface as if they had been sunk under water and rose, filmed with red, orange, purple like the bloom on the skin of ripe fruit. The veins on the glaze of the china, the grain of the wood, the fibres of the matting became more and more finely engraved. Everything was without shadow. A jar was so green that the eye seemed sucked up through a funnel by its intensity and stuck to it like a limpet. Then shapes took on mass and edge. Here was the boss of a chair; here the bulk of a cupboard. And as the light increased, flocks of shadow were driven before it and conglomerated and hung in many-pleated folds in the background.

'How fair, how strange,' said Bernard, 'glittering, many-pointed and many-domed London lies before me under mist. Guarded by gasometers, by factory chimneys, she lies sleeping as we approach. She folds the ant-heap to her breast. All cries, all clamour, are softly enveloped in silence. Not Rome herself looks more majestic. But we are aimed at her. Already her maternal somnolence is uneasy. Ridges, fledged with houses rise from the mist. Factories, cathedrals, glass domes, institutions and theatres erect themselves. The early train from the north is hurled at her like a missile. We draw a curtain as we pass. Blank expectant faces stare at us as we rattle and flash through stations. Men clutch their newspapers a little tighter, as our wind sweeps them, envisaging death. But we roar on. We are about to explode in the flanks of the city like a shell in the side of some ponderous, maternal, majestic animal. She hums and murmurs; she awaits us.

'Meanwhile as I stand looking from the train window, I feel strangely, persuasively, that because of my great happiness (being engaged to be married) I am become part of this speed, this missile hurled at the city. I am numbed to tolerance and acquiescence. My dear sir, I could say, why do you fidget, taking down your suitcase and pressing into it the cap that you have worn all night? Nothing we can do will avail. Over us all broods a splendid unanimity. We are enlarged and solemnized and brushed into uniformity as with the grey wing of some enormous goose (it is a fine but colourless morning) because we have only one desire—to arrive at the station. I do not want the train to stop with a thud. I do not want the connection which has bound us together sitting opposite each other all night long to be broken. I do not want to feel that hate and rivalry have resumed their sway; and different desires. Our community in the rushing train, sitting together with only one wish, to arrive at Euston, was very welcome. But behold! It is over. We have attained our desire. We have drawn up at the platform. Hurry and confusion and the wish to be first through the gate into the lift assert themselves. But I do not wish to be first through the gate, to assume the burden of individual life. I, who have been since Monday, when she accepted me, charged in every nerve with a sense of identity, who could not see a tooth-brush in a glass without saying, "My toothbrush", now wish to unclasp my hands and let fall my possessions, and merely stand here in the street, taking no part, watching the omnibuses, without desire; without envy; with what would be boundless curiosity about human destiny if there were any longer an edge to my mind. But it has none. I have arrived; am accepted. I ask nothing.

'Having dropped off satisfied like a child from the breast, I am at liberty now to sink down, deep, into what passes, this omnipresent, general life. (How much, let me note, depends upon trousers; the intelligent head is entirely handicapped by shabby trousers.) One observes curious hesitations at the door of the lift. This way, that way, the other? Then individuality asserts itself. They are off. They are all impelled by some necessity. Some miserable affair of keeping an appointment, of buying a hat, severs these beautiful human beings once so united. For myself, I have no aim. I have no ambition. I will let myself be carried on by the general impulse. The surface of my mind slips along like a pale-grey stream, reflecting what passes. I cannot remember my past, my nose, or the colour of my eyes, or what my general opinion of myself is. Only in moments of emergency, at a crossing, at a kerb, the wish to preserve my body springs out and seizes me and stops me, here, before this omnibus. We insist, it seems, on living. Then again, indifference descends. The roar of the traffic, the passage of undifferentiated faces, this way and that way, drugs me into dreams; rubs the features from faces. People might walk through me. And, what is this moment of time, this particular day in which I have found myself caught? The growl of traffic might be any uproar—forest trees or the roar of wild beasts. Time has whizzed back an inch or two on its reel; our short progress has been cancelled. I think also that our bodies are in truth naked. We are only lightly covered with buttoned cloth; and beneath these pavements are shells, bones and silence.

'It is, however, true that my dreaming, my tentative advance like one carried beneath the surface of a stream, is interrupted, torn, pricked and plucked at by sensations, spontaneous and irrelevant, of curiosity, greed, desire, irresponsible as in sleep. (I covet that bag—etc.) No, but I wish to go under; to visit the profound depths; once in a while to exercise my prerogative not always to act, but to explore; to hear vague, ancestral sounds of boughs creaking, of mammoths; to indulge impossible desires to embrace the whole world with the arms of understanding— impossible to those who act. Am I not, as I walk, trembling with strange oscillations and vibrations of sympathy, which, unmoored as I am from a private being, bid me embrace these engrossed flocks; these starers and trippers; these errand-boys and furtive and fugitive girls who, ignoring their doom, look in at shop-windows? But I am aware of our ephemeral passage.

'It is, however, true that I cannot deny a sense that life for me is now mysteriously prolonged. Is it that I may have children, may cast a fling of seed wider, beyond this generation, this doom-encircled population, shuffling each other in endless competition along the street? My daughters shall come here, in other summers; my sons shall turn new fields. Hence we are not raindrops, soon dried by the wind; we make gardens blow and forests roar; we come up differently, for ever and ever. This, then, serves to explain my confidence, my central stability, otherwise so monstrously absurd as I breast the stream of this crowded thoroughfare, making always a passage for myself between people's bodies, taking advantage of safe moments to cross. It is not vanity; for I am emptied of ambition; I do not remember my special gifts, or idiosyncrasy, or the marks I bear on my person; eyes, nose or mouth. I am not, at this moment, myself.

'Yet behold, it returns. One cannot extinguish that persistent smell. It steals in through some crack in the structure—one's identity. I am not part of the street—no, I observe the street. One splits off, therefore. For instance, up that back street a girl stands waiting; for whom? A romantic story. On the wall of that shop is fixed a small crane, and for what reason, I ask, was that crane fixed there? and invent a purple lady swelling, circumambient, hauled from a barouche landau by a perspiring husband sometime in the sixties. A grotesque story. That is, I am a natural coiner of words, a blower of bubbles through one thing and another. And, striking off these observations spontaneously, I elaborate myself; differentiate myself and, listening to the voice that says as I stroll past, "Look! Take note of that!" I conceive myself called upon to provide, some winter's night, a meaning for all my observations—a line that runs from one to another, a summing up that completes. But soliloquies in back streets soon pall. I need an audience. That is my downfall. That always ruffles the edge of the final statement and prevents it from forming. I cannot seat myself in some sordid eating-house and order the same glass day after day and imbue myself entirely in one fluid—this life. I make my phrase and run off with it to some furnished room where it will be lit by dozens of candles. I need eyes on me to draw out these frills and furbelows. To be myself (I note) I need the illumination of other people's eyes, and therefore cannot be entirely sure what is my self. The authentics, like Louis, like Rhoda, exist most completely in solitude. They resent illumination, reduplication. They toss their pictures once painted face downward on the field. On Louis' words the ice is packed thick. His words issue pressed, condensed, enduring.

'I wish, then, after this somnolence to sparkle, many-faceted under the light of my friends' faces. I have been traversing the sunless territory of non-identity. A strange land. I have heard in my moment of appeasement, in my moment of obliterating satisfaction, the sigh, as it goes in, comes out, of the tide that draws beyond this circle of bright light, this drumming of insensate fury. I have had one moment of enormous peace. This perhaps is happiness. Now I am drawn back by pricking sensations; by curiosity, greed (I am hungry) and the irresistible desire to be myself. I think of people to whom I could say things: Louis, Neville, Susan, Jinny and Rhoda. With them I am many-sided. They retrieve me from darkness. We shall meet tonight, thank Heaven. Thank Heaven, I need not be alone. We shall dine together. We shall say good-bye to Percival, who goes to India. The hour is still distant, but I feel already those harbingers, those outriders, figures of one's friends in absence. I see Louis, stone-carved, sculpturesque; Neville, scissor-cutting, exact; Susan with eyes like lumps of crystal; Jinny dancing like a flame, febrile, hot, over dry earth; and Rhoda the nymph of the fountain always wet. These are fantastic pictures—these are figments, these visions of friends in absence, grotesque, dropsical, vanishing at the first touch of the toe of a real boot. Yet they drum me alive. They brush off these vapours. I begin to be impatient of solitude—to feel its draperies hang sweltering, unwholesome about me. Oh, to toss them off and be active! Anybody will do. I am not fastidious. The crossing-sweeper will do; the postman; the waiter in this French restaurant; better still the genial proprietor, whose geniality seems reserved for oneself. He mixes the salad with his own hands for some privileged guest. Which is the privileged guest, I ask, and why? And what is he saying to the lady in ear-rings; is she a friend or a customer? I feel at once, as I sit down at a table, the delicious jostle of confusion, of uncertainty, of possibility, of speculation. Images breed instantly. I am embarrassed by my own fertility. I could describe every chair, table, luncher here copiously, freely. My mind hums hither and thither with its veil of words for everything. To speak, about wine even to the waiter, is to bring about an explosion. Up goes the rocket. Its golden grain falls, fertilizing, upon the rich soil of my imagination. The entirely unexpected nature of this explosion—that is the joy of intercourse. I, mixed with an unknown Italian waiter—what am I? There is no stability in this world. Who is to say what meaning there is in anything? Who is to foretell the flight of a word? It is a balloon that sails over tree-tops. To speak of knowledge is futile. All is experiment and adventure. We are for ever mixing ourselves with unknown quantities. What is to come? I know not. But as I put down my glass I remember: I am engaged to be married. I am to dine with my friends tonight. I am Bernard, myself.'

'It is now five minutes to eight,' said Neville. 'I have come early. I have taken my place at the table ten minutes before the time in order to taste every moment of anticipation; to see the door open and to say, "Is it Percival? No; it is not Percival." There is a morbid pleasure in saying: "No, it is not Percival." I have seen the door open and shut twenty times already; each time the suspense sharpens. This is the place to which he is coming. This is the table at which he will sit. Here, incredible as it seems, will be his actual body. This table, these chairs, this metal vase with its three red flowers are about to undergo an extraordinary transformation. Already the room, with its swing-doors, its tables heaped with fruit, with cold joints, wears the wavering, unreal appearance of a place where one waits expecting something to happen. Things quiver as if not yet in being. The blankness of the white table-cloth glares. The hostility, the indifference of other people dining here is oppressive. We look at each other; see that we do not know each other, stare, and go off. Such looks are lashes. I feel the whole cruelty and indifference of the world in them. If he should not come I could not bear it. I should go. Yet somebody must be seeing him now. He must be in some cab; he must be passing some shop. And every moment he seems to pump into this room this prickly light, this intensity of being, so that things have lost their normal uses—this knife-blade is only a flash of light, not a thing to cut with. The normal is abolished.

'The door opens, but he does not come. That is Louis hesitating there. That is his strange mixture of assurance and timidity. He looks at himself in the looking-glass as he comes in; he touches his hair; he is dissatisfied with his appearance. He says, "I am a Duke—the last of an ancient race." He is acrid, suspicious, domineering, difficult (I am comparing him with Percival). At the same time he is formidable, for there is laughter in his eyes.

He has seen me. Here he is.'

'There is Susan,' said Louis. 'She does not see us. She has not dressed, because she despises the futility of London. She stands for a moment at the swing-door, looking about her like a creature dazed by the light of a lamp. Now she moves. She has the stealthy yet assured movements (even among tables and chairs) of a wild beast. She seems to find her way by instinct in and out among these little tables, touching no one, disregarding waiters, yet comes straight to our table in the corner. When she sees us (Neville, and myself) her face assumes a certainty which is alarming, as if she had what she wanted. To be loved by Susan would be to be impaled by a bird's sharp beak, to be nailed to a barnyard door. Yet there are moments when I could wish to be speared by a beak, to be nailed to a barnyard door, positively, once and for all.

'Rhoda comes now, from nowhere, having slipped in while we were not looking. She must have made a tortuous course, taking cover now behind a waiter, now behind some ornamental pillar, so as to put off as long as possible the shock of recognition, so as to be secure for one more moment to rock her petals in her basin. We wake her. We torture her. She dreads us, she despises us, yet comes cringing to our sides because for all our cruelty there is always some name, some face, which sheds a radiance, which lights up her pavements and makes it possible for her to replenish her dreams.'

'The door opens, the door goes on opening,' said Neville, 'yet he does not come.'

'There is Jinny,' said Susan. 'She stands in the door. Everything seems stayed. The waiter stops. The diners at the table by the door look. She seems to centre everything; round her tables, lines of doors, windows, ceilings, ray themselves, like rays round the star in the middle of a smashed window-pane. She brings things to a point, to order. Now she sees us, and moves, and all the rays ripple and flow and waver over us, bringing in new tides of sensation. We change. Louis puts his hand to his tie. Neville, who sits waiting with agonized intensity, nervously straightens the forks in front of him. Rhoda sees her with surprise, as if on some far horizon a fire blazed. And I, though I pile my mind with damp grass, with wet fields, with the sound of rain on the roof and the gusts of wind that batter at the house in winter and so protect my soul against her, feel her derision steal round me, feel her laughter curl its tongues of fire round me and light up unsparingly my shabby dress, my square-tipped finger-nails, which I at once hide under the table-cloth.'

'He has not come,' said Neville. The door opens and he does not come. That is Bernard. As he pulls off his coat he shows, of course, the blue shirt under his arm-pits. And then, unlike the rest of us, he comes in without pushing open a door, without knowing that he comes into a room full of strangers. He does not look in the glass. His hair is untidy, but he does not know it. He has no perception that we differ, or that this table is his goal. He hesitates on his way here. Who is that? he asks himself, as he half knows a woman in an opera cloak. He half knows everybody; he knows nobody (I compare him with Percival). But now, perceiving us, he waves a benevolent salute; he bears down with such benignity, with such love of mankind (crossed with humour at the futility of "loving mankind"), that, if it were not for Percival, who turns all this to vapour, one would feel, as the others already feel: Now is our festival; now we are together. But without Percival there is no solidity. We are silhouettes, hollow phantoms moving mistily without a background.'

'The swing-door goes on opening,' said Rhoda. 'Strangers keep on coming, people we shall never see again, people who brush us disagreeably with their familiarity, their indifference, and the sense of a world continuing without us. We cannot sink down, we cannot forget our faces. Even I who have no face, who make no difference when I come in (Susan and Jinny change bodies and faces), flutter unattached, without anchorage anywhere, unconsolidated, incapable of composing

465

any blankness or continuity or wall against which these bodies move. It is because of Neville and his misery. The sharp breath of his misery scatters my being. Nothing can settle; nothing can subside. Every time the door opens he looks fixedly at the table—he dare not raise his eyes—then looks for one second and says, "He has not come." But here he is.'

'Now,' said Neville, 'my tree flowers. My heart rises. All oppression is relieved. All impediment is removed. The reign of chaos is over. He has imposed order. Knives cut again.'

'Here is Percival,' said Jinny. 'He has not dressed.'

'Here is Percival,' said Bernard, 'smoothing his hair, not from vanity (he does not look in the glass), but to propitiate the god of decency. He is conventional; he is a hero. The little boys trooped after him across the playing-fields. They blew their noses as he blew his nose, but unsuccessfully, for he is Percival. Now, when he is about to leave us, to go to India, all these trifles come together. He is a hero. Oh yes, that is not to be denied, and when he takes his seat by Susan, whom he loves, the occasion is crowned. We who yelped like jackals biting at each other's heels now assume the sober and confident air of soldiers in the presence of their captain. We who have been separated by our youth (the oldest is not yet twenty-five), who have sung like eager birds each his own song and tapped with the remorseless and savage egotism of the young our own snail-shell till it cracked (I am engaged), or perched solitary outside some bedroom window and sang of love, of fame and other single experiences so dear to the callow bird with a yellow tuft on its beak, now come nearer; and shuffling closer on our perch in this restaurant where everybody's interests are at variance, and the incessant passage of traffic chafes us with distractions, and the door opening perpetually its glass cage solicits us with myriad temptations and offers insults and wounds to our confidence—sitting together here we love each other and believe in our own endurance.'

'Now let us issue from the darkness of solitude,' said Louis.

'Now let us say, brutally and directly, what is in our minds,' said Neville. 'Our isolation, our preparation, is over. The furtive days of secrecy and hiding, the revelations on staircases, moments of terror and ecstasy.'

'Old Mrs Constable lifted her sponge and warmth poured over us,' said Bernard. 'We became clothed in this changing, this feeling garment of flesh.'

'The boot-boy made love to the scullery-maid in the kitchen garden,' said Susan, 'among the blown-out washing.'

'The breath of the wind was like a tiger panting,' said Rhoda.

'The man lay livid with his throat cut in the gutter,' said Neville. 'And going upstairs I could not raise my foot against the immitigable apple tree with its silver leaves held stiff.'

'The leaf danced in the hedge without anyone to blow it,' said Jinny.

'In the sun-baked corner,' said Louis, 'the petals swam on depths of green.'

'At Elvedon the gardeners swept and swept with their great brooms, and the woman sat at a table writing,' said Bernard.

'From these close-furled balls of string we draw now every filament,' said Louis, 'remembering, when we meet.'

'And then,' said Bernard, 'the cab came to the door, and, pressing our new bowler hats tightly over our eyes to hide our unmanly tears, we drove through streets in which even the housemaids looked at us, and our names painted in white letters on our boxes proclaimed to all the world that we were going to school with the regulation number of socks and drawers, on which our mothers for some nights previously had stitched our initials, in our boxes. A second severance from the body of our mother.'

'And Miss Lambert, Miss Cutting and Miss Bard,' said Jinny, 'monumental ladies, white-ruffed, stone-coloured, enigmatic, with amethyst rings moving like virginal tapers, dim glow-worms over the pages of French, geography and arithmetic, presided; and there were maps, green-baize boards, and rows of

467

shoes on a shelf.'

'Bells rang punctually,' said Susan, 'maids scuffled and giggled. There was a drawing in of chairs and a drawing out of chairs on the linoleum. But from one attic there was a blue view, a distant view of a field unstained by the corruption of this regimented, unreal existence.'

'Down from our heads veils fell,' said Rhoda. 'We clasped the flowers with their green leaves rustling in garlands.'

'We changed, we became unrecognizable,' said Louis. 'Exposed to all these different lights, what we had in us (for we are all so different) came intermittently, in violent patches, spaced by blank voids, to the surface as if some acid had dropped unequally on the plate. I was this, Neville that, Rhoda different again, and Bernard too.'

'Then canoes slipped through palely tinted yellow branches,' said Neville, 'and Bernard, advancing in his casual way against breadths of green, against houses of very ancient foundation, tumbled in a heap on the ground beside me. In an access of emotion—winds are not more raving, nor lightning more sudden—I took my poem, I flung my poem, I slammed the door behind me.'

'I, however,' said Louis, 'losing sight of you, sat in my office and tore the date from the calendar, and announced to the world of ship-brokers, corn-chandlers and actuaries that Friday the tenth, or Tuesday the eighteenth, had dawned on the city of London.'

'Then,' said Jinny, 'Rhoda and I, exposed in bright dresses, with a few precious stones nestling on a cold ring round our throats, bowed, shook hands and took a sandwich from a plate with a smile.'

'The tiger leapt, and the swallow dipped her wings in dark pools on the other side of the world,' said Rhoda.

'But here and now we are together,' said Bernard. 'We have come together, at a particular time, to this particular spot. We are drawn into this communion by some deep, some common emotion. Shall we call it, conveniently, "love"? Shall we say "love of Percival" because Percival is going to India?

'No, that is too small, too particular a name. We cannot attach the width and spread of our feelings to so small a mark. We have come together (from the North, from the South, from Susan's farm, from Louis' house of business) to make one thing, not enduring—for what endures?—but seen by many eyes simultaneously. There is a red carnation in that vase. A single flower as we sat here waiting, but now a seven-sided flower, many-petalled, red, puce, purple-shaded, stiff with silver-tinted leaves—a whole flower to which every eye brings its own contribution.

'After the capricious fires, the abysmal dullness of youth,' said Neville, 'the light falls upon real objects now. Here are knives and forks. The world is displayed, and we too, so that we can talk.'

'We differ, it may be too profoundly,' said Louis, 'for explanation. But let us attempt it. I smoothed my hair when I came in, hoping to look like the rest of you. But I cannot, for I am not single and entire as you are. I have lived a thousand lives already. Every day I unbury—I dig up. I find relics of myself in the sand that women made thousands of years ago, when I heard songs by the Nile and the chained beast stamping. What you see beside you, this man, this Louis, is only the cinders and refuse of something once splendid. I was an Arab prince; behold my free gestures. I was a great poet in the time of Elizabeth. I was a Duke at the court of Louis the Fourteenth. I am very vain, very confident; I have an immeasurable desire that women should sigh in sympathy. I have eaten no lunch today in order that Susan may think me cadaverous and that Jinny may extend to me the exquisite balm of her sympathy. But while I admire Susan and Percival, I hate the others, because it is for them that I do these antics, smoothing my hair, concealing my accent. I am the little ape who chatters over a nut, and you are the dowdy women with shiny bags of stale buns; I am also the caged tiger, and you are the keepers with red-hot bars. That is, I am fiercer

469

and stronger than you are, yet the apparition that appears above ground after ages of nonentity will be spent in terror lest you should laugh at me, in veerings with the wind against the soot storms, in efforts to make a steel ring of clear poetry that shall connect the gulls and the women with bad teeth, the church spire and the bobbing billycock hats as I see them when I take my luncheon and prop my poet—is it Lucretius?—against a cruet and the gravy-splashed bill of fare.'

'But you will never hate me,' said Jinny. 'You will never see me, even across a room full of gilt chairs and ambassadors, without coming to me across the room to seek my sympathy. When I came in just now everything stood still in a pattern. Waiters stopped, diners raised their forks and held them. I had the air of being prepared for what would happen. When I sat down you put your hands to your ties, you hid them under the table. But I hide nothing. I am prepared. Every time the door opens I cry "More!" But my imagination is the bodies. I can imagine nothing beyond the circle cast by my body. My body goes before me, like a lantern down a dark lane, bringing one thing after another out of darkness into a ring of light. I dazzle you; I make you believe that this is all.'

'But when you stand in the door,' said Neville, 'you inflict stillness, demanding admiration, and that is a great impediment to the freedom of intercourse. You stand in the door making us notice you. But none of you saw me approach. I came early; I came quickly and directly, *here,* to sit by the person whom I love. My life has a rapidity that yours lack. I am like a hound on the scent. I hunt from dawn to dusk. Nothing, not the pursuit of perfection through the sand, nor fame, nor money, has meaning for me. I shall have riches; I shall have fame. But I shall never have what I want, for I lack bodily grace and the courage that comes with it. The swiftness of my mind is too strong for my body. I fail before I reach the end and fall in a heap, damp, perhaps disgusting. I excite pity in the crises of life, not love. Therefore I suffer horribly. But I do not suffer, as Louis does, to make myself a spectacle. I have too fine a sense of fact to allow myself these juggleries, these pretences. I see everything— except one thing—with complete clarity. That is my saving. That is what gives my suffering an unceasing excitement. That is what makes me dictate, even when I am silent. And since I am, in one respect, deluded, since the person is always changing, though not the desire, and I do not know in the morning by whom I shall sit at night, I am never stagnant; I rise from my worst disasters, I turn, I change. Pebbles bounce off the mail of my muscular, my extended body. In this pursuit I shall grow old.'

'If I could believe,' said Rhoda, 'that I should grow old in pursuit and change, I should be rid of my fear: nothing persists. One moment does not lead to another. The door opens and the tiger leaps. You did not see me come. I circled round the chairs to avoid the horror of the spring. I am afraid of you all. I am afraid of the shock of sensation that leaps upon me, because I cannot deal with it as you do—I cannot make one moment merge in the next. To me they are all violent, all separate; and if I fall under the shock of the leap of the moment you will be on me, tearing me to pieces. I have no end in view. I do not know how to run minute to minute and hour to hour, solving them by some natural force until they make the whole and indivisible mass that you call life. Because you have an end in view—one person, is it, to sit beside, an idea is it, your beauty is it? I do not know—your days and hours pass like the boughs of forest trees and the smooth green of forest rides to a hound running on the scent. But there is no single scent, no single body for me to follow. And I have no face. I am like the foam that races over the beach or the moonlight that falls arrowlike here on a tin can, here on a spike of the mailed sea holly, or a bone or a half-eaten boat. I am whirled down caverns, and flap like paper against endless corridors, and must press my hand against the wall to draw myself back.

'But since I wish above all things to have lodgment, I pretend, as I go upstairs lagging behind Jinny and Susan, to have an end

471

in view. I pull on my stockings as I see them pull on theirs. I wait for you to speak and then speak like you. I am drawn here across London to a particular spot, to a particular place, not to see you or you or you, but to light my fire at the general blaze of you who live wholly, indivisibly and without caring.'

'When I came into the room tonight,' said Susan, 'I stopped, I peered about like an animal with its eyes near to the ground. The smell of carpets and furniture and scent disgusts me. I like to walk through the wet fields alone, or to stop at a gate and watch my setter nose in a circle, and to ask: Where is the hare? I like to be with people who twist herbs, and spit into the fire, and shuffle down long passages in slippers like my father. The only sayings I understand are cries of love, hate, rage and pain. This talking is undressing an old woman whose dress had seemed to be part of her, but now, as we talk, she turns pinkish underneath, and has wrinkled thighs and sagging breasts. When you are silent you are again beautiful. I shall never have anything but natural happiness. It will almost content me. I shall go to bed tired. I shall lie like a field bearing crops in rotation; in the summer heat will dance over me; in the winter I shall be cracked with the cold. But heat and cold will follow each other naturally without my willing or unwilling. My children will carry me on; their teething, their crying, their going to school and coming back will be like the waves of the sea under me. No day will be without its movement. I shall be lifted higher than any of you on the backs of the seasons. I shall possess more than Jinny, more than Rhoda, by the time I die. But on the other hand, where you are various and dimple a million times to the ideas and laughter of others, I shall be sullen, storm-tinted and all one purple. I shall be debased and hide-bound by the bestial and beautiful passion of maternity. I shall push the fortunes of my children unscrupulously. I shall hate those who see their faults. I shall lie basely to help them. I shall let them wall me away from you, from you and from you. Also, I am torn with jealousy. I hate Jinny because she shows me that my hands are red, my nails bitten. I love with such ferocity that it kills me when the object of my love shows by a phrase that he can escape. He escapes, and I am left clutching at a string that slips in and out among the leaves on the tree-tops. I do not understand phrases.'

'Had I been born,' said Bernard, 'not knowing that one word follows another I might have been, who knows, perhaps anything. As it is, finding sequences everywhere, I cannot bear the pressure of solitude. When I cannot see words curling like rings of smoke round me I am in darkness—I am nothing. When I am alone I fall into lethargy, and say to myself dismally as I poke the cinders through the bars of the grate, Mrs Moffat will come. She will come and sweep it all up. When Louis is alone he sees with astonishing intensity, and will write some words that may outlast us all. Rhoda loves to be alone. She fears us because we shatter the sense of being which is so extreme in solitude—see how she grasps her fork—her weapon against us. But I only come into existence when the plumber, or the horse-dealer, or whoever it may be, says something which sets me alight. Then how lovely the smoke of my phrase is, rising and falling, flaunting and falling, upon red lobsters and yellow fruit, wreathing them into one beauty. But observe how meretricious the phrase is—made up of what evasions and old lies. Thus my character is in part made of the stimulus which other people provide, and is not mine, as yours are. There is some fatal streak, some wandering and irregular vein of silver, weakening it. Hence the fact that used to enrage Neville at school, that I left him. I went with the boasting boys with little caps and badges, driving off in big brakes—there are some here tonight, dining together, correctly dressed, before they go off in perfect concord to the music hall; I loved them. For they bring me into existence as certainly as you do. Hence, too, when I am leaving you and the train is going, you feel that it is not the train that is going, but I, Bernard, who does not care, who does not feel, who has no ticket, and has lost perhaps his purse. Susan, staring at the string that slips in and out among the leaves of the beech trees, cries: "He is gone! He has escaped me!" For there is nothing to lay hold of. I am made and remade continually. Different people draw different words from me.

'Thus there is not one person but fifty people whom I want to sit beside tonight. But I am the only one of you who is at home here without taking liberties. I am not gross; I am not a snob. If I lie open to the pressure of society I often succeed with the dexterity of my tongue in putting something difficult into the currency. See my little toys, twisted out of nothing in a second, how they entertain. I am no hoarder—I shall leave only a cupboard of old clothes when I die—and I am almost indifferent to the minor vanities of life which cause Louis so much torture. But I have sacrificed much. Veined as I am with iron, with silver and streaks of common mud, I cannot contract into the firm fist which those clench who do not depend upon stimulus. I am incapable of the denials, the heroisms of Louis and Rhoda. I shall never succeed, even in talk, in making a perfect phrase. But I shall have contributed more to the passing moment than any of you; I shall go into more rooms, more different rooms, than any of you. But because there is something that comes from outside and not from within I shall be forgotten; when my voice is silent you will not remember me, save as the echo of a voice that once wreathed the fruit into phrases.'

'Look,' said Rhoda; 'listen. Look how the light becomes richer, second by second, and bloom and ripeness lie everywhere; and our eyes, as they range round this room with all its tables, seem to push through curtains of colour, red, orange, umber and queer ambiguous tints, which yield like veils and close behind them, and one thing melts into another.'

'Yes,' said Jinny, 'our senses have widened. Membranes, webs of nerve that lay white and limp, have filled and spread themselves and float round us like filaments, making the air tangible and catching in them far-away sounds unheard before.'

'The roar of London,' said Louis, 'is round us. Motor-cars, vans, omnibuses pass and repass continuously. All are merged in one turning wheel of single sound. All separate sounds—wheels, bells, the cries of drunkards, of merrymakers—are churned into one sound, steel blue, circular. Then a siren hoots. At that shores slip away, chimneys flatten themselves, the ship makes for the open sea.'

'Percival is going,' said Neville. 'We sit here, surrounded, lit up, many coloured; all things—hands, curtains, knives and forks, other people dining—run into each other. We are walled in here. But India lies outside.'

'I see India,' said Bernard. 'I see the low, long shore; I see the tortuous lanes of stamped mud that lead in and out among ramshackle pagodas; I see the gilt and crenellated buildings which have an air of fragility and decay as if they were temporarily run up buildings in some Oriental exhibition. I see a pair of bullocks who drag a low cart along the sun-baked road. The cart sways incompetently from side to side. Now one wheel sticks in the rut, and at once innumerable natives in loin-cloths swarm round it, chattering excitedly. But they do nothing. Time seems endless, ambition vain. Over all broods a sense of the uselessness of human exertion. There are strange sour smells. An old man in a ditch continues to chew betel and to contemplate his navel. But now, behold, Percival advances; Percival rides a flea-bitten mare, and wears a sun-helmet. By applying the standards of the West, by using the violent language that is natural to him, the bullock-cart is righted in less than five minutes. The Oriental problem is solved. He rides on; the multitude cluster round him, regarding him as if he were—what indeed he is—a God.'

'Unknown, with or without a secret, it does not matter,' said Rhoda, 'he is like a stone fallen into a pond round which minnows swarm. Like minnows, we who had been shooting this way, that way, all shot round him when he came. Like minnows, conscious of the presence of a great stone, we undulate and eddy contentedly. Comfort steals over us. Gold runs in our blood. One, two; one, two; the heart beats in serenity, in confidence, in some trance of well-being, in some rapture of benignity;

and look—the outermost parts of the earth—pale shadows on the utmost horizon, India for instance, rise into our purview. The world that had been shrivelled, rounds itself; remote provinces are fetched up out of darkness; we see muddy roads, twisted jungle, swarms of men, and the vulture that feeds on some bloated carcass as within our scope, part of our proud and splendid province, since Percival, riding alone on a flea-bitten mare, advances down a solitary path, has his camp pitched among desolate trees, and sits alone, looking at the enormous mountains.'

'It is Percival,' said Louis, 'sitting silent as he sat among the tickling grasses when the breeze parted the clouds and they formed again, who makes us aware that these attempts to say, "I am this, I am that," which we make, coming together, like separated parts of one body and soul, are false. Something has been left out from fear. Something has been altered, from vanity. We have tried to accentuate differences. From the desire to be separate we have laid stress upon our faults, and what is particular to us. But there is a chain whirling round, round, in a steel-blue circle beneath.'

'It is hate, it is love,' said Susan. That is the furious coal-black stream that makes us dizzy if we look down into it. We stand on a ledge here, but if we look down we turn giddy.'

'It is love,' said Jinny, 'it is hate, such as Susan feels for me because I kissed Louis once in the garden; because equipped as I am, I make her think when I come in, "My hands are red," and hide them. But our hatred is almost indistinguishable from our love.'

'Yet these roaring waters,' said Neville, 'upon which we build our crazy platforms are more stable than the wild, the weak and inconsequent cries that we utter when, trying to speak, we rise; when we reason and jerk out these false sayings, "I am this; I am that!" Speech is false.

'But I eat. I gradually lose all knowledge of particulars as I eat. I am becoming weighed down with food. These delicious mouthfuls of roast duck, fitly piled with vegetables, following each other in exquisite rotation of warmth, weight, sweet and bitter, past my palate, down my gullet, into my stomach, have stabilized my body. I feel quiet, gravity, control. All is solid now. Instinctively my palate now requires and anticipates sweetness and lightness, something sugared and evanescent; and cool wine, fitting glove-like over those finer nerves that seem to tremble from the roof of my mouth and make it spread (as I drink) into a domed cavern, green with vine leaves, musk-scented, purple with grapes. Now I can look steadily into the mill-race that foams beneath. By what particular name are we to call it? Let Rhoda speak, whose face I see reflected mistily in the looking-glass opposite; Rhoda whom I interrupted when she rocked her petals in a brown basin, asking for the pocket-knife that Bernard had stolen. Love is not a whirlpool to her. She is not giddy when she looks down. She looks far away over our heads, beyond India.'

'Yes, between your shoulders, over your heads, to a landscape,' said Rhoda, 'to a hollow where the many-backed steep hills come down like birds' wings folded. There, on the short, firm turf, are bushes, dark leaved, and against their darkness I see a shape, white, but not of stone, moving, perhaps alive. But it is not you, it is not you, it is not you; not Percival, Susan, Jinny, Neville or Louis. When the white arm rests upon the knee it is a triangle; now it is upright—a column; now a fountain, falling. It makes no sign, it does not beckon, it does not see us. Behind it roars the sea. It is beyond our reach. Yet there I venture. There I go to replenish my emptiness, to stretch my nights and fill them fuller and fuller with dreams. And for a second even now, even here, I reach my object and say, "Wander no more. All else is trial and make-believe. Here is the end." But these pilgrimages, these moments of departure, start always in your presence, from this table, these lights from Percival and Susan, here and now. Always I see the grove over your heads, between your shoulders, or from a window when I have crossed the room at a party and stand looking down into the street.'

'But his slippers?' said Neville. 'And his voice downstairs in the hall? And catching sight of him when he does not see one? One waits and he does not come. It gets later and later. He has forgotten. He is with someone else. He is faithless, his love meant nothing. Oh, then the agony—then the intolerable despair! And then the door opens. He is here.'

'Ripping gold, I say to him, "Come",' said Jinny. 'And he comes; he crosses the room to where I sit, with my dress like a veil billowing round me on the gilt chair. Our hands touch, our bodies burst into fire. The chair, the cup, the table—nothing remains unlit. All quivers, all kindles, all burns clear.'

('Look, Rhoda,' said Louis, 'they have become nocturnal, rapt. Their eyes are like moths' wings moving so quickly that they do not seem to move at all.'

'Horns and trumpets,' said Rhoda, 'ring out. Leaves unfold; the stags blare in the thicket. There is a dancing and a drumming, like the dancing and the drumming of naked men with assegais.'

'Like the dance of savages,' said Louis, 'round the camp-fire. They are savage; they are ruthless. They dance in a circle, flapping bladders. The flames leap over their painted faces, over the leopard skins and the bleeding limbs which they have torn from the living body.'

'The flames of the festival rise high,' said Rhoda. 'The great procession passes, flinging green boughs and flowering branches. Their horns spill blue smoke; their skins are dappled red and yellow in the torchlight. They throw violets. They deck the beloved with garlands and with laurel leaves, there on the ring of turf where the steep-backed hills come down. The procession passes. And while it passes, Louis, we are aware of downfalling, we forebode decay. The shadow slants. We who are conspirators, withdrawn together to lean over some cold urn, note how the purple flame flows downwards.'

'Death is woven in with the violets,' said Louis. 'Death and again death.')

'How proudly we sit here,' said Jinny, 'we who are not yet twenty-five! Outside the trees flower; outside the women linger; outside the cabs swerve and sweep. Emerged from the tentative ways, the obscurities and dazzle of youth, we look straight in front of us, ready for what may come (the door opens, the door keeps on opening). All is real; all is firm without shadow or illusion. Beauty rides our brows. There is mine, there is Susan's. Our flesh is firm and cool. Our differences are clear-cut as the shadows of rocks in full sunlight. Beside us lie crisp rolls, yellow-glazed and hard; the table-cloth is white; and our hands lie half curled, ready to contract. Days and days are to come; winter days, summer days; we have scarcely broken into our hoard. Now the fruit is swollen beneath the leaf. The room is golden, and I say to him, "Come".'

'He has red ears,' said Louis, 'and the smell of meat hangs down in a damp net while the city clerks take snacks at the lunch bar.'

'With infinite time before us,' said Neville, 'we ask what shall we do? Shall we loiter down Bond Street, looking here and there, and buying perhaps a fountain-pen because it is green, or asking how much is the ring with the blue stone? Or shall we sit indoors and watch the coals turn crimson? Shall we stretch our hands for books and read here a passage and there a passage? Shall we shout with laughter for no reason? Shall we push through flowering meadows and make daisy chains? Shall we find out when the next train starts for the Hebrides and engage a reserved compartment? All is to come.'

'For you,' said Bernard, 'but yesterday I walked bang into a pillar-box. Yesterday I became engaged.'

'How strange,' said Susan, 'the little heaps of sugar look by the side of our plates. Also the mottled peelings of pears, and the plush rims to the looking-glasses. I had not seen them before. Everything is now set; everything is fixed. Bernard is engaged. Something irrevocable has happened. A circle has been cast on the waters; a chain is imposed. We shall never flow freely again.'

'For one moment only,' said Louis. 'Before the chain breaks, before disorder returns, see us fixed, see us displayed, see us held in a vice.

'But now the circle breaks. Now the current flows. Now we rush faster than before. Now passions that lay in wait down there in the dark weeds which grow at the bottom rise and pound us with their waves. Pain and jealousy, envy and desire, and something deeper than they are, stronger than love and more subterranean. The voice of action speaks. Listen, Rhoda (for we are conspirators, with our hands on the cold urn), to the casual, quick, exciting voice of action, of hounds running on the scent. They speak now without troubling to finish their sentences. They talk a little language such as lovers use. An imperious brute possesses them. The nerves thrill in their thighs. Their hearts pound and churn in their sides. Susan screws her pocket-handkerchief. Jinny's eyes dance with fire.'

'They are immune,' said Rhoda, 'from picking fingers and searching eyes. How easily they turn and glance; what poses they take of energy and pride! What life shines in Jinny's eyes; how fell, how entire Susan's glance is, searching for insects at the roots! Their hair shines lustrous. Their eyes burn like the eyes of animals brushing through leaves on the scent of the prey. The circle is destroyed. We are thrown asunder.'

'But soon, too soon,' said Bernard, 'this egotistic exultation fails. Too soon the moment of ravenous identity is over, and the appetite for happiness, and happiness, and still more happiness is glutted. The stone is sunk; the moment is over. Round me there spreads a wide margin of indifference. Now open in my eyes a thousand eyes of curiosity. Anyone now is at liberty to murder Bernard, who is engaged to be married, so long as they leave untouched this margin of unknown territory, this forest of the unknown world. Why, I ask (whispering discreetly), do women dine alone together there? Who are they? And what has brought them on this particular evening to this particular spot? The youth in the corner, judging from the nervous way in which he puts his hand from time to time to the back of his head, is from the country. He is suppliant, and so anxious to respond suitably to the kindness of his father's friend, his host, that he can scarcely enjoy now what he will enjoy very much at about half-past eleven tomorrow morning. I have also seen that lady powder her nose three times in the midst of an absorbing conversation—about love, perhaps, about the unhappiness of their dearest friend perhaps. "Ah, but the state of my nose!" she thinks, and out comes her powder-puff, obliterating in its passage all the most fervent feelings of the human heart. There remains, however, the insoluble problem of the solitary man with the eyeglass; of the elderly lady drinking champagne alone. Who and what are these unknown people? I ask. I could make a dozen stories of what he said, of what she said—I can see a dozen pictures. But what are stories? Toys I twist, bubbles I blow, one ring passing through another. And sometimes I begin to doubt if there are stories. What is my story? What is Rhoda's? What is Neville's? There are facts, as, for example: "The handsome young man in the grey suit, whose reserve contrasted so strangely with the loquacity of the others, now brushed the crumbs from his waistcoat and, with a characteristic gesture at once commanding and benign, made a sign to the waiter, who came instantly and returned a moment later with the bill discreetly folded upon a plate." That is the truth; that is a fact, but beyond it all is darkness and conjecture.'

'Now once more,' said Louis, 'as we are about to part, having paid our bill, the circle in our blood, broken so often, so sharply, for we are so different, closes in a ring. Something is made. Yes, as we rise and fidget, a little nervously, we pray, holding in our hands this common feeling, "Do not move, do not let the swing door cut to pieces the thing that we have made, that globes itself here, among these lights, these peelings, this litter of bread crumbs and people passing. Do not move, do not go. Hold it for ever."'

'Let us hold it for one moment,' said Jinny; 'love, hatred, by whatever name we call it, this globe whose walls are made of Percival, of youth and beauty, and something so deep sunk within us that we shall perhaps never make this moment out of one man again.'

'Forests and far countries on the other side of the world,' said Rhoda, 'are in it; seas and jungles; the howlings of jackals and moonlight falling upon some high peak where the eagle soars.'

'Happiness is in it,' said Neville, 'and the quiet of ordinary things. A table, a chair, a book with a paper-knife stuck between the pages. And the petal falling from the rose, and the light flickering as we sit silent, or, perhaps, bethinking us of some trifle, suddenly speak.'

'Week-days are in it,' said Susan, 'Monday, Tuesday, Wednesday; the horses going up to the fields, and the horses returning; the rooks rising and falling, and catching the elm-trees in their net, whether it is April, whether it is November.'

'What is to come is in it,' said Bernard. 'That is the last drop and the brightest that we let fall like some supernal quicksilver into the swelling and splendid moment created by us from Percival. What is to come? I ask, brushing the crumbs from my waistcoat, what is outside? We have proved, sitting eating, sitting talking, that we can add to the treasury of moments. We are not slaves bound to suffer incessantly unrecorded petty blows on our bent backs. We are not sheep either, following a master. We are creators. We too have made something that will join the innumerable congregations of past time. We too, as we put on our hats and push open the door, stride not into chaos, but into a world that our own force can subjugate and make part of the illumined and everlasting road.

'Look, Percival, while they fetch the taxi, at the prospect which you are so soon to lose. The street is hard and burnished with the churning of innumerable wheels. The yellow canopy of our tremendous energy hangs like a burning cloth above our heads. Theatres, music halls and lamps in private houses make that light.'

'Peaked clouds,' said Rhoda, 'voyage over a sky dark like polished whalebone.'

'Now the agony begins; now the horror has seized me with its fangs,' said Neville. 'Now the cab comes; now Percival goes. What can we do to keep him? How bridge the distance between us? How fan the fire so that it blazes for ever? How signal to all time to come that we, who stand in the street, in the lamplight, loved Percival? Now Percival is gone.'

The sun had risen to its full height. It was no longer half seen and guessed at, from hints and gleams, as if a girl couched on her green-sea mattress tired her brows with water-globed jewels that sent lances of opal-tinted light falling and flashing in the uncertain air like the flanks of a dolphin leaping, or the flash of a falling blade. Now the sun burnt uncompromising, undeniable. It struck upon the hard sand, and the rocks became furnaces of red heat; it searched each pool and caught the minnow hiding in the cranny, and showed the rusty cartwheel, the white bone, or the boot without laces stuck, black as iron, in the sand. It gave to everything its exact measure of colour; to the sandhills their innumerable glitter, to the wild grasses their glancing green; or it fell upon the arid waste of the desert, here wind-scourged into furrows, here swept into desolate cairns, here sprinkled with stunted dark-green jungle trees. It lit up the smooth gilt mosque, the frail pink-and-white card houses of the southern village, and the long-breasted, white-haired women who knelt in the river bed beating wrinkled cloths upon stones. Steamers thudding slowly over the sea were caught in the level stare of the sun, and it beat through the yellow awnings upon passengers who dozed or paced the deck, shading their eyes to look for the land, while day after day, compressed in its oily throbbing sides, the ship bore them on monotonously over the waters.

The sun beat on the crowded pinnacles of southern hills and glared into deep, stony river beds where the water was shrunk beneath the high slung bridge so that washerwomen kneeling on hot stones could scarcely wet their linen; and lean mules went picking their way among the chattering grey stones with panniers slung across their narrow shoulders. At midday the heat of the sun made the hills grey as if shaved and singed in an explosion, while, further north, in cloudier and rainier countries hills smoothed into slabs as with the back of a spade had a light in them as if a warder, deep within, went from chamber to chamber carrying a green lamp. Through atoms of grey-blue air the sun struck at English fields and lit up marshes and pools, a white gull on a stake, the slow sail of shadows over blunt-headed woods and young corn and flowing hayfields. It beat on the orchard wall, and every pit and grain of the brick was silver pointed, purple, fiery as if soft to touch, as if touched it must melt into hot-baked grains of dust. The currants hung against the wall in ripples and cascades of polished red; plums swelled out their leaves, and all the blades of the grass were run together in one fluent green blaze. The trees' shadow was sunk to a dark pool at the root. Light descending in floods dissolved the separate foliation into one green mound.

The birds sang passionate songs addressed to one ear only and then stopped. Bubbling and chuckling they carried little bits of straw and twig to the dark knots in the higher branches of the trees. Gilt and purpled they perched in the garden where cones of laburnum and purple shook down gold and lilac, for now at midday the garden was all blossom and profusion and even the tunnels under the plants were green and purple and tawny as the sun beat through the red petal, or the broad yellow petal, or was barred by some thickly furred green stalk.

The sun struck straight upon the house, making the white walls glare between the dark windows. Their panes, woven thickly with green branches, held circles of impenetrable darkness. Sharp-edged wedges of light lay upon the window-sill and showed inside the room plates with blue rings, cups with curved handles, the bulge of a great bowl, the crisscross pattern in the rug, and the formidable corners and lines of cabinets and bookcases. Behind *their conglomeration hung a zone of shadow in which might be a further shape to be disencumbered of shadow or still denser depths of darkness.*

The waves broke and spread their waters swiftly over the shore. One after another they massed themselves and fell; the spray tossed itself back with the energy of their fall. The waves were steeped deep-blue save for a pattern of diamond-pointed light on their backs which rippled as the backs of great horses ripple with muscles as they move. The waves fell; withdrew and fell again, like the thud of a great beast stamping.

'He is dead,' said Neville. 'He fell. His horse tripped. He was thrown. The sails of the world have swung round and caught me on the head. All is over. The lights of the world have gone out. There stands the tree which I cannot pass.

'Oh, to crumple this telegram in my fingers—to let the light of the world flood back—to say this has not happened! But why turn one's head hither and thither? This is the truth. This is the fact. His horse stumbled; he was thrown. The flashing trees and white rails went up in a shower. There was a surge; a drumming in his ears. Then the blow; the world crashed; he breathed heavily. He died where he fell.

'Barns and summer days in the country, rooms where we sat—all now lie in the unreal world which is gone. My past is cut from me. They came running. They carried him to some pavilion, men in riding-boots, men in sun helmets; among unknown men he died. Loneliness and silence often surrounded him. He often left me. And then, returning, "See where he comes!" I said.

'Women shuffle past the window as if there were no gulf cut in the street, no tree with stiff leaves which we cannot pass. We deserve then to be tripped by molehills. We are infinitely abject, shuffling past with our eyes shut. But why should I submit? Why try to lift my foot and mount the stair? This is where I stand; here, holding the telegram. The past, summer days and rooms where we sat, stream away like burnt paper with red eyes in it.

485

Why meet and resume? Why talk and eat and make up other combinations with other people? From this moment I am solitary. No one will know me now. I have three letters, "I am about to play quoits with a colonel, so no more," thus he ends our friendship, shouldering his way through the crowd with a wave of his hand. This farce is worth no more formal celebration. Yet if someone had but said: "Wait"; had pulled the strap three holes tighter—he would have done justice for fifty years, and sat in Court and ridden alone at the head of troops and denounced some monstrous tyranny, and come back to us.

'Now I say there is a grinning, there is a subterfuge. There is something sneering behind our backs. That boy almost lost his footing as he leapt on the bus. Percival fell; was killed; is buried; and I watch people passing; holding tight to the rails of omnibuses; determined to save their lives.

'I will not lift my foot to climb the stair. I will stand for one moment beneath the immitigable tree, alone with the man whose throat is cut, while downstairs the cook shoves in and out the dampers. I will not climb the stair. We are doomed, all of us. Women shuffle past with shopping-bags. People keep on passing. Yet you shall not destroy me. For this moment, this one moment, we are together. I press you to me. Come, pain, feed on me. Bury your fangs in my flesh. Tear me asunder. I sob, I sob.'

'Such is the incomprehensible combination,' said Bernard, 'such is the complexity of things, that as I descend the staircase I do not know which is sorrow, which joy. My son is born; Percival is dead. I am upheld by pillars, shored up on either side by stark emotions; but which is sorrow, which is joy? I ask, and do not know, only that I need silence, and to be alone and to go out, and to save one hour to consider what has happened to my world, what death has done to my world.

'This then is the world that Percival sees no longer. Let me look. The butcher delivers meat next door; two old men stumble along the pavement; sparrows alight. The machine then works; I note the rhythm, the throb, but as a thing in which I have no part, since he sees it no longer. (He lies pale and bandaged in some room.) Now then is my chance to find out what is of great importance, and I must be careful, and tell no lies. About him my feeling was: he sat there in the centre. Now I go to that spot no longer. The place is empty.

'Oh yes, I can assure you, men in felt hats and women carrying baskets—you have lost something that would have been very valuable to you. You have lost a leader whom you would have followed; and one of you has lost happiness and children. He is dead who would have given you that. He lies on a camp-bed, bandaged, in some hot Indian hospital while coolies squatted on the floor agitate those fans—I forget how they call them. But this is important; "You are well out of it," I said, while the doves descended over the roofs and my son was born, as if it were a fact. I remember, as a boy, his curious air of detachment. And I go on to say (my eyes fill with tears and then are dry), "But this is better than one had dared to hope." I say, addressing what is abstract, facing me eyeless at the end of the avenue, in the sky, "Is this the utmost you can do?" Then we have triumphed. You have done your utmost, I say, addressing that blank and brutal face (for he was twenty-five and should have lived to be eighty) without avail. I am not going to lie down and weep away a life of care. (An entry to be made in my pocket-book; contempt for those who inflict meaningless death.) Further, this is important; that I should be able to place him in trifling and ridiculous situations, so that he may not feel himself absurd, perched on a great horse. I must be able to say, "Percival, a ridiculous name." At the same time let me tell you, men and women, hurrying to the tube station, you would have had to respect him. You would have had to form up and follow behind him. How strange to oar one's way through crowds seeing life through hollow eyes, burning eyes.

'Yet already signals begin, beckonings, attempts to lure me back. Curiosity is knocked out for only a short time. One cannot live outside the machine for more perhaps than half an hour. Bodies, I note, already begin to look ordinary; but what is behind them differs—the perspective. Behind that newspaper placard is the hospital; the long room with black men pulling ropes; and then they bury him. Yet since it says a famous actress has been divorced, I ask instantly Which? Yet I cannot take out my penny; I cannot buy a paper; I cannot suffer interruption yet.

'I ask, if I shall never see you again and fix my eyes on that solidity, what form will our communication take? You have gone across the court, further and further, drawing finer and finer the thread between us. But you exist somewhere. Something of you remains. A judge. That is, if I discover a new vein in myself I shall submit it to you privately. I shall ask, What is your verdict? You shall remain the arbiter. But for how long? Things will become too difficult to explain: there will be new things; already my son. I am now at the zenith of an experience. It will decline. Already I no longer cry with conviction, "What luck!" Exaltation, the flight of doves descending, is over. Chaos, detail return. I am no longer amazed by names written over shop-windows. I do not feel Why hurry? Why catch trains? The sequence returns; one thing leads to another—the usual order.

'Yes, but I still resent the usual order. I will not let myself be made yet to accept the sequence of things. I will walk; I will not change the rhythm of my mind by stopping, by looking; I will walk. I will go up these steps into the gallery and submit myself to the influence of minds like mine outside the sequence. There is little time left to answer the question; my powers flag; I become torpid. Here are pictures. Here are cold madonnas among their pillars. Let them lay to rest the incessant activity of the mind's eye, the bandaged head, the men with ropes, so that I may find something unvisual beneath. Here are gardens; and Venus among her flowers; here are saints and blue madonnas. Mercifully these pictures make no reference; they do not nudge; they do not point. Thus they expand my consciousness of him and bring him back to me differently. I remember his beauty. "Look, where he comes," I said.

'Lines and colours almost persuade me that I too can be heroic, I, who make phrases so easily, am so soon seduced, love what comes next, and cannot clench my fist, but vacillate weakly making phrases according to my circumstances. Now, through my own infirmity I recover what he was to me: my opposite. Being naturally truthful, he did not see the point of these exaggerations, and was borne on by a natural sense of the fitting, was indeed a great master of the art of living so that he seems to have lived long, and to have spread calm round him, indifference one might almost say, certainly to his own advancement, save that he had also great compassion. A child playing—a summer evening—doors will open and shut, will keep opening and shutting, through which I see sights that make me weep. For they cannot be imparted. Hence our loneliness; hence our desolation. I turn to that spot in my mind and find it empty. My own infirmities oppress me. There is no longer him to oppose them.

'Behold, then, the blue madonna streaked with tears. This is my funeral service. We have no ceremonies, only private dirges and no conclusions, only violent sensations, each separate. Nothing that has been said meets our case. We sit in the Italian room at the National Gallery picking up fragments. I doubt that Titian ever felt this rat gnaw. Painters live lives of methodical absorption, adding stroke to stroke. They are not like poets—scapegoats; they are not chained to the rock. Hence the silence, the sublimity. Yet that crimson must have burnt in Titian's gizzard. No doubt he rose with the great arms holding the cornucopia, and fell, in that descent. But the silence weighs on me—the perpetual solicitation of the eye. The pressure is intermittent and muffled. I distinguish too little and too vaguely. The bell is pressed and I do not ring or give out irrelevant clamours all jangled. I am titillated inordinately by some splendour; the ruffled crimson against the green lining; the march of pillars: the orange light behind the black, pricked ears of the olive trees. Arrows of sensation strike from my spine, but without order.

'Yet something is added to my interpretation. Something lies deeply buried. For one moment I thought to grasp it. But bury it, bury it; let it breed, hidden in the depths of my mind some day to fructify. After a long lifetime, loosely, in a moment of revelation, I may lay hands on it, but now the idea breaks in my hand. Ideas break a thousand times for once that they globe themselves entire. They break: they fall over me. "Line and colours they survive, therefore . . ."

'I am yawning. I am glutted with sensations. I am exhausted with the strain and the long, long time—twenty-five minutes, half an hour—that I have held myself alone outside the machine. I grow numb; I grow stiff. How shall I break up this numbness which discredits my sympathetic heart? There are others suffering—multitudes of people suffering. Neville suffers. He loved Percival. But I can no longer endure extremities; I want someone with whom to laugh, with whom to yawn, with whom to remember how he scratched his head; someone he was at ease with and liked (not Susan, whom he loved, but Jinny rather). In her room also I could do penance. I could ask, Did he tell you how I refused him when he asked me to go to Hampton Court that day? Those are the thoughts that will wake me leaping in anguish in the middle of the night—the crimes for which one would do penance in all the markets of the world bareheaded; that one did not go to Hampton Court that day.

'But now I want life round me, and books and little ornaments, and the usual sounds of tradesmen calling on which to pillow my head after this exhaustion, and shut my eyes after this revelation. I will go straight, then, down the stairs, and hail the first taxi and drive to Jinny.'

'There is the puddle,' said Rhoda, 'and I cannot cross it. I hear the rush of the great grindstone within an inch of my head. Its wind roars in my face. All palpable forms of life have failed me. Unless I can stretch and touch something hard, I shall be blown down the eternal corridors for ever. What, then, can I touch? What brick, what stone? and so draw myself across the enormous gulf into my body safely?

'Now the shadow has fallen and the purple light slants downwards. The figure that was robed in beauty is now clothed in ruin. The figure that stood in the grove where the steep-backed hills come down falls in ruin, as I told them when they said they loved his voice on the stair, and his old shoes and moments of being together.

'Now I will walk down Oxford Street envisaging a world rent by lightning; I will look at oaks cracked asunder and red where the flowering branch has fallen. I will go to Oxford Street and buy stockings for a party. I will do the usual things under the lightning flash. On the bare ground I will pick violets and bind them together and offer them to Percival, something given him by me. Look now at what Percival has given me. Look at the street now that Percival is dead. The houses are lightly founded to be puffed over by a breath of air. Reckless and random the cars race and roar and hunt us to death like bloodhounds. I am alone in a hostile world. The human face is hideous. This is to my liking. I want publicity and violence and to be dashed like a stone on the rocks. I like factory chimneys and cranes and lorries. I like the passing of face and face and face, deformed, indifferent. I am sick of prettiness; I am sick of privacy. I ride rough waters and shall sink with no one to save me.

'Percival, by his death, has made me this present, has revealed this terror, has left me to undergo this humiliation—faces and faces, served out like soup-plates by scullions; coarse, greedy, casual; looking in at shop-windows with pendent parcels; ogling, brushing, destroying everything, leaving even our love impure, touched now by their dirty fingers.

'Here is the shop where they sell stockings. And I could believe that beauty is once more set flowing. Its whisper comes down these aisles, through these laces, breathing among baskets of coloured ribbons. There are then warm hollows grooved in the heart of the uproar; alcoves of silence where we can shelter under the wing of beauty from truth which I desire. Pain is suspended as a girl silently slides open a drawer. And then, she speaks; her voice wakes me. I shoot to the bottom among the weeds and see envy, jealousy, hatred and spite scuttle like crabs over the sand as she speaks. These are our companion's. I will pay my bill and take my parcel.

'This is Oxford Street. Here are hate, jealousy, hurry, and indifference frothed into the wild semblance of life. These are our companions. Consider the friends with whom we sit and eat. I think of Louis, reading the sporting column of an evening newspaper, afraid of ridicule; a snob. He says, looking at the people passing, he will shepherd us if we will follow. If we submit he will reduce us to order. Thus he will smooth out the death of Percival to his satisfaction, looking fixedly over the cruet, past the houses at the sky. Bernard, meanwhile, flops red-eyed into some arm-chair. He will have out his notebook; under D, he will enter "Phrases to be used on the deaths of friends". Jinny, pirouetting across the room, will perch on the arm of his chair and ask, "Did he love me?" "More than he loved Susan?" Susan, engaged to her farmer in the country, will stand for a second with the telegram before her, holding a plate; and then, with a kick of her heel, slam to the oven door. Neville, after staring at the window through his tears, will see through his tears, and ask, "Who passes the window?"—"What lovely boy?" This is my tribute to Percival; withered violets, blackened violets.

'Where shall I go then? To some museum, where they keep rings under glass cases, where there are cabinets, and the dresses that queens have worn? Or shall I go to Hampton Court and look at the red walls and courtyards and the seemliness of herded yew trees making black pyramids symmetrically on the grass among flowers? There shall I recover beauty, and impose order upon my raked, my dishevelled soul? But what can one make in loneliness? Alone I should stand on the empty grass and say, Rooks fly; somebody passes with a bag; there is a gardener with a wheelbarrow. I should stand in a queue and smell sweat, and scent as horrible as sweat; and be hung with other people like a joint of meat among other joints of meat.

'Here is a hall where one pays money and goes in, where one hears music among somnolent people who have come here after lunch on a hot afternoon. We have eaten beef and pudding enough to live for a week without tasting food. Therefore we cluster like maggots on the back of something that will carry us on. Decorous, portly—we have white hair waved under our hats; slim shoes; little bags; clean-shaven cheeks; here and there a military moustache; not a speck of dust has been allowed to settle anywhere on our broadcloth. Swaying and opening programmes, with a few words of greeting to friends, we settle down, like walruses stranded on rocks, like heavy bodies incapable of waddling to the sea, hoping for a wave to lift us, but we are too heavy, and too much dry shingle lies between us and the sea. We lie gorged with food, torpid in the heat. Then, swollen but contained in slippery satin, the seagreen woman comes to our rescue. She sucks in her lips, assumes an air of intensity, inflates herself and hurls herself precisely at the right moment as if she saw an apple and her voice was the arrow into the note, "Ah!"

'An axe has split a tree to the core; the core is warm; sound quivers within the bark. "Ah!" cried a woman to her lover, leaning from her window in Venice. "Ah, ah!" she cried, and again she cries "Ah!" She has provided us with a cry. But only a cry. And what is a cry? Then the beetle-shaped men come with their violins; wait; count; nod; down come their bows. And there is ripple and laughter like the dance of olive trees and their myriad-tongued grey leaves when a seafarer, biting a twig between his lips where the many-backed steep hills come down, leaps on shore.

'"Like" and "like" and "like"—but what is the thing that lies beneath the semblance of the thing? Now that lightning has gashed the tree and the flowering branch has fallen and Percival, by his death, has made me this gift, let me see the thing. There is a square; there is an oblong. The players take the square and place it upon the oblong. They place it very accurately; they make a perfect dwelling-place. Very little is left outside. The structure is now visible; what is inchoate is here stated; we are not so various or so mean; we have made oblongs and stood them upon squares. This is our triumph; this is our consolation.

The sweetness of this content overflowing runs down the walls of my mind, and liberates understanding. Wander no more, I say; this is the end. The oblong has been set upon the square; the spiral is on top. We have been hauled over the shingle, down to the sea. The players come again. But they are mopping their faces. They are no longer so spruce or so debonair. I will go. I will set aside this afternoon. I will make a pilgrimage. I will go to Greenwich. I will fling myself fearlessly into trams, into omnibuses. As we lurch down Regent Street, and I am flung upon this woman, upon this man, I am not injured, I am not outraged by the collision. A square stands upon an oblong. Here are mean streets where chaffering goes on in street markets, and every sort of iron rod, bolt and screw is laid out, and people swarm off the pavement, pinching raw meat with thick fingers. The structure is visible. We have made a dwelling-place.

'These, then, are the flowers that grow among the rough grasses of the field which the cows trample, wind-bitten, almost deformed, without fruit or blossom. These are what I bring, torn up by the roots from the pavement of Oxford Street, my penny bunch, my penny bunch of violets. Now from the window of the tram I see masts among chimneys; there is the river; there are ships that sail to India. I will walk by the river. I will pace this embankment, where an old man reads a newspaper in a glass shelter. I will pace this terrace and watch the ships bowling down the tide. A woman walks on deck, with a dog barking round her. Her skirts are blown; her hair is blown; they are going out to sea; they are leaving us; they are vanishing this summer evening. Now I will relinquish; now I will let loose. Now I will at last free the checked, the jerked-back desire to be spent, to be consumed.

We will gallop together over desert hills where the swallow dips her wings in dark pools and the pillars stand entire. Into the wave that dashes upon the shore, into the wave that flings its white foam to the uttermost corners of the earth, I throw my violets, my offering to Percival.'

The sun no longer stood in the middle of the sky. Its light slanted, falling obliquely. Here it caught on the edge of a cloud and burnt it into a slice of light, a blazing island on which no foot could rest. Then another cloud was caught in the light and another and another, so that the waves beneath were arrow-struck with fiery feathered darts that shot erratically across the quivering blue.

The topmost leaves of the tree were crisped in the sun. They rustled stiffly in the random breeze. The birds sat still save that they flicked their heads sharply from side to side. Now they paused in their song as if glutted with sound, as if the fullness of midday had gorged them. The dragon-fly poised motionless over a reed, then shot its blue stitch further through the air. The far hum in the distance seemed made of the broken tremor of fine wings dancing up and down on the horizon. The river water held the reeds now fixed as if glass had hardened round them; and then the glass wavered and the reeds swept low. Pondering, sunken headed, the cattle stood in the fields and cumbrously moved one foot and then another. In the bucket near the house the tap stopped dripping, as if the bucket were full, and then the tap dripped one, two, three separate drops in succession.

The windows showed erratically spots of burning fire, the elbow of one branch, and then some tranquil space of pure clarity. The blind hung red at the window's edge and within the room daggers of light fell upon chairs and tables making cracks across their lacquer and polish. The green pot bulged enormously, with its white window elongated in its side. Light driving darkness before it spilt itself profusely upon the corners and bosses; and yet heaped up darkness in mounds of unmoulded shape.

The waves massed themselves, curved their backs and crashed.
Up spurted stones and shingle. They swept round the rocks, and
the spray, leaping high, spattered the walls of a cave that had been
dry before, and left pools inland, where some fish stranded lashed
its tail as the wave drew back.

'I have signed my name,' said Louis, 'already twenty times. I, and again I, and again I. Clear, firm, unequivocal, there it stands, my name. Clear-cut and unequivocal am I too. Yet a vast inheritance of experience is packed in me. I have lived thousands of years. I am like a worm that has eaten its way through the wood of a very old oak beam. But now I am compact; now I am gathered together this fine morning.

'The sun shines from a clear sky. But twelve o'clock brings neither rain nor sunshine. It is the hour when Miss Johnson brings me my letters in a wire tray. Upon these white sheets I indent my name. The whisper of leaves, water running down gutters, green depths flecked with dahlias or zinnias; I, now a duke, now Plato, companion of Socrates; the tramp of dark men and yellow men migrating east, west, north and south; the eternal procession, women going with attaché cases down the Strand as they went once with pitchers to the Nile; all the furled and close-packed leaves of my many-folded life are now summed in my name; incised cleanly and barely on the sheet. Now a full-grown man; now upright standing in sun or rain. I must drop heavy as a hatchet and cut the oak with my sheer weight, for if I deviate, glancing this way, or that way, I shall fall like snow and be wasted.

'I am half in love with the typewriter and the telephone. With letters and cables and brief but courteous commands on the telephone to Paris, Berlin, New York, I have fused my many lives into one; I have helped by my assiduity and decision to score those lines on the map there by which the different parts of the world are laced together. I love punctually at ten to come into my room; I love the purple glow of the dark mahogany; I love the table and its sharp edge; and the smooth-running drawers. I love the telephone with its lip stretched to my whisper, and the date on the wall; and the engagement book. Mr Prentice at four; Mr Eyres sharp at four-thirty.

'I like to be asked to come to Mr Burchard's private room and report on our commitments to China. I hope to inherit an arm-chair and a Turkey carpet. My shoulder is to the wheel; I roll the dark before me, spreading commerce where there was chaos in the far parts of the world. If I press on,—from chaos making order, I shall find myself where Chatham stood, and Pitt, Burke and Sir Robert Peel. Thus I expunge certain stains, and erase old defilements; the woman who gave me a flag from the top of the Christmas tree; my accent; beatings and other tortures; the boasting boys; my father, a banker at Brisbane.

'I have read my poet in an eating-house, and, stirring my coffee, listened to the clerks making bets at the little tables, watched the women hesitating at the counter. I said that nothing should be irrelevant, like a piece of brown paper dropped casually on the floor. I said their journeys should have an end in view; they should earn their two pound ten a week at the command of an august master; some hand, some robe, should fold us about in the evening. When I have healed these fractures and comprehended these monstrosities so that they need neither excuse nor apology, which both waste our strength, I shall give back to the street and the eating-shop what they lost when they fell on these hard times and broke on these stony beaches. I shall assemble a few words and forge round us a hammered ring of beaten steel.

'But now I have not a moment to spare. There is no respite here, no shadow made of quivering leaves, or alcove to which one can retreat from the sun, to sit, with a lover, in the cool of the evening. The weight of the world is on our shoulders; its vision is through our eyes; if we blink or look aside, or turn back to finger what Plato said or remember Napoleon and his conquests, we inflict on the world the injury of some obliquity. This is life; Mr

Prentice at four; Mr Eyres at four-thirty. I like to hear the soft rush of the lift and the thud with which it stops on my landing and the heavy male tread of responsible feet down the corridors. So by dint of our united exertions we send ships to the remotest parts of the globe; replete with lavatories and gymnasiums. The weight of the world is on our shoulders. This is life. If I press on, I shall inherit a chair and a rug; a place in Surrey with glass houses, and some rare conifer, melon or flowering tree which other merchants will envy.

'Yet I still keep my attic room. There I open the usual little book; there I watch the rain glisten on the tiles till they shine like a policeman's waterproof; there I see the broken windows in poor people's houses; the lean cats; some slattern squinting in a cracked looking-glass as she arranges her face for the street corner; there Rhoda sometimes comes. For we are lovers.

'Percival has died (he died in Egypt; he died in Greece; all deaths are one death). Susan has children; Neville mounts rapidly to the conspicuous heights. Life passes. The clouds change perpetually over our houses. I do this, do that, and again do this and then that. Meeting and parting, we assemble different forms, make different patterns. But if I do not nail these impressions to the board and out of the many men in me make one; exist here and now and not in streaks and patches, like scattered snow wreaths on far mountains; and ask Miss Johnson as I pass through the office about the movies and take my cup of tea and accept also my favourite biscuit, then I shall fall like snow and be wasted.

'Yet when six o'clock comes and I touch my hat to the commissionaire, being always too effusive in ceremony since I desire so much to be accepted; and struggle, leaning against the wind, buttoned up, with my jaws blue and my eyes running water, I wish that a little typist would cuddle on my knees; I think that my favourite dish is liver and bacon; and so am apt to wander to the river, to the narrow streets where there are frequent public-houses, and the shadows of ships passing at the end of the street, and women fighting. But I say to myself, recovering my sanity, Mr Prentice at four; Mr Eyres at four-thirty. The hatchet must fall on the block; the oak must be cleft to the centre. The weight of the world is on my shoulders. Here is the pen and the paper; on the letters in the wire basket I sign my name, I, I, and again I.'

'Summer comes, and winter,' said Susan. 'The seasons pass. The pear fills itself and drops from the tree. The dead leaf rests on its edge. But steam has obscured the window. I sit by the fire watching the kettle boil. I see the pear tree through the streaked steam on the window-pane.

'Sleep, sleep, I croon, whether it is summer or winter, May or November. Sleep I sing—I, who am unmelodious and hear no music save rustic music when a dog barks, a bell tinkles, or wheels crunch upon the gravel. I sing my song by the fire like an old shell murmuring on the beach. Sleep, sleep, I say, warning off with my voice all who rattle milk-cans, fire at rooks, shoot rabbits, or in any way bring the shock of destruction near this wicker cradle, laden with soft limbs, curled under a pink coverlet.

'I have lost my indifference, my blank eyes, my pear-shaped eyes that saw to the root. I am no longer January, May or any other season, but am all spun to a fine thread round the cradle, wrapping in a cocoon made of my own blood the delicate limbs of my baby. Sleep, I say, and feel within me uprush some wilder, darker violence, so that I would fell down with one blow any intruder, any snatcher, who should break into this room and wake the sleeper.

'I pad about the house all day long in apron and slippers, like my mother who died of cancer. Whether it is summer, whether it is winter, I no longer know by the moor grass, and the heath flower; only by the steam on the window-pane, or the frost on the window-pane. When the lark peels high his ring of sound and it falls through the air like an apple paring, I stoop; I feed my baby. I, who used to walk through beech woods noting the jay's feather turning blue as it falls, past the shepherd and the tramp, who stared at the woman squatted beside a tilted cart in a ditch, go from room to room with a duster. Sleep, I say, desiring sleep to fall like a blanket of down and cover these weak limbs; demanding that life shall sheathe its claws and gird its lightning and pass by, making of my own body a hollow, a warm shelter for my child to sleep in. Sleep, I say, sleep. Or I go to the window, I look at the rook's high nest; and the pear tree. "His eyes will see when mine are shut," I think. "I shall go mixed with them beyond my body and shall see India. He will come home, bringing trophies to be laid at my feet. He will increase my possessions."

'But I never rise at dawn and see the purple drops in the cabbage leaves; the red drops in the roses. I do not watch the setter nose in a circle, or lie at night watching the leaves hide the stars and the stars move and the leaves hang still. The butcher calls; the milk has to be stood under a shade lest it should sour.

'Sleep, I say, sleep, as the kettle boils and its breath comes thicker and thicker issuing in one jet from the spout. So life fills my veins. So life pours through my limbs. So I am driven forward, till I could cry, as I move from dawn to dusk opening and shutting, "No more. I am glutted with natural happiness." Yet more will come, more children; more cradles, more baskets in the kitchen and hams ripening; and onions glistening; and more beds of lettuce and potatoes. I am blown like a leaf by the gale; now brushing the wet grass, now whirled up. I am glutted with natural happiness; and wish sometimes that the fullness would pass from me and the weight of the sleeping house rise, when we sit reading, and I stay the thread at the eye of my needle. The lamp kindles a fire in the dark pane. A fire burns in the heart of the ivy. I see a lit-up street in the evergreens. I hear traffic in the brush of the wind down the lane, and broken voices, and laughter, and Jinny who cries as the door opens, "Come! Come!"

'But no sound breaks the silence of our house, where the fields sigh close to the door. The wind washes through the elm trees; a moth hits the lamp; a cow lows; a crack of sound starts in the rafter, and I push my head through the needle and murmur, "Sleep".'

'Now is the moment,' said Jinny. 'Now we have met, and have come together. Now let us talk, let us tell stories. Who is he? Who is she? I am infinitely curious and do not know what is to come. If you, whom I meet for the first time, were to say to me, "The coach starts at four from Piccadilly," I would not stay to fling a few necessaries in a bandbox, but would come at once.

'Let us sit here under the cut flowers, on the sofa by the picture. Let us decorate our Christmas tree with facts and again with facts. People are so soon gone; let us catch them. That man there, by the cabinet; he lives you say, surrounded by china pots. Break one and you shatter a thousand pounds. And he loved a girl in Rome and she left him. Hence the pots, old junk found in lodging-houses or dug from the desert sands. And since beauty must be broken daily to remain beautiful, and he is static, his life stagnates in a china sea. It is strange though; for once as a young man, he sat on damp ground and drank rum with soldiers.

'One must be quick and add facts deftly, like toys to a tree, fixing them with a twist of the fingers. He stoops, how he stoops, even over an azalea. He stoops over the old woman even, because she wears diamonds in her ears, and, bundling about her estate in a pony carriage, directs who is to be helped, what tree felled, and who turned out tomorrow. (I have lived my life, I must tell you, all these years, and I am now past thirty, perilously, like a mountain goat, leaping from crag to crag; I do not settle long anywhere; I do not attach myself to one person in particular; but you will find that if I raise my arm, some figure at once breaks off and will come.) And that man is a judge; and that man is a millionaire, and that man, with the eyeglass, shot his governess through the heart with an arrow when he was ten years old. Afterwards he rode through deserts with despatches, took part in revolutions and now collects materials for a history of his mother's family, long settled in Norfolk. That little man with a blue chin has a right hand that is withered. But why? We do not know. That woman, you whisper discreetly, with the pearl pagodas hanging from her ears, was the pure flame who lit the life of one of our statesmen; now since his death she sees ghosts, tells fortunes, and has adopted a coffee-coloured youth whom she calls the Messiah. That man with the drooping moustache, like a cavalry officer, lived a life of the utmost debauchery (it is all in some memoir) until one day he met a stranger in a train who converted him between Edinburgh and Carlisle by reading the Bible.

'Thus, in a few seconds, deftly, adroitly, we decipher the hieroglyphs written on other people's faces. Here, in this room, are the abraded and battered shells cast on the shore. The door goes on opening. The room fills and fills with knowledge, anguish, many kinds of ambition, much indifference, some despair. Between us, you say, we could build cathedrals, dictate policies, condemn men to death, and administer the affairs of several public offices. The common fund of experience is very deep. We have between us scores of children of both sexes, whom we are educating, going to see at school with the measles, and bringing up to inherit our houses. In one way or another we make this day, this Friday, some by going to the Law Courts; others to the city; others to the nursery; others by marching and forming fours. A million hands stitch, raise hods with bricks. The activity is endless. And tomorrow it begins again; tomorrow we make Saturday. Some take train for France; others ship for India. Some will never come into this room again. One may die tonight. Another will beget a child. From us every sort of building, policy, venture, picture, poem, child, factory, will spring. Life comes; life goes; we make life. So you say.

'But we who live in the body see with the body's imagination things in outline. I see rocks in bright sunshine. I cannot take these facts into some cave and, shading my eyes, grade their yellows, blues, umbers into one substance. I cannot remain seated for long. I must jump up and go. The coach may start from Piccadilly. I drop all these facts—diamonds, withered hands, china pots and the rest of it—as a monkey drops nuts from its naked paws. I cannot tell you if life is this or that. I am going to push out into the heterogeneous crowd. I am going to be buffeted; to be flung up, and flung down, among men, like a ship on the sea.

'For now my body, my companion, which is always sending its signals, the rough black "No", the golden "Come", in rapid running arrows of sensation, beckons. Someone moves. Did I raise my arm? Did I look? Did my yellow scarf with the strawberry spots float and signal? He has broken from the wall. He follows. I am pursued through the forest. All is rapt, all is nocturnal, and the parrots go screaming through the branches. All my senses stand erect. Now I feel the roughness of the fibre of the curtain through which I push; now I feel the cold iron railing and its blistered paint beneath my palm. Now the cool tide of darkness breaks its waters over me. We are out of doors. Night opens; night traversed by wandering moths; night hiding lovers roaming to adventure. I smell roses; I smell violets; I see red and blue just hidden. Now gravel is under my shoes; now grass. Up reel the tall backs of houses guilty with lights. All London is uneasy with flashing lights. Now let us sing our love song—Come, come, come. Now my gold signal is like a dragonfly flying taut. Jug, jug, jug, I sing like the nightingale whose melody is crowded in the too narrow passage of her throat. Now I hear crash and rending of boughs and the crack of antlers as if the beasts of the forest were all hunting, all rearing high and plunging down among the thorns. One has pierced me. One is driven deep within me.

'And velvet flowers and leaves whose coolness has been stood in water wash me round, and sheathe me, embalming me.'

'Why, look,' said Neville, 'at the clock ticking on the mantelpiece? Time passes, yes. And we grow old. But to sit with you, alone with you, here in London, in this firelit room, you there, I here, is all. The world ransacked to its uttermost ends, and all its heights stripped and gathered of their flowers, holds no more. Look at the firelight running up and down the gold thread in the curtain. The fruit it circles droops heavy. It falls on the toe of your boot, it gives your face a red rim—I think it is the firelight and not your face; I think those are books against the wall, and that a curtain, and that perhaps an armchair. But when you come everything changes. The cups and saucers changed when you came in this morning. There can be no doubt, I thought, pushing aside the newspaper, that our mean lives, unsightly as they are, put on splendour and have meaning only under the eyes of love.

'I rose. I had done my breakfast. There was the whole day before us, and as it was fine, tender, non-committal, we walked through the Park to the Embankment, along the Strand to St Paul's, then to the shop where I bought an umbrella, always talking, and now and then stopping to look. But can this last? I said to myself, by a lion in Trafalgar Square, by the lion seen once and for ever;—so I revisit my past life, scene by scene; there is an elm tree, and there lies Percival. For ever and ever, I swore. Then darted in the usual doubt. I clutched your hand. You left me. The descent into the Tube was like death. We were cut up, we were dissevered by all those faces and the hollow wind that seemed to roar down there over desert boulders. I sat staring in my own room. By five I knew that you were faithless. I snatched the telephone and the buzz, buzz, buzz of its stupid voice in your empty room battered my heart down, when the door opened and there you stood. That was the most perfect of our meetings. But these meetings, these partings, finally destroy us.

'Now this room seems to me central, something scooped out of the eternal night. Outside lines twist and intersect, but round us, wrapping us about. Here we are centred. Here we can be silent, or speak without raising our voices. Did you notice that and then that? we say. He said that, meaning. . . . She hesitated, and I believe suspected. Anyhow, I heard voices, a sob on the stair late at night. It is the end of their relationship. Thus we spin round us infinitely fine filaments and construct a system. Plato and Shakespeare are included, also quite obscure people, people of no importance whatsoever. I hate men who wear crucifixes on the left side of their waistcoats. I hate ceremonies and lamentations and the sad figure of Christ trembling beside another trembling and sad figure. Also the pomp and the indifference and the emphasis, always on the wrong place, of people holding forth under chandeliers in full evening dress, wearing stars and decorations. Some spray in a hedge, though, or a sunset over a flat winter field, or again the way some old woman sits, arms akimbo, in an omnibus with a basket—those we point at for the other to look at. It is so vast an alleviation to be able to point for another to look at. And then not to talk. To follow the dark paths of the mind and enter the past, to visit books, to brush aside their branches and break off some fruit. And you take it and marvel, as I take the careless movements of your body and marvel at its ease, its power—how you fling open windows and are dexterous with your hands. For alas! my mind is a little impeded, it soon tires; I fall damp, perhaps disgusting, at the goal.

'Alas! I could not ride about India in a sun helmet and return to a bungalow. I cannot tumble, as you do, like half-naked boys on the deck of a ship, squirting each other with hose-pipes. I want this fire, I want this chair. I want someone to sit beside me after the day's pursuit and all its anguish, after its listenings, and its waitings, and its suspicions. After quarrelling and reconciliation I need privacy—to be alone with you, to set this hubbub in order. For I am as neat as a cat in my habits. We must oppose the waste and deformity of the world, its crowds eddying round and round disgorged and trampling. One must slip paper-knives, even, exactly through the pages of novels, and tie up packets of letters neatly with green silk, and brush up the cinders with a hearth broom. Everything must be done to rebuke the horror of deformity. Let us read writers of Roman severity and virtue; let us seek perfection through the sand. Yes, but I love to slip the virtue and severity of the noble Romans under the grey light of your eyes, and dancing grasses and summer breezes and the laughter and shouts of boys at play—of naked cabin-boys squirting each other with hosepipes on the decks of ships. Hence I am not a disinterested seeker, like Louis, after perfection through the sand. Colours always stain the page; clouds pass over it. And the poem, I think, is only your voice speaking. Alcibiades, Ajax, Hector and Percival are also you. They loved riding, they risked their lives wantonly, they were not great readers either. But you are not Ajax or Percival. They did not wrinkle their noses and scratch their foreheads with your precise gesture. You are you. That is what consoles me for the lack of many things—I am ugly, I am weak—and the depravity of the world, and the flight of youth and Percival's death, and bitterness and rancour and envies innumerable.

'But if one day you do not come after breakfast, if one day I see you in some looking-glass perhaps looking after another, if the telephone buzzes and buzzes in your empty room, I shall then, after unspeakable anguish, I shall then—for there is no end to the folly of the human heart—seek another, find another, you. Meanwhile, let us abolish the ticking of time's clock with one blow. Come closer.'

The sun had now sunk lower in the sky. The islands of cloud had gained in density and drew themselves across the sun so that the rocks went suddenly black, and the trembling sea holly lost its blue and turned silver, and shadows were blown like grey cloths over the sea. The waves no longer visited the further pools or reached the dotted black line which lay irregularly upon the beach. The sand was pearl white, smoothed and shining. Birds swooped and circled high up in the air. Some raced in the furrows of the wind and turned and sliced through them as if they were one body cut into a thousand shreds. Birds fell like a net descending on the tree-tops. Here one bird taking its way alone made wing for the marsh and sat solitary on a white stake, opening its wings and shutting them.

Some petals had fallen in the garden. They lay shell-shaped on the earth. The dead leaf no longer stood upon its edge, but had been blown, now running, now pausing, against some stalk. Through all the flowers the same wave of light passed in a sudden flaunt and flash as if a fin cut the green glass of a lake. Now and again some level and masterly blast blew the multitudinous leaves up and down and then, as the wind flagged, each blade regained its identity. The flowers, burning their bright discs in the sun, flung aside the sunlight as the wind tossed them, and then some heads too heavy to rise again drooped slightly.

The afternoon sun warmed the fields, poured blue into the shadows and reddened the corn. A deep varnish was laid like a lacquer over the fields. A cart, a horse, a flock of rooks—whatever moved in it was rolled round in gold. If a cow moved a leg it stirred ripples of red gold, and its horns seemed lined with light. Sprays of flaxen-haired corn lay on the hedges, brushed from the shaggy carts that came up from the meadows short legged and primeval looking. The round-headed clouds never dwindled as they bowled along, but kept every atom of their rotundity. Now, as they passed, they caught a whole village in the fling of their net and, passing, let it fly free again. Far away on the horizon, among the million grains of blue-grey dust, burnt one pane, or stood the single line of one steeple or one tree.

The red curtains and the white blinds blew in and out, flapping against the edge of the window, and the light which entered by flaps and breadths unequally had in it some brown tinge, and some abandonment as it blew through the blowing curtains in gusts. Here it browned a cabinet, there reddened a chair, here it made the window waver in the side of the green jar.

All for a moment wavered and bent in uncertainty and ambiguity, as if a great moth sailing through the room had shadowed the immense solidity of chairs and tables with floating wings.

'And time,' said Bernard, 'lets fall its drop. The drop that has formed on the roof of the soul falls. On the roof of my mind time, forming, lets fall its drop. Last week, as I stood shaving, the drop fell. I, standing with my razor in my hand, became suddenly aware of the merely habitual nature of my action (this is the drop forming) and congratulated my hands, ironically, for keeping at it. Shave, shave, shave, I said. Go on shaving. The drop fell. All through the day's work, at intervals, my mind went to an empty place, saying, "What is lost? What is over?" And "Over and done with," I muttered, "over and done with," solacing myself with words. People noticed the vacuity of my face and the aimlessness of my conversation. The last words of my sentence tailed away. And as I buttoned on my coat to go home I said more dramatically, "I have lost my youth."

'It is curious how, at every crisis, some phrase which does not fit insists upon coming to the rescue—the penalty of living in an old civilization with a notebook. This drop falling has nothing to do with losing my youth. This drop falling is time tapering to a point. Time, which is a sunny pasture covered with a dancing light, time, which is widespread as a field at midday, becomes pendant. Time tapers to a point. As a drop falls from a glass heavy with some sediment, time falls. These are the true cycles, these are the true events. Then as if all the luminosity of the atmosphere were withdrawn I see to the bare bottom. I see what habit covers. I lie sluggish in bed for days. I dine out and gape like a codfish. I do not trouble to finish my sentences, and my actions, usually so uncertain, acquire a mechanical precision. On this occasion, passing an office, I went in and bought, with all the composure of a mechanical figure, a ticket for Rome.

'Now I sit on a stone seat in these gardens surveying the eternal city, and the little man who was shaving in London five days ago looks already like a heap of old clothes. London has also crumbled. London consists of fallen factories and a few gasometers. At the same time I am not involved in this pageantry. I see the violet-sashed priests and the picturesque nursemaids; I notice externals only. I sit here like a convalescent, like a very simple man who knows only words of one syllable. "The sun is hot," I say. "The wind is cold." I feel myself carried round like an insect on top of the earth and could swear that, sitting here, I feel its hardness, its turning movement. I have no desire to go the opposite way from the earth. Could I prolong this sense another six inches I have a foreboding that I should touch some queer territory. But I have a very limited proboscis. I never wish to prolong these states of detachment; I dislike them; I also despise them. I do not wish to be a man who sits for fifty years on the same spot thinking of his navel. I wish to be harnessed to a cart, a vegetable-cart that rattles over the cobbles.

"The truth is that I am not one of those who find their satisfaction in one person, or in infinity. The private room bores me, also the sky. My being only glitters when all its facets are exposed to many people. Let them fail and I am full of holes, dwindling like burnt paper. Oh, Mrs Moffat, Mrs Moffat, I say, come and sweep it all up. Things have dropped from me. I have outlived certain desires; I have lost friends, some by death—Percival—others through sheer inability to cross the street. I am not so gifted as at one time seemed likely. Certain things lie beyond my scope. I shall never understand the harder problems of philosophy. Rome is the limit of my travelling. As I drop asleep at night it strikes me sometimes with a pang that I shall never see savages in Tahiti spearing fish by the light of a blazing cresset, or a lion spring in the jungle, or a naked man eating raw flesh. Nor shall I learn Russian or read the Vedas. I shall never again walk bang into the pillar-box. (But still a few stars fall through my night, beautifully, from the violence of that concussion.) But as I think, truth has come nearer. For many years I crooned complacently, "My children . . . my wife . . . my house . . . my dog." As I let myself in with the latch-key I would go through that familiar ritual and wrap myself in those warm coverings. Now that lovely veil has fallen. I do not want possessions now. (Note: an Italian washer-woman stands on the same rung of physical refinement as the daughter of an English duke.)

'But let me consider. The drop falls; another stage has been reached. Stage upon stage. And why should there be an end of stages? and where do they lead? To what conclusion? For they come wearing robes of solemnity. In these dilemmas the devout consult those violet-sashed and sensual-looking gentry who are trooping past me. But for ourselves, we resent teachers. Let a man get up and say, "Behold, this is the truth," and instantly I perceive a sandy cat filching a piece of fish in the background. Look, you have forgotten the cat, I say. So Neville, at school, in the dim chapel, raged at the sight of the doctor's crucifix. I, who am always distracted, whether by a cat or by a bee buzzing round the bouquet that Lady Hampden keeps so diligently pressed to her nose, at once make up a story and so obliterate the angles of the crucifix. I have made up thousands of stories; I have filled innumerable notebooks with phrases to be used when I have found the true story, the one story to which all these phrases refer. But I have never yet found that story. And I begin to ask, Are there stories?

'Look now from this terrace at the swarming population beneath. Look at the general activity and clamour. That man is in difficulties with his mule. Half a dozen good-natured loafers offer their services. Others pass by without looking. They have as many interests as there are threads in a skein. Look at the sweep of the sky, bowled over by round white clouds. Imagine the leagues of level land and the aqueducts and the broken Roman pavement and the tombstones in the Campagna, and beyond the Campagna, the sea, then again more land, then the sea. I could break off any detail in all that prospect—say the mule-cart—and describe it with the greatest ease. But why describe a man in trouble with his mule? Again, I could invent stories about that girl coming up the steps. "She met him under the dark archway. . . . 'It is over,' he said, turning from the cage where the china parrot hangs." Or simply, "That was all." But why impose my arbitrary design? Why stress this and shape that and twist up little figures like the toys men sell in trays in the street? Why select this, out of all that—one detail?

'Here am I shedding one of my life-skins, and all they will say is, "Bernard is spending ten days in Rome." Here am I marching up and down this terrace alone, unoriented. But observe how dots and dashes are beginning, as I walk, to run themselves into continuous lines, how things are losing the bald, the separate identity that they had as I walked up those steps. The great red pot is now a reddish streak in a wave of yellowish green. The world is beginning to move past me like the banks of a hedge when the train starts, like the waves of the sea when a steamer moves. I am moving too, am becoming involved in the general sequence when one thing follows another and it seems inevitable that the tree should come, then the telegraph-pole, then the break in the hedge. And as I move, surrounded, included and taking part, the usual phrases begin to bubble up, and I wish to free these bubbles from the trap-door in my head, and direct my steps therefore towards that man, the back of whose head is half familiar to me. We were together at school. We shall undoubtedly meet. We shall certainly lunch together. We shall talk. But wait, one moment wait.

'These moments of escape are not to be despised. They come too seldom. Tahiti becomes possible. Leaning over this parapet I see far out a waste of water. A fin turns. This bare visual impression is unattached to any line of reason, it springs up as one might see the fin of a porpoise on the horizon. Visual impressions often communicate thus briefly statements that we shall in time to come uncover and coax into words. I note under F., therefore, "Fin in a waste of waters." I, who am perpetually making notes in the margin of my mind for some final statement, make this mark, waiting for some winter's evening.

'Now I shall go and lunch somewhere, I shall hold my glass up, I shall look through the wine, I shall observe with more than my usual detachment, and when a pretty woman enters the restaurant and comes down the room between the tables I shall say to myself, "Look where she comes against a waste of waters." A meaningless observation, but to me, solemn, slate-coloured, with a fatal sound of ruining worlds and waters falling to destruction.

'So, Bernard (I recall you, you the usual partner in my enterprises), let us begin this new chapter, and observe the formation of this new, this unknown, strange, altogether unidentified and terrifying experience—the new drop—which is about to shape itself. Larpent is that man's name.'

'In this hot afternoon,' said Susan, 'here in this garden, here in this field where I walk with my son, I have reached the summit of my desires. The hinge of the gate is rusty; he heaves it open. The violent passions of childhood, my tears in the garden when Jinny kissed Louis, my rage in the schoolroom, which smelt of pine, my loneliness in foreign places, when the mules came clattering in on their pointed hoofs and the Italian women chattered at the fountain, shawled, with carnations twisted in their hair, are rewarded by security, possession, familiarity. I have had peaceful, productive years. I possess all I see. I have grown trees from the seed. I have made ponds in which goldfish hide under the broad-leaved lilies. I have netted over strawberry beds and lettuce beds, and stitched the pears and the plums into white bags to keep them safe from the wasps. I have seen my sons and daughters, once netted over like fruit in their cots, break the meshes and walk with me, taller than I am, casting shadows on the grass.

'I am fenced in, planted here like one of my own trees. I say, "My son," I say, "My daughter," and even the ironmonger looking up from his counter strewn with nails, paint and wire-fencing respects the shabby car at the door with its butterfly nets, pads and bee-hives. We hang mistletoe over the clock at Christmas, weigh our blackberries and mushrooms, count out jam-pots, and stand year by year to be measured against the shutter in the drawing-room window. I also make wreaths of white flowers, twisting silver-leaved plants among them for the dead, attaching my card with sorrow for the dead shepherd, with sympathy for the wife of the dead carter; and sit by the beds of dying women, who murmur their last terrors, who clutch my hand; frequenting rooms intolerable except to one born as I was and early acquainted with the farmyard and the dung-heap and the hens straying in and out, and the mother with two rooms and growing children. I have seen the windows run with heat, I have smelt the sink.

'I ask now, standing with my scissors among my flowers, Where can the shadow enter? What shock can loosen my laboriously gathered, relentlessly pressed down life? Yet sometimes I am sick of natural happiness, and fruit growing, and children scattering the house with oars, guns, skulls, books won for prizes and other trophies. I am sick of the body, I am sick of my own craft, industry and cunning, of the unscrupulous ways of the mother who protects, who collects under her jealous eyes at one long table her own children, always her own.

'It is when spring comes, cold showery, with sudden yellow flowers—then as I look at the meat under the blue shade and press the heavy silver bags of tea, of sultanas, I remember how the sun rose, and the swallows skimmed the grass, and phrases that Bernard made when we were children, and the leaves shook over us, many-folded, very light, breaking the blue of the sky, scattering wandering lights upon the skeleton roots of the beech trees where I sat, sobbing. The pigeon rose. I jumped up and ran after the words that trailed like the dangling string from an air ball, up and up, from branch to branch escaping. Then like a cracked bowl the fixity of my morning broke, and putting down the bags of flour I thought, Life stands round me like a glass round the imprisoned reed.

'I hold some scissors and snip off the hollyhocks, who went to Elvedon and trod on rotten oak-apples, and saw the lady writing and the gardeners with their great brooms. We ran back panting lest we should be shot and nailed like stoats to the wall. Now I measure, I preserve. At night I sit in the arm-chair and stretch my arm for my sewing; and hear my husband snore; and look up when the light from a passing car dazzles the windows and feel the waves of my life tossed, broken, round me who am rooted; and hear cries, and see other's lives eddying like straws round the piers of a bridge while I push my needle in and out and draw my thread through the calico.

'I think sometimes of Percival who loved me. He rode and fell in India. I think sometimes of Rhoda. Uneasy cries wake me at dead of night. But for the most part I walk content with my sons. I cut the dead petals from hollyhocks. Rather squat, grey before my time, but with clear eyes, pear-shaped eyes, I pace my fields.'

'Here I stand,' said Jinny, 'in the Tube station where everything that is desirable meets—Piccadilly South Side, Piccadilly North Side, Regent Street and the Haymarket. I stand for a moment under the pavement in the heart of London. Innumerable wheels rush and feet press just over my head. The great avenues of civilization meet here and strike this way and that. I am in the heart of life. But look—there is my body in that looking glass. How solitary, how shrunk, how aged! I am no longer young. I am no longer part of the procession. Millions descend those stairs in a terrible descent. Great wheels churn inexorably urging them downwards. Millions have died. Percival died. I still move. I still live. But who will come if I signal?

'Little animal that I am, sucking my flanks in and out with fear, I stand here, palpitating, trembling. But I will not be afraid. I will bring the whip down on my flanks. I am not a whimpering little animal making for the shadow. It was only for a moment, catching sight of myself before I had time to prepare myself as I always prepare myself for the sight of myself, that I quailed. It is true; I am not young—I shall soon raise my arm in vain and my scarf will fall to my side without having signalled. I shall not hear the sudden sigh in the night and feel through the dark someone coming. There will be no reflections in window-panes in dark tunnels. I shall look into faces, and I shall see them seek some other face. I admit for one moment the soundless flight of upright bodies down the moving stairs like the pinioned and terrible descent of some army of the dead downwards and the churning of the great engines remorselessly forwarding us, all of us, onwards, made me cower and run for shelter.

'But now I swear, making deliberately in front of the glass those slight preparations that equip me, I will not be afraid. Think of the superb omnibuses, red and yellow, stopping and starting, punctually in order. Think of the powerful and beautiful cars that now slow to a foot's pace and now shoot forward; think of men, think of women, equipped, prepared, driving onward. This is the triumphant procession; this is the army of victory with banners and brass eagles and heads crowned with laurel-leaves won in battle. They are better than savages in loin-cloths, and women whose hair is dank, whose long breasts sag, with children tugging at their long breasts. These broad thoroughfares—Piccadilly South, Piccadilly North, Regent Street and the Haymarket—are sanded paths of victory driven through the jungle. I too, with my little patent-leather shoes, my handkerchief that is but a film of gauze, my reddened lips and my finely pencilled eyebrows, march to victory with the band.

'Look how they show off clothes here even under ground in a perpetual radiance. They will not let the earth even lie wormy and sodden. There are gauzes and silks illumined in glass cases and underclothes trimmed with a million close stitches of fine embroidery. Crimson, green, violet, they are dyed all colours. Think how they organize, roll out, smooth, dip in dyes, and drive tunnels blasting the rock. Lifts rise and fall; trains stop, trams start as regularly as the waves of the sea. This is what has my adhesion. I am a native of this world, I follow its banners. How could I run for shelter when they are so magnificently adventurous, daring, curious, too, and strong enough in the midst of effort to pause and scrawl with a free hand a joke upon the wall? Therefore I will powder my face and redden my lips. I will make the angle of my eyebrows sharper than usual. I will rise to the surface, standing erect with the others in Piccadilly Circus. I will sign with a sharp gesture to a cab whose driver will signify by some indescribable alacrity his understanding of my signals. For I still excite eagerness. I still feel the bowing of men in the street like the silent stoop of the corn when the light wind blows, ruffling it red.

'I will drive to my own house. I will fill the vases with lavish, with luxurious, with extravagant flowers nodding in great bunches. I will place one chair there, another here. I will put ready cigarettes, glasses and some gaily covered new unread book in case Bernard comes, or Neville or Louis. But perhaps it will not be Bernard, Neville or Louis, but somebody new, somebody unknown, somebody I passed on a staircase and, just turning as we passed, I murmured, "Come." He will come this afternoon; somebody I do not know, somebody new. Let the silent army of the dead descend. I march forward.'

'I no longer need a room now,' said Neville, 'or walls and firelight. I am no longer young. I pass Jinny's house without envy, and smile at the young man who arranges his tie a little nervously on the door-step. Let the dapper young man ring the bell; let him find her. I shall find her if I want her; if not, I pass on. The old corrosion has lost its bite—envy, intrigue and bitterness have been washed out. We have lost our glory too. When we were young we sat anywhere, on bare benches in draughty halls with the doors always banging. We tumbled about half naked like boys on the deck of a ship squirting each other with hose-pipes. Now I could swear that I like people pouring profusely out of the Tube when the day's work is done, unanimous, indiscriminate, uncounted. I have picked my own fruit. I look dispassionately.

'After all, we are not responsible. We are not judges. We are not called upon to torture our fellows with thumb-screws and irons; we are not called upon to mount pulpits and lecture them on pale Sunday afternoons. It is better to look at a rose, or to read

Shakespeare as I read him here in Shaftesbury Avenue. Here's the fool, here's the villain, here in a car comes Cleopatra, burning on her barge. Here are figures of the damned too, noseless men by the police-court wall, standing with their feet in fire, howling. This is poetry if we do not write it. They act their parts infallibly, and almost before they open their lips I know what they are going to say, and wait the divine moment when they speak the word that must have been written. If it were only for the sake of the play, I could walk Shaftesbury Avenue for ever.

'Then coming from the street, entering some room, there are people talking, or hardly troubling to talk. He says, she says, somebody else says things have been said so often that one word is now enough to lift a whole weight. Argument, laughter, old grievances—they fall through the air, thickening it. I take a book and read half a page of anything. They have not mended the spout of the teapot yet. The child dances, dressed in her mother's clothes.

'But then Rhoda, or it may be Louis, some fasting and anguished spirit, passes through and out again. They want a plot, do they? They want a reason? It is not enough for them, this ordinary scene. It is not enough to wait for the thing to be said as if it were written; to see the sentence lay its dab of clay precisely on the right place, making character; to perceive, suddenly, some group in outline against the sky. Yet if they want violence, I have seen death and murder and suicide all in one room. One comes in, one goes out. There are sobs on the staircase. I have heard threads broken and knots tied and the quiet stitching of white cambric going on and on on the knees of a woman. Why ask, like Louis, for a reason, or fly like Rhoda to some far grove and part the leaves of the laurels and look for statues? They say that one must beat one's wings against the storm in the belief that beyond this welter the sun shines; the sun falls sheer into pools that are fledged with willows. (Here it is November; the poor hold out matchboxes in wind-bitten fingers.) They say truth is to be found there entire, and virtue, that shuffles along here, down blind alleys, is to be had there perfect. Rhoda flies with her neck outstretched and blind fanatic eyes, past us. Louis, now so opulent, goes to his attic window among the blistered roofs and gazes where she has vanished, but must sit down in his office among the typewriters and the telephone and work it all out for our instruction, for our regeneration, and the reform of an unborn world.

'But now in this room, which I enter without knocking, things are said as if they had been written. I go to the bookcase. If I choose, I read half a page of anything. I need not speak. But I listen. I am marvellously on the alert. Certainly, one cannot read this poem without effort. The page is often corrupt and mud-stained, and torn and stuck together with faded leaves, with scraps of verbena or geranium. To read this poem one must have myriad eyes, like one of those lamps that turn on slabs of racing water at midnight in the Atlantic, when perhaps only a spray of seaweed pricks the surface, or suddenly the waves gape and up shoulders a monster. One must put aside antipathies and jealousies and not interrupt. One must have patience and infinite care and let the light sound, whether of spiders' delicate feet on a leaf or the chuckle of water in some irrelevant drain-pipe, unfold too. Nothing is to be rejected in fear or horror. The poet who has written this page (what I read with people talking) has withdrawn. There are no commas or semi-colons. The lines do not run in convenient lengths. Much is sheer nonsense. One must be sceptical, but throw caution to the winds and when the door opens accept absolutely. Also sometimes weep; also cut away ruthlessly with a slice of the blade soot, bark, hard accretions of all sorts. And so (while they talk) let down one's net deeper and deeper and gently draw in and bring to the surface what he said and she said and make poetry.

'Now I have listened to them talking. They have gone now. I am alone. I could be content to watch the fire burn for ever, like a dome, like a furnace; now some spike of wood takes the look of a scaffold, or pit, or happy valley; now it is a serpent curled crimson with white scales. The fruit on the curtain swells beneath the parrot's beak. Cheep, cheep, creaks the fire, like the cheep of insects in the middle of a forest. Cheep, cheep, it clicks while out there the branches thrash the air, and now, like a volley of shot, a tree falls. These are the sounds of a London night. Then I hear the one sound I wait for. Up and up it comes, approaches, hesitates, stops at my door. I cry, "Come in. Sit by me. Sit on the edge of the chair." Swept away by the old hallucination, I cry, "Come closer, closer".'

'I come back from the office,' said Louis. 'I hang my coat here, place my stick there—I like to fancy that Richelieu walked with such a cane. Thus I divest myself of my authority. I have been sitting at the right hand of a director at a varnished table. The maps of our successful undertakings confront us on the wall. We have laced the world together with our ships. The globe is strung with our lines. I am immensely respectable. All the young ladies in the office acknowledge my entrance. I can dine where I like now, and without vanity may suppose that I shall soon acquire a house in Surrey, two cars, a conservatory and some rare species of melon. But I still return, I still come back to my attic, hang up my hat and resume in solitude that curious attempt which I have made since I brought down my fist on my master's grained oak door. I open a little book. I read one poem. One poem is enough.

O western wind . . .

O western wind, you are at enmity with my mahogany table and spats, and also, alas, with the vulgarity of my mistress, the little actress, who has never been able to speak English correctly—

O western wind, when wilt thou blow . . .

Rhoda, with her intense abstraction, with her unseeing eyes the colour of snail's flesh, does not destroy you, western wind, whether she comes at midnight when the stars blaze or at the most prosaic hour of midday. She stands at the window and looks at the chimney-pots and the broken windows in the houses of poor people—

O western wind, when wilt thou blow . . .

'My task, my burden, has always been greater than other people's. A pyramid has been set on my shoulders. I have tried to do a colossal labour. I have driven a violent, an unruly, a vicious team. With my Australian accent I have sat in eating-shops and tried to make the clerks accept me, yet never forgotten my solemn and severe convictions and the discrepancies and incoherences that must be resolved. As a boy I dreamt of the Nile, was reluctant to awake, yet brought down my fist on the grained oak door. It would have been happier to have been born without a destiny, like Susan, like Percival, whom I most admire.

O western wind, when wilt thou blow.
That the small rain down can rain?

'Life has been a terrible affair for me. I am like some vast sucker, some glutinous, some adhesive, some insatiable mouth. I have tried to draw from the living flesh the stone lodged at the centre. I have known little natural happiness, thought I chose my mistress in order that, with her cockney accent, she might make me feel at my ease. But she only tumbled the floor with dirty under-linen, and the charwoman and the shop-boys called after me a dozen times a day, mocking my prim and supercilious gait.

O western wind, when wilt thou blow,
That the small rain down can rain?

'What has my destiny been, the sharp-pointed pyramid that has pressed on my ribs all these years? That I remember the Nile and the women carrying pitchers on their heads; that I feel myself woven in and out of the long summers and winters that have made the corn flow and have frozen the streams. I am not a single and passing being. My life is not a moment's bright spark like that on the surface of a diamond. I go beneath ground tortuously, as if a warder carried a lamp from cell to cell. My destiny has been that I remember and must weave together, must plait into one cable the many threads, the thin, the thick, the broken, the enduring of our long history, of our tumultuous and varied day. There is always more to be understood; a discord to be listened for; a falsity to be reprimanded. Broken and soot-stained are these roofs with their chimney cowls, their loose slates, their slinking cats and attic windows. I pick my way over broken glass, among blistered tiles, and see only vile and famished faces.

'Let us suppose that I make reason of it all—one poem on a page, and then die. I can assure you it will not be unwillingly. Percival died. Rhoda left me. But I shall live to be gaunt and sere, to tap my way, much respected, with my gold-headed cane along the pavements of the city. Perhaps I shall never die, shall never attain even that continuity and permanence—

O western wind, when wilt thou blow,
That the small rain down can rain?

'Percival was flowering with green leaves and was laid in the earth with all his branches still sighing in the summer wind. Rhoda, with whom I shared silence when the others spoke, she who hung back and turned aside when the herd assembled and galloped with orderly, sleek backs over the rich pastures, has gone now like the desert heat. When the sun blisters the roofs of the city I think of her; when the dry leaves patter to the ground; when the old men come with pointed sticks and pierce little bits of paper as we pierced her—

O western wind, when wilt thou blow,
That the small rain down can rain?
Christ, that my love were in my arms,
And I in my bed again!

I return now to my book; I return now to my attempt.'

'Oh, life, how I have dreaded you,' said Rhoda, 'oh, human beings, how I have hated you! How you have nudged, how you have interrupted, how hideous you have looked in Oxford Street, how squalid sitting opposite each other staring in the Tube! Now as I climb this mountain, from the top of which I shall see Africa, my mind is printed with brown-paper parcels and your faces. I have been stained by you and corrupted. You smelt so unpleasant too, lining up outside doors to buy tickets. All were dressed in indeterminate shades of grey and brown, never even a blue feather pinned to a hat. None had the courage to be one thing rather than another. What dissolution of the soul you demanded in order to get through one day, what lies, bowings, scrapings, fluency and servility! How you chained me to one spot, one hour, one chair, and sat yourselves down opposite! How you snatched from me the white spaces that lie between hour and hour and rolled them into dirty pellets and tossed them into the waste-paper basket with your greasy paws. Yet those were my life.

'But I yielded. Sneers and yawns were covered with my hand. I did not go out into the street and break a bottle in the gutter as a sign of rage. Trembling with ardour, I pretended that I was not surprised. What you did, I did. If Susan and Jinny pulled up their stockings like that, I pulled mine up like that also. So terrible was life that I held up shade after shade. Look at life through this, look at life through that; let there be rose leaves, let there be vine leaves—I covered the whole street, Oxford Street, Piccadilly Circus, with the blaze and ripple of my mind, with vine leaves and rose leaves. There were boxes too, standing in the passage when the school broke up. I stole secretly to read the labels and dream of names and faces. Harrogate, perhaps, Edinburgh, perhaps, was ruffled with golden glory where some girl whose name I forget stood on the pavement. But it was the name only. I left Louis; I feared embraces. With fleeces, with vestments, I have tried to cover the blue-black blade. I implored day to break into night. I have longed to see the cupboard dwindle, to feel the bed soften, to float suspended, to perceive lengthened trees, lengthened faces, a green bank on a moor and two figures in distress saying good-bye. I flung words in fans like those the sower throws over the ploughed fields when the earth is bare. I desired always to stretch the night and fill it fuller and fuller with dreams.

'Then in some Hall I parted the boughs of music and saw the house we have made; the square stood upon the oblong. "The house which contains all," I said, lurching against people's shoulders in an omnibus after Percival died; yet I went to Greenwich. Walking on the embankment, I prayed that I might thunder for ever on the verge of the world where there is no vegetation, but here and there a marble pillar. I threw my bunch into the spreading wave. I said, "Consume me, carry me to the furthest limit." The wave has broken; the bunch is withered. I seldom think of Percival now.

'Now I climb this Spanish hill; and I will suppose that this mule-back is my bed and that I lie dying. There is only a thin sheet between me now and the infinite depths. The lumps in the mattress soften beneath me. We stumble up—we stumble on. My path has been up and up, towards some solitary tree with a pool beside it on the very top. I have sliced the waters of beauty in the evening when the hills close themselves like birds' wings folded. I have picked sometimes a red carnation, and wisps of hay. I have sunk alone on the turf and fingered some old bone and thought: When the wind stoops to brush this height, may there be nothing found but a pinch of dust.

'The mule stumbles up and on. The ridge of the hill rises like mist, but from the top I shall see Africa. Now the bed gives under me. The sheets spotted with yellow holes let me fall through. The good woman with a face like a white horse at the end of the bed makes a valedictory movement and turns to go. Who then comes with me? Flowers only, the cowbind and the moonlight-coloured May. Gathering them loosely in a sheaf I made of them a garland and gave them—Oh, to whom? We launch out now over the precipice. Beneath us lie the lights of the herring fleet. The cliffs vanish. Rippling small, rippling grey, innumerable waves spread beneath us. I touch nothing. I see nothing. We may sink and settle on the waves. The sea will drum in my ears. The white petals will be darkened with sea water. They will float for a moment and then sink. Rolling me over the waves will shoulder me under. Everything falls in a tremendous shower, dissolving me.

'Yet that tree has bristling branches; that is the hard line of a cottage roof. Those bladder shapes painted red and yellow are faces. Putting my foot to the ground I step gingerly and press my hand against the hard door of a Spanish inn.'

The sun was sinking. The hard stone of the day was cracked and light poured through its splinters. Red and gold shot through the waves, in rapid running arrows, feathered with darkness. Erratically rays of light flashed and wandered, like signals from sunken islands, or darts shot through laurel groves by shameless, laughing boys. But the waves, as they neared the shore, were robbed of light, and fell in one long concussion, like a wall falling, a wall of grey stone, unpierced by any chink of light.

A breeze rose; a shiver ran through the leaves; and thus stirred they lost their brown density and became grey or white as the tree shifted its mass, winked and lost its domed uniformity. The hawk poised on the topmost branch flicked its eyelids and rose and sailed and soared far away. The wild plover cried in the marshes, evading, circling, and crying further off in loneliness. The smoke of trains and chimneys was stretched and torn and became part of the fleecy canopy that hung over the sea and the fields.

Now the corn was cut. Now only a brisk stubble was left of all its flowing and waving. Slowly a great owl launched itself from the elm tree and swung and rose, as if on a line that dipped, to the height of the cedar. On the hills the slow shadows now broadened, now shrank, as they passed over. The pool on the top of the moor looked blank. No furry face looked there, or hoof splashed, or hot muzzle seethed in the water. A bird, perched on an ash-coloured twig, sipped a beak full of cold water. There was no sound of cropping, and no sound of wheels, but only the sudden roar of the wind letting its sails fill and brushing the tops of the grasses. One bone lay rain-pocked and sun-bleached till it shone like a twig that the sea has polished. The tree, that had burnt foxy red in spring and in midsummer bent pliant leaves to the south wind, was now black as iron, and as bare.

The land was so distant that no shining roof or glittering window could be any longer seen. The tremendous weight of the shadowed earth had engulfed such frail fetters, such snail-shell encumbrances. Now there was only the liquid shadow of the cloud, the buffeting of the rain, a single darting spear of sunshine, or the sudden bruise of the rainstorm. Solitary trees marked distant hills like obelisks.

The evening sun, whose heat had gone out of it and whose burning spot of intensity had been diffused, made chairs and tables mellower and inlaid them with lozenges of brown and yellow. Lined with shadows their weight seemed more ponderous, as if colour, tilted, had run to one side. Here lay knife, fork and glass, but lengthened, swollen, and made portentous. Rimmed in a gold circle the looking-glass held the scene immobile as if everlasting in its eye.

Meanwhile the shadows lengthened on the beach; the blackness deepened. The iron black boot became a pool of deep blue. The *rocks lost their hardness. The water that stood round the old boat was dark as if mussels had been steeped in it. The foam had turned livid and left here and there a white gleam of pearl on the misty sand.*

'Hampton Court,' said Bernard. 'Hampton Court. This is our meeting-place. Behold the red chimneys, the square battlements of Hampton Court. The tone of my voice as I say "Hampton Court" proves that I am middle-aged. Ten years, fifteen years ago, I should have said "Hampton Court?" with interrogation—what will it be like? Will there be lakes, mazes? Or with anticipation, What is going to happen to me here? Whom shall I meet? Now, Hampton Court—Hampton Court—the words beat a gong in the space which I have so laboriously cleared with half a dozen telephone messages and post cards, give off ring after ring of sound, booming, sonorous: and pictures rise—summer afternoons, boats, old ladies holding their skirts up, one urn in winter, some daffodils in March—these all float to the top of the waters that now lie deep on every scene.

There at the door by the Inn, our meeting-place, they are already standing—Susan, Louis, Rhoda, Jinny and Neville. They have come together already. In a moment, when I have joined them, another arrangement will form, another pattern. What now runs to waste, forming scenes profusely, will be checked, stated. I am reluctant to suffer that compulsion. Already at fifty yards distance I feel the order of my being changed. The tug of the magnet of their society tells upon me. I come nearer. They do not see me. Now Rhoda sees me, but she pretends, with her horror of the shock of meeting, that I am a stranger. Now Neville turns. Suddenly, raising my hand, saluting Neville I cry, "I too have pressed flowers between the pages of Shakespeare's sonnets," and am churned up. My little boat bobs unsteadily upon the chopped and tossing waves. There is no panacea (let me note) against the shock of meeting.

'It is uncomfortable too, joining ragged edges, raw edges; only gradually, as we shuffle and trample into the Inn, taking coats and hats off, does meeting become agreeable. Now we assemble in the long, bare dining-room that overlooks some park, some green space still fantastically lit by the setting sun so that there is a gold bar between the trees, and sit ourselves down.'

'Now sitting side by side,' said Neville, 'at this narrow table, now before the first emotion is worn smooth, what do we feel? Honestly now, openly and directly as befits old friends meeting with difficulty, what do we feel on meeting? Sorrow. The door will not open; he will not come. And we are laden. Being now all of us middle-aged, loads are on us. Let us put down our loads. What have you made of life, we ask, and I? You, Bernard; you, Susan; you, Jinny; and Rhoda and Louis? The lists have been posted on the doors. Before we break these rolls, and help ourselves to fish and salad, I feel in my private pocket and find my credentials—what I carry to prove my superiority. I have passed. I have papers in my private pocket that prove it. But your eyes, Susan, full of turnips and cornfields, disturb me. These papers in my private pocket—the clamour that proves that I have passed—make a faint sound like that of a man clapping in an empty field to scare away rooks. Now it has died down altogether, under Susan's stare (the clapping, the reverberation that I have made), and I hear only the wind sweeping over the ploughed land and some bird singing—perhaps some intoxicated lark. Has the waiter heard of me, or those furtive everlasting couples, now loitering, now holding back and looking at the trees which are not yet dark enough to shelter their prostrate bodies? No; the sound of clapping has failed.

'What then remains, when I cannot pull out my papers and make you believe by reading aloud my credentials that I have passed? What remains is what Susan brings to light under the acid of her green eyes, her crystal, pear-shaped eyes. There is always somebody, when we come together, and the edges of meeting are still sharp, who refuses to be submerged; whose identity therefore one wishes to make crouch beneath one's own. For me now, it is Susan. I talk to impress Susan. Listen to me, Susan.

'When someone comes in at breakfast, even the embroidered fruit on my curtain swells so that parrots can peck it; one can break it off between one's thumb and finger. The thin, skimmed milk of early morning turns opal, blue, rose. At that hour your husband—the man who slapped his gaiters, pointing with his whip at the barren cow—grumbles. You say nothing. You see nothing. Custom blinds your eyes. At that hour your relationship is mute, null, dun-coloured. Mine at that hour is warm and various. There are no repetitions for me. Each day is dangerous. Smooth on the surface, we are all bone beneath like snakes coiling. Suppose we read *The Times;* suppose we argue. It is an experience. Suppose it is winter. The snow falling loads down the roof and seals us together in a red cave. The pipes have burst. We stand a yellow tin bath in the middle of the room. We rush helter-skelter for basins. Look there—it has burst again over the bookcase. We shout with laughter at the sight of ruin. Let solidity be destroyed. Let us have no possessions. Or is it summer? We may wander to a lake and watch Chinese geese waddling flat-footed to the water's edge or see a bone-like city church with young green trembling before it. (I choose at random; I choose the obvious.) Each sight is an arabesque scrawled suddenly to illustrate some hazard and marvel of intimacy. The snow, the burst pipe, the tin bath, the Chinese goose—these are signs swung high aloft upon which, looking back, I read the character of each love; how each was different.

'You meanwhile—for I want to diminish your hostility, your green eyes fixed on mine, and your shabby dress, your rough hands, and all the other emblems of your maternal splendour—have stuck like a limpet to the same rock. Yet it is true, I do not want to hurt you; only to refresh and furbish up my own belief in myself that failed at your entry. Change is no longer possible. We are committed. Before, when we met in a restaurant in London with Percival, all simmered and shook; we could have been anything. We have chosen now, or sometimes it seems the choice was made for us—a pair of tongs pinched us between the shoulders. I chose. I took the print of life not outwardly, but inwardly upon the raw, the white, the unprotected fibre. I am clouded and bruised with the print of minds and faces and things so subtle that they have smell, colour, texture, substance, but no name. I am merely "Neville" to you, who see the narrow limits of my life and the line it cannot pass. But to myself I am immeasurable; a net whose fibres pass imperceptibly beneath the world. My net is almost indistinguishable from that which it surrounds. It lifts whales—huge leviathans and white jellies, what is amorphous and wandering; I detect, I perceive. Beneath my eyes opens—a book; I see to the bottom; the heart—I see to the depths. I know what loves are trembling into fire; how jealousy shoots its green flashes hither and thither; how intricately love crosses love; love makes knots; love brutally tears them apart. I have been knotted; I have been torn apart.

'But there was another glory once, when we watched for the door to open, and Percival came; when we flung ourselves unattached on the edge of a hard bench in a public room.'

'There was the beech wood,' said Susan, 'Elvedon, and the gilt hands of the clock sparkling among the trees. The pigeons broke the leaves. The changing travelling lights wandered over me. They escaped me. Yet look, Neville, whom I discredit in order to be myself, at my hand on the table. Look at the gradations of healthy colour here on the knuckles, here on the palm. My body has been used daily, rightly, like a tool by a good workman, all over. The blade is clean, sharp, worn in the centre. (We battle together like beasts fighting in a field, like stags making their horns clash.) Seen through your pale and yielding flesh, even apples and bunches of fruit must have a filmed look as if they stood under glass. Lying deep in a chair with one person, one person only, but one person who changes, you see one inch of flesh only; its nerves, fibres, the sullen or quick flow of blood on it; but nothing entire. You do not see a house in a garden; a horse in a field; a town laid out, as you bend like an old woman straining her eyes over her darning. But I have seen life in blocks, substantial, huge; its battlements and towers, factories and gasometers; a dwelling-place made from time immemorial after an hereditary pattern. These things remain square, prominent, undissolved in my mind. I am not sinuous or suave; I sit among you abrading your softness with my hardness, quenching the silver-grey flickering moth-wing quiver of words with the green spurt of my clear eyes.

'Now we have clashed our antlers. This is the necessary prelude; the salute of old friends.'

'The gold has faded between the trees,' said Rhoda, 'and a slice of green lies behind them, elongated like the blade of a knife seen in dreams, or some tapering island on which nobody sets foot. Now the cars begin to wink and flicker, coming down the avenue. Lovers can draw into the darkness now; the boles of the trees are swollen, are obscene with lovers.'

'It was different once,' said Bernard. 'Once we could break the current as we chose. How many telephone calls, how many post cards, are now needed to cut this hole through which we come together, united, at Hampton Court? How swift life runs from January to December! We are all swept on by the torrent of things grown so familiar that they cast no shade; we make no comparisons; think scarcely ever of I or of you; and in this unconsciousness attain the utmost freedom from friction and part the weeds that grow over the mouths of sunken channels. We have to leap like fish, high in the air, in order to catch the train from Waterloo. And however high we leap we fall back again into the stream. I shall never now take ship for the South Sea Islands. A journey to Rome is the limit of my travelling. I have sons and daughters. I am wedged into my place in the puzzle.

'But it is only my body—this elderly man here whom you call Bernard—that is fixed irrevocably—so I desire to believe. I think more disinterestedly than I could when I was young and must

530

dig furiously like a child rummaging in a bran-pie to discover my self. "Look, what is this? And this? Is this going to be a fine present? Is that all?" and so on. Now I know what the parcels hold; and do not care much. I throw my mind out in the air as a man throws seeds in great fan-flights, falling through the purple sunset, falling on the pressed and shining ploughland which is bare.

'A phrase. An imperfect phrase. And what are phrases? They have left me very little to lay on the table, beside Susan's hand; to take from my pocket, with Neville's credentials. I am not an authority on law, or medicine, or finance. I am wrapped round with phrases, like damp straw; I glow, phosphorescent. And each of you feels when I speak, "I am lit up. I am glowing." The little boys used to feel "That's a good one, that's a good one", as the phrases bubbled up from my lips under the elm trees in the playing-fields. They too bubbled up; they also escaped with my phrases. But I pine in solitude. Solitude is my undoing.

'I pass from house to house like the friars in the Middle Ages who cozened the wives and girls with beads and ballads. I am a traveller, a pedlar, paying for my lodging with a ballad; I am an indiscriminate, an easily pleased guest; often putting up in the best room in a four-poster; then lying in a barn on a haystack. I don't mind the fleas and find no fault with silk either. I am very tolerant. I am not a moralist. I have too great a sense of the shortness of life and its temptations to rule red lines. Yet I am not so indiscriminate as you think, judging me—as you judge me—from my fluency. I have a little dagger of contempt and severity hidden up my sleeve. But I am apt to be deflected. I make stories. I twist up toys out of anything. A girl sits at a cottage door; she is waiting; for whom? Seduced, or not seduced? The headmaster sees the hole in the carpet. He sighs. His wife, drawing her fingers through the waves of her still abundant hair, reflects—et cetera. Waves of hands, hesitations at street corners, someone dropping a cigarette into the gutter—all are stories. But which is the true story? That I do not know. Hence I keep my phrases hung like clothes in a cupboard, waiting for someone to wear them. Thus waiting, thus speculating, making this note and then another, I do not cling to life. I shall be brushed like a bee from a sunflower. My philosophy, always accumulating, welling up moment by moment, runs like quicksilver a dozen ways at once. But Louis, wild-eyed but severe, in his attic, in his office, has formed unalterable conclusions upon the true nature of what is to be known.'

'It breaks,' said Louis, 'the thread I try to spin; your laughter breaks it, your indifference, also your beauty. Jinny broke the thread when she kissed me in the garden years ago. The boasting boys mocked me at school for my Australian accent and broke it. "This is the meaning," I say; and then start with a pang—vanity. "Listen," I say, "to the nightingale, who sings among the trampling feet; the conquests and migrations. Believe—" and then am twitched asunder. Over broken tiles and splinters of glass I pick my way. Different lights fall, making the ordinary leopard spotted and strange. This moment of reconciliation, when we meet together united, this evening moment, with its wine and shaking leaves, and youth coming up from the river in white flannels, carrying cushions, is to me black with the shadows of dungeons and the tortures and infamies practised by man upon man. So imperfect are my senses that they never blot out with one purple the serious charge that my reason adds and adds against us, even as we sit here. What is the solution, I ask myself, and the bridge? How can I reduce these dazzling, these dancing apparitions to one line capable of linking all in one? So I ponder; and you meanwhile observe maliciously my pursed lips, my sallow cheeks and my invariable frown.

'But I beg you also to notice my cane and my waistcoat. I have inherited a desk of solid mahogany in a room hung with maps. Our steamers have won an enviable reputation for their cabins replete with luxury. We supply swimming-baths and gymnasiums. I wear a white waistcoat now and consult a little book before I make an engagement.

'This is the arch and ironical manner in which I hope to distract you from my shivering, my tender, and infinitely young and unprotected soul. For I am always the youngest; the most naïvely surprised; the one who runs in advance in apprehension and sympathy with discomfort or ridicule—should there be a smut on a nose, or a button undone. I suffer for all humiliations. Yet I am also ruthless, marmoreal. I do not see how you can say that it is fortunate to have lived. Your little excitements, your childish transports, when a kettle boils, when the soft air lifts Jinny's spotted scarf and it floats web-like, are to me like silk streamers thrown in the eyes of the charging bull. I condemn you. Yet my heart yearns towards you. I would go with you through the fires of death. Yet am happiest alone. I luxuriate in gold and purple vestments. Yet I prefer a view over chimneypots; cats scraping their mangy sides upon blistered chimney-stacks; broken windows; and the hoarse clangour of bells from the steeple of some brick chapel.'

'I see what is before me,' said Jinny. 'This scarf, these wine-coloured spots. This glass. This mustard pot. This flower. I like what one touches, what one tastes. I like rain when it has turned to snow and become palatable. And being rash, and much more courageous than you are, I do not temper my beauty with meanness lest it should scorch me. I gulp it down entire. It is made of flesh; it is made of stuff. My imagination is the body's. Its visions are not fine-spun and white with purity like Louis'. I do not like your lean cats and your blistered chimney-pots. The scrannel beauties of your roof-tops repel me. Men and women, in uniforms, wigs and gowns, bowler hats and tennis shirts beautifully open at the neck, the infinite variety of women's dresses (I note all clothes always) delight me. I eddy with them, in and out, in and out, into rooms, into halls, here, there, everywhere, wherever they go. This man lifts the hoof of a horse. This man shoves in and out the drawers of his private collection. I am never alone. I am attended by a regiment of my fellows. My mother must have followed the drum, my father the sea. I am like a little dog that trots down the road after the regimental band, but stops to snuff a tree-trunk, to sniff some brown stain, and suddenly careers across the street after some mongrel cur and then holds one paw up while it sniffs an entrancing whiff of meat from the butcher's shop. My traffics have led me into strange places. Men, how many, have broken from the wall and come to me. I have only to hold my hand up. Straight as a dart they have come to the place of assignation—perhaps a chair on a balcony, perhaps a shop at a street corner. The torments, the divisions of your lives have been solved for me night after night, sometimes only by the touch of a finger under the table-cloth as we sat dining—so fluid has my body become, forming even at the touch of a finger into one full drop, which fills itself, which quivers, which flashes, which falls in ecstasy.

'I have sat before a looking-glass as you sit writing, adding up figures at desks. So, before the looking-glass in the temple of my bedroom, I have judged my nose and my chin; my lips that open too wide and show too much gum. I have looked. I have noted. I have chosen what yellow or white, what shine or dullness, what loop or straightness suits. I am volatile for one, rigid for another, angular as an icicle in silver, or voluptuous as a candle flame in gold. I have run violently like a whip flung out to the extreme end of my tether. His shirt front, there in the corner, has been white; then purple; smoke and flame have wrapped us about; after a furious conflagration—yet we scarcely raised our voices, sitting on the hearth-rug, as we murmured all the secrets of our hearts as into shells so that nobody might hear in the sleeping-house, but I heard the cook stir once, and once we thought the ticking of the clock was a footfall—we have sunk to ashes, leaving no relics, no unburnt bones, no wisps of hair to be kept in lockets such as your intimacies leave behind them. Now I turn grey; now I turn gaunt; but I look at my face at midday sitting in front of the looking-glass in broad daylight, and note precisely my nose, my chin, my lips that open too wide and show too much gum. But I am not afraid.'

'There were lamp-posts,' said Rhoda, 'and trees that had not yet shed their leaves on the way from the station. The leaves might have hidden me still. But I did not hide behind them. I walked straight up to you instead of circling round to avoid the shock of sensation as I used. But it is only that I have taught my body to do a certain trick. Inwardly I am not taught; I fear, I hate, I love, I envy and despise you, but I never join you happily. Coming up from the station, refusing to accept the shadow of the trees and the pillar-boxes, I perceived, from your coats and umbrellas, even at a distance, how you stand embedded in a substance made of repeated moments run together; are committed, have an attitude, with children, authority, fame, love, society; where I have nothing. I have no face.

'Here in this dining-room you see the antlers and the tumblers; the salt-cellars; the yellow stains on the tablecloth. "Waiter!" says Bernard. "Bread!" says Susan. And the waiter comes; he brings bread. But I see the side of a cup like a mountain and only parts of antlers, and the brightness on the side of that jug like a crack in darkness with wonder and terror. Your voices sound like trees creaking in a forest. So with your faces and their prominences and hollows. How beautiful, standing at a distance immobile at midnight against the railings of some square! Behind you is a white crescent of foam, and fishermen on the verge of the world are drawing in nets and casting them. A wind ruffles the topmost leaves of primeval trees. (Yet here we sit at Hampton Court.) Parrots shrieking break the intense stillness of the jungle. (Here the trams start.) The swallow dips her wings in midnight pools. (Here we talk.) That is the circumference that I try to grasp as we sit together. Thus I must undergo the penance of Hampton Court at seven thirty precisely.

'But since these rolls of bread and wine bottles are needed by me, and your faces with their hollows and prominences are beautiful, and the table-cloth and its yellow stain, far from being allowed to spread in wider and wider circles of

535

understanding that may at last (so I dream, falling off the edge of the earth at night when my bed floats suspended) embrace the entire world, I must go through the antics of the individual. I must start when you pluck at me with your children, your poems, your chilblains or whatever it is that you do and suffer. But I am not deluded. After all these callings hither and thither, these pluckings and searchings, I shall fall alone through this thin sheet into gulfs of fire. And you will not help me. More cruel than the old torturers, you will let me fall, and will tear me to pieces when I am fallen. Yet there are moments when the walls of the mind grow thin; when nothing is unabsorbed, and I could fancy that we might blow so vast a bubble that the sun might set and rise in it and we might take the blue of midday and the black of midnight and be cast off and escape from here and now.'

'Drop upon drop,' said Bernard, 'silence falls. It forms on the roof of the mind and falls into pools beneath. For ever alone, alone, alone,—hear silence fall and sweep its rings to the farthest edges. Gorged and replete, solid with middle-aged content, I, whom loneliness destroys, let silence fall, drop by drop.

'But now silence falling pits my face, wastes my nose like a snowman stood out in a yard in the rain. As silence falls I am dissolved utterly and become featureless and scarcely to be distinguished from another. It does not matter. What matters? We have dined well. The fish, the veal cutlets, the wine have blunted the sharp tooth of egotism. Anxiety is at rest. The vainest of us, Louis perhaps, does not care what people think. Neville's tortures are at rest. Let others prosper—that is what he thinks. Susan hears the breathing of all her children safe asleep. Sleep, sleep, she murmurs. Rhoda has rocked her ships to shore. Whether they have foundered, whether they have anchored, she cares no longer. We are ready to consider any suggestion that the world may offer quite impartially. I reflect now that the earth is only a pebble flicked off accidentally from the face of the sun and that there is no life anywhere in the abysses of space.'

'In this silence,' said Susan, 'it seems as if no leaf would ever fall, or bird fly.'

'As if the miracle had happened,' said Jinny, 'and life were stayed here and now.'

'And,' said Rhoda, 'we had no more to live.'

'But listen,' said Louis, 'to the world moving through abysses of infinite space. It roars; the lighted strip of history is past and our Kings and Queens; we are gone; our civilization; the Nile; and all life. Our separate drops are dissolved; we are extinct, lost in the abysses of time, in the darkness.'

'Silence falls; silence falls,' said Bernard. 'But now listen; tick, tick; hoot, hoot; the world has hailed us back to it. I heard for one moment the howling winds of darkness as we passed beyond life. Then tick, tick (the clock); then hoot, hoot (the cars). We are landed; we are on shore; we are sitting, six of us, at a table. It is the memory of my nose that recalls me. I rise; "Fight," I cry, "fight!" remembering the shape of my own nose, and strike with this spoon upon this table pugnaciously.'

'Oppose ourselves to this illimitable chaos,' said Neville, 'this formless imbecility. Making love to a nursemaid behind a tree, that soldier is more admirable than all the stars. Yet sometimes one trembling star comes in the clear sky and makes me think the world beautiful and we maggots deforming even the trees with our lust.'

('Yet, Louis,' said Rhoda, 'how short a time silence lasts. Already they are beginning to smooth their napkins by the side of their plates. "Who comes?" says Jinny; and Neville sighs, remembering that Percival comes no more. Jinny has taken out her looking-glass. Surveying her face like an artist, she draws a powder-puff down her nose, and after one moment of deliberation has given precisely that red to the lips that the lips need. Susan, who feels scorn and fear at the sight of these preparations, fastens the top button of her coat, and unfastens it. What is she making ready for? For something, but something different.'

'They are saying to themselves,' said Louis, '"It is time. I am still vigorous," they are saying. "My face shall be cut against the black of infinite space." They do not finish their sentences. "It is time," they keep saying. "The gardens will be shut." And going with them, Rhoda, swept into their current, we shall perhaps drop a little behind.'

'Like conspirators who have something to whisper,' said Rhoda.)

'It is true, and I know for a fact,' said Bernard, 'as we walk down this avenue, that a King, riding, fell over a molehill here. But how strange it seems to set against the whirling abysses of infinite space a little figure with a golden teapot on his head. Soon one recovers belief in figures: but not at once in what they put on their heads. Our English past—one inch of light. Then people put teapots on their heads and say, "I am a King!" No, I try to recover, as we walk, the sense of time, but with that streaming darkness in my eyes I have lost my grip. This Palace seems light as a cloud set for a moment on the sky. It is a trick of the mind— to put Kings on their thrones, one following another, with crowns on their heads. And we ourselves, walking six abreast, what do we oppose, with this random flicker of light in us that we call brain and feeling, how can we do battle against this flood; what has permanence? Our lives too stream away, down the unlighted avenues, past the strip of time, unidentified. Once Neville threw a poem at my head. Feeling a sudden conviction of immortality, I said, "I too know what Shakespeare knew." But that has gone.'

'Unreasonably, ridiculously,' said Neville, 'as we walk, time comes back. A dog does it, prancing. The machine works. Age makes hoary that gateway. Three hundred years now seem no more than a moment vanished against that dog. King William mounts his horse wearing a wig, and the court ladies sweep the turf with their embroidered panniers. I am beginning to be convinced, as we walk, that the fate of Europe is of immense importance, and, ridiculous as it still seems, that all depends upon the battle of Blenheim. Yes; I declare, as we pass through this gateway, it is the present moment; I am become a subject of King George.'

'While we advance down this avenue,' said Louis, 'I leaning slightly upon Jinny, Bernard arm-in-arm with Neville, and Susan with her hand in mine, it is difficult not to weep, calling ourselves little children, praying that God may keep us safe while we sleep. It is sweet to sing together, clasping hands, afraid of the dark, while Miss Curry plays the harmonium.'

'The iron gates have rolled back,' said Jinny. 'Time's fangs have ceased their devouring. We have triumphed over the abysses of space, with rouge, with powder, with flimsy pocket-handkerchiefs.'

'I grasp, I hold fast,' said Susan. 'I hold firmly to this hand, anyone's, with love, with hatred; it does not matter which.'

'The still mood, the disembodied mood is on us,' said Rhoda, 'and we enjoy this momentary alleviation (it is not often that one has no anxiety) when the walls of the mind become transparent. Wren's palace, like the quartet played to the dry and stranded people in the stalls, makes an oblong. A square is stood upon the oblong and we say, "This is our dwelling-place. The structure is now visible. Very little is left outside."'

'The flower,' said Bernard, 'the red carnation that stood in the vase on the table of the restaurant when we dined together with Percival, is become a six-sided flower; made of six lives.'

'A mysterious illumination,' said Louis, 'visible against those yew trees.'

'Built up with much pain, many strokes,' said Jinny.

'Marriage, death, travel, friendship,' said Bernard; 'town and country; children and all that; a many-sided substance cut out of this dark; a many-faceted flower. Let us stop for a moment; let us behold what we have made. Let it blaze against the yew trees. One life. There. It is over. Gone out.'

'Now they vanish,' said Louis. 'Susan with Bernard. Neville with Jinny. You and I, Rhoda, stop for a moment by this stone urn. What song shall we hear now that these couples have sought the groves, and Jinny, pointing with her gloved hand, pretends to notice the water-lilies, and Susan, who has always loved Bernard, says to him, "My ruined life, my wasted life." And Neville, taking Jinny's little hand, with the cherry-coloured finger-nails, by the lake, by the moonlit water, cries, "Love, love," and she answers, imitating the bird, "Love, love?" What song do we hear?'

'They vanish, towards the lake,' said Rhoda. 'They slink away over the grass furtively, yet with assurance as if they asked of our pity their ancient privilege—not to be disturbed. The tide in the soul, tipped, flows that way; they cannot help deserting us. The dark has closed over their bodies. What song do we hear— the owl's, the nightingale's, the wren's? The steamer hoots; the light on the electric rails flashes; the trees gravely bow and bend. The flare hangs over London. Here is an old woman, quietly returning, and a man, a late fisherman, comes down the terrace with his rod. Not a sound, not a movement must escape us.'

'A bird flies homeward,' said Louis. 'Evening opens her eyes and gives one quick glance among the bushes before she sleeps. How shall we put it together, the confused and composite message that they send back to us, and not they only, but many dead, boys and girls, grown men and women, who have wandered here, under one king or another?'

'A weight has dropped into the night,' said Rhoda, 'dragging it down. Every tree is big with a shadow that is not the shadow of the tree behind it. We hear a drumming on the roofs of a fasting city when the Turks are hungry and uncertain tempered. We hear them crying with sharp, stag-like barks, "Open, open." Listen to the trams squealing and to the flashes from the electric rails. We hear the beech trees and the birch trees raise their branches as if the bride had let her silken nightdress fall and come to the doorway saying "Open, open".'

'All seems alive,' said Louis. 'I cannot hear death anywhere tonight. Stupidity, on that man's face, age, on that woman's, would be strong enough, one would think, to resist the incantation, and bring in death. But where is death tonight? All the crudity, odds and ends, this and that, have been crushed like glass splinters into the blue, the red-fringed tide, which, drawing into the shore, fertile with innumerable fish, breaks at our feet.'

'If we could mount together, if we could perceive from a sufficient height,' said Rhoda, 'if we could remain untouched without any support—but you, disturbed by faint clapping sounds of praise and laughter, and I, resenting compromise and right and wrong on human lips, trust only in solitude and the violence of death and thus are divided.'

'For ever,' said Louis, 'divided. We have sacrificed the embrace among the ferns, and love, love, love by the lake, standing, like conspirators who have drawn apart to share some secret, by the urn. But now look, as we stand here, a ripple breaks on the horizon. The net is raised higher and higher. It comes to the top of the water. The water is broken by silver, by quivering little fish. Now leaping, now lashing, they are laid on shore. Life tumbles its catch upon the grass. There are figures coming towards us. Are they men or are they women? They still wear the ambiguous draperies of the flowing tide in which they have been immersed.'

'Now,' said Rhoda, 'as they pass that tree, they regain their natural size. They are only men, only women. Wonder and awe change as they put off the draperies of the flowing tide. Pity returns, as they emerge into the moonlight, like the relics of an army, our representatives, going every night (here or in Greece) to battle, and coming back every night with their wounds, their ravaged faces. Now light falls on them again. They have faces. They become Susan and Bernard, Jinny and Neville, people we know. Now what a shrinkage takes place! Now what a shrivelling, what an humiliation! The old shivers run through me, hatred and terror, as I feel myself grappled to one spot by these hooks they cast on us; these greetings, recognitions, pluckings of the finger and searchings of the eyes. Yet they have only to speak, and their first words, with the remembered tone and the perpetual deviation from what one expects, and their hands moving and making a thousand past days rise again in the darkness, shake my purpose.'

'Something flickers and dances,' said Louis. 'Illusion returns as they approach down the avenue. Rippling and questioning begin. What do I think of you—what do you think of me? Who are you? Who am I?—that quivers again its uneasy air over us, and the pulse quickens and the eye brightens and all the insanity of personal existence without which life would fall flat and die, begins again. They are on us. The southern sun flickers over this urn; we push off in to the tide of the violent and cruel sea. Lord help us to act our parts as we greet them returning—Susan and Bernard, Neville and Jinny.'

'We have destroyed something by our presence,' said Bernard, 'a world perhaps.'

'Yet we scarcely breathe,' said Neville, 'spent as we are. We are in that passive and exhausted frame of mind when we only wish to rejoin the body of our mother from whom we have been severed. All else is distasteful, forced and fatiguing. Jinny's yellow scarf is moth-coloured in this light; Susan's eyes are quenched. We are scarcely to be distinguished from the river. One cigarette end is the only point of emphasis among us. And sadness tinges our content, that we should have left you, torn the fabric; yielded to the desire to press out, alone, some bitterer, some blacker juice, which was sweet too. But now we are worn out.'

'After our fire,' said Jinny, 'there is nothing left to put in lockets.'

'Still I gape,' said Susan, 'like a young bird, unsatisfied, for something that has escaped me.'

'Let us stay for a moment,' said Bernard, 'before we go. Let us pace the terrace by the river almost alone. It is nearly bed-time. People have gone home. Now how comforting it is to watch the lights coming out in the bedrooms of small shopkeepers on the other side of the river. There is one—there is another. What do you think their takings have been today? Only just enough to pay for the rent, for light and food and the children's clothing. But just enough. What a sense of the tolerableness of life the lights in the bedrooms of small shopkeepers give us! Saturday comes, and there is just enough to pay perhaps for seats at the Pictures. Perhaps before they put out the light they go into the little garden and look at the giant rabbit couched in its wooden hut. That is the rabbit they will have for Sunday dinner. Then they put out the light. Then they sleep. And for thousands of people sleep is nothing but warmth and silence and one moment's sport with some fantastic dream. "I have posted my letter," the greengrocer thinks, "to the Sunday newspaper. Suppose I win five hundred pounds in the football competition? And we shall kill the rabbit. Life is pleasant. Life is good. I have posted the letter. We shall kill the rabbit." And he sleeps.

'That goes on. Listen. There is a sound like the knocking of railway trucks in a siding. That is the happy concatenation of one event following another in our lives. Knock, knock, knock. Must, must, must. Must go, must sleep, must wake, must get up—sober, merciful word which we pretend to revile, which we press tight to our hearts, without which we should be undone. How we worship that sound like the knocking together of trucks in a siding!

'Now far off down the river I hear the chorus; the song of the boasting boys, who are coming back in large charabancs from a day's outing on the decks of crowded steamers. Still they are singing as they used to sing, across the court, on winters' nights, or with the windows open in summer, getting drunk, breaking the furniture, wearing little striped caps, all turning their heads the same way as the brake rounded the corner; and I wished to be with them.

'What with the chorus, and the spinning water and the just perceptible murmur of the breeze we are slipping away. Little bits of ourselves are crumbling. There! Something very important fell then. I cannot keep myself together. I shall sleep.

But we must go; must catch our train; must walk back to the station—must, must, must. We are only bodies jogging along side by side. I exist only in the soles of my feet and in the tired muscles of my thighs. We have been walking for hours it seems. But where? I cannot remember. I am like a log slipping smoothly over some waterfall. I am not a judge. I am not called upon to give my opinion. Houses and trees are all the same in this grey light. Is that a post? Is that a woman walking? Here is the station, and if the train were to cut me in two, I should come together on the further side, being one, being indivisible. But what is odd is that I still clasp the return half of my ticket to Waterloo firmly between the fingers of my right hand, even now, even sleeping.'

Now the sun had sunk. Sky and sea were indistinguishable. The waves breaking spread their white fans far out over the shore, sent white shadows into the recesses of sonorous caves and then rolled back sighing over the shingle.

The tree shook its branches and a scattering of leaves fell to the ground. There they settled with perfect composure on the precise spot where they would await dissolution. Black and grey were shot into the garden from the broken vessel that had once held red light. Dark shadows blackened the tunnels between the stalks. The thrush was silent and the worm sucked itself back into its narrow hole. Now and again a whitened and hollow straw was blown from an old nest and fell into the dark grasses among the rotten apples. The light had faded from the tool-house wall and the adder's skin hung from the nail empty. All the colours in the room had overflown their banks. The precise brush stroke was swollen and lop-sided; cupboards and chairs melted their brown masses into one huge obscurity. The height from floor to ceiling was hung with vast curtains of shaking darkness. The looking-glass was pale as the mouth of a cave shadowed by hanging creepers.

The substance had gone from the solidity of the hills. Travelling lights drove a plumy wedge among unseen and sunken roads, but no lights opened among the folded wings of the hills, and there was no sound save the cry of a bird seeking some lonelier tree. At the cliff's edge there was an equal murmur of air that had been brushed through forests, of water that had been cooled in a thousand glassy hollows of mid-ocean.

As if there were waves of darkness in the air, darkness moved on, covering houses, hills, trees, as waves of water wash round the sides of some sunken ship. Darkness washed down streets, eddying round single figures, engulfing them; blotting out couples clasped under the showery darkness of elm trees in full summer foliage. Darkness rolled its waves along grassy rides and over the wrinkled skin of the turf, enveloping the solitary thorn tree and the empty snail shells at its foot. Mounting higher, darkness blew along the bare upland slopes, and met the fretted and abraded pinnacles of the mountain where the snow lodges for ever on the hard rock even when the valleys are full of running streams and yellow vine leaves, and girls, sitting on verandahs, look up at the snow, shading their faces with their fans. Them, too, darkness covered.

'Now to sum up,' said Bernard. 'Now to explain to you the meaning of my life. Since we do not know each other (though I met you once, I think, on board a ship going to Africa), we can talk freely. The illusion is upon me that something adheres for a moment, has roundness, weight, depth, is completed. This, for the moment, seems to be my life. If it were possible, I would hand it to you entire. I would break it off as one breaks off a bunch of grapes. I would say, "Take it. This is my life."

'But unfortunately, what I see (this globe, full of figures) you do not see. You see me, sitting at a table opposite you, a rather heavy, elderly man, grey at the temples. You see me take my napkin and unfold it. You see me pour myself out a glass of wine. And you see behind me the door opening, and people passing. But in order to make you understand, to give you my life, I must tell you a story—and there are so many, and so many—stories of childhood, stories of school, love, marriage, death, and so on; and none of them are true. Yet like children we

545

tell each other stories, and to decorate them we make up these ridiculous, flamboyant, beautiful phrases. How tired I am of stories, how tired I am of phrases that come down beautifully with all their feet on the ground! Also, how I distrust neat designs of life that are drawn upon half-sheets of note-paper. I begin to long for some little language such as lovers use, broken words, inarticulate words, like the shuffling of feet on the pavement. I begin to seek some design more in accordance with those moments of humiliation and triumph that come now and then undeniably. Lying in a ditch on a stormy day, when it has been raining, then enormous clouds come marching over the sky, tattered clouds, wisps of cloud. What delights me then is the confusion, the height, the indifference and the fury. Great clouds always changing, and movement; something sulphurous and sinister, bowled up, helter-skelter; towering, trailing, broken off, lost, and I forgotten, minute, in a ditch. Of story, of design, I do not see a trace then.

'But meanwhile, while we eat, let us turn over these scenes as children turn over the pages of a picture-book and the nurse says, pointing: "That's a cow. That's a boat." Let us turn over the pages, and I will add, for your amusement, a comment in the margin.

'In the beginning, there was the nursery, with windows opening on to a garden, and beyond that the sea. I saw something brighten—no doubt the brass handle of a cupboard. Then Mrs Constable raised the sponge above her head, squeezed it, and out shot, right, left, all down the spine, arrows of sensation. And so, as long as we draw breath, for the rest of time, if we knock against a chair, a table, or a woman, we are pierced with arrows of sensation—if we walk in a garden, if we drink this wine. Sometimes indeed, when I pass a cottage with a light in the window where a child has been born, I could implore them not to squeeze the sponge over that new body. Then, there was the garden and the canopy of the currant leaves which seemed to enclose everything; flowers, burning like sparks upon the depths of green; a rat wreathing with maggots under a rhubarb leaf; the fly going buzz, buzz, buzz upon the nursery ceiling, and plates upon plates of innocent bread and butter. All these things happen in one second and last for ever. Faces loom. Dashing round the corner. "Hullo," one says, "there's Jinny. That's Neville. That's Louis in grey flannel with a snake belt. That's Rhoda." She had a basin in which she sailed petals of white flowers. It was Susan who cried, that day when I was in the tool-house with Neville; and I felt my indifference melt. Neville did not melt. "Therefore," I said, "I am myself, not Neville", a wonderful discovery. Susan cried and I followed her. Her wet pocket-handkerchief, and the sight of her little back heaving up and down like a pump-handle, sobbing for what was denied her, screwed my nerves up. "That is not to be borne," I said, as I sat beside her on the roots that were hard as skeletons. I then first became aware of the presence of those enemies who change, but are always there; the forces we fight against. To let oneself be carried on passively is unthinkable. "That's your course, world," one says, "mine is this." So, "Let's explore," I cried, and jumped up, and ran downhill with Susan and saw the stable-boy clattering about the yard in great boots. Down below, through the depths of the leaves, the gardeners swept the lawns with great brooms. The lady sat writing. Transfixed, stopped dead, I thought, "I cannot interfere with a single stroke of those brooms. They sweep and they sweep. Nor with the fixity of that woman writing." It is strange that one cannot stop gardeners sweeping nor dislodge a woman. There they have remained all my life. It is as if one had woken in Stonehenge surrounded by a circle of great stones, these enemies, these presences. Then a wood-pigeon flew out of the trees. And being in love for the first time, I made a phrase—a poem about a wood-pigeon—a single phrase, for a hole had been knocked in my mind, one of those sudden transparencies through which one sees everything. Then more bread and butter and more flies droning round the nursery ceiling on which quivered islands of light, ruffled, opalescent, while the pointed fingers of the lustre dripped blue pools on the corner of the mantelpiece. Day after day as we sat at tea we observed these sights.

'But we were all different. The wax—the virginal wax that coats the spine melted in different patches for each of us. The growl of the boot-boy making love to the tweeny among the gooseberry bushes; the clothes blown out hard on the line; the dead man in the gutter; the apple tree, stark in the moonlight; the rat swarming with maggots; the lustre dripping blue—our white wax was streaked and stained by each of these differently. Louis was disgusted by the nature of human flesh; Rhoda by our cruelty; Susan could not share; Neville wanted order; Jinny love; and so on. We suffered terribly as we became separate bodies.

'Yet I was preserved from these excesses and have survived many of my friends, am a little stout, grey, rubbed on the thorax as it were, because it is the panorama of life, seen not from the roof, but from the third-storey window, that delights me, not what one woman says to one man, even if that man is myself. How could I be bullied at school therefore? How could they make things hot for me? There was the Doctor lurching into chapel, as if he trod a battleship in a gale of wind, shouting out his commands through a megaphone, since people in authority always become melodramatic—I did not hate him like Neville, or revere him like Louis. I took notes as we sat together in chapel. There were pillars, shadows, memorial brasses, boys scuffling and swopping stamps behind Prayer Books; the sound of a rusty pump; the Doctor booming, about immortality and quitting ourselves like men; and Percival scratching his thigh. I made notes for stories; drew portraits in the margin of my pocket-book and thus became still more separate. Here are one or two of the figures I saw.

'Percival sat staring straight ahead of him that day in chapel. He also had a way of flicking his hand to the back of his neck. His movements were always remarkable. We all flicked our hands to the backs of our heads—unsuccessfully. He had the kind of beauty which defends itself from any caress. As he was not in the least precocious, he read whatever was written up for our edification without any comment, and thought with that magnificent equanimity (Latin words come naturally) that was to preserve him from so many meannesses and humiliations, that Lucy's flaxen pigtails and pink cheeks were the height of female beauty. Thus preserved, his taste later was of extreme fineness. But there should be music, some wild carol. Through the window should come a hunting-song from some rapid unapprehended life—a sound that shouts among the hills and dies away. What is startling, what is unexpected, what we cannot account for, what turns symmetry to nonsense—that comes suddenly to my mind, thinking of him. The little apparatus of observation is unhinged. Pillars go down; the Doctor floats off; some sudden exaltation possesses me. He was thrown, riding in a race, and when I came along Shaftesbury Avenue tonight, those insignificant and scarcely formulated faces that bubble up out of the doors of the Tube, and many obscure Indians, and people dying of famine and disease, and women who have been cheated, and whipped dogs and crying children—all these seemed to me bereft. He would have done justice. He would have protected. About the age of forty he would have shocked the authorities. No lullaby has ever occurred to me capable of singing him to rest.

'But let me dip again and bring up in my spoon another of these minute objects which we call optimistically, "characters of our friends"—Louis. He sat staring at the preacher. His being seemed conglobulated in his brow, his lips were pressed; his eyes were fixed, but suddenly they flashed with laughter. Also he suffered from chilblains, the penalty of an imperfect circulation. Unhappy, unfriended, in exile he would sometimes, in moments of confidence, describe how the surf swept over the beaches of his home. The remorseless eye of youth fixed itself upon his swollen joints. Yes, but we were also quick to perceive how cutting, how apt, how severe he was, how naturally, when we lay under the elm trees pretending to watch cricket, we waited his approval, seldom given. His ascendancy was resented, as Percival's was adored. Prim, suspicious, lifting his feet like a crane, there was yet a legend that he had smashed a door with his naked fist. But his peak was too bare, too stony for that kind of mist to cling to it. He was without those simple attachments by which one is connected with another. He remained aloof; enigmatic; a scholar capable of that inspired accuracy which has something formidable about it. My phrases (how to describe the moon) did not meet with his approval. On the other hand, he envied me to the point of desperation for being at my ease with servants. Not that the sense of his own deserts failed him. That was commensurate with his respect for discipline. Hence his success, finally. His life, though, was not happy. But look—his eye turns white as he lies in the palm of my hand. Suddenly the sense of what people are leaves one. I return him to the pool where he will acquire lustre.

'Neville next—lying on his back staring up at the summer sky. He floated among us like a piece of thistledown, indolently haunting the sunny corner of the playing-field, not listening, yet not remote. It was through him that I have nosed round without ever precisely touching the Latin classics and have also derived some of those persistent habits of thought which make us irredeemably lop-sided—for instance about crucifixes, that they are the mark of the devil. Our half-loves and half-hates and ambiguities on these points were to him indefensible treacheries. The swaying and sonorous Doctor, whom I made to sit swinging his braces over a gas-fire, was to him nothing but an instrument of the inquisition. So he turned with a passion that made up for his indolence upon Catullus, Horace, Lucretius, lying lazily dormant, yes, but regardant, noticing, with rapture, cricketers, while with a mind like the tongue of an ant-eater, rapid, dexterous, glutinous, he searched out every curl and twist of those Roman sentences, and sought out one person, always one person to sit beside.

'And the long skirts of the masters' wives would come swishing by, mountainous, menacing; and our hands would fly to our caps. And immense dullness would descend unbroken, monotonous. Nothing, nothing, nothing broke with its fin that leaden waste of waters. Nothing would happen to lift that weight of intolerable boredom. The terms went on. We grew; we changed; for, of course, we are animals. We are not always aware by any means; we breathe, eat, sleep automatically. We exist not only separately but in undifferentiated blobs of matter. With one scoop a whole brakeful of boys is swept up and goes cricketing, footballing. An army marches across Europe. We assemble in parks and halls and sedulously oppose any renegade (Neville, Louis, Rhoda) who sets up a separate existence. And I am so made that, while I hear one or two distinct melodies, such as Louis sings, or Neville, I am also drawn irresistibly to the sound of the chorus chanting its old, chanting its almost wordless, almost senseless song that comes across courts at night; which we hear now booming round us as cars and omnibuses take people to theatres. (Listen; the cars rush past this restaurant; now and then, down the river, a siren hoots, as a steamer makes for the sea.) If a bagman offers me snuff in a train I accept. I like the copious, shapeless, warm, not so very clever, but extremely easy and rather coarse aspect of things; the talk of men in clubs and public-houses, of miners half naked in drawers— the forthright, perfectly unassuming, and without end in view except dinner, love, money and getting along tolerably; that which is without great hopes, ideals or anything of that kind; what is unassuming except to make a tolerably good job of it. I like all that. So I joined them, when Neville sulked or Louis, as I quite agree sublimely, turned on his heel.

'Thus, not equally by any means or with order, but in great streaks my waxen waistcoat melted, here one drop, there another. Now through this transparency became visible those wondrous pastures, at first so moon-white, radiant, where no foot has been; meadows of the rose, the crocus, of the rock and the snake too; of the spotted and swart; the embarrassing, the binding and tripping up. One leaps out of bed, throws up the window; with what a whirr the birds rise! You know that sudden rush of wings, that exclamation, carol, and confusion; the riot and babble of voices; and all the drops are sparkling, trembling, as if the garden were a splintered mosaic, vanishing, twinkling; not yet formed into one whole; and a bird sings close to the window. I heard those songs. I followed those phantoms. I saw Joans, Dorothys, Miriams, I forget their names, passing down avenues, stopping on the crest of bridges to look down into the river. And from among them rise one or two distinct figures, birds who sang with the rapt egotism of youth by the window; broke their snails on stones, dipped their beaks in sticky, viscous matter; hard, avid, remorseless; Jinny, Susan, Rhoda. They had been educated on the east coast or on the south coast. They had grown long pigtails and acquired the look of startled foals, which is the mark of adolescence.

'Jinny was the first to come sidling up to the gate to eat sugar. She nipped it off the palms of one's hands very cleverly, but her ears were laid back as if she might bite. Rhoda was wild—Rhoda one never could catch. She was both frightened and clumsy. It was Susan who first became wholly woman, purely feminine. It was she who dropped on my face those scalding tears which are terrible, beautiful; both, neither. She was born to be the adored of poets, since poets require safety; someone who sits sewing, who says, "I hate, I love," who is neither comfortable nor prosperous, but has some quality in accordance with the high but unemphatic beauty of pure style which those who create poetry so particularly admire. Her father trailed from room to room and down flagged corridors in his flapping dressing-gown and worn slippers. On still nights a wall of water fell with a roar a mile off. The ancient dog could scarcely heave himself up on to his chair. And some witless servant could be heard laughing at the top of the house as she whirred the wheel of the sewing-machine round and round.

'That I observed even in the midst of my anguish when, twisting her pocket-handkerchief, Susan cried, "I love; I hate." "A worthless servant," I observed, "laughs upstairs in the attic," and that little piece of dramatization shows how incompletely we are merged in our own experiences. On the outskirts of every agony sits some observant fellow who points; who whispers as he whispered to me that summer morning in the house where the corn comes up to the window, "The willow grows on the turf by the river. The gardeners sweep with great brooms and the lady sits writing." Thus he directed me to that which is beyond and outside our own predicament; to that which is symbolic, and thus perhaps permanent, if there is any permanence in our sleeping, eating, breathing, so animal, so spiritual and tumultuous lives.

'The willow tree grew by the river. I sat on the smooth turf with Neville, with Larpent, with Baker, Romsey, Hughes, Percival and Jinny. Through its fine plumes specked with little pricked ears of green in spring, of orange in autumn, I saw boats; buildings; I saw hurrying, decrepit women. I buried match after match in the turf decidedly to mark this or that stage in the process of understanding (it might be philosophy; science; it might be myself) while the fringe of my intelligence floating unattached caught those distant sensations which after a time the mind draws in and works upon; the chime of bells; general murmurs; vanishing figures; one girl on a bicycle who, as she rode, seemed to lift the corner of a curtain concealing the populous undifferentiated chaos of life which surged behind the outlines of my friends and the willow tree.

'The tree alone resisted our eternal flux. For I changed and changed; was Hamlet, was Shelley, was the hero, whose name I now forget, of a novel by Dostoevsky; was for a whole term, incredibly, Napoleon; but was Byron chiefly. For many weeks at a time it was my part to stride into rooms and fling gloves and coat on the back of chairs, scowling slightly. I was always going to the bookcase for another sip of the divine specific. Therefore,

I let fly my tremendous battery of phrases upon somebody quite inappropriate—a girl now married, now buried; every book, every window-seat was littered with the sheets of my unfinished letters to the woman who made me Byron. For it is difficult to finish a letter in somebody else's style. I arrived all in a lather at her house; exchanged tokens but did not marry her, being no doubt unripe for that intensity.

'Here again there should be music. Not that wild hunting-song, Percival's music; but a painful, guttural, visceral, also soaring, lark-like, pealing song to replace these flagging, foolish transcripts—how much too deliberate! how much too reasonable!—which attempt to describe the flying moment of first love. A purple slide is slipped over the day. Look at a room before she comes and after. Look at the innocents outside pursuing their way. They neither see nor hear; yet on they go. Moving oneself in this radiant yet gummy atmosphere how conscious one is of every movement—something adheres, something sticks to one's hands, taking up a newspaper even. Then there is the being eviscerated—drawn out, spun like a spider's web and twisted in agony round a thorn. Then a thunder-clap of complete indifference; the light blown out; then the return of measureless irresponsible joy; certain fields seem to glow green for ever, and innocent landscapes appear as if in the light of the first dawn—one patch of green, for example, up at Hampstead; and all faces are lit up, all conspire in a hush of tender joy; and then the mystic sense of completion and then that rasping, dog-fish skin-like roughness—those black arrows of shivering sensation, when she misses the post, when she does not come. Out rush a bristle of horned suspicions, horror, horror, horror—but what is the use of painfully elaborating these consecutive sentences when what one needs is nothing consecutive but a bark, a groan? And years later to see a middle-aged woman in a restaurant taking off her cloak.

'But to return. Let us again pretend that life is a solid substance, shaped like a globe, which we turn about in our fingers. Let us pretend that we can make out a plain and logical story, so that when one matter is despatched—love for instance—we go on, in an orderly manner, to the next. I was saying there was a willow tree. Its shower of falling branches, its creased and crooked bark had the effect of what remains outside our illusions yet cannot stay them, is changed by them for the moment, yet shows through stable, still, and with a sternness that our lives lack. Hence the comment it makes; the standard it supplies, and the reason why, as we flow and change, it seems to measure. Neville, for example, sat with me on the turf. But can anything be as clear as all that, I would say, following his gaze, through the branches, to a punt on the river, and a young man eating bananas from a paper bag? The scene was cut out with such intensity and so permeated with the quality of his vision that for a moment I could see it too; the punt, the bananas, the young man, through the branches of the willow tree. Then it faded.

'Rhoda came wandering vaguely. She would take advantage of any scholar in a blowing gown, or donkey rolling the turf with slippered feet to hide behind. What fear wavered and hid itself and blew to a flame in the depths of her grey, her startled, her dreaming eyes? Cruel and vindictive as we are, we are not bad to that extent. We have our fundamental goodness surely or to talk as I talk freely to someone I hardly know would be impossible—we should cease. The willow as she saw it grew on the verge of a grey desert where no bird sang. The leaves shrivelled as she looked at them, tossed in agony as she passed them. The trams and omnibuses roared hoarse in the street ran over rocks and sped foaming away. Perhaps one pillar, sunlit, stood in her desert by a pool where wild beasts come down stealthily to drink.

'Then Jinny came. She flashed her fire over the tree. She was like a crinkled poppy, febrile, thirsty with the desire to drink dry dust. Darting, angular, not in the least impulsive, she came prepared. So little flames zigzag over the cracks in the dry earth. She made the willows dance, but not with illusion; for she saw nothing that was not there. It was a tree; there was the river; it was afternoon; here we were; I in my serge suit; she in green. There was no past, no future; merely the moment in its ring of light, and our bodies; and the inevitable climax, the ecstasy.

'Louis, when he let himself down on the grass, cautiously spreading (I do not exaggerate) a mackintosh square, made one acknowledge his presence. It was formidable. I had the intelligence to salute his integrity; his research with bony fingers wrapped in rags because of chilblains for some diamond of indissoluble veracity. I buried boxes of burnt matches in holes in the turf at his feet. His grim and caustic tongue reproved my indolence. He fascinated me with his sordid imagination. His heroes wore bowler-hats and talked about selling pianos for tenners. Through his landscape the tram squealed; the factory poured its acrid fumes. He haunted mean streets and towns where women lay drunk, naked, on counterpanes on Christmas day. His words falling from a shot-tower hit the water and up it spurted. He found one word, one only for the moon. Then he got up and went; we all got up; we all went. But I, pausing, looked at the tree, and as I looked in autumn at the fiery and yellow branches, some sediment formed; I formed; a drop fell; I fell—that is, from some completed experience I had emerged.

'I rose and walked away—I, I, I; not Byron, Shelley, Dostoevsky, but I, Bernard. I even repeated my own name once or twice. I went, swinging my stick, into a shop, and bought—not that I love music—a picture of Beethoven in a silver frame. Not that I love music, but because the whole of life, its masters, its adventurers, then appeared in long ranks of magnificent human beings behind me; and I was the inheritor; I, the continuer; I, the person miraculously appointed to carry it on. So, swinging my stick, with my eyes filmed, not with pride, but with humility rather, I walked down the street. The first whirr of wings had gone up, the carol, the exclamation; and now one enters; one goes into the house, the dry, uncompromising, inhabited house, the place with all its traditions, its objects, its accumulations of rubbish, and treasures displayed upon tables. I visited the family tailor, who remembered my uncle. People turned up in great quantities, not cut out, like the first faces (Neville, Louis, Jinny, Susan, Rhoda), but confused, featureless, or changed their features so fast that they seemed to have none. And blushing yet scornful, in the oddest condition of raw rapture and scepticism, I took the blow; the mixed sensations; the complex and disturbing and utterly unprepared for impacts of life all over, in all places, at the same time. How upsetting! How humiliating never to be sure what to say next, and those painful silences, glaring as dry deserts, with every pebble apparent; and then to say what one ought not to have said, and then to be conscious of a ramrod of incorruptible sincerity which one would willingly exchange for a shower of smooth pence, but could not, there at that party, where Jinny sat quite at her ease, rayed out on a gilt chair.

'Then says some lady with an impressive gesture, "Come with me." She leads one into a private alcove and admits one to the honour of her intimacy. Surnames change to Christian names; Christian names to nicknames. What is to be done about India, Ireland or Morocco? Old gentlemen answer the question standing decorated under chandeliers. One finds oneself surprisingly supplied with information. Outside the undifferentiated forces roar; inside we are very private, very explicit, have a sense indeed, that it is here, in this little room, that we make whatever day of the week it may be. Friday or Saturday. A shell forms upon the soft soul, nacreous, shiny, upon which sensations tap their beaks in vain. On me it formed earlier than on most. Soon I could carve my pear when other people had done dessert. I could bring my sentence to a close in a hush of complete silence. It is at that season too that perfection has a lure. One can learn Spanish, one thinks, by tying a string to the right toe and waking early. One fills up the little compartments of one's engagement book with dinner at eight; luncheon at one-thirty. One has shirts, socks, ties laid out on one's bed.

'But it is a mistake, this extreme precision, this orderly and military progress; a convenience, a lie. There is always deep below it, even when we arrive punctually at the appointed time with our white waistcoats and polite formalities, a rushing stream of broken dreams, nursery rhymes, street cries, half-finished sentences and sights—elm trees, willow trees, gardeners sweeping, women writing—that rise and sink even as we hand a lady down to dinner. While one straightens the fork so precisely on the table-cloth, a thousand faces mop and mow. There is nothing one can fish up in a spoon; nothing one can call an event. Yet it is alive too and deep, this stream. Immersed in it I would stop between one mouthful and the next, and look intently at a vase, perhaps with one red flower, while a reason struck me, a sudden revelation. Or I would say, walking along the Strand, "That's the phrase I want", as some beautiful, fabulous phantom bird, fish or cloud with fiery edges swam up to enclose once and for all some notion haunting me, after which on I trotted taking stock with renewed delight of ties and things in shop-windows.

'The crystal, the globe of life as one calls it, far from being hard and cold to the touch, has walls of thinnest air. If I press them all will burst. Whatever sentence I extract whole and entire from this cauldron is only a string of six little fish that let themselves be caught while a million others leap and sizzle, making the cauldron bubble like boiling silver, and slip through my fingers. Faces recur, faces and faces—they press their beauty to the walls of my bubble—Neville, Susan, Louis, Jinny, Rhoda and a thousand others. How impossible to order them rightly; to detach one separately, or to give the effect of the whole—again like music. What a symphony with its concord and its discord, and its tunes on top and its complicated bass beneath, then grew up! Each played his own tune, fiddle, flute, trumpet, drum or whatever the instrument might be. With Neville, "Let's discuss Hamlet." With Louis, science. With Jinny, love. Then suddenly, in a moment of exasperation, off to Cumberland with a quiet man for a whole week in an inn, with the rain running down the window-panes and nothing but mutton and mutton and again mutton for dinner. Yet that week remains a solid stone in the welter of unrecorded sensation. It was then we played dominoes; then we quarrelled about tough mutton. Then we walked on the fell. And a little girl, peeping round the door, gave me that letter, written on blue paper, in which I learnt that the girl who had made me Byron was to marry a squire. A man in gaiters, a man with a whip, a man who made speeches about fat oxen at dinner—I exclaimed derisively and looked at the racing clouds, and felt my own failure; my desire to be free; to escape; to be bound; to make an end; to continue; to be Louis; to be myself; and walked out in my mackintosh alone, and felt grumpy under the eternal hills and not in the least sublime; and came home and blamed the meat and packed and so back again to the welter; to the torture.

'Nevertheless, life is pleasant, life is tolerable. Tuesday follows Monday; then comes Wednesday. The mind grows rings; the identity becomes robust; pain is absorbed in growth. Opening and shutting, shutting and opening, with increasing hum and sturdiness, the haste and fever of youth are drawn into service until the whole being seems to expand in and out like the mainspring of a clock. How fast the stream flows from January to December! We are swept on by the torrent of things grown so familiar that they cast no shadow. We float, we float . . .

'However, since one must leap (to tell you this story), I leap, here, at this point, and alight now upon some perfectly commonplace object—say the poker and tongs, as I saw them sometime later, after that lady who had made me Byron had married, under the light of one whom I will call the third Miss Jones. She is the girl who wears a certain dress expecting one at dinner, who picks a certain rose, who makes one feel "Steady, steady, this is a matter of some importance", as one shaves. Then one asks, "How does she behave to children?" One observes that she is a little clumsy with her umbrella; but minded when the mole was caught in the trap; and finally, would not make the loaf at breakfast (I was thinking of the interminable breakfasts of married life as I shaved) altogether prosaic—it would not surprise one sitting opposite this girl to see a dragon-fly perched on the loaf at breakfast. Also she inspired me with a desire to rise in the world; also she made me look with curiosity at the hitherto repulsive faces of new-born babies. And the little fierce beat—tick-tack, tick-tack—of the pulse of one's mind took on a more majestic rhythm. I roamed down Oxford Street. We are the continuers, we are the inheritors, I said, thinking of my sons and daughters; and if the feeling is so grandiose as to be absurd and one conceals it by jumping on to a bus or buying the evening paper, it is still a curious element in the ardour with which one laces up one's boots, with which one now addresses old friends committed to different careers. Louis, the attic dweller; Rhoda, the nymph of the fountain always wet; both contradicted what was then so positive to me; both gave the other side of what seemed to me so evident (that we marry, that we domesticate); for which I loved them, pitied them, and also deeply envied them their different lot.

'Once I had a biographer, dead long since, but if he still followed my footsteps with his old flattering intensity he would here say, "About this time Bernard married and bought a house . . . His friends observed in him a growing tendency to domesticity . . . The birth of children made it highly desirable that he should augment his income." That is the biographic style, and it does to tack together torn bits of stuff, stuff with raw edges. After all, one cannot find fault with the biographic style if one begins letters "Dear Sir", ends them "your faithfully"; one cannot despise these phrases laid like Roman roads across the tumult of our lives, since they compel us to walk in step like civilized people with the slow and measured tread of policemen though one may be humming any nonsense under one's breath at the same time—"Hark, hark, the dogs do bark", "Come away, come away, death", "Let me not to the marriage of true minds", and so on. "He attained some success in his profession . . . He inherited a small sum of money from an uncle"—that is how the biographer continues, and if one wears trousers and hitches them up with braces, one has to say that, though it is tempting now and then to go blackberrying; tempting to play ducks and drakes with all these phrases. But one has to say that.

'I became, I mean, a certain kind of man, scoring my path across life as one treads a path across the fields. My boots became worn a little on the left side. When I came in, certain re-arrangements took place. "Here's Bernard!" How differently different people say that! There are many rooms—many Bernards. There was the charming, but weak; the strong, but supercilious; the brilliant, but remorseless; the very good fellow, but, I make no doubt, the awful bore; the sympathetic, but cold; the shabby, but—go into the next room—the foppish, worldly, and too well dressed. What I was to myself was different; was none of these. I am inclined to pin myself down most firmly there before the loaf at breakfast with my wife, who being now entirely my wife and not at all the girl who wore when she hoped to meet me a certain rose, gave me that feeling of existing in the midst of unconsciousness such as the tree-frog must have couched on the right shade of green leaf. "Pass" . . . I would say. "Milk" . . . she might answer, or "Mary's coming" . . . —simple words for those who have inherited the spoils of all the ages but not as said then, day after day, in the full tide of life, when one feels complete, entire, at breakfast. Muscles, nerves, intestines, blood-vessels, all that makes the coil and spring of our being, the unconscious hum of the engine, as well as the dart and flicker of the tongue, functioned superbly. Opening, shutting; shutting, opening; eating, drinking; sometimes speaking— the whole mechanism seemed to expand, to contract, like the mainspring of a clock. Toast and butter, coffee and bacon. *The Times* and letters—suddenly the telephone rang with urgency and I rose deliberately and went to the telephone. I took up the black mouth. I marked the ease with which my mind adjusted itself to assimilate the message—it might be (one has these fancies) to assume command of the British Empire; I observed my composure; I remarked with what magnificent vitality the atoms of my attention dispersed, swarmed round the interruption, assimilated the message, adapted themselves to a new state of affairs and had created, by the time I put back the receiver, a richer, stronger, a more complicated world in which I was called upon to act my part and had no doubt whatever that I could do it. Clapping my hat on my head, I strode into a world inhabited by vast numbers of men who had also clapped their hats on their heads, and as we jostled and encountered in trains and tubes we exchanged the knowing wink of competitors and comrades braced with a thousand snares and dodges to achieve the same end—to earn our livings.

'Life is pleasant. Life is good. The mere process of life is satisfactory. Take the ordinary man in good health. He likes eating and sleeping. He likes the snuff of fresh air and walking at a brisk pace down the Strand. Or in the country there's a cock crowing on a gate; there's a foal galloping round a field. Something always has to be done next. Tuesday follows Monday; Wednesday Tuesday. Each spreads the same ripple of wellbeing, repeats the same curve of rhythm; covers fresh sand with a chill or ebbs a little slackly without. So the being grows rings; identity becomes robust. What was fiery and furtive like a fling of grain cast into the air and blown hither and thither by wild gusts of life from every quarter is now methodical and orderly and flung with a purpose—so it seems.

'Lord, how pleasant! Lord, how good! How tolerable is the life of little shopkeepers, I would say, as the train drew through the suburbs and one saw lights in bedroom windows. Active, energetic as a swarm of ants, I said, as I stood at the window and watched workers, bag in hand, stream into town. What hardness, what energy and violence of limb, I thought, seeing men in white drawers' scouring after a football on a patch of snow in January. Now being grumpy about some small matter— it might be the meat—it seemed luxurious to disturb with a little ripple the enormous stability, whose quiver, for our child was about to be born, increased its joy, of our married life. I snapped at dinner. I spoke unreasonably as if, being a millionaire, I could throw away five shillings; or, being a perfect steeple-jack, stumbled over a footstool on purpose. Going up to bed we settled our quarrel on the stairs, and standing by the window looking at a sky clear like the inside of a blue stone, "Heaven be praised," I said, "we need not whip this prose into poetry. The little language is enough." For the space of the prospect and its clarity seemed to offer no impediment whatsoever, but to allow our lives to spread out and out beyond all bristling of roofs and chimneys to the flawless verge.

'Into this crashed death—Percival's. "Which is happiness?" I said (our child had been born), "which pain?" referring to the two sides of my body, as I came downstairs, making a purely physical statement. Also I made note of the state of the house; the curtain blowing; the cook singing; the wardrobe showing through the half-opened door. I said, "Give him (myself) another moment's respite" as I went downstairs. "Now in this drawing-room he is going to suffer. There is no escape." But for pain words are lacking. There should be cries, cracks, fissures, whiteness passing over chintz covers, interference with the sense of time, of space; the sense also of extreme fixity in passing objects; and sounds very remote and then very close; flesh being gashed and blood spurting, a joint suddenly twisted—beneath all of which appears something very important, yet remote, to be just held in solitude. So I went out. I saw the first morning he would never see—the sparrows were like toys dangled from a string by a child. To see things without attachment, from the outside, and to realize their beauty in itself—how strange! And then the sense that a burden has been removed; pretence and make-believe and unreality are gone, and lightness has come with a kind of transparency, making oneself invisible and things seen through as one walks—how strange. "And now what other discovery will there be?" I said, and in order to hold it tight ignored newspaper placards and went and looked at pictures. Madonnas and pillars, arches and orange trees, still as on the first day of creation, but acquainted with grief, there they hung, and I gazed at them. "Here," I said, "we are together without interruption." This freedom, this immunity, seemed then a conquest, and stirred in me such exaltation that I sometimes go there, even now, to bring back exaltation and Percival. But it did not last. What torments one is the horrible activity of the mind's eye—how he fell, how he looked, where they carried him; men in loin-cloths, pulling ropes; the bandages and the mud. Then comes the terrible pounce of memory, not to be foretold, not to be warded off—that I did not go with him to Hampton Court. That claw scratched; that fang tore; I did not go. In spite of his impatiently protesting that it did not matter; why interrupt, why spoil our moment of uninterrupted community?—Still, I repeated sullenly, I did not go, and so, driven out of the sanctuary by these officious devils, went to Jinny because she had a room; a room with little tables, with little ornaments scattered on little tables. There I confessed, with tears—I had not gone to Hampton Court. And she, remembering other things, to me trifles but torturing to her, showed me how life withers when there are things we cannot share. Soon, too, a maid came in with a note, and as she turned to answer it and I felt my own curiosity to know what she was writing and to whom, I saw the first leaf fall on his grave. I saw us push beyond this moment, and leave it behind us for ever. And then sitting side by side on the sofa we remembered inevitably what had been said by others; "the lily of the day is fairer far in May"; we compared Percival to a lily—Percival whom I wanted to lose his hair, to shock the authorities, to grow old with me; he was already covered with lilies.

'So the sincerity of the moment passed; so it became symbolical; and that I could not stand. Let us commit any blasphemy of laughter and criticism rather than exude this lily-sweet glue; and cover him with phrases, I cried. Therefore I broke off, and Jinny, who was without future, or speculation, but respected the moment with complete integrity, gave her body a flick with the whip, powdered her face (for which I loved her), and waved to me as she stood on the doorstep, pressing her hand to her hair so that the wind might not disorder it, a gesture for which I honoured her, as if it confirmed our determination—not to let lilies grow.

'I observed with disillusioned clarity the despicable nonentity of the street; its porches; its window curtains; the drab clothes, the cupidity and complacency of shopping women; and old men taking the air in comforters; the caution of people crossing; the universal determination to go on living, when really, fools and gulls that you are, I said, any slate may fly from a roof, any car may swerve, for there is neither rhyme nor reason when a drunk man staggers about with a club in his hand—that is all. I was like one admitted behind the scenes: like one shown how the effects are produced. I returned, however, to my own snug home and was warned by the parlourmaid to creep upstairs in my stockings. The child was asleep. I went to my room.

'Was there no sword, nothing with which to batter down these walls, this protection, this begetting of children and living behind curtains, and becoming daily more involved and committed, with books and pictures? Better burn one's life out like Louis, desiring perfection; or like Rhoda leave us, flying past us to the desert; or choose one out of millions and one only like Neville; better be like Susan and love and hate the heat of the sun or the frost-bitten grass; or be like Jinny, honest, an animal. All had their rapture; their common feeling with death; something that stood them in stead. Thus I visited each of my friends in turn, trying, with fumbling fingers, to prise open their locked caskets. I went from one to the other holding my sorrow—no, not my sorrow but the incomprehensible nature of this our life—for their inspection. Some people go to priests; others to poetry; I to my friends, I to my own heart, I to seek among phrases and fragments something unbroken—I to whom there is not beauty enough in moon or tree; to whom the touch of one person with another is all, yet who cannot grasp even that, who am so imperfect, so weak, so unspeakably lonely. There I sat.

'Should this be the end of the story? a kind of sigh? a last ripple of the wave? A trickle of water in some gutter where, burbling, it dies away? Let me touch the table—so—and thus recover my sense of the moment. A sideboard covered with cruets; a basket full of rolls; a plate of bananas—these are comfortable sights. But if there are no stories, what end can there be, or what beginning? Life is not susceptible perhaps to the treatment we give it when we try to tell it. Sitting up late at night it seems strange not to have more control. Pigeon-holes are not then very useful. It is strange how force ebbs away and away into some dry creek. Sitting alone, it seems we are spent; our waters can only just surround feebly that spike of sea-holly; we cannot reach that further pebble so as to wet it. It is over, we are ended. But wait—I sat all night waiting—an impulse again runs through us; we rise, we toss back a mane of white spray; we pound on the shore; we are not to be confined. That is, I shaved and washed; did not wake my wife, and had breakfast; put on my hat, and went out to earn my living. After Monday, Tuesday comes.

'Yet some doubt remained, some note of interrogation. I was surprised, opening a door, to find people thus occupied; I hesitated, taking a cup of tea, whether one said milk or sugar. And the light of the stars falling, as it falls now, on my hand after travelling for millions upon millions of years—I could get a cold shock from that for a moment—not more, my imagination is too feeble. But some doubt remained. A shadow flitted through my mind like moths' wings among chairs and tables in a room in the evening. When, for example, I went to Lincolnshire that summer to see Susan and she advanced towards me across the garden with the lazy movement of a half-filled sail, with the swaying movement of a woman with child, I thought, "It goes on; but why?" We sat in the garden; the farm carts came up dripping with hay; there was the usual gabble of rooks and doves; fruit was netted and covered over; the gardener dug. Bees boomed down the purple tunnels of flowers; bees embedded themselves on the golden shields of sunflowers. Little twigs were blown across the grass. How rhythmical, and half conscious and like something wrapped in mist it was; but to me hateful, like a net folding one's limbs in its meshes, cramping. She who had refused Percival lent herself to this, to this covering over.

'Sitting down on a bank to wait for my train, I thought then how we surrender, how we submit to the stupidity of nature. Woods covered in thick green leafage lay in front of me. And by some flick of a scent or a sound on a nerve, the old image—the gardeners sweeping, the lady writing—returned. I saw the figures beneath the beech trees at Elvedon. The gardeners swept; the lady at the table sat writing. But I now made the contribution of maturity to childhood's intuitions—satiety and doom; the sense of what is unescapable in our lot; death; the knowledge of limitations; how life is more obdurate than one had thought it. Then, when I was a child, the presence of an enemy had asserted itself; the need for opposition had stung me. I had jumped up and cried, "Let's explore." The horror of the situation was ended.

'Now what situation was there to end? Dullness and doom. And what to explore? The leaves and the wood concealed nothing. If a bird rose I should no longer make a poem—I should repeat what I had seen before. Thus if I had a stick with which to point to indentations in the curve of being, this is the lowest; here it coils useless on the mud where no tide comes—here, where I sit with my back to a hedge, and my hat over my eyes, while the sheep advanced remorselessly in that wooden way of theirs, step by step on stiff, pointed legs. But if you hold a blunt blade to a grindstone long enough, something spurts—a jagged edge of fire; so held to lack of reason, aimlessness, the usual, all massed together, out spurted in one flame hatred, contempt. I took my mind, my being, the old dejected, almost inanimate object, and lashed it about among these odds and ends, sticks and straws, detestable little bits of wreckage, flotsam and jetsam, floating on the oily surface. I jumped up. I said, "Fight! Fight!" I repeated. It is the effort and the struggle, it is the perpetual warfare, it is the shattering and piecing together—this is the daily battle, defeat or victory, the absorbing pursuit. The trees, scattered, put on order; the thick green of the leaves thinned itself to a dancing light. I netted them under with a sudden phrase. I retrieved them from formlessness with words.

'The train came in. Lengthening down the platform, the train came to a stop. I caught my train. And so back to London in the evening. How satisfactory, the atmosphere of common sense and tobacco; old women clambering into the third-class carriage with their baskets; the sucking at pipes; the good-nights and see you tomorrows of friends parting at wayside stations, and then the lights of London—not the flaring ecstasy of youth, not that tattered violet banner, but still the lights of London all the same; hard, electric lights, high up in offices; street lamps laced along dry pavements; flares roaring above street markets. I like all this when I have despatched the enemy for a moment.

'Also I like to find the pageant of existence roaring, in a theatre for instance. The clay-coloured, earthy nondescript animal of the field here erects himself and with infinite ingenuity and effort puts up a fight against the green woods and green fields and sheep advancing with measured tread, munching. And, of course, windows in the long grey streets were lit up; strips of carpet cut the pavement; there were swept and garnished rooms, fire, food, wine, talk. Men with withered hands, women with pearl pagodas hanging from their ears, came in and went out. I saw old men's faces carved into wrinkles and sneers by the work of the world; beauty cherished so that it seemed newly sprung even in age; and youth so apt for pleasure that pleasure, one thought, must exist; it seemed that grass-lands must roll for it; and the sea be chopped up into little waves; and the woods rustle with bright-coloured birds for youth, for youth expectant. There one met Jinny and Hal, Tom and Betty; there we had our jokes and shared our secrets; and never parted in the doorway without arranging to meet again in some other room as the occasion, as the time of the year, suggested. Life is pleasant; life is good. After Monday comes Tuesday, and Wednesday follows.

'Yes, but after a time with a difference. It may be that something in the look of the room one night, in the arrangement of the chairs, suggests it. It seems comfortable to sink down on a sofa in a corner, to look, to listen. Then it happens that two figures standing with their backs to the window appear against the branches of a spreading willow. With a shock of emotion one feels "There are figures without features robed in beauty." In the pause that follows while the ripples spread, the girl to whom one should be talking says to herself, "He is old." But she is wrong. It is not age; it is that a drop has fallen; another drop. Time has given the arrangement another shake. Out we creep from the arch of the currant leaves, out into a wider world. The true order of things—this is our perpetual illusion—is now apparent. Thus in a moment, in a drawing-room, our life adjusts itself to the majestic march of day across the sky.

'It was for this reason that instead of pulling on my patent-leather shoes and finding a tolerable tie, I sought Neville. I sought my oldest friend, who had known me when I was Byron; when I was Meredith's young man, and also that hero in a book by Dostoevsky whose name I have forgotten. I found him alone, reading. A perfectly neat table; a curtain pulled methodically straight; a paper-knife dividing a French volume—nobody, I thought, ever changes the attitude in which we saw them first, or the clothes. Here he has sat in this chair, in these clothes, ever since we first met. Here was freedom; here was intimacy; the firelight broke off some round apple on the curtain. There we talked; sat talking; sauntered down that avenue, the avenue which runs under the trees, under the thick-leaved murmuring trees, the trees that are hung with fruit, which we have trodden so often together, so that now the turf is bare round some of those trees, round certain plays and poems, certain favourites of ours—the turf is trodden bare by our incessant unmethodical pacing. If I have to wait, I read; if I wake in the night, I feel along the shelf for a book. Swelling, perpetually augmented, there is a vast accumulation of unrecorded matter in my head. Now and then I break off a lump, Shakespeare it may be, it may be some old woman called Peck; and say to myself, smoking a cigarette in bed, "That's Shakespeare. That's Peck"—with a certainty of recognition and a shock of knowledge which is endlessly delightful, though not to be imparted. So we shared our Pecks, our Shakespeares; compared each other's versions; allowed each other's insight to set our own Peck or Shakespeare in a better light; and then sank into one of those silences which are now and again broken by a few words, as if a fin rose in the wastes of silence; and then the fin, the thought, sinks back into the depths, spreading round it a little ripple of satisfaction, content.

'Yes, but suddenly one hears a clock tick. We who had been immersed in this world became aware of another. It is painful. It was Neville who changed our time. He, who had been thinking with the unlimited time of the mind, which stretches in a flash from Shakespeare to ourselves, poked the fire and began to live by that other clock which marks the approach of a particular person. The wide and dignified sweep of his mind contracted. He became on the alert. I could feel him listening to sounds in the street. I noted how he touched a cushion. From the myriads of mankind and all time past he had chosen one person, one moment in particular. A sound was heard in the hall. What he was saying wavered in the air like an uneasy flame. I watched him disentangle one footstep from other footsteps; wait for some particular mark of identification and glance with the swiftness of a snake at the handle of the door. (Hence the astonishing acuteness of his perceptions; he has been trained always by one person.) So concentrated a passion shot out others like foreign matter from a still, sparkling fluid. I became aware of my own vague and cloudy nature full of sediment, full of doubt, full of phrases and notes to be made in pocket-books. The folds of the curtain became still, statuesque; the paperweight on the table hardened; the threads on the curtain sparkled; everything became definite, external, a scene in which I had no part. I rose, therefore; I left him.

'Heavens! how they caught me as I left the room, the fangs of that old pain! the desire for someone not there. For whom? I did not know at first; then remembered Percival. I had not thought of him for months. Now to laugh with him, to laugh with him at Neville—that was what I wanted, to walk off arm-in-arm together laughing. But he was not there. The place was empty.

'It is strange how the dead leap out on us at street corners, or in dreams.

'This fitful gust blowing so sharp and cold upon me sent me that night across London to visit other friends, Rhoda and Louis, desiring company, certainty, contact. I wondered, as I mounted the stairs, what was their relationship? What did they say alone? I figured her awkward with the tea-kettle. She gazed over the slate roofs—the nymph of the fountain always wet, obsessed with visions, dreaming. She parted the curtain to look at the night. "Away!" she said. "The moor is dark beneath the moon." I rang; I waited. Louis perhaps poured out milk in a saucer for the cat; Louis, whose bony hands shut like the sides of a dock closing themselves with a slow anguish of effort upon an enormous tumult of waters, who knew what has been said by the Egyptian, the Indian, by men with high cheek-bones and solitaires in hair shirts. I knocked: I waited; there was no answer. I tramped down the stone stairs again. Our friends—how distant, how mute, how seldom visited and little known. And I, too, am dim to my friends and unknown; a phantom, sometimes seen, often not. Life is a dream surely. Our flame, the will-o'-the-wisp that dances in a few eyes, is soon to be blown out and all will fade. I recalled my friends. I thought of Susan. She had bought fields. Cucumbers and tomatoes ripened in her hothouses. The vine that had been killed by last year's frost was putting out a leaf or two. She walked heavily with her sons across her meadows. She went about the land attended by men in gaiters, pointing with her stick at a roof, at hedges, at walls fallen into disrepair. The pigeons followed her, waddling, for the grain that she let fall from her capable, earthy fingers. "But I no longer rise at dawn," she said. Then Jinny—entertaining, no doubt, some new young man. They reached the crisis of the usual conversation. The room would be darkened; chairs arranged. For she still sought the moment. Without illusions, hard and clear as crystal, she rode at the day with her breast bared. She let its spikes pierce her. When the lock whitened on her forehead she twisted it fearlessly among the rest. So when they come to bury her nothing will be out of order. Bits of ribbons will be found curled up. But still the door opens. Who is coming in? she asks, and rises to meet him, prepared, as on those first spring nights when the tree under the big London houses where respectable citizens were going soberly to bed scarcely sheltered her love; and the squeak of trams mixed with her cry of delight and the rippling of leaves had to shade her languor, her delicious lassitude as she sank down cooled by all the sweetness of nature satisfied. Our friends, how seldom visited, how little known—it is true; and yet, when I meet an unknown person, and try to break off, here at this table, what I call "my life", it is not one life that I look back upon; I am not one person; I am many people; I do not altogether know who I am— Jinny, Susan, Neville, Rhoda, or Louis; or how to distinguish my life from theirs.

'So I thought that night in early autumn when we came together and dined once more at Hampton Court. Our discomfort was at first considerable, for each by that time was committed to a statement, and the other person coming along the road to the meeting-place dressed like this or that, with a stick or without, seemed to contradict it. I saw Jinny look at Susan's earthy fingers and then hide her own; I, considering Neville, so neat and exact, felt the nebulosity of my own life blurred with all these phrases. He then boasted, because he was ashamed of one room and one person and his own success. Louis and Rhoda, the conspirators, the spies at table, who take notes, felt, "After all, Bernard can make the waiter fetch us rolls—a contact denied us." We saw for a moment laid out among us the body of the complete human being whom we have failed to be, but at the same time, cannot forget. All that we might have been we saw; all that we had missed, and we grudged for a moment the other's claim, as children when the cake is cut, the one cake, the only cake, watch their slice diminishing.

'However, we had our bottle of wine, and under that seduction lost our enmity, and stopped comparing. And, half-way through dinner, we felt enlarge itself round us the huge blackness of what is outside us, of what we are not. The wind, the rush of wheels became the roar of time, and we rushed—where? And who were we? We were extinguished for a moment, went out like sparks in burnt paper and the blackness roared. Past time, past history we went. For me this lasts but one second. It is ended by my own pugnacity. I strike the table with a spoon. If I could measure things with compasses I would, but since my only measure is a phrase, I make phrases—I forget what, on this occasion. We became six people at a table in Hampton Court. We rose and walked together down the avenue. In the thin, the unreal twilight, fitfully like the echo of voices laughing down some alley, geniality returned to me and flesh. Against the gateway, against some cedar tree I saw blaze bright, Neville, Jinny, Rhoda, Louis, Susan, and myself, our life, our identity. Still King William seemed an unreal monarch and his crown mere tinsel. But we—against the brick, against the branches, we six, out of how many million millions, for one moment out of what measureless abundance of past time and time to come, burnt there triumphant. The moment was all; the moment was enough. And then Neville, Jinny, Susan and I, as a wave breaks, burst asunder, surrendered—to the next leaf, to the precise bird, to a child with a hoop, to a prancing dog, to the warmth that is hoarded in woods after a hot day, to the lights twisted like white ribbon on rippled waters. We drew apart; we were consumed in the darkness of the trees, leaving Rhoda and Louis to stand on the terrace by the urn.

'When we emerged from that immersion—how sweet, how deep!—and came to the surface and saw the conspirators still standing there it was with some compunction. We had lost what they had kept. We interrupted. But we were tired, and whether it had been good or bad, accomplished or left undone, the dusky veil was falling upon our endeavours; the lights were sinking as we paused for a moment upon the terrace that overlooks the river. The steamers were landing their trippers on the bank; there was a distant cheering, the sound of singing, as if people waved their hats and joined in some last song. The sound of the chorus came across the water and I felt leap up that old impulse, which has moved me all my life, to be thrown up and down on the roar of other people's voices, singing the same song; to be tossed up and down on the roar of almost senseless merriment, sentiment, triumph, desire. But not now. No! I could not collect myself; I could not distinguish myself; I could not help letting fall the things that had made me a minute ago eager, amused, jealous, vigilant, and hosts of other things, into the water. I could not recover myself from that endless throwing away, dissipation, flooding forth without our willing it and rushing soundlessly away out there under the arches of the bridge, round some clump of trees or an island, out where sea-birds sit on stakes, over the roughened water to become waves in the sea—I could not recover myself from that dissipation. So we parted.

'Was this, then, this streaming away mixed with Susan, Jinny, Neville, Rhoda, Louis, a sort of death? A new assembly of elements? Some hint of what was to come? The note was scribbled, the book shut, for I am an intermittent student. I do not say my lessons by any means at the stated hour. Later, walking down Fleet Street at the rush hour, I recalled that moment; I continued it. "Must I for ever," I said, "beat my spoon on the table-cloth? Shall I not, too, consent?" The omnibuses were clogged; one came up behind another and stopped with a click, like a link added to a stone chain. People passed.

'Multitudinous, carrying attaché-cases, dodging with incredible celerity in and out, they went past like a river in spate. They went past roaring like a train in a tunnel. Seizing my chance

I crossed; dived down a dark passage and entered the shop where they cut my hair. I leant my head back and was swathed in a sheet. Looking-glasses confronted me in which I could see my pinioned body and people passing; stopping, looking, and going on indifferent. The hairdresser began to move his scissors to and fro. I felt myself powerless to stop the oscillations of the cold steel. So we are cut and laid in swaths, I said; so we lie side by side on the damp meadows, withered branches and flowering. We have no more to expose ourselves on the bare hedges to the wind and snow; no more to carry ourselves erect when the gale sweeps, to bear our burden upheld; or stay, unmurmuring, on those pallid noondays when the bird creeps close to the bough and the damp whitens the leaf. We are cut, we are fallen. We are become part of that unfeeling universe that sleeps when we are at our quickest and burns red when we lie asleep. We have renounced our station and lie now flat, withered and how soon forgotten! Upon which I saw an expression in the tail of the eye of the hairdresser as if something interested him in the street.

'What interested the hairdresser? What did the hairdresser see in the street? It is thus that I am recalled. (For I am no mystic; something always plucks at me—curiosity, envy, admiration, interest in hairdressers and the like bring me to the surface.) While he brushed the fluff from my coat I took pains to assure myself of his identity, and then, swinging my stick, I went into the Strand, and evoked to serve as opposite to myself the figure of Rhoda, always so furtive, always with fear in her eyes, always seeking some pillar in the desert, to find which she had gone; she had killed herself. "Wait," I said, putting my arm in imagination (thus we consort with our friends) through her arm. "Wait until these omnibuses have gone by. Do not cross so dangerously. These men are your brothers." In persuading her I was also persuading my own soul. For this is not one life; nor do I always know if I am man or woman, Bernard or Neville, Louis, Susan, Jinny, or Rhoda—so strange is the contact of one with another.

'Swinging my stick, with my hair newly cut and the nape of my neck tingling, I went past all those trays of penny toys imported from Germany that men hold out in the street by St Paul's—St Paul's, the brooding hen with spread wings from whose shelter run omnibuses and streams of men and women at the rush hour. I thought how Louis would mount those steps in his neat suit with his cane in his hand and his angular, rather detached gait. With his Australian accent ("My father, a banker at Brisbane") he would come, I thought, with greater respect to these old ceremonies than I do, who have heard the same lullabies for a thousand years. I am always impressed, as I enter, by the rubbed roses; the polished brasses; the flapping and the chanting, while one boy's voice wails round the dome like some lost and wandering dove. The recumbency and the peace of the dead impress me—warriors at rest under their old banners. Then I scoff at the floridity and absurdity of some scrolloping tomb; and the trumpets and the victories and the coats of arms and the certainty, so sonorously repeated, of resurrection, of eternal life. My wandering and inquisitive eye then shows me an awe-stricken child; a shuffling pensioner; or the obeisances of tired shop-girls burdened with heaven knows what strife in their poor thin breasts come to solace themselves in the rush hour. I stray and look and wonder, and sometimes, rather furtively, try to rise on the shaft of somebody else's prayer into the dome, out, beyond, wherever they go. But then like the lost and wailing dove, I find myself failing, fluttering, descending and perching upon some curious gargoyle, some battered nose or absurd tombstone, with humour, with wonder, and so again watch the sightseers with their Baedekers shuffling past, while the boy's voice soars in the dome and the organ now and then indulges in a moment of elephantine triumph. How then, I asked, would Louis roof us all in? How would he confine us, make us one, with his red ink, with his very fine nib? The voice petered out in the dome, wailing.

'So into the street again, swinging my stick, looking at wire trays in stationers' shop-windows, at baskets of fruit grown in the colonies, murmuring Pillicock sat on Pillicock's hill, or Hark, hark, the dogs do bark, or The World's great age begins anew, or Come away, come away, death—mingling nonsense and poetry, floating in the stream. Something always has to be done next. Tuesday follows Monday: Wednesday, Tuesday. Each spreads the same ripple. The being grows rings, like a tree. Like a tree, leaves fall.

'For one day as I leant over a gate that led into a field, the rhythm stopped; the rhymes and the hummings, the nonsense and the poetry. A space was cleared in my mind. I saw through the thick leaves of habit. Leaning over the gate I regretted so much litter, so much unaccomplishment and separation, for one cannot cross London to see a friend, life being so full of engagements; nor take ship to India and see a naked man spearing fish in blue water. I said life had been imperfect, an unfinishing phrase. It had been impossible for me, taking snuff as I do from any bagman met in a train, to keep coherency— that sense of the generations, of women carrying red pitchers to the Nile, of the nightingale who sings among conquests and migrations. It had been too vast an undertaking, I said, and how can I go on lifting my foot perpetually to climb the stair? I addressed myself as one would speak to a companion with whom one is voyaging to the North Pole.

'I spoke to that self who had been with me in many tremendous adventures; the faithful man who sits over the fire when everybody has gone to bed, stirring the cinders with a poker; the man who has been so mysteriously and with sudden accretions of being built up, in a beech wood, sitting by a willow tree on a bank, leaning over a parapet at Hampton Court; the man who has collected himself in moments of emergency and banged his spoon on the table, saying, "I will not consent."

'This self now as I leant over the gate looking down over fields rolling in waves of colour beneath me made no answer. He threw up no opposition. He attempted no phrase. His fist did not form. I waited. I listened. Nothing came, nothing. I cried then with a sudden conviction of complete desertion, Now there is nothing. No fin breaks the waste of this immeasurable sea. Life has destroyed me. No echo comes when I speak, no varied words. This is more truly death than the death of friends, than the death of youth. I am the swathed figure in the hairdresser's shop taking up only so much space.

'The scene beneath me withered. It was like the eclipse when the sun went out and left the earth, flourishing in full summer foliage, withered, brittle, false. Also I saw on a winding road in a dust dance the groups we had made, how they came together, how they ate together, how they met in this room or that. I saw my own indefatigable busyness—how I had rushed from one to the other, fetched and carried, travelled and returned, joined this group and that, here kissed, here withdrawn; always kept hard at it by some extraordinary purpose, with my nose to the ground like a dog on the scent; with an occasional toss of the head, an occasional cry of amazement, despair and then back again with my nose to the scent. What a litter—what a confusion; with here birth, here death; succulence and sweetness; effort and anguish; and myself always running hither and thither. Now it was done with. I had no more appetites to glut; no more stings in me with which to poison people; no more sharp teeth and clutching hands or desire to feel the pear and the grape and the sun beating down from the orchard wall.

'The woods had vanished; the earth was a waste of shadow. No sound broke the silence of the wintry landscape. No cock crowed; no smoke rose; no train moved. A man without a self, I said. A heavy body leaning on a gate. A dead man. With dispassionate despair, with entire disillusionment, I surveyed the dust dance; my life, my friends' lives, and those fabulous presences, men with brooms, women writing, the willow tree by the river—clouds and phantoms made of dust too, of dust that changed, as clouds lose and gain and take gold or red and lose their summits and billow this way and that, mutable, vain.

I, carrying a notebook, making phrases, had recorded mere changes; a shadow. I had been sedulous to take note of shadows. How can I proceed now, I said, without a self, weightless and visionless, through a world weightless, without illusion?

'The heaviness of my despondency thrust open the gate I leant on and pushed me, an elderly man, a heavy man with grey hair, through the colourless field, the empty field. No more to hear echoes, no more to see phantoms, to conjure up no opposition, but to walk always unshadowed, making no impress upon the dead earth. If even there had been sheep munching, pushing one foot after another, or a bird, or a man driving a spade into the earth, had there been a bramble to trip me, or a ditch, damp with soaked leaves, into which to fall—but no, the melancholy path led along the level, to more wintriness and pallor and the equal and uninteresting view of the same landscape.

'How then does light return to the world after the eclipse of the sun? Miraculously. Frailly. In thin stripes. It hangs like a glass cage. It is a hoop to be fractured by a tiny jar. There is a spark there. Next moment a flush of dun. Then a vapour as if earth were breathing in and out, once, twice, for the first time. Then under the dullness someone walks with a green light. Then off twists a white wraith. The woods throb blue and green, and gradually the fields drink in red, gold, brown. Suddenly a river snatches a blue light. The earth absorbs colour like a sponge slowly drinking water. It puts on weight; rounds itself; hangs pendent; settles and swings beneath our feet.

'So the landscape returned to me; so I saw the fields rolling in waves of colour beneath me, but now with this difference; I saw but was not seen. I walked unshadowed; I came unheralded. From me had dropped the old cloak, the old response; the hollowed hand that beats back sounds. Thin as a ghost, leaving no trace where I trod, perceiving merely, I walked alone in a new world, never trodden; brushing new flowers, unable to speak save in a child's words of one syllable; without shelter from phrases—I who have made so many; unattended, I who have always gone with my kind; solitary, I who have always had someone to share the empty grate, or the cupboard with its hanging loop of gold.

'But how describe the world seen without a self? There are no words. Blue, red—even they distract, even they hide with thickness instead of letting the light through. How describe or say anything in articulate words again?—save that it fades, save that it undergoes a gradual transformation, becomes, even in the course of one short walk, habitual—this scene also. Blindness returns as one moves and one leaf repeats another. Loveliness returns as one looks, with all its train of phantom phrases. One breathes in and out substantial breath; down in the valley the train draws across the fields lop-eared with smoke.

'But for a moment I had sat on the turf somewhere high above the flow of the sea and the sound of the woods, had seen the house, the garden, and the waves breaking. The old nurse who turns the pages of the picture-book had stopped and had said, "Look. This is the truth."

'So I was thinking as I came along Shaftesbury Avenue to-night. I was thinking of that page in the picture-book. And when I met you in the place where one goes to hang up one's coat I said to myself, "It does not matter whom I meet. All this little affair of 'being' is over. Who this is I do not know; nor care; we will dine together." So I hung up my coat, tapped you on the shoulder, and said, "Sit with me."

'Now the meal is finished; we are surrounded by peelings and breadcrumbs. I have tried to break off this bunch and hand it you; but whether there is substance or truth in it I do not know. Nor do I know exactly where we are. What city does that stretch of sky look down upon? Is it Paris, is it London where we sit, or some southern city of pink-washed houses lying under cypresses, under high mountains, where eagles soar? I do not at this moment feel certain.

'I begin now to forget; I begin to doubt the fixity of tables, the reality of here and now, to tap my knuckles smartly upon the edges of apparently solid objects and say, "Are you hard?" I have seen so many different things, have made so many different sentences. I have lost in the process of eating and drinking and rubbing my eyes along surfaces that thin, hard shell which cases the soul, which, in youth, shuts one in—hence the fierceness, and the tap, tap, tap of the remorseless beaks of the young. And now I ask, "Who am I?" I have been talking of Bernard, Neville, Jinny, Susan, Rhoda and Louis. Am I all of them? Am I one and distinct? I do not know. We sat here together. But now Percival is dead, and Rhoda is dead; we are divided; we are not here. Yet I cannot find any obstacle separating us. There is no division between me and them. As I talked I felt "I am you". This difference we make so much of, this identity we so feverishly cherish, was overcome. Yes, ever since old Mrs Constable lifted her sponge and pouring warm water over me covered me with flesh I have been sensitive, percipient. Here on my brow is the blow I got when Percival fell. Here on the nape of my neck is the kiss Jinny gave Louis. My eyes fill with Susan's tears. I see far away, quivering like a gold thread, the pillar Rhoda saw, and feel the rush of the wind of her flight when she leapt.

'Thus when I come to shape here at this table between my hands the story of my life and set it before you as a complete thing, I have to recall things gone far, gone deep, sunk into this life or that and become part of it; dreams, too, things surrounding me, and the inmates, those old half-articulate ghosts who keep up their hauntings by day and night; who turn over in their sleep, who utter their confused cries, who put out their phantom fingers and clutch at me as I try to escape—shadows of people one might have been; unborn selves. There is the old brute, too, the savage, the hairy man who dabbles his fingers in ropes of entrails; and gobbles and belches; whose speech is guttural, visceral—well, he is here. He squats in me. To-night he has been feasted on quails, salad, and sweetbread. He now holds a glass of fine old brandy in his paw. He brindles, purrs and shoots warm thrills all down my spine as I sip. It is true, he washes his hands before dinner, but they are still hairy. He buttons on trousers and waistcoats, but they contain the same organs. He jibs if I keep him waiting for dinner. He mops and mows perpetually, pointing with his half-idiot gestures of greed and covetousness at what he desires. I assure you, I have great difficulty sometimes in controlling him. That man, the hairy, the ape-like, has contributed his part to my life. He has given a greener glow to green things, has held his torch with its red flames, its thick and smarting smoke, behind every leaf. He has lit up the cool garden even. He has brandished his torch in murky by-streets where girls suddenly seem to shine with a red and intoxicating translucency. Oh, he has tossed his torch high! He has led me wild dances!

'But no more. Now to-night, my body rises tier upon tier like some cool temple whose floor is strewn with carpets and murmurs rise and the altars stand smoking; but up above, here in my serene head, comes only fine gusts of melody, waves of incense, while the lost dove wails, and the banners tremble above tombs, and the dark airs of midnight shake trees outside the open windows. When I look down from this transcendency, how beautiful are even the crumbled relics of bread! What shapely spirals the peelings of pears make—how thin, and mottled like some sea-bird's egg. Even the forks laid straight side by side appear lucid, logical, exact; and the horns of the rolls which we have left are glazed, yellow-plated, hard. I could worship my hand even, with its fan of bones laced by blue mysterious veins and its astonishing look of aptness, suppleness and ability to curl softly or suddenly crush—its infinite sensibility.

'Immeasurably receptive, holding everything, trembling with fullness, yet clear, contained—so my being seems, now that desire urges it no more out and away; now that curiosity no longer dyes it a thousand colours. It lies deep, tideless, immune, now that he is dead, the man I called "Bernard", the man who kept a book in his pocket in which he made notes—phrases for the moon, notes of features; how people looked, turned, dropped their cigarette ends; under B, butterfly powder, under D, ways of naming death. But now let the door open, the glass door that is for ever turning on its hinges. Let a woman come, let a young man in evening-dress with a moustache sit down: is there anything that they can tell me? No! I know all that, too. And if she suddenly gets up and goes, "My dear," I say, "you no longer make me look after you." The shock of the falling wave which has sounded all my life, which woke me so that I saw the gold loop on the cupboard, no longer makes quiver what I hold.

'So now, taking upon me the mystery of things, I could go like a spy without leaving this place, without stirring from my chair. I can visit the remote verges of the desert lands where the savage sits by the camp-fire. Day rises; the girl lifts the watery fire-hearted jewels to her brow; the sun levels his beams straight at the sleeping house; the waves deepen their bars; they fling themselves on shore; back blows the spray; sweeping their waters they surround the boat and the sea-holly. The birds sing in chorus; deep tunnels run between the stalks of flowers; the house is whitened; the sleeper stretches; gradually all is astir. Light floods the room and drives shadow beyond shadow to where they hang in folds inscrutable. What does the central shadow hold? Something? Nothing? I do not know.

'Oh, but there is your face. I catch your eye. I, who had been thinking myself so vast, a temple, a church, a whole universe, unconfined and capable of being everywhere on the verge of things and here too, am now nothing but what you see—an elderly man, rather heavy, grey above the ears, who (I see myself in the glass) leans one elbow on the table, and holds in his left hand a glass of old brandy. That is the blow you have dealt me. I have walked bang into the pillar-box. I reel from side to side. I put my hands to my head. My hat is off—I have dropped my stick. I have made an awful ass of myself and am justly laughed at by any passer-by.

'Lord, how unutterably disgusting life is! What dirty tricks it plays us, one moment free; the next, this. Here we are among the breadcrumbs and the stained napkins again. That knife is already congealing with grease. Disorder, sordidity and corruption surround us. We have been taking into our mouths the bodies of dead birds. It is with these greasy crumbs, slobbered over napkins, and little corpses that we have to build. Always it begins again; always there is the enemy; eyes meeting ours; fingers twitching ours; the effort waiting. Call the waiter. Pay the bill. We must pull ourselves up out of our chairs. We must find our coats. We must go. Must, must, must—detestable word. Once more, I who had thought myself immune, who had said, "Now I am rid of all that," find that the wave has tumbled me over, head over heels, scattering my possessions, leaving me to collect, to assemble, to heap together, summon my forces, rise and confront the enemy.

'It is strange that we, who are capable of so much suffering, should inflict so much suffering. Strange that the face of a person whom I scarcely know save that I think we met once on the gangway of a ship bound for Africa—a mere adumbration of eyes, cheeks, nostrils—should have power to inflict this insult. You look, eat, smile, are bored, pleased, annoyed—that is all I know. Yet this shadow which has sat by me for an hour or two, this mask from which peep two eyes, has power to drive me back, to pinion me down among all those other faces, to shut me in a hot room; to send me dashing like a moth from candle to candle.

'But wait. While they add up the bill behind the screen, wait one moment. Now that I have reviled you for the blow that sent me staggering among peelings and crumblings and old scraps of meat, I will record in words of one syllable how also under your gaze with that compulsion on me I begin to perceive this, that and the other. The clock ticks; the woman sneezes; the waiter comes—there is a gradual coming together, running into one, acceleration and unification. Listen: a whistle sounds, wheels rush, the door creaks on its hinges. I regain the sense of the complexity and the reality and the struggle, for which I thank you. And with some pity, some envy and much good will, take your hand and bid you good night.

'Heaven be praised for solitude! I am alone now. That almost unknown person has gone, to catch some train, to take some cab, to go to some place or person whom I do not know. The face looking at me has gone. The pressure is removed. Here are empty coffee-cups. Here are chairs turned but nobody sits on them. Here are empty tables and nobody any more coming to dine at them to-night.

'Let me now raise my song of glory. Heaven be praised for solitude. Let me be alone. Let me cast and throw away this veil of being, this cloud that changes with the least breath, night and day, and all night and all day. While I sat here I have been changing. I have watched the sky change. I have seen clouds cover the stars, then free the stars, then cover the stars again. Now I look at their changing no more. Now no one sees me and I change no more. Heaven be praised for solitude that has removed the pressure of the eye, the solicitation of the body, and all need of lies and phrases.

'My book, stuffed with phrases, has dropped to the floor. It lies under the table, to be swept up by the charwoman when she comes wearily at dawn looking for scraps of paper, old tram tickets, and here and there a note screwed into a ball and left with the litter to be swept up. What is the phrase for the moon? And the phrase for love? By what name are we to call death? I do not know. I need a little language such as lovers use, words of one syllable such as children speak when they come into the room and find their mother sewing and pick up some scrap of bright wool, a feather, or a shred of chintz. I need a howl; a cry. When the storm crosses the marsh and sweeps over me where I lie in the ditch unregarded I need no words. Nothing neat. Nothing that comes down with all its feet on the floor. None of those resonances and lovely echoes that break and chime from nerve to nerve in our breasts, making wild music, false phrases. I have done with phrases.

'How much better is silence; the coffee-cup, the table. How much better to sit by myself like the solitary sea-bird that opens its wings on the stake. Let me sit here for ever with bare things, this coffee-cup, this knife, this fork, things in themselves, myself being myself. Do not come and worry me with your hints that it is time to shut the shop and be gone. I would willingly give all my money that you should not disturb me but will let me sit on and on, silent, alone.

'But now the head waiter, who has finished his own meal, appears and frowns; he takes his muffler from his pocket and ostentatiously makes ready to go. They must go; must put up the shutters, most fold the table-cloths, and give one brush with a wet mop under the tables.

'Curse you then. However beat and done with it all I am, I must haul myself up, and find the particular coat that belongs to me; must push my arms into the sleeves; must muffle myself up against the night air and be off. I, I, I, tired as I am, spent as I am, and almost worn out with all this rubbing of my nose along the surfaces of things, even I, an elderly man who is getting rather heavy and dislikes exertion, must take myself off and catch some last train.

'Again I see before me the usual street. The canopy of civilization is burnt out. The sky is dark as polished whalebone. But there is a kindling in the sky whether of lamplight or of dawn. There is a stir of some sort—sparrows on plane trees somewhere chirping. There is a sense of the break of day. I will not call it dawn. What is dawn in the city to an elderly man standing in the street looking up rather dizzily at the sky? Dawn is some sort of whitening of the sky; some sort of renewal. Another day; another Friday; another twentieth of March, January, or September. Another general awakening. The stars draw back and are extinguished. The bars deepen themselves between the waves. The film of mist thickens on the fields. A redness gathers on the roses, even on the pale rose that hangs by the bedroom window. A bird chirps. Cottagers light their early candles. Yes, this is the eternal renewal, the incessant rise and fall and fall and rise again.

'And in me too the wave rises. It swells; it arches its back. I am aware once more of a new desire, something rising beneath me like the proud horse whose rider first spurs and then pulls him back. What enemy do we now perceive advancing against us, you whom I ride now, as we stand pawing this stretch of pavement? It is death. Death is the enemy. It is death against whom I ride with my spear couched and my hair flying back like a young man's, like Percival's, when he galloped in India. I strike spurs into my horse. Against you I will fling myself, unvanquished and unyielding, O Death!'

The waves broke on the shore.

Lightning Source UK Ltd.
Milton Keynes UK
UKHW010952130622
404345UK00002B/405